# LAW, GENDER, AND INJUSTICE

**FEMINIST CROSSCURRENTS**
EDITED BY KATHLEEN BARRY

American Feminism: A Contemporary History
GINETTE CASTRO
TRANSLATED FROM THE FRENCH BY ELIZABETH LOVERDE-BAGWELL

Lesbian Texts and Contexts: Radical Revisions
EDITED BY KARLA JAY AND JOANNE GLASGOW

Fraternity Gang Rape: Sex, Brotherhood, and Privilege on Campus
PEGGY REEVES SANDAY

Sexuality and War: Literary Masks of the Middle East
EVELYNE ACCAD

Law, Gender, and Injustice: A Legal History of U.S. Women
JOAN HOFF

# LAW, GENDER, AND INJUSTICE

## A Legal History of U.S. Women

## Joan Hoff

NEW YORK UNIVERSITY PRESS
New York and London

*To Terry, for always being there.*

Copyright © 1991 by New York University
All rights reserved
Manufactured in the United States of America

Library of Congress Cataloging-in-Publication Data
Hoff, Joan, 1937–
Law, gender, and injustice: a legal history
of U.S. women
American Revolution to the present / Joan Hoff.
p. cm. — (Feminist crosscurrents)
Includes bibliographical references and index.
ISBN 0-8147-3467-7 (cloth)
1. Sex discrimination against women—Law and legislation—United
States—History. 2. Women—Legal status, laws, etc.—United States—
History. I. Title. II. Series.
KF4758.H64 1990
346.7301'34—dc20
[347.306134]        90-40553
                    CIP

New York University Press books are printed on acid-free paper,
and their binding materials are chosen for strength and durability.

*Book design by Ken Venezio*

# Contents

# Foreword

The current women's movement of the 1990s is more vigorous than ever. But despite all of its creative energy and political determinism, for the last twenty years the "prophets of doom" in the media have continually proclaimed it dead while academicians designate our demise in terms such as *postfeminism*. Yet feminism has expanded to encompass the global dimensions of patriarchal oppression with theories and actions that reveal a sharpened politics and deeper analysis of sex class conditions. The racial, cultural, and national diversities among women make the work of international feminism all the more profound as it carves out and celebrates that which women share in common and politically unifies us against patriarchal domination.

Since the late 1960s, the women's movement has proven itself to be the most viable social movement of those years and the 1970s, the most urgently necessary of the 1980s, and now is one of our strongest hopes in the 1990s. Feminism has refused the conservative and Fundamentalist efforts to reduce women to their reproductive functions and has contested the liberal ideal of women as pornographic sexual objects. Feminist scholarship, at its best, is charting its own course and emerging from women's lives to define theory and shape research around the globe.

The Feminist Crosscurrent Series is committed to emphasizing the critical links between scholarly research and theory and feminist politics and practice. This series recognizes that radicalism is critical to any movement of feminist thought and that women's oppression constitutes a class condition. We are concerned with theory and analysis that enlightens research and activism on how sex, class, gender stratification, and race interface in the lives of women; yet, we do not invalidate white, middle-class women's experience by reducing it, as many have tried, to "privileged" or "bourgeois." And we do not avoid works that may be considered "too hostile" because they expose systems of male privileges and awards as class conditions of domination over women. We seek to present works from a diverse, international community of feminist scholars in a broad range of academic disciplines that speak to the fullest dimensions of the condition of women. Our series has been launched with a range of works that reflect this goal and includes works on women, sexuality, war in the Middle East, an anthology of lesbian literary criticism, a French study of the women's movement in the United States, and an anthropology of fraternity gang rape.

Joan Hoff's book, *Unequal before the Law: A Legal History of Women from the American Revolution to the Present,* is the first comprehensive legal history of women in the United States and their struggle for the full rights and protections of the law. Under the yoke of a Constitution that launched a new republic while rationalizing slavery, it is not surprising, but perhaps awesome, to face the full extent of legal jeopardy in which women have been placed by always being granted "too little, too late." Hoff illuminates the legal texts of U.S. patriarchy by reperiodizing them according to the historical deprivation women experienced under each succeeding epoch of history. But legal harms can only be understood in their concrete, experiential realities. Hoff grounds her theories and her reperiodization of constitutional history in the lives, events, and actions of women — black and white. *Unequal before the Law* is a challenge to women to not settle for less than the most radical demands that full equality can yield. Only uncompromising equality can compensate for the historical losses women have suffered as a class, making this work a call for nothing short of a legal revolution.

Kathleen Barry
*Pennsylvania State University*

# Acknowledgments

Since beginning this book ten years ago, it has assumed a life of its own. I owe much to the many friends and colleagues who continued to advise and encourage me throughout a decade in which I made several professional decisions and experienced personal events that also helped to shape this study of the second-class citizenship of women in the United States into a more broadly synthetic and theoretical work than it started out to be. As the book became more intertwined with my own life and with my former position as executive secretary of the Organization of American Historians (OAH), I began to realize that the single-minded pursuit of equality over the course of two hundred years had not made U.S. women full citizens, any more than it had ensured them equal status or treatment with men despite all the recent juridical and legislative rhetoric to the contrary. Most importantly, I came to the conclusion that even if de jure equality had been achieved as a result of the First and Second Women's movements, it would not have been enough because, as historian Mary Ritter Beard noted almost a half-century ago, making "man the measure" of female equality was such an inadequate standard that it could only perpetuate women's de facto inequality in society.

My work on this book began when I was a Project '87 fellow at the Brookings Institution in the fall of 1979 and at the Woodrow Wilson International Center for Scholars in the spring of 1980. It continued with the help of a Guggenheim Foundation Fellowship in 1981–82. My research for the sections on pornography originated when I coordinated the 1985–86 Multidisciplinary Faculty Seminar on Pornography and Violence in American Society sponsored by the Dean of Faculties at Indiana University and greatly profited from a 1986 Summer Faculty Research Stipend granted by the Indiana University Dean of Research and Graduate Development that allowed me to utilize relevant sexually explicit works of the past and present at the Kinsey Institute on the Indiana University campus and the Widener Library at Harvard. Additionally, archivists and librarians at the following institutions aided me with various legal and historical aspects of this project: the Manuscript Division and Law Library of the Library of Congress; the Law School Library at Indiana University; the Arthur and Elizabeth Schlesinger Library at Radcliffe College; the Manuscript Division of the New York Public Library Annex; the Sophia Smith Collection at Smith College; the microfilm collection on women at the National Museum of History in Washington, D.C.; the Archives of De Pauw University in the Roy O. West Library; the Lilly Library at Indiana University; the South Carolina Department of Archives and History in Columbia; the Bancroft Library at the University of California, Berkeley; and the Franklin D. Roosevelt Presidential Library at Hyde Park.

Most importantly, however, a synthetic work of this nature depends on the monographic efforts of others writing in the fields of U.S. legal and social history, such as Judith A. Baer, Norma Basch, Susan D. Becker, Ruth H. Block, Lois Green Carr, Nancy Cott, Richard Chused, Elaine Forman Crane, Elizabeth Fox-Genovese, Joan R. Gunderson, Michael Grossberg, Linda K. Kerber, Alexander Keyssar, Suzanne Lebsock, Gloria L. Main, Mary Beth Norton, Peggy A. Rabkin, Carole Shammas, Daniel Scott Smith, Marylynn Salmon, Linda E. Speth, Laurel Thatcher Ulrich, and Judith Wellman. I have also drawn somewhat eclectically from the legal studies and interpretations of the law by Barbara Babcock, Andrea Dworkin, Zillah R. Eisenstein, Ruth Bader Ginsburg, Robert W. Gordon, Herma Hill Kay, Kenneth L. Karst, Hendrik Hartog, George L. Haskins, Morton J. Horwitz, Catharine MacKinnon, Isabel Marcus, Sylvia A. Law, William E. Nelson, Frances Olsen, Carole Pateman, Ann C. Scales, Lenore J. Weitzman, Robin West, Stephanie M. Wildman, and Wendy Williams. Obviously, none of these specialists are responsible for the conclusions I have drawn from their published or unpublished works in writing this book. Basch and Chused, in addition to Mary Frances Berry, Nancy F. Cott, Jane Sherron De Hart, Christie Farnham, Susanne Kappeler, Gerda Lerner, Elyce Rotella, and Louise Tilly read and commented on portions of this manuscript as chapters or papers prepared for anthologies or delivered at conferences.

As helpful as various librarians, archivists, and the works and advice of lawyers and other historians have been in my research on the changing legal status of women since the American Revolution, three people are primarily responsible for this work. Elizabeth Defeis, former dean of Seton Hall Law School, introduced me to the study of women and law over fifteen years ago. Defeis also initiated my collaboration with English barrister Albie Sachs on an earlier comparative study of the legal status of women in the United States and England, and she has critiqued most of my publications dealing with contemporary Supreme Court decisions, including this one. Sachs's quietly determined pursuit of justice and equality for blacks in South Africa and Mozambique has been a constant reminder and standard by which I judged my own political activism and legal writings. Without the support, comments, and advice of Kathleen Barry, however, this work would not have been completed. Seven years of professional administrative work at the OAH had sharpened my own personal and professional sense of the covert discrimination women academics, especially those in administrative positions, still experience but had both dulled and fragmented my incentive for finishing this lengthy study. During my 1989 sabbatical leave from Indiana University, Barry most unselfishly provided an atmosphere of encouragement, intellectual stimulation, and friendship that allowed me to think through to complete the technical and theoretical aspects of the original manuscript that another old friend, Dee Scriven, had previously edited and commented on for me.

Finally, Deborah Hall, as a graduate student at Indiana University, assembled data for the tables on Married Women's Property Acts, and William Hamm persevered for a number of years in entering and reorganizing the various sections of this work, using a variety of computer systems and software, as it progressively became longer and more complicated. The OAH staff in Bloomington also graciously and steadfastly accommodated my research and writing schedule. In particular, I am indebted to OAH staff members Mary Belding, Sharon Caughill, Jeanette Chafin, Ginger Foutz, Kara Hamm, Howard McMains, Michael Regoli, and Sheri Sherrill. It was with a sense of both relief and rejoicing that I turned this manuscript over to New York University Press and Senior Editor Kitty Moore's capable hands after Indiana University law student Heidi Henderson and history graduate students Michael Fitzsimmons and Liann Tsoukas with good humor and efficiency checked and corrected its numerous citations. Realizing the problems that radical feminist analyses face in the publishing and academic worlds, I am most grateful that New York University Press chose to publish this long work in its entirety without trying to second-guess either its audience or its author.

I am also grateful to the following for permission to quote or reprint from their publications:

The Women's Foreign Policy Council for permission to reprint its Declaration of Interdependence.

The *University of Chicago Law Review* for permission to quote from "Jurisprudence and Gender," by Robin West, *University of Chicago Law Review* 55, no. 1 (Winter 1988): 1–72.

The publishers and The Massachusetts Historical Society for permission to reprint letters from *Adams Family Correspondence,* vol. 1, December 1761–May 1776, L. H. Butterfield, editor, Cambridge, Mass.: The Belknap Press of Harvard University Press, Copyright © 1963, Massachusetts Historical Society. All rights reserved.

# LAW, GENDER, AND INJUSTICE

# Toward a Theory of Women's Legal History

This book, which started out as a monograph on eighteenth- and nineteenth-century dower and equity procedures ten years ago, has become a study of U.S. women's legal history extending from the War of Independence to the present. From the narrow focus of my earlier quantitative work on dower rights in South Carolina and interest in Mary Ritter Beard's legal theories, I came to the conclusion that the colonial period, however important, simply did not set in motion major national trends affecting the legal status of all women as did the drafting of the Constitution, institutionalization of a legal system following the American Revolution, and codification of law in the age of Jackson. During their two-hundred-year quest to become full citizens under the law, women in the United States have not yet completely displaced, let alone replaced, these postrevolutionary juridical trends based on male legal texts and discourses.

So this became a synthetic work—an attempt to interpret and inform—in the hope of persuading the general reader that the legal status of U.S. women in the United States, while improved, is not and never has been based on other than assimilationist or pluralist male standards of justice and equality. I have also written it to suggest legal and political action in the future that goes beyond the pursuit of traditional forms of equality. More of the same liberal "advances" combined with conservative foot dragging, especially as occurred during the Reagan administrations, has produced a two-steps-forward, one-step-backward historical and legal dance in which the participants are too engaged in the complicated footwork to think about adopting a new choreography with different partners and new steps. The stream of self-congratulatory statements and continuing feigned sparring on the part of liberal and conservatives has resulted in a stalemate that will not fundamentally alter the legal status of women because they are too well ensconced within an adversarial system of law that supports both capitalism and patriarchy. The only hope on the horizon is a feminist jurisprudence based on radical feminism.[1]

When I first began to work in the field of legal history with Albie Sachs in the late 1970s, I brought to my research methodologies I had employed as a revisionist foreign-policy specialist—namely, a healthy skepticism about structural-functional and modernization theories, but with a basic acceptance of the idea that military parity between the two superpowers was a better way to deal with the cold war than continued U.S. insistence on superiority in the arms race. My suspicion about modernization gave me insights into the position of colonial and early republican women that I would not otherwise have had. However, when I applied my belief in parity to U.S. women (and minorities) in their attempts to obtain equality with men, I temporarily forgot that parity can only occur between equal entities. (Before the USSR actually became equal in power to the United States, our cold war diplomats talked in terms of superiority, not parity.) Unlike parity between two essentially equal superpowers, the granting of parity to women or other disadvantaged groups in American society could not automatically be interpreted as unqualified improvement or progress in their actual, as opposed to theoretical, legal status vis-à-vis white men.

This work began, therefore, by my questioning certain standard assumptions about the position of women during the late eighteenth and early nineteenth centuries when the United States was still a developing nation. These were reinforced once I reevaluated the juridical results obtained by women in the last two hundred years as they pursued equality—or what in diplomatic terms would amount to increasing parity under the law. At the same time, the writings of feminists associated with the Critical Legal Studies (CLS) movement and radical feminist lawyers who distance themselves from both liberal legalism and critical legal theory convinced me of the limitations of past and present liberal legalism that has rationalized so many arguments in favor of women obtaining equality on male terms under the First and Second Women's movements. Poststructural theories also enticed me for a while and Foucauldian theories about the relationship between power and sexuality in modern society, along with deconstructionist modes of gender analysis, still do.

All of these diverse intellectual forays, in turn, pushed me beyond my belief that parity was enough for women, but they also led me to scrutinize the negative implications when some of these innovative methodologies and theories of the last twenty years were carried to their logical extremes. Thus, I will note throughout this book that the excessive use of poststructural techniques can nullify the reality of women's oppression and collective identity by overstressing female differences, because of its emphasis on the elimination of fixed binary oppositions. At the same time, CLS criticism of liberal legal changes in women's legal status can result in the ahistorical and political paralyzing idea that women are hopeless victims of unending, unequal sexual relations interacting in multiple force fields or discursive levels. Neither interpretative approach bodes well for a feminist restructuring of U.S. society between now and the end of the century. The same can be said of the continued, albeit increasingly fragmented, attempt by main-stream feminists to obtain equality—that is, parity—with men in the United States.

My intention in stressing the negative in this introduction is not to give solace or ammunition to conservatives, in general, or to antiaffirmative-action lawyers, in particular. Nor is it to discourage the current plethora of piecemeal state and federal legislative reforms affecting women recommended by mainstream liberals (as if liberals can ever be discouraged from making the world incrementally better, but not different). Instead, this book is an attempt to synthesize into an interpretative narrative the last two hundred years of the legal history of women in the United States, suggesting why the Second Women's movement, like the First Women's movement, may also end up settling for too little, too late and hence, in retrospect, may also reflect no more than the sum of its achievements in behalf of individual female rights. It is also a call for revolutionary reform of the U.S. legal system through a feminist demystification and reinterpretation of legal texts and the reassertion of the relevance of history in that process.

## Women as the "Broken Barometers" of U.S. Legal History

Only in the last twenty-five years have women begun to be accorded juridical equality with men and the scholarly attention their historical legal status deserves. Although the legal status of women has changed more rapidly in the last two decades than in the previous two hundred years, the fact remains that the U.S. Constitution still does not explicitly protect women against discrimination. Consequently, radical feminists now question whether equality based on traditional individual rights and assimilationist values is really what will most improve conditions for women for the remainder of the twentieth century. In retrospect, many of these hard-won battles have resulted in unintended negative consequences or in gains that became less important over time because they took so long to achieve. Moreover, in the last two hundred years, the basic pattern that laws concerning women reveal in relation to the power of the liberal state and the changing U.S. political socioeconomy is how out of sync women's rights have been with actual economic and political developments. Almost without exception each legal change or improvement, despite the arguments used by women (and men) to rationalize them, has reflected the American past, not its future. I call this time-lag phenomenon the "broken-barometer" theory of historical legal interpretation.

From the most severe colonial coverture restrictions on married women's legal existence to postrevolutionary changes in dower, divorce, and equity rights; from republican motherhood to the cult of true womanhood; from married women's property acts to protective legislation; from suffrage to sexual liberation; from no divorce to no-fault divorce; from equal pay and the ERA to comparable worth and pregnancy-disability acts—all these changes in the legal status of women and their own and society's perceptions about them occurred as policy and opinion makers were moving on to other "more important" and innovative activities. Thus, women "missed" becoming full citizens of the new republic (along with most white, male mechanics and artisans, slaves, free African-Americans, and native American Indians), despite praise for female patriotism and their contributions to the War of Independence, because the Founding Fathers believed in the necessity of limiting legal equality primarily to white, male property owners.

Women also were not included in the male definition of certain revolutionary terms until the original meaning of these words began to change for men. For example, at the beginning of the American Revolution the prevailing concept of virtue was based on eighteenth-century classical and republican usage referring to the "manly" attribute that placed limits on individualism in the name of the common good. Then, as this male concept of "disinterested public virtue" changed, especially after the drafting of the Constitution of 1787, women increasingly found themselves the proud recipients and embodiment of civic morality, with the privately virtuous task of raising patriotic children. When the rhetoric about male virtue in the form of self-restraint ran headlong into the reality of economic opportunity in the 1780s and 1790s, the solution to this moral dilemma, in retrospect, appears quick and simple: assign virtue to the private sphere of women where it could do the least harm to the economy and individual self-interest.[2]

These postrevolutionary legacies of virtue and second-class legal status meant that republican wives and mothers became private, but not public, citizens of the United States without completely understanding why. Privatization (or feminization) of virtue came at the very moment when postrevolutionary leaders were getting on with the business of carving out political privileges and economic opportunities for themselves and for many succeeding generations of white males. Just as male revolutionary symbols of virtue and morality were turning into female ones, women were being systematically relegated by the new laws of the land to peripheral positions outside the political and economic developments that shaped the country's destiny during the first half of the nineteenth century.

It was not until Elizabeth Cady Stanton's generation, symbolized by the Declaration of Sentiments in 1848, that some women broke out of their state of "privatized morality" and came to understand and collectively demand the legal status secured by privileged white males almost a century earlier.[3] Moreover, it was only after the Civil War that they fully realized the extent to which they would have to struggle and organize to achieve the additional rights that most free white men had obtained under Jacksonian democracy in the 1830s and 1840s. By that time, however, the American political economy was moving from republican, agrarian, manufacturing, and commercial structures to early corporate and industrialized principles of power and politics, making eighteenth-century enlightenment theories about natural law obsolete for most white males. Likewise, family demographics and sexual mores evolved in ways between the 1790s and 1890s that could not be fully understood, let alone resolved with the century-old ideas the women of 1848 advocated. As early republican ideals became less important to men in the United States in the course of the nineteenth century, they became *more* important to women reformers. Despite the fact that such theories no longer reflected mainstream socioeconomic or cultural conditions, they happened to perfectly reflect the time-lag in which women lived compared to men.

Additionally, to the degree that women increasingly entered the public realm in the 1830s and 1840s through the temperance and abolitionist movements, their own claim to being private paragons of virtue both in the family and society gradually diminished. Later, after the Civil War, as they became even more vocal reformers their virtuous "nature" became more suspect, despite all the Victorian praise they continued to receive (and heap upon themselves) as the repositories of social purity. Inevitably, this gradual and subtle loss of a monopoly on virtue contributed to the failure of female reformers at the end of the nineteenth century to obtain legislation and court decisions protecting women from physical abuse. Since the "entire premise of social purity rested upon the protection of female sexual virtue from ruin," according to Elizabeth Pleck,[4] once *all* women were perceived as less virtuous because of *some* women's entrance into professional and political activities, legal safeguards against battering and abandonment did not rank high among social reforms among men in power by 1900.

The transformation of sex into sexuality in the late nineteenth and early twentieth centuries[5] also made the medical profession, the courts, and legislatures less sensitive to women's somatic and psychic suffering within their private spheres. Moving into the public realm, therefore, made the socioeconomic construction of the private one more dangerous for women, although leaders of the First Women's movement did not realize this at the time because they could not anticipate the negative implications that the discursive development, known as the "science of sexuality," would hold for the female half of the population.[6] Likewise, as women moved further and further away from puritanical, Victorian, and, finally, Freudian notions about their sexuality in the twentieth century, they encountered even more indifference about how much protection from physical harm they actually "deserved." As a heretofore ignored by-product of their liberation, fear has become a constant factor in the intellectual and physical lives of contemporary women. Like their predecessors, the leaders of the Second Women's movement did not anticipate the most virulent current form of this negative and fearful backlash—violent pornography directed against women. They also have yet to resolve society's continuing indifference to the private "consensual" sufferings and fears of females or the continued effectiveness of legal and socioeconomic mechanisms for "silencing" women who try to speak other than in a male voice.[7]

Another thing women reformers of the 1870s could not have anticipated was the way they and their successors would have to persevere for *another half-century* until some of their pre– and post–Civil War demands were achieved, culminating with one—the right to vote in 1920. (If one dates the beginning of the suffrage movement from the 1848 Seneca Falls Convention, seventy-two years elapsed before the passage of the Nineteenth Amendment. A less known lapse of time is the ninety-three years between 1870, when the first equal pay bill for working women was introduced in Congress, and the Equal Pay Act of 1963. Forty-nine years intervened between the initial introduction of the first Equal Rights Amendment in 1923 and congressional approval in 1972, or a total of fifty-nine years before the defeat of the proposed Twenty-seventh Amendment in 1982, after a three-year extension of the original time limit.) Such enormous time-lags usually mean that when women finally achieve improvements in their legal status, the changes often no longer accurately reflect their present needs because of intervening developments in the political economy, family demographics, and technology.

Consequently, women obtained suffrage not in the nineteenth century, when it would have been truly significant in terms of the grass-roots legacy of Jacksonian democracy (and when most white males were enfranchised), but in the twentieth century at the very time when electoral politics in the United States was breaking down into increasingly meaningless electoral choices. This was due in part to certain progressive reforms and in part to the manipulation of public opinion through new developments in advertising and in mass-media communication, so that by the end of the 1920s political experts assumed that "packaged" candidates and campaigns were necessary for the smooth and efficient operation of an American political system inherited from the nineteenth century.[8] Television and more recent "progressive" reforms of the electoral process since the 1970s have simply exacerbated this tendency in modern electoral politics—they did not create it.

And so it goes. Women received equal pay for equal work in the 1960s on the eve of declining productivity rates and permanently high unemployment; enforcement of affirmative action beginning for educational and other traditionally female service occupations in the 1970s occurred when these markets were glutted and fewer hirings were taking place; the constitutional right to abortion (as tenuous as this may now be) was granted *after* effective means and mass distribution of contraception existed; ease of no-fault divorce, so quickly enacted by male-dominated legislatures, has contributed to the impoverishment of female heads of households in the 1980s; agitation in behalf of comparable worth began in the 1980s just as computer technology had begun to make those clerical and service jobs traditionally occupied by women more and more obsolete or "dangerous" to their reproductive systems, in what is being called the dawning "information age";[9] debates about child care and parental leaves began not at the height of the baby-boom births following World War II but now that the average birth rate is half what it was in 1964; and, finally, an ambiguous tripartite definition of obscenity, indicating when sexually explicit material should be considered legally obscene under criminal law, was handed down by the Supreme Court in 1973— the same decade in which violence against women in multimedia pornographic representations increased dramatically. This essential male definition of obscenity is now meaningless for regulating the current flood of sexually violent pornography on the market and for figuring out whether this kind of material harms women in contemporary American society.[10]

Application of my "broken-barometer" theory to the dramatic change in the legal status of women during the past quarter-century indicates that white women have received many of the individual equal rights white men have enjoyed for almost two hundred years, often without adequate consideration or compensation for the institutionalized inequality women continue to experience in marriage and the work force. Moreover, these changes have taken place at the very moment when the material and pop cultural excesses of individuality and relativism of postmodern society are under attack from the right and left; when high-technology industry is replacing many female jobs with computers or using "genetic screening" to argue that women are more susceptible than men to occupational hazards resulting from environmental pollutants; and when violence against women is implicitly legitimized through mass distribution of pornographic print and audiovisual materials.

Whenever the American power structure has relinquished something in the form of legal rights or other improvements for women or minorities (usually after years of struggle on the part of activists), it has been because that "something" was no longer as important or useful to those in power. For example, in the 1950s and 1960s case law and legislative statutes began to grant previously denied individual rights and privileges to disadvantaged groups. Therefore, instead of presuming that each successful step in the struggles for full female citizenship has led the United States in new directions, the opposite may well be true as the nation shifts from an independent national industrial economy to a much more interdependent global information–service economy. Such "advances" for women should probably be viewed as inverse barometric indicators of where society has been and not where it is going. In other words, improvements in the constitutional status of women and minority groups are almost always problematic, in part because improved objective conditions within the public sphere are often confused (or equated) with improved subjective conditions of the private sphere and vice versa.

I am not arguing that history has stood still for American women since the American Revolution or that women have not benefited from improved legal status in the last twenty-five years. It is simply that most women exist in a subjective experiential time frame that has never quite "caught up" with the changing objective conditions they have faced in the last two hundred years. Nonetheless, many female reformers continue to act as though their latest (or next) legislative achievement or court decision will at last make them equal with men. (At the moment, federal child-care and parental-leave legislation and fewer state restrictions on abortion, along with future Supreme Court decisions continuing to support abortion and in favor of comparable worth head most feminists' lists of "must achieve" for equality.) Like the frog in the math problem who keeps jumping half the distance each time to reach an unstated and vague point in time and space, American women will never "catch up" unless they literally leapfrog over their present legal status into a future one—from equality to equity. To do this they must anticipate the underlying socioeconomic changes that belated improvements in their legal status reflect at any given time.

Thus, the rapidly changing legal status of women between 1963 and 1989 constitutes an unfinished revolution because of the ambiguity of certain Supreme Court decisions since 1972 and because of increased hostility toward affirmative action and abortion since the country entered what should have been a typical period of postwar conservatism following the end of the U.S. involvement in the conflict in Indochina. Unfortunately, that conservatism was exacerbated and prolonged by the unprecedented resignation of Richard Nixon in 1974 and the equally untoward "failure" of the presidency of Jimmy Carter, leading to the election of Ronald Reagan accompanied by a resurgence of the radical Right riding high on the tide of impending millennialism. Moreover, this heightened conservatism in the country at large since 1974 has seen the reemergence of an old but basically unresolved cultural conflict and legalistic confusion among women activists over the question of special treatment versus equal treatment on such diverse issues as pregnancy-related benefits, pornography, and comparable worth.

Women can no longer settle for what is being offered as finally their "due" or because of stereotypic views of female "responsibilities," as in the case of child care. Instead, women must ask themselves over and over again whether the latest liberal improvements are actually empowering them as women or simply placating them with the false hope of assimilation with men. They must begin to use the growing body of critical historical and legal studies to see beyond illusory liberal legalism and the ever–self-correcting aspects of capitalism and patriarchy. Otherwise, women still remain the "broken barometers" of U.S. history. This "no-win" situation results from the fact that leaders of both the First and Second Women's movements have almost never been able to project themselves as women, their causes, or vision of change beyond past and present liberal ideas about advances in individual rights based on obtaining equality with men into the future, where emancipation instead of traditional liberation lies—like an ever-receding line on the horizon. (Throughout this book I am using *emancipation* to mean equitable treatment that is not grounded, as equal treatment is, in dominant male values of any time period and that does not violate women's sense of community, commonality, and/or culture by demanding assimilation or acceptance of stereotypic "feminine" roles as the price for full participation in U.S society.)

*mean what?*

## From Patriarchal to Poststructural History

Twenty years ago a synthetic interpretation such as this one about the changing legal status of women could not have been written because too little primary research had been conducted in either the new social history, with its subfield of women, or the new legal history, with its subfield of sex discrimination. The content of both subfields reflected the revitalized scholarly interest in feminist topics due to the Second Women's movement, giving woman's history in the United States an important moral and political relevance to activists inside and outside academe.[11] The methodology of both subfields also reflects interdisciplinary and quantitative techniques developed in this country and abroad since the mid-1960s.

The new social history, which directly challenged traditional patriarchal history by concerning itself with the affairs of ordinary people and private, rather than public, matters, paralleled the new legal history as it turned from describing "aristocratic detail" and appellate case law to assessing the actual impact of law on the average citizen.[12] But initially neither the new social history nor the new legal history showed much concern for women. From the beginning of the new legal history in 1942, J. Willard Hurst instructed classes to "deal with the security and values of individual personality in a world increasingly marked by centralized, large-scale power arrangements. The emphasis [should] be on the small man,—laborer, white-collar worker, farmer, small businessman."[13] Until recently, most of the new legal historians clearly ignored women.[14] The same can be said of exponents of the new social history, especially those who first wrote family history without any gender analysis—implausible as this may seem. For example, early

scholarship in family history most frequently dealt with categories such as "household," "single parents," "children," "adolescents," and "the aged," without recognizing that each of these is fundamentally divided by sex. The result [was] history that either ignore[d] women or [gave] the false impression that female and male experiences with the primary institution of the family were the same.[15]

When the new social history and the new legal history emerged in the late 1960s, they did not use gender to differentiate women as a separate social class. Thus, two subfields—women's history and sex discrimination—were misnamed. Their subjects should be called the history of gender evolution and the history of gender discrimination. Gender is at the heart of all socialized behavior and perceived differences between the sexes, but twenty years ago the word *gender* was vaguely perceived as too radical to be used effectively on campuses establishing women's studies programs or by historians beginning to take a fresh look at the history of one-half of the human race. Hence, both widely used terms— women's history and the history of sex discrimination—are misnomers.

In the early years of the Second Women's movement, the words *woman, women,* and *sex* became common usage in historical and legal writings, while *gender, feminism,* or *feminist* did not because they were considered too confrontational and subversive even within supposedly liberated intellectual circles during the early development of the new social history and the new legal history. Only the most self-conscious feminists insisted on distinguishing between the meanings of *sex* and *gender.* For example, the first edition of a national published list of readings and course outlines in women's history, used largely in the 1970s, did not carry the word *gender* in any of the titles. However, in the 1987 edition, *gender* appeared "as an organizing principle in one out of nine" entries and dominated papers given at the Eighth Berkshire Conference on the History of Women in 1990.[16]

A similar, although by no means identical, semantic evolution has taken place inside the legal profession and law schools. That is why the early law classes, decisions, and casebooks talked about sex discrimination or women and the law, rather than gender discrimination or gender and the law. For the most part, "Women and the Law" classes did not do much more than describe the weak juridical arguments behind most past and present case-law rationalizing and maintaining past legal disabilities of women, with recommendations about how they could now obtain equality with men.[17] These early law-school classes were like so many early women's history classes—primarily remedial and compensatory in nature—designed to prove that women and men experienced historical events similarly and that once women were accorded the same equal socioeconomic and political opportunity as men, society would somehow be transformed. Only recently has the study of gender appeared in a few (very few) law-school curricula. For example, courses on feminist jurisprudence and feminist legal theory or thought are intended to question traditional assumptions about the presumed transformational aspects of advocating equality that encourages women to act like men.

At the very least, these new titles reflect the limitation of a male-equality model for women stressed in the women and the law, or sex-discrimination, classes of the 1970s. In the process of exposing the biased and unneutral aspects of masculine jurisprudence, the terminology and content of feminist jurisprudence classes (and monographs) of the 1980s often projected essentialist theories designed to substitute equally ahistorical and absolutist legal truths for the traditional justice-and-equality theories of the Enlightenment, upon which most law-school education rests. Commonly, this type of feminist jurisprudential essentialism is based on "women-as-mother" or "women-as-victims" theories, which purport to speak for all women without differentiating female experiences. This type of feminist legal essentialism will ultimately flounder (as has masculinist essentialism) in a sea of deconstructionist criticism and radical scholarship. Therefore, the introduction of poststructural gender analysis into legal theory was initially encouraging because it directly challenged the binary extremes of our adversarial system of law, which traditionally "assumes a radical separation between what women want and the [legal] principles upon which they can justify what they want." [18] A similarly encouraging but ultimately problematic move toward poststructural analysis and definitions of the words *gender* and *feminist* has occurred among academic historians.

However, these postmodern developments in law schools and academic circles are not representative of societal trends in general. Compare, for example, a 1970 and 1980 dictionary definition of *feminist*. In 1970, the *American Heritage Dictionary* defined *feminism* as "militant advocacy of equal rights and status for women." In 1980, the definition read: "a doctrine that advocates or demands for women the same rights granted men, as in political or economic status." Even this downgrading of the militancy of the word *feminism* has not made the word more acceptable inside or outside academe among young women or business women. At the beginning of 1988, the Australian editor of *Ms.* magazine announced that "extensive marketing research" had shown that "younger women don't like the word feminism." Consequently, this sixteen-year-old publication of mainstream feminism implied that it would not alienate them by using even the watered-down meaning of this eight-letter *f* word unnecessarily in the future. Fortunately, Robin Morgan, after becoming editor of *Ms.* in 1990, resurrected the term *feminism* to its most radical and meaningful place in that publication. Unfortunately, banks and career-placement and counseling services that had originally used the words *women* or *feminist* in their names a decade earlier began dropping them in the late 1980s in favor of unisex titles, on the grounds that they "do not attract affluent women [and] repelled some men."[19]

Equally disturbing as this linguistic and political downgrading and/or avoidance of the terms *feminist* and *women* in nonacademic circles is the possibility that this may also happen to the word *gender* within academe. Poststructural gender analysis supposedly represents a "methodological and theoretical reformulation" that is changing the organization of knowledge of the humanities and the social sciences, "especially in the areas of symbolic representations and theories of language." But some feminist historians and lawyers, who effectively employ gender as a category of analysis to deconstruct both male and female essentialism, are now focusing so much on the existence of multiple "masculinities" that they are "implicitly denying the existence of patriarchy" and espousing theories about the predominance of differences among women in which "the voice of gender risks being lost entirely." In other words, deconstructionist techniques that focus increasingly on "male sensitivity and male persecution" downplay male privilege and, hence, not only depoliticize gender but also deny that feminism can or should be a coherent philosophy or ideology in the writing of women's history.[20]

## Historical Manifestations of Feminism

Although historians of women have variously defined feminism in their research, Karen Offen has distinguished two basic historical types: equal rights feminism, based on the liberal individualism predominant in England and the United States since the late nineteenth century, and relational feminism, which in France and other Western countries is often called the doctrine of "equality in difference."[21] Most of the historiographic debate in the United States has focused on the first type because by the turn of the century, leaders of the First Women's movement had decided that they wanted the individual political and civil rights enjoyed by white men. By contrast, relational feminism not only accepts the notion of biological differences between women and men but also emphasizes the traditional cultural distinctions between the sexes that presumably are based on these biological differences. Hence, relational feminists oppose a quest for equal rights that would eliminate cultural distinctions. Relational feminism is based on a strong claim for the "moral equality of women and men with an explicit acknowledgement of differences in women's and men's sexual functions in society."[22]

These two groups reenact the historical split between those who advocate the equality or sameness of women and men and those who advocate equity (or fairness) in their treatment.[23] After 1972, feminist efforts to pass the Equal

Rights Amendment blurred this distinction. Through the early 1980s, reformists (including both liberals and socialists) dominated the Second Women's movement in its efforts in behalf of the ERA. Since its defeat, radical feminism has reemerged in the United States and given its attention to arguments for a relational, rather than an equal rights, approach to reform. With the exception of the United States and possibly England, relational feminism is more widespread (and controversial) in the Western world than is equal rights feminism.

Consequently, any comprehensive historical definition of feminism must encompass both types and must come to terms with the various claims and methods of poststructuralist analysis. Such analysis, when carried to a deconstructionist extreme, threatens not only to deny the historical realities represented by these two types of feminism but also to dissolve textually the socially constructed dualities that continue experientially to characterize relations between women and men in the United States. Clearly, the postfeminist claims of the poststructuralists are premature; yet, relational and equal rights feminisms must continue to be studied until we understand how their different concerns have confounded both the First and Second Women's movements over such issues as protective legislation and the Equal Rights Amendment.

In historical and legal literature, this conflict has been variously described as a battle between private female and public male spheres of activities; between radical (sometimes erroneously referred to as cultural) feminists and political (including both reformist and socialist) feminists; between group rights and individual rights; between equality of results and equality of opportunity; between relational or familial feminism and individualistic feminism; and between pluralist or assimilationist concepts of justice. Finally, this division is sometimes referred to as a conflict between "equality in difference" and "equality in sameness." Among certain mainstream feminist attorneys in the 1980s, this debate is still most commonly referred to as the difference between equal treatment and special treatment. In this book I develop a concept of equity based on feminist jurisprudence in order to begin to bridge the gap between these traditional binary oppositions. Whatever terminology has been (or will be) employed to describe the dilemmas these subjective and objective dichotomies have created for women in the past, they have not been satisfactorily resolved or plausibly deconstructed in the present. Until they are, the hope for restructuring American society or public policy based on feminist, rather than masculinist, values remains remote.

From a relational feminist point of view, for instance, those who supported protective legislation in the early twentieth century may resemble those contemporary feminists who advocate a group approach to improving the socioeconomic conditions of working women. Another segment of the female population since the Progressive Era that has appeared to espouse relational feminism can be found among certain antiratificationalists in the battle over the Equal Rights Amendment.[24] Despite the cooptation of relational feminists by governments in Nazi Germany, in the USSR, in China, and by the Christian Right in the United States today, the broad appeal of relational views to U.S. women cannot be ignored. Unfortunately, NOW and other pro-ERA groups learned this historical lesson too late. Only political theory and action based on the best characteristics of both equal rights and relational feminisms will allow the Second Women's movement to move into the twenty-first century with viable feminist public policies.

Women must be studied and represented in both litigation and legislation as a socially constructed gender—neither hopelessly particularized nor completely essentialized. To conclude, as Nancy Hewitt has, that "diversity, discontinuity, and conflict were as much a part of the historical agency of women as of men" is to ignore the degree to which women experience the same events and time periods differently than men.[25] More importantly, to stress diversity for diversity's sake hinders rather than helps in the contemporary formulation of public policy aimed at ameliorating the harmful gender-constricting aspects affecting women's public and private activities in contemporary society, by implicitly precluding effective political activism.

To deny women a collective historical identity with theoretical attempts to deconstruct all socially constructed dualities is to dissipate any analysis of the impact that various forms of patriarchy have had on women in the United States. Moreover, with its obsession for eliminating binary oppositions, deconstruction can lead historians away from recounting the historical and contemporary circumstances of women's collective identity and oppression. Male domination of women in the United States is not merely a discourse. Yet contemporary critics of political sisterhood often suggest that writing or speaking collectively against the common sufferings of women is theoretically naive or culturally insensitive. However, if historians follow deconstructionists in disregarding the material conditions that permeate society and in shattering the categorical differences in the moral development of women and men, then they will find it difficult to write histories of the legal, political, and material manifestations of a gendered social reality.

My legal and historical interpretations, therefore, are based on the currently contested assumption that *women are women.* For purposes of this book, their biological, legal, and socioeconomic commonality as women is more important for understanding their common treatment under law and the masculinity of U.S. constitutionalism than any of the many differences among them. I nonetheless believe that deconstructionist methodology can be used profitably to view the Constitution and other legal documents as symbolic texts of patriarchy. This does not mean, however, that, having researched their way from patriarchal to post-structuralist history, modern feminist historians should now weaken their focus on women or forget the political potential of historical works to shape feminist public policy in the future.

The following tripartite definition of feminism is meant to apply across time periods. In other words, using a "timeless" standard for evaluating female activity in the ageless struggle toward emancipation, my definition begins with the recognition that while all feminists are for equal rights women advocating *only* equal rights with men are, at most, partial feminists. Equal rights for women in the United States simply means obtaining those rights men already have when they are no longer as highly valued or important to the legal, political, and economic power elites. This equality based on presumed sameness is, after all, what suffrage, equal pay, and the ERA were all about. Calling women from the past or the present feminists is not justified if their only—or primary—activity was or is to obtain equality for women based on male legal standards. Obviously, such activity is an example of *raised* consciousness among women, but it is not necessarily an indication of *changed* or anticipatory consciousness on the part of those women who struggle for equal rights.

I also believe that women can obtain levels of liberation *but not true emancipation* unless they perceive of themselves as agents for societal change in other than patriarchal, individualistic terms. This means that to be a feminist in the United States, contemporary women must not simply use traditionally liberal means to achieve public reform and personal success. While I agree with Offen that feminists must recognize or be aware of the "institutionalized injustice (or inequity) toward women as a group by men as a group in a given society," I would add that to be personally and politically meaningful the struggle for equal rights requires a *changed,* not simply a *raised,* consciousness. Janice Raymond calls this the *"essential tension* of feminism"—namely, a "nearsighted," materialistic view of "the conditions of female expression" and a "farsighted" idealistic vision of the future.[26]

This second component, or "test," for feminism is that its practitioners demonstrate an awareness of what constitutes antipatriarchal behavior in whatever time period they happen to have lived. They should have a sense of women being a separate, independent sex with a distinctly different, although no less socialized, worldview than the men around them. Or, as Offen has put it: they must "recognize the validity of women's own interpretations of their lived experiences and needs and acknowledge the values women claim publicly as their own (as distinct from an aesthetic ideal of womanhood invented by men) in assessing their status in society relative to that of men."[27] The limitations placed on women by patriarchal structures in any time period can only be perceived by feminists who are consciously female in thought and action and not simply men in disguise. Such assertive "femaleness" has become more important to my definition of feminism since I developed the "broken-barometer" theory of U.S. women's history, because it must become a part of women's worldview if they are to transcend not only standard historical periodization but also liberal illusions about accepting "legal rights" as representing linear progress. Often such rights may simply be liberating traps based on socialized gender concepts of "other" disguised as "self." Conscious antipatriarchal female behavior is, therefore, essential for women to overcome the normal time-lag from which so many of their legal tactics and political strategies have suffered.

The third and final component of my definition of feminism focuses on the active and collective cultivation and preservation of female culture. In other words, the "complete feminist" of the past and present is not only a person who fought or fights for equal rights while perceiving women as being socialized by, and yet outside, patriarchy but also a person who works to produce and/or preserve female culture in the hope of someday defining the "self" of women in female, not male, terms. If one is fortunate enough to be feminist artist or writer, it is relatively easy to fulfill this last requirement. However, it is also possible to preserve female culture outside the world of art and literature. In one sense, women can all become preservers of female culture by simply keeping diaries, writing letters, or saving relevant documentation about themselves and encouraging others to do likewise. The importance of this component of my definition is that it forces women to recognize that if their socialized female sensibilities are keeping them on the periphery of mainstream society, perhaps that mainstream is not worth emulating. It is a constant reminder not to forget or abandon their female "roots" in order that they may radically alter, not simply reform, society.

## Full Citizenship and Reperiodization of Constitutional History

In addition to documenting my "broken-barometer" theory of women's legal history, this book also places various historiographical and juridical questions into perspective by discussing the changing legal status of women in the United States for a little over two hundred years—from the American Revolution to 1990—in terms of several underlying themes. I begin with a general discussion of the inherently conservative limitations of historical and liberal legalism with respect to analyzing and advocating women's rights and feminism. I then proceed to (1) reperiodize U.S. constitutional history from the standpoint of women's own understanding of their legal status, relating these periods to major socioeconomic changes in the country's political economy; (2) criticize the categorical nature of the debate over whether women should have separate or the same rights as men, or a combination of both; and (3) review the antiquated nature of the historical and legal debate over the equal and special treatment of women. Finally, I reinterpret the latest civil rights gains for women in the context not only of equality *and* equity but also in poststructural terms of *going beyond* the binary politics of assimilation and pluralism.

Major subthemes of this book analyze the legal relationship between public and private spheres of activity. In particular, I focus on the ways in which male politicians and lawyers of the last two hundred years have imposed dominance upon, and expected deference from, women by translating objective social conditions of their private domestic sphere into subjective legal constructs—fooling themselves some of the time but fooling the vast majority of women almost always. When such legal constructs mask continued liberal and patriarchal domination in the form of "false protection" or "false equality,"[28] they should not be confused with either eliminating or creating new private/public relationships. For example, as women in the United States and abroad moved from private to public sphere activity in the late nineteenth and early twentieth centuries, they followed the "model of the mother"—that is, "a woman teacher or nurse was seen primarily as mother, and female professions exploited the image of feminine devotion and sacrifice." Such an extension of motherhood rationalizations to certain professions, social-welfare activities, and suffrage, especially during the Progressive Era in the United States, created exaggerated expectations and ultimate disappointment or confusion when the changes finally achieved proved superficial, "bringing about no revolution, either in legislation or practice."[29]

More often than not, the law and its accompanying legal texts both contributed to the insidious opposition between public and private spheres and then exploited the multiple variations of female/male stereotypes upon which the separate-spheres concept was based to perpetuate the legal status quo of public and private activities in different historical time periods. *"The master's tools,"* as Audre Lorde has so cogently remarked, *"will never dismantle the master's house."*[30] This is not to say that the judicial system created the inequality between female and male spheres; but to the degree it continues to condone such inequality with gendered case law, it reveals serious limitations for reforming itself, let alone reconstructing society. As the capstone of the American legal structure, the U.S. Supreme Court remains what it has always been—a politically conservative institution that must be endlessly cajoled into granting full citizenship rights to those groups long denied them.

Changing female perceptions about the actual, as opposed to theoretical, equality of the private sphere (usually in the form of various ideas about citizenship) and men's reluctance to grant their own equal status within the public sphere to women over the past two hundred years cries out for radical feminist legal analysis of the improvements in women's legal status over the last twenty years. Therefore, in the last chapters I discuss the dangers involved for both women and minorities to be suddenly declared "factually" equal by the very people who previously construed the subordination of such disadvantaged groups. Instant proclamations of legal equality do not eliminate inequality nor immediately result in interpretations by the courts or statutes in ways that ameliorate lingering inequalities.[31] Consequently, another subtheme of this book addresses the various meanings of female citizenship over the last two hundred years. I will demonstrate that it was only in those brief time periods when women have demanded that citizenship rights *include* rather than *exclude* the private sphere that they have come close to escaping their "broken-barometer" legal status.

Since "citizenship is a form of power," the liberal premise that government should be based on the consent of the governed citizens has been particularly problematic for women and African-Americans for a number of reasons. First, neither group chose or consented to be second-class citizens before or after the American Revolution. Both were accorded that inferior legal status without consultation. Second, the legal definition of "consensual freedom" for women and racial minorities has always been different and accorded less legal status or social esteem than for white men. When certain white women and black reformers tried to become full citizens following the Civil War, they were rebuffed by the courts in proof that U.S. citizenship continued to reflect two related power concepts—namely, the contradiction between the theoretical rights of national citizens of the United States and the actual freedom to exercise those rights at the state level by traditionally disadvantaged groups of citizens.[32] Citizenship status in the name of womanhood, that is, the political significance of the private sphere, was central to the First Women's movement before the Civil War. It was less so in post–Civil War court cases arguing for women's constitutional and professional rights, except to the degree that such suits questioned female "consent" to certain legal procedures carried over from the colonial and early national periods. Unfortunately, full rights of citizenship for women as women were not a major theoretical concern of progressive female activists at the turn of the century. They simply assumed it would somehow result from suffrage.

Full citizenship rights became an active concern of the early supporters of the ERA in the 1920s, but by then it had become a method for obtaining male status by individual women, not equal respect or esteem for womanhood. It again became an important issue for those early feminists of the Second Women's movement who cut their teeth on the "participatory-democracy" rhetoric of the civil rights and antiwar movements of the 1960s and 1970s. The rhetoric of "participatory democracy" temporarily challenged the presumed "consent" of the governed to racism, militarism, and sexism. Subsequently, in the 1970s some American socialists coopted the concept of "participatory democracy"; combined it with Foucauldian theories about the dispersement of power; and transformed it into notions about radical political pluralism that usually lacked a sexual, woman-focused component. At the same time, however, the "consensuality" of sexual acts among adults increasingly became a major concern of radical feminists. Yet many feminists, ranging from moderates to Marxists, continued to insist that "pornography and other sexual diversions . . . do not affect most women's lives," or that "the pervasive discourse on sexuality . . . confuses our understanding of the deeper changes that are occurring and the most serious challenges we face." [33]

Most mainstream feminists of the 1980s have not, for example, explored the multiple contradictions of citizenship, individualism, equal rights, sexuality, consent of the governed, and pluralism in their pursuit of what I call "one-size-fits-all" equality, or "unisex" parity with men. Some radical feminists, such as Andrea Dworkin and Carole Pateman, have begun to question whether women can ever obtain (or should want) full citizenship because of the masculinist and misogynist notions upon which it originated and has manifested itself under all patriarchal forms of the state over time. Still others, such as Robin West and Catharine MacKinnon, have repeatedly examined the subtle silencing of women that occurs in myriad legal ways because the "engendered nature of law privileges men." [34] Unfortunately, the ideas and influence of radical feminists remain on the periphery of the Second Women's movement as it prepares to enter its third decade.

Since changes in the legal status of women over the last two hundred years seldom fit the standard periods and categories of analysis found in most constitutional textbooks, this book includes a discussion of the common-law and equity procedures affecting women during and immediately following the American Revolution. It also divides female constitutional experiences into five basic periods: ranging from constitutional neglect (1787–1872) and constitutional discrimination (1872–1908) to constitutional protection (1908–63) and constitutional equality (1963–87). The fifth period, which will last at least through the end of this century, may determine whether women can break the bonds of liberal legalism and go beyond the traditional notions of equality to more equitable treatment under the law. [35]

In summary, this study of women's legal history argues that women have obtained rights in the United States on a too-little-too-late basis. A truly visionary radical feminist history and radical feminist jurisprudence would anticipate the future needs of women as women, not as men. Women's legal history must be able to overcome and transcend *both* the paralysis often produced by poststructural theories about difference and the false hopes generated by the repressive tolerance of equality based on male assimilationist or pluralist standards. Instead, feminist scholars and activists interested in emancipating rather than simply liberating women must abandon liberal legalism and, on some issues affecting women, abandon legal remedies altogether, in the realization that on the outer fringes of societal change the law—with its propensity to uphold simplistic, categorical arguments—remains more a bulwark for, than a battering ram against, the remnants of late twentieth-century patriarchy in the United States.

# CHAPTER ONE

# The Masculinity of U.S. Constitutionalism

During the bicentenary of the U.S. Constitution in 1987, an orgy of praise and pomp and circumstance celebrating "We the People" exploded under the watchful guidance of retired chief justice Warren Burger. Only a few isolated voices like that of former Texas congresswoman Barbara Jordan could be heard saying, "as grand as it sounds, it is not true." Amid uncritical praise for the wisdom of the framers and their concept of equality, Justice Thurgood Marshall, in a bicentennial address on 6 May 1987, courageously pointed out that the government created by the U.S. Constitution "was defective from the start, requiring several amendments, a civil war, and momentous social transformation to attain the system of constitutional government, and its respect for individual freedoms and human rights, we hold fundamental today."[1]

To the degree that constitutional government has evolved to compensate for the Constitution's original defects of exclusivity and inequality, the legal status of women also changed in the last two hundred years. Progress has been erratic and slow, in part because "We the People" did not include women or a majority of other Americans. These words from the preamble to the Constitution have no legally binding effect, yet the myth about their original inclusiveness persists. Contrary to conventional historical and legal wisdom, therefore, I do not think that major improvements in women's legal status have occurred often, or always, in a progressively linear fashion. Instead, since the American Revolution the history of women is replete with examples of them obtaining too little, too late through the legal and legislative systems. This is why it is still necessary to reexamine the topic of women *and* the Constitution because women are still not *in* that hallowed document except for the 1920 suffrage amendment.

American women's history and American legal history continue to be dominated by the broadest kind of political and theoretical liberalism reflecting binary views of reality. The most familiar dualisms include traditional Lockean power relationships: between public and private spheres; between the authority of the state and individual freedom; and between individual equality and group rights. Legal scholars have documented several trends in this basically liberal process from postrevolutionary judicial instrumentalism, to judicial formalism, to legal progressivism, to pragmatic instrumentalism and realism,[2] and now to the Critical Legal Studies movement (CLS),[3] which has influenced most, but not all, of the contemporary radical feminist legal scholars attempting to go beyond the assumptions of all these previous schools of liberal legal interpretation.[4]

Even those liberal legal historians whose works include more than passing reference to, and concern for, women often reflect a basic conservatism from a feminist point of view because liberal legalism, according to Judith Shklar, has always embodied a

> dislike of vague generalities, the preference for case by case treatment to all social issues, the structuring of all possible human relations into the form of claims and counterclaims under established rules and belief that rules are there. . . . As law serves ideally to promote the security of established expectations, so legalism with its concentration on specific cases and rules is, essentially conservative. . . . [it] is no mask for anything. It is an openly, intrinsically, and quite specifically conservative view because law is itself a conservatizing idea. In its epitome, the judicial ethos, it becomes clear that this is the conservatism of consensus. It relies on what appears already to have been established and accepted. . . . For the judiciary to remain uncontroversial is the mark of neutral impartiality. Adjustment is therefore its natural policy, whenever possible.[5]

If legal discourse is a rationale for patriarchy, then the very texts of the law cannot help but reflect that same male-dominated reality. The "very structure of the assumptions underpinning liberalism," according to Isabel Marcus, "is a manifestation of a gendered social construction of reality." This simple assertion is essential for understanding why liberal historicity and liberal legalism have until recently ignored the experiences of women or assumed they were identical with those of men. Consequently, until the emergence of the new legal history and the new social history movements of the 1960s, the "view of the law [and history] as highly political [and gendered] in itself" was uncommon, as critical legal studies advocates have noted. This helps explain why legal procedures and legal documents have so easily been utilized to deny women (and minorities) full rights of citizenship during most of U.S. history by simply declaring that the issues raised in their charges of discrimination are not cognizable or within the jurisdiction of the law.[6] For example, the eighteenth- and nineteenth-century courts routinely denied married women ownership and contractual, dispositional, professional, and civil rights with lengthy discourses about their lack of legal personality or legal existence separate from that of their husbands.

Such legal texts do not simply exist to communicate the order of power relationships in society. Additionally, they turn patriarchy and liberal legalism normative into immutable "myths" or functional "givens." Hence, such documents have been (and remain) problematic symbols for both women and minorities. Like all other patriarchal legal texts, the Constitution possesses potential for both oppressing *and* liberating all those disadvantaged persons and segments of society who were not represented at (or in) its creation. This is also a basic feature of most liberal legal texts: they engender "contradictory feelings of [both] oppression and liberation" in disadvantaged groups, such as women, because they assist in the construction of legal discourses that define the parameters of both sides of the argument, thus permitting discussion but not questioning of the basic premises of liberal legalism. Along with other patriarchal legal texts over the last two hundred years, the Constitution has been not only legitimized in the minds of an increasing number of Americans but also has been mystified, especially for those groups for whom it has not always been a benevolent juridical authority. This reifying process has taken place largely through the creation of a maze of "legalistic mechanisms of authoritative texts" that serve to enforce the socioeconomic and political hierarchy of any particular time period.[7] Thus, legal documents and legal discourse become self-fulfilling in that they legitimate and mystify themselves along with the powers of the state.

Because most individual men remain more societally sovereign than most individual women, this line of feminist legal argument asserts that male freedoms under various liberal forms of patriarchy were first primarily dependent upon the socioeconomic inequality (dominance) of women and that they now continue to be dependent upon the sexual and psychological inequality of women. Only "feminists take women's humanity seriously," according to Robin West, "jurisprudence does not, because the law does not." Such an assertion leads to the conclusion that women's freedom (and the creation of a feminist jurisprudence) can only come at the expense of the two sovereigns women have served for so long, that is, various hegemonic (and still masculinist) forms of state power and widely dispersed individual male power.[8]

In this sense, the Constitution is not only the legal text of patriarchy but also has increasingly become the legal text of prevailing sexual mores because so many of the most controversial interpretative constitutional issues today involving women's legal status are related to sexuality. Here I refer to such issues as evidence admissible in rape cases, pornography, prostitution, abortion, surrogate motherhood, and pregnancy disability. Even when Congress began a much-belated discussion of child care in the last half of the 1980s, the statutory debate turned into a "working women's" issue, premised largely on unstated assumptions about the primacy of female responsibility for all offspring produced by human sexual activity.

The process of mystifying the Constitution and making it the guardian of sexuality, promoted by the existence of complex juridical procedures and promises of the good life, has led women and minorities to have contradictory and ambivalent feelings about it and other legal texts. The "price" such groups have had to pay for past and present inclusion in these texts has been an assimilationist brand of equality based on white, male standards—whether they be those of the Founding Fathers or those of contemporary white males. The questions raised by the last twenty years of successfully pursuing "unisex" parity with men, based on "one-size" sameness or assimilation, has led radical feminists to unravel the way in which other gendered legal and political texts have contributed to the Constitution's mystification and subtle role in "legitimizing" the socioeconomic and political system. The result has been a linguistic and metaphorical level of analysis that redefines legal and political terms from a female, rather than male, point of view.

Many other feminist authors,[9] for example, have already detailed the androcentric, misogynistic, and heterosexual qualities of liberalism present in the political theories of John Locke and Jean-Jacques Rousseau. I will build upon, but not reiterate, them here except to note that I agree with Carole Pateman that when Locke offered the social contract as a substitute for the classic patriarchal theories of Sir Robert Filmer, he did not intend or expect contractualism to benefit women. Instead, in denying Filmer's assertion that male procreative power was the origin of political power, Locke did not refute masculinist notions about political rights. Instead, he separated paternal power from political power, relegating the former to a status outside the boundaries of civil society and politics.

In other words, the liberal Lockean civil state reflected traditional sexual divisions of society more subtly and insidiously than had been the case with conservative patriarchalists of the seventeenth century. Moreover, both were "fraternal" systems based on the sexist assumption that only male children would mature into independent adults capable of exercising individual political power in the public sphere. Despite "the emancipatory potential of contract doctrine," it contained a basic gendered contradiction—namely, that all men but not all women were born equal, and, hence, only men were capable of giving their consent to be governed. Mary Astell, Mary Wollstonecraft, Harriet Martineau, and other isolated feminist critics of the seventeenth and eighteenth centuries pointed out the speciousness of this assumption, but their voices were drowned out by a chorus of fraternal contractualism that continues in subtly disguised ways to echo in academic and political settings across this country. Thus, Locke (and most liberal contractualists since him) simply ignored the private conjugal contract that accepted the subordination of women as "natural" and "nonpolitical."[10]

It has taken two hundred years for women in the United States to overcome their unequal public political status under Lockean contract theory. They still have not overcome their private subordination under liberal contractualism. To the degree that male freedoms under modern liberalism remain dependent upon the sexual and psychological inequality of women, and as long as the basic freedom of speech is still primarily a male monopoly, women will not experience full equality or parity under the law. Unless such remaining conservative and sexist constraints from past and present liberal legalism are recognized and changed, it will be impossible to transcend either the male language or male standards by which progress in the historical and legal status of women continues to be judged. While many of the lingering legal restrictions on women have been exposed and remedied in the last twenty-five years, many remain to be amelio- rated. Progress should not be confused with cooptation.

Women are discovering that a "raised" consciousness about *equal* treatment and liberation is quite different from having a "changed" consciousness about *equitable* treatment and emancipation when it comes not only to analyzing court decisions but also to understanding women's perceptions of themselves and their needs in any particular time period. Such terms as *equality, progress, liberation, equity, justice, happiness,* and *emancipation* have yet to be redefined by women for women, based on their actual, as opposed to prescribed, constitutional and histor- ical experiences. In essence, therefore, women can only be emancipated when they are finally accorded equity—justice—not simply equality under the law, although equality is a precondition for equitable justice.[11]

Needless to say, traditional historical studies based on liberal legalism do not usually make these essential semantic distinctions. Several acclaimed histories of constitutionalism published in connection with the bicentennial, for example, contain few references to women in their indexes, let alone their texts, confirm- ing the continued marginality of half of the U.S. population in the minds of major scholars in this field.[12] Little wonder that there have been increasing incidents of conflict and disagreements between radical legal feminists and civil libertarians in the 1980s. Many of these differences are, like the issue of pornography, *related to sexuality,* such as prostitution, battery, abortion, surrogate motherhood, sexual harassment, and evidence admissible in rape trials. This should not come as a surprise because civil libertarians and socialist feminists obdurately refuse to admit that these sexual issues are "central to women's survival," continuing to insist that feminism is simply "a traditional civil liberties quest for constitutional and legislative equality." Thus, they argue that since the middle of the nine- teenth century, the term *women's rights* has simply meant "the equality of women with men," often ignoring issues of sexuality altogether.[13]

Equating women's rights and civil rights symbolizes the degree to which the liberal state has utilized the law to institutionalize male power relationships without considering alternatives based on female concepts of justice and morality that could lead to a feminist jurisprudence.[14] While feminism in the United States has historically overlapped on occasion with the goals of liberal legalism, its most radical and comprehensive forms since 1848 have always gone beyond the male model of civil libertarianism in its quest to transform society's attitudes and treatment of women. And this is why in the twentieth century, more and more of these transformational issues dividing mainstream liberal/socialist and radical feminists focus on sexuality—an issue which in its many complex manifestations does not lend itself to standard case-law solutions based on fixed binary oppositions, mainstream politics, or socioeconomic class analysis.

In particular, radical feminist lawyers are reevaluating the rapidly changing legal status of women between 1963 and 1990. Most of these improvements were based on traditional views of progress, which stress women's obtaining the same rights as men. Instead, radical feminists are positing female, rather than male, standards for progress and justice. Ideas about relational, nonadversarial concepts of morality and equitable justice, rather than strict adherence to rule of law in the name of masculine notions about legal neutrality and objectivity, constitute some of the nontraditional legal views that stand the very essence of liberal legalism on its head. Consequently, the ERA, which is based on traditional equality with men, may not remain the epitome of legal stature for women in the last years of the twentieth century that it was for many between 1923 and 1982, since it was first introduced as an amendment to the Constitution and finally failed to achieve ratification at the state level. To better understand the potential importance of such a shift in emphasis from equality to equity and from individualism to interconnectedness, I have posed the following legal and historical questions and suggested answers here and in subsequent chapters.

## Why Are Some More Equal Than Others?

The subject of equality often brings to mind George Orwell's *Animal Farm,* in which all the animals were declared to be equal but some, notably the pigs, were more equal than all the others. And, indeed, this fictionalized and cynical version of equality is not that far from reality when one takes a hard look at the *application* of equality—as opposed to the *theories* about equality—in most contemporary industrialized nations, regardless of their political economies. The reason that the reality of equality usually differs so markedly from its theoretical constructs in any historical period stems from the fact that, at best, equality remains an elusive concept despite all that has been written about it.

The basic problem with equality is that, unlike liberty, it *is* a divisible concept. The origins of this divisibility and, hence, elusiveness vary from country to country; but in the United States, at least, unequal status among individuals and groups goes back to the colonial period when the majority of whites enjoyed liberty without equality or power. Following the American Revolution, and continuing throughout the nineteenth and into the early twentieth centuries, more and more white males were accorded equality and some access to power far outstripping that of white women. At the same time African-Americans, other racial minority groups, and many immigrant or ethnic groups were just beginning to experience liberty without being accorded equality or power. Gradually, however, in the course of the twentieth century many individual members of these groups were granted limited equality, but this usually did not result, especially in the case of women and African-Americans, in their exercise of any meaningful individual (or collective) political or economic power until the last quarter of the twentieth century.

It has always been possible in the United States, therefore, to have liberty without having either equality or power. It is even possible to enjoy liberty and certain types of equality without having power. What this means is that freedom and liberty have traditionally been considered indivisible—at least for white women and men—but the concept of equality has always been divisible. The primary beneficiaries of this inequitable distribution of equality have been white males. The most commonly cited liberal justification for this divisibility is rooted in Lockean respect for individual diversity and equal opportunity for each individual under the law. Thus, "equality is one of the foundation values of America." But both Barbara Jordan and Eleanor Holmes Norton have noted that it is "a tough word" because it "has been defined and redefined almost exclusively by the Supreme Court." Consequently, even though there are at least four types of recognizable equality today in the United States, the Supreme Court has had a "disproportionate influence" on ranking and legitimizing some forms of equality but not others.[15]

First, there is *equality of rights*, which is the idea that each citizen is entitled to equal protection before the law. Contrary to conventional wisdom, however, the equal-protection doctrine does not offer any broad guarantee of equality except to people who are "similarly situated." Thus, equality of rights can keep women and minorities in subordinate positions because they are "different."[16] The second type of equality is *equality of opportunity,* and it is most often discussed today in terms of access to educational and economic opportunities. This type of equality is usually associated with affirmative action, for which there were at the end of the 1980s five distinct models. The purpose of affirmative action is to offset the inequality generated through the equal-protection doctrine by providing temporary, remedial legal mechanisms for eliminating the discriminatory preferences under the law that have for two hundred years facilitated the rise of white males to positions of power, wealth, and privilege in the United States.[17]

3　　Third, there is *equality of esteem,* which usually comes about through the application of unwritten, informal, and often moral concepts about membership or belonging in society, rather than strictly legal aspects of citizenship. Obviously, equality of esteem, or equal respect as it is sometimes called, "depends ultimately on how citizens treat one another" and is still beyond the grasp of most women and minorities in this country. The most controversial, and putatively most

4　　radical, type of equality is referred to as *equality of results.*[18] American women and minorities are also very far from achieving this type of equality. The goal of equality of results is to provide the maximum benefits for the greatest number. This concept of equality is diametrically opposed to all types of equality that are based primarily on recognizing the rights of individuals rather than those of groups. Therefore, equality of results stands in stark relief to equality of opportunity because the latter is posited on the liberal belief that unfettered individualism leads to "natural" inequalities among people and accounts for the unequal distribution of goods and services in this and other Western countries.

As a legal text of eighteenth-century patriarchy, the Constitution originally provided very few specific protections for either individual or group rights. The Bill of Rights partially compensated for the Constitution's lack of individual rights, as have other amendments to the Constitution accompanied by copious court decisions and legal interpretations. In addition, the Supreme Court has protected the individual against government infringement through a growing list of civil liberties. These are fundamental values not explicitly designated in the Constitution or Bill of Rights. Many personal rights, some referred to collectively as the "right of privacy," for example, constitute unwritten civil liberties that exist, nonetheless, as the result of judicial interpretation. These civil liberties are often called "basic liberties" or "fundamental freedoms." The best known of these unwritten civil liberties now include voting, interstate travel, reproductive freedom, and privacy. It has taken the Supreme Court two hundred years of reviewing cases involving state or federal statutes restricting or permitting certain public and private activities to evolve the existing set of basic liberties.

Since the Civil War, generally speaking, the Court has responded in one of two ways when deciding questions involving the constitutional jurisprudence of rights: with "judicial activism," (the presumption of unconstitutionality), meaning the justices have intervened through the use of constitutional adjudication to strike down such legislation; or with "judicial deference," or "judicial self-restraint" (the presumption of constitutionality), by bowing to the majority will of Congress or state legislatures. The terms *activism* and *deference*, or *self-restraint,* have little to do with prevailing conservative or liberal standards in political terms because there are numerous examples of conservative judicial "activism" and liberal "self-restraint" on the part of individual justices. From the Civil War until the New Deal, "conservative" judicial intervention tended to prevail on such issues as property rights and states' rights. Then the Great Depression forced the Court to change its interpretation of both the due-process clauses of the Fifth and Fourteenth amendments, as well as the commerce clause, in favor of expanding federal power to regulate rather than protect interstate commerce. The result was "liberal" self-restraint, or deference, toward the flood of depression legislation from Congress and the states that accompanied the creation of the U.S. social-service system.[19]

Increasingly, after World War II the Supreme Court turned from passively defending increased federal power and began to use constitutional adjudication to expand "individual human liberty, dignity, and equality." For the first time liberal or progressive justices became judicial activists in the name of eliminating "invidious" distinctions or classifications affecting access to certain fundamental rights associated with civil and religious freedom of expression and personal equality.[20] By the end of the 1980s, the constitutional jurisprudence seemed to be moving in the direction of "conservative" judicial activism on such issues as affirmative action, abortion, prayer in schools, and regulation of the life style of pregnant women, while more liberal justices were trying to hold on to the human rights revolution of the last three decades by relying on *stare decisis*—that is, on case-law precedent from former decisions—to prevent any backsliding on affirmative action, in general, and on these other specific issues, in particular.

Before the 1950s, for example, Congress, as well as the Supreme Court, deferred to state legislatures in matters involving racial and sex discrimination. While the Fourteenth Amendment says that states cannot "deny to any person within its jurisdiction the equal protection of the laws," it does not mean that states cannot discriminate among categories of individuals. Technically, there has to be a reasonable connection (or "minimum rationality") between a blanket classification and the public policy or purpose for which any law has been enacted. In most instances, the burden of proof rests with the person who charges that any particular classification discriminates unfairly among different groups of people. Blue-eyed people cannot be prevented from driving cars, but people with poor eyesight can be required to wear glasses when driving because the latter is considered a reasonable classification, while the former is not.

To restrict those activities, however, designated as fundamental freedoms, the state must show some "compelling public purpose" why it is differentiating among classes of individuals with respect to these basic problems. Such state legislation is subjected to "strict scrutiny" by the courts. Therefore, in these instances it is not enough for a state to argue that its discriminatory classification is reasonable. In other words, there is no presumption of constitutionality. Not only certain rights but also certain groups have been accorded the constitutional protection through strict scrutiny by being designated as "suspect" classes. The initial groupings were based on race, religion, and national origin. Sex would seem to be similarly deserving of "suspect" categorization, since women belong to a "class victimized by arbitrary prejudice" because they can almost always be distinguished by physical characteristics and often by their socioeconomic and cultural conditioning as well.[21] Obviously, other groups also come to mind: migrant workers, children, older people, indigents, and homosexuals. To date, however, the Supreme Court has not accorded any other groups "suspect classification," which would automatically make all state laws discriminating against them subject to active review—that is, strict scrutiny.

Since equality of results is based on improving the collective status of people as groups, rather than individual by individual, it is not based on the traditional Lockean acceptance of the inequalities inherent in the practice of equality of opportunity. Consequently, equality of results, in particular, and affirmative action, in general, pose several interesting and difficult dilemmas for liberal legalism and democracy. Those liberals who ostensibly defend equality of results, such as John Rawls, Isaiah Berlin, and Ronald Dworkin, argue "that only those inequalities are justified which are to the greatest benefit of the least advantaged." While their use of the terms *common good* or *distributive justice* appears to be a collectivist—not an individualistic—approach to the question of equality, it is not. Their language is also misleading because it masks continuing support for the premises of white, male individualism, which makes it difficult for them to discuss the constitutionality of class-action suits under affirmative-action programs for minorities or women.[22] Therefore, the need to find "particularized violation(s) of law. . . . based on specific acts of deliberate discrimination by the immediate parties to the lawsuit" often limits or embarrasses the arguments not only of liberal constitutional theorists but also of Supreme Court justices in behalf of affirmative action.[23]

Consequently, the constitutional jurisprudence of rights in the United States remains based on individual, not group or community concepts about equality of opportunity. Since affirmative action and equality of results are about collectivist rights that would expand and not simply maintain the current exclusivity of citizenship rights, even the most liberal lawyers and judges are hard put to find within their masculinist and individualistic vocabulary words to turn equality of opportunity into equality of results by making it more inclusive. As a result, affirmative action in the United States has been juridically based on viewing first blacks (and other minorities) as "basically the same as whites" and then women as "basically the same as men." This comparative approach is designed to ensure that affirmative action is a transitional remedy for dislodging discrimination based on the assumption that someday the need for it will disappear. "By definition then, affirmative action is a temporary, remedial effort, designed to hasten equals to their rightful place," according to feminist attorney Wendy W. Williams. "It becomes obsolete (and legally and morally unjustifiable) when the discrimination-engendered displacement of the group at which it is aimed has been eliminated."[24]

Theoretically, therefore, this current comparative basis of affirmative action is not designed to deal with permanent racial or gender differences (whether biological or socially conditioned). As noted in chapter 10, this comparison-based definition of affirmative action cannot resolve the contemporary debate within the Second Women's movement over how to adjudicate cases involving a variety of noncomparative physical and psychological differences among women and men. And yet the hard fact remains that the constitutionality of affirmative action has primarily been upheld in using comparative analogies, and even this moderate approach remains a matter of concern and controversy in the Supreme Court.

Given their Lockean origins, the Constitution, the Bill of Rights, many other constitutional amendments, and most Supreme Court decisions before the 1950s did not support the idea of equality of results or affirmative action (even when disguised in liberal legalese) because these legal texts were at best designed to extend equal protection to unequal individuals. Moreover, since traditional adversarial lawsuits constitute zero-sum games in which litigants win or lose, court actions do not generally seek cooperative or collectivist solutions to legal problems. Prior to the last twenty years the Supreme Court did not condone differential or special-group treatment except, as one 1938 decision stated, "to protect [a] discrete and insular minority."[25] The basic liberal assumption at the beginning of this century has been that only special categories of people requiring protection, such as native American Indians and working-class women, collectively qualified for group status—separate and usually inferior—to that of individuals meeting the standards of mainstream male life in America. Despite overwhelming evidence to the contrary, constitutional jurisprudence continues to rest primarily on the Lockean-inspired legal fiction that all citizens have equal access to equal opportunity.

## Can There Be Equality among Unequals?

White males have understandably and quite rightly argued that divisibility of equality is imbedded in the federal Constitution of 1787 (which they drafted), and other amendments to the Constitution. All these documents have since been interpreted to embody respect for individual diversity and equal opportunity for every individual under the law. In other words, the Constitution, with its slowly expanding list of amendments and accompanying Supreme Court and lower-court decisions, generally supports the notion of extending uniform equal protection under the law *to all Americans as individuals—not as members of racial, ethnic, religious, or gender groupings—regardless of how unequal those individuals may be.* This is what is meant by such phrases as the Constitution of the United States is "neutral as to persons"; or that "it applies to individuals without distinguishing between classes"; or that it is "color-blind" and "gender-neutral." It is, unfortunately, also what Justice John Marshal Harlan had in mind when he wrote his brave, sole dissent in *Plessy v. Ferguson* in 1896: "Our Constitution is color-blind and neither knows nor tolerates classes among citizens." Equality may be a "synonym for uniformity" in the guarantee of rights by the state, but people are not uniform.[26]

While all such phrases sound well and good, at the heart of equality of rights and equality of opportunity is the simple and, some would say, insidious legal guarantee that *unequal individuals have the absolute right in American society to compete with one another, regardless of class, sex, race, ethnicity, or religion.* This is why for over a century after the American Revolution a white, male legal and political system kept women from voting and out of most professions and why for almost two hundred years this system did not grant basic civil rights to African-Americans or other racial minorities. It is also why U.S. penal institutions are populated primarily by the poor and uneducated; why women are more disadvantaged by divorce than men; why racial minorities are disproportionately discriminated against in the application of the death penalty; and why white-collar crime is seldom punished as severely as crimes committed by blue-collar workers or the unemployed.

J. R. Pole has pointed out that there is a "co-ordinate" to this extreme form of legal and moral individualism that has been "widely accepted throughout a large part of American history." He calls it the "doctrine of interchangeable individual rights," or the "interchangeability principle." While Pole insisted in 1978 that the "interchangeability principle has inspired generations of Americans to hold faith with their society and country," he could not ignore the obvious—namely, that "the actual equality of the sexes still tended to elude the kind of classification required by the principle of interchangeability" to a greater degree than similar exclusion based on race or religion. Pole saw hope in some differential treatment of women in order for them to obtain equal rights based on their obviously experiential and biological differences. But like so many other advocates of liberal legalism, Pole remained convinced that this differentiation would only be needed in special cases because "experience and experiment" had demonstrated "that *when women were properly trained,* socially encouraged, and acting from choice, *they could in fact operate interchangeably with men* in all those walks of life to which men had traditionally been called" (emphasis added).[27]

Unequal individuals competing as equals in order to become more like the dominant white males is by no means simply a semantic conundrum. Such individualized inequality or one-sided competition in which the losers lose their collective identity is not normally tolerated in professional athletic contests or political campaigns, for example. Yet, such unequal competition for justice among unequal citizens has been extolled by mainstream liberal jurists in the United States for the better part of two centuries. Equality of rights guaranteed to unequal individuals is a harsh model upon which to base a system of justice. Along with the individual freedoms that it ensures, it also condones excessive socioeconomic disparities in the name of democracy and equal opportunity. The discrepancy between our ideals and their application may appear more glaring as the twentieth century draws to a close; nonetheless, the United States probably came closer to practicing, as opposed to merely advocating, political and legal pluralism in the 1960s and early 1970s before the end of the Vietnam War than at any other time in its history.[28]

Simultaneously, most mainstream women reformers decided it was time to focus realistically on obtaining only individual rights with men—that is, to abandon both the rhetoric and politics of protection and domesticity that had resulted from so much of the First Women's movement's emphasis on the special nature of women. Thus, both the civil rights movement and women's movement after World War II focused first on obtaining individual equal rights with all of its assimilationist overtones. Protectionism and special status based on race or gender had simply backfired on minorities and women in the past. With the emergence of affirmative-action and class-action suits, however, native American Indians and then African-American and Hispanic leaders "began to question whether civil rights without an awareness of community were adequate." Women also experienced this shift in consciousness from individualistic, assimilationist views to more collective, pluralistic ones, reflected in the earlier civil rights activities on the part of racial and ethnic groups, when, in the late 1960s and again in the 1980s, radical feminists, in particular, questioned the premise upon which traditional equality of opportunity was based.[29]

When most twentieth-century feminists tried to reinterpret the Constitution, however, they almost always talked about obtaining equality *with* white men rather than constructing equitable treatment *for* women. Only after women obtained a certain amount of white, male equality, as has been the case in the last twenty years, have more of them been in a better position to assess whether such reinterpretation based on continued expansion of patriarchal jurisprudence and traditional rhetoric about individual rights is in their collective best interests. Consequently, they are now not only in a better position to assess whether this type of equality benefits all women (or only those who are best able to act like men), but also to determine whether the potential loss of culturally and structurally determined female behavioral patterns and values is not perhaps too high a price to pay for equality based on assimilation.

Employing this kind of feminist gender analysis to reexamine these attempts to include women in the Constitution, it becomes apparent that perhaps more unequal competition among unequal individuals is not what will benefit most women in the future. Moreover, women cannot simplistically emulate the collective cultural and compensatory civil rights approach of racial minority groups. Women have always lost when the courts granted them special or remedial laws based on traditional gender stereotypes. The special treatment accorded women as a group under the law still continues to reflect gender-based male perceptions of "female" as inferior and unequal to a greater degree than this is now true of males from racially or ethnically disadvantaged groups, especially in politics, where women, in particular, continue to play an insignificant role given their numbers, education, and availability.

Women and African-Americans both started out their respective movements for liberation with theories about their own inequality, only to find that "judges gave them back an ideology of equality which was all too often translated into a formula for penalizing them for all of the ways in which they are not equal to white men." Women and racial groups must find ways in the future to avoid this "equality with a vengeance." At the same time, their unequal subjective and objective conditions when compared with white men must somehow be transformed into a basis for feminist jurisprudence, if women and all minorities are to move from liberation to emancipation—meaning more equitable treatment in society. To accomplish this ideational breakthrough, however, feminist historians and lawyers must honestly assert and detail the ways in which women's personal and professional lives remain unequal, so that female issues no longer seem irrational by the prevailing masculine standards of equality under liberal legalism. This means developing a linguistic and theoretical critique that "enables feminists to expose and deconstruct idealist modes of domination."[30]

The difficulty of such a radical intellectual undertaking is obvious, however, because women still have difficulty presenting certain issues in ways that are cognizable in courts of law instead of being implicitly dismissed as "crazy" or "insane." I stress the use of the words *insanity* and *craziness* because scrutiny of the legal issues raised by feminists today and in the past has often led the male establishment to declare such issues beyond juridical redress. Although there are numerous contemporary examples of the "irrationality" of women's legal concerns, such as those associated with reproductive freedom, pornography, surrogate motherhood, and rape,[31] we should not forget that the newspaper attacks on the Declaration of Sentiments of 1848 were so excessive that many of the original one hundred signers withdrew their names from that "insane" legal document, prompting Elizabeth Cady Stanton to remark: "No words could express our astonishment on finding that what seemed to us so timely, so rational, and so sacred, should be a subject for sarcasm and ridicule to the entire press of the nation."[32]

By the end of 1980s, women have not yet been able to articulate adequately a female definition of equality in the face of continued efforts to silence their "crazy" legal ideas and needs. But let us suppose at some point in the future women do succeed in obtaining equality as it is currently defined for, and by, men. What would it mean? In 1877, for example, Susan B. Anthony questioned whether such male equality could be legislated in a society where women's and men's gendered realities made them so different in the eyes of society and the law. "Even when man's intellectual convictions shall be sincerely and fully on the side of Freedom and equality to woman," Anthony insisted, "the force of long existing customs and laws will impel him to exert authority over her. . . . Not even amended constitutions and law can revolutionize the practical relations of men and women . . . any more than did the Constitutional freedom and franchise of Black men. . . . Constitutional equality only gives to all the aid and protection of the law. . . . It simply allows equality of *chances*." Because she also doubted the "adequacy of sheer equality," Mary Beard echoed Anthony's views in the 1930s and 1940s when she proclaimed that "man" should not be made the "measure" of women's status in society.[33] And today, feminist lawyers frequently point out that it is simply not enough to identify the inequality of relationships under capitalist or socialist forms of patriarchy by comparing women and minorities to white men, and then automatically assuming that antisexist or antipaternalistic legislation and case law will create equality among individuals who are not, in fact, equal. Inequality masquerading as equality does not constitute a constitutional advance in women's legal status, as the results of no-fault divorce have so clearly revealed.

Little wonder that contemporary professional women continue to find it difficult to articulate how their own legal needs, let alone those of the average woman, differ from those of white males. The silence imposed upon women by custom and legally enforced societal norms about the very nature of the pain and pleasure in their public and private lives is not automatically alleviated when they speak out because women are not always encouraged or allowed to speak the truth, especially about when they do and do not "consent" to a wide variety of professional, political, and sexual activities. As a result, women have developed a "seemingly endless capacity to lie" to themselves and to others. "It is now commonplace," according to Robin West, "that women 'don't feel at home' with male language—but this is no wonder, when what we've mainly learned to do with it is lie . . . about the quality of our internal lives." Even if West has exaggerated her point, Carroll Smith-Rosenberg has demonstrated that after an elite group of women began adopting male scientific and literary language in the 1920s, they began communicating less effectively with other women across class and cultural barriers, not only about themselves personally but also about public feminist issues. This communication problem became painfully evident during the futile struggle for ratification of the ERA between 1972 and 1982.[34]

## Private and Public Spheres, or When Is the Personal Political?

While the quality of women's internal lives has always been associated with their private activities, it has only recently been shown to be related to their public endeavors as well. Full citizenship carries with it the "power to influence matters that are personal without interference from the state."[35] These "personal zones of noninterference," or what is also called "negative liberty," have traditionally been the private prerequisite of only white males who possessed full citizenship rights. In contrast, imposed silence, the charge of irrationality, and false or misleading articulation of their legal needs remain discursive symbols of women's second-class citizenship as they have battled from their private spheres for space in the male-dominated public one during the last two hundred years. Traditional legal discussions about the distinction between the private and public spheres of women and men often assume that only the latter is governed by law, when in fact both are. In this sense, the private has always been public for women and men—underneath the guise of the constitutional principle of noninterference. Public law has always formally confirmed and reinforced the private constraints informally imposed by mainstream ideology and culture.

To a very large degree, therefore, the law serves to define the legal parameters of what is private or personal in all societies. First common law and then modern case-law precedent have operated not only to keep middle-class women in their private spheres but also to force poor women of all races into the "public sphere of the marketplace." Additionally, the law has "disguised the role of the 'public' in the creation of the definition 'private,' " according to Anne E. Simon, "[making] 'the personal is political' . . . more than a clever slogan of the Second Women's Movement."[36] The loss of legal identity for married women under eighteenth- and nineteenth-century law and, until recently, the unquestioned legality of rape in marriage are but two examples of the law creating private conditions of existence. Not surprisingly, the most effective hierarchical systems are those in which both the "haves" and the "have-nots" are convinced that "the existing order, with perhaps marginal changes, is satisfactory, or at least represents the most that anyone could expect, because things pretty much have to be the way they are."[37]

Assigning domesticity to women as their primary function is not new in Western society; but in the United States following the American Revolution, it has been particularly virulent. In the 1830s Alexis de Tocqueville positively described "the quiet sphere of domestic duties" that characterized American women's lives in contrast with his perception of what was happening abroad.

There are people in Europe who, confounding together the different characteristics of the sexes, would make man and woman into beings not only equal, but alike. . . . *It may readily be conceived, that, by thus attempting to make one sex equal to the other, both are degraded;* and from so preposterous a medley of the works of nature, nothing could ever result but weak men and disorderly women.

It is not thus that the Americans understand that species of democratic equality which may be established between the sexes. . . . The Americans have applied to *the sexes the great principle of political economy which governs the manufactures of our age, by carefully dividing the duties of man from those of woman, in order that the great work of society may be the better carried on.* . . .

I never observed that the women of America consider conjugal authority as a fortunate usurpation of their rights, not that they thought themselves degraded by submitting to it. It *appeared to me, on the contrary, that they attach a sort of pride to the voluntary surrender of their own will, and make it their boast to bend themselves to the yoke,—not to shake it off.* Such, at least, is the feeling expressed by the most virtuous of their sex; *the others are silent;* and, in the United States, it is not the practice for a *guilty wife* to clamor for the rights of women, whilst she is trampling on her own holiest duties. . . .

*Thus, then, whilst they have allowed the social inferiority of woman to subsist, they have done all they could to raise her morally and intellectually to the level of man;* and in this respect they appear to me to have excellently understood the true principle of democratic improvement (emphasis added throughout).

While the usually prescient de Tocqueville can be faulted for not questioning why so many women were "silent" about the ostensibly "natural" and "consensual" aspects of their "voluntary" subordination, it is anachronistic to say that his portrayal has been made irrelevant by deconstructionist analysis because his inadvertent description of the inequality of women's self-sacrificing roles within marriage and the family still resonates as "truth" in the hearts and minds of many Americans—including many jurists.[38]

From the earliest colonial days, the proper sphere for women in preindustrial America was characterized by the practice of private and sometimes public virtue. For colonial men, it was the exercise of much private and complete public power. While these two spheres of virtue and power overlapped more in the seventeenth and eighteenth centuries than they did in the nineteenth and twentieth, they were—and are—based on gender distinctions. As important as the work of women inside and outside the home was in colonial times, it always represented a compromised form of power. Conversely, as important as the power of men was, it represented a compromised form of virtue. Rather than "encroaching regularly on each other's domain," under British rule both spheres represented a more complementary mix of such male-defined and societally enforced characteristics as authority, deference, dependence, duty, privilege, virtue, power, corruption, responsibility, and ambition than was the case after the American Revolution.[39]

While postrevolutionary republicanism enhanced the colonial meaning of personal morality and virtue for women in the United States, the same does not appear true for men. Instead, the classical male definition of public virtue became an increasingly irrelevant concept to the young nation's ambitious male leaders, especially after the drafting of the Constitution of 1787. In its place a private female version of patriotic virtue suited to the existing socialization of women came into vogue in the 1780s, which helped to ensure that women's work would continue to be objectified and isolated in a separate sphere. This private sphere, despite its infusion of civic virtue, did not foster any "constitutional consciousness of a morality of mutual responsibility" because as second-class citizens postrevolutionary women did not possess the constitutional rights capable of influencing the public sphere.[40]

These postrevolutionary legacies of virtue and second-class legal status meant that republican wives and mothers became private, but not public, citizens of the United States without completely understanding why. Privatization and patriotic feminization of virtue came at the very moment when postrevolutionary leaders were getting on with the business of carving out political privileges and economic opportunities for themselves and for many succeeding generations of white males. Just as the most self-sacrificing, community-oriented male revolutionary symbols of virtue and morality were turned over to the care of females, women were being systematically relegated by the new laws of the land to peripheral positions outside the political and economic developments that were shaping the country's destiny.

No matter how much historians tout republican motherhood (or republican wifehood) as a form of civic virtue, it did not expand postrevolutionary women's citizenship rights or wrench them out of a historical frame of mind and experiential level that was to keep them locked in step behind the legal status of men from the late eighteenth century to the present. Most important, the terms *republican wife* and *republican mother* obfuscate how male ideology and the law upon which it functioned confined women to their private sphere. According to popular postrevolutionary literature, the "loving partnership of man and wife" represented the ideal republican model and alternative to patriarchal political relationships. Thus, republican wives primarily became "political creatures," only in the sense that it was their duty to "seduce" their husbands into virtuous ways during their courtship period and to keep them there after marriage.[41]

Making married women's domesticity sentimentally patriotic by turning the home into a "nursery of citizenship" and encouraging better, but woefully unequal, education for these mothers of freedom did not bring women intellectually anywhere near the threshold of modernity and individualism in the immediate postrevolutionary decades. An understanding of what the American Revolution had been all about for men did not become a conscious, motivating reality for women until just before and after the Civil War because their experiential level lagged so far behind men's on the eve of the War of Independence. Thus, in the endless game of "catch up" that women in all patriarchal cultures play, the American Revolution did not have the constitutional or other forms of consciousness-raising impact on women that the American Civil War had over a half-century later. Rather, it left them with an odd contextual combination of aspects of the classical concept of public virtue that men were abandoning and a type of "maternal virtue" that presaged both the development of the "cult of true womanhood" and the service roles as teachers and reformers that middle- and upper-middle-class women were to play before the Civil War.

Moreover, it was the Second Great Awakening and the sentimentalization of both motherhood and children in the early decades of the nineteenth century that first encouraged women to mature with a sense of private identity, self worth, and personal importance as individualistic adults from their earlier arrested state of development based on ascribed and dependent private status as generic republican wives or mothers. Nascent liberal individualism, not early republican ideas of subordination of self for the common good, nurtured this heightened private consciousness and confidence. Such burgeoning individualism prompted later generations of female temperance and abolitionist advocates to overcome their internalized sense of eighteenth-century virtue and morality (which the American Revolution had reinforced and not diminished in them). Liberalism—not republicanism—encouraged some nineteenth-century women to enter the professional and political worlds of men before, but especially after, the Civil War.

Republican wifehood and motherhood could not and did not do anything similar for several generations of revolutionary and postrevolutionary women. Neither Abigail Adams nor Mercy Otis Warren, two of the best educated and most astute observers of the American Revolution, conceived of any potential political (or other) role for women in the public sphere of power. Although the Enlightenment theories with which elite colonial women were familiar held out hope of equality for all based on natural law, they also strongly reinforced the separate-spheres doctrine. While such women shared certain Enlightenment ideas with men, even they lived literally in a different conceptual frame of mind (and time) from their husbands and male relatives. As republican wives and mothers, their consciousness (and actions) remained circumscribed by feudalistic views about female private morality, dependence, and deference.[42]

In the course of the nineteenth century as the new nation became more democratic and a land of economic opportunity for white males, a smaller, nuclear middle-class family began to emerge. In classical Greece and early modern Europe when the "small household emerged as the productive unit of the society," the male heads of such households automatically became the most privileged citizens of the state. Both these classical Greek theories about the *polis* and Lockean political notions accorded equality and "fraternity" to men in the public realm and gave them autonomous dominant private status as heads of households. Women's private roles were determined by their dependent (and primarily sexual) relationship to men in both the Greek *polis* and the ideal Lockean state. Both sets of political theories were inherently more misogynistic than the ones they replaced in preclassical Greece and prerevolutionary America—a fact disguised in part because in each of these widely separated time periods there was exaggerated praise for the virtues and civic contributions of married women.[43]

This confluence of the democratic state, the nuclearized conjugal unit, and economic development that individualized the public sphere at the expense of the family is often called *modernization*. Both Marilyn Arthur and Lawrence Stone have suggested that modernization in the form of a "more individualized household unit . . . was on the whole bad for women" in the eighteenth and nineteenth centuries because it increased male dominance over women whose primary self-identity came from within the weakened family unit. In the twentieth century, it has become abundantly evident that modernization does not initially benefit women in Third World countries. While this point should not be exaggerated, there are many contemporary theories about (and examples of) democratization and modernization in developing countries lowering the status of women by removing them from clan and amorphous kinship relationships and subjecting them to the more direct authority of the state or their husbands. Likewise, in Western, developed nations married women's presumed legal dependence has prevented most adult females from obtaining full citizenship status.[44]

Certain conditions ameliorated the worst features of modernization for women in the United States following the American Revolution. There were, for example, the increasing stress placed on affection and partnership in marriage and the assumption that such a marital union freely entered into was "the republican model for social and political relationships." The image of women as virtuous "temptresses" and then as patriotic wives and mothers abounded in many postrevolutionary sermons and articles.[45] These postrevolutionary views about the virtuous role of women in marital relationships mitigated in part the social, more than the legal, harshness of modernization on women in the United States in the late eighteenth century. Such patriotic idealization of marriage evolved either into companionate or romantic concepts of marriage in the early nineteenth century. To the degree that wives in the early republic became the repositories of marital virtue and patriotism, their status in the eyes of the state can be differentiated from that of classical Greece. While Locke's original liberal theories did not include women in the public sphere of "fraternal" power and actually downgraded women's authority within the private sphere of the family, revolutionary-inspired notions about female-centered virtue and patriotism rescued the women in the United States from at least a modicum of the sexism inherent in both liberalism and modernization.

Because women until recently have remained "unsolvable mysteries" for those studying liberalism and modernization, few attempts have been made to analyze the impact of these theories on women in the United States in the eighteenth and nineteenth centuries. Women were not, for example, the focus of influential works applying liberal or modernization theories[46]—especially those analyzing self-interested individualism—to the American Revolution.[47] One reason is that early specialists in Lockean liberalism and particularly modernization seldom asked themselves whether women were subjected to the same set of transitional economic forces and sociopsychological pressures as men on the so-called road to modernity. Most history texts and monographs about early American history implicitly answer this question affirmatively. Indeed, this continues to be one of the best-preserved illusions of most scholarship dealing with the revolutionary and early national periods. Yet, even in the United States, the first leg of the journey for women into the modern, liberal world contained some distinctly different emotional and intellectual experiences, a decrease in certain socioeconomic functions, and fewer liberalizing political-legal benefits than it did for men.

Consequently, women of the early national period were far from immune to all of the negative legal and political implications of modernization. White men became privileged citizens as heads of households under Jacksonian democracy; the private became more separated from the public as economic independence became inextricable with political independence following the American Revolution; romantic concepts about companionate marriages initially decreased women's discretionary rights over property, making them more legally dependent upon their husbands, despite their greater control over household affairs; and, finally, married women entered the nineteenth century with fewer opportunities than their colonial predecessors to act as "deputy" husbands in the public realm.[48] Instead, as the middle-class home became a "haven from the heartless world" for men who worked outside the private sphere, the personal became separated even more from the political for women.

In a word, the private became more private for most women in the first half of the nineteenth century. This increased privatization thrived on praise for the domestic and patriotic functions of republican mothers following the American Revolution and the emergence of the "cult of domesticity" among middle-class families. Religious and social change for women continued to reside, as it had before and during the War of Independence, on private, personal conversion and the one-on-one reform of individuals. As such, the personal was not really political at all for most women until the middle of the nineteenth century, when some of them developed a collective consciousness outside the private and stopped trying to reform society individual by individual.

One of the best examples of this strategic, psychological, and ideological breakthrough can be seen in the history of the Temperance movement. It began with largely private attempts by individual women to change the drinking habits of the men in their lives, whether they were husbands, in-laws, or blood relatives. Not only was this labor-intensive approach doomed to fail, but it also left the institutionalized social abuse of women, within the private sphere resulting from alcoholism, completely intact. Temperance became a collective and truly radical reform when its adherents went to the courts and state legislatures to obtain rulings and statutes to punish the psychic and somatic battering of women by the alcoholics in their lives, and to provide legal procedures whereby women could leave homes and marriages tormented by excessive drinking. Likewise, when women adopted a collective approach to political reform based on Enlightenment theories about natural law, it led them ultimately to question the masculinity of both constitutionalism and Lockean contractualism in their demand for structural, socioeconomic, and political changes in American society—but especially the institution of marriage. When a growing number of educated, single women, such as Susan B. Anthony, began to act as "surrogate" husbands for married women and as they organized themselves to function outside of their private spheres, the personal assumed its first public, political dimensions for women.[49]

Progress in the process of making the political collectively personal has not been linear. In part this was because of the legal fiction that the private sphere was beyond the law or, at best, governed by a jurisprudence of rights based on equalitarian theories about "negative liberty"—that is, private, individual "zones of noninterference."[50] Progress has also not followed a steadily upward historical path because women reformers did not initially distinguish (or understand the differences) between obtaining special or equal rights in the public sphere. When they finally did in the 1920s, they disagreed so fundamentally that the First Women's movement lost its national coherence and collective momentum.[51] Even the Second Women's movement did not systematically begin to address this divisive (and often falsely diverting) political and legal question of reconciling special and equal treatment until after the defeat of the ERA in 1982.

The question of whether private relations mirror or create public ones remains unresolved because contemporary women in the United States probably remain less emancipated inside their own homes than outside them. Most households in the United States still impose dual working loads on women who are also employed outside the home, in terms of housework, meal preparation, and child care. Liberal laws and litigation that have given women gains in equal treatment with men have not ended the sex-segregated labor market or the disparity in wages between women and men.[52] In both the public and private spheres, the expectation of female subordination remains the flip side of equal rights liberation theories because of the male values they embody. Thus, the private/public sphere debate is far from settled after two hundred years of erratic improvement in the legal status of women in the United States and recent historiographical and poststructural attempts to diminish the debate's importance.

## Self/Other, or When Is Progress Really Progress?

Stripped of their reification by historical liberal legalism, these private/public oppositions can be viewed for what they really are: not figments of radical feminist imagination but male in origin and institutionalized by a gendered legal system that perpetuates the objectification of women through the dyadic concepts of self and other. Thinkers as diverse as Simone de Beauvoir, Michel Foucault, Jane Flax, Susanne Kappeler, Evelyn Keller, Jean Bethke Elshtain, Nancy Chodorow, Dorothy Dinnerstein, and many others from various disciplines have delineated the psychological, economic, and political sources of gender-stereotyped "modelings" of self/other relationships in all societies with similar asymmetric divisions of labor by gender as they are found in America down to the present day.[53]

The self/other model I employ here is one used by radical feminist lawyers and is based on the "selfness" and selfish consensual acts associated with men that can be found dominating the public sphere, in contrast to the "selflessness" and self-giving consensual acts of women that have been traditionally relegated to the private sphere. The "otherness" of women as a group is not meant as a universal, as some cultural feminists insist it is, but as a statistical, socially constructed set of characteristics. Not only is the "other" construed to be naturally dependent and contingent in the gendered social reality of the world of liberal legalism, but the "other," as two such different contemporary authors as Carol Gilligan and Mary Daly have noted, also speaks in a different language—making legal action in behalf of women's needs difficult at best and sometimes impossible. Given the experiential time-lag between women and men described in the Introduction and the difficulty women have overcoming both imposed silence or the label of "crazy" or irrational when they express themselves on the subject of feminist reforms, the legal obstacles posed by traditional constitutional language for female litigants are to be expected.[54]

The criticism of theories of "otherness," in general, and of Gilligan's work on female moral development, in particular, is much more common among feminist historians than among feminist lawyers. This distinctly different reaction between the two disciplines is difficult to explain. Historians usually fault Gilligan's small, sex-segregated sample (her study is based primarily on a group of women who decided whether to have abortions), her reinforcement of women's separate sphere as representative of a rigid cultural dualism separating the sexes, and the self-righteousness and essentialism implicit in the idea that women by nature and culture are more caring and nurturing than men. Thus, poststructural historians are particularly concerned that Gilligan's material and phenomenological explanations are too speculative and that they are having unwarranted impact despite their ahistorical, "self-reproducing binary opposition[s]" and insistence on "fixed differences . . . [which] contribute to the kind of thinking [feminists] want to oppose."[55]

In summary, deconstructionist methodology has led some historians to dismiss all experiential binary oppositions, including self/other, public/private, and male/female, as Western constructs that disallow recognition of other (and, presumably, more important) nonexperiential differences among women rather than between women and men.[56] The rejection of the objective reality of certain dualities and of cognitive notions about moral development makes it difficult for poststructuralists to focus on the political and patriarchal implications of historical and liberal legalism as a "manifestation of a gendered social construction of reality" and also "to forgo existing standards of historical inquiry" in order to question other fundamental discursive assumptions. Little wonder that it is those radical feminist attorneys—who have *disassociated* themselves from the masculinity of both the CLS movement and liberal legal theorists—who are leaders in questioning claims to neutrality and universality on the part of historical interpretations of male jurisprudence—not feminist poststructural historians. Such radical feminists posit the need for a feminist jurisprudence and feminist language that reflect more accurately both the relational female approach to morality (or what Gilligan has described as a sense of justice based on a web of interdependence and connection) and honest articulation of the most private female hedonic experiences (what Robin West has called a woman's redefinition of herself as "self-regarding" rather than "self-giving").[57]

Nonetheless, I do not think that these poststructural rationalizations entirely explain the differences between historians and lawyers on the question of the "otherness" of women as evidenced in works like Gilligan's. Lawyers, for one thing, are not interested in the methodological reliability or empirical historicity of a study purporting to document very disturbing and different moral and relational imperatives among women and men. They need winning arguments in courtrooms—not historical hair splitting over causality. Most important, perhaps, is that lawyers who have represented black female welfare recipients in any legal context come in daily contact with the differing attitudinal and juridical treatment accorded women and men. For some constitutional specialists Gilligan's theory has a "ring of truth" about it because they realize how much the public sphere of law impinges (and actually creates) the parameters of the private sphere, resulting in the fact that until recently "men [got] to do more or less whatever they want[ed]" within the most private unit of the private sphere—the family. Because many feminist lawyers and legal scholars deal with the objective conditions of oppression, they may intuitively accept a subjective theory like Gilligan's, which seems to explain the "highly interwoven" nature of the objective discrimination against women by a judicial system that does not basically reflect their socially constructed position in, and/or ethical view of, society.[58] Historians do not generally have such "hands-on" experience, nor the sense of immediacy or responsibility for improving the lives of the disadvantaged connected with their work as do most social-service lawyers and some who specialize in constitutional jurisprudence.

I also suspect that many professional women, especially those in academe, are uncomfortable with a theory that challenges whether they have been able to overcome their own social conditioning as well as they would like to believe because they pride themselves on their ability to assimilate within their respective disciplines by speaking in accepted male terms. While linguistic assimilation is even a stronger prerequisite in legal than historical circles, given the highly specialized nature of jurisprudential language, the most radical feminist legal scholars have begun to use more female terminology than their counterparts in history departments, especially those where poststructuralist interpretations tend to prevail among the faculty. Perhaps this slight linguistic "edge" is what makes some radical feminist lawyers appear more optimistic about their ability to change the current "male voice" of the law into a "female voice" once their numbers in the profession reach critical-mass proportions.[59]

Finally, since academic women historians have participated in their discipline in significant numbers much longer than women lawyers have in their profession, they are perhaps both more jaded and more realistic about bringing about change through their presence alone; hence, they are personally more skeptical about Gilligan's idea that women, indeed, speak in a voice different enough to transform a profession or discipline. As Hilda Smith has noted about historians, "all of us ground our theoretical insight more securely in a limited concrete experiential base than, perhaps, we would like to admit." After all, most female professionals who succeed do so on male terms. While this is as true of lawyers as historians, the latter are experientially further removed from the day-to-day examples of discrimination and the hopelessness that some critical theory lawyers express about ever achieving equality of results through legal remedies.[60] Therefore, for all of these reasons most feminist historians appear less willing than most feminist legal academicians to question the underlying male prerequisites of success for women in American society. Gilligan may well touch a chord in these historians that they have long since learned to repress or ignore, while radical female attorneys face the overwhelming masculinity of the U.S. adversarial legal system not only as students but also in court through their female clients.

Until the different socioeconomic expectations of girls and women are recognized as equal to those of boys and men—or until men want what women "are" (not just certain things women "have")—social, political, legal, and economic reality will remain rooted in a gendered concept of "self" that is explicitly or implicitly defined as male.[61] Until then, the masculinity of public law and U.S. constitutionalism will continue to define both the public and private spheres of women's activities in changing but, nonetheless, gender-constricting terms. Regardless of the theoretical attempts to demystify and deconstruct all socially constructed binary dualities, practical reality will out. Most women and men continue to function in separate subjective time frames and under different objective conditions, however much more blurred their respective spheres have become in the twentieth century.

Thus, progress or regression for women must be measured by the relationship among multiple "selves" and "others" within the remaining private and public spheres of activities that prevail today or within the less complex and more clearly defined notions about "self" and "other" of a past time period. As men's work literally left the home in the late eighteenth and early nineteenth centuries, these two gender-based and socially conditioned spheres became more separate. In the nineteenth century, for example, the legal "otherness" of women was so complete that the courts could refuse to recognize their political and professional existence. This extreme manifestation of contingent and dependent status corresponded with the period in which separate spheres of women and men were also the most distinct in U.S. history. Some historians maintain that this separateness, by increasing women's domestic autonomy, actually empowered them despite their constitutional and political neglect. Why? I suggest it is because they are confusing liberal " 'progress' within 'otherness' " for a "qualitative transformation" of female status. It is not. Nor is it even a "preamble to profound change" of society itself.[62] Whether the state interferes to reinforce a gendered construction of a separate sphere of reality, such as it did in denying women the right to vote or whether it refuses to interfere into family matters because they are beyond the "rule of law," the action or nonaction is determined by the dominant "selfness" or maleness of the legal construct of society.

Unless feminist historians and lawyers consciously recognize the continued existence of separate spheres in the United States in the form of the dual, gendered cultures of "self" and "other," they will forget that (1) progress within the parameters of the self-giving "other" is limited progress at best, and possibly even a regression for women, if it means that society at large pays less attention or accords even less value to such segregated change in women's status; (2) progress in the form of obtaining the male status of self-serving "self" at the expense of self-giving "other" likewise represents problematic progress for women; and (3) only progress that accords the "self-regarding" female equitable but different status with the male "self" is significant progress because it offers the possibility of restructuring a society where social conditioning still produces two distinctly different types of human beings—women and men.

The question that these different definitions of progress raises from a legal point of view, according to attorney Wendy W. Williams, is, "Do we want equality of the sexes—or do we want justice for two kinds of human beings who are fundamentally different?"[63] From a historical point of view the question is, Do we want to define progress for women as change that takes place only within the private sphere of self-giving "otherness"; or only at the expense of self-regarding female in exchange for self-serving male "self"; or do we want to analyze at least different kinds of progress (or regression) for women based on the recognition that women and men have been, and will continue for some time to be, socialized in distinctly different ways? Without radically different socialization, separate female/male spheres, especially at the most personal, private level of existence, will continue to exist despite the theoretical claims by deconstructionists to the contrary.

It is possible to look at Supreme Court cases from the last quarter of the nineteenth century to the present and see that liberal legalism has not reconstructed American society.[64] The most liberal decisions simply expanded the standards of the "self"—that is, expanded the rights and privileges of white males to other segments of society. If this is understood, then it should be possible to analyze progress or regression of women's status over time from a historical and legal perspective, rather than continuing to debate the issue without even defining the terms or overcoming the "present-mindedness" that now dominates the discussion. As long as progress remains rooted in the socialized male concept of the self-serving "self" rather than in the self-regarding female, such progress will simplistically be interpreted to mean obtaining equal rights with men. As a result, there will be no "serious redefinition or reconstruction of social reality which feminists seek."[65]

Using this view of progress, which transcends the masculinist limitations of liberalism, the historical and legal status of American women can be interpreted at best as a case of erratic progress and at worst as a case of circular progress—that is, from an amorphous private female sphere that overlapped with a male public one in the seventeenth and eighteenth centuries, to a precisely defined separate sphere in the nineteenth century, to yet another amorphous sphere, which in this century is no longer recognized as either public or private and, therefore, places women in a state of legal limbo (where they are free to act individually like men but not always able to protect their collective interests and needs as women). If contemporary historiography and jurisprudence continue to ignore the relationship between full citizenship and female "otherness" or between equity and the self-regarding female, they will ensure that the male "self" remains the major standard of progress and equality for both women and men. This, in turn, will perpetuate the too-little-too-late pattern already so characteristic of the legal history of U.S. women and minorities.

# CHAPTER TWO

# Women and the American Revolution

The impact of the American Revolution on women remains a controversial topic among colonial specialists. Much of the current historiographical debate hinges on two related but separate questions: had the political and personal perceptions of women changed significantly by 1787; and regardless of whether their subjective perceptions had been altered by the American Revolution, did the successful end to that conflict directly result in meaningful objective improvement in their actual socioeconomic and legal status? Answers to both revolve around whether the concepts of citizenship and private identity for women were enhanced or retarded by the American Revolution.

Gender analysis has made it easy to discern that postrevolutionary treatment of women, in general, and single women, in particular, contradicted the basic political and economic tenets of the War of Independence. Nowhere was this more evident than in the economic overtones associated with the words *liberty* and *independence*. The American Revolution came about in large measure because male leaders rejected economic dependence of the colonies as a form of slavery. Yet after the American Revolution, married women remained economically dependent and even those single women who were economically independent could not vote or exercise political rights associated with full citizenship. To the extent that political participation in postrevolutionary society came to be based on the prerevolutionary notion about unencumbered title to property, there is no conclusive evidence that the War of Independence made married women bona-fide citizens of the new republic or that the legal status of married or single women improved significantly in other less-tangible areas of civil life in the first three or four decades following the end of the War of Independence.

In the course of the nineteenth century, this traditional concept of property changed radically from "the physicalist and absolutist elements of Blackstone" to modern, "less protected forms of property," representing "legal relations among persons" rather than complete "dominion over things." Married women ultimately benefited from this "dephysicalization" of property but not in the immediate wake of the American Revolution. During and right after the War of Independence, both individual rights and personal virtue remained tied to "unencumbered ownership of hereditary and transmissable land. . . . to lose title was to lose one's personal identity and political liberty."[1] The American Revolution did not make women citizens in terms of property. Common-law restrictions on property ownership prevailed for all but the wealthiest of married women well into the nineteenth century.

If postrevolutionary women did not immediately obtain citizen status by acquiring absolute (fee simple) property rights, what about the claim that republican motherhood (and republican wifehood) became the female equivalent of male citizenship but *without* all of the latter's attendant political and legal rights, as discussed in chapter 1. This position hinges on the idea that the revolutionary ideology of women found expression through republican wives and mothers in combination with complementary romantic notions about domesticity. Proponents of republican wifehood and motherhood argue that in the immediate postwar years, these terms assumed a temporarily inflated importance because women were assigned the roles of raising patriotic sons and keeping husbands on the straight and narrow path of republican virtue.[2] The consequence was, indeed, a heightened privatized sense of personal morality and virtue for women. At the same time, the classical definition of public virtue became an increasingly irrelevant concept to the young nation's ambitious male leaders, especially after the drafting of the Constitution of 1787.[3] In its place a private female version came into vogue in the 1780s that helped to ensure that women's work would continue to operate in a separate sphere from men's. This private sphere, despite its infusion of civic virtue, insulated postrevolutionary women from the present, just as the public one occupied by postrevolutionary men propelled them toward the future.

## From Virtuous Men to Virtuous Women

Until very recently historians assumed that the attitudes and experiences among the female members of this revolutionary generation were the same as their male contemporaries. Comparative cross-cultural studies on revolutions and wars since the eighteenth century, however, reveal that women's socioeconomic and legal status is often only rhetorically improved immediately following the cessation of such dramatic changes in national power.[4] Why women in the United States following the American Revolution should be considered an exception to this well-established international pattern has never made sense to me. Nevertheless, some colonial and early national-period historians have gone to great lengths to portray the American Revolution as unique because of its purported positive impact on free, white women.

The very poorest women—particularly those in urban areas—had no resources to fall back on when confronted with the personal or economic traumas caused by the War of Independence. This was especially evident in the case of women wage earners, who, regardless of race or class, had always received lower pay than free men or hired-out slaves and had suffered severely during the war from the runaway inflation. Women's services were more likely to be paid for in Continental currency than with specie. Fees for male "doctors," for example, according to one Maryland family account book, were made in specie payment after the middle of 1780, while midwives had to accept the depreciated Continental currency for a longer period of time. Thus, the American Revolution hastened the appearance of greater class-based activities among "daughters of the new republic," with poor women undertaking the least desirable tasks—often forced by poverty to become camp followers.[5] It is easy to imagine the impact that the inflationary spiral had on the rural and urban poor, but it even affected those in the middle and upper-middle classes who were left at home to manage businesses, estates, plantations, or farms. Their activities often meant the difference between bankruptcy and solvency for male revolutionary leaders.

Perhaps the most significant and long-lasting legacy of the supportive activities among women for the patriot cause was the increase in class and social distinctions that they symbolized. For example, it appears unlikely that poor white or black women joined Daughters of Liberty groups, actively boycotted English goods, or participated in any significant numbers in those associations of "Ladies of the highest rank and influence" who raised money and supplies for the Continental army by ostentatiously organized spinning meetings and other charitable activities. On the contrary, it may well have been primarily "young female spinsters" from prominent families and well-to-do widows and wives who could afford the time or the luxury of such highly publicized and possibly somewhat self-indulgent activities. However, the vast majority of middle-class female patriots (as well as female Loyalists, for that matter), whether single or married, performed such necessary volunteer roles as seamstresses, nurses, hostesses, and sometimes spies, whenever the fighting shifted to their locales, without any undue fanfare or praise. The same was true of poorer women, with one important difference: they had no choice. They had all they could do to survive on wages that were estimated to have been 30 to 50 percent lower than men's.[6]

During the War of Independence, colonial women's attitudes had been molded by a complex variety of modernization trends they encountered in the course of the eighteenth century. Out of the necessities wrought by the conflict with England, women at all levels of society performed certain tasks that appeared revolutionary in nature, just as they performed other nonfamilial tasks out of necessity throughout the colonial period when circumstance required. This seemingly atypical behavior, however, should not be viewed as proof that the vast majority of these women understood abstract revolutionary principles or that they accepted their performance in these nontraditional roles.

One of the most poignant of the extant memorabilia about women's attitudes toward the American Revolution is the 1779 broadside entitled "New Touch on the Times" issued "By a Daughter of Liberty, living in Marblehead," named Molly Coutridge. Three years into the War of Independence, this twenty-stanza "song" addressed the "distressing Situation in very Sea-port Town," describing with less than patriotic fervor the difficulties women were having trying to take care of their families in "hard and cruel times" with food shortages, inflated money, and "our best beloved" men away at war or on the high seas. The right-hand corner of this engraving carried the picture of a woman with a powder horn and a musket, and has been reprinted numerous times in this century, especially during the 1976 bicentenary of the American Revolution, as an example of female patriotism. However, in the left-hand corner there is a partial woodcut of a barren room with a woman and children huddled in one corner, while another woman appears to be guarding the door.

This contrasting image is seldom mentioned or displayed, except, as in this instance, when the entire broadside is reproduced. Yet all of the couplets lament the war and describe in religious, not militant terms, the plight of women as they are pathetically depicted by the left-corner illustration—not by the determined-looking, musket-wielding woman on the right. Most telling are those stanzas in which the war is attributed to the "sin" and "crimes" of the colonists, specifically noting that "Wan't it for our polluted tongues / This cruel war would ne'er begun." Lamenting both the causes and the effects of the war, this particular Daughter of Liberty chose to end her "song" with an appeal for an immediate end to the conflict, with the words "Then gracious GOD, now cause to cease / This bloody war and give us peace!" These despairing and disparaging religious views of the origins of the American Revolution were not uncommon at the time because they "allowed women to comment on public events even though they were excluded from the world of practical politics."[7]

Despite their participation in somewhat more economic specialization; despite their experiences with a slightly smaller conjugal household where power relations were changing; and despite the limited expansion of the legal rights and somewhat improved educational opportunities for free, white females, the revolutionary generation of women was less prepared than most men for the modern political implications of independence. The religious caste to so many of their statements and poetry about the War of Independence testifies to an ambivalence and tension about the way old values and ideas were being replaced by new ones.

For example, Kenneth A. Lockridge has argued that modernization requires a diversity of worldly experience on the part of individual members of society.[8] There is no doubt that before and after 1776 women did not participate enough in conflicts over land, religion, taxes, local politics, or commercial transactions to be as prepared as men for the modernizing forces set in motion by the American Revolution.

Their distinctly different experiential level, combined with the limited intellectual and psychological impact of the First Great Awakening and the Enlightenment on women, made it literally impossible for even the best-educated colonial females to understand the political intent or legal principles behind the inflated rhetoric of the revolutionary era. Words like *virtue, veracity, morality, tyranny,* and *corruption* were ultimately given public political meanings by male revolutionary leaders—meanings that were either incomprehensible or, more likely, misunderstood by most women who continued to interpret and define the key revolutionary words in private, religious, and domestic contexts. Such words, in fact, had distinctly *gendered meanings* that historians are only beginning to explore.[9]

As the rhetoric of the Revolution began to assume dynamic, emotional proportions, its obsession with "virtue" versus "corruption" struck a particularly responsive chord among literate women, as evidenced, for example, in their patriotic statements as individuals and in voluntary groups when supporting the boycott of English goods between 1765 and 1774. While these statements are impressive both in number and intensity of telling, it can be questioned whether the idea of taking "their country back on the path of virtue" and away from "the oppression of corrupt outside forces" was understood in the same way by female and male patriots, when even men of varying Whig persuasions could not agree on it.[10]

In the writings of male revolutionary activists, virtue was almost always associated or linked with the idea of what Thomas Paine called "public esteem." In fact, most Founding Fathers assumed that public service was a necessary condition and obligation of the virtuous life for men. This assumption was a natural reflection of the classical and early modern republican idea that virtue referred "not to female private morality but to male public spirit, that is to the willingness of citizens to engage actively in civil life and to sacrifice individual interests for the common good." Yet, as Paine also pointed out, virtuous women from the Greeks forward were depicted as those who were "least talked of," as though "in exacting virtues from them would make it a crime [for women] to aspire to honour."[11] Consequently, although male leaders combined the word *virtue* with *public service* in their speeches before and during the American Revolution, potential female activists could not—at least in any realistic way. Instead, such women accepted the two concepts of private virtue and public esteem—claiming only the first for themselves—not realizing this implicitly relegated future generations of U.S. women to a political and legal time-lag behind all white men.

Unlike Mary Wollstonecraft, who argued later in the 1790s that since "liberty is the mother of virtue and if women be, by their very constitution slaves . . . they must ever languish like exotics, and be reckoned beautiful flaws in nature," the best-educated revolutionary women remained fearful of moving out of their separate, virtuous sphere. Wollstonecraft was convinced that "as sound politics diffuse liberty, mankind, including woman, will become more wise and virtuous." Sounding very much like someone writing in the 1970s rather than the 1790s, she urged in A *Vindication of the Rights of Woman* that if men allowed women to share their socioeconomic and political rights, they would then "emulate the virtues of man." This emulation could only take place, however, if women received the same education as men because they too needed a "civil" existence *before* obtaining a "social" one.[12]

While there was a nascent, female concept of internalized private virtue by the time of the American Revolution, it did not receive much attention until after the drafting of the Constitution of 1787. Its origins, according to Ruth H. Bloch, lay less in classical or republican thought than in three underlying religious, educational, and literary trends already manifest well before the War of Independence. At best, the American Revolution accelerated but did not originate this long-term cultural process. Therefore, as men abandoned the notion of manly virtue, based on "self-sacrificial public spirit," for "enlightened" self-interest, the private virtue of women assumed some very tenuous "civic" overtones, primarily in the form of educating future generations of patriots.[13]

My problem with the recent emphasis on the importance of republican motherhood, the feminization of morality, and the domestication of *virtù* is that outside of exhortations by a few male novelists, ministers, and politicians in the immediate postrevolutionary period, there is very little evidence that even the best-educated upper-class women believed that the heightened importance of the second-hand virtue, which had been bestowed on them primarily after the drafting of the Constitution of 1787, had, in fact, improved or changed their socioeconomic or legal status in society. That the term had considerable moral and religious significance for them I do not deny.

Abigail Adams, for example, grasped the limitations of the educational function of virtuous upper-class women and of the inadequacy of their education. Writing in the summer of 1782 to both her husband and her cousin John Thaxter, she first pointed out that "patriotism in the female Sex is the most disinterested of all virtues" because women had no political rights. Hence, their patriotism consisted of the unheralded act of surviving the loss in battle of "those whom we

Love most." Adams most astutely noted that given the increase in political corruption and private vice during the war, she did not see how women could effectively transfer their private virtues to the public realm. How could they possibly control the virtue of society, as Rousseau had recommended, when their distinctly inferior female education and socialization had instilled in them ideas of morality that males increasingly did not share in the immediate postrevolutionary period? Indeed, what means did they have at their disposal for such an enormously pretentious task? It was obvious, at least to Abigail Adams, that education conducted in the home was not the way to preserve uncorrupted republicanism.[14]

Adams's friend Mercy Otis Warren elaborated on some of these thoughts in 1800 when she said that education was as unnecessary for a woman as virtue was for a gentleman. In 1805, in her three-volume *History of the Rise, Progress, and Termination of the American Revolution,* Warren commented negatively on the decline in virtue of the "Children of Columbia," nowhere indicating that women could stem this counterrevolutionary tide.[15] It should be noted, however, that Warren's views on the value of female education had not always been so cynical. *Before* the American Revolution she had written to Abigail Adams on 25 July 1773 of the importance of teaching "many . . . virtues to children, particularly the "Law of truth." Warren also advised her niece Rebecca Otis in 1776 about the desirability of combining "attention to the economy of domestic life . . . [with] cultivat[ing] your mind, and . . . your understanding by reading . . . those useful lessons of virtue and science . . . exhibited in the faithful pages of authentic history." Additionally, Warren's early letters to Catherine Macaulay, the republican sympathizer and British political philosopher, indicate that she was initially exposed to Macaulay's much stronger and more secular views about equal education for women and men.[16]

By the turn of the century, however, Mercy Otis Warren no longer appeared to believe in the efficacy of education for women under the new republic. Her discouragement (along with that of Abigail Adams) stands out in stark relief when compared to the standard renditions of the significant change in self-perception that republican wifehood and motherhood supposedly brought about among postrevolutionary American women. If anything, the changed perceptions of these two remarkable women seem to have gone from prewar optimism to postwar pessimism, not only about female education but also about women's general ability to influence the course of history.

## The Roles of Republican Wives and Mothers

Nonetheless, by the mid-1980s some historians do not hesitate to assert that "ultimately the concept of 'republican motherhood' altered the character of the family and of American society. . . . [and] many married women used their moral position as 'guardians of virtue' to achieve a position of near-equality in the home."[17] At the very most, this description applies to "the rapid rise in consciousness" of a few women in the 1830s and 1840s who realized (along with African-American activists) that they "had in fact been excluded from full participation in the republican experiments." Women only began to address their own legitimate grievances after they obtained a greater sense of private identity and personal confidence because of their private religious experiences during the Second Great Awakening and their experience with public participation in the temperance and abolitionist movements. As noted in chapter 1, the revolutionary and immediate postrevolutionary generation of American women did not exhibit even the early stages of transformation of passive, private piety into assertive demands for public participation in American society.[18]

Women of the revolution, when not described collectively in platitudinous phrases as paragons of virtue and patriotism—which they supposedly transmitted through their household roles as educators—were usually damned with faint praise, even by those among them who were in a position to know better. Thus, Mercy Warren in her history, as in her earlier patriotic plays and poetry, ignored entirely the significant contributions of women to the American Revolution—an indication of the limits of her "feminism." Instead, her most direct comment on the subject came during the war, when she wrote: "Be it known unto Britain even American daughters are politicians and patriots, and will aid the good work with their feeble efforts."[19]

Clinging to the presumed safety of older, familiar concepts of virtue and morality, the vast majority of Americans (but particularly women) were not prepared for the "acceptance of diversity, the commitment to individual action in pursuit of individual goals, the conception of politics as an arena where these goals contest and the awareness of a national government which is at once the source of political power and the framework for an orderly clash of interest." These are characteristics of "modern man."[20] And during the course of the American Revolution the few modern men around happened to be concentrated in that elite group known as the Founding Fathers, whose definitions of certain revolutionary words and political concepts did not represent those of most men, let alone of most women, by the time they drafted the Constitution in 1787.

Even more important from the standpoint of the several generations of American women whose lives spanned the revolutionary and postrevolutionary periods from 1765 to 1800 was the double-edged dimension of the word *virtue*. It simultaneously allowed them to respond to the rhetoric of the Revolution, while understanding it only within the confines of their private sphere of domesticity and religious beliefs. Public virtue remained a male attribute before, during, and following the American Revolution. After virtue became a female attribute in the 1780s and 1790s, it remained private and "outside politics," thus effectively excluding women from "institutionalized public life."[21]

To understand how little the equalitarian ideals of the Revolution changed the legal status of women, the restrictive private parameters within which such independent women as Abigail Adams, Margaret Livingston, Sarah Jay, Judith Sargent Murray, Elizabeth Southgate Browne, Elizabeth Drinker, and Mercy Otis Warren operated have to be separated from the excessive praise lavished upon them. Like most of the better organized, but ultimately unsuccessful, Républicaines of France, they did not aspire to equality with men except occasionally when discussing the deficiencies of education. Moreover, none challenged the institution of marriage or defined themselves "as other than mothers and potential mothers." They simply could not conceive of a society the standards of which were not set by male, patriarchal institutions, nor should they be expected to have done so. Instead of organizing for equal rights, the most articulate and politically conscious women of this generation asked at most for individual privileges and at least for favors—not for an absolute expansion of their legal or political functions, which they considered beyond their proper womanly sphere.[22] Man was, indeed, the measure of equality to these women; and, given their societal conditioning, male status was beyond their conception of themselves as individuals.

How does one test such a generalization about the attitudes behind the female understanding of virtue and the behavior of women during the Revolution? Few poor white or black women left records revealing how they felt about the war. Such women, whether Loyalists or patriots, conveyed their sentiments silently with their physical labor. Among the more articulate and educated women there is written testimony to at least an initial sense of pride and importance involved in their participation in the war effort, and they were exhorted to support the enlistment of their men at public gatherings. Thus, Abigail Foote, a young Connecticut woman, wrote in her diary in 1775 that carding two pounds of whole wool had made her feel "Nationaly [sic]," while others recorded their contributions in similarly patriotic terms—often at the same time complaining about the hardships of being separated from their husbands or male relatives, urging them to resign and come home.[23]

But the question remains, Did their supportive actions that were so clearly orchestrated and publicized by patriotic men prepare them to accept a secular vision of society anywhere near the one ultimately conveyed by James Madison's *Federalist Papers* (number 10) in the debate over the 1787 Constitution? To date, there is little evidence that this type of sophisticated political or legal thought was present, either in the writings of women about the Revolution and its results or in the appeals made to them during or immediately following the war. From the popular 1767 statement of advice to the Daughters of Liberty to the 1787 one urging women to use "their influence over their husbands, brothers and sons to draw them from those dreams of liberty under a simple democratical form of government, which are so unfriendly to . . . order and decency," it is difficult to conclude that women were being prepared to understand the pluralistic political ramifications of the Revolution, let alone partake of its legal and economic opportunities.[24]

This same lack of political (let alone legal) astuteness appears to underlie even the least traditional and most overtly political activities of women, such as the fifty-one individuals who signed the Anti-Tea Declaration in Edenton, North Carolina, on 25 October 1774 (later immortalized in a London cartoon). The same could be said of the more than five hundred Boston women who agreed on 31 January 1770 to support the radical male boycott of tea; of the Daughters of Liberty in general; and of the sixteen hundred Philadelphia women who raised $7,500 in gold for the Continental army. Even the anti-Federalist historian Mercy Otis Warren never envisioned the modern public system that evolved from the Revolution; nor did she project any public roles for even the most patriotic women in her many satirical and serious writings in the 1770s and 1780s. Instead, in religious terms she ambiguously viewed the war and its aftermath as an exercise in the practice of virtue, which became an "instrument of Providence that sparked a world movement, changing thought and habit of men to complete the divine plan for human happiness."[25]

To the degree that republican wives and mothers succeeded in maintaining some consistency among their emotional, physical, and intellectual commitments to one side or the other, the moral consciousness of this particular generation of late eighteenth-century women suffered most from their unrequited loyalty when it became apparent that neither side had a monopoly on virtue or righteousness. Like the rank and file of American men, they were psychologically and experientially unprepared to accept the many compromises that public life forced upon male revolutionary leaders. In addition, their individual self-perceptions and economic, legal, and political notions were so underdeveloped by modernization standards that the American women who experienced the war never attempted, as French women later did, to organize in their own behalf when their specific needs and mild material requests were not satisfied.

Their familial duties, particularly child bearing, were still so demanding and obviously important that they were nowhere near what Chalmers Johnson has referred to as the conscious condition of "multiple dysfunctionalism," or what Anthony F. C. Wallace has described as that condition of "panic stricken anxiety, shame, guilt, depression or apathy" so characteristic of those "culturally disillusioned" people who are the catalyst of revolutionary change. Indeed, it has taken most of the twentieth century for even middle-class American women to recognize the decline in their functional status, to obtain the necessary prerequisites for their own emancipation, and to begin to envision a society based on other than patriarchal terms.[26] As a result, with the exception of the few military heroines who received pensions from the United States government, none of the supportive actions of women during the Revolution was monetarily rewarded. Nor was there any organized feminist demand that they should be.

If anything, the War of Independence and the subsequent trials of the new republic between 1776 and 1800 strengthened belief in the separate-sphere concept. The idea that men and women existed in two separate spheres, or orbits, was commonly accepted in the last half of the eighteenth century as one of the natural laws of the universe. While European Enlightenment theories underscored the inferiority of the natural and proper sphere occupied by women, in colonial America these theories were tacitly challenged and modified by experience—as were so many other aspects of natural-law doctrines—but their original gendered meanings became more pronounced after the American Revolution.[27] Therefore, the degree to which a few educated upper-class women might have thought that their private sphere of activity was in fact equal, and the degree to which it actually was accorded such status by the male-dominated culture, is all important. Historians have tended to place greater emphasis on the former rather than the latter, resulting in misleading interpretations about the roles played by both colonial and revolutionary women. Instead of evaluating the real legal status of such women, there has been a tendency to rationalize about them.

## Abigail Adams: "Remembering the Ladies" and Separate Spheres

It is usually overlooked, for example, that in the famous letter of 31 March 1776, in which Abigail Adams asked John Adams to "Remember the Ladies," she was not asking for anything like equality *or* even the right to vote (although her husband chose to interpret her words as meaning the latter). Since this letter and John Adams's response to it have been subject to widely varying interpretations, it is worth quoting from the originals at length. Abigail's words to John can be found at the end of a letter that contrasted wartime conditions in Boston (and the dirty state that one of the "Doctors of the Regiment" had left their house) with the hopeful signs of spring in the countryside that made her heart "gay":

I long to hear that you have declared an independancy—and by the way in the new Code of Laws which I suppose it will be necessary for you to make I desire you would Remember the Ladies, and be more generous and favourable to them than your ancestors. Do not put such unlimited power into the hands of the Husbands. Remember all Men would be tyrants if they could. If perticular care and attention is not paid to the Laidies we are determined to foment a Rebelion, and will not hold ourselves bound by any Laws in which we have no voice, or Representation.

That your Sex are Naturally Tyrannical is a Truth so thoroughly established as to admit of no dispute, but such of you as wish to be happy willingly give up the harsh title of Master for the more tender and endearing one of Friend. Why then, not put it out of the power of the vicious and the Lawless to use us with cruelty and indignity with impunity. Men of Sense in all Ages abhor those customs which treat us only as vassals of your Sex. Regard us then as Beings placed by providence under your protection and in immitation of the Supreem Being make use of that power only for our happiness.[28]

Abigail Adams justified this mild request for "more generous and favourable" treatment on the grounds that married women were then subjected to the "unlimited power" of their husbands. She was not asking her husband for the right to vote, only for some legal protection of wives from abuses under common-law practices. Despite her statement in this letter about "laidies" being "determined to foment a Rebelion" and refusing to be "bound by any Laws in which we have no voice, or Representation," Abigail Adams was not specifically demanding legal equality with men at the beginning of the American Revolution, yet her request does show legal acumen on her part with respect to the common-law disabilities of married women. However, her husband was not contemplating changing her legal status or that of other women. On 14 April 1776 Adams accorded a supercilious answer to his wife's polite, if somewhat lighthearted, request for limits on the power of husbands.

As to your extraordinary Code of Laws, I cannot but laugh. We have been told that our Struggle has loosened the bands of Government every where. That Children and Apprentices were disobedient—that schools and Colledges were grown turbulent—that Indians slighted their Guardians and Negroes grew insolent to their Masters. But your Letter was the first Intimation that another Tribe more numerous and powerfull [sic] than all the rest were grown discontented.—This is rather too coarse a Compliment but you are so saucy, I wont blot it out.

Depend upon it, We know better than to repeal our Masculine systems. Altho they are in full Force, you know they are little more than Theory. We dare not exert our Power in its full Latitude. We are obliged to go fair, and softly, and in Practice you know We are the subjects. We have only the Name of Masters, and rather than give up this, which would compleatly subject Us to the Despotism of the Peticoat, I hope General Washington, and all our brave Heroes would fight. I am sure every good Politician would plot, as long as he would against Despotism, Empire, Monarchy, Aristocracy, Oligarchy, or Ochlocracy.[29]

By comparing women to other dependent and disobedient "tribes," such as Indians, children, apprentices, and African-Americans, John Adams's words presaged later legal briefs and court decisions throughout the nineteenth century that routinely categorized women with children, lunatics, and criminals as dependent groups without full citizenship. When he concluded that because women were the "more numerous and powerful" of all these "tribes"—they already ruled their men from behind the scenes—he was simply reiterating a stereotypic view of women of the last quarter of the eighteenth century—one that can still be found lingering in certain dark corners in the last quarter of the twentieth. However, on 26 May 1776 Adams wrote to his friend and colleague James Sullivan a more serious letter addressing the dangers in his wife's now-famous request that he and the other Founding Fathers "Remember the Ladies," with more seriousness than he earlier had accorded her.

It is certain in Theory, that the only moral Foundation of Government is the Consent of the People. But to what an Extent Shall We carry this Principle? Shall We Say, that every Individual of the Community, old and young, male and female, as well as rich and poor, must consent, expressly to every Act of Legislation? No, you will Say, this is impossible. How then does the Right arise in the Majority to govern the Minority, against their Will? Whence arises the Right of the Men to govern the Women, without their Consent? Whence the Right of the old to bind the Young, without theirs?

But let us first Suppose, that the whole Community of every Age, Rank, Sex, and Condition, has a Right to vote—This Community is assembled—a Motion is made and carried by a Majority of one Voice. The Minority will not agree to this. Whence arises the Right of the Majority to govern, and the obligation of the Minority to obey? From Necessity, you will Say, because there can be no other rule. But why exclude Women? You will Say, because their Delicacy renders them unfit for Practice and Experience, in the great Businesses of Life, and the hardy Enterprises of War, as well as the arduous Cares of State. Besides, their attention is so much engaged with the necessary Nurture of their Children, that Nature has made them fittest for domestic Cares. And Children have not Judgment or Will of their own. True. But will not these Reasons apply to others? Is it not equally true, that Men in general in every Society, who are wholly destitute of Property, are also too little acquainted with public affairs to form a Right Judgment, and too dependent upon other Men to have a Will of their own? If this is a Fact, if you give to every man, who has no Property, a Vote, will you not make a fine encouraging Provision for Corruption by your fundamental Law? Such is the Frailty of the human Heart, that very few Men, who have no Property, have any Judgment of their own. They talk and vote as they are directed by Some Man of Property, who has attached their Minds to his Interest. . . .

The Same Reasoning, which will induce you to admit all Men, who have no Property, to vote, with those who have, for those Laws, which affect the Person will prove that you ought to admit Women and Children: for generally Speaking, Women and Children have as good Judgment, and as independent Minds as those Men who are wholly destitute of Property: these last being to all Intents and Purposes as much dependent upon others, who will please to feed, cloath, and employ them, as Women are upon their Husbands, or Children on their Parents. . . .

Depend upon it, Sir, it is dangerous to open so fruitfull a Source of Controversy and altercation; as would be opened by attempting to alter the Qualifications of Voters. There will be no End of it. New Claims will arise. Women will demand a Vote. Lads from 12 to 21 will think their Rights not enough attended to, and every Man, who has not a Farthing, will demand an equal Voice with any other in all Acts of State. It tends to confound and destroy all Distinctions, and prostrate all Ranks, to one common Levell.[30]

In summary, to grant women voting rights (which Abigail Adams had not requested, but which John Adams assumed to be implicit in her 1776 letter) would open up the possibility of propertyless men and other dependent groups who lacked the experience and judgment (which came from owning and managing property) from demanding the same right. Thus, in the final analysis for John Adams and other Founding Fathers, such as Jefferson, the presumed dependency of all women was enough to disqualify them from voting—even those who were single and whose ownership of property presumably gave them temporary independence of mind.[31] Whether Abigail Adams ever became aware of her husband's serious response to Sullivan about her original request is not known. Subsequently, however, she wrote both him and Mercy Otis Warren about his "very sausy [sic]" response to her "List of Female Grievances." Significantly, Abigail's interpretation of John's words to her friend represented an early indication that the revolutionary generation of educated women would ultimately conclude that male leaders were not adhering to the same concepts of virtue as their female counterparts (if they ever had) in the course of the War of Independence and in the establishment of the new national and state governments. "I will tell him I have only been making trial of the Disintresstedness of his Virtue," Abigail Adams wrote Warren on 27 April 1776, "and when weigh'd in the balance have found it wanting."[32] In a curt 7 May reply to her husband, she said:

I can not say that I think you very generous to the Ladies, for whilst you are proclaiming peace and good will to Men, Emancipating all Nations, you insist upon retaining an absolute power over Wives. But you must remember that Arbitrary power is like most other things which are very hard, very liable to be broken—and notwithstanding all your wise Laws and Maxims we have it in our power not only to free ourselves but to subdue our Masters, and without voilence [sic] throw both your natural and legal authority at our feet—

> "Charm by accepting, by submitting sway
> Yet have our Humour most when we obey."[33]

Although there is no indication that Abigail Adams ever again requested that her husband consider modifying common-law restrictions on married women, in 1777 Hanna Lee Corbin of Virginia actually did ask her brother, Richard Henry Lee, to support voting rights for widows who paid taxes, arguing that otherwise it would be another example of taxation without representation. As a member of the Continental Congress, Lee indicated that he favored such a measure, but that it was not necessary because women already had "as legal a right to vote as any other person." Obviously, this right was one that few women in Virginia knew about or exercised. Not until 5 July 1780 did Abigail Adams admit to John that he had turned her into a "politician." Despite the fact that "I cannot be a voter upon this occasion, I will be a writer of votes," Adams told her husband. Two years later, on 17 June 1782, she again raised the question of married women's civil rights with him, but by then she appears to have accepted female exclusion from the political process as a given that made any interest women might take in "publick Welfare . . . most Heroick."[34] Much later, on 15 November 1797, Adams indicated to her sister Mary Cranch that she was aware that women had the suffrage vote in New Jersey: "If our State constitution had been equally liberal, . . . I should have certainly exercised it [the right to vote]." However, earlier that same year she had expressed outrage that her behind-the-scenes political activity had resulted in a "Gentleman . . . [who] must have lost his senses" referring to her as an authority at a Quincy town meeting.[35]

Abigail Adams's correspondence with others about other female roles in post-revolutionary America was not as ambivalent as on the question of women's political rights and responsibilities. On these subjects her opinions did not vacillate. For example, she firmly criticized books by foreign authors who subordinated the female sphere to that of the male. As she wrote in 1799 to her sister Elizabeth Shaw Peabody, she would "not consent to have our sex considered in an inferior point of light. Let each planet shine in their [sic] own orbit. God and nature designed it so—if man is Lord, woman is Lordess—that is what I contend for." Thus, when her husband was away she deemed it was within her proper sphere to act as head of the household in all matters, including the decision to have her children inoculated against smallpox without his permission. At the same time, however, she always deferred to his ambitions and his societal superiority because the theoretical equality of their two separate spheres did not make them actually equal as individuals. In general, Abigail Adams and other women of her class and education accepted the notion that while they were mentally equal to men their sphere of activity was entirely private in nature, except on those occasions when they substituted for their absent husbands as "deputies." "Government of States and Kingdoms, tho' God knows badly enough managed," she asserted in 1796, "I am willing should be solely administered by the lords of creation. I should contend for Domestic Government, and think that best administered by the female."[36]

Mercy Otis Warren also believed that male and female spheres should be equal. On several occasions, for example, she strongly denied that women should be considered only "indifferent politician[s] or unconcerned and silent spectator[s]." Yet in explaining these remarks, she seemed at worst to be referring to a "pillow-talk" type of politics, or at best to a "power-behind-the-scenes" political role for her sex. "When observations are just and honorary to the heart and character," she wrote Macaulay on 29 December 1774, "I think it very immaterial whether they flow from a female life in the soft whispers of private friendship, or thundered in the Senate. . . . Nor will one be more influential than the other . . . so long as the private interest is the spring of action which is indeed too often the Sole Star that governs mankind from the King to the Cottage."[37]

In the final analysis, the belief of Abigail Adams and Mercy Otis Warren in equal, but separate, spheres was indeed admirable for the times, but it should not be confused with feminism.[38] Ironically it is this same sense of the equality of their "proper sphere" that explains why the most politically astute female patriots did not feel obliged to organize for the purpose of demanding more from the Founding Fathers. However, their lives and letters clearly indicated to other educated women that they were not obliged to remain ignorant of politics taking place in the public realm outside their domestic sphere. In 1779 Eliza Wilkinson, a wealthy South Carolina widow, wrote:

Never were [there] greater politicians than the several knots of ladies, who met together. . . . All trifling discourse of fashions . . . was thrown by, and we commenced perfect statesmen. Indeed, I don't know but if we had taken a little pains, we should have been qualified for prime ministers, so well could we discuss several important matters in hand. . . . I won't have it thought, that because we are the weaker sex as to bodily strength, my dear, we are capable of nothing more than minding the dairy, visiting the poultry-house, and all such domestic concerns; our thoughts can soar aloft, we . . . have as just a sense of honor glory, and great actions, as the 'Lords of Creation'. . . . They won't even allow us the liberty of thought, and that is all I want. I would not wish that we should meddle in what is unbecoming female delicacy, but sure we have sense enough to give our opinions . . . without being reminded of our spinning and household affairs as the only matter we are capable of thinking or speaking of with justness or propriety. I won't allow it, positively won't.[39]

Wilkinson concluded this portion of her letter, only to ruefully reflect a few pages later: "What will the men say if they should see this? I am really out of *my sphere* now, and must fly to Homer for direction and instruction on household matters."[40]

For women to have asked for individual or political equality with men would not only have violated their belief in two separate, but equal, spheres of duty but also would have automatically meant asking for a role in the public realm that was literally considered a physical impossibility by most eighteenth-century women. Their dawn-to-dusk domestic duties as household managers and their health problems from frequent childbirth and inadequate diets relegated all classes of colonial women to lives of domesticity in the broadest sense of the term. This was philosophically reinforced by the political theories and physical laws of the universe associated with the Enlightenment that deemed it "natural" for public affairs to be conducted exclusively by men.[41]

Only a most-radical male revolutionary like Thomas Paine asserted that revolutionary women be treated like men when, in his famous 1775 "An Occasional Letter on the Female Sex," he had a hypothetical female speaker proclaim: "If we have an equal right to virtue, why should we not have an equal right to praise?" Moreover, it was Paine—not the female patriots—who also took advantage of American revolutionary conditions to attack the institution of marriage. Later, in the 1790s, only a few isolated women in the United States supported Mary Wollstonecraft's "the-personal-is-political" demand for the right of woman to public as well as private fulfillment on the grounds that "private duties are never properly fulfilled unless the understanding enlarges the heart and that public virtue is only an aggregate of private." Like Paine's, Wollstonecraft's criticisms of marital bondage were never seriously considered by American women in the postrevolutionary decade.[42]

The reasons for this unresponsiveness to the feminism of both Paine and Wollstonecraft are complex, for it was opposed not only by the patriarchal Founding Fathers but also by most women themselves. Again we must ask, Why? The physical and mental hardships endured by most women during the war continued to varying degrees during the economic dislocation following in its wake. Sheer personal survival, not rising social or material expectations, dominated the thinking and activities of lower- and even some middle- and upper-class women. Probably more important, the few well-educated American women fortunate enough to have had the leisure time to reflect clearly realized the discrepancy that had occurred between the theory and practice of virtue in the course of the war and its aftermath. While it was discouraging for them to witness the corruption of their privatized sense of morality and virtue by the society at large and particularly among men in public life, they could take some satisfaction in the greater consistency between the theory and practice of virtue in their own private lives. In a word, Paine and Wollstonecraft were too secular and public about matters better left to providence or privacy. Such postrevolutionary women found their familial duties and homosocial relationships untainted by the corruption of public life. They considered themselves most fortunate—and they *were,* compared to their nineteenth-century descendants who had to pay a much higher price for similar private virtuous consistency and spiritual purity.[43]

It was natural, therefore, for the educated among this generation to express disillusionment with politics, as they saw republican principles corrupted or distorted, and then to enter a stage of relative quiescence that marked the beginning of the transitional period between their war-related activities and a later generation of female reformers who emerged in the 1830s. They cannot be held responsible for their failure to realize the full extent of the potentially debilitating features of their withdrawal to the safety of traditional domesticity and self-sacrifice—where virtue often becomes its own punishment instead of reward. Mercy Otis Warren's revolutionary career poignantly reflects the dilemma of this privileged group of white women.

## Mercy Otis Warren's Circumscribed Intellect

Mercy Otis Warren grew up in a farmhouse that was often visited by leaders of the English colonies, and she had access to a wide selection of the latest pamphlets, journals, and newspapers. She formed a close bond with her brother James, with whom she frequently exchanged letters after he left home to attend Harvard. In addition, James guided her reading, recommending that she study Milton, Shakespeare, Dryden, Pope, and Locke. Later, her poetry would be reminiscent of Pope's, while her prose recalled the writings of Raleigh. Warren combined such reading with experiments in writing verse and lessons in household skills, such as making soap, cheese, and candles. While she appeared well trained in all of the traditional domestic duties, her efficiency as a household and land manager never approached that of Abigail Adams. Unlike her friend, Mercy Otis Warren led a secluded life, keeping in touch with the world at large vicariously. She rarely left her home in Barnstable, except for a 1744 trip to Harvard at age fifteen to attend the graduation ceremonies for her brother James. It was during this visit to Cambridge that she met James Warren of Plymouth, her future husband.[44] The years immediately preceding the American Revolution found Mercy Otis Warren closer to the center of the political action because of her husband's and son's revolutionary activities than she would be following the war, because neither of them achieved prominence in the new government.

Because of her frequent contact with these leaders, Warren had the opportunity to gather letters, newspapers, and books outlining the political positions of many colonial rebels. Much of the information she collected would later be incorporated into her three-volume *History of the Rise, Progress, and Termination of the American Revolution* (1805). As early as December 1775, for example, she unsuccessfully attempted to obtain from Abigail Adams "[c]ertain private Journals as you dare trust me, With. I have a curiosity to know a Little More about Certain public Characters and perticular [*sic*] transactions than I am in a Way of being Acquainted with. It Would be an agreeable Entertainment to my Lonely hours."[45] Adams later refused to turn over her husband's diary volumes to Warren, saying that she could not comply with the request because "unless I knew the hand by which I sent them I am afraid to write any thing which ought not to come to the public Eye."[46] Undaunted, Warren continued to solicit confidential information about American leaders from the Adamses and other prominent revolutionary families. That she succeeded more often than she failed in obtaining information in this fashion is proved by the personal insights and characterizations contained in her *History*.

Responding to rising anti-British sentiment, Mercy Otis Warren took up her pen and did not lay it down again for the next thirty-five years. While continuing to keep her duties as a wife and mother foremost in her life, Warren began composing poems and plays voicing her political philosophy. She had been composing poetry since 1759, but in the early 1770s turned increasingly to political satire. Her first revolutionary verses reflected what would later become a major theme of her interpretation of American independence—namely, the absence or presence of virtue. Thus, in "A Political Reverie," a poem about how the colonists vacillated over whether or not to resort to arms, she predicted revolution because freedom no longer existed in England; its people had stopped emulating Locke. She wrote, "Virtue turned pale, and freedom left the isle."[47]

In the aftermath of the Boston Tea Party, John Adams, in a letter to Warren's husband, urged her to write about the "equity" of the event that he described as the "late frolic among the Sea Nymphs and Goddesses." Adams even sketched the highly classical outline he had in mind for such a work, and on 21 March 1774, "The Squabble of the Sea Nymphs; or, the Sacrifice of the Tuscararoes [*sic*]" appeared on the front page of the Boston *Gazette*. In an unusually positive reference to the contemporary attitudes of women, she wrote that "the virtuous daughters of the neighboring mead / In graceful smiles approved the glorious deed."[48] Typically she chided women in these propaganda poems "to check [their] wanton pride / And lay [their] female ornaments aside." At the instigation of Dr. John Winthrop, the husband of her friend Hannah Winthrop, she urged women to support various boycotts of British goods. Accordingly, she once proclaimed: "[A]nd be it known unto Britain, even American daughters are politicians and patriots, and will aid the good work with their female efforts."[49]

Warren's reliance on the encouragement and praise of men, such as her husband, John Adams, Alexander Hamilton, and later Thomas Jefferson, emerged as an early pattern in her literary career. After publishing her poem about the Boston Tea Party, she was not disappointed when John Adams excessively praised "the skirmish of the sea deities." Warren ingenuously expressed surprise, claiming that she never realized that she could "amuse, much less . . . benefit the world by [her] unstudied composition." Of course, she disclaimed any desire for public esteem or eminence. Her correspondence contains many apologies for going "so much out of the road of female attention" because she realized it was "not altogether consonant with Female Genius."[50] However, she constantly sought private approval from her male friends. This tendency was particularly evident in her early correspondence with John Adams during the height of her poetic output before and during the American Revolution.

Virtue, however, remained uppermost in her mind. Thus, she advised a young American male residing in France during the War of Independence to remember to practice private virtue in the midst of foreign corruption. In 1778, after her eldest son had lost a leg in battle, she began to lament the disappearance of virtue from the revolutionary cause. On 5 October 1778 her poem "O Tempora! O Mores!" made the front page of the Boston *Gazette* with a prose comment that read: "This piece was written when a most remarkable depravity of manners pervaded the cities of the United States, in consequence of a state of war; a relaxation of government; a sudden acquisition of fortune; a depreciating currency; and a new intercourse with foreign nations." In the course of the poem, she asked:

> Shall freedom's cause by vice be thus betray'd
> Our country bleeds and bleeds at every pore,
> Yet gold's the deity whom all adore;
> All public faith, and private justice dead,
> and patriot zeal by patriots betray'd.[51]

Warren's growing moral disillusionment with what she perceived as the diminished virtue of American political leaders is reflected in the satiric focus of five plays published anonymously between 1773 and 1779. In *The Adulateur* (1772) and *The Defeat* (1773), she castigated Governor Thomas Hutchinson, attacking him as mediocre and unprincipled. In her best-known play, *The Group* (1775), she attacked the British-appointed officials ruling Massachusetts. After the war began, she published *The Blockheads* (1776), her only prose play, which satirized the grand treatment Loyalist Bostonians gave the captured British general, John Burgoyne. In this play, Warren startled her readers by using rough street language to emphasize her disenchantment with those who did not support the Revolution. By 1779, in *The Motley Assembly,* she had turned her satire on another group of Americans, the moderate Whigs, who were beginning to emerge as leaders of the new nation.

Her stultified, classical style, although highly regarded at the time, seems unduly artificial to the modern reader. Later, her three-volume history was to read like a narrative prose version of these early poems. In retrospect, it is difficult to perceive any significant development in her writing. Her style has been described as a pseudoelegant "flowery mode of expression."[52] Only *The Blockheads,* renowned at the time for its "vulgarity," stands out from the rest because she used terms such as "prig," and "pimp" and described one character as having "shit his breeches." As a result, some scholars question her authorship of this play and *The Motley Assembly*.[53] However, the sentiments in both plays are surely hers. Their vocabulary and broad sexual humor afford a glimpse of a considerably less staid and protected homebody than her portraits and private correspondence would lead us to expect.

*The Blockheads*, interesting because of its sexual innuendos, is distinguished by unusual demographic insight. As in all her satires, she portrayed the British as more degenerate and avaricious then they were; however, she also depicted American Loyalists as stupid, pretentious, lower-class farmers interested mainly in rising socially among their new-found British friends. Most standard accounts of Loyalists have stressed their wealth, education, and cultural refinement. While she exaggerated both their social ambitions and uncouthness, she was demographically correct in describing the American Loyalists as primarily poor farmers dissatisfied with their lot in life. For what it is worth, Warren's satire comes closer to the collective biographical truth about rank-and-file native American Loyalists than most standard accounts since that time. Thus, Mr. and Mrs. Simple and their daughter Tabitha leave their "filthy farm" because "it is all dirty stuff, only fit for Yankees," in response to false promises from the British (including the propositioning of their daughter by Lord Dapper). Their humiliation and suffering as refugees is approved by a woman in good radical Whig (later Jeffersonian Republican) fashion in the last soliloquy of the play:

Good enough for them, they have brought it upon themselves; they had better have minded their farms. . . . If I had a good farm, I would see government to the devil, before they should catch me here, to be froz'd, famish'd, ridiculed'd—curse them and their spiritless protectors, and let's conclude with huzzas for America.[54]

*The Group* is more traditional in both style and subject matter. Concentrating on wealthier Loyalist leaders after Hutchinson's departure for England, Warren paints a devastating picture of them as ambitious, greedy, petty traitors compared to the patriots who are represented only at the end of the play interestingly by a woman. Lady Patriot predicted full-scale war because of the stupid tenacity of the Loyalists, although it is implied that she may have been married to one. Her patriotic views are all the more interesting, therefore, because they represent an independence of mind, but her monologue is laced with vintage female virtuousness that depicts "Freedom" weeping at the death of patriots whose memorial would bear the inscription "Virtue's sons lie here!" In comparison to the two other Tory wives in *The Group*, who are mistreated by their husbands, Lady Patriot seems modeled after Warren herself.[55]

It has been suggested that the presence of such strong, virtuous women in a number of her plays and poems made Warren "something of a feminist for her time."[56] More often than not, however, the politically astute women she depicted fared no better than their weaker or abused sisters, regardless of the fact that they always had virtue on their side. Warren was no more a feminist than she was a typical republican wife and mother. Her gender circumscribed her intellect to such a degree that she, like most of her female characters, acted only within prescribed male parameters—pushing their limits on occasion but never crossing over into the public sphere without permission, and then often at their own or their husbands' expense. In 1933, Clifford K. Shipton captured Warren's plight with this sexist but probably accurate description:

She was a woman whose strong character and never-quiet pen made her more famous than her husband. Untroubled by logic, reason, or perspective, furious in her prejudices, she poured upon the leading men of the times a confident and assertive correspondence which caused many a pitying glance to be cast toward her husband.[57]

Warren's lifelong insecurity about her abilities and achievements is nowhere more evident than in the motivations she attributes to her literary efforts. These are usually contained in introductions or letters and, in retrospect, are more interesting than the historical contents of her works because almost all of them represented male-inspired projects. Although she wrote *The Blockheads* upon the "particular desire" of her husband, Warren worried that she might have violated good taste and her proper sphere with her "satirical propensity." So she asked John Adams on 30 January 1775 if she should curb her talent and remain entirely within her proper sphere. Adams, who already had been sent a partial manuscript by Warren's husband and had published it anonymously in the Boston *Gazette* on 23 January, replied through James Warren that "it would be criminal to neglect" her talent and concluded with words he would not remember later when she dared to criticize him in her *History:* "The faithful Historian delineates Characters truly, let the Censure fall where it will."[58]

Abigail Adams also reassured Warren that she need not worry about her writing being incompatible with her "female character" because "when it is so happily blended with benevolence, and is awakened by the love of virtue and the abhorrence of vice . . . it is so far from blameable that it is certainly meritorious." Nonetheless, after the entire play had been published as an anonymous pamphlet in April 1775, Warren was upset by the immediate rumors that she had written it. Her claim to anonymity, always tenuous at best, disappeared after the play had become a success. John Adams even drew up a list identifying the characters in *The Group* as leading Tories.[59]

It must be remembered that plays written in the eighteenth century were for readers, not theater-goers, since a law in Massachusetts actually prohibited all public performances. The authorities believed the theater to be "the highway to hell." Warren's plays, however, appeared in newspapers and reached a wide audience. Although she wrote anonymously and ostensibly behind the scenes, her friends knew which works she authored. Both they, and a large segment of the public, also knew which fictional characters represented actual Bostonians.

Warren's two dramatic poems, *The Ladies of Castile* (1784) and *The Sack of Rome* (1785), were both written immediately after the War of Independence but were not published until 1790 in a collection of her poetry dedicated to George Washington. On 4 January 1787 she had asked John Adams if he could get *The Sack of Rome* (which was then dedicated to him) published; if not, she wanted him to "dispose of this little WORK to the most advantage of your friends." This letter clearly reflected Warren's use of feminine flattery at its best (or worst, depending on one's point of view). Lauding his judgment, his national prominence as U.S. minister to England, and his friendship, she disclaimed any serious desire to see the work in print and any attempt to influence him with undue praise. Most important for their later relationship, she casually informed him at the end of this classic example of female persuasion that she had begun to write "a concise History of the American Revolution."[60] Although Adams heartily approved of *The Sack of Rome*, he failed to get it produced or printed in London.

Both blank-verse tragedies were inspired by her son Winslow, and both focus on the conflict between love and duty, virtue and corruption, responsibility and ambition. Both contain introductions anticipating the rather gender-conscious, semiapologetic way in which Warren would twenty years later introduce her history. Both were thinly disguised analogies about postrevolutionary America. *The Ladies of Castile*, the first of her two blank-verse tragedies, concerns the tyrannical successors of Charles V in Spain; however, it begins with unadulterated praise of the uniqueness of the newly created United States:

America stands alone:—May she long stand, independent of every foreign policy; superior to the spirit of intrigue, or the corrupt principles of usurpation that may spring from successful exertions of her own sons . . . whose valour completed a revolution that will be the wonder of the ages. What a field day for genius: What a difference of capacity . . . in science, in business, and in politics does this revolution exhibit! Certain enough to fire the ambition, and light every noble spark in the bosoms of those who are in the morning of life.[61]

In spite of these confident words, Warren apologized because *The Ladies of Castile* was a dramatic poem rather than an epic, saying that "the candor of the public will be exercised not so much for the sake of the sex, as the design of the writer, who wishes only to cultivate the sentiments of public and private virtue in whatsoever falls from her pen."[62] *The Sack of Rome* begins more pessimistically, focusing on the intrigues of the Roman court under Petronius Maximus. Warren claims here that her aim is to improve morals in the United States "by an exhibition of the tumult and misery into which mankind are often plunged by an unwarrantable indulgence of the discordant passion of the human mind." She asked to be forgiven if the play is distasteful, and in an epilogue she describes herself as a "female bard" asking the public for a "candid eye."[63]

Between the writing of these two dramatic poems Warren's evaluation of the American Revolution changed, as did perhaps her estimation of herself. She seems more self-assertive and desirous of private or public approval in the second tragedy. Both poems have stronger female characters than her previous plays, even though the most virtuous women are doomed to suffer and often die with their virtuous fathers, husbands, lovers, brothers, or sons. Nonetheless, strong patriotic women emerge in the two poems, both of which end with death-scene statements either by or about women. Thus, *The Ladies of Castile* concludes with the words "To virtue bend the wayward mind of men," which *The Sack of Rome* echoes with "[v]irtue, sublim'd by piety and truth, now beckons to the skies."[64]

## Mercy Otis Warren as Historian

By 1785, when *The Sack of Rome* was written, Warren's poetry already presaged that all was not well with the new American republic. Soon she would find herself swept into postrevolutionary politics. Finally, she would write a three-volume history, in part to justify those politics. During the hostilities with Britain, American political leaders formed a government under the Articles of Confederation. When the Articles were judged to be unworkable and the Constitution of 1787 was subsequently written, Warren found herself ideologically on the side of the Antifederalists. In 1788, anonymous objections to the Constitution were published as a pamphlet entitled *Observations on the New Constitution and on the Federal and State Conventions. By a Columbian Patriot.* Originally attributed to Elbridge Gerry, scholars now assign authorship to Warren.[65]

The opinions Warren expressed in *Observations* certainly corresponded to the political and ideological stance she took in her previous literary works and in her unfinished *History.* She called the Constitution a "heterogeneous phantom" and a "many-headed monster; of such motley mixture that its enemies cannot trace a feature of Democratic or Republican extract" from it. Warren predicted a loss of liberty would follow its ratification and made references to loss of virtue over a dozen times in this twenty-two-page pamphlet. After reiterating Lockean doctrines regarding sovereignty and inalienable rights, Warren warned that the new document might promote tyranny and listed eighteen specific objections to the Constitution. Some were based on what she considered critical omissions in its text. For example, she noted the lack of specific provisions for direct annual elections and freedom of the press, as well as the absence of a general bill of rights. Warren also was not convinced that the new Constitution provided for a clear separation of executive and legislative powers, concluding:

the ratification of a Constitution, which, by the undefined meaning of some parts, and the ambiguities of expression in others, is dangerously adapted to the purposes of an immediate *aristocratic tyranny;* that from the difficulty, if not impracticability of its operation, must soon terminate in the most *uncontrouled despotism.* [66]

In addition to being concerned about omissions, Warren also thought the document contained several dangerous provisions. Her list of the Constitution's objectionable segments included the power over a standing army given to the president; the resources for taxation; the appellate jurisdiction given to the Supreme Court; the excessive length of the term of office for senators; and the power of the electoral college to take freedom of choice away from the people. She also questioned the practicality of the Constitution, arguing that the United States was too large to be governed by one legislative body, even if divided into two different representative bodies. Warren even questioned the legality of the Constitution by charging that the Constitutional Committee went beyond its authorized duties (which it had). In conclusion, she pointed out that the mode of ratification appeared to deny the people enough time for reasonable consideration of the new document, and she objected as well to the provision stipulating ratification by only nine states before the Constitution became effective. [67]

Warren's passionate Antifederalist attitudes, first exhibited in the 1788 debates over ratification of the Constitution, later led her to emphasize her own political philosophy in the last volume of her own *History* based on a sophisticated, but now antiquated, amalgamation of ideology and religious ethics, in which the latter ultimately prevails. Republican ideals could only survive if people remained ethical and mutually reinforced one another. For Warren, virtue remained a basic principle of society and history, as well as a personal characteristic. In her *History,* however, unlike in some of her earlier writings, vice and corruption tend to overwhelm virtue in the new republic. As a radical republican, this, of course, was a source of concern for her because she did not believe that the Revolution could be permanently institutionalized. The country's future would ultimately rise or fall on the moral character of its leaders and people, not on the structure of the government. [68]

Warren began writing her three-volume work in 1775 and labored over the text intermittently until it was nearly finished in 1791. The delay in completing the manuscript was perhaps fortunate because during this period publishers worked from subscription lists, taking orders from those who indicated a willingness to purchase a forthcoming publication. There is little doubt that Warren's political stance would have precluded a healthy subscription list during the 1780s, the decade when conservative Federalist views tended to dominate national politics. However, Warren made one concession in light of possible sales by restraining her public views about the Constitution of 1787 in her book. However, her personal fears and doubts about it remained as strong as ever. Although three of her contemporaries, notably William Gordon, David Ramsay, and John Marshall, already had published their views of the revolutionary period, they had championed the more popular Federalist cause. Mercy Otis Warren's work remains the *only* multivolume Antifederalist history of the American Revolution written by an eyewitness.[69]

As in the case of her other publications, Warren felt compelled to apologize for her intrusion into the public sphere of men by becoming a historian. She acknowledged overstepping prescribed boundaries, stating in her introduction to the *History:* "It is true there are certain appropriate duties assigned to each sex; and doubtless it is the more peculiar province of masculine strength . . . to describe the blood-stained field, and relate the story of slaughtered armies."[70] Her preoccupation with the preservation of virtue and her belief in the duty of all citizens to combat vice led her to write: "yet, recollecting that every domestic enjoyment depends on the unimpaired possession of civil and religious liberty, that a concern for the welfare of society ought equally to glow in every human breast, the work was not relinquished."[71]

The encouragement of both her husband and son played an important role in the completion of the *History,* as Warren admitted, "the trembling heart has recoiled at the magnitude of the undertaking, and the hand often shrunk back from the task."[72] Her eldest son, James Warren Jr., copied the manuscript before it went to press and probably compiled the index. She also received critical assistance and praise from the Reverend James Freeman, who conducted negotiations with the publishers and arranged for proofreading.[73] Thus, once again private approval and encouragement from men gave her the courage to step outside the domestic sphere.

Mercy Otis Warren's writing career constitutes an early example of what Sandra Gilbert and Susan Gubar have called the "anxiety of authorship"[74] expressed by female writers later in the nineteenth century because of the harsh judgments imposed on their thoughts and writing style by patriarchal literary traditions. The same has remained true of patriarchal historical evaluations of Warren's *History of the Rise, Progress, and Termination of the American Revolution.* Comments on Warren's *History* have fluctuated through the years from praise to criticism, from enthusiasm to boredom. In their evaluation of the work of American historians, Mary and Charles Beard discussed Warren's work with even-handed and fair criticism and concluded that her attempts to give meaning to the history of an emerging nation deserve attention, even praise. As they pointed out,

Warren found herself at odds with both Thomas Jefferson and John Adams, espousing the ideal of ethical, revolutionary progress, while they realized that much more mundane and less virtuous motivation was needed to organize the country after independence from England was achieved.[75]

From our vantage point it is possible to see in Warren a distant precursor of the late nineteenth-century historian Frederick Jackson Turner, who developed the "frontier thesis," because she seems to have had an environmental sense about the country's potential and future. In 1779, long before she composed her *History*, Warren had written Abigail Adams about the United States with sentiments very similar to those made famous by Turner:

America is a theatre just erected—the drama is here but begun, while the actors of the old world have run through every species of pride, luxury, venality, and vice—their characters will become less interesting, and the western wilds which for ages have been little known, may exhibit those striking traits of wisdom, and grandeur and magnificence, which the Divine economist may have reserved to crown the closing scene.[76]

From this letter, and her other writings as well, it is clear that Warren, like Turner a century later, saw American society as distinctly different from European society and attributed the democratic principles evident in the emerging American society to the equality of conditions existing on this continent, especially on the frontier. She warned her readers that freedom could be lost as it had been in other democratic experiments and urged them to oppose the constitutional provision of a standing army. She likewise idealistically called for the conquest of poverty, an end to servility, and respect for the dignity of native American Indians.[77]

Although Warren concentrated on the divine plan for humankind and the virtuous origins of both the Revolution and the formation of the new nation, she also emphasized a unifying patriotic theme. In this way she thought she had explained how Americans could gain a sense of their nationality through a common history and tradition, despite her serious doubts about the conservative nature and undemocratic potential of the 1787 Constitution. She almost succeeded in synthesizing two basic ideas—republican ideology as a part of the national character and the special moral destiny of the nation—into a portrayal of not only a new nation but also a new society.[78] She failed in this attempt because her commitment to radical republicanism led her to concentrate on the absence of these ideological principles in the postwar period. This persistent commitment to freedom based on virtue and the fear of corruption ultimately contradicted her patriotic appeal for national unity.

Yet development of the new nation required a patriotic commitment to national unity. Warren understood this but insisted on implementing only the broadest possible aspects of freedom and equality. However in tune this may be with the present, it was out of step with the times in which she lived and among postrevolutionary leaders. She advocated, for example, the humane treatment of native American Indians at the expense of western expansion.[79] No wonder her *History* so quickly became obsolete for those interested in conquering the continent. Thus she prophetically, but unpopularly, wrote:

But if the lust of domination, which takes hold of the ambitious and the powerful in all ages and nations, should be indulged by the authority of the United States, and those simple tribes of men, contented with the gifts of nature, that had filled their forest with game sufficient for their subsistence, should be invaded, it will probably be a source of most cruel warfare and bloodshed, until the extermination of the original possessors.[80]

Warren's *History of the Rise, Progress, and Termination of the American Revolution* was the work of a keen mind and painstaking scholar, but it was neither a brilliant nor a practical political document for its time. It is, nonetheless, a synthetic work of substance that reveals a distinctly female perspective about the American Revolution. As the first U.S. woman historian, Warren never anticipated the modern political or legal system that evolved from the Revolution in secular or pluralistic terms. It is ironic that John Adams accused her of having written for the nineteenth century. If anything, her belief in virtue and her conviction that God, or providence, had used the American experiment to further an ultimate plan for humankind seems closer to religious beliefs of the seventeenth century than to the emerging scientific views of the eighteenth-century Enlightenment. Although she seems to have accepted the Lockean concept that men were created equal in nature as well as in the sight of God, she continued to stress the opposite: that each man must search his inner being, overcome selfishness, and act in accordance with God's will, not as a self-contained individual without ethical moorings. Her insistence on the vice and corruption that characterized postrevolutionary developments prevented her from accepting secular or scientific concepts about historical progress. Warren viewed the Revolution as a defense of the divinely inspired principles that Americans had discovered and practiced throughout their colonial experience. That other countries learned from the American example and instigated their own revolutions was evidence to her of the success of God's plan, rather than of liberal individualism at work.[81]

Although Warren acknowledged that men were basically selfish, she remained convinced that if they allowed reason and conscience to control their actions they could further God's plan and thereby promote equality and ensure their own happiness and virtue. Because she regarded those who conspired illegally to write the Constitution as monarchists, she argued that merely revising the Articles of Confederation would have been sufficient, and she believed that they were attempting to undermine the original ideology of the Revolution. In contrast, she viewed those who opposed ratification, herself included, as radical republicans who were continuing to carry on the moral and political principles for which the war with England had been fought.[82] In her *History* Warren reluctantly concluded that although the Constitution was thought by many to be too strongly marked with the features of monarchy, it was, after much discussion, adopted by the majority of the states.[83]

Warren had praised George Washington and the patriot forces during the War of Independence, but she became critical of many of the peacetime leaders who emerged after the fighting stopped. During the administrations of both Washington and Adams, she felt sure that there was a decline in the principles of republicanism because of the influence of Hamilton's policies; his views seemed to her to violate both constitutional law and God's plan. Each attempt by the Federalists to increase the power of the central government in the 1790s appeared to her an assault on republicanism based on a "simple, virtuous and free people," with the long-term intent of establishing an American monarchy, "corrupted by wealth, effeminated by luxury, impoverished by licentiousness, and . . . the *automatons* of intoxicated ambition." And she predicted that "some unborn historian" would document this "unpleasing part of history," should it continue.[84]

Although John Adams had encouraged Warren to write her *History,* her ultimate evaluation of him and his political allies enraged him. Fortunately, the letters that passed between John Adams and Warren discussing the *History* have survived. From them we get the full impact of her formidable and independent mind, circumscribed as it was by her gender. Adams began the correspondence on 11 July 1807 by taking issue with Warren's historical assessment of his temperament: "Mr. Adams was undoubtedly a statesman of penetration and ability, but his prejudices and his passions were sometimes too strong for his sagacity and judgment." Fixing on only the last part of Warren's sentence, Adams asked her to supply instances when his "passion" and "prejudice" were even too strong for his "sagacity" and "judgment." Not in the least mollified by Warren's tribute to the unimpeachable character of his private life, Adams was furious with her for suggesting that he had returned from Europe with a partiality for monarchy. Asserting that he had always opposed "despotism, absolute monarchy, absolute aristocracy, and absolute democracy," Adams adds that "a mixed government is the only one that can preserve liberty.[85]

It is possible to read the first few letters that passed between Adams and Warren with some detachment, but in a few months Adams begins to sound so condescending and petulant that one is tempted to conclude that Warren's assessment of his temperament in her history was overly flattering, in light of his remarks to her that today would be viewed as sexist. In his letter of 3 August 1807, for example, he attacked her on the very issue she had dreaded and confided to him years before—transgressing her proper womanly sphere—by insisting that she had exposed herself to "eternal ridicule by her unladylike insinuations and assertions." Warren replied calmly considering her lifelong anxiety on this point. Perhaps this response represents her use of feminine reserve and intellectual subterfuge at its best:

On what point of ridicule would Mrs. Warren's character stand, were she to write her History over again and correct her *errors*. . . . She must tell the world that Mr. Adams was no monarchist; that he had no partiality for the habits, manners, or government of England; that he was a man of fashion, that his polite accomplishment rendered him completely qualified for the refinements of Parisian taste. . . . that he was beloved of every man, woman, and child in France; that he had neither ambition nor pride of talents, and that he "had no talents to be proud of"; . . . that he was a favorite of the administrators of the affairs of France; that they loved him for his yielding, compliant temper and manners; that he was always a republican, though he has asserted that there was no possibility of understanding or defining the term republicanism; that in France he was always happy.[86]

Although the breach between Mercy Otis Warren and John Adams was ostensibly healed in 1812 through the arbitration of a mutual friend, Elbridge Gerry, governor of Massachusetts at the time, John Adams could not resist one more attack on Warren when he said in 1813 that "history is not the Province of the Ladies."[87] The friendly correspondence between Abigail Adams and Mercy Warren resumed, however, and continued until Warren's death in 1814. The reconciliation between the families seems to have pleased both Abigail Adams and Mercy Warren, with the latter writing in January 1813: "A visit from two such aged friends would be gratifying indeed. Mr. Adams with yourself will accept the respect and regard of your friend."[88]

Neither Abigail Adams nor Mercy Otis Warren were feminists; nor, given their historical context, should we expect them to have been. Warren, in particular, opposed many of the views of Mary Wollstonecraft, whose A *Vindication of the Rights of Women* advocated political and economic equality for women. She supported education for women only as long as it did not interfere with their domestic duties, and in her letters she repeatedly stated that care for husband and family must remain a woman's prime objective. Moreover, she never acknowledged other than a classical republican view of male virtue. Although Warren did not always practice what she preached—once describing herself as a "politician" in a private letter to one of her sons—there is no convincing evidence that her brand of female politics included even as much moderate concern for, and limited commitment to, the legal rights of married women as that demonstrated by Abigail Adams. For example, Abigail Adams unsuccessfully urged Warren to champion the cause of removing certain common-law restrictions on married women during the first months of the American Revolution.[89]

In advice to women other than of Adams's and Macauley's stature, Warren repeatedly stressed that "the duties of . . . family affairs" came before self-indulgence or self-improvement. Yet she obviously did not follow this advice herself. She also told these same women to justify any "impertinent" political views "much out of the road of female attention" in the name of their legitimate domestic concerns as mothers and wives, "who tremble lest [their] dearest connections should fall victims of lawless power." It is conceivable that she gave such advice because she thought that this behavior and rationalization more appropriate for all those women who did not possess her "typically Masculine Genius."[90] But nowhere in her surviving letters or literary writings did Warren advocate suffrage or any other political rights for women, as had her brother James Otis, Jr., as early as 1764 in his prerevolutionary pamphlet, *The Rights of the British Colonies Asserted and Proved.* In that work, he had argued more directly than his sister ever did:

> Are not women born as free as men? Would it not be infamous to assert that the ladies are all slaves by nature? If every man and woman born or to be born has and will have a right to be consulted and must accede to the original compact before they can with any kind of justice be said to be bound by it, will not the compact be ever forming and never finished? If upon abdication all were reduced to a state of nature, had not the apple women and orange girls as good a right to give their respectable suffrages for a new King as the philosopher, courtier, and politician?[91]

The question remains if women of the stature and caliber of Adams and Warren did not show significant appreciation of enhanced self-importance or confidence in their new roles as the private keepers of postrevolutionary virtue — who did? Presumably, men of the period did because it allowed them in good conscience to abandon virtue for themselves and pursue their own legal, economic, and political self-interest. At the same time, even these two most perceptive revolutionary women chose to interpret their independent thoughts and actions "as a form of dependency." This was not false consciousness *or* false modesty on their part; it was their individual awareness and acceptance that postrevolutionary culture had pointedly reinforced the colonial tradition that politics was beyond the proper and private sphere of women's activities.[92] Trapped in a time warp not of their making, women of the American Revolution became U.S. citizens with their colonial dependency and deference in tact, despite their much-lauded positions as republican wives and mothers. Their lack of collective consciousness prevented them from making any effective legal or political demands and/or from impeding the progress of the "too-little, too-late" constitutional syndrome from which women in the United States have not yet completely emerged.

# CHAPTER THREE

# From British Subjects
# to U.S. Citizens

Before the War of Independence colonists existed in a collective condition of dependency, reflecting the feudal origins of the English state. All British colonial subjects, regardless of gender, occupied dependent positions in relation to the Crown. English subjectship meant certain obligations to the state, but it also carried with it certain rights and privileges that were mutually binding on women and men in ways that muted, rather than drew attention to, sex stereotyping. Not all English subjects were equal before the Crown, but under the English system class deference and dependence carried with them a personal and community sense of allegiance, as opposed to strictly individual and political features. This concept preceded seventeenth-century "social-compact" theories about government by consent.

In retrospect, gender inequality did not become an overt civic problem for women until the revolutionary war, when the Founding Fathers' more modern Lockean concepts about the individual rights and duties of citizenship finally placed them in a gender-specific category of dependency—one "emphasizing powerlessness and stripping the word [citizen] of its voluntary connotations."[1] With the American Revolution, citizenship became race, gender, and class specific. While British subjecthood had not prevented upper-class English and colonial women from exercising vestigial feudal and fiduciary authority over lower-class men, U.S. citizenship eliminated the possibility of even this limited form of class-based female power. Moreover, instead of assuming collective loyalty, as Britain did for subjectship, American revolutionary leaders required *individual* loyalty for citizenship.[2] There is evidence of women being required to take loyalty oaths in at least three states—Massachusetts, New York, and Connecticut.

Therefore, citizenship and *consent* or *assent* of the governed were closely associated in early liberal republican theory following the American Revolution. Yet the groups not consulted in the drafting of the U.S. Constitution were the same people whose consent had always carried the least legal weight and social esteem under English rule and subjectship. The same proved true under U.S. citizenship because full citizenship for a privileged group of white males carried with it full membership in society as well. Full societal membership in turn conferred equal esteem, or equal respect, upon such men but not upon even the women they were married to, as had been the case under English subjectship. Following the American Revolution, consent to citizenship did not mean for women that they were equal citizens in the public realm, let alone accorded full citizenship in the private one. Yet, if "the essence of equal citizenship is the dignity of full membership in society," including the sense of "belonging," as Kenneth Karst has maintained, then this definitely is not the type of citizenship women in the United States consented to after 1776.[3]

Even the minimal type of "consent" required of women during the colonial period in certain legal common-law and equity legal procedures diminished under the type of citizenship granted to women by 1800. The socioeconomic and political construction of postrevolutionary America eliminated all but white, male, middle-class consent from the legal and, even the more popular, notions about citizenship. This discursive development left women and other disadvantaged groups to play what up to now has proven a hopeless game of catch-up to obtain the latest liberal versions of citizenship and to "consent" to the latest liberal trends in politics, economics, and sexuality. But in the 1770s and 1780s, no collective voices were raised to protest this form of second-class citizenship for the vast majority of Americans.

At best, white women were "citizens" by 1800 only in the sense that they were native-born or naturalized free inhabitants of the United States whose civil rights and responsibilities had yet to be defined.[4] As largely "nonlegal" entities, several generations of postrevolutionary women were neglected as they groped toward a conscious collective sense of belonging, citizenship, and their own civil rights in the first half of the nineteenth century. As a social and legal construct, U.S. citizenship was defined several times in the nineteenth century, using the rhetoric of "republicanism." While the republicanism of that time period should not be simplistically equated with classic liberalism, its communal and equalitarian political and economic aspects seldom affected women. Instead, each time white men redefined republicanism for themselves it contained glaring contradictions for those few educated and propertied white and free black women, especially those who remained or became unmarried (*femes soles*) during their lifetimes. Thus, early republican citizenship reinforced the inferiority of the private sphere and linked personal behavior with a civic life that was not offered as the model of excellence for less-than-equal citizens to emulate.[5] In the process, the good life, good government, and good citizenship became more, rather than less, white and masculine by definition in both its individualistic and collective manifestations.

## Colonial Women under Common-Law and Equity Jurisprudence

This is not to say that the colonial period represented a millennium for women's rights compared to the immediate postrevolutionary years. What legal leniency and county-court accessibility under common law existed before 1776 arose out of economic necessity and the numerical scarcity of women in the New World— not any fundamental change in the patriarchal attitudes that had been transplanted from Europe. Moreover, while equity jurisprudence theoretically offered an alternative to common law in determining of the civil capacities of women, it was not officially sanctioned by colonial or state legislatures before the 1820s. Among other things, equity procedures provided a means for bypassing "the rules comprising the common-law status of married women [*femes coverts*] whose irrationality became increasingly clear as the economy became more commercial." Only relatively few wealthier women benefited from this separate form of jurisprudence by taking advantage of equity rules, before or after they married, to establish separate estates. There were other equity procedures, however, in addition to those used in marriage settlements to create property trusts for upper-class married women that directly affected many female civil actions during the colonial period.[6]

Equity jurisprudence arose from the application of an Aristotelian sense of proportion to unique or individual legal questions. Its Roman equivalent, *aequalitas,* conveyed the idea of social justice, rather than our modern definition of equality. Equity jurisprudence often assumed informal forms of legal redress, constituting customary or ecclesiastical law, in contrast to the word-for-word transcript of court arguments and decisions kept in common-law cases and referred to as *precedents.* For centuries in England, and to a lesser degree in colonial America, equity courts offered a major means of compensating for the injustices that arose under common law as a result of the attempt to apply case law uniformly to all legal situations. Equity law brought an element of fairness to justice by allowing for the individualistic settlement of legal disputes or the moderation of legal disabilities of certain (often privileged) individuals, such as wealthy women who wanted to continue to have some financial independence after marrying or who wanted to assume fiduciary guardianship or other legal functions not normally permitted females under common law.

In essence, equity jurisprudence represented a potential vehicle for law reform both before and after the American Revolution because it allowed for the "defeudalization" of real property by removing common-law disabilities for both men and women.[7] Unfortunately for married colonial women equity procedures remained suspect, and then several postrevolutionary generations of lawyers and judges, in their haste to reform the laws of the new nation, ignored the importance of equity as an agent for change and justice as they turned from the original natural-law foundation of the common law to a unitary and instrumental foundation for both statute law and common law.

The early colonial period in the New World was characterized by an absence of strict adherence to English statutory and common laws because of the primacy of local customs, demographic and economic considerations that did not pertain in the Old World, or because of individual colonial legislative actions. This *sometimes* meant greater legal leniency in the application of common and equity law in the New World and *sometimes* it did not. These negative and positive variations, as far as women's proprietary, contractual, testamentary, and evidentiary capacities were concerned, often were the accident of residence or birth (as is still the case in certain legal matters today in the United States). That is, the legal status of women depended on the location of the colony in which they happened to reside and the degree to which it followed or strayed from English practice. The testamentary and evidentiary behavior of colonial and nineteenth-century women remain the least studied aspects of female legal capacities, yet these may prove to have had more bearing on their societal and legal status than did their meager property holdings.

The very earliest settlements in the seventeenth century tended to be more lenient toward women with respect to a limited number of assorted economic functions and inheritance or dower rights, although there were many exceptions to even this generalization. The number of colonial women, for example, who died with enough property to be probated—both testates (those leaving wills) and intestates (those who did not write a will)—seldom exceeded more than 10 percent of all probate records in most counties for the entire period before the American Revolution and probably averaged no more than 7 percent by 1774 for all thirteen colonies. Moreover, the small amount of total colonial wealth that was ever owned by women ranged from 1 to 11 percent at most in various locations before 1776 to below 7 percent by 1800. Although the percentage of female probates increased between the American Revolution and the end of the eighteenth century, their proportion of the total wealth actually declined. Thus, scarcity of data, lack of significant economic power for women, and "tremendous variation evident in early American rules on married women's property rights" make it difficult to talk about trends in female proprietary capacities that apply to all thirteen original colonies and states before 1800. It is now possible, however, to document a few regional patterns from existing records.[8]

While Massachusetts and Connecticut tended to limit married women's property rights in the course of the eighteenth century by restricting dower interest and such traditional equity devices as separate estates and pre- or antenuptial agreements, the Chesapeake area colonies of Maryland, Virginia, and South

Carolina created chancery (equity) courts (as did New York) and were much more generous in granting women more dower and inheritance portions in both personalty as well as realty. Pennsylvania, on the other hand, tended to be a unique colony in the sense that it tried to administer equity procedures through common-law courts exclusively and honored very limited dower or separate estate rights until the 1790s when the colony's original settlers placed the rights of creditors above those of married women. The other colonies fell in between these extremes.

The question of whether women during the colonial and early national periods were treated poorly or well under the law can only begin to be answered by determining their access to, and participation in, the particular court system of the time and their utilization of any less formal equity proceedings (both are discussed later in this chapter), in addition to the impact on them of formal law and informal customs of succession (intestacy). Succession law determines inheritance patterns and, hence, constitutes an indication of the socioeconomic standing of women in the past and present. Although a complex legal topic, the law of succession reflects more about the economic, demographic, and social structures of a period than it does the state of law in general. In fact, reform of succession laws usually lags behind reform in other fields of law because it is determined by changes in the economy and the status of women within the family and society due to slowly evolving demographic and interpersonal relationships between women and men. When people will property to one another it is often more a matter of personal volition or personal reaction to economic and familial conditions than it is a matter of complying with the law. The writing of wills (testamentary behavior) cannot be predicted precisely on the basis of statutory or common law governing succession. It was and is a highly idiosyncratic and personal aspect of legal behavior that changes only slowly over time.

In colonial America, for example, the strict family-settlement practice that existed in England based on equity law was not followed. Strict family land settlements were intended to keep estates together by precisely indicating how much wives, daughters, and sons would inherit as a life tenant or custodian (not outright owner) of patrilineal holdings. Because of the abundance of land in the New World compared to England, because there were far fewer equity courts or equity rules in most of the colonies, and because some of the colonies did not generally follow the statutory changes in England that by the end of the seventeenth century granted husbands wide-ranging testamentary power over personalty (moveable) as well as real (unmoveable) property, such as land and things attached to such realty, a more equalitarian treatment of children as heirs evolved by the time of the American Revolution than for widows. For example, the English primogeniture practice (making the eldest son the sole inheritor) had not been strictly followed before 1776 in most colonies (and was completely abolished after 1776), so there was greater testamentary freedom among colonial men to will their property outside of lineage, but also to daughters on a more equal basis with sons. What in fact happened, however, was that it became more common in the New World for eldest sons to receive double shares of realty and for the widows to inherit less and less property compared to children. Although daughters may have inherited more, they never achieved anywhere near equality with sons by 1800, despite some postrevolutionary state legislation that attempted to abolish the practice of double shares for eldest sons. Widows were increasingly excluded from executrixships in the course of the eighteenth century, with a new low in both inheritances and executrixes occurring between the colonial period and the American Revolution that continued into the early nineteenth century.[9]

In Virginia, for example, throughout the seventeenth-century men clearly favored their wives as executrixes and often provided them with more than one-third of their estates as dower law required. Because of the initially higher male mortality rates in the South, wills in that region generally favored women more than those written in New England. Increasingly, however, in both geographical areas eighteenth-century wills began to relegate widows to share part of a house with the surviving son who, as executor, also received the bulk of the inheritance. This trend developed even though there is some indication that widows wanted to administer their husbands' estates and would have preferred (or been expected, as today) to live with their daughters and sons-in-law. It may have reflected a distinct, yet tacit, disagreement between husbands and wives over patrilineal or matrilineal inheritance. If so, this was a basic disagreement over power (in terms of property inheritance) that women lost in the course of the eighteenth-century. This loss became statistically significant in certain regions during the decades immediately preceding and following the American Revolution, according to a study of Hingham, Massachusetts, by Daniel Scott Smith. Prior to 1720 no less than 27 percent of colonial wives with adult sons were named sole executrixes of their husbands' property. This figure dropped to 6 percent between 1761 and 1800, with 85 percent of the wills written by males naming sons as executors. Also, before 1700 in Hingham, 95.5 percent of all families with three or more daughters named one of them after the mother. By 1780, this name-sharing had dropped to 53.2 percent, and the practice was to decrease even more into the early nineteenth century, although less rapidly for boys than girls because of the potential inheritance value of having the same name as one's father or another close male relative. These law-of-succession figures are roughly approximated in other colonies, with the exception of Maryland and New York, where exclusion of widows as executrixes rose from less than 20 percent in the seventeenth and early eighteenth centuries to 30 to 45 percent or more by 1776.[10]

In fact, widows' inheritance percentages continued to decline until the 1820s. This indicated a significant loss in the legal and economic status of middle- and upper-class women, who had more commonly exercised such executory responsibility and testamentary power in the early colonial period. As women's inheritances declined proportionately, there is evidence that as primogeniture faded male (and female) children began to inherit some land, making widows' dower rights become more and more difficult to claim in real property. Obviously, breaking up family estates also forced changes in how widows were awarded their dower shares, which was not always advantageous for them depending on the law governing partitions of land in the various states.[11] While this inheritance pattern with respect to married women would gradually change for the better in the course of the nineteenth century, dower-right law did not. Since the law of succession in any time period reflects the slowly changing demographic and economic conditions, as well as family dynamics, it does not cause change in the socioeconomic structure nor can it be juridically or politically "reformed" very easily—if at all. In this sense, the inheritance patterns remain obdurately "conservative" and always "behind" fundamental shifts in private and public changes in the political economy. For example, dower law was much more immediately and negatively affected by changes in the economy during the first half of the nineteenth century than was the law of succession.

This deterioration in the proprietary and testamentary capacities of widows cannot completely be explained by the presence of more living adult children when husbands died at the end of the eighteenth century rather than earlier. There is no single explanation for this "meaner" legal treatment of wives by husbands. Carole Shammas, after studying a select group of counties, primarily Bucks County in Pennsylvania, has suggested that it reflected basic changes in the infrastructure of the American economy as capitalism was transformed from a family operation to a commercial and finally an industrial one. This was accompanied by less availability of land for inheritance purposes in the more populated areas during the late colonial and early national periods, as well as by affective responses to demographic changes in the family before 1800. While the exact reasons for the negative treatment of widows remain obscure, it was a statistical reality that only improved gradually from the 1820s to the end of the nineteenth century. The inheritance and testamentary capacities of women continued to improve in the "more conjugally oriented" twentieth century. In other words, eighteenth- and nineteenth-century lineal inheritance patterns did not favor wives, but twentieth-century conjugal ones do.[12]

At the same time the colonies also made niggardly use of marriage settlements compared to England, out of suspicions about and the existence of fewer courts for the dispensation of equity procedures. No colony or state specifically denied women the right to create such equity trusts, but not all had courts or other legal bodies to enforce them before 1800. This meant that wealthy colonial women were statistically less likely than their English counterparts to benefit from marriage settlements granting them separate estates or to overcome their other property-right disabilities under common law. However, as will be noted later, what early colonial women lost through uncertainty about equitable rules providing for the establishment of marriage settlements they sometimes partially made up for because of more generous inheritance or dower rights in certain regions of the New World.[13]

Many of even these ameliorating factors in the property-owning capabilities of colonial women had deteriorated by the time of the American Revolution and were not resuscitated until several decades into the nineteenth century. Thus, to the degree that the legal status of married women before and immediately following the American Revolution is looked upon primarily in terms of property rights obtained through equity procedures or statutory and common law, the historical and legal record remains a bleak one until the 1830s. Today, as in the past, economic inequality for women and other disadvantaged groups is produced largely by the fact that the vast majority of household wealth in the United States is inherited rather than earned through work. If this condition did not prevail, women still would not have been full citizens in the past—any more than they are now. Improved inheritance and property rights are a necessary but not exclusive prerequisite of citizenship and improved legal status for women, despite the emphasis placed upon them by legal historians.

From the beginning of the colonial period, however, English common law was modified in other ways to fit New World conditions. Often these modifications came about through the legal principle known as *tacit consent*. They were most apparent in urban, commercial areas where some married women obtained the status of *feme-sole traders*—a title that gave them the right to sue, conduct businesses, be sued, enter into contracts, sell real property, and have the power of attorney in the absence of their husbands. Whether single or married, seventeenth- or eighteenth-century women could not act as attorneys-at-law, but they did on occasion temporarily become attorneys-in-fact. This quasi power of attorney to act as the agent of their husbands was conferred by local colonial political bodies or legislatures in advance, but was usually upheld by the courts relying on the doctrine of necessities. Thus, necessity or prominence sometimes informally allowed wives to assume such legal power when their husbands were incapacitated or unavailable. Nonetheless, an individual married woman (*feme covert*) could not expect to experience equal legal status with the single or widowed woman (*feme sole*) because she was technically under the "cover" of her husband's legal status.[14] Hence, the term *coverture* refers to the common-law restriction that prevented married women from acting as their own agents at law or to have independent property rights because their legal "personalities were merged with and, therefore, subsumed by their husbands' legal standing because only the husbands had full membership in the judicial and political community."[15]

Yet throughout the colonial period there is an impressive, if exceptional, array of women workers and entrepreneurs because of the general labor shortage and the resulting circumvention of common-law restrictions on female activities. In Philadelphia, for example, women engaged in roughly thirty different trades, ranging from essential to luxury services. They included female silversmiths, tinworkers, barbers, bakers, fish picklers, brewers, tanners, ropemakers, lumberjacks, gunsmiths, butchers, milliners, harnessmakers, potash manufacturers, upholsterers, printers, morticians, chandlers, coach-makers, embroiderers, dry cleaners and dyers, woodworkers, stay-makers, tailors, flour processors, seamstresses, netbraziers, and founders. It is this diversity of female labor in Philadelphia, Boston, and other colonial towns that has led to the conclusion that work for women was much less sex-stereotyped in the seventeenth and eighteenth centuries than it was to become in the nineteenth—although, as noted in chapter 2, women were never paid anywhere near the wages men were even when hired to do the same work.[16]

Therefore, there is no doubt that some colonial women lawfully worked for wages or in family businesses, but it must be remembered that they often found themselves in these essential and nonfamilial roles not because the colonial period was less patriarchal but because they were substituting for dead or absent husbands or other male relatives. It was simply not considered "inappropriate" according to prevailing socioeconomic norms for women to engage in this wide variety of occupations, carry on the family business if widowed, or become skilled artisans while still married or if single.

This relatively lenient attitude toward all working women was beginning to change by the end of the eighteenth century, however, for demographic, socioeconomic, and legal reasons. As the percentage of women in the population increased and greater class lines developed, it was no longer so acceptable or necessary for middle-class women to fill in for their husbands. More standardized law practices came to prevail over local ones. Increased mercantile specialization demanded greater economic stability and, hence, a closer application of the more conservative aspects of English common law. While bar associations and professional training for lawyers were evident before the Revolution, their influence expanded after the war, contributing to the development of even greater legal conservatism with respect to the "proper" roles for women after 1776 (except for those women at the bottom of the economic scale—female factory workers, indentured servants, and slaves). Reliance on Blackstone's *Commentaries* as a guide both in training attorneys and in codifying American law also increased. Not only were free white women more stringently prevented from acting in a variety of legal capacities because of the greater professionalization of law following the Revolution, but the new law codes also explicitly barred them from engaging in activities that, though not formally authorized previously, had not been expressly forbidden.

Even before the Revolution, however, a regressive change in the socioeconomic and legal status of women was in progress, especially for widows. One of the major informal legal functions women had exercised from the beginning of the colonial period was the writing of wills. In addition, they were often the beneficiaries of wills, dowries, or dowers. Yet under common law, widows could not be heirs—that is, they could not be accorded the full property rights of their deceased husbands as heads of households nor could they legally write wills. But they could be named sole executrixes of their husbands' property and were often accorded dower rights (traditionally one-third of the husband's real property), which were "interpreted by the courts in a manner which was in many instances at variance with common law rules." Although they usually only inherited a life interest in any inherited property, widows of the early colonial period appear to have exercised slightly more inheritance and testimonial control over transmission of property from one colonial generation to another than their ancestors by the time of the American Revolution. Widows were "considered a community responsibility" since their dower rights or inheritances seldom provided them with sufficient income, especially during wars or inflationary periods. Technically, women whose husbands had died could not sell any real property that they had not already possessed at the time of marriage (and protected by registering it through an equity trust). In practice, both their proprietary and contractual rights were given limited recognition out of necessity in the course of the seventeenth and first half of the eighteenth centuries in order to provide them with a modicum of greater economic independence. [17]

Although some of the most debilitating aspects of English common law restrictions on married women had been modified before 1776 through equity procedures, under remaining coverture rules the vast majority of married women in 1800 still could not be parties to litigation or own property in their own names. Even the few wealthy colonial women who had succeeded in taking advantage of equity jurisprudence to create separate estates did not usually receive transfer, management, or devising rights over such property. Thus, improvements of married women's status under common law before the American Revolution and up through the 1820s did not include the simple ability to write wills unless the pre- or antenuptial deeds creating the separate estates specifically provided the wife with the power to dispose of her property after death (which had the same effect as a will). Under these and many other remaining disabling conditions of coverture, married women in the United States entered the nineteenth century.[18] The Revolution did not immediately foster any more lenient colonial trends toward improving the legal rights of women than had existed before 1776, with the possible, but problematic, exception in the number of divorces granted. Most important, their political status as citizens did not improve.

## Loyalist Cases Affirm Dependence of Married Women

During and immediately following the American Revolution, married Loyalist women brought out all of the political and legal contradictions in republican theory regarding gender and citizenship. The new state legislatures contended with these contradictions, rather than the Continental Congress. The legal problem appeared simple on the face of it: British and colonial equity jurisprudence had long recognized the separate estates and dower rights of wealthy married women *without* negating or even challenging the common-law dictum that wives were the legal dependents of their husbands. In the course of the War of Independence, the obvious question became, How could a dependent Loyalist wife exercise independent judgment from her husband about her own citizenship without endangering both the family unit and the common-law fiction about the unity of husband and wife?[19] The juridical answer to this question would set the pattern for dealing with the postwar legal status of republican wives and mothers as well.

States passed a variety of confiscation acts to accompany treason statutes so that Loyalist property could be legally seized. If a wife did not join her Tory husband in exile, most states honored her traditional dower right to one-third of his real and personal property. If she left the country, these absentee statutes were much less generous with respect to the amount of property on which she could claim dower rights. While many Loyalist women petitioned for their dower rights following the American Revolution, few made their way into legal history through the court system and then usually only at the lowest (often only summarily) recorded levels. Two of note are *Martin v. Commonwealth of Massachusetts*, and *Kempe's Lessee v. Kennedy*.

Theoretically, marital status (or lack thereof) did not prevent women from being prosecuted for treason under federal and state statutes; practically speaking, because of prevailing coverture restrictions on married women at the beginning of the Revolution, only widows and spinsters were prosecuted. In other words, only single women were considered capable of choosing their own allegiance because state legislatures thought that married women's first allegiance was to their husbands. Therefore, it was generally assumed by the legal system that married women and children could not make a conscious choice in behalf of their own citizenship. Later, as independence proved successful, the elite group of white males who constituted "We the People" placed greater "emphasis on [all] women as dependents." They abandoned the more complex British tradition of female and male dependency based on an ostensibly more transparent and voluntary "web of mutual obligations, privileges, and rights," as well as the colonial legal view that single women could exercise independent judgment.[20]

If "citizenship was an individual act," how could a married woman prove her loyalty if her person and property were merged with that of her husband's under common law? Honoring the property rights of women whose husbands became Loyalists, therefore, became a litmus test for recognizing or not recognizing the separate status of females as U.S. citizens. Could a woman married to a Tory hold political views independent of her husband? Although case law can be cited on both sides of this question,[21] in general the new states did not break with years of legal tradition that subordinated married women's rights to those of their husbands. Thus, the new individualistic definition of U.S. citizenship placed women theoretically, at least, in a more dependent position from judicial, political, and economic points of view than had been the case when they were British subjects.

Wives of Loyalists may have been the first to experience the ambiguous legal position created by citizenship in the new republic, but all married women ultimately fell into the limbo of partial citizenship because of their legally dependent status in a country founded on liberty and independence. Revolutionary rhetoric may have replaced virtual representation with direct representation for the United States in relation to England; but it contradicted itself by excluding women from the franchise, thus relegating them with all other dependent groups who could not vote because they presumably lacked an independent will—that is, children, African-Americans, native American Indians, and propertyless men. Because single women (and some married women who took advantage of equity procedures) could own enough property to qualify to vote, revolutionary leaders had to stress their dependency and, in some cases, their lack of an independent will. Ultimately, the Founding Fathers were prepared to argue the irrationality of *all* women following the War of Independence to eliminate the possibility of even qualified single ones expecting or exercising the franchise or other rights.

Although the Articles of Confederation had recognized "free inhabitants" as citizens, the precise definition of *citizenship* varied, especially with respect to women who, if they were married, did not have a recognized legal or national status other than that of their husbands. And since most women did not officially participate in the War of Independence as combatants, they could not claim citizenship on those grounds. Male concepts about property, military obligation, and "political personality" characterized early republican descriptions of citizenship, regardless of whether local or state statutes referred to "persons," "members," or "inhabitants." Not until the 1820s did the dictionary definition of a U.S. citizen drop military service and stress voting rights based on the ability to own property, but notions of masculinity continued to dominate thinking about citizenship and the national character well into the twentieth century—and some would say down to the present time.[22] With few exceptions, females were not required to take any direct action to change their status from British subjects to U.S. citizens during the course of the American Revolution, on the assumption that their political interests were not independently held but simply reflected those of the males upon whom they were dependent. (It appears that only three states—Massachusetts, New York, and Connecticut—required women to take loyalty oaths.)[23] This is one of the reasons that there were so few treason charges brought against women, even when they were married to men considered traitors during the War of Independence.

While marital dependency sometimes provided legal protection to Loyalist women, it did not always prevent the confiscation of property in which they had dower rights, as litigation following the Revolution indicates. The basic legal issue in postrevolutionary cases involving women Loyalists whose husbands supported England during the American Revolution was: Could married women be independent citizens? The first time that the new state legislatures recognized gender in passing statutes during the War of Independence occurred when they defined treasonable activity. For example, one of the earliest examples of legislators referring to women, as well as men, in relation to citizenship came in 1780 when New Jersey legislators stated that those supplying the enemy "shall from the Day of passing Judgment against *him, her or them*, become disfranchised, and shall lose all Privileges, Rights and Immunities which otherwise *he or she* might have enjoyed as a free Citizen of the State" (emphasis added).[24] But this was an innovative wording whose time had not arrived, as demonstrated when Loyalist women tested the linguistic and legal limitations of the postrevolutionary jurisprudence by claiming their dower or other property rights.

One of the most discursively symbolic cases was Martin v. Commonwealth of Massachusetts, 1 Mass. 347 (1805). When Loyalists William and Anna Martin left the United States for England during the War of Independence, they left property that the state of Massachusetts confiscated in 1781. Their son William returned twenty years later to claim his mother's dower rights, on the grounds that as a *feme covert* her one-third portion of his father's estates could not have been legally confiscated. Attorneys for Massachusetts argued in *Martin* that as an "inhabitant of Massachusetts," a state that had required loyalty oaths, Anna Martin was also a "member" of the body politic during the revolutionary period.

Therefore, she "chose" to accompany her husband to England and this deliberate political choice voided any dower claims she (and now her son) may have had to confiscated property. This argument struck at the heart of coverture—the cloak of nonpersonhood women assumed upon marrying under British and U.S. common law.[25]

William Martin's attorney was prominent Federalist Theophilus Parsons, and his procoverture argument carried the day. Parsons asserted that the mother's share of the property should be returned because as a married woman she had "no political relation to the state any more than an alien." Distinguishing between passive "inhabitants" and active "members" of the state, he insisted that married women, like infants and the insane, had "no will, [and] cannot act freely." The judge agreed, saying that a married woman "is viewed in such a state of subjection and so under the control of her husband, that she acts merely as his instrument." Clearly, the Supreme Judicial Court of Massachusetts thought it dangerous to encourage women to disobey their husbands and in so doing lose property. "When lawmakers chose coverture over independence and dependence over autonomy," according to Linda K. Kerber, "they set down clear limits on the transformation of the political culture."[26]

Four years later in 1809, the first postrevolutionary separate-estate case, *Kempe's Lessee v. Kennedy*, reached the U.S. Supreme Court. It involved Grace Kempe, the widow of John Tabor Kempe, a legal representative of the king of England in New York City before the War of Independence. New Jersey had confiscated and sold the land Grace Kempe owned when she married. After her husband died in exile, she claimed her New Jersey property should not have been included in the confiscatory action taken against her husband. When a lower court ruled against Grace Kempe's claim, her lawyer, Richard Stockton, appealed the case to the Supreme Court. In trying to recover property for this Loyalist widow, Stockton went even further than Parsons had in making an argument at the expense of Kempe's citizenship rights, by saying that a *feme covert* "cannot be properly called [even] an inhabitant of a state: the husband is the inhabitant. By the constitution of New Jersey, all inhabitants are entitled to vote; but it has never been supposed that a *feme covert* was a legal voter. Single women have been allowed to vote, because the law supposes them to have wills of their own." The Supreme Court chose not to hear the case; thus, no national precedent with respect to the property versus the citizenship rights of married women was set until later in the century. However, Chief Justice John Marshall tacitly agreed with the earlier procoverture state ruling in *Martin* when he summarily indicated *obiter dicta* that he thought the New Jersey lower court had erred in denying Grace Kempe her confiscated lands.[27]

In addition to the ideological embarrassment that rational, property-owning women represented to the Founding Fathers and the case law involving property rights of former Loyalist women that denied married women full citizenship because they were simply passive representatives of their husbands' political views, there were other juridical and political indications of women's official postrevolutionary subordination. These consisted of various forms of individual supplication in which postrevolutionary women engaged. Outside of the numerous private letters of widows and other single women pleading for support money from male relatives—often as a result of the economic dislocation caused by the War of Independence—perhaps the two types that contained the most public evidence of the "rhetoric of humility" can be found in divorce and other forms of postwar petitions that women presented to state legislatures or to the Continental Congress. The language of these pleadings on the part of individual women by and large reflected their dependent, rather than independent, status in the new republic. Whether they were pleading for divorces, pensions as wartime widows, compensation for wartime financial goods and services, or simply funds for burial plots, most were ignored or not acted upon. Even when a determined woman, such as Rachel Wells of Bordentown, New Jersey, insisted repeatedly in the name of "Liberty" that in lending money to the war effort she had "bin a good Soger . . .[and] don as much to Carrey on the Warr as maney that Sett Now at ye healm of government," her plea for restitution went unheeded.[28]

The pathetic (and usually ignored) formal postwar petitions of other individual female patriots also reflected the inadvertent ways in which the Founding Fathers' definition of citizenship worked against women's postrevolutionary political and economic rights. Moreover, during the period from 1750 to 1825, in addition to the negative implications of less than full citizenship for women, there were two other major underlying legal trends that affected their legal and socioeconomic status: the changing role of county courts and the slow but steady undermining of dower rights. All these developments made the transition from British subjects to U.S. citizens juridically problematic for women, especially the vast majority who chose to marry.

## The Changing Role of County Courts

In the Western world, the legal status of women cannot be disassociated from meaningful access to the services provided by the prevailing judicial system. Under modern concepts of citizenship, laws affecting women and other dependent groups constitute the lowest common intersect between the public power of the state and the private lives of average individuals. In fact, accessibility of legal redress determines the outer parameters of judicial standing in any time period. Without ease of legal entrée, the guarantee of equal or equitable treatment of women cannot begin to ameliorate their traditional state of dependence and deference in most Western countries.[29]

For most of the colonial period, independent, local courts constituted the "lowest"—that is, the basic—access level to the legal system for disadvantaged individuals. These county bodies were gradually transformed, first into courts of law in the 1750s and 1760s and then, after the Revolution, into specialized governmental agencies performing limited routine, standardized functions.[30] The modern legal system—based on centralized authority, specialization, and adherence to common-law standards of judicability—ultimately replaced the undifferentiated community-controlled judicial means of "conserving the peace" represented by the county courts of the colonial period. Consequently, it is entirely possible that the subjective and often informal functions of the colonial county courts better met the legal needs of women (and other disadvantaged groups) for a century *before* the American Revolution than did the more bureaucratized and less multifacetized courts for a century afterward.

Because county, or sessions, courts existed in all of the original colonies except South Carolina, they tended to assume similar functions up and down the eastern seaboard. They had both appellate and original jurisdiction and were originally staffed by "commissioners" and later by so-called justices of the peace who, before the middle of the eighteenth century, were not necessarily men with formal legal training. This probably posed no great disadvantage because these courts often performed more administrative functions than common-law and equity actions. They not only handled the probate matters historians began studying with renewed vigor in the 1970s but also made a variety of regulatory and licensing decisions, including those affecting community morals.[31] One study of early justice in Massachusetts lists the duties of the county courts as

probate and administration, apportionment of charges for the repair of bridges, provision for the maintenance of the ministry, punishment of interference with church elections, punishment of heretics, ordering highways laid out, licensing of ordinaries, violations of town orders, regulating wages, settlement of the poor, settlement of houses of correction, licensing of new meeting houses and punishment of vendors charging excessive prices.[32]

In considering the specific duties of the colonial county courts, it is necessary to read between the lines because such bodies also functioned in general as moral guardians of the community, hearing a variety of civil cases involving defamation and sexual misconduct, in which women served as witnesses and in other evidentiary capacities.[33] It is also necessary to determine the significance to women of any changes over time in the functions and accessibility of these judicial bodies. During the first half of the eighteenth century, for example, some colonies automatically assigned court costs to criminal defendants whether or not they were found guilty. Naturally, such a practice encouraged greater use of local courts, both as a substitute for gratuitous private violence and for legitimate self-help. From a structural point of view there is little doubt that by the first half of the eighteenth century the voluntary, community-oriented county-court system, steeped in the English concept of subjectship, offered women more opportunity to initiate civil actions and to utilize civil procedures than did the more stream-lined, impersonal, and professionalized modern legal system that began to emerge after 1787.[34] It is estimated that "up until 1720 women appeared as a principle party in one-fifth to one-quarter of all the cases," when criminal and civil dockets are counted together.[35]

Hendrik Hartog, for example, has documented in detail how the "concept of undifferentiated judicial government that underwrote the power of a sessions court over county affairs gradually unravelled and was replaced by a modern conception of county government as an administrative agency." He further noted how the transformation was "in seemingly direct opposition to the ideological and constitutional struggle of revolutionary America to confirm the independent authority of local institutions against the will of the sovereign." There was no place, he concluded, in postrevolutionary America "for a discretionary problem solv-er. . . . committed to an undifferentiated conservation of the peace." The work of the county courts prior to 1750 "stands as a public manifestation of the private needs of its public" and, as such, "depended on the allegiance of a local public. But by the late eighteenth century that allegiance was not forthcoming. . . . . A local public had grown unresponsive to the values represented by an undifferen-tiated judicial government. And so that older conception of a judicial government of county life was replaced by a bureaucratic model of county government, by a conception of an institution responsible only for specific categories of county action and administration."[36]

According to Hartog, the integrated jurisdiction of the average county court had been a continuum:

At one extreme stood each purely administrative business as petitions to build roads or the repair of county buildings, at the other extreme were particular cases of violent or economic crime. But in the middle lay the great majority of the business of the court; and in the middle categories like administrative or criminal were mixed and had only a technical meaning. *Much of what we think of as the criminal practice of the court fell directly within this middle ground of moral and regulatory "order"* (emphasis added).[37]

This continuum gradually disintegrated after 1750 and was completely disrupted in postrevolutionary legal reform. Women lost most in this process. Their access to the legal system, as well as to redress on moral and other extralegal cultural issues that bound colonial communities together, disappeared into an amorphous, gender-limited citizenship based on highly touted roles as republican wives and mothers.

Consequently, one of the least noticed structural changes affecting the legal standing (if not status) of women came with juridical modernization, induced by new private and public laws that appeared in the United States in the first three decades of the nineteenth century. Relying largely, but not exclusively, on Blackstone's *Commentaries* as a guide in the training of professional lawyers in reaching court decisions and in drafting new laws, the American legal profession began to construct a new rationale for the common law because the Revolution had undermined some of its former legitimacy. Morton J. Horwitz has noted that from 1780 to 1820 judges began to abandon the eighteenth-century, natural-law concept of law and to view it as an instrument for achieving policy goals.[38] (This theoretical development took place at approximately the same time that the county courts were undergoing their final transformation into administrative units with limited legal functions. It constituted, in essence, the ideological analogue to the structural changes then occurring in the American legal system.)

During the course of early nineteenth-century changing legal reforms, this abandonment of natural law as a theoretical base for reforming postrevolutionary American law also ensured the likelihood that woman's legal rights would not be given much attention by lawyers or judges. Natural-law and other Enlightenment theories, which had played such an important role in justifying rebellion against England, had also allowed such writers as Condorcet and Mary Wollstonecraft to argue for equality of the sexes. Simultaneously, the legal profession abandoned natural-law theories in favor of an instrumental approach, just as educational reformers and those few advocates of women's rights at home and abroad adopted them to argue for greater equality between men and women.[39]

Horwitz has argued that "an instrumental perspective on law did not simply emerge as a response to new economic forces in the nineteenth century. Rather, judges began to use law in order to encourage social change." At the same time, lawyers began to play a more important role than juries in private lawmaking through their influence over state legislatures and judicial decisions. Lawyers thus "defeudalized social relations among men but left inter-gender social relations feudal." This development temporarily created legal conditions that may have been slightly worse for women than they were during the colonial period, in part because of the increased disdain with which postrevolutionary leaders viewed equity procedures and in part because of their support for the newly reorganized and sanitized county-court system.[40] Consequently, legal reforms of first private and then public law were considerably less liberalizing for female than for male citizens, especially in the area of contractual relationships.

At the same time, the conditions that already severely limited political rights women had possessed before 1776 were also specifically or implicitly enforced by the American Revolution as the new states drafted their own constitutions. Even though unmarried women with enough property technically had been able to qualify to vote on local issues throughout the colonial period, few had exercised this right except for a handful of strongly independent Dutch, English, or Quaker women in Massachusetts, New York, New Jersey, Rhode Island, and Pennsylvania. Without formal political rights, colonial women had obviously been quite limited in exercising political influence and had fulfilled any civic aspirations vicariously through their husbands or other male members of their families. In 1777, for example, New York became the first state to disfranchise women voters by inserting the word *male* into its constitution, and most of the remaining original states soon followed suit by specifically forbidding women or actively discouraging them from voting. While New Jersey resisted this trend initially, it finally rescinded suffrage for women in 1807 as the result of an amendment introduced, interestingly enough, by a *liberal* Republican member of the state legislature.[41]

## Voting in New Jersey: A Case Study in Citizenship

There is inadequate historical documentation to determine exactly why New Jersey women were granted the constitutional right to vote in 1776, and why they were finally denied that right thirty-one years later. In neither instance, however, did women themselves organize or request that right. It was given to them and taken away from them by men. Unprecedented as these voting rights were in the postrevolutionary era, they became even more important just before and after the Civil War because early leaders of the First Women's movement began to refer to the New Jersey example in speeches and court cases.[42] What little is known about women's suffrage in New Jersey following the American Revolution reflects characteristic early republican ambivalence toward female civic rights.

This single example of postrevolutionary enfranchisement of women has been discussed more after the fact than it was at the time. In other words, the right of women in New Jersey to vote came and went without much publicity, although there was more discussion of it between 1796 and 1807 than between 1776 and 1796 (as emotional and fraudulent election practices came into existence because of political campaigns between the emerging Federalist and Republican political factions at the turn of the century). Additionally, there is every indication that the long-standing liberal attitude of the Quakers toward women had a good deal to do with the response of the New Jersey state convention to the call from the Second Continental Congress in 1776 to create a state government. While the new state constitution was drafted in haste with many provisions that later proved to be ill-considered (it was drafted in two days and finally approved six days later),[43] the same was true of the constitutions of other colonies-turned-states in that same time period—none of which granted women the right to vote.

Although this action, granting suffrage to women, by those men who met in secret to draft the New Jersey Constitution from 26 May to 2 July 1776 appeared unusual both then and now, it was in keeping with both Quaker and traditional colonial practice. In essence, therefore, it confirmed the status quo in New Jersey, with respect to *femes soles*, instead of breaking new ground. Another way of saying this is that when New York and Massachusetts later specifically excluded women as voters (and, hence, as full citizens), they were attempting to alter custom or tradition that had at least on occasion allowed single women, who had been variously referred to as "inhabitants, persons, commoners, and house-holders or heads of families, proprietors, and [even] freemen," to participate in local property and taxation matters (if not actually to vote). Colonial custom and tradition had also provided these unmarried women considerable access to minor litigation in the county-court system. New Jersey, however, because of Quaker views about women, had a stronger tradition than most colonies of specifically referring in its early land-grant laws to "freemen" and "freewomen." Thus, when New Jersey's 1776 state constitution extended the franchise to "all inhabitants of this State of full age who are worth *fifty pounds*, Proclamation Money, clear Estate in the same and have resided within the county in which they claim their Vote for twelve Months," New Jersey was carrying out the mandate of the Second Continental Congress in a manner that was most true to its liberal tradition—unlike other "revolutionary" bodies that drafted state constitutions around the same time.[44]

Even the liberal Quakers, however, could not overcome traditional patriarchal and postrevolutionary republican attitudes about women for very long, despite several attempts to bolster franchise for women. While only a few female names can be found in county records in the first dozen years following the adoption of the New Jersey Constitution on 2 July 1776, in 1787 the legislature specifically designated that women could cast proxy ballots as landowners in elections to decide whether to improve "tide swamps and marshes."[45] In 1797, however, the New Jersey legislature passed a new election law to make voting procedures across the state more uniform. This statute declared that only "free inhabitants properly qualified" were allowed to vote. While the phrase continued to include women in the definition of "inhabitants," it specifically eliminated slaves for the first time. That same year, the legislators also reinforced the right of free women to vote at the local level by specifically indicating that "all persons" twenty-one years old who paid taxes could elect township officers and that "no person shall be entitled to vote in any other township or precinct than in which *he or she* doth actually reside at the time of the election" (emphasis added).[46]

Such specific pronouns first appeared in the electoral rules of certain counties and townships in 1790 and were made part of the general election law in 1797, which stated that "every voter shall openly and in full view deliver *his or her* ballot which shall be a single ticket containing the names of the person or persons for whom *he or she* votes" (emphasis added). Only four out of almost forty votes cast were against this unusually explicit 1797 wording. This election law also carelessly left out the words *clear estate* when referring to property qualifications, thus opening up the possibility (contrary to the wording of the 1776 constitution) that married women who did not have fee simple property rights under common law might vote.[47] It was also in 1797, however, that the seeds of partisan discontent were sown that would contribute to denying the women of New Jersey the right to vote a decade later.

A controversial, but basically innocuous, election took place in Essex County in October 1797 in which the Republican John Condict of Newark narrowly defeated Federalist William Crane. Local newspapers reported that Condict had almost been defeated when approximately seventy-five women in the town of Elizabeth voted for Crane at the last moment. These contemporary accounts leave the impression that this was the first year that women had voted in any number in New Jersey, although the 1797 newspaper stories were not as explicit on the subject at the time as they became a decade later. In any case, local newspapers began to comment on women voting in this and other 1797 elections. At least one song was composed to commemorate what historians have described as a "throng of women" being "literally herded to the polls" and was published in the pro-Republican Newark paper, *Sentinel of Freedom,* on 18 October 1797. The final stanza read:

Then Freedom hail—thy powers prevail
    O'er prejudice and error
No longer shall man tyrannize
    and rule the world in terror.
Now one and all, proclaim the fall
    Of tyrants! Open wide your throats,
And welcome in the peaceful scene
    Of government in petticoats ! ! ![48]

Not all comments were positive or lighthearted. In particular, in 1798 the *True American* of Trenton reported that balloting places sometimes did not allow women to vote when they presented themselves, noting that female voters gave an advantage to more populated areas because they could be more easily marshaled to vote than was possible in more rural, isolated areas. Subsequently, in 1800 the New Jersey House of Assembly was asked to reiterate that "inspectors of elections . . . shall not refuse the vote of any widow or unmarried woman of full age." The legislature decided that such wording was unnecessary since the state constitution already "gives this right to maids, widows, black or white." By 1800, the year Jefferson was elected president, newspaper accounts documented that unmarried women had voted in a variety of places and that many toasts, according to the *Sentinel of Freedom,* were offered to them by celebrating Republicans, such as "May their patriotic conduct at the late elections add an irresistible zest to their charms . . . may they stand unrivalled in their love of freedom and justice."[49]

During the first years of the new century as confusion reigned over the role that nascent political parties were beginning to play in the nation's life, attitudes in New Jersey began to sour on the question of women's suffrage. First, there were vague comments about the "inconvenience" in accommodating female voters; then there were rumors about how easily Federalists in particular began to take unfair advantage in local elections by encouraging women to vote. In 1802, residents of Hunterdon County brought specific complaints to the state legislature about married women voting only to have them dismissed. This was also the year that the state legislature was so evenly divided among Republican and Federalist factions that no governor was chosen for the next twelve months (a political embarrassment later blamed on women!).[50]

On 18 October 1802, the *True American* printed an article, signed by "Friend to the Ladies" attacking the practice of women voting that sounded very much like some of the arguments John Adams had made earlier in 1776 when discussing the issue with his friend John Sullivan—namely, the general dependence of women on men that robbed them of independent judgment. "The man who bring[s] his two daughters, his mother and his aunt to the elections, this "Friend to the Ladies" asserted, "gives five votes instead of one." Moreover, the article questioned whether partisan strife made female suffrage not only inconvenient but also dangerous because "from the moment when party spirit began to rear its hideous head the female vote became its passive tools, and the ill consequences of their admission have increased yearly." The article concluded (both echoing Adams and anticipating the opinions of Supreme Court justices later in the nineteenth century) that "female reserve and delicacy are incompatible with the duties of a free elector."[51]

Ironically, the issue that brought about the demise of women's suffrage in New Jersey arose over where to build a new courthouse—the symbol of legal access for women to both formal and informal forms of justice before the American Revolution. The denouement for women's suffrage in New Jersey came after a hotly contested election that went on for several days, the details of which have never been completely documented. Partisan emotions over the location of the new Essex County courthouse became so inflamed before the vote beginning on

10 February 1807 that inhabitants of Newark and Elizabeth could not safely visit each others' towns. The initial results indicated that Newark had won, but both sides charged the other with fraud once it was determined that almost three times as many votes (fourteen thousand compared to forty-five hundred) were cast in the election. This was half the number usually recorded in statewide elections and more than had ever been recorded before in the county, the population of which was only 22,000. One township, for example, with 350 voters recorded approximately nineteen hundred votes. Clearly the electoral process had gone awry, and, in November 1807, the election was declared void.[52]

The exact nature of the fraudulent voting is unclear. Not only was it charged that unqualified women and boys voted repeatedly, but also that African-Americans and aliens had voted. Interestingly, some men and boys dressed as women purportedly voted more than once in what is possibly the only example of political transvestism in U.S. history. Obviously, women were not responsible for anywhere near the majority of the fraudulent votes cast; but they, along with aliens and African-Americans, were implicitly blamed for the electoral farce that primitive political factionalism had precipitated. In the fall, John Condict, the Republican legislator who had narrowly won against his Federalist opponent in 1797, recommended changing the election law that limited the franchise to "free white male citizen[s]," arguing that the use of the words "all inhabitants" in the state constitution "did not intend to give the right to vote to married women, aliens and negroes, if so, they would have the right to hold office." The preamble to the new state statute passed in November 1807 rationalized the disfranchisement of these three groups on the grounds that it was "highly necessary to the safety, quiet, good order and dignity of the state, to clear up the said doubts . . . declaratory of the true sense and meaning of the constitution, and to ensure its just execution . . . according to the intent of the framers."[53]

Thus, the postrevolutionary liberal legalism of the political faction whose adherents called themselves Republicans prevailed over the traditional egalitarianism of the prerevolutionary Quakerism to deny women and other disadvantaged groups the right to vote. This precedent of antifemale attitudes and activity on the part of liberal males would be repeated again and again down to the present day. Each time it occurs to the surprise and dismay of those mainstream women activists who have never learned the political lessons of female disfranchisement in New Jersey at the beginning of the nineteenth century—namely, that the enemy is not always the conservatives. Because full U.S. citizenship originated with white, native males, significant areas of civic activity (such as female voting and then, after 1920, holding high public office) still remain dominated by notions of masculinity.

Even with these conscious acts of disfranchisement at the state level, it cannot be said that the political status or power of women deteriorated drastically as a direct result of the Revolution because it must be remembered that few had voted or stood for office in the colonial period or even requested such political rights. The significant decline in the political position of women came a few decades later in the nineteenth century, when the franchise was extended to virtually every white male, regardless of property holdings. The precedents set in the new revolutionary state constitutions only prepared the way for the Jacksonian era of the 1820s and 1830s, which, according to Harriet Martineau, "witnessed the completion of the retrograde and anti-democratic tendency that had commenced a half century earlier," as far as female suffrage was concerned, and resulted in the "political non-existence" of women in the North and the "degradation" of women in the South. No female equivalent to the "myth of self-reliant American man" emerged under Jacksonian democracy—an era in U.S. history that proved as masculinist in terms of political and legal developments as had early republicanism with respect to the concept of citizenship.[54]

Since women were more often ignored in the formation of the new laws and courts of the nation than they were consciously discriminated against by the paternalistic Founding Fathers, the ultimate determinants of the impact of the American Revolution on the legal status of women in the United States does not rest exclusively with doctrinal analysis of isolated court decisions or random state laws, which often prove the exception rather than the rule. Instead, the legal significance for women of the American Revolution also lies in the gendered symbolism of the text and context of early cases; the incremental impact of the erosion of certain equity procedures; the transformation of oral legal practices into printed legal documents; increased dower renunciations; and the narrowing of county-court functions as the modern U.S. legal system emerged. In any case, before 1800 discernible national trends in the legal status of women are difficult to document on the basis of meaningful aggregate data, except with respect to dower rights. Such early legal documents pertaining to women remain as important as general societal artifacts as they do for the juridical and statistical information that they contain.[55]

## Examples of Equity Jurisprudence

Even though only seven colonies had separate chancery courts, women utilized equity-law documents or equity bodies, such as writs or commissions of *dedimus protestatem*.[56] These were issued or established in the colonies by chancery courts, or their equivalents, enjoining the person or persons named to perform certain functions based on equity procedures. In other words, marriage settlements were neither the most common nor the most frequently used equity-law devices affecting the property rights of colonial women. For example, most of the numerous renunciations of dower, which took place in the eighteenth century, were heard by commissions established through the equity procedure of *dedimus protestatem*.

Divorce also evolved out of equity law before being given statutory legitimacy by colonial or state legislatures. Therefore, the structural origins of, as well as the revolutionary hostility toward, those colonial bodies performing such quasi-chancery court functions in the New World are factors to consider when analyzing changes in divorce patterns from 1750 through the first quarter of the nineteenth century. Increases in divorces after the Revolution did not, therefore, necessarily reflect any more progress in the legal status of women than did the increases in renunciations of dower. Instead, as Stanley N. Katz has pointed out, it was not equity law that was disputed in the last half of the eighteenth century as much as it was the courts or ad hoc legal bodies that dispensed equity.[57]

Equity jurisprudence operated like a two-edged sword as far as women were concerned. It provided them with some redress from the injustices of the common law, but it could be utilized in negative ways as well. Decline in equity procedures in the immediate postwar decades constituted a particular hardship on widows who were more likely to take advantage of antenuptial agreements upon remarrying than were young women marrying for the first time. The virtual elimination of certain equity trusts (and dower rights) in some states led inexorably to the Married Women's Property Acts beginning in the second quarter of the nineteenth century.

An examination of the evolution of the legal fiction of marital unity leads to a similar constitutional pattern. For example, Supreme Court references to state divorce laws in Dartmouth College v. Woodward, 17 U.S. 518 (1819), contain a general review of the common-law marital prototype that appears to have prevailed both before and after the American Revolution. *Dartmouth College* was a precedent-setting contract-law case involving the legal question of whether a private corporation like Dartmouth was subject to the control of the state legislature, thus violating obligations under the original contract with the king of England that had established the college. Among other things, the state of New Hampshire argued that the Dartmouth College contract was no more immune from state action than was the marriage contract, which the legislature could abrogate by granting a divorce. Chief Justice Marshall, in delivering the opinion of the Supreme Court, ignored the divorce issue and simply stated that the Dartmouth contract could not be "impaired [by the state], without violating the constitution of the United States."[58]

In a lengthy concurring opinion, Justice Story went out of his way to note that it was difficult to distinguish between this type of private contract, involving property, and the civil contract of marriage. "A man has just as good a right to his wife, as to *the property* acquired under a marriage contract," Story argued. "He has a legal right to her society and her fortune; to devest [*sic*] such right without his default, and against his will, would be as flagrant a violation of the principles of justice, as the confiscation of his own estate. I leave this case, however, to be settled, when it shall arise."[59] The implication of Justice Story's remarks in 1819 casts doubt on arguments about how the increased number of divorces during and immediately following the American Revolution had created a more positive postwar attitude toward women's rights within marriage and, hence, a more lenient legal climate for granting divorces.

This one Supreme Court decision highlights how difficult it is to discern national juridical trends affecting the legal status of women in the early decades of the nineteenth century from one or two cases or sporadic state legislation. As a legal text, therefore, *Dartmouth College* is more important as a general reflection of how entrenched the social construction of married women according to Black-stonian views on their common-law disabilities was within the top echelon of the judicial system than it is a specific precedent for divorce-case law. State practices on divorce continued to vary widely from the most liberal in Connecticut to the most conservative in South Carolina. Linda K. Kerber has persuasively argued that "the function of divorce [during and after the American Revolution] was emphatically not to make both individuals happy, but to eliminate sources of social disorder."[60]

Therefore, to conclude on the basis of the increased number in divorces that greater independence and legal autonomy existed for postrevolutionary women is to project figures from one or two New England states onto the rest of the country and to ignore the role economic dislocation and societal mores played in fostering what appears on the surface to be liberal leniency in the handling of a few divorce cases after 1776. Sexual bias in favor of men and the traditional views of the family unit almost always prevailed in early divorce decrees, and this bias was clearly reflected in Story's historic concurring opinion in the *Dartmouth College* decision. In fact, states began to exercise more rather than less patriarchal control over marriage, divorce, and child custody in the course of the nineteenth century. Most of the "new" family rights for women and children that Michael Grossberg and others have pointed out were the rights of dependents "based on judicial discretion."[61]

Constitutional attitudes toward women seldom emerged full-blown from Supreme Court decisions such as *Dartmouth College* until after the Civil War. Before then they evolved structurally and substantively at local and state levels. The private and informal nature of the subsystem of extralegal or ad hoc equity procedures, within which American women operated from colonial times, mandated to them an inferior status that was later reinforced by the masculinist nature of postrevolutionary citizenship and of early constitutional developments.[62] Most of this subsystem was reflected in the multifaceted aspects of equity jurisprudence and other structural considerations, such as the changing status in, and accessibility of, the county courts; and they hold the key to understanding the changing legal rights of colonial women as they evolved from British subjects to U.S. citizens.

Civil regulations touched the lives of many more married and single women than did the criminal codes between 1750 and 1825.[63] Since these years were also ones of periodic economic, as well as political, upheaval, there was a tendency in all of the colonies for criminal actions to take a back seat to the marked increase in civil litigation that began in the 1790s. In particular, there is one specific kind of civil action that colonial women engaged in more often than any other except marriage—the act of renouncing their dower rights at some point during marriage before the death of their husbands. These renunciations head any list of civil actions in which a substantial number of women engaged and, hence, can be considered a quantifiably and qualitatively significant "gendered" aspect of early American law.

## Without "Compulsion, Dread, or Fear"

From the perspective of the 1990s, dower rights appear to have constituted a type of limited marriage insurance, which applied not in the case of divorce or separation but only upon the death of the husband (much like life insurance today). In reality, dower was a much more convoluted concept than insurance but, nonetheless, a form of automatic payment for services rendered by wives during the lifetimes of their husbands. Technically, under common law the dower came to be defined as

an estate for life—in the third part—of the lands and tenements—of which the husband was solely seised either in deed or in law—at any time during the coverture—of a legal estate of inheritance—in possession—to which the issue of the wife might by possibility inherit and which the law gives—to every married woman . . . who survives her husband —to be enjoyed by such woman . . . from the death of her husband—whether she have issue by him or not—having for its object the sustenance of herself, and the nurture and education of her children, if any;—and the right to which attaches upon the land immediately upon the marriage, or as soon after the husband becomes seised—and is incapable of being discharged by the husband without her concurrence.[64]

Traditionally, under English common law dower meant that a widow was entitled to a life interest "in one-third of the land held by her husband *at any time during the marriage*" (emphasis added). In actual practice in colonial America, however, dower rights were usually abrogated or limited to one-third of the real property held by the husband at the time of his death.[65] As noted, dower rights suffered indirectly from the strong revolutionary rhetoric against equity-dispensing courts as a form of British tyranny.

Calculating "widows' thirds" in terms of real estate became an increasingly complex process in the postrevolutionary period. Consequently, Maryland and South Carolina regularly began to grant cash equivalents to widows; other states, such as Pennyslvania and New York, did on occasion. But unless there was considerable wealth in the family, the value of land or money obtained through dower rights was not usually adequate for the family's support. Cash dower settlements also often benefited creditors more than widows and almost always ignored "emotional attachment to a certain piece of property." The dower became an even less adequate source of basic support for widows in the course of the late eighteenth and early nineteenth centuries as renunciations increased, and more legal estoppels were placed on the types of land and transactions subject to dower-right claims. Moreover, from the middle of the eighteenth century, dower rights were increasingly regarded as "a dormant incumbrance on a title"—that is, as hindrances to land development.[66]

A series of obscure, but effective, state-court decisions generally undermined the right of dower in the first quarter of the nineteenth century because the right operated "as a clog upon estates designed to be the subject of transfer."[67] One of the earliest antidower decisions came in Pennsylvania, which had an unusual colonial history of *not* guaranteeing women their dowers if their husbands died in debt. While it can be argued that in Graff v. Smith's Administrations, 1 Dallas 481 (1789), the Pennsylvania Supreme Court presaged other findings undermining dower rights in Massachusetts, Virginia, and New York, it must be remembered that as a Quaker colony Pennsylvania had always granted dower rights less generously than any of the other colonies.[68] A negative trend did develop in the new republic with respect to honoring dower rights, but it was not necessarily set in motion by the *Graff* decision, which reflected an extreme example of Pennsylvania—as both a colony and a state—favoring the rights of creditors over those of widows.

Connecticut was the only other colony and state to severely restrict dower rights before 1800. The economic rationales behind the antidower legal sentiments in Pennsylvania and Connecticut were diametrically opposed: the former being a "primitive economy" in which most of the wealth was in real property and the latter being a highly successful commercial economy.[69] The point being that whenever and for whatever economic reasons, case law limited dower rights because they did not facilitate commerce, land utilization, payment of debts, or early industrialization, especially after 1800 as the American economy began to develop at an accelerated pace.

Following *Graff*, decisions in other states were not, however, uniformly against the traditional common-law dower rights of wives; but slowly a negative, national pattern began to emerge. Most state and federal decisions handed down between the 1780s and 1850s purported to uphold dower rights but within ever-narrowing boundaries. If these judicial limitations (often based on state laws) are combined with the increasing number of renunciations of dower across the new nation, they amount to a serious loss of economic holdings and economic influence of wives over the business dealings of their husbands. *Graff*, for example, constituted a strong statement defending the wife's dower when creditors and surviving children made claims against the estate of the wife's late husband. One portion of this opinion stated that "a widow's right of dower . . . is held so sacred . . . that no judgement, recognisance, mortgage, or any encumbrance whatever, may be made by the husband after marriage, can, at common law, affect her right of dower." Yet the final decision in *Graff* held that "under our acts of assembly" Pennsylvania could deny widows their dowers if creditors claimed the land was needed to pay debts.[70]

While not all late eighteenth- and early nineteenth-century dower decisions were as Janus-faced as *Graff*, many began to hedge on the common-law assumption that "dower is an equitable, moral, and legal right in the wife [and] . . . highly favored by the law either in its original nature of its statutory equivalent or substitute."[71] Thus, in Braxton v. Codeman, 9 Virginia 433 (1805); Ayer v. Spring, 9 Mass. 8 (1812); and Thompson v. Morrow, 5 Serg. & R 289 (PA) (1819), a widow could not claim dower rights in improvements on land sold by her husband that were otherwise "dowable." *Thompson* also negated the need for a private examination of a wife when she had otherwise agreed to the sale of land in which she had legitimate dower rights. Although as late as 1833 in Combs v. Young, 12 Tenn. (4 Yerg.) 218 (1833); and Bray v. Lamb, 17 N.C. (2 Dev. Eq.) (1833), the right of dower (like women's separate estates) was held to be superior to the right of creditors, loopholes abounded in other decisions. In Greene v. Greene, 1 Ohio 535 (1824), lands purchased with Partnership funds were placed beyond the reach of dower rights if needed to pay off debts. Likewise, in Den ex dem. Davidson v. Frew, 14 N.C. (3 Dev. L.) 1 (1831), land that was in the process of being sold at the time of the husband's death fell outside the wife's dower claims.

Increasingly, following the precedent set in Conner v. Shephard, 15 Mass. 164 (1818), "waste" land that had not been brought under cultivation before the husband's death was declared "not dowable."[72] The *Conner* decision is a particularly important one because Massachusetts Chief Justice Parker chose to delineate in detail why he was "protecting" the economic well-being of the widow by limiting her dower right in undeveloped land. First, he argued that "no possible benefit" could accrue to the widow in the form of rents and profits or income of the estate if such property were included in her dower. The original English common-law interpretation of waste provisions preventing the clearing, tilling, or mining of land had been considerably loosened in Massachusetts and other states by the time of Justice Parker's 1818 decision. Yet, he held strictly to traditional common law and presented a contradictory set of economic arguments, in an almost perfect example of false protection, or what Frances Olsen has called "false paternalism." Noting that timberlands "in a state of nature may, in a country fast increasing its population, be more valuable than the same land would be with . . . cultivation" by a widow with only a life interest, Judge Parker concluded that making such land "dowable" would constitute a "waste of inheritance." Then he claimed in a series of related statements, which contradicted his first premise, that dower rights in timberland would hamper the speculative activity of potential purchasers because it could not be transferred (sold) during the life of the widow by insisting that successful cultivation and speculative use of land demanded that it be easily transferable and unencumbered by dower claims. Hence, the conclusion in *Conner* was that widows were better off if uncultivated land were not included in their dower rights.[73]

The issue of dower proved of such importance that the Supreme Court agreed three times between 1800 and 1850 to hear such cases. Not surprisingly, when the Supreme Court agreed to hear dower cases, it relied heavily on precedents set in state decisions. The first dower decision handed down by the justices was Herbert v. Wren, 7 Cranch 368, 3 L. Ed. 374 (1813). Until this ruling, no fewer than a dozen different states had held that wives could take both their widows' provision *in addition to* any property their husbands may have designated for them in their wills, provided the husbands did not also specifically exclude their wives' dower rights. *Herbert* represented an attempt by the Supreme Court to come to terms with the emerging impact of both postrevolutionary codification of U.S. law and commercialization of the economy on traditional dower rights under equity. It is considered an "election" case because the widow had to choose between a devise of land (a gift of property from her husband's will) and land that she would receive under equity from her dower rights. In this instance, Susanna Wren's husband Lewis left a devise of land to his wife to be held in trust for his sons until they came of age. Unlike the dower land that she had received, the property left specifically for the maintenance of her sons contained a watermill and so had commercial rental potential. Before her husband died she had entered into a joint deed of property with him, and, beginning in 1794, they agreed to lease to Philip R. Fendall for thirteen years the land devised to her in trust for her sons. Lewis Hipkins specifically indicated in his will that the rental monies from this transaction were to be used to educate and care for their sons. Any other land was to be sold, if necessary, to pay his debts.

In 1797, three years after her husband died, his widow conveyed both her dower share in her late husband's unsold property and in the devised life interest he had left her in trust for their sons. She took this action just before she married a man named Richard Wren. Fendall continued to pay Susanna Hipkins Wren her dower one-third of the rent from the water-mill land until 1803. In that year he brought suit against the estate, and a Virginia court ordered that the entire estate be sold. However, the deed of conveyance for this sale contained the proviso that the property thus sold was "subject to dower." [74]

Initially E. I. Lee purchased the land in trust for Fendall (who had died), and Lee then sold it to Joseph Deane. If a court upheld the dower claim on the property that Richard and Susanna Wren had initiated through equity procedures, Deane indicated that he would pay it in cash. In other words, Susanna Hipkins Wren was attempting to use equity procedures to claim one-third of the sale price of the entire estate. She had already been receiving one-third of the rental payments on the devised portion of it up to 1803 as part of her dower share. Wren was claiming, in other words, her right to both dower and devise. Her claim to dower was strong because she had created a premarital trust for herself before remarrying and, indeed, the Circuit Court of Alexandria had upheld both her dower and devise claims at the time of the sale of the estate. However, the Supreme Court, headed by John Marshall, said that Wren had to choose between the two, despite the fact that her late husband had not specifically indicated that he had intended for her to make such a choice. The ruling specifically stated that the circuit court had erred in not forcing her "to elect between her dower and the provision made for her in the will of her late husband" for two reasons: First, her husband Lewis Hipkins had left her a life estate "which appears by various provisions in his will to have been intended to be in lieu of dower," although it was not "expressly" stated.

Chief Justice Marshall delivered the decision in *Herbert* saying that Susanna Wren could choose either dower or estate land but not both because Hipkins had made only a limited fund available for the care of his five children. This meant, according to Marshall, that "the presumption is much against his intending that this fund should be diminished by being charged with dower." [75] The Circuit Court of Alexandria had erred, therefore, in not requiring her to decide between the two before awarding her profits from both dating back to the 1803 sale. Moreover, Marshall insisted that all profits Susanna Wren had received from the estate lands bestowed to her over and above her legitimate dower lands had to be *subtracted* from her dower claims if she chose the latter and vice versa. Commonly cited as a prodower case, *Herbert* has all the earmarks of a Solomonic decision on dower, complicating at best and undermining at worst its original significance to widows by arbitrarily interpreting husbands' intent to exclude dower rights when they had not expressly denied such rights.

Twenty-five years after *Herbert v. Wren* when the Supreme Court, now headed by Chief Justice Roger B. Taney, decided the case of Stelle v. Carroll, 12 Pet. 200, 9 L. Ed. 1056 (1838), an even more strict common-law attitude toward dower rights had taken place. This was a District of Columbia case, but the court relied upon Maryland state law in 1804—the year that Pontius D. Stelle had received a deed to certain lots from William Turnicliffe. Within a day Stelle mortgaged this same property back to Turnicliffe (in order to secure money to pay for the lots) *without* asking his wife Beulah specifically to renounce her dower claim to one-third. Then in 1808 Stelle sold another lot to Peter Miller. In this instance, his wife did formally relinquish her dower claim "upon privy examination."[76]

In 1811 Stelle mortgaged the lots already mortgaged to Turnicliffe back to Miller, and again his wife agreed to renounce her dower rights in this transaction. At the same time, Stelle asked Miller to pay off his debt to Turnicliffe in return for selling all of his remaining property to Miller. For this transaction Beulah Stelle *was not asked* to relinquish her dower rights, and her attorney later argued that she retained those rights in the lots originally mortgaged to Turnicliffe in 1804 because she had not been asked to deny them. Miller later sold the property to Daniel Carroll, against whom Beulah Stelle brought her dower claims. Her case rested on whether as a widow she could receive dower from the equity of redemptions created by her husband's various mortgages. Since her husband had not paid off these mortgages before his death, he had left no clear claim to the title, although an equity of redemption was usually considered to represent an interest in the property and, thus, was subject to the normal common laws of conveyancing. Thus, even if her husband had devised a share of these mortgaged lands to her, they would have been subject to payment of the debt owed on them. However, if Beulah Stelle succeeded in claiming dower rights to them, her share would have been beyond the grasp of her husband's creditors.

In 1804 in the state of Maryland, case law and statutes denied widows any dower interest in an equity of redemption. However, in 1818 legislation was passed that allowed dower claims against an equity of redemption. Beulah Stelle's case was caught in the middle of the codification process; therefore, the decision rested on how the Supreme Court would choose to interpret the changing legal horizon and whether it would honor the fact that she had formally renounced some, but not all, of her dower rights in the land mortgaged by her late husband. The court opted for the most strict and least lenient interpretation in keeping with the national trend on dower by the 1830s. Regardless of whether she had consented to the various sales, Chief Justice Taney ruled that "a widow is not dowable in her husband's equity of redemption . . . [and so] it was unnecessary for the wife to join in, or to acknowledge the deed." In other words, Beulah Stelle "had no [dower] interest to relinquish" because the property had been legally mortgaged by her husband at a time when Maryland did not recognize such claims by widows.[77]

The last dower case reviewed by the U.S. Supreme Court before the Civil War, Mayburry v. Brien, 15 Pet 21 10 L. Ed. 646 (1841), contained an excellent review of how codification interacted with dower since the American Revolution. The case involved a partnership case dating back to an 1812 sale. The decision held that dower did not apply in cases where the husband owned land in joint tenancy with a business partner. In this instance, the widow of Willoughby Mayburry claimed dower rights in a steel-producing furnace and the land around it on the grounds that only a tenancy in common had been created, not a joint tenancy. According to the attorney for Willoughby Mayburry's widow, Susan, the property in question was valued primarily for its industrial potential. Such land was usually held by partners as tenants in common, not as joint tenants. Most important for her dower claim was the fact that under English common law, dower rights came with tenancy in common because there were no rights of survivorship for the partners, as there was with joint tenancy. A final factor that should have strengthened Susan Mayburry's dower claim was the 1822 Maryland statute that for all intents and purposes abolished the device of joint tenancy.

This complicated case began when Willoughby Mayburry and his brother Thomas purchased an estate jointly (including the land surrounding and on which the furnace stood) on 5 March 1812. Fourteen days later they mortgaged it to John Brien, retaining joint tenancy only in the equity of redemption used to purchase the furnace and property. Subsequently, in 1813 Thomas "conveyed to Willoughby his undivided moiety [one-half] in the estate"; Willoughby, in turn, immediately "mortgaged to Thomas all his . . . interest in the Catoctin Furnace." The details of the 1813 deed between Thomas and Willoughby Mayburry were vague and did not explicitly indicate that they "meant to carry on the furnace as partners" or whether they had ever operated the furnace before or after they purchased it. Even though the state of Maryland passed a law in 1822 requiring that deeds or wills could only create joint tenancy by expressly stating it, the justices finally agreed with Brien's counsel that a joint tenancy had, indeed, been created. In reaching this conclusion, they disagreed with the logical argument of Susan Mayburry's attorney that the property was obviously "useful only for trade or business; and in no instance could it apply more forcibly than to the instance of the furnace."[78] Moreover, the Supreme Court ruled that with their 1813 transaction, Thomas passed his half of the equity of redemption to Willoughby, thus vesting the whole of the equity of redemption in Willoughby.

Susan Mayburry would have had dower claim to her late husband's equity of redemption had he died before redeeming the property in question because of the 1818 Maryland statute that made widows "dowable of equity estates," subject to claims of creditors. But in this instance the mortgage was foreclosed while her husband was still alive, and so her belated dower claim to the estate of John Brien (who also died in the course of this lengthy litigation) was denied. As in *Stelle*, the Supreme Court refused to liberally apply either the 1818, or 1822, state law to earlier transactions. The justices preferred, instead, to retreat to a strict common-law interpretation of dower rights. Legislative relief—the product of codification—came too late to benefit most women before the Civil War, even if the Supreme Court had been predisposed to liberalize dower rights in an age of burgeoning commercial and industrial development—which it was not. Once again, as in *Stelle*, the justices chose to interpret unstated intent, concluding that the deed between Thomas and Willoughby Mayburry "meant what the legal importance of the conveyances does not show." And so they ruled that a joint tenancy had been created for property that was *not* primarily designed for industrial purposes; thereby giving Brien's heirs the benefit of the doubt over Susan Mayburry's dower claims.[79]

Language in one part of this decision, which like *Herbert* is also cited as upholding dower rights, is extremely important for its discussion of a common error committed in previous dower cases involving the simultaneous transference of property. Susan Mayburry's attorney pointed out that while it had been assumed that the wife was a party to such simultaneous transactions, whether or not her permission had been obtained, "the truth is *that she should be regarded as a stranger*, so far as the law takes care of her interest and endows her; *and as utterly independent of the husband*" (emphasis added).[80] With these words, the attorney for the widow conferred false equality (using the terms "stranger" and "independent") upon Susan Mayburry in order to obtain her dower rights, when such terms implying false equality almost never applied to married women under other legal circumstances because of coverture restrictions that still prevailed in the 1840s. This ruse did not prevail with the Supreme Court in 1841. Instead, like Beulah Stelle, Susan Mayburry found her right to dower defended in general but denied in the particular.[81]

If dower was, indeed, a "gift of the law," it became an increasingly less generous one in the first half of the nineteenth century, and this trend continued after the Civil War. Three Supreme Court cases in the 1870s,[82] for example, confirmed state-court decisions limiting the "inchoate or contingent dower as a valid right or interest" prior to the death of the husband. Two of these three

Supreme Court decisions in 1871 and 1874 upheld a "minimizing view" of inchoate dower, relegating it to "a mere expectancy or possibility, contingent rather than vested . . . before the death of the [husband]." The third decision in 1873 was slightly more lenient, granting that "an inchoate right of dower . . . is a valuable right . . . of the wife possessing attributes of property and constitutes an encumbrance on the husband's title."[83] Yet this was a far cry from how dower had been interpreted and valued by most colonies as necessary public policy to help prevent widows and children from becoming destitute wards of the community.

Having said this about the declining favor in which dower rights were viewed by the legal profession in the United States, what additional insights can be obtained from quantitative analysis of the numerous cases of renunciation of dower, which occurred in the original colonies and new states?[84] A random sampling and computer analysis of over five thousand cases of renunciations of dower from representative areas (an estimated twenty to thirty thousand such documents were recorded between the middle of the eighteenth century and the end of the first quarter of the nineteenth century) reveals an alarming tendency on the part of women to convey to others property in which they would have had a vested right to a life estate if their husbands had predeceased them. Dower records continue to represent the largest existing data base about the involvement of pre- and postrevolutionary women in property transactions. Their renunciation indicates a general decline in female economic power—a decline that took place through apparently voluntary, legal means.

For example, from 1726 to 1787 there were 1,931 recorded cases of women renouncing their dower rights in South Carolina alone. Fifty-two percent of all these renunciations took place between 1761 and 1787—the years of greatest revolutionary upheaval. All of these conveyances by women were made, according to official testimony, without "compulsion, dread or fear from their husbands." Yet the procedure had become so informal on the eve of the Revolution that few of the new states required more than *pro forma* compliance, often not even the requirement that the examination take place on neutral ground—that is, other than in the home and on the property of the husband.[85]

While it is unclear how many women underwent these examinations and agreed to these transactions completely voluntarily, there is no doubt that they represented a dramatic decline in the property controlled by wealthier women in South Carolina (and most other colonies) by the end of the revolutionary period. There is strong indication, from a regional and town-lot breakdown, that many of the large South Carolinian estates controlled by men as of 1800 were built on the basis of these renunciations. Less conclusive figures suggest that, in the case of the Loyalists, they tried to preserve their land from confiscation by the Patriots through conveyance by renunciation of dower rights to those not suspected of disloyalty to the revolutionary cause.

Not all of the dower-right lands went to men, however. Between 1726 and 1787, 124 women received land from other women through dower renunciations. While this is only 6 percent of the total number for these years, some female kinship patterns emerge from these figures. Most of these female recipients of renounced acreage and town-lots turned out to be sisters-in-law, widowed mothers, and unmarried sisters—in that order, with sisters-in-law clearly the dominant group. These ostensibly voluntary conveyances of property from married women to married or single women should not be interpreted exclusively as an example of affective female disposition of property. Rather, the estate patterns, which are reflected even in these few cases where land is conveyed to women, seem to be dominated by the male members of the two families involved. Widowed mothers and unmarried sisters received scattered portions of town-lots exclusively, while sisters-in-law received contiguous improved and unimproved acreage.

The economic reality is clear, even if the exact state of mind of the women who were renouncing their dower rights is not. Linda K. Kerber has noted that private examinations should not be automatically viewed as a procedure protecting a woman from renouncing her dower claims under duress, because the average wife "could not very well say that she was selling property against her will without putting her own security at risk."[86] How much duress or pressure they were under remains open to speculation. By renouncing such lands while their husbands were alive and relatively young, these women were reducing what they were entitled to inherit upon their spouses' deaths, except for what was provided them through wills on intestacy laws. No amount of dowry that they brought with them or marriage settlement could make up for this kind of property loss during marriage. Although there is some indication that women amassing their dowers took precautions to see that they were provided for in their husbands' wills or through the establishment of separate estates, quantitative enunciations far outnumber other such extant documents, such as wills, probate inventories, and pre- or antenuptial agreements. Whether undertaken under duress, the fact remains that "the erosion of dower rights was the most important legal development directly affecting the women of the early Republic."[87]

Yet the legal and cultural fiction that the interests of husband and wife were one masked this enormous loss of property and potential economic influence of early republican wives and mothers. As state statutes modified dower rights, decision after decision tried in various ways to rationalize the situation, by stating in essence that "statutes which have made substitutions for dower show, it is not dower and its purpose which have fallen into disrepute; *it is the administration of dower which has come into conflicts with modern conditions*" (emphasis added).[88] It is this kind of legal double-talk that allowed nineteenth-century courts to continue to pretend to protect widows with increasingly meaningless circumscribed dower rights. Combined with figures showing diminished inheritance patterns for widows throughout the eighteenth and early nineteenth centuries, these ostensibly innocuous renunciations produce, on the basis of legal and quantitative analysis, an impressive amount of information about the economic condition of an important group of colonial women.

At one level, therefore, the initial postrevolutionary period was one of declining legal status for women, brought about either by an increase of citizenship rights and duties for men without equivalent civil status for women or by inadvertent or intentional restrictions or elimination of the limited rights and economic functions that colonial women had informally exercised—often through equity procedures. Legislatures, lawyers, land speculators, and business conditions in general all contributed to this relative decline in legal and economic status between 1776 and the 1820s and 1830s. At another level, however, women's legal status improved on a state-by-state basis as the nineteenth century wore on, indicating that from the colonial period to the present female rights have varied depending on geographical location, cultural climate, and political or socioeconomic events. For example, although dower renunciations increased dramatically and the kinds of land held "dowable" narrowed, the Married Women's Property Acts contributed to a decline in coverture restrictions and, hence, to greater control over property by married women.

Despite these conflicting patterns, national trends developed affecting women's legal position in U.S. society between 1800 and 1900 that were more significant both statistically and doctrinally than can be documented for the entire colonial and revolutionary periods.

# CHAPTER FOUR

# Constitutional Neglect, 1787–1872

The first period in the development of the legal status of women in the United States lasted from 1787 to 1872. It can be characterized as one of constitutional neglect resulting, in part, from the fact that the Founding Fathers did not have women's rights on their collective minds when they met in Philadelphia in 1787 to draft a new constitution. Nor were the Federalists and Antifederalists thinking about women when the Bill of Rights later came into existence during the battle over ratification. While neither document specifically denied equal rights to women, the Constitution and Bill of Rights created an exclusively masculine system of justice based on English common law and eighteenth-century ideals of liberty, justice, and equality.

The framers of these documents made relatively frequent use of *persons, people,* and *electors*—terms that today are considered gender-neutral. On these grounds, it has been argued that the Constitution and the original Bill of Rights left open at least the possibility that women might be able to qualify to vote and to run for federal office at some time in the future. Theoretically true, in retrospect, it most definitely was not the original intent of the Founding Fathers.[1] Other dependent groups, such as slaves and indentured servants, are euphemistically referred to; and native American Indians are specifically cited twice by name in the Constitution, but *women are not mentioned at all.*

A possible explanation for the total neglect of women by the framers of the Constitution (and it can only be a conjecture given the absence of discussion of women even in the *correspondence* of the delegates to the Philadelphia convention) lies in the antifemale contract theories of Locke, whose liberal ideas about the social organization of the state gave representation only to male heads of households.[2] Unlike the older English feudal model of the family and state, the "more democratic and . . . more nuclearized family unit" did not grant even single women head-of-household status, regardless of class, because such a position carried with it more rights of citizenship than the framers of the Constitution were willing to accord to patriotic and virtuous postrevolutionary females.[3]

Moreover, women would have been entirely left out of the *Federalist Papers*

117

debate over ratification had Alexander Hamilton not made several negative references to them in the *Federalist Papers*, number 6. First, he noted that Pericles destroyed the city of the Samnians "in compliance with the resentment of a prostitute." Then, in quick succession he deplored the influence of the "bigotry" of Madame de Maintenon, the "petulancies" of the Duchess of Marlborough, and the "cabals" of Madame de Pompadour over "contemporary policy, ferments and pacifications of a considerable part of Europe." Hamilton's references starkly contrasted with the praise being accorded patriotic and virtuous women in the sermons and popular postrevolutionary literature of the day.[4]

Yet even semantic exclusion from these documents and the *Federalist Papers* does not entirely explain the state of constitutional neglect from which women initially suffered under the new republic. Since the Founding Fathers were simply the patriarchal and Lockean products of their time—nothing more and nothing less—for them to have considered granting political or other civil rights to women would have opened up possibilities that for even enlightened revolutionary leaders went beyond the pale of their Western concepts of justice and politics. Whatever the new Constitution and Bill of Rights might have done theoretically to transform colonial women from British subjects into U.S. citizens, they did little concretely to strengthen their civil or political rights vis-à-vis men.

For all these reasons, it is anachronistic to conclude that the presence of putative gender-neutral words in the Constitution and Bill of Rights indicated that the Founding Fathers "intended" for women to occupy significant political or professional positions in U.S. society. In fact, the exact opposite was most likely true, making original-intent arguments attempting to rationalize women's current constitutional status in the 1990s exercises in futility. Thus, the wording of these documents reflects the philosophical reasons behind the omission of women from the 1787 Constitution and the Bill of Rights, and the words remain important determinants of why after two hundred years women still have not obtained the same treatment as men under the law. This is why these documents should be given a feminist reinterpretation. If such documents are thereby demystified and comprehended as juridical artifacts that encapsulate the culture and mentality of their framers at a precise moment in time, then it will be easier to comprehend the constitutional neglect that women experienced from 1787 until 1872. The words of the Constitution and Bill of Rights did not recognize women as legal historical entities because they constituted symbolic representations of a male political and legal mind-set that, we now know in retrospect, would have excluded women from full citizenship regardless of how patriotically or disloyally they participated in the American Revolution.

## Ways to Overcome Constitutional Neglect

Constitutional neglect plagued women for almost one hundred years following the drafting of the Constitution—from 1787 until the early 1870s. It was reinforced not only by the fact that "liberty" and "independence" had unmistakable masculine and economic overtones during and after the American Revolution but also by the fact that throughout the nineteenth century there were only three traditional ways in which any disadvantaged group had been able to achieve formal change in legal status since the colonial period: the use of legal fictions to decide cases under common law, equity exceptions to common law, and statutory reform of common law. The debate over these three means for changing common law intensified after 1800 among the men who led the postrevolutionary generation of legal practitioners.

The major legal fiction applied to women had been the debilitating one of coverture, discussed in chapter 3, which assumed the unity of the wife within the husband. This particular legal fiction was at the heart of Blackstone's famous common-law dictum about the "civil death" of married women.[5] Two other related legal fictions gained prominence in the course of the nineteenth century: One was the old patriarchal assumption about the inherently inferior or unfit position of women because their biological make-up and private function as childbearers made them unfit for most public tasks of importance. The other reflected a somewhat more modern assumption about the inherently superior, or pedestal position, assigned to women because of their moral purity, feminine delicacy, and sense of civil propriety. These last two legal fictions about the nature of women represented the opposite sides of the same coin; however, the first, or biologically determined view of women, came full-blown into postrevolutionary America from the colonial period, while the latter, based on the moral superiority of women, was just beginning to come into vogue with the rise of a nascent middle class during the Jackson era. Lawyers and judges of the new republic ascribed both assumptions to women without thinking about the unwarranted gender stereotyping they represented. Instead, in the nineteenth century they were considered "common knowledge" within (and outside) the legal profession. None of these legal fictions enhanced women's legal status in the nineteenth century.

Equity jurisprudence provided a second traditional way women had achieved change in their legal status. Although twenty-five of the thirty-three states admitted to the Union before 1860 at some time allowed for the exercise of equity jurisprudence or equity procedures, and eighteen of these twenty-five states at some time had constitutions calling for the establishment of special chancery courts, equity was on its way out as a *separate* form of jurisprudence in the United

States. This is not to say that its principles were eliminated from American juridical practices. Rather, they were combined in the course of the nineteenth century with common-law jurisdiction at both the state- and federal-court levels. Jurisprudential difference still exists in the United States between equity and common law, but today they are part of a single system of law.

The final and third way women had improved their legal status in the colonial period was through statutory changes; and of the three traditional means of achieving legal reform for women, only this last one—legislation at the state level —proved a viable alternative in the course of the nineteenth century. Improvement in female legal status through legislation came in large measure as the result of the codification of public law in the first half of the nineteenth century. In adapting private law to the economic needs of those white males who had benefited most from the War of Independence, reformers on the state level began to commercialize and simplify the law of real property. This was certainly a step forward for a young nation that was rapidly becoming industrialized. The Married Women's Property Acts before the Civil War represented a necessary afterthought in the ensuing codification process that was based on protecting, not granting, equality to females. By the end of the nineteenth century, it was clear that the dominant agents of law reform in the United States would be statutes passed by state legislatures, new amendments to the federal Constitution, and subsequent judicial interpretation of these state laws and of the Constitution.

Such statutory improvement for women came about, however, through a circuitously delayed process. Immediately following the American Revolution, the arguments of legal practitioners favored few statutory improvements (or any other improvements in women's legal status) for a very basic philosophical reason: In establishing new private and public laws of the United States in the first three decades of the nineteenth century, judges and lawyers abandoned natural law and other Enlightenment concepts as a theoretical base for reforming the American legal system. Aside from small and isolated improvements in the property rights of postrevolutionary women noted by Marylynn Salmon, especially in South Carolina and Connecticut, little statistically or statutorily verifiable change appears to have occurred before the 1830s. Most important, there is little evidence of improvements in women's day-to-day experiences with the law as they corresponded with male relatives about their insecure economic situations.[6] This is because private law, in particular, began to reflect a conscious tendency on the part of the first generations of postrevolutionary lawyers and state and federal judges in the early republic to use the legal system as an instrument of economic reform. The system almost always facilitated the needs of early American entrepreneurs—but did not necessarily improve the socioeconomic status of all men, let alone women.

Consequently, under Jacksonian democracy a popular antipathy developed toward both the legal profession and its instrumental manipulation of common law in the courts. This sentiment gave rise to the codification movement. Instead of democratizing American contract law or the legal system, however, all codification did was freeze or institutionalize the process where it was around 1850. Women suffered most from such a lock-in-step procedure because their legal status already lagged far behind that of men. While the power of judges and lawyers to influence private law through court decisions may have been reduced by the codification process, the result was that laws in the form of state statutes misleadingly appeared impartial and above petty political and economic interests. In fact, this *public law* simply institutionalized the existence of a legal and economic elite that had already been created by the early instrumental changes in *private law*.[7]

Rather than achieving a redistribution of wealth or even more testamentary, proprietary, and contractual rights for women, Jacksonian codification concretized existing inequalities between rich and poor men and between women and men in general. Most of the legislative reform and codification of the law that took place through the 1850s primarily benefited white males, although women experienced some improvement in property rights through the Married Women's Property Acts and an expansion of "familial privileges"—if not always an expansion of formal legal rights—through a variety of rulings, statutes, and decisions involving divorce, custody, and adoption. Even before the Civil War, however, access to abortion became increasingly restricted, and newly emerging ideas about female sexuality in general did not bode well for women's collective emancipation.[8]

## The Demise of Coverture

By 1900, however, common-law coverture restrictions (and their antithesis, separate equity procedures) had almost entirely disappeared because they had been replaced by state statutes and private law purporting to create more equal property arrangements between wives and husbands. While the nineteenth century deserves credit as the time period in which common-law coverture rules gradually disappeared, the process was complex and uneven—and, as always, too little or too late given the rapid economic and social changes that occurred in the country during those one hundred years.

This century-long, torturous demise of coverture took place against a confusing and changing backdrop of a political and economic drama in which women played consistently secondary and reactive roles. The larger stage was occupied by male actors trying to understand, and take advantage of, political reform and burgeoning industrialization—initially during the period characterized by Jacksonian democracy and later during the Reconstruction era following the American Civil War. Coverture languished and diminished in these traumatic times for several basic reasons: first, there was the need to expand special equity treatment as a privilege of only the wealthy to a growing number of middle-class women. Although this "extension of the privileges of the few to the many" was in keeping with the general political tenets of Jacksonian democracy, when it came to women such democratization had little to do with political rights; and the limited improvements in female legal status in the 1830s and 1840s were rooted in the country's past—not its future. Thus, the first Married Women's Property Acts in the 1830s and 1840s usually only imitated through codification the "simplest separate estates [protecting] . . . married women from the debts of their husbands" that had been characteristic of eighteenth-century equity cases.[9]

While some early nineteenth-century marital statutes went beyond these colonial-established boundaries, most did not because they were largely the product of male responses to such major economic dislocations as panics and depressions. Consequently, the second reason contributing to the decline of coverture was the seesaw relationship of nineteenth-century women to their husband's creditors. A developing nation like the United States had to foster economic growth based on land transfers and facilitation of entrepreneurial transactions. This is why the kind of land and business agreements subject to dower rights narrowed so rapidly following the American Revolution. Once dower and other impediments to rapid development were resolved, speculation fostered by the economic policies of the Jackson administration resulted in a bust-and-boom economy.

A third factor working against coverture was the responsiveness of state legislatures to various conservative coalitions advocating legal changes in time of economic unrest. The first and most long-lasting depression of the nineteenth century began in 1837 and did not end until 1843. Its severity prompted legislators and judges to protect married women's separate property (in the name of the family economy) *from* creditors in time of economic hardship. While land developers and entrepreneurs had prevailed over dower rights following the American Revolution, creditors initially *did not* triumph over the special treatment accorded women's separate estates in the pre–Civil War Married Women's Property Acts.[10]

## Constitutional Neglect and Codification

Changes in the legal status of women so evident by the end of the first half of the nineteenth century appear to have been caused primarily by the codification of American law at the state level beginning in the 1820s and 1830s—not by significant Supreme Court cases, except those addressing dower rights. This codification process reflected a movement in the direction of public law based on state statutes, which sometimes resulted in a more strict application of common law to women in private litigations. Codification consolidated both the negative and positive aspects of the changing legal status of colonial women that had become evident by the middle of the eighteenth century. These changes were subtle and complex because there was a stage between the end of the Revolution and the beginning of codification in which private contract law, in particular, began to reflect the breakdown of customary law and conduct. At this same time, increased commercialization, speculation, and the beginning of industrialization in the United States produced unstable conditions leading to the panic of 1819.

Regardless of the exact motivation or arguments of legal practitioners, the results were the same: the customary, ad hoc legal circumventions or lax applications of common law for both women and men became a less likely means of settling disputes, especially those involving property, as the courts literally began to make new private laws. By 1800 women had already lost a number of property rights through diminishing access to equity procedures, renunciations of dower, and lower inheritance patterns. Some of these trends were reversed by 1850; others were not.[11] Reversals were most evident in the increase in the number of female beneficiaries in wills, in the percentage of women writing wills, and in state statutes incorporating equity procedures that allowed married women to protect their own property through the creation of separate estates.[12]

Some of the original postrevolutionary moves to reform property law in New York, for example, actually made the laws governing the property of married women more complex and uncertain. Especially in the area of uses and trusts, equity procedures were restricted or eliminated without replacing them with other proprietary or contractual rights. When New York legal codifiers defeudalized and commercialized property in 1828 and again in 1836, with specific state laws governing transactions between white males, they inadvertently made intergender property relations more ambiguous than they had been under equity. The incompleteness of property reform, the narrowing of dower rights through court decisions, and the growing demand and concern of a number of women and men in a burgeoning industrial society for stable and clear-cut inheritance procedures led to the Married Women's Property Acts in various states both before and after (but not during) the American Civil War.

Some legal historians have maintained that most of these acts were no more than codification of equity jurisprudence, which had never provided a parity of legal status between men and women in any case because it was based on the traditional notion that women needed to be protected through special treatment.

Judge Joseph Story accurately summarized this paternalistically protective function of equity courts in the years between the American Revolution and the Civil War when he wrote in his 1839 *Commentaries on Equity Jurisprudence:*

And here, on the subject of married women as well as in the exercise of the jurisdiction in regard to infants and lunatics, we cannot fail to observe the parental solicitude with which Courts of Equity administer to the wants and guard the interests, and succor the weakness of those who are left without any other protectors, in a manner which common law was too rigid to consider or too indifferent to provide for.[13]

Other legal historians have maintained that equity was too complicated to codify and that, at best, some of the first Married Women's Property Acts, like that of 1848 in New York, actually protected the common-law property rights of fathers who were worried that their sons-in-law might squander their daughters' dowries or inheritances. They were usually not designed to shelter any wages or gifts women might acquire independently during marriage or to give women functional control over the property obtained by dower or inheritance.

## Mary Ritter Beard's Views on Equity

One of the few women historians to consider the complicated concept of equity in relation to the legal status of American women was Mary Ritter Beard. Mary Beard belonged to a generation of women historians who were not afraid to make path-breaking generalizations.[14] Her own provocative theories and comments about women's legal rights have been widely quoted out of context, often criticized, increasingly ignored by contemporary legal historians, but seldom subjected to systematic analysis.[15] Beard's research on women and the law ranged widely from Roman times through the first half of the twentieth century. In order to understand and evaluate her views on equity, it is necessary to come to terms with her concept of equality. The minimum degree of equality of legal treatment Beard found tolerable can be traced to her historical interpretation of the legal rights possessed by women before and immediately following the American Revolution. Her interpretation denied many of the inequalities nineteenth-century female activists had attributed to a strict application of English common law during the colonial and early national periods.[16]

In rightly opposing the exaggerated rhetoric of early women's rights advocates about the negative impact of Blackstone's *Commentaries,* particularly on the rights of married women under common law, Beard wrongly asserted her own equally exaggerated interpretation of the role of equity jurisprudence. I do not mean that she was wrong in pointing out that equity was a traditional means of mitigating the inequalities arising from indiscriminant adherence to legal precedents establishing under common law.[17] Equity is, after all, what Beard said it was—a concept of justice through fairness, not uniformity based on case law. Nonetheless, Beard realized that equity could provide relief not only from legal uniformity but also that on occasion equity procedures could be generalized—that is, codified usually through state legislation, thus extending justice from a wronged individual to an entire group of legally underprivileged people. This is how she simplistically viewed the early Married Women's Property Acts—as direct translations of equitable procedures into legislative acts. Always consistent, however, she was quick to point out that as beneficial as these acts were, their obvious limitations confirmed her idea that absolute equality could and should never be formally legislated between husband and wife.[18]

Beard's eagerness to correct the historical record led her to overstate the case for equity jurisprudence. While her views on the history of equity were basically sound, she did not have the details to document precisely the role equity jurisprudence played in establishing the early legal status of women in the United States in the eighteenth and nineteenth centuries. Consequently, Beard claimed both *too much and too little* for equity procedures through misplaced historical and legal emphasis. More reprehensible than her inadequate research, however, is that until very recently few legal historians of women took her insights seriously enough to investigate their strengths as well as their obvious weaknesses.

Characteristically, Beard also used excessive rhetoric to present her point of view. For example, because she was so convinced that Blackstone willfully intended to disadvantage women by making equity procedures a subordinate part of the English law, she ignored all the less harsh remarks he made about the legal status of married women.[19] Thus, Beard, along with the leaders of the First Women's movement whom she criticized, accepted at face value Blackstone's comments about the "civil death" of married women, insisting that he deliberately concealed "the revolution wrought by equity in this domain of marital relations."[20]

Beard did not acknowledge any common ground with leading nineteenth-century feminists, wrongly insisting that they remained ignorant of Blackstone's insidious descriptions of common law and equity procedures. Among other things, too many of them were married to lawyers; were lawyers themselves; or, like Susan B. Anthony, were self-taught experts in constitutional law for Beard to write as she did in her 1946 work, *Woman as Force in History*:

Equity had long been shooting holes in the list of the married woman's disabilities, but leaders of the woman movement in the U.S. did not take these facts into full account. . . . If possible, the dictation which Blackstone's oversimplification of English jurisprudence exercised over the leaders of the woman movement in the course of the 19th century was even more autocratic than it was in the case of most competent lawyers.[21]

Beard was also either unaware or ignored a crucial fact about trusts established under equity: they did not give women legal ownership and use of such property. Under colonial equity, the legal owner or owners remained the trustee or trustees. A woman only had equitable or beneficial ownership of the use or trust established in her name. This is why women's rights advocates in the last half of the nineteenth century supported the Married Women's Property Acts instead. These at least gave women limited rights to own property and to control their own legal estates. Equity procedures had never provided such legal ownership and, in fact, often allowed for fraud on the part of the trustee. Thus, to have simply codified equity, as Beard recommended, would not have eliminated these disabilities. Many nineteenth-century women reformers realized this, and it is why they tried to reform the first Married Women's Property Acts. It was not because they misunderstood equity, as Beard claimed.[22] It was she who misunderstood, when she said:

About 1830 [before even the earliest Married Women's Property Act had been passed], long after Equity had emancipated millions of women from the rigidities of the Common Law so admired by Blackstone and his disciples, a widespread demand arose for married women's property acts. . . . In upshot, the distinction between Common Law and Equity, which had led to so much misunderstanding in relation to married women's rights was eliminated by legislative acts. . . . In this way the doctrine of the separate estate for married women, which had been the creation of Equity, was embodied in the express terms of statutory law and put beyond the reach of the Blackstone Lawyers.[23]

Obviously, only a small portion of colonial women ever benefited from equitable trusts, namely, the wealthier ones. In ignoring this discriminatory socioeconomic application of equity, Beard also ignored such aspects of equity procedures as injunctions and the variety of specific equity relief provided by colonial county courts that cut across class lines as far as women were concerned. She also appears unaware that new state legislatures did not begin to officially sanction equity marriage settlements until 1818. Therefore, for a time after 1776, all women, regardless of wealth, were less able to take advantage of traditional colonial equity procedures because of their uncertain standing with postrevolutionary legislators who viewed these unique and often quasi-legal processes as monarchical legacies.[24] In correctly identifying at least one important aspect of equity jurisprudence, Beard incorrectly emphasized that its greatest impact on women took place in the first decade of the nineteenth century, instead of just before the Civil War. It is simply not true, as she overstated, that "from decade to decade, as the nineteenth century advanced . . . thousands of courts . . . applied Equity to the correction of common-law discriminations against married women, establishing more and more the equality of rights which had prevailed in civil law of Rome in the age of Roman enlightenment." She also ignored the constitutional neglect of women following 1787 by indicating that "impetus to the spread of equity in the U.S. was given by the adoption of the Federal Constitution and the establishment of the federal judiciary in 1789," indicating that a "high volume of state legislation" had been enacted before 1848.[25]

Despite these shortcomings, Mary Ritter Beard both accurately perceived and actually underestimated the influence of equity procedures in a number of ways. For example, she correctly identified equity as a major means in England of both mitigating and reforming common law to the advantage of married women with property to protect. Beard also rightly noted that "nearly all the states recognized Equity in some measure" after the American Revolution. Ironically, what Beard failed to perceive was that there were more equity procedures available to women (not all of them positive) before 1776, even though only seven of the original colonies had separate chancery courts because of the multifaceted functions of the county courts and ad hoc legal means for settling minor legal questions.[26]

Because husband and wife were, indeed, not equal at law or equity, Beard correctly predicted the difficulty of devising truly gender-neutral family law—a problem that continues to confound most lawyers and legislators to the present day. However, we have come a long way in answering many of the difficult questions she posed about marital relations. Although she made the common misassumption that married women were legally entitled to support by their husbands, her emphasis on the difficulty of legislating equality between husband and wife remains quite correct. In addition, Beard was the first historian to point out that "the agitations of women . . . had little to do" with the passage of the *first significant* Married Women's Property Act in New York in 1848. Most important, Beard noted that the conservative, economic nature of this and other similar pieces of legislation had little to do with the early tenets of nineteenth-century feminism.[27]

## Changes in the Legal Status of Married Women

In retrospect, there appears to have been a variety of laws passed affecting female legal status in the nineteenth century, not simply the well-known Married Women's Property Acts. Moreover, there were at least two distinct types of marital-property statutes: ones before the Civil War stressing equity procedures and those after the Civil War stressing more equal property relations between wives and husbands. Of the approximately two dozen Married Women's Property Acts passed by states *before* the Civil War (beginning with Arkansas's in 1835), none significantly expanded the legal rights of wealthier women from what they had been under equity trusts. The 1848 New York state statute became the model for many others, thus making equity procedures available through statutory means to the growing number of middle-class women. A few isolated voices like that of New York judge Thomas Herttell made strong arguments for equalizing the property rights of men and women, but most state legislators voted for the Married Women's Property Acts on the basis of conservative economic reasoning designed to protect, not to liberate, women.[28]

Unlike the equity procedures they replaced, these state acts passed during the first half of the nineteenth century did not explicitly classify women with lunatics, idiots, charities, and infants; neither did they do much to alter or reform prevailing gender-based customs and stereotypic attitudes. They covered six broadly defined testamentary, contractual, and inheritance rights but most commonly established simpler statutory procedures for protecting married women's separate property while changing "as little as possible the underlying institution of marriage." This legislation also tended to adhere to traditional ideas of patriarchal common law by denying women the right to sell, sue, or contract without their husbands' or other male relatives' approval. As one legal article noted in 1886 after such acts had become law in most states *and* in England: "There is recognition in these acts of the inherent incapacity of women, as a rule, to deal judiciously with their own property or to act with even ordinary wisdom in the making of contracts." This type of pre–Civil War statute left most noneconomic privileges of husbands completely intact, and the restrictive judicial interpretation of these laws minimized progress toward other improvements in women's rights.[29]

After the Civil War, however, these same six broad legal functions of women dramatically improved in quantity and quality through new legislation or case law. They ranged from the simple ability of wives to write wills with or without their husbands' consent, to granting *feme sole* status to abandoned women, to allowing women some control over their own wages, to establishing separate estates for women, to protecting land inherited by widows from their husbands' creditors, to allowing widows' legal access to their husbands' personal estates. The accompanying charts can only approximate how women living in four separate regions of the country fared under these new statutes and, in some instances, court decisions in the course of the nineteenth century because they do not distinguish between the law and practice.[30] A comparison of figures before and after the Civil War for these six categories of legal functions in declining order of percentages for all regions combined reveals the following national percentages.

It would appear from this table and the one showing national percentages by decade for the entire nineteenth century on page 129 that poor women's needs (assuming more of them were working outside the home and were more likely to be abandoned than their wealthier sisters) were least well met in the course of the nineteenth century, as was to be expected since the motivation for much of

**Percentage of States with Laws Affecting Property Rights of Married Women before and after the Civil War**

| 1860 | | 1900 | |
|---|---|---|---|
| Debt-free estates | 67% | Debt-free estates | 91% |
| Separate estates | 58% | Separate estates | 87% |
| Wills | 42% | Wills | 70% |
| Personal estate access | 42% | Personal estate access | 67% |
| *Feme sole* status | 36% | *Feme sole* status | 63% |
| Earnings acts | 21% | Earnings acts | 39% |

this legislation came from the burgeoning middle classes. Consequently, the fact that fewer coverture restrictions existed by 1900 meant that middle- and upper-middle-class women benefited most, as was also to be expected. Interestingly, fewer statutory improvements in the legal status of women in the United States occurred during the depressions of the 1880s and 1890s than in the earlier ones of the 1830s and 1840s. In part, this was because the later depressions hit agricultural areas harder and longer, causing less immediate concern among the urban middle class about female property rights. It also was the consequence, however, of the time-lag between the demands women activists had made before the Civil War and new ones that would not appear until the turn of the century and the general narrowing of the goals of the First Women's movement following the Civil War. When significant new legislation affecting large numbers of

**National Percentages[a] by Decade for Laws Affecting the Legal Status of Married Women from 1800 to 1900**

| Year | Wills | Debt-free estates | Feme sole status | Personal estate access | Separate estates | Earnings acts |
|---|---|---|---|---|---|---|
| 1800 | — | 4 | — | 4 | — | — |
| 1810 | 9 | 4 | — | 4 | — | — |
| 1820 | 13 | 4 | 4 | 13 | — | — |
| 1830 | 21 | 4 | 13 | 33 | — | — |
| 1840 | 23 | 15 | 23 | 50 | — | — |
| 1850 | 32 | 68 | 39 | 45 | 52 | — |
| 1860 | 46 | 67 | 36 | 42 | 61 | 24 |
| 1870 | 51 | 73 | 41 | 51 | 73 | 38 |
| 1880 | 68 | 84 | 53 | 55 | 90 | 63 |
| 1890 | 71 | 86 | 62 | 64 | 93 | 64 |
| 1900 | 72 | 85 | 65 | 63 | 89 | 61 |

[a]Calculations for each year were made according to the number of states admitted; 1800–1820 = 23, 1830 = 24, 1840 = 26, 1850 = 31, 1860 = 33, 1870 = 37, 1880 = 38, 1890 = 42, 1900 = 46. Declining national percentages in some categories between 1890 and 1900 reflect the increase in the number of states admitted rather than recisions of legislation or reversal of court decisions. (See appendix 1 for supporting data on the four regions.)

women occurred again in the early twentieth century, it would be undertaken for the protection of working-class women through special treatment, such as setting maximum hours for a day's work.

According to the charts in appendix 1, legal status appears to have improved more for women living in the Northeast/Mid-Atlantic and Midwest than in the South and West (except that seven, or over half, of all twelve western states had granted suffrage by 1911 and eight before 1920). Northeastern and Mid-Atlantic states passed more legislation in all six categories than southern ones. Midwestern states came in second, with western states slowly gaining and surpassing southern states in all but two categories by 1900 (debt-free estates and widows' access to personal estates of their husbands). The South was also slower than other established areas, such as the Northeast/Mid-Atlantic and Midwest in granting improved legal status to women before the Civil War, especially in the area of wage legislation. The Midwest, for example, was behind the 33 percent of the Northeast/Mid-Atlantic states in this category but ahead of both the South and the West when it came to passing laws granting women more control over their earnings before the Civil War (33 percent to 22 percent to 0 percent to 0 percent). By 1880 the Midwest jumped into the lead with respect to wage legislation and held that position in 1900. By then, the West was second, the Northeast/Mid-Atlantic states third, and the South last (78 percent to 75 percent to 58 percent to 46 percent). Working women generally had to wait until after the Civil War for passage of the majority of statutes allowing them some control over their wages. By 1900 eight out of the forty-six states, or 17 percent of all wage legislation in the country, only applied if the wife was no longer living with her husband.

The Midwest was slightly better than the South, and both regions far outstripped the West when it came to establishing separate estates for women before the Civil War (44 percent to 31 percent to 8 percent). The South remained greatly behind the 91 percent of the Northeast/Mid-Atlantic. The South continued to move ahead in the category of separate-estate legislation after the Civil War until it peaked in 1900 at 85 percent, still not reaching the 100 percentage levels of the Northeast/Mid-Atlantic and West. By the turn of the century, only 78 percent of midwestern states had passed such legislation.

The biggest percentage gain for women in all categories before the Civil War was in their ability to inherit estates free from their husbands' debts. Such legislation, mainly in the form of Married Women's Property Acts, which often allowed women to create separate estates for themselves as well, reflected various economic dislocations in the first half of the nineteenth century, but particularly the panic of 1837 and the resulting six-year depression. Roughly the same proportion of separate and debt-free estates should have been permitted in these four respective regions of the country because they were usually combined in the same legislation. However, the percentage of separate-estates legislation in the Northeast/Mid-Atlantic (83 percent before the Civil War) was slightly higher than its percentage of debt-free estate legislation (75 percent). For the remainder of the century after the Civil War, the discrepancy increased: 100 percent to 75 percent. By 1900 the West duplicated the same imbalance. This imbalance between separate estates and debt-free estates was reversed in the Midwest in both time periods: 44 percent to 67 percent before the Civil War and 78 percent to 100 percent after. Southern states also passed more debt-free legislation than separate debt-free estates legislation before 1860 (46 to 31 percent) and again in 1900 (92 to 85 percent).

In the southern and midwestern sections of the country, larger parcels of land and an essentially agrarian economy prevailed, making the need for women to inherit real property free from their husbands' debts more important than in the more commercial and industrial Northeast/Mid-Atlantic region. The amount of legislation affecting married women's property rights in the West was insignificant before the Civil War but matched the pattern of the Northeast/Mid-Atlantic region by 1900, where 100 percent of the states permitted separate estates, while only 75 percent ensured that these inherited or separate female estates would be free from their husbands' debts. Despite claims about widespread ownership of land by western women, as this newly settled area of the country developed economically it is probable that few frontier women inherited large ranches or farms. Hence, western states that were quick to grant suffrage to women did not reinforce female political rights with comprehensive property rights. This was particularly evident in Idaho and Wyoming (the first to allow women the right to vote)—the only two states that by 1900 had not passed any legislation protecting wives' estates from their husbands' creditors or legislation protecting women's earnings. Moreover, only three western states permitted widows' access to their husbands' personal estates before 1900.

Demographic, as well as economic, changes also affected the legal status of nineteenth-century women. The number of children under the age of five per one thousand women in their childbearing years (ages 20 to 44) dropped almost 50 percent between 1800 and 1900 (from 1,342 per thousand to 688), compared to a 37 percent drop in the eighty years from 1900 to 1980. Eighty years into the nineteenth century the drop was similar to that which has taken place in this century, or 39 percent. By the time of the Civil War, the decline was already 31 percent. From 1800 to the 1980s, the decline in the number of children under the age of five per thousand childbearing women was 67 percent. For both nineteenth- and twentieth-century women, these demographic changes in the size of the nuclear family cannot be underestimated. Among other things, these changes related to the increasing number of women in the work force.[31]

Ostensibly, fewer children made it somewhat easier for more married women to work outside their homes in the nineteenth century. But only a small percentage of married women entered the labor market in the course of the nineteenth century. Although women made up 10 percent of the total working population just before the Civil War and 18 percent by 1900, almost 90 percent of them were single and half were under the age of twenty-five. A startling increase in the number of never-married single women also constituted an important demographic fact at the turn of the century when it reached 8.8 percent of all women over forty.[32] Whether single or married, however, women worked out of necessity, and improvements in working women's overall legal status did not match their needs even in those states that passed earnings legislation. Moreover, certain female gains in child-custody and divorce law were more than offset by inadequate alimony awards and the criminalization of birth control in 1873.

Interestingly, these new custody and guardianship rights evolved at the same time married women's property rights were being conservatively increased in the course of the nineteenth century. Under traditional common law, fathers automatically received custody of children. This began to change with the "tender-years" doctrine established in Commonwealth v. Addicks, 5 Binney (Pa.) 519 (1813), in which a man who had not supported his children during their marriage sued for their custody after he divorced his wife on grounds of adultery. Although *Addicks* gave temporary custody to the mother, it upheld the notion that the father had primary rights to the child, including unlimited visitation. Later, in Barry v. Mercein, 3 Hill (N.Y.) 339 (1842), a common-law court of New York finally granted custody to John A. Barry after the chancery court had affirmed *Addicks* in four previous actions by the husband between 1839 and 1842. *Barry v. Mercein* was quite a complicated case involving a Pennsylvania wife and husband who had made an agreement to separate because she did not move to Nova Scotia. He kept an infant son and she an infant daughter. He finally prevailed over the newly established "tender-years" doctrine because the last court decided not to recognize the validity of the agreement (contract) between them and simply upheld the primacy of paternal custody rights. Barry's litigious perseverance, as well as the court's reluctance to apply the "will theory of contract" to a domestic-relations situation seemed to determine the outcome of this case. Not until thirty-five years later, with McKim v. McKim, 12 (R.I.) 462 (1879), did the courts generally begin to view mothers as separate legal individuals from their husbands who could best provide for the emotional needs of children.

According to Michael Grossberg, "judicial patriarchy" prevailed rather than diminished with the establishment of the "best-interests-of-the-child" doctrine in *McKim.* By 1900, family-law courts awarded most children to their mothers in divorce or separation suits. Likewise, the legitimization of illegitimate children that also took place by the end of the century was not intended to disrupt traditional family inheritance patterns or condone promiscuity. Through a series of carefully analyzed legal decisions, Grossberg has illustrated that these divorce and custody cases constitute a valuable source of juridical artifacts for determining the strength—not the weakness—of male domination of family law that continues down to the present day through the acceptance of the family as a "collection of separate legal individuals rather than an organic part of the body politic." However, in the nineteenth century the courts did not view the custody claims by mothers to be a legal right, but instead they based decisions on what had become a gendered ideological and cultural theory about which parent could best see to the needs of the children. In one particular case, involving an upper-class Bostonian woman Ellen Sears and a Swiss nobleman Daniel d'Hauteville, Grossberg conclusively demonstrates that even when women "won" custody suits, they did so only "according to specific nineteenth-century values" that "emphasized duty over independence." Thus this evolution in custody law by 1900 should not be viewed as unqualified linear progress in women's legal status but rather the cooptation of gender into constitutional jurisprudence as a natural, rather than a suspect, classification, thus empowering women to take legal action only within very circumscribed limits of their private sphere of activities.[33]

Similarly, in the course of the nineteenth century divorce rates increased without any significant change in divorce laws or the gendered view under the law that women needed to be protected, not liberated. Marriage remained a "hard bargain" for women in 1900, even though they constituted the majority of those seeking and receiving divorces, because contract law was used primarily to preserve marriages, not to end them equitably. As courts also granted alimony and child support to more women, then as today, the amounts were inadequate and payments erratic. Likewise, cases concerning cruelty to women and children broke little new juridical ground before 1900, despite all the efforts of the First Women's movement to make this a major legal and social issue. Acceptance by the courts of a gendered principle of marital happiness meant more rather than less state interference into that most private of spheres—marriage—even when, as in the case of battered women, the courts refused to take action. For example, a clear indication of the general indifference to violence against women is the fact that there were hundreds of societies for the protection of children (and animals) in Victorian America, only one, in 1886 in Chicago, was established to specifically protect battered women.[34] Statistics, statutes, and case law, however, only tell part of the story about the slowly changing domestic-relations status of women during this period of basic constitutional neglect as dependent legal entities who required sporadic special treatment rather than full rights as citizens.

At no time in the course of the nineteenth century were Married Women's Property Acts or new custody, guardianship, and divorce laws liberally interpreted by the lower courts in behalf of female independence. Yet these legally limited and narrowly interpreted acts remain major instruments whereby the legal status of women improved following independence from England. By 1900, Married Women's Property Acts in particular constituted the most significant means of advance for women with respect to marital property rights, thus contributing to the demise of coverture. Despite the failure of the Married Women's Property Acts to enhance women's formal constitutional status after 1848, wherever the First Women's movement was particularly active property and other legal reforms affecting women, though still quite limited by modern standards, were more comprehensive than in those states with few female activists.[35] This suggests a connection, however tenuous, between the emergence of new domestic-relations, marital-property, and inheritance laws and the early women's movement. Nonetheless, the relationship between women's reform groups and changes in intestacy laws and testamentary behavior appears to be stronger in the twentieth century, but succession law by nature is still very resistant to political influence.[36]

Women reformers were only marginally involved, for example, in the passage of the Married Women's Property Acts in the 1830s and 1840s. In New York, marital-property legislation was passed in 1848 three months *before* the gathering at Seneca Falls. Elizabeth Cady Stanton later recalled that the debate over the New York married women's property bill gave "rise to some discussion of women's rights" and that its passage "encouraged action on the part of women." Stanton also noted the logical relationship between property rights for married women and suffrage in an 1854 decleration to the New York state legislature, when she said that "the right to property will, of necessity, compel us *in due time* to the exercise [of] our right to the elective franchise, and then naturally follows the right to hold office" (emphasis added). But she was not stressing suffrage or other *constitutional* rights *over* property rights in this talk or in any other before the Civil War—no more than she was claiming the immediate right of women to run for office. Her and Susan B. Anthony's activities in the 1850s to improve the 1848 and 1849 Married Women's Property Acts in New York State make this quite clear, as do their recollections and those of Ernestine Rose about the impact on their thinking of the original 1848 New York legislation passed three months before the Seneca Falls Convention.[37]

Just as legislation in the 1960s calling for equal pay for equal work and no-fault divorce antedated the emergence of an organized women's movement, so did the first Married Women's Property Acts in the 1830s and 1840s. In their respective time periods, both the first and second wave of feminists tried to improve upon these statutes in the subsequent decades. They often used tactically such "excessive" demands for suffrage and office holding in the 1850s to make their proposals for better property and wage rights for married women appear more reasonable—that is, less "insane." This tactical ploy of threatening the most "radical" in order to make their main objectives palatable to the male power structure was also utilized by some feminists before passage of the Nineteenth Amendment and again in the 1960s and 1970s to improve upon state and federal statutes, particularly if they had not been integrally involved in their original drafting or passage.

## The First Feminists and Seneca Falls

By the middle of the nineteenth century most of the major female abolitionists in the United States, such as Lucretia Mott, Sarah and Angelina Grimke, Lucy Stone, Sojourner Truth, Antoinette Brown, Susan B. Anthony, and Elizabeth Cady Stanton, were simultaneously working for the emancipation of African-Americans and of themselves as women. (Many of them had begun their reform activity as members of the temperance movement.) By 1850, women constituted a majority in Northern abolition societies and were the leading organizers of antislavery petition drives. Unfortunately, but not too surprisingly, most male abolitionists both before and after the Civil War opposed women taking up their own cause along with that of African-Americans. Such sexism was to reveal itself in full force after the Civil War when the leaders of the First Women's movement, having subordinated the cause of women to fighting the war at the behest of their male colleagues in the abolitionist movement, tried to return to the work of their own emancipation.

While their oratorical and organizational skills may have been honed by participation in temperance and abolitionist work, it should not be assumed that the First Feminists took up their own cause as an afterthought or simply to emulate other groups. The objective conditions of women in the United States by the 1840s were such that they would have spoken out in any case, as they slowly awakened from the deep sleep that decades of privatized morality and constitutional neglect had induced. The Second Great Awakening, improvements in female education, debates in state legislatures over married women's property rights, and participation in temperance and abolitionist crusades all hastened their awakening to the possibility of both improving and moving out of their private spheres by playing more public political roles. This metamorphosis had been gradual and was not complete by the time the Civil War started in 1862—

not because the women's cause was weak or their needs unsubstantiated, but because male political opposition was so intransigent and male domination of the legal and political systems so pervasive.

Prior to the war, however, this small group of activists finally overcame the one-on-one approach to reform that had characterized their early temperance and abolitionist work. They finally asserted their own collective right as well as that of slaves to equal and humane treatment under natural law. The famous Declaration of Sentiments and resolutions passed at the Seneca Falls Convention in 1848 represented, therefore, not a sudden beginning but the thoughtful product of several decades of individual reform work at the state level on the part of women reformers (especially in New York) who coalesced in 1848 with a vision for women and society that transcended their individual selves and self-interest on particular issues. The female legal document produced at Seneca Falls has yet to be duplicated because its major emphasis was not primarily about obtaining individual male rights. It was about the general subordination of all women, and married women in particular, in mid-nineteenth-century American society. Later generations of female activists settled for the single individual right to vote in the name of traditional motherhood and the patriarchal family. [38]

Participants in the Seneca Falls Convention did not, and women in the United States have yet, to achieve the "feminized," as Mary Beard described it, universal human rights and happiness demanded in 1848. The Declaration of Sentiments "looked back to 1776 rather than forward." It was steeped in the "ethical" and "humanistically" progressive language of the republican ideology of the American Revolution. Therefore, what is important about the Seneca Falls meeting is not simply that the major statement was patterned after the Declaration of Independence and became the first postrevolutionary female legal text or that one of the resolutions called for the enfranchisement of women. (This was the only resolution that was not passed unanimously because almost half of the one hundred men and women attending feared that a demand for the right to vote would defeat the other resolutions by making the convention look ridiculous.) While the right to vote may have been the most emotionally controversial and tactically radical resolution passed at the 1848 meeting, it did not specifically address the basic purposes of the gathering: the legal disabilities of most married women and the religious and educational discrimination suffered by all women, regardless of marital status. This was a collective natural-rights vision of equality that called for far more than specific individual rights; it was a feminist demand for the long-overdue reconciliation of republican theory with republican practice. [39]

The lasting significance of the Seneca Falls Declaration of Sentiments lay in its attack on the institutions of religion and modern marriage—both of which fostered the stifling domesticity of the nascent nuclear family and the rise of the privatization of true womanhood with industrialization and urbanization. These first-generation feminists were demanding the complete and collective emancipation of married women in their churches and homes in the name of God, justice, and humanity. Although disfranchisement is mentioned three times in the declaration segment of the 1848 document, it was not its "central idea," as Ellen DuBois has maintained. What was central to both the declaration and the attached resolutions was the statement of the many other ways in which men had "oppressed [women] on all sides."[40] Oppression from "all sides" in the declaration referred to marital, educational, moral, economic, professional, and religious subordination experienced by women that could not exclusively or primarily at that time (or now) be remedied simply through obtaining the political right to vote. This lack of central emphasis on suffrage, in particular, and on an individual rights-centered drive for political equality, in general, is especially evident in the twelve resolutions passed at Seneca Falls.

In many ways Seneca Falls (and the surrounding area) was ripe for such a historic meeting, situated as it was in the religious-revival and reform area of central New York, known as the "Burned-Over District." All that was missing from the mills, factories, and three thousand inhabitants living in the approximately four hundred houses of Seneca Falls near the "psychic highway" of the Erie Canal was a strong woman leader to produce a feminist synergism of momentous proportions.[41] When Elizabeth Cady Stanton and her husband moved to Seneca Falls in 1847, previous religious and political dissent, particularly as manifested in the temperance and antislavery movements, had already produced splits among the Methodists and New York Democrats. At the same time, both Seneca Falls and the nearby town of Waterloo were experiencing rapid transformations—with the establishment of factory manufacturing and the arrival of the railroad—from agricultural, transportation, and milling areas into industrial centers. Social and economic ferment prevailed in the area, and the Wesleyan Chapel, newly constructed in 1843, already had served as a free-speech haven for female activists, abolitionists, and opponents of alcohol.[42]

Stanton and Lucretia Mott's choice of the chapel for their 1848 meeting was not unusual nor was their concern for "sex equality" a sudden or whimsical idea. They had been thinking along these lines since at least 1840 and 1841 as they discussed the refusal of a majority of both British and American representatives to the World Anti-Slavery Convention in London to seat the U.S. women who had been sent as official delegates. In the intervening years, Mott had continued to devote most of her time to abolitionism and Stanton to raising a family in Boston, where she was in contact with radical abolitionists and other reformers of the day. Compared to life in Boston, where "all my immediate friends were reformers," Stanton became bored and depressed on the outskirts of Seneca Falls with her husband absent for long periods of time and without "modern conveniences and well-trained servants." In July 1848, Stanton took advantage of an invitation to meet with Mott and a few other women in nearby Waterloo. "I poured out the torrent of my long-accumulated discontent with such a vehemence and indignation," Stanton later recalled, "that I stirred myself, as well as the rest of the party, to do and dare anything." The result was a notice in several local newspapers calling for a "WOMAN'S RIGHTS CONVENTION . . . to discuss the social, civil, and religious condition and rights of woman."[43]

The year 1848 also proved momentous for economic theories and political developments abroad. Not only was it the year that Karl Marx wrote the *Communist Manifesto* and John Stuart Mill published *Principles of Political Economy*, but there were also a series of uprisings beginning in France on February 22 that ultimately changed European politics and boundaries. While Stanton and many of the other women and men gathering in Wesleyan Chapel were aware of these foreign political events, it is not evident that they understood the advanced political theories behind them. Instead, they were more discontented over the U.S. presidential nominees for 1848. Stanton later recalled the importance of certain contemporary international and national influences on their thinking but related all of them to Enlightenment theories and to the earlier revolutions in America and France, noting the overall impact these eighteenth-century events had on the nineteenth-century "minds of women of the highest culture." After rejecting several reform documents by their male contemporaries that proved "too tame . . . for the inauguration of a Rebellion such as the world had never seen before," the women decided at a planning meeting a few days before the Seneca Falls Convention to go back to the words of the Founding Fathers, by using the Declaration of Independence as a model.[44]

This clever imitation of Jefferson's Declaration of Independence was not purely an accident (nor was it as slavish as is usually assumed).[45] Its ideas against British domination of the colonies more readily reflected nineteenth-century women's domination within the family and society than those contained in temperance or even abolitionist tracts. The Seneca Falls Declaration of Sentiments became the first female legal text in U.S. history. As such, over time it has suffered almost as much from mystification and reification as the Constitution and Bill of Rights, because contemporary scholars and feminists have taken its exact wording too literally from a liberal legal point of view and not symbolically enough from the standpoint of the Enlightenment mentality it represented when written. At the time, however, its meaning appeared—at least to women activists —rather straightforward. In the minds of Elizabeth Cady Stanton's generation of reformers, for example, the Declaration of Sentiments was their collective attempt to address the socioeconomic disadvantages of married women (primarily), as Abigail Adams had so tentatively tried to do on her own seventy-two years earlier. It symbolized their realization that their legal situation was considerably more complex and in a greater state of flux than hers, but it was still not that much different from the standpoint of full citizenship.

Uppermost in the minds of women at Seneca Falls, however, was the general pursuit of "true and substantial happiness" for themselves within the private sphere of marriage, not individual political rights identified with the public sphere. Words about happiness can be found in both the declaration and the preamble to the twelve resolutions passed in 1848. The preamble justified happiness not by directly quoting Jefferson, as the author of the declaration they had decided to emulate, but with a surprising paraphrase from Blackstone's infamous *Commentaries*—a paraphrase noting that "God himself" had dictated "the great precept of nature . . . that "man shall pursue his own true and substantial happiness.' " This is important because it allowed these women to present their ideas about their own happiness and legal status in the 1848 declaration and resolutions in "higher-law" rhetoric that placed them above the secular and theistic practices that they wanted changed. (Religious concerns were noted in half of the twelve resolutions, natural or human rights in four resolutions, and specific civil or economic rights in only two.) It is the general and sweeping nonsecular nature of these 1848 statements that make them so radical for their time (and ours), not their socioeconomic or political specificity. As a legal text, the words are more significant as an act of collective feminist consciousness than they are as an assertion of individual rights.

What were the other important, collective demands made at Seneca Falls? There was the general assumption that since women were created equal to men, they deserved "equality of human rights," encouragement to partake of educational and religious opportunities, and "equal participation with men in the various trades, professions, and commerce." Most of the more specific grievances cited dwelled not on the question of individual enfranchisement but on legal and socioeconomic questions concerning the subordination of all women within the family. Thus, the Seneca Falls Declaration of Sentiments stressed wife beating, dual standards of morality, divorce, child custody, and control over property and wages—all problems stemming from the institution of marriage as it had evolved by the middle of the nineteenth century. As Stanton said in 1853, "the right idea of marriage is at the foundation of all reforms."[46] Both Anthony and Stanton and other radical feminists of their time reasserted for the remainder of the century that "marital bondage" was "woman's chief discontent." As their militant newspaper, *The Revolution,* would later proclaim on 27 October 1870:

But we are not dreamers or fanatics; and we know that the ballot when we get it, will achieve for woman no more than it has achieved for man. . . . the ballot is not even half the loaf; it is only a crust, a crumb. The ballot touches only those interests, either of men or women, which take their root in political questions. But woman's chief discontent is not with her political, but with her social, and particularly her marital bondage. The solemn and profound question of marriage . . . is of more vital consequence to woman's welfare, reaches down to a deeper depth in woman's heart, and more thoroughly constitutes the core of the woman's movement, than any such superficial and fragmentary question as woman's suffrage.[47]

Although the First Women's movement in the United States is usually said to have begun with the Seneca Falls Convention of 1848, this beginning did not have a specific *individual*-rights political agenda. In general, the annual women's conventions between 1848 and the Civil War also attacked women's general subordination within the institutions of religion and marriage—a condition that antebellum female activists were not trying to ameliorate or eliminate primarily through the franchise or other political rights enjoyed by most white males at the time. To interpret these pre–Civil War statements and resolutions as examples of "the supremacy of individual rights" is to misread these original texts as legal documents and to skew both the ideological strategy and political tactics of these early feminists. Instead, they often equated happiness with a good private life rather than with exercising political rights in the public sphere. As a hedonist, Stanton probably talked more about happiness than Anthony or other more stoic early leaders of the First Women's movement. As late as 1860, in her discussions of marriage and divorce when Stanton asserted that it was the "inalienable right of all to be happy," her words were generic and collectively inclusive for women as a group, not "radically individualistic."[48] It took the Civil War and the reconstruction amendments before leaders of the First Women's movement began to think individually about rights.

Elizabeth Cady Stanton saw and expressed more clearly than most feminists then (or today) that the meaning of happiness and equality for women (and, in her time, for black slaves) was not the same as for white men. She later asked and answered the following set of questions in 1857: "When we talk of women's rights, is not the right to her person, to her happiness, to her life, the first on the lists? If you go to a southern plantation and speak to a slave of his right to property, to the elective franchise, to a thorough education, his response will be a vacant stare. . . . The great idea of his right to himself, to his personal dignity, must first take possession of his soul."[49] Equality for women and slaves obviously started from different points in time and culture, but both had to do with individual happiness as articulated by racial or gender conditioning—making their happiness different from happiness for white males.

Moreover, Stanton's much-quoted and misunderstood comments to the 1860 Woman's Rights Convention about marriage and divorce focused not only on marriage as a contract but also on the general subordination of women within the family. Because Stanton's attempt to reformulate marriage by insisting that it should be viewed as no more than a civil contract between two consenting adults received the most attention (and criticism) at the time, there has been a tendency among historians to ignore or downplay how radical a reformulation of marriage and divorce her position and Anthony's was in the 1860s. The legal contract aspects of her argument pale beside her condemnation of "marital feudalism." To the degree that the essence of female happiness rested on transforming the institution of marriage to meet female needs, Stanton and Anthony resorted to natural rights and Enlightenment theories that transcended their argument about contract rights.

Oppressed as a group, these First Feminists initially realized they could not be emancipated as individuals. Only in the early 1870s did they begin to settle for individual liberation in place of collective emancipation. Only then did they edge toward considering inclusion in the U.S. Constitution exclusively on the same terms as men. Only then did they abandon their ideological radicalism for liberal legalism. Even after they had become more legalistically male oriented on the questions of civil and political rights for women, Stanton and Anthony, despite the overwhelmingly negative reaction to their dramatic reformulation of marriage and divorce, never abandoned their belief that it was "folly to talk of the sacredness of marriage and maternity, while the wife is practically regarded as an inferior, a subject, a slave." They also did not abandon their view that "the highest good and happiness of the individual and society lie in the same direction." In their heart of hearts, these two women never severed the connection between the collective and the individual. Their views on marriage and divorce best exemplify how far they were from simplistically advocating individual rights before and after the Civil War. [50]

The 1840s not only marked the time in which women began to organize in their own behalf and to take more of their legal grievances to state courts and legislatures but was also a period in which African-Americans took to the courts for redress. Dred Scott began his doomed eleven-year struggle for freedom in 1846; and in 1848 Benjamin Roberts, a black printer in Boston, sued the city for the right of his four-year-old daughter to attend a white public school. This case initiated a struggle over integration of the Boston school system that lasted until 1855. Roberts's suit reached the Massachusetts Supreme Court, headed by Chief Justice Lemuel Shaw, in December 1849. Shaw defended segregation under a separate-but-equal concept that became woven into state supreme court decisions for the next one hundred years. Ironically, while the case Roberts v. The City of Boston, 59 Mass. 198 (1849), set in motion a national legal precedent for all forms of state-enforced segregation, Boston reformers reacted to it by launching a successful integration drive that culminated in 1855 with a state law banning segregation in public schools.[51]

On the face of it, the case was simple enough. Roberts had tried four times to enter his daughter in one of Boston's white primary schools before he finally brought suit. Also, free African-Americans in Boston, with the support of the Massachusetts Anti-Slavery Society, had attempted to abolish the exclusively black schools in Boston only to be told by the primary-school committee in 1846 that "the distinction is one which the Almighty has seen fit to establish, and it is founded deep in the physical, mental and moral natures of the two races. No legislature, no social customs, can efface this distinction." In the opinion of the committee, "the continuance of the separate schools for colored children . . . is not only legal and just, but is best adapted to promote the education of that class of our population."[52] The fact that Sarah Roberts passed five white primary schools on her way to the designated black one was not considered relevant in Roberts's previous petitions nor ultimately by the Supreme Court of Massachusetts.

The decision is worth noting for several reasons: First, a brief by the renowned abolitionist Charles Sumner argued eloquently for "equality of men before the law" and, in anticipation of the later "separate-but-equal" ruling in *Plessy v. Ferguson,* asserted that "whites themselves are injured by the separation. . . . The school is the little world in which the child is trained for the larger world of life. . . . Prejudice is the child of ignorance. It is sure to prevail where people do not know each other." Second, although Judge Shaw's decision was almost totally "unreasoned" in terms of case law, it became the legal precedent that would prevail in post–Civil War cases upholding discrimination against women and African-Americans and against other racial groups for the first half of the twentieth century.[53] "The great principle . . . [that] all persons without distinction of age or sex, birth or color, origin or condition, are equal before the law . . . ought to appear in a declaration of rights," Shaw noted in presenting the unanimous opinion of the court.

But when this great principle comes to be applied to the actual and various conditions of persons in society *it will not warrant the assertion that men and women are legally clothed with the same civic and political powers, and that children and adults are legally to have the same functions and be subject to the same treatment, but only that the rights of all, as they are settled and regulated by law, are equally entitled to the paternal consideration and protection of the law, for their maintenance and security.* What those rights are, to which individuals, in the infinite variety of circumstances by which they are surrounded in society, are entitled, must depend on laws adapted to their respective relations and conditions (emphasis added).[54]

With equal juridical abandon, Shaw concluded his decision by denying that desegregated education could ameliorate "distinction of caste." This prejudice, "*if it exists,* is not created by law, and probably cannot be changed by law. Whether this distinction and prejudice . . . would not be as effectively fostered by compelling colored and white children to associate together in the same schools, may well be doubted, [but the decision of the school committee] is founded on just grounds of reason and experience" (emphasis added).[55] As a leading state jurist of the 1840s, Shaw had little trouble distinguishing without the benefit of case-law precedent among African-Americans and whites, women and men, and children and adults. Neither would other state and federal judges in the 1870s and 1880s.

## The First Feminists and the Civil War: Unrequited Patriotism

In retrospect, there is no doubt that the Civil War effectively killed the initial collectivity behind the broadly based humanitarian goals of the Seneca Falls Convention. By 1869, the First Women's movement had split into two wings, represented by the National Woman Suffrage Association (NWSA) and the American Woman's Suffrage Association (AWSA). Ostensibly, this division, which remained for twenty years, was caused by the dispute over whether or not women, as well as black males, should be granted the right to vote. However, it involved much more: strategy, socioeconomic tensions within the movement, commitment to a visionary feminism, and the conflict between radical and mainstream reform of American society.

Having supported war at the expense of their own movement and other reforms, leading feminists, such as Anthony, Stanton, and Lucy Stone, unlike their revolutionary sisters almost a century earlier, were politically conscious of the collective significance of their contributions to the war effort. Not until the introduction of the reconstruction amendments (beginning in 1865 with the Thirteenth Amendment and ending in 1870 with the Fifteenth Amendment), however, did the vote replace all other possible modes of recognition for their patriotic actions. Only these three amendments finally convinced the most radical women reformers that the conclusion of the war preserved the union, freed the slaves, but did nothing to enhance women's rights.

During the Civil War, as in the War of Independence and the War of 1812, women were called upon in even greater numbers, particularly in the South, to carry on with farm work and to feed and clothe soldiers. Unlike these earlier wars, however, few wives of officers were permitted to join their husbands. Female nurses and cooks replaced the unofficial wives of enlisted men of previous wars and traveled officially to military encampments only to be labeled camp followers or prostitutes by the soldiers they served. Both groups of women on each side were treated inhumanely as health rather than moral problems. Women also entered mills in the North in greater numbers than ever before and made significant contributions as teachers and as retail store clerks while the fighting continued. For the first time in the North they began to do secretarial work in the offices of the federal government; some of them were even permitted, because of the male labor shortage, to take up occupations that some of their female colonial ancestors had also engaged in, such as those of innkeeper, steamboat captain, teamster, and mortician. Confederate women found fewer job opportunities and, in general, suffered more from shortages, inflation, and military occupation than their Northern sisters. Few, however, participated in food riots and the looting of military warehouses.[56]

Approximately four hundred women actually served as soldiers on both sides during the Civil War. Some, like Franny Wilson, Ellen Goodridge, Sarah Emma Edmonds, and Amy Clark, used male names and cross-dressed in order to engage in combat; but most served without disguising their sex in the roles of spies, saboteurs, scouts, and couriers—blowing up bridges and arsenals and helping prisoners and slaves to escape. A few, such as Harriet Tubman and Anna Ella Carroll, devised military strategy and suggested battle plans (Tubman for Colonel James Montgomery and his three hundred black soldiers in the campaign along the Combahee River in South Carolina and Carroll for Grant's Tennessee campaign, which was one of the turning points in the war). Other black women, such as Susie King Taylor and Charlotte Forten, despite hardship and ridicule, served as teachers in the South for black civilians or soldiers.

Most women on both sides, however, served behind the lines: at least thirty-two hundred became nurses, despite the hostility of army doctors; others raised over $50 million in the North for training more nurses, for care of the wounded, and for hospital supplies. Women worked in a variety of capacities in all medical facilities, but the number of women doctors did not increase during the war as might have been expected. Northern women successfully organized seven thousand local societies of the Sanitary Commission to raise money and supplies for soldiers, widows, and orphans, in addition to training nurses. Finally, Susan B. Anthony personally created the Woman's National Loyal League in New York, working for $12 a week during the duration of the war and facing the sporadic violence of racist draft riots that occurred in the city. Under her dogged leadership, by August 1864 this organization had collected approximately four hundred thousand signatures on petitions for the unconditional emancipation of the slaves, which was finally achieved with passage of the Thirteenth Amendment in 1865.[57]

As Anthony viewed the battlefield of the First Women's movement in the wake of the Civil War, she found the old enthusiasm and collectivity had waned. The 1860s and 1870s would have probably been a typical one of postwar conservatism for women and men had it not been for the passage of two reconstruction amendments to the U.S. Constitution. It would have been difficult, if not impossible, to resurrect the First Women's movement (as it proved impossible in the first decades after the two world wars) had it not been for the passage of the Fourteenth and Fifteenth amendments. Because these amendments rallied the most radical of the First Feminists, they also separated such women from their more moderate sisters. Thus, the reconstruction amendments simultaneously acted *both* as a catalyst and as a check on postwar feminism. They provided organizational motivation; but, at the same time, they first split and then skewed the goals of the revitalized movement more and more in the direction of individual litigation and single-issue politics.

When a small group of postwar feminists headed by Anthony and Stanton were told by Republicans to accept voting rights for black men as part of the Fourteenth and Fifteenth amendments because it was "the [male] Negroes' hour," they expressed shock, anger, and dismay. Elizabeth Cady Stanton repeatedly and eloquently denied the justice of this partisan claim because before the war radical reformers had talked about universal, not gender-specific, suffrage. Again and again in her speeches on reconstruction, Stanton returned to the Declaration of Independence as she had at Seneca Falls in 1848. What had gone wrong with the Declaration of Independence, she insisted with feminist clarity about the patriarchal meaning of legal texts, had been the drafting of the Constitution:

Our Fathers declared all men equal, then placed the power in the hands of the few. They declared no just government could be formed without the consent of the governed, then denied the elective franchise to men without property and education, to clergymen, women and negroes. They declared taxation without representation tyranny, then taxed all these dis-enfranchised classes. Through a century of discord, friction and injustice, these violations of the republican idea have culminated at last in a four years bloody war. And now we stand once more debating with ourselves the fundamental principles of government. From the baptism of this second revolution, with a century of added experience, shall we repeat the blunder of the Fathers and build again on the old foundation whose corner stone is class and caste?[58]

In opposing Republican reconstruction legislation and amendments, Stanton noted that they were all too little, too sectional, and too partial, saying:

This is not reconstruction, it is whitewashing, it is patching, it is propping up what cannot stand. This is not the negroes' hour. We have passed from him to the broader question of the life of the Republic. In the discussion of his rights we have gone back to first principles and learned that the safety and durability of a nation demand that the least right of the humblest citizen be secured. . . . The demand of the hour is equal rights to all, that the ideal republic of the Fathers be now made a fact of life.[59]

Stanton's prediction proved all too correct. Positive application of the equal-protection clause of the Fourteenth Amendment to women did not materialize until the last quarter of the twentieth century and is still not complete.

## The First Feminists and the "New Departure"

By the end of 1865, it was clear to Anthony and Stanton that the proposed Fourteenth Amendment would have to be opposed politically if it ever was approved by Congress and sent to the states for ratification. This meant, however, that they would have to enter into political alliances of a different nature from those they had experienced when supporting the Married Women's Property Acts, child custody, or divorce-reform legislation before the Civil War. This time they would be entering into a coalition with the male-led American Anti-Slavery Society (later, the American Equal Rights Association) to obtain improved legal and political status for women, as well as blacks. When Theodore Tildon proposed in December 1865 the formation of the National Equal Rights Society, Anthony decided the time was right to consolidate the American Anti-Slavery Society with various state women's rights groups into this new organization, even though Wendell Phillips, who supported the Fourteenth Amendment, would be its first president. The "New Departure" began, therefore, with a conscious but dangerous political decision on the part of Anthony and Stanton—dangerous because of the possibility of cooptation or betrayal.

In 1866, however, when Anthony formally supported the formulation of a National Equal Rights Association in order to keep universal suffrage (not simply the vote for black males) a goal of postwar politics, Phillips, as president of the American Anti-Slavery Society, killed the consolidation idea. He later proposed that the women should be passively content with the "intellectual theory" of women's suffrage, while actively fighting to remove "white"—but not "male"—from the New York Constitution in order to ensure the vote for all men. While Anthony understood the significance of this ploy before Stanton, both realized that women would have to continue to fight for their own enfranchisement with or without the support of former male abolitionists.[60]

Their next foray into postwar establishment politics proved even more discouraging as they battled in vain from June 1866 through July 1867 to alter the wording of the Fourteenth Amendment. Female activists of the late 1860s interpreted the legal meaning of the text of the Fourteenth Amendment in two distinct ways. They initiated litigation in their own behalf under Section 1 in the hope that its emphasis and broad wording would aid them in their postwar campaign for constitutional equality and full citizenship. At the same time, they reacted negatively to Section 2, in which the states were specifically informed that if they denied the right to vote to any "male" citizen over twenty-one, the basis of their representation in the electoral college, in the House of Representatives, among state executive and judicial offices and legislatures would be "reduced in the proportion which the number of such male citizens shall bear to the whole number of male citizens twenty-one years of age."[61]

While some constitutional specialists have since argued that this second section of the Fourteenth Amendment did not really guarantee or confer voting rights on black men because postwar Republicans did not have the power or the will to enforce the penalty clause, few post–Civil War feminists could afford the luxury of interpreting the Fourteenth Amendment this way. Moreover, despite the fact that it conferred "no [enforcement] power whatever on Congress," the Fifteenth Amendment also appeared to such women at the time to confirm the voting rights of black men by stating that no citizen could be denied the right to vote because of "race, color or previous condition of servitude,"[62] thereby reaffirming their own subordinate political status in relation to universal *man*hood suffrage.

These feminists had unsuccessfully employed every effort to get Republican leaders to eliminate the word *male* from the Fourteenth Amendment and to add the word *sex* to the Fifteenth Amendment. Taken together these two amendments implied that women were not citizens of the United States, and female activists wasted no time testing both in the courts. In a very real sense, therefore, passage of the Fourteenth and Fifteenth amendments forced most postwar women reformers—whether they considered themselves radicals or moderates—to concentrate on what had never been their primary prewar goal: women's suffrage. That both amendments are now viewed as narrow and negatively worded textual examples of the "constitutional conservatism" of radical reconstruction was no consolation to the post–Civil War generation of American feminists. The fact that the Fourteenth and Fifteenth amendments told the states "what may *not* be done, rather than what must be done on behalf of the freedmen" was lost both on most Democrats, who incorrectly viewed them as a radical trampling of states rights, and on most female activists, who correctly interpreted them as reinforcing a gendered political hierarchy in which women of all races remained "slaves."[63]

Just as Anthony and Stanton had lost their fight to change the wording of the Fourteenth Amendment in the summer of 1868, the Kansas legislature submitted a referendum calling for female and black suffrage to its citizens for consideration. They decided to carry the politics of the "New Departure" to the state level, only to find themselves "sold out" by Lucy Stone's husband, Henry Blackwell. After convincing Anthony that Kansas state senator Samuel Wood was a friend of women's suffrage, Blackwell plotted with Wood to bring the antiblack Democrat George Francis Train into Kansas to campaign with Anthony in order to win

Democratic votes in the lost cause that Kansas Republicans were waging in behalf of the referendum. Anthony knew nothing of this strategy to link her impeccable reputation and strong character with Train, in order to keep his flamboyant character and racism in line. Historians ignored this "male betrayal" of Anthony and other postwar women suffragists until sociologist Kathleen Barry pointed it out in 1989. At the time, however, Blackwell succeeded in discrediting Anthony and Stanton's wing of the First Women's movement as racist, among other things, because of its brief association with Train. And so the third political effort of women to enter into male postwar politics failed and, as noted in chapter 5, the "New Departure" took on a distinctly legal overtone after 1869.[64]

Neither the Democrats nor women could anticipate in the late 1860s that the Republicans would never use federal power to ensure the civil rights of African-Americans or that they would use *both* the state and federal power of courts and legislatures to keep women from exercising civil rights during the reconstruction decades. But this is exactly what happened. Republican commitment to federalism was exercised in contradictory, but equally negative, ways when dealing with the individual rights of these two individually powerless groups. In other words, fear that Radical Republicans would exercise arbitrary national power over the defeated South proved unfounded; instead, they exercised it over those women who were staunch abolitionists and who had remained loyal during the Civil War —namely, northern feminists. Differing feminist responses to such overt discrimination produced a split in the First Women's movement, represented by the NWSA and the AWSA. Their differences lasted until 1890, when these two groups came together in the National American Woman Suffrage Association (NAWSA).[65]

Male opposition to female rights following the Civil War remains one of the major reasons behind this split in the First Women's movement in 1869 because most married feminists refused to oppose the views of their liberal husbands and male friends during the turbulent Reconstruction years. Of the leading male abolitionists before the war, only four—Samuel J. May, Robert Purvis, Parker Pillsbury, and Stephen S. Foster—remained even minimally loyal to women's rights after the war by insisting on their enfranchisement. All the rest, including Wendell Phillips, George William Curtis, Thomas Wentworth Higginson, Horace Greeley, William Lloyd Garrison, Gerrit Smith, Theodore Tilton, Frederick Douglass, and the brothers Samuel and Henry Blackwell, did not want any aspect of the "women's question" to complicate their work of putting the country back together. Ultimately, Tilton and Henry Blackwell headed moderate suffrage associations designed to diffuse the female opposition to the Fourteenth and Fifteenth amendments, which the Republican party had expediently made keystones of their reconstruction program for the nation.[66] Together these two amendments and the results of the initial litigation arising from them personally and legally humiliated some, but not all, in their determination to be recognized as full citizens of the United States.

These two reconstruction amendments convinced certain women that the right to vote should be obtained through widespread, but low-profile, state-level political activity. AWSA women preferred this more moderate form of activity, compared to court battles and agitation for a federal suffrage amendment. The more militant women of NWSA, led by Anthony and Stanton, continued to reject most male politicians as turncoats when it came to the rights of women. They also continued to fight for a broad range of collective female rights in the courts, as well as in the political arena at the grass-roots level. They even supported one of the many short-lived attempts by free-love advocate Virginia Woodhull to capture the national political spotlight by petitioning Congress to pass a declaratory act granting women the vote. This only further alienated the AWSA women's (and their men's) sense of postwar propriety. Although Woodhull had not consulted the NWSA about her petition, Anthony and Stanton came to her defense by pointing out that "women had enough sacrificed to this sentimental, hypocritical prating about [sexual] purity." But the damage had been done.[67]

NWSA leaders opposed these two reconstruction amendments, therefore, with a variety of quickly devised political tactics, including temporary association with Train and Woodhull. By doing so, they left themselves open not only to the charge of racism but also of questionable morals. (More recently, these same charges were made against those women who turned from the male-dominated civil rights and antiwar activities of the 1960s to join the women's movement.) It made no difference that both charges against Anthony and Stanton reeked of hypocrisy. The more moderate post–Civil War female reformers (and most of their male colleagues), on the other hand, were quite willing to place moral purity and the vote for black men ahead of the vote for women—black and white. Their uncompromising stand was grounded in principle and received the support from such prominent black leaders as Sojourner Truth and Robert Purvis.[68]

In retrospect, the Fourteenth and Fifteenth amendments were predicated more on political expediency than any belief in the equality of the races and a constitutional conservatism typical of liberal legalism. Most simply stated, the Northern-based Republican party saw the political potential of two million black male votes in the South and had no intention of letting the controversial women's question stand in the way of creating a power base in the formerly rebellious states. More tragically for black civil rights, while making proclamations implying an expansion of national power, most Radical Republicans "intended to keep that expansion to the absolute minimum" when it came to enforcing voting standards or any other "sweeping alterations in national-state relations." Apparently, some unrealistically hoped that the enforcement clause of the Fourteenth Amendment and the other conditions they set for the restoration of statehood would somehow be "self-enforcing."[69]

Few, if any, Americans could rise above the prevailing racism of the day; and this included the former male abolitionists, the suffragists, and members of the legal profession. Although the Constitution of the United States gives the courts interpretive powers to assert prescribed fundamental rights, judges have been able to maintain massive social, sexual, and racial subordination employing the rhetoric of equality for most of this document's two-hundred-year existence. The greatest self-sustaining aspect of liberal legalism in the United States is that it can convert significant social issues relating to power into a zero-sum game based on a series of ad hoc disputes concerned with individual rights, while maintaining at all times the appearance of procedural and, therefore, ostensibly neutral justice.[70]

The postwar maelstrom created by rising rights-consciousness expectations, hypocritical charges of racism, and outrage over the Fourteenth Amendment forced the First Feminists into developing some hastily conceived political (and subsequently, constitutional) tactics known as the "New Departure." Increasingly, these tactics were narrowly designed to obtain the right to vote. Consequently, although the "New Departure" appeared to have failed during Reconstruction, its political and juridical legacies ultimately transformed the First Women's movement from a radical to a mainstream phenomenon as female reformers began to act and talk more like men in their political and litigious activities.

# CHAPTER FIVE

# Constitutional Discrimination, 1872–1908

The second period in the development of women's legal status in the United States lasted from 1872 until 1908. During these years, the legal discourse relating to women changed dramatically in response to their demands based on a heightened sense of rights consciousness. During Reconstruction, courts and state houses stopped benignly or malignly neglecting women and began to discriminate actively against those who wanted to vote or enter certain previously all-male professions, such as law and medicine. Legal fictions, false-protection arguments (and, occasionally, false-equality ones) reinforcing certain female common-law disabilities abounded during this period of overt constitutional discrimination against women.

While there were nominal gains during these years in property rights for wealthier women and more wage legislation for poorer women, little overall improvement took place in the legal status or working conditions of the increasing number of working women (many of them immigrants) who flocked to American factories. And even the most white, privileged women experienced the negative force of federal constitutional power as they tried to invoke it in their behalf.

For the first time beginning in the early 1870s, women systematically tried to obtain constitutional equality and full citizenship from the courts by challenging the remaining common-law restrictions on them. While this rights-consciousness campaign of the First Feminists did not succeed, their attempts in retrospect are significant for a number of reasons. First, the major female reconstruction cases indicate that women altered not only the texts but also the contexts of legal discourse in their briefs and legislative appeals to be included as part of "We, the people." They found judges and elected officials unresponsive to their awakened sense of constitutionalism not only because it threatened their patriarchal hegemony, but also because it exposed the inherent contradictions in liberal legalism that had relegated women to second-class citizenship since the American Revolution. Second, judicial patterns or preferences that emerged by 1900 from these negative reconstruction decisions lingered for many years—some down to the present. Third, as I first pointed out in 1976, there was also a subtle interaction (and potential contradiction) between the collective political and individualistic legal activities of women reformers during this period, which new scholarship since then has helped to disentangle.[1]

It is now possible to trace how these two types of activity on the part of women varied *according to the intensity of their legal-rights consciousness at any given time.* In fact, it can be argued that to the degree that the courts discouraged women from pursuing full citizenship through constitutional equality, they took political action as a form of compensation. Such compensatory political actions, although better organized and orchestrated than some of their legal initiatives, were often more typically conservative in nature than their court cases appeared to be. However, the litigation of these early feminists in behalf of specific individual rights also represented a compromise with the male legal system, rather than a frontal attack on it. A similar, but possibly less obvious, seesaw relationship between political and legal action continues to exist today because women have still to find acceptance for a feminist jurisprudence that does not require their assimilation as a group in return for equality as individual citizens. Reconstruction provided the first opportunity for women to try to reconcile the "inherited libertarian rhetoric" of "possessive individualism" with "collective organization and collective identities."[2] In retrospect, their failure is not as much a surprise as is the degree to which they succeeded in reviving the First Women's movement and in laying a legal discursive foundation from which to argue for their own equality.

The legal system in this second period of constitutional discrimination successfully thwarted the newly articulated rights struggle on the part of post–Civil War feminists by simply refusing to address the central issue: to what extent should women be regarded as persons and, therefore, full citizens in the eyes of the Constitution? Instead, judges evaded this legal determination by handing down decisions based on traditional pre- and postrevolutionary stereotypes about women. Supreme Court decisions following the Civil War specifically classified women as other than full citizens of the United States and cast serious doubt on their legal capacities as persons. Both juridical developments underscored how little the very narrowly interpreted Married Women's Property Acts passed before and after the Civil War had changed the citizenship status of married women, even though such statutes and case law based on them had improved their property, testamentary, contractual, and fiduciary rights.

### The Case of *United States of America v. Susan B. Anthony*

"Now Register?" asked the editorial headline that Susan B. Anthony read in the Rochester, New York, morning newspaper on 1 November 1872. "If you were not permitted to vote, you would fight for the right, undergo all privation for it, face death for it." [3] With these words firmly in mind, Anthony walked down to the local registration office and after considerable argument convinced three inexperienced male inspectors that she should be allowed to register as a Republican in the forthcoming presidential election, in part by promising to aid them legally if they were prosecuted. Her bold and well-publicized action prompted approximately fifty other women to register to vote in Rochester; and, on 5 November, fifteen of them, including Anthony, actually did cast ballots. Within two weeks all were arrested under a provision of the federal Civil Rights Act of 1870 that was designed to prevent white men from canceling out black male votes by casting more than one ballot. Obviously, the 1870 law was never intended to apply to women trying to vote only once. Its enforcement against the Rochester women was a clear indication of the gendered nature of their arrests. In addition to gender bias, a suspicious political aspect of Anthony's subsequent trial in June 1873 was the presence of President Ulysses S. Grant's political aide and senator from New York, Roscoe Conkling, an avowed opponent of women's suffrage.

Between the time of her release on bail in November 1872 and her trial on 18 June 1873, Susan B. Anthony made numerous speeches in her own behalf in Monroe and Ontario counties, trying to influence prospective jurors. It was perspicacious of her to have done this because, as it turned out, she was not allowed to testify in her own defense. These speeches constitute the legal text she was not able to create as part of the court record. In approximately fifty pretrial talks, her theme remained the same: "Is it a crime for a United States citizen to vote?" This and most of the other legal questions that Anthony raised before her trial took place were not considered by the United States Circuit Court of New York that heard her case, nor were they dealt with by any American court in a gender-neutral fashion until the last quarter of the twentieth century. The Circuit Court ignored such questions as whether the Fourteenth Amendment included women as citizens and therefore as persons; whether women had the right to a jury of their peers; and whether women should continue to submit to taxation without representation. [4] Anthony's basic argument against the crime of having voted was the following:

For any State to make sex a qualification that must ever result in the disfranchisement of one entire half of the people, is to pass a bill of attainder, or an *ex post facto* law, and is therefore a violation of the supreme law of the land. By it, the blessings of liberty are forever withheld from women and their female posterity. To them, this government has not just powers derived from the consent of the governed. To them this government is not a democracy. It is not a republic. It is an odious aristocracy: a hateful oligarchy; the most hateful ever established on the face of the globe. An oligarchy of wealth, where the rich govern the poor; an oligarchy of learning, where the educated govern the ignorant; or even an oligarchy of race, where the Saxon rules the African, might be endured; but surely this oligarchy of sex, which makes the men of every household sovereigns, masters; the women subjects, slaves; carrying dissension, rebellion into every home of the Nation, can not be endured.[5]

While the First Feminists had independently developed some of these legal and political arguments before the Civil War when supporting property rights for married women, Anthony now increasingly defended this position by resorting primarily to the first section of the Fourteenth Amendment, which specifically stated: "No State shall make or enforce any law which shall abridge the privileges or immunities of citizens of the United States; nor shall any State deprive any person of life, liberty or property, without due process of law; nor deny to any person within its jurisdiction the equal protection of the laws." Anthony logically raised the rhetorically simple question about this historic section of the Fourteenth Amendment, *Are women persons?* Her answer was equally simple and rhetorical:

I hardly believe any of our opponents will have the hardihood to say they are not. Being persons, then, women are citizens, and no State has a right to make any new law, or to enforce any old law, that shall abridge their privileges or immunities. Hence, every discrimination against women in the constitutions and laws of the several States, is to-day null and void, precisely as is every one against negroes. Is the right to vote one of the privileges or immunities of citizens? I think the disfranchised ex-rebels, and the ex-state prisoners will all agree with me, that it is not only one of them, but *the one without which all the others are nothing.*[6]

Anthony even anticipated a revival of the section of Dred Scott v. Sandford, 60 U.S. 394 (1857), in which Justice Roger B. Taney, called upon to decide the citizenship rights of African-Americans taken into free territory, had reiterated the traditional republican notion that placed women and children into a "special category" of nonvoting citizens. Ignoring the portion of the majority decision that had excluded African-Americans from even this type of second-class citizenship, Anthony focused on another section of *Dred Scott,* which stated: "The words 'People of the United States' and 'citizens,' are synonymous terms, and mean the same thing. They both describe the political body, who, according to our republican institutions, form the sovereignty, and who hold the power and conduct the government, through their representatives." She vehemently opposed the legal precedent that allowed the infamous *Dred Scott* decision (which had been voided for African-Americans by the Civil War and reconstruction amendments) to continue to be used "against the women of the entire nation, vast numbers of whom are the peers of those honorable gentlemen themselves, in morals, intellect, culture, wealth, family—paying taxes on large estates, and contributing equally with them and their sex, in every direction, to the growth, prosperity, and well-being of the Republic."[7]

She further buttressed her point of view by pointing out that at least two U.S. judges had recently asserted that the Fourteenth Amendment did indeed grant women the right to vote. Anthony believed that if the Fourteenth Amendment did not grant all citizens the right to vote, then it had no purpose because black males were already entitled to all other constitutional privileges and immunities of the Constitution under the terms of the Thirteenth Amendment, which had granted them (and black women) freedom from slavery.

Thus, you see, those newly-made freed men were in possession of every possible right, privilege, and immunity of the Government, except that of suffrage, and hence, needed no constitutional amendment for any other purpose. What right, I ask you, has the Irishman the day after he receives his naturalization papers that he did not possess the day before, save the right to vote and hold office? And the Chinamen, now crowding our Pacific coast, are in precisely the same position. What privilege or immunity has California or Oregon the constitutional right to deny them, save that of the ballot? Clearly, then, if the XIV. Amendment was not to secure to black men their right to vote, it did nothing for them, since they possessed everything else before. But if it was meant to be a prohibition of the States to deny or abridge their right to vote—which I fully believe—then it did the same for all persons, white women included, born or naturalized in the United States, for the amendment does not say all male persons of African descent, but all persons are citizens.[8]

At this point, however, Anthony had to face up to the existence of the last of the three famous reconstruction amendments following the Civil War—namely, the Fifteenth Amendment, which stated that "the right of citizens of the United States to vote shall not be abridged on account of race, color or previous condition of servitude." On the surface, this amendment seemed to contradict her arguments about the Fourteenth Amendment conferring the franchise on *all* citizens. Why then was the Fifteenth Amendment necessary? She explained away this apparent contradiction by interpreting the language of the amendment to her rhetorical advantage. "How can the State deny or abridge the right of a citizen," she asked, "if the citizen does not possess it?" Then she proceeded to attribute the passage of this last reconstruction amendment to purely partisan politics. Since the Southern states under the domination of the Democratic party were not honoring the Fourteenth Amendment, it was necessary for the Republican party of President Grant to compel compliance (in order to ensure his reelection in 1872) with "this positive prohibition of the Fifteenth Amendment."[9]

Finally, in the event that none of the above arguments convinced her audiences, Anthony carried her case to its logical extreme by saying that women, in general, and married women, in particular, despite the passage of the Married Women's Property Acts, existed in a state of servitude.

But if you will insist that the XV. Amendment's emphatic interdiction against robbing United States citizens of their right to vote, "on account of race, color, or previous condition of servitude," is a recognition of the right, either of the United States or any State, to rob citizens of that right for any or all other reasons, I will prove to you that the class of citizens for which I now plead, and to which I belong, may be, and are, by all the principles of our Government, and many of the laws of the States, included under the term "previous condition of servitude."

First. — The married women and their legal status. What is servitude? "The condition of a slave." What is a slave? "A person who is robbed of the proceeds of his labor; a person who is subject to the will of another." . . . There is an old saying that "a rose by any other name would smell as sweet," and I submit if the deprivation by law of the ownership of one's own person, wages, property, children, the denial of the right as an individual, to sue and be sued, and to testify in the courts, is not a condition of servitude most bitter and absolute, though under the sacred name of marriage?

Does any lawyer doubt my statement of the legal status of married women? I will remind him of the fact that the old common law of England prevails in every State in this Union, except where the Legislature has enacted special Laws annulling it. And I am ashamed that not one State has yet blotted from its statute books the old common law of marriage, by which Blackstone, summed up in the fewest words possible, is made to say: "Husband and wife are one, and that one is the husband."

Thus may all married women, wives, and widows, by the laws of the several States, be technically included in the XV. Amendment's specification of "condition of servitude," present or previous. And not only married women, but I will also prove to you that by all the great fundamental principles of our free government, the entire womanhood of the nation is in a "condition of servitude" as surely as were our revolutionary fathers, when they rebelled against old King George. Women are taxed without representation, governed without their consent, tried, convicted, and punished without a jury of their peers. And is all this tyranny any less humiliating and degrading to women under our democratic — republican government to-day than it was to men under their aristocratic, monarchical government one hundred years ago?[10]

Having proven women's condition of servitude to her own satisfaction, Anthony left no stone unturned in her public defense of herself. She went on to attack the presence of masculine pronouns in all state and federal statutes. If the legal profession insisted on a literal interpretation by sex, then consistency would dictate that women would be exempt from all the tax laws, among others. "There is no she, or her, or hers, in the tax laws," she provocatively told her listeners. She also noted that all the pronouns in the section of the Civil Rights Act of 1870 she was charged with having violated were male. Then she cited the 1868 Supreme Court case of *Silver v. Ladd,* in which it had been held that the words *single man* and *unmarried man* should be interpreted in a generic sense. In this case, involving a widow's right to land under the Oregon donation law of 1850, the Court said that "embraced within the term single man [was] an unmarried woman."[11]

Anthony closed most of her pretrial speeches by warning that if the legal system did not respond women would battle for the ballot and other kinds of remedial legislation in order to bring about the day "when all United States citizens shall be recognized as equals before the law." Anthony never lived to see this "complete triumph," as she called it, and neither has any other generation of American women.[12]

On 18 June 1873 Anthony could not repeat her pretrial statements in court because Judge Ward Hunt refused her the right to testify in her own behalf. Moreover, Hunt, described in the *History of Woman Suffrage* as "small-brained," delivered a previously prepared written opinion immediately following three hours of argument by Anthony's attorney Henry R. Seldon. Finally, he summarily instructed the all-male jury to bring in a verdict of guilty. When Anthony's lawyer questioned the constitutionality of this directed verdict in what was, after all, a criminal case, Judge Hunt simply discharged the jurors and denied a motion for retrial. Seldon told Anthony as they were leaving the courtroom that the judge "had as much right to order me hung from the nearest tree, as to take this case from the jury and render the decision he did."[13] In the opinion he had written before hearing the defendant's case, Judge Hunt ruled that the Fourteenth Amendment could not be used as a basis for defense because of the recent Supreme Court rulings in the *Slaughter-House Cases* and the *Bradwell v. Illinois* case, in which it had been determined that "the rights referred to in the XIV Amendment are those belonging to a person as a citizen of the United States and not as a citizen of a State." He further argued that even if Anthony honestly believed that she had the right to vote, such a belief did not excuse the act. Judge Hunt relied almost exclusively on U.S. District Attorney Richard Crowley's opening remarks, in which he said that when Anthony voted on 5 November 1872, "she was a woman. I suppose there will be no question about that." Therefore, being "a person of the female sex," the act of voting was automatically "against the peace of the United States of America and their dignity." Judge Hunt simply echoed this circular reasoning in his summary when he said that only "two principles apply here: First, ignorance of the law excuses no one; second, every person is presumed to understand and to intend the necessary effects of his own acts. Miss Anthony knew that she was a woman, and that the constitution of this state prohibits her from voting."[14]

Seldon, Anthony's attorney, had pointed out in his brief that he had personally told her "that she was as lawful a voter as I am, or as any other man is, and advised her to go and offer her vote."[15] He argued, therefore, that she had the right to vote, believed she had the right to vote, and that female voting was not a crime under the Civil Rights Act of 1870. Most of his defense of the first point was based on improvements in the inheritance and testamentary rights of women under some of the Married Women's Property Acts. In making this argument, however, he was using these acts in a manner that contradicted Anthony's pretrial statements about them. Seldon also used a standard male interpretation of this specific kind of legislation and of the right to vote in general, which was anathema to Anthony's brand of radical feminism. There is no documentary evidence indicating how she reacted when she heard her attorney tell the court:

On the one hand it is supposed by some that the character of women would be radically changed—that they would be unsexed, as it were, by clothing them with political rights, and that instead of modest, amiable, and graceful beings, we should have bold, noisy, and disgusting political demagogues, or something worse, if anything worse can be imagined. I think those who entertain such opinions are in error. The innate character of women is the result of God's laws, not of man's, nor can the laws of man affect that character beyond a very slight degree. Whatever rights may be given to them, and whatever duties may be charged upon them by human laws, their general character will remain unchanged. Their modesty, their delicacy, and intuitive sense of propriety, will never desert them, into whatever new positions their added rights or duties may carry them.

So far as women, without change of character as women, are qualified to discharge the duties of citizenship, they will discharge them if called upon to do so, and beyond that they will not go. Nature has put barriers in the way of any excessive devotion of women to public affairs, and it is not necessary that nature's work in that respect should be supplemented by additional barriers invented by men. Such offices as women are qualified to fill will be sought by those who do not find other employment, and others they will not seek, or if they do, will seek in vain.[16]

Seldon also employed elaborate constitutional and historical arguments about the positive implications for women of the Fourteenth Amendment, but by the time he argued the case the *Bradwell* decision had legally foreclosed most of them. His primary defense remained, therefore, that his famous client had acted in "perfect good faith, with motives as pure and impulses as noble as any which can find place in your honor's breast in the administration of justice." To condemn her as a criminal for voting when she had been advised it was legal "would only add another most weighty reason to those which I have already advanced, to show that women need the aid of the ballot for their protection."[17]

In a final attempt to defend herself, Anthony tried to speak in court before being sentenced. Although her remarks were ultimately cut short by Judge Hunt, she did manage to question whether she had indeed been tried by her peers and to express her defiance of the entire male-dominated legal system. The exchange that took place between the judge and the feminist is one of the most dramatic examples of an extemporaneous female legal text.

May it please the Court to remember that since the day of my arrest last November, this is the first time that either myself or any person of my disfranchised class has been allowed a word of defense before judge or jury—

Judge *HUNT*: The prisoner must sit down; the Court can not allow it.

Miss *ANTHONY*: All my prosecutors, from the 8th Ward corner grocery politician, who entered the complaint, to the United States Marshal, Commissioner, District Attorney, District Judge, your honor on the bench, not one is my peer, but each and all are my political sovereigns; and had your honor submitted my case to the jury, as was clearly your duty, even then I should have had just cause of protest, for not one of those men was my peer; but, native or foreign, white or black, rich or poor, educated or ignorant, awake or asleep, sober or drunk, each and every man of them was my political superior; hence, in no sense, my peer. . . . precisely as no disfranchised person is entitled to sit upon a jury, and no woman is entitled to the franchise, so, none but a regularly admitted lawyer is allowed to practice in the courts, and no woman can gain admission to the bar—hence jury, judge, counsel, must all be of the superior class.

Judge *HUNT*: The Court must insist—the prisoner has been tried according to the established forms of law.

Miss *ANTHONY*: Yes, your honor, but by forms of law all made by men, interpreted by men, administered by men, in favor of men, and against women; and hence, your honor's ordered verdict of guilty, against a United States citizen for the exercise of, "that citizen's right to vote," simply because that citizen was a woman and not a man. . . . As then the slaves who got their freedom must take it over, or under, or through the unjust forms of law, precisely so now must women, to get their right to a voice in this Government, take it; and I have taken mine, and mean to take it at every possible opportunity.

Judge *HUNT*: The Court orders the prisoner to sit down. It will not allow another word.

Miss *ANTHONY*: When I was brought before your honor for trial, I hoped for a broad and liberal interpretation of the Constitution and its recent amendments, that should declare all United States citizens under its protecting aegis—that should declare equality of rights the national guarantee to all persons born or naturalized in the United States. But failing to get this justice—failing, even to get a trial by a jury *not* of my peers—I ask not leniency at your hands—but rather the full rigors of the law.

Judge *HUNT*: The Court must insist—(Here the prisoner sat down.)

Judge *HUNT*: The prisoner will stand up. (Here Miss Anthony arose again.) The sentence of the Court is that you pay a fine of one hundred dollars and the costs of the prosecution.

Miss *ANTHONY*: May it please your honor, I shall never pay a dollar of your unjust penalty. All the stock in trade I possess is a $10,000 debt, incurred by publishing my paper the *Revolution*—four years ago, the sole object of which was to educate all women to do precisely as I have done, rebel against your manmade, unjust, unconstitutional forms of law, that tax, fine, imprison, and hang women, while they deny them the right of representation in the Government; and I shall work on with might and main to pay every dollar of that honest debt, but not a penny shall go to this unjust claim. And I shall earnestly and persistently continue to urge all women to the practical recognition of the old revolutionary maxim, that "Resistance to tyranny is obedience to God."

Judge *HUNT*: Madam, the Court will not order you committed until the fine is paid.[18]

Anthony's words have continued to ring in the ears of later generations of feminists down to the present. Matilda Joslyn Gage, who gave seventeen pretrial talks in Anthony's behalf, wrote a letter to the editor of the *Syracuse Journal*, printed on 30 July 1874, responding to the Albany *Law Journal* that had suggested that if Anthony was dissatisfied with "our laws . . . she would better adopt the methods of reform that men use, or, better still, migrate." Gage correctly noted that, first, "our laws" meant "man-made laws"; and, second, that Anthony had very determinedly employed male reform tactics in speaking out before the trial only to be denied justice anyway. Although even Gage had to admit that "Judge Hunt did what he had the power to do, but not the right to do," she implied that his action was "senile" and contradicted the view of "man [as] a reasoning animal." Earlier, Anthony's attorney had said immediately after the trial that "the war [between the states] has abolished some things besides slavery, it has abolished jury trial."[19]

A *nolle prosequi* was entered for the other fourteen women who voted with Anthony and the charges against them were dropped, but the three male inspectors stood trial under the same Civil Rights Act of 1870. Unlike Anthony, these men were allowed to testify in their own behalf. Anthony was called as a witness for the defendants, but as soon as she asserted that she had presented herself at the voters' registration *not* as a female but as a citizen with the right to vote, she was summarily dismissed from the witness stand by the same Judge Hunt. The three registration inspectors were found guilty and fined twenty-five dollars each. Their attorneys advised against payment, and after a nine-month delay they were sentenced to jail in February 1874. Fulfilling her prevote promise to them, Anthony helped to secure their release by indirectly appealing to President Grant through the New York senator, A. A. Sargent. Grant officially pardoned them on 3 March 1874. In the intervening days, hundreds of Rochester people visited them in the local jail; and the fifteen women who had voted, including Anthony, brought them daily meals.[20]

Although Anthony never paid her own fine, she was not sentenced to jail; thus, her case ended anticlimactically for a number of reasons. Most important was the fact that it never reached the United States Supreme Court because of two legal technicalities—both beyond her control. First, she would have been able to take her case directly to the Supreme Court by writ of *habeas corpus* if her counsel had not independently decided, over her protests, to pay her bail of one thousand dollars to prevent her from actually being imprisoned before her trial. Likewise, presiding Judge Hunt later refused to enforce his judgment against her, which carried with it the fine of one hundred dollars plus court costs. Prevented in this manner from going to jail a second time, she could not seek direct Supreme Court review of the adverse directed verdict.

No doubt this inability to appeal the circuit court decision was a great disappointment to Anthony. So she appealed to Congress instead. On 22 January 1874, Anthony petitioned Congress for remission of the fine imposed by the New York court. On 20 June 1874, the Senate Committee on the Judiciary turned down her request.[21] And so ended *United States of America v. Susan B. Anthony*. In retrospect, the literal and figurative significance of her defeat cannot be underestimated. Not only had Anthony's arguments before the trial begun to reflect a more male-identified, individualistic concept of voting rights, but after losing this case her tactical and strategic views also naturally began to focus more narrowly on obtaining suffrage. While Anthony and others argued ostensibly for universal suffrage, their rhetoric increasingly sounded like white, middle-class liberalism.

To a degree, this linguistic change was inevitable because the "New Departure" of the early postwar years dictated that feminists play the established political and legal game by petitioning Congress and state legislatures and litigating in court. Once they entered this all-male atmosphere, however, they began to sound more like men than they had before the Civil War. Their anger over the Fourteenth and Fifteenth amendments was justifiable, but these women could not have anticipated how quickly co-opting the use of male constitutional language would prove and how quickly collective demands in behalf of womanhood could deteriorate into individualistic pursuits and political fragmentation.

From the distance of over one hundred years, it is difficult to reconstruct why Anthony and other feminists harbored any hope that the post–Civil War cases involving the right of women to vote would result in new constitutional precedents. Yet right after she had voted on 5 November 1872, Anthony wrote her old friend, Elizabeth Cady Stanton: "Well, I have been and gone and done it! Positively voted the Republican ticket—straight—this *A.M.* at seven o'clock. . . . How I wish you were here to write up the funny things said and done. . . . If only now *all the Woman Suffrage women* would work to *this* end of *enforcing the existing Constitutional* supremacy of national law over State law, what strides we might make this very winter!"[22] Within a very few years, however, she realized how negative a precedent her case and others like it had set, when she wrote in the Declaration of Rights in 1876 that the trials of women who had tried to vote under the Fourteenth Amendment added up to the same thing: "making sex [being female] a crime in the eye of United States laws."[23] By that time, however, suffrage was beginning to assume a life of its own—something that the First Feminists had not anticipated in 1848.

## Women Lawyers and the American Bar, 1865–1908

The case most damaging to the arguments of Anthony's attorney was that of Bradwell v. Illinois, 83 U.S. 130 (1873). This decision had a double significance. In the first place, it dealt with the extent to which the individual states could abridge the privileges and immunities of local citizens, including women. Secondly, since *Bradwell* also addressed the question of the right of women to practice as lawyers, it indicated the degree of willingness of the legal profession and judiciary to open their ranks to women.

As U.S. women attempted to become lawyers following the Civil War, they soon discovered that state laws and courts revealed erratic patterns on this subject. A few allowed women to practice as attorneys; but most required a court decision, an act of the legislature, or *both* before a woman could be admitted to the bar. Although a few women had been granted power-of-attorney in colonial times, post–Civil War judges went to great lengths to ban them from the legal profession and other "gainful occupations." Sometimes it was argued that this was in keeping with traditional common law, which did not recognize married women as legal entities. These state courts also argued that statutes setting up requirements for admission of attorneys were never intended to apply to women. But then, neither the federal Constitution nor the Fourteenth Amendment were originally "intended" to apply to women.[24]

The argument about the intentions of the Founding Fathers, or the drafters of a constitutional amendment, or of state legislators was obviously a non sequitur because attitudes change over time; and the original intentions of one generation, even when possible to determine, constitute a questionable basis for action several generations later. The intention of the framers of the Constitution in 1787 concerning African-Americans was clearly questioned and superseded by the Thirteenth, Fourteenth, and Fifteenth amendments, which freed and technically granted all constitutional rights to this segment of the population. By 1920 (the first year women voted in a presidential election), a similar reversal of popular and legal opinion had occurred. All states by then admitted women to the bar. By that time, the American Bar Association also allowed female members. It was not until 1957, however, that the Supreme Court officially disallowed certain state regulations discriminating against women in bar admissions.[25] Female participation in the legal profession remained at a token level from 1920 until the 1970s. The long struggle of female attorneys to advance from exclusion to tokenism is not atypical of the fight by American women to gain entrance into other professions in which they have been systematically discriminated against, such as medicine, higher education, engineering, and the ministry.[26]

In June 1869, the first woman was admitted to the practice of law in the United States. This occurred in the state of Iowa when Arabella ("Bell") Babb Mansfield applied for a law license. Under the Iowa Code of 1851, admission to the bar had been specifically limited to "any white male person." The Iowa Supreme Court ruled in the case of Mansfield that an "affirmative [declaration of gender] is not any implied denial of the right of females."[27] As a result of this precedent, the Iowa Code of 1870 deleted the words *white male* as a bar-admission requirement. Apparently, however, the deletion occurred fortuitously and should not be viewed as a conscious act favoring women's liberation. (As noted in chapter 7, the same thing occurred later in 1964, when the word *sex* was added to the

Civil Rights Act.) In this 1870 instance, a Republican member of the Iowa state legislature had recommended that the word *white* be eliminated in the bar-admission bill, and a Democrat sarcastically suggested that the word *male* should be removed as well. It cannot be said that the intent of the legislature was to strike a blow against either racism or sexism within the legal profession. But this was the unexpected result of the ruling of Iowa justice Francis Springer. Mansfield, however, never actually practiced law. She became a professor of history instead.[28]

In the same year that Mansfield was admitted to the Iowa bar, two women were admitted to study law at Washington University in St. Louis. This was the first law school in the United States to accept students regardless of sex. Mansfield had obtained her legal knowledge essentially through an apprenticeship system by studying in her brother's law office—not in a law school. Of the two women who matriculated at Washington University in 1869, Lemma Barkaloo became the first woman to try a case in an American court in 1870, although she never finished her course work. Tragically, she died a few months later from typhoid fever. Barkaloo's application to law school had earlier been rejected by both Columbia and Harvard. In 1870 when Columbia denied admission to three more female applicants, one male member of the Board of Trustees of the Law School exercised his prerogative of protective paternalism when he reportedly said: "No woman shall degrade herself by practicing law in New York, especially if I can save her. . . . I think that the clack of these possible Portias will never be heard in Dwight's Moot Courts." The other Washington University Law School student, Phoebe Couzins, who entered with Mansfield, did graduate. Although she handled cases in several states, she never established a successful practice.[29]

The same was true of Ada H. Kepley, who became the first American woman to receive an accredited law degree from Union College of Law in Chicago in 1870 (before Couzins). All of these legal pioneers had studied law privately as apprentices before attempting to enter such schools. Around the same time similarly qualified women in Connecticut, California, Colorado, and Indiana were being denied admission to schools of law and to the bar. Sometimes states would deny admission only to reverse this opinion a few years later by new statutes. Such statutory and juridical reversals usually avoided addressing the question of women's constitutional rights as citizens. Perhaps the best example of this kind of arbitrary about-face occurred in Wisconsin, when Lavinia Goodell was denied admission to the bar in 1875 and then granted a license to practice by that same state in 1879. In that four-year period, the Wisconsin Supreme Court completely reversed itself—without using reasoned legal arguments in either case. In 1875, Chief Justice C. J. Ryan had carried the day with the argument that to construe the masculine pronoun in the state law governing bar admissions to include women would constitute a "judicial revolution." Speaking for the entire court, he further argued:

Nature has tempered woman as little for the judicial conflicts of the court room as for the physical conflicts of the battlefield. Woman is modeled for gentler and better things . . . [Our] profession has essentially and habitually to do with all that is selfish and extortionate, knavish and criminal, coarse and brutal, repulsive and obscene in human life. It would be revolting to all female sense of innocence and sanctity of their sex, shocking to man's reverence for womanhood and faith in woman on which hinge all the better affections and humanities of life, that woman should be permitted to mix professionally in all the nastiness of the world which finds its way into the courts of justice. . . . Discussions are habitually necessary which are unfit for female ears. The habitual presence of women at these would tend to relax the public sense of decency and propriety. If these things are to come, we will take no voluntary part in bringing them about.[30]

In 1879, after state law specifically forbade this sex barrier, Chief Justice Ryan continued to dissent. However, the majority opinion now read:

We are satisfied that the applicant possesses all the requisite qualifications as to learning, ability, and moral character to entitle her to admission, no objection existing thereto except that founded upon her sex alone. Under the circumstances, a majority think that objection must be disregarded. Miss Goodell will therefore be admitted to practice in this court upon signing the roll and taking the prescribed oath.[31]

This same sporadic and often capricious pattern continued until 1920, when only Delaware and Rhode Island did not admit women to the bar. Both relented after the passage that year of the Nineteenth Amendment, which granted suffrage to women. The issue of women's right to practice law and the constitutionality of state prohibitions on such a right was the first to reach the Supreme Court after the adoption of the Fourteenth Amendment.

### Married Women Cannot Be Lawyers

From 1865 to 1908, only two cases involving the exclusion of women from the practice of law reached the Supreme Court of the United States. The best known was Bradwell v. Illinois, 83 U.S. (16 Wall) 130 (1873), which Judge Hunt had referred to in his decision in the *Anthony* case. Myra Colby Bradwell, an avowed suffragist and champion of women's legal rights, had studied law under her husband, Judge James B. Bradwell, and passed the Illinois bar examination in 1869 only to be denied admission to that bar because she was married. Myra Bradwell specifically sought redress through the benefit of the privileges-and-immunities clause of the first section of the Fourteenth Amendment. Despite the precedent that had been set earlier in the year by the *Mansfield* case in Iowa, courts in Illinois based their refusal to allow her to practice law on Blackstone's idea that a married woman was not competent to perform such duties as making contracts, which an attorney would have to do. This argument about her common-law disabilities was totally inapplicable because Myra Bradwell had been making contracts and acting in other official, legal capacities as president of a publishing company in Illinois and as founder and editor of the most important legal publication in the West and Midwest, the *Chicago Legal News*. In fact, the state had granted her a special charter to engage in such legal activities. Yet, the Illinois Supreme Court said she was not qualified to act in a similar capacity as a lawyer.[32]

When the case came before the Supreme Court of the United States, Justice Miller, writing for the majority, ignored the lower-court opinions about her common-law disabilities as a married woman and held that the right to practice law was not a privilege and immunity of citizenship. (This, of course, was the same argument that would later be used against female voting rights.) He based his position on the well-known Slaughter-House Cases, 16 Wall 36 (1873), a decision delivered the day before, on 14 April 1873. Miller's decision placed such severe limitations on the scope and meaning of the privileges-and-immunities clause of the Fourteenth Amendment that it has been virtually unused since. While this majority opinion was bad enough as far as Bradwell's right to practice law was concerned, the concurring opinion of Justice Bradley was even more damaging because of the overtly sexist language and attitudes it contained based on common-law precedent. In the Blackstone tradition, Bradley insisted that women had no legal existence separate from their husbands despite the passage of a number of Married Women's Property Acts. His opinion stated:

. . . the civil law, as well as nature herself, has always recognized a wide difference in the respective spheres and destinies of man and woman. Man is, or should be, woman's protector and defender. The natural and proper timidity and delicacy which belongs to the female sex evidently unfits it for many of the occupations of civil life. The constitution of the family organization, which is founded in the divine ordinance, as well as in the nature of things, indicates the domestic sphere as that which properly belongs to the domain and functions of womanhood. The harmony, not to say identity, of interests and views which belong or should belong to the family institution is repugnant to the idea of a woman adopting a distinct and independent career from that of her husband. So firmly fixed was this sentiment in the founders of the common law that it became a maxim of that system of jurisprudence that a woman had no legal existence separate from her husband, who was regarded as her head and representative in the social state.[33]

Bradley conceded that some women remained single and not affected by any of the duties, complications, and incapacities arising from marriage, but these were exceptions to the general rule. "The paramount destiny and mission of women

[was] to fulfill the noble and benign offices of wife and mother," according to Bradley. "This is the law of the Creator. And the rules of civil society must be adapted to the general constitution of things, and cannot be based upon exceptional cases."[34]

Bradley heartily supported women's participation in those reform movements that opened up avenues for their advancement into occupations that he assumed were suitable for their legal condition and gendered societal functions. But he was not prepared to say that women had the fundamental right and privilege to be admitted into every office and position, including those requiring highly special qualifications and demanding special responsibilities. In the nature of things, Bradley argued, not every citizen of every age, sex, and condition was qualified for every calling and position. It was the prerogative of the legislator to prescribe regulations founded on nature, reason, and experience for the due admission of qualified persons to professions and callings demanding special skill and confidence. Thus, he concluded:

This fairly belongs to the police power of the state; and, in my opinion, in view of the peculiar characteristics, destiny, and mission of woman, it is within the province of the legislature to ordain what offices, positions, and callings shall be filled and discharged by men, and shall receive the benefit of those energies and responsibilities, and that decision and firmness which are presumed to predominate in the sterner sex.[35]

While Bradley's often-quoted concurring sexist remarks did not decide the case in *Bradwell* because the ruling on law in the *Slaughter-House Cases* prevailed, his words remain a classic example of "false paternalism," according to Frances Olsen. His opinion was not benignly paternalistic, as is usually claimed, because Bradley was not trying "to promote Myra Bradwell's true best interests." Instead, Olsen argues that Bradley was being "disingenuous" by claiming that for Bradwell and other women to practice as lawyers would somehow "harm" them as women. When demystifying Bradley's (and countless other jurists') detrimental or false paternalism, it is also necessary to project what would be "good" for women in a particular time period in order to take collective action in behalf of women. Thus, Olsen uses *Bradwell* to caution contemporary feminists who similarly do not distinguish false paternalism (or, to use my term, false protection) from beneficial paternalism (protection) under the law.[36]

Conversely, Olsen notes that women can also suffer from being granted false equality. For example, in 1895 in *Ritchie v. People,* the Illinois Supreme Court said that a state statute limiting women to working eight hours a day in sweatshops violated their constitutional rights as both "persons" and "citizens" under the Fourteenth Amendment. Anticipating the 1905 Supreme Court decision in *Lochner v. New York,* discussed in the next chapter, the decision in *Ritchie* proclaimed that "woman is entitled to the same rights, under the constitution, to make contracts with reference to her labor as are secured thereby to men. . . . her right to a choice of vocations cannot be said to be denied or abridged on account of sex." While this decision was in keeping with an 1872 state law ostensibly granting women equal-employment rights with men, it is a clear example of "false equality," according to Olsen, because women in Illinois in 1872 and 1895 did not enjoy "formal juridical equality." Thus, the Supreme Court of the state was not benefiting women working in sweatshops by saying they had the right to contract for as many hours as they pleased.[37] Today, as well as in the last quarter of the nineteenth century, false protection and false equality can harm women because the courts of the 1990s will very likely continue to grant women individualistic equality in socioeconomic areas where they remain collectively unequal—just as they began to do a century ago in the 1890s.

It is also worth noting several other interrelationships between *Bradwell* and the *Slaughter-House Cases*. First, they were both argued in January 1872, and the two opinions were scheduled to be announced on the same day in April 1873. It has been suggested that, because the cases were *sub judice* during the fourteen-month period of decision, the narrow interpretation of privileges and immunities with respect to choice of occupations in the *Slaughter-House Cases* was probably "influenced by the court's realization that a broad interpretation would necessarily change the status of women."[38] While this may be true, much more was involved in this decision. The *Slaughter-House Cases* involved an attempt by butchers in Louisiana to obtain federal protection under the privileges-and-immunities clause from state legislation, which had created a private monopoly of the slaughterhouse trade. The majority opinion, however, did not limit itself to denying butchers the right to choose an occupation under the privileges-and-immunities clause. It also addressed itself to the "original intent" of the equal-protection clause of the Fourteenth Amendment and said that it could only be applied to class distinctions based upon race. The exact wording of the majority opinion was "We doubt very much whether any action of a state not directed by way of discrimination against the negroes as a class, or on account of their race, will be held to come within the purview of this provision."[39]

Justice Bradley's position on these two cases is also noteworthy. In his concurring opinion, he argued *against* Myra Bradwell's right of choice of occupation, but he was not in the majority when he argued *for* the butchers having that same right. In his dissenting opinion in the *Slaughter-House Cases*, Bradley said that "a law which prohibits a large class of citizens from adopting a lawful employment . . . does deprive them of liberty as well as property, without due process of law. Their right of choice is a portion of their liberty; their occupation is their property. Such a law also deprives those citizens of the equal protection of the laws."[40] He held to a diametrically opposed viewpoint in *Bradwell*.

Matthew Carpenter, one of the best-known advocates of the day, also took similarly irreconcilable positions in these two cases. He was, unlike Bradley, arguing *against* the butchers and *for* Bradwell as her attorney and a family friend. His positions were as inconsistent as Bradley's, albeit for different legal reasons. Nonetheless, both men used standard sexist arguments. Carpenter, for example, tried in *Bradwell* to trade the right to follow an occupation for the right to vote. He assured the Court that if they granted women their choice of profession it would not lead to granting them suffrage, for this was simply a political right that could be infringed or abridged while an occupation was a right of citizenship. Furthermore, he assured the Court of this by noting that "female suffrage . . . would overthrow Christianity, defeat the ends of modern civilization and upturn the world," and no one wanted this—except Myra Bradwell and her feminist supporters.[41]

Such inconsistencies on the part of Carpenter and Bradley were never seriously questioned by the Court or by any lawyer or legal historian until recently. Was the *Bradwell* case simply considered less important because of prevailing "natural-male-dominance" theories of the time? Did the general political climate of the Reconstruction play a more important role than sexism or capitalism in the *Bradwell* and *Slaughter-House Cases* decisions? It should be remembered that this was a time of political and constitutional uncertainty as Northern Republicans tried to assert federal authority over Southern Democrats and the power of individual states in general. The Supreme Court ended up the referee in this sectional and constitutional struggle between congressional and state power. Both decisions asserted that the Court "knew" what the original intent was. Both decisions also ostensibly upheld state legislation, but often in surprising and contradictory ways. For example, in *Bradwell* the decision second-guessed (thus expanded) what Illinois legislators had "intended"; in the *Slaughter-House Cases,* the decision exercised judicial restraint that favored a wealthy minority of businessmen over a powerful group of independent butchers by accepting (thus restricting) the "original intent" of the drafters of the Fourteenth Amendment.

Thus federalism, in the form of states' rights, and judicial restraint versus judicial activism were clearly issues—at least in the *Slaughter-House Cases.* If instead of exercising restraint the Supreme Court had countered the arguments of the four dissenting justices who wanted to protect citizens from legislative threats to such basic rights as the one to work, it would have had to have based its decision on a broad, activist interpretation of state police power. Since the state's defense rested in part on the argument that it created the Slaughter-House corporate monopoly as a health measure, had the justices used this approach in the butchers' case they could have possibly reached a decision favoring Myra Bradwell since Illinois could not argue as Louisiana did that its discriminatory legislation was motivated by health considerations. Instead, they simply applied their narrow interpretation of the privileges-and-immunities clause in the *Slaughter-House Cases* to *Bradwell* without having to compare or rethink anything about the police power of states. Thus, Carpenter's victory as an attorney in the former seems to have set the stage for defeat in the latter. Logically, the four dissenting justices in the *Slaughter-House Cases* should have supported Bradwell's right to practice law as they had supported the butchers' right to work where they wanted, but only one did—Chief Justice Salmon P. Chase. Moreover, three of these four justices were a part of the majority on the Court later in *Minor v. Happersett* (discussed later): Noah Swayne, Joseph Bradley, and Stephen J. Field (Chase having died was replaced by Waite.) Still later when these four justices again found themselves in the majority, they began to use their belief in basic individual rights to strike down early reform legislation of the Progressive Era. This is a classic example of where judicial activism as represented by the dissenters in the *Slaughter-House Cases* did not promote liberal reform when it became the majority position of the Supreme Court.[42]

Regardless of how the justices reached their decision in the *Slaughter-House Cases*, it is clear that neither Myra Bradwell nor her legal battle was taken seriously by the legal profession. One history of the United States Supreme Court has suggested: "While Chicago lawyers could not fail to respect " 'our Myra's' " remarkable attainments . . . her serious effort to win recognition as a lawyer was commonly treated as somewhat whimsical." She did not again apply for admission to the bar, even though the Illinois legislature passed an act in 1872 giving all persons, regardless of sex, freedom in selecting an occupation. Thus by the time the Supreme Court decided against Bradwell in 1873, the decision had no impact in Illinois because it had passed a law making it illegal to bar any person from employment on account of sex. In 1890, four years before her death, the Illinois Supreme Court admitted Bradwell to the practice of law; two years later, she was admitted to practice before the Supreme Court of the United States.[43]

Myra Bradwell never practiced law, although most of her professional and political activities were closely related to the law and she remained an outspoken advocate of women's rights. When she heard of the negative and arbitrary decision in the *Anthony* case, she wrote in her newspaper, the *Chicago Legal News*, that Judge Hunt "violated the Constitution of the United States more, to convict her of illegal voting, than she did in voting, for he had sworn to support it, she had not."[44] Perhaps there is some poetic justice in the fact that both Bradwell's daughter and son became attorneys. Even in death, however, Bradwell could not escape the same male condescension that had greeted her earlier attempt to be recognized as a lawyer. Thus, according to a memorial in the *American Law Review* in 1894, she was described as "a gentle and noiseless woman, her tenderness and refinement making her character all the more effective. Mrs. Bradwell was one of those who live their creed instead of preaching it. She did not spend her days proclaiming on the rostrum the rights of women but quietly, none the less effectively, set to work to clear the barriers."[45]

One point of immediate interest that emerges from Myra Bradwell's case is that, despite the great differences in the constitutional jurisprudence in the United States and England by the 1870s, the judges in both countries were expressing roughly similar sentiments and arriving at substantially the same results, even though the technical routes they followed were considerably different. The major difference was that judges in the United States articulated policy issues far more freely than did their English counterparts, for the Constitution encouraged them to do so. Consequently, the inconsistency and judicial confusion over female citizenship created by such decisions as the *Slaughter-House Cases* and *Bradwell v. Illinois* were more readily apparent in this country than in Britain, and these decisions did not bode well for a broadening of women's legal rights in the post–Civil War years. This was true not only with respect to choice of occupation but also, as the *Anthony* decision already demonstrated, with respect to the franchise. In both *Bradwell* and *Anthony,* the New York State Circuit Court and the Supreme Court had admitted that women were "citizens" under the Fourteenth Amendment. It still remained to be determined what kind of citizens they were and if they were also "persons" in the language of that amendment. Clearly, they did not yet have full citizenship, let alone full membership, in U.S. society.

## "Citizens" and "Persons" but Not Voters

The only case to reach the Supreme Court out of all the attempts women made to vote in the 1870s was Minor v. Happersett, 88 U.S. 162 (1875). Virginia Minor tried to vote at the same time that Anthony did in the fall of 1872. Unlike Anthony, however, she was not even allowed to register in St. Louis, Missouri, and so never did cast a ballot. Also unlike the Anthony trial, Minor's was a civil, not a criminal, case. Finally, as a married woman she could not sue independently under Missouri law, as Anthony had been able to do in New York as a single woman. Instead, she and her husband, as co-plaintiff and counsel, first filed suit against the local registrar, Reese Happersett; they then appealed the case to the Missouri Supreme Court and finally to the United States Supreme Court in 1874.

As part of its short-lived "New Departure" tactics, NAWSA had endorsed a resolution at the beginning of 1870 declaring that the privileges-and-immunities clause of the Fourteenth Amendment had enfranchised women to vote in state as well as federal elections. It is not without significance that Francis Minor provided the constitutional arguments in favor of this resolution. In October of the year before, Minor had written a letter to *The Revolution* (enclosing resolutions he had drafted for the 1869 statewide woman suffrage convention in St. Louis). His letter and these resolutions provided the basic legal rationale for asserting that the Fourteenth Amendment gave women the right to vote. His wife, Virginia Minor, who was president of the Missouri National Woman Suffrage Association, had already indicated her intention to vote in the form of a resolution to that state's suffrage group in October 1869. Her opening address to its convention was also published in *The Revolution*. Minor never actually cast a ballot because the local registrar said she was "not a 'male' citizen but a woman!"[46]

Rather than turning to Congress for redress of the disfranchisement of women, as Virginia Woodhull had in 1870–71, or deciding to vote somewhat spontaneously, as Anthony would later in 1872, the Minors carefully planned their constitutional-rights campaign to broaden the discursive meaning and constitutional interpretation of the first section of the Fourteenth Amendment. Francis Minor's resolutions to *The Revolution* anticipated a number of the arguments he and his attorneys later made in behalf of his wife in their 1872 brief before the Supreme Court. In addition to sophisticated constitutional arguments, Francis Minor's letter and state and federal briefs all made the political assertion that when only half the population could vote the United States could not claim to be a republic but rather was a despotic form of government.[47]

The language in all the Minors' briefs is both so constitutionally and politically extreme for the time that it leads one to wonder whether the briefs were written to win in court or for posterity.[48] By 1874 in particular, it is hard to believe that either Virginia or Francis Minor harbored much hope about the outcome of their case before the Supreme Court, given previous reconstruction decisions at the state and federal levels. In fact, like the state of Illinois in the *Bradwell* case, Missouri did not even bother to file a counterbrief before the Supreme Court.[49] Consequently, there is none of the immediacy or urgency conveyed by Anthony's pretrial talks or her lawyer's earnest, if somewhat sexist, defense of her. Probably sensing their case was lost, the Minors were free to range widely in their arguments and indulge in their own liberal individualism, hoping perhaps to goad the justices into a landmark decision even if it were negative. And to that degree they succeeded. While their defeat affected all women, their brief was personally calculated to serve their own needs.

The Minors' Supreme Court brief began with an elaborate political and constitutional argument that "there can be no half-way citizenship" under the Constitution. This was dismissed by the Court out of hand, as were the arguments about female disfranchisement being a bill of attainder and, therefore, a violation of due process. The Court entertained only those arguments based on the rights of citizens to vote under the First Amendment (voting was a form of free expression), the Thirteenth Amendment (not voting was a form of involuntary servitude), and the Fourteenth Amendment (voting for officials of the federal government was a privilege and immunity of national citizenship rather than simply state citizenship because these offices would not exist to vote for if the federal government did not).[50] Of these arguments, the Supreme Court chose only to consider whether voting was a privilege and immunity of citizenship. It most noticeably failed to address the question of why voting for *national* officers did not constitute a form of *national* citizenship that could not be abridged arbitrarily by individual states.

Writing for a unanimous court, Chief Justice Morrison Waite began by noting that "disputes have arisen as to whether or not *certain persons or certain classes of persons* were part of the people at the time [of the adoption of the Constitution of 1787]" (emphasis added), concluding that there was never any question of their being citizens. Since the Court had already held that "there is no doubt that women may be citizens because sex has never been made one of the elements of citizenship in the United States," it concluded that in this respect "men have never had an advantage over women." Chief Justice Waite argued that women, like children, were also legally "persons" because they were counted as part of the total population.[51] Then, the Court presented a simplistic historical summary to prove that it had never been the "intent" of the framers of the federal or state constitutions to enfranchise women, despite the fact that they were *both* "citizens" and "persons." "For nearly ninety years the people have acted upon the idea that the Constitution when it conferred citizenship did not necessarily confer the right of suffrage. . . . Our province is to decide what the law is, not to declare what it should be.[52]

Rather than simply relying on the narrow constitutional precedent set in the *Slaughter-House Cases* about national citizenship under the Fourteenth Amendment, as the Court had in *Bradwell,* Chief Justice Waite proceeded to discuss the political implications of the sweeping charge of despotism made by the Minors in their brief.[53] Although the unanimous opinion of the Supreme Court ignored most of the legitimate constitutional questions raised in the Minors' brief, it could not afford to let the one political challenge to republican government go unanswered. This is why half of the fourteen-page decision consists of a historical recitation demonstrating that the framers of the Constitution did *not* intend "to make all citizens of the United States voters." Therefore, "women were excluded from suffrage in nearly all the States by the express provision of their constitutions and laws."[54]

Chief Justice Waite and his colleagues were clearly disturbed by the idea that their "common understanding" about women as second-class citizens might some-how be construed as unrepublican or that female disfranchisement was somehow antirepublican. While the Court summarily dismissed most of the constitutional arguments of the Minors, the justices seemed compelled by their political arguments to engage in a debate over what constituted citizenship and republicanism in Victorian America. Like all women who sued in the courts over political or professional discrimination following the Civil War, Virginia Minor through her attorneys had been forced to adopt masculine language about individual rights to argue for national citizenship under the Fourteenth Amendment. In turn, the justices of the Supreme Court were forced into a discussion about why women had never been accorded full citizenship.[55] Gendered constitutional discourse changed with this decision in October 1874, despite the fact that constitutional specialists have yet to accord *Minor v. Happersett* such jurisprudential importance.

Using parallel reasoning to the *Dred Scott* decision, the *Minor* decision declared that historically women constituted a special category of citizens whose inability to vote did not infringe upon their rights as citizens or persons. Thus, it avoided the constitutional question raised by the Minors of whether voting for national officials was a privilege and immunity of national citizenship. The *Minor* decision, like the *Dred Scott* one twenty years before, could only be overruled by constitutional amendment. In other words, it took the Thirteenth Amendment to abolish the special category of slavehood for African-Americans by granting them citizenship, and it finally took the Nineteenth Amendment to abolish in part the special category of citizenship for women by granting them the right to vote.

What is curious is that the *Dred Scott* decision has for some time been considered a blot on constitutional law, but the *Minor* decision and the related *Bradwell* one have yet to receive the same deserved castigation by the legal profession. Why? One reason is that *Minor* did not receive anywhere near the publicity and national attention that the *Dred Scott* decision had because it was not related to any *important* historic or constitutional events, such as the Missouri Compromise or legality of slavery in territories where it was legally prohibited. Men were not about to fight and die over whether women could vote—domestic or national security was not at stake. However, it should be noted that Plessy v. Ferguson, 163 U.S. 537 (1896), did not make any more headlines in 1898 than *Roberts v. The City of Boston* had in 1848 or *Minor* in 1874. Since *Plessy* was a Supreme Court decision and *Roberts* was not, constitutional specialists of a later time simply raised *Plessy*'s status and Justice John Marshall Harlan's dissent from obscurity to landmark status.[56] One would have thought that this same arbitrary case-law approbrium would have been accorded the unanimous opinion in *Minor* by the 1990s, but such has not been the case except in contemporary feminist legal circles. Had Susan B. Anthony been the plaintiff the decision would have received national attention in the 1870s, but this in itself would have been no guarantee that a Supreme Court case involving Anthony would have been recognized as "bad" case law—then or now.

## Constitutional Legacy of the "New Departure"

The "New Departure" had, therefore, a strong constitutional element as well as the political one discussed in chapter 4. It was on constitutional grounds that it finally floundered and failed in the 1870s, not only for women but also for African-Americans. Like the *Bradwell* and *Anthony* decisions, the one in *Minor* was grounded in the post–Civil War constitutional interpretation of the Fourteenth Amendment in the *Slaughter-House Cases*. Although prevailing sex-stereotyped language abounds in both, *Minor* is the only one of the three cases in which the male legal and political system responded to a direct challenge posed by the Minors to the peculiar Victorian brand of liberal republicanism. Women had denounced the tyranny of their disfranchisement and argued for full citizenship rights under the Fourteenth Amendment in all three, but not until the arguments put forth by the Minors did the Supreme Court deign to defend itself and the country from the charge of despotism. In doing so, it simultaneously *accepted* its own male-rights language as employed by women (or their attorneys) and *rejected* their claim to such rights.

The constitutional significance of this contradiction between the discourse and the decision in *Minor* went largely unnoticed at the time, or was thought of as an advancement in the women's legal tactics because they finally forced the courts to *listen* to their arguments. However, it is a mistake to interpret the litigious ideas and actions of post–Civil War women reformers as more radical than they had been before that conflict unless one believes that radicalism for women consists of acting and sounding like men. While their juridical arguments may have sounded radical from the standpoint of the prevailing constitutionalism of the period, it was so only because *women* (and *blacks*) dared to ask for the basic individual right that white males already possessed. Voting rights are necessary for disadvantaged groups to begin to fulfill hopes of full citizenship, but it has not proven a "radical" way to alter society in the United States. Calls for divorce reform before and after the Civil War constituted a much more radical legal issue because these struck at the heart of women's subordination in both the public and private spheres. Suffrage did not, as U.S. women have gradually realized since the 1920s.

From a juridical point of view, nevertheless, half the battle was won with these post–Civil War cases, but only because women started to use male legal standards and male constitutional terminology because of the passage of the

Fourteenth Amendment. To win the other half of the battle would require an amendment to the Constitution in 1919 and case-law precedents that would not materialize until the 1970s. Gendered law prevailed against Virginia Minor, but her brief contained language and arguments that paradoxically contained the seeds of destruction for pre–Civil War radical feminism, while at the same time it presaged a diminishing of discrimination against women in the far distant future. When reconstruction politics and constitutionalism combined with the Victorian views that female moral superiority would be diminished by participation in public affairs, the only way that women could claim full citizenship was in a masculine voice. (This male voice of liberal legalism used *without* arguments about the moral superiority of women would not begin to prevail in the courts until a century later.) The response of the legal system to *Minor* in the 1870s was masculinist and probably racist, as well as sexist, for it has been suggested that Justice Waite had Justice Taney's infamous *Dred Scott* decision before him when preparing the *Minor* one and that this was no mere coincidence. It was, according to this theory, absolutely essential for judges to deal as summarily and as harshly as possible with the question of increased legal rights for women following the Civil War in order that they might proceed to keep to a minimum any rights implicit in the newly gained legal status of African-Americans.[57]

Once second-class citizenship had been unequivocally reinforced for women (who, after all, had been second-class citizens of the United States since the American Revolution), the white, male-dominated judiciary could then use this as a legal precedent to build a rationalization for Jim Crow laws. As Susan B. Anthony had predicted during her pretrial talks in behalf of her own voting rights case, once the courts established that U.S. citizenship did "not carry with it the right to vote in every State, . . . there is no end to the . . . cunning devices that will be resorted to, to exclude one and another class of citizens from the right of suffrage." Disfranchisement of black men did follow on the heels of *Minor* but so did other forms of racial discrimination.[58] Just as advances in civil rights for African-Americans in the 1960s provided women with legal precedents with which to fight for greater legal rights, it is possible that one hundred years earlier the reverse had taken place. For example, the first significant Supreme Court decision refusing to allow blacks to ride with whites in public transportation systems was handed down in 1869 in *Hall v. De Cuir*.

This case involved a black woman, Mrs. De Cuir, who was ejected from accommodations reserved for whites when she was traveling by steamboat through Louisiana. The state had passed a reconstruction law requiring all public carriers to provide equal accommodations for all travelers, "without distinction or discrimination on account of race or color." Chief Justice Waite also delivered this opinion, declaring the Louisiana statute to be an unconstitutional violation of the

Commerce Clause of the U.S. Constitution. He said: "If each State was at liberty to regulate the conduct of carriers while within its jurisdiction, the confusion likely to follow could not but be productive of great inconvenience and unnecessary hardship. . . . If the public good requires such legislation, it must come from Congress and not from the States."[59] In a concurring opinion, Justice Nathan Clifford noted the proliferation of such cases at the state level in the 1870s and concluded that most of them decided it was not "an unreasonable regulation to seat passengers so as to preserve order and decorum . . . arising from natural or well-known customary repugnancies . . . when white and colored persons are huddled together without their consent." Clifford also used state school-segregation cases, including *Roberts v. The City of Boston,* to bolster the Court's decision.[60]

*De Cuir* set the stage for numerous late nineteenth-century decisions denying equal protection of the law to African-Americans as a matter of course, as did a number of post–Civil War cases involving the legitimacy of pre–Civil War marriages among slaves. It is also interesting to note the number of these early civil and domestic rights cases that were brought by, or on behalf of, black women— *Roberts* and *De Cuir* being only the first of many.[61] Sex bias paved the way for increased racial bias within the American legal system in the last quarter of the nineteenth century. In each instance of gender and race discrimination, judges could and did argue, as in *Minor,* that "if the law is wrong, it ought to be changed; but the power for that is not with us. . . . No argument as to women's need of suffrage can be considered. We can only act upon her rights as they exist. It is not for us to look at the hardship of withholding [privileges and immunities of citizenship]. Our duty is at an end if we find it is within the power of a State to withhold."[62]

Feminists reacted to the 1874 Supreme Court decision in *Minor* that upheld disfranchisement of women with a volley of angry letters-to-the-editor and articles. One read in part:

As long as there were no women who demanded the ballot, and by tacit consent it was relinquished, the fraud practiced by debarring them from it was merely of a negative character but the privilege should have been left open; but from the moment that one woman demanded it, an outrage was practiced upon her by the entire people in denying it her, and the pleas that it is not woman's sphere . . . is the most subterfuge of any, for it is not for men, but for woman alone, to determine what the sphere is, or is not.[63]

All such protests were to no avail. The Supreme Court of the United States had not only upheld the police power of the states through the most narrow interpretation possible of the privileges-and-immunities clause of the Fourteenth Amendment but also had placed women on the confining pedestal known as "special category of citizen," using historical sex stereotypes rather than reasoned legal arguments. In addition, since congressional debates of the late 1860s made it clear that Congress had not anticipated the enfranchisement of women with the passage of the Fourteenth Amendment, the Court in the *Minor* case tacitly upheld the original "intent" of the drafters of the Fourteenth Amendment.[64]

The *History of Woman Suffrage* in two different volumes credits Francis Minor with initiating the "New Departure" of postwar female reformers into the realm of heretofore exclusively male constitutionalism. It also made it crystal clear that NWSA thought the first phase of the "New Departure" ended in 1875 with the Supreme Court decision in Virginia Minor's case because that was also the last year the organization went before Congress to obtain a declaratory act permitting women to vote under the Fourteenth Amendment. Following 1875, NWSA began to fight for a national suffrage amendment, which started as the Sixteenth and finally ended up as the Nineteenth Amendment to the Constitution forty-five years later. In this sense, the "New Departure" was really a "male departure" on the part of women following the Civil War as far as both types of its major constitutional aspects were concerned: suffrage petitions to Congress independently initiated by Virginia Woodhull in December 1870 and litigation based on the right of women to vote under the Fourteenth and Fifteenth Amendments. Both were based on constitutional arguments largely composed by men. In the case of Woodhull, her initial petition (memorial), if not her later address to Congress on 11 January 1871, primarily reflected the constitutionalism of Representative Benjamin F. Butler from Massachusetts and other supportive members of the House of Representatives. As noted previously, Francis Minor provided the much more sophisticated arguments about the meaning of the Fourteenth Amendment as early as October 1869.[65]

In fact, a chapter in the second volume of *The History of Woman Suffrage,* entitled "The New Departure," consists almost exclusively of detailing the two ways in which these male-inspired constitutional arguments were utilized by women between 1870 and 1872. Although Francis Minor's ideas were described "as the first ray of hope," by the time the *Minor* decision was handed down, women realized that they could not secure "all the powers and rights of citizens" under the Fourteenth or Fifteenth Amendments. Matilda Gage went so far as to predict that "in the near future these trials of women under the XIV. Amendment will be looked upon as the great State trials of the world; trials on which a republic, founded upon the acknowledged rights of all persons to self-government, through its courts decided against the right of one half of its citizens on the ground that sex was a barrier and a crime."[66] Both this recognition of the defeat of the "New Departure" and the determination to carry on with other forms of the male constitutionalism and politics that it represented can be found in the 1876 Declaration of Rights.

## The First Feminists and the 1876 Declaration of Rights

The centennial celebration of the American Revolution in 1876 symbolized a turning point in the discursive, theoretical, and tactical realignment of the priorities of the First Women's movement. After being refused a place on the Philadelphia commemorative program, Anthony and four other NWSA women insisted on formally presenting a "Women's Declaration of Rights" during the official proceedings and on passing out copies to the centennial audience. Beginning with the words "The history of our country the past 100 years has been a series of assumptions and usurpations of power over women, in the direct opposition to the principles of just government," the 1876 Declaration of Rights called for the impeachment of all American leaders. With this declaration, the original generation of women reformers and their younger followers turned more and more to political activities—in part, out of the realization that they had failed to improve their post–Civil War legal status through the courts and, in part, to cope with postwar conservatism.[67]

This reorientation on the part of the First Feminists is reflected in the textual contrasts between the 1876 and the 1848 declarations. Even the titles of the two documents are significantly different. The word *sentiment* was definitely not chosen in 1848 because of its emotional, attitudinal, and sentimental connotations about feelings and love, but rather because it conveyed to the authors the sense of reflection, observation, opinion, and theory. As noted in chapter 4, the wording of the 1848 document also *does not* convey any specific notion of "equal rights for all, with franchise as the crowning jewel of individual freedom," if for no other reason than the obvious fact that the Declaration of Independence on which it was formatted did not.[68] Even the Declaration of Rights twenty-eight years later, in 1876, did not use the word *rights* in the modern sense of individual constitutional rights as we know them today because the juridical interpretations of the Constitution, and the Bill of Rights, had not yet evolved to that point for men, let alone for women. The "constitutional rights consciousness" that appeared among women and African-Americans after the Civil War was still emotionally rooted in the "emancipatory vision of natural rights" for groups denied such rights by the Founding Fathers, even though their arguments and language were increasingly moving away from the "subversive and disruptive utopian message" of the prewar period.[69]

In other words, the "happiness" that Jefferson had meant in the Declaration of Independence and the "happiness" of the Declaration of Sentiments was based on a consciousness of community stemming from natural-law theories of the eighteenth century and early republican ideas that stressed group dependency and responsibility even as they encouraged some individual autonomy—but always in the name of the common good following the Civil War. These collective political and legal ideas had fragmented to the point that the pursuit of happiness meant "individual autonomy—the freedom to be left alone and to lead a "private life."[70] This was a far cry from the concept of collective responsibilities for the good of the community that had initially inspired revolutionary leaders. But it is also a far cry from the materialistic and self-centered "constitutional rights consciousness" of today.

Thus, the Declaration of Rights of 1876 is more like the Bill of Rights in its listings of desired legal protections against the power of the state than it is like the Constitution. It tried to balance a limited notion of individual rights with natural rights collectivity in an uneasy tension that was over a century old. Between 1776 and 1876, American men had gone on to develop industrial capitalism rooted in a sense of liberal individualism for themselves, which women were only beginning to understand and apply to themselves without the same theoretical base or practical stake in the political economy. This individualistic breakthrough in political and legal consciousness, however, could not (and did not) take place until some of the initial demands made at Seneca Falls based on Enlightenment theories had been achieved. Only from this belatedly improved status could feminism in the United States begin to disintegrate into fragmented liberal legal thought and individualistic actions beginning in the 1870s—reaching a debilitating high point in the 1920s and again in the 1980s.

Some of the most general basic demands in 1848 had been granted by women by 1876. For example, they no longer had to insist upon the right to speak in public or to participate in most religious and educational institutions. The difference between the original Seneca Falls Declaration of Sentiments and the 1876 Declaration of Rights symbolizes most clearly not only the initial defeats that women had suffered in the hands of the courts following the Civil War but also the gains women as a group had made on largely nonconstitutional grounds since 1848. Consequently, the 1876 declaration stressed the need for specific political and civil rights still denied women collectively, but it did so using post–Civil War individual rights language. Yet, the philosophical and theoretical framework of the women who drafted both these documents remained rooted in the eighteenth, not the nineteenth, century—where their legal status also largely still resided. Naturally, therefore, lingering ideas of the Enlightenment still dominated their theories more than those of Jacksonian democracy as they created these two female legal documents. But their language was much more masculine in 1876 than in 1848 because of the constitutional maelstrom created by the reconstruction amendments.

In retrospect, the 1876 Declaration of Rights, much more than its 1848 predecessor, should be viewed as an emulation of earlier eighteenth-century male legal thinking—not as a unique, original female vision of society and law or even a mid-nineteenth-century version because "women were living through a different history than men."[71] In particular, trial without a jury of peers, bills of attainder, writs of *habeas corpus,* and taxation without representation duplicated exactly prerevolutionary controversies with England. As had Abigail Adams in 1776, the 1876 statement also noted the "unequal codes for men and women." In both documents, but especially in the 1876 one, women symbolically took the place of the colonies—with white men playing the role of England. Well over half of the Declaration of Rights deals with 1776 issues. The only references to issues reflecting nineteenth-century legal or political conditions were those that mentioned married women's statutes, certain nativistic remarks against Asian immigrants, and criticism of universal *man*hood suffrage that established an "aristocracy of sex," which was described as worse than European aristocracy where at least upper-class women held some authority and power. Other social and cultural issues representing women's continued subordination in society, such as the double standard of morality, male dominance in marriage, and inequitable divorce and child-custody settlements, were given passing notice in the 1876 Declaration of Rights but not the prominence they had been accorded in the 1848 Declaration of Sentiments.

Because it so specifically referred back to 1776 issues, the Declaration of Rights has been less mystified over time as a feminist text than the Declaration of Sentiments, the goals of which were more woman oriented and, hence, more distinctive with the passage of time as differences between female and male rights have diminished. Although both documents called for the right to vote, the essential radicalism of the 1848 declaration was its pointed emphasis on female happiness—a concept only tagged on to the end of the 1876 declaration (with a rhetorical flourish reminiscent of 1848) that has never been accorded its rightful place of recognition among nineteenth-century legal oratory:

And now, at the close of a hundred years, as the hour-hand of the great clock that marks the centuries points to 1876, we declare our faith in the principles of self-government; our full equality with man in natural rights; that woman was made first for her own happiness, with the absolute right to herself—to all the opportunities and advantages life affords for her complete development; and we deny that dogma of the centuries, incorporated in the codes of all nations—that woman was made for man—her best interests . . . to be sacrificed to his will. We ask of our rulers, at this hour, no special privileges, no special legislation. We ask justice, we ask equality, we ask that all the civil and political rights that belong to citizens of the United States be guaranteed to us and our daughters forever.

When the "natural rights of each individual" was advocated at the centenary of the Constitution, it was not in the name of the "Creator," as in 1848, but in reference to the "broad principles of human rights proclaimed in 1776." Specific male standards of equality were stressed in 1876 to a greater degree than they had been in 1848. Not only did this reflect the constitutional rights language used in reconstruction cases and the failure of the "New Departure" in the courts but also the Declaration of Rights' more traditionally liberal and, hence, male legalistic and political approach compared to the earlier Declaration of Sentiments. The organizational and litigious experiences of the "New Departure" retarded, rather than enhanced, the original radical militancy of the First Women's movement, despite the argument by some historians that the acquiring of mainstream political and legal tactics should be viewed as radical in this time period.[72] Instead, such tactics invariably dimmed the broader vision of a society transformed by womanhood to accommodate female happiness based on collective natural rights by deferring to, or actively emulating, the increasingly individualistic concept of rights typically enjoyed by white males.

Clearly, this was a sign of the post–Civil War times. It was becoming increasingly evident even to the most militant female reformers that they could not oppose the prevailing male Victorian standards of morality and socioeconomic mores, especially those associated with industrialization, the modern nuclear family, and sexuality. Feminist radicalism was slowly being eased out of the First Women's movement as male mainstream political organization with all its inevitably narrowing compromises took over. In 1878 when Stanton talked about the "numerous demands by people for national protection in many rights not specified in the constitution," proving that "the people have outgrown the compact that satisfied the fathers," she was specifically criticizing constitutional jurisprudence as it had evolved during Reconstruction. Far from having "outgrown" that hallowed document, women were finally demanding entrance into it—a demand that has continued down to the present. They could not frame their demands, however, in terms critical of constitutional jurisprudence until the passage and interpretations of the reconstruction amendments following the Civil War had awakened their "constitutional rights consciousness" in the modern sense of that concept.[73]

Although the reconstruction amendments had created a primitive "constitutional rights consciousness" among the First Feminists, in the process it had begun to dim their vision of female happiness, with its radical restructuring of American society. This vision would not die officially, however, until 1890, when the American and National leaders finally overcame their differences and formed the National American Woman Suffrage Association (NAWSA). With this formal act of unity, they tacitly settled for much less than some of them had advocated in 1848, making the individual right to vote with men—not the collective concerns of women—the single goal of the new hybrid organization. Immediacy and militancy inexorably gave way to patience and reformism.

This reorientation meant, among other things, that the pervasive inequality of all women in the institution of marriage and in the capitalist work force received less juridical and discursive attention by the turn of the century as single and married women alike emphasized their roles as mothers and supporters of the nuclear family—although the plight of working women was addressed during the Progressive Era with the passage of protective legislation. It also meant that obtaining full citizenship dimmed as a feminist goal. When women finally achieved the right to vote in 1920, little had been done to improve the legal status of married or working women beyond the nineteenth-century Married Women's Property Acts and minimum-hour statutes. Questions of personhood; credit; equal pay; jury duty; exclusion from certain occupations, professions, and elite educational institutions; domicile rights; divorce settlements; access to contraception and abortion; child custody—even the right to retain a birth name once married—all remained neglected, ignored, or peripheral rights of citizenship during the single-issue fight for suffrage.

A Second Women's movement would not emerge to continue the battle for female happiness as full citizens of the United States until the late 1960s. Repeating history, however, the sweeping attack on the general subordination of all women to most men in society, made by the radical feminists of the late 1960s, would subsequently take a back seat again to another narrow and single constitutional rights crusade—the Equal Rights Amendment.

## More "Unreasoned" Decisions

The Supreme Court continued to issue decisions for the remainder of the nineteenth century based on arguments that muddied constitutional waters more than they cleared them because of the resulting legal inconsistencies between cases involving women and those that did not. Ten years later, for example, in Ex parte Yarbrough, 1 10 U.S. 651 (1884), a voting case involving personal intimidation of a black male, the Court ruled that the right to vote for a member of Congress did have its origins in the Constitution and, therefore, could not be abridged by the states. Later decisions interpreted this to mean that voting for a national official was, therefore, a privilege and immunity of national citizenship. This was the question the Court had refused to address when the Minors had raised it in 1874. While the *Yarbrough* decision did not technically overrule the position taken by the *Minor* court, by any logical determination it was overruled *sub silentio*. Yet the Court argued unconvincingly that *Yarbrough* could be distinguished from *Minor* because private actions of intimidation were involved, not state qualifications for voting, and because somehow the requirement by states that electors be male was a lawful state qualification for voting and not an abridgement of the rights of females to vote. Thus, the crucial, if questionable, distinction that the Courts made between *Yarbrough* and *Minor* was based in part on the difference between the right of a state to set qualifications for voting and the actual abridgement of a citizen's right to vote. A sex qualification was by implication not an abridgement.

As if *Yarbrough* had not confused matters enough, the Supreme Court then proceeded in 1886 to declare that corporations were "persons" under the Fourteenth Amendment. This possibility had been raised during the original congressional debates over the amendment; and, at the time, a majority of congressmen had clearly indicated that they did not "intend" to have businesses qualify as persons. Two decades later a burgeoning corporate structure prevailed over one of the most specific "original-intent" arguments, but the "original intent" of the framers of the Fourteenth Amendment *not* to enfranchise women remained an inviolate aspect of constitutional jurisprudence. Finally, twenty-one years after *Bradwell,* the Supreme Court's contradicting array of decisions over women as persons, women as voters, and women as lawyers reached a logical extreme with In re Lockwood, 154 U.S. 116 (1894). This was the only case other than Myra Bradwell's to reach the Supreme Court because of a state's refusal to license a woman lawyer.

Belva A. Lockwood's legal career had a stormy history long before her appeal to the Supreme Court in 1894. As one of the first women to complete her law studies at National University Law School in Washington, D.C., she was denied her degree until she protested to President Ulysses S. Grant, who was *ex officio* president of the law school as well. "You are, or you are not the President of the National University Law School," she wrote in 1873. "If you are its President I wish to say to you that I have been passed through the curriculum of study of that school, and am entitled to, and demand my Diploma."[74] Her imperious manner was dutifully rewarded by Grant that same year when Lockwood was forty-three years old. While she was then admitted to the bar of the District of Columbia, in 1876 she was denied permission to practice before the Supreme Court of the United States. She overcame this obstacle by lobbying for federal legislation enabling all women lawyers the right to appear before the Supreme Court. In 1879, she became the first woman to benefit from the passage of this landmark statute. An avid suffragist, she ran for president of the United States as a candidate of the National Equal Rights party in 1884 and 1888.

Against this formidable background and reputation, the state of Virginia denied Lockwood the right to practice law, although she had already been admitted to the bars of several other states in addition to the District of Columbia and the Supreme Court. The state's bar admission act indicated that any "person" who had been licensed to practice in any other state or in the District of Columbia could practice in Virginia. In this instance, the Supreme Court of Appeals of Virginia decided that "person" meant "male," even though the Court in *Minor* had stated that women were both "persons" and "citizens." It affirmed this position by refusing to issue a writ of *mandamus* ordering the state to admit Lockwood to practice. As in *Bradwell,* there was no mention of equal protection; and, since *Bradwell* was based on a very narrow interpretation of the privileges-and-immunities clause, it could not be used effectively here. The historical and legal importance of *Lockwood* lies in the fact that the Supreme Court chose to allow states to confine their definition of a "person" to males only. This, of course, was exactly the same question that Anthony had first posed in Rochester, New York, when she had voted in 1872. From 1894 until 1971, states could maintain that women were not legally "persons" by virtue of this single Supreme Court decision. [75]

Three years after her "persons" case had made Supreme Court history, negative as that was, Belva Lockwood, at the age of sixty-seven, enigmatically responded when asked if she considered herself a "new woman":

As a rule I do not consider myself at all. I am, and always have been a progressive woman, and while never directly attacking the conventionalities of society, have always done, or attempted to do those things which I have considered conducive to my health, convenience or emolument, as for instance: Attended college and graduated when the general sentiment of the people was against it, and this after I had been a married woman [cites legal battles]. . . . I was the first woman to ride a wheel [bicycle] in the District of Columbia, which I persisted in doing notwithstanding newspaper comments. . . . I do not believe in sex distinction in literature, law, politics, or trade; or that modesty and virtue are more becoming to women than to men; but wish we had more of it everywhere. I was new about 60 years ago, but did not then appreciate my privileges. [76]

Despite these later reservations about her own accomplishments, Lockwood's life clearly represented a "new way" for American women at the turn of the century. However, only the hardiest would follow in her footsteps.

## Legacy of Reconstruction Constitutionalism for Women

The *Lockwood* decision clearly indicated that judicial neutrality had not prevailed in post–Civil War gender cases nor had Radical Republican "constitutional conservatism"—in the states' rights sense that this phrase is usually employed by constitutional specialists writing about the reconstruction decades. As women attempted to improve their legal status through various interpretations of the reconstruction amendments, their efforts were rebuffed by what in retrospect was overtly sexist "judicial activism" at the state and federal levels. The politicization of the entire legal system but especially the Supreme Court during the years between the 1857 *Dred Scott* decision and the 1883 death of the reconstruction civil rights acts[77] constitute almost exactly the same period of time that women began first collectively and then more and more individualistically to question the major U.S. legal texts and their gendered interpretations since the American Revolution.

The result of the thwarted "constitutional rights consciousness" on the part of women and African-Americans following the Civil War and erratic examples of judicial activism resulted in a sense of "constitutional deterioration," not only among members of these disadvantaged groups but also among the American public in general because of the acrimonious debates that had erupted in the wake of ambiguous and sometimes contradictory decisions during Reconstruction.[78] Therefore, by contradictorily interpreting the broad language of the Fourteenth Amendment so that it extended to only one of two groups normally denied equal rights under the law—African-Americans—the Supreme Court ensured continuation for almost a century of the artificial distinction between the legal status of women and the legal status of African-Americans. Both groups were now accorded inferior citizenship status that did not include equality before the law, or even equality as second-class citizens with each other—a condition that continued racism reinforced until countered by the Civil Rights movement of the 1950s and 1960s.

The passage of the Fourteenth and Fifteenth amendments figuratively as well as literally separated the rights of women and the rights of African-Americans and contributed to the split within the women's movement in 1869. Indeed, the rights of these two legally inferior groups had been separate political issues all along, even though they were logically and morally similar. After all, the existence of slavery had caused a Civil War; the women's question was never accorded such status or intensity of feeling in the nineteenth century except on a personal, private level. It was one thing for Northern male abolitionists to free southern slaves—little would change in their personal lives as a result, especially if black civil rights were not forced on the former confederate states. It was entirely another matter for them to free their own women from common-law and other socioeconomic restraints.

The constitutionalism that the First Feminists began to develop then (and that feminists continue to use today) to try to overcome these disabilities was not radical to the degree that it was safely within the paradigm of legal discourse of their respective time periods. Constitutionalism has seldom been a lever for radical social change in the United States, despite claims of some constitutional specialists to the contrary.[79] Radicals always start out appealing to "higher laws" of God, or nature, or technology but usually end up tailoring their original demands to meet the requirements of liberal constitutionalism. That post–Civil

War women reformers fell into this familiar pattern is not surprising. By taking their cause to the courts, however, they forced a change in legal discourse that makes these late nineteenth-century decisions sound hopelessly gendered and obsolete in retrospect.

In the last quarter of the nineteenth century, the Supreme Court negatively and narrowly interpreted the Fourteenth Amendment in cases involving not only women but also all minority groups. In its initial interpretation of the privileges-and-immunities clause of the Fourteenth Amendment, the Supreme Court adhered to procedural due process, assigning to the states broad authority to pass laws regulating the health, safety, welfare, and morals of the public. This type of due process remained for three decades following the Civil War, "simply an assurance of fair procedures." Not until the 1880s did Supreme Court justices begin to succumb to pressures for broadening the realm of due process from strictly procedural to more ambiguous substantive grounds. It was not until substantive due process subsequently supplemented procedural due process that the Fourteenth (and earlier the Fifth) Amendment offered greater hope against arbitrary state regulations. Under substantive due process, all federal and state legislation is judged by how "reasonably" it furthers a legitimate governmental objective.[80] Originally, however, women, minorities, and occupational groups failed to obtain a broad or substantive interpretation of the privileges-and-immunities clause of Section 1, which covers all citizens and the entire spectrum of civil rights, including the right to choose one's livelihood freely and to vote. As noted, the Supreme Court in the *Bradwell v. Illinois* and the *Slaughter-House Cases* of 1873 limited the privileges and immunities of United States' citizens to only those rights that owed their existence to the federal government, its national character, its constitution, or its laws. Hence, the right to choose and follow one's occupation and the right to vote were not held to be privileges and immunities of federal citizenship and, accordingly, could be constrained or eliminated by state legislation.

This narrow, procedural interpretation of Section 1 of the Fourteenth Amendment implied that the states had the broadest kind of power to enact laws governing the health, welfare, safety, and morals of the public—as interpreted by each state legislature and not by the Supreme Court. However, when reform legislation was passed during the Progressive Era that did not favor capitalistic monopoly, as the *Slaughter-House Cases,* then the justices conveniently reversed themselves on the question of state police powers. Due process was viewed simply in terms of the procedures used to pass and the means used to enforce the laws of the land. Substantive due process, the concept that was employed to override states' rights primarily in the first quarter of this century, first entered the legal scene in 1897 and was of no benefit to the original generation of feminists, although their immediate successors in the Progressive movement tried to use it to obtain protective legislation for all workers—men, women, and children— succeeding only with women and children. Substantive due process fell into jurisprudential disrepute in the 1940s and 1950s, only to be revived in post– World War II cases involving the right to privacy. [81]

## Legal Status of Women by 1900

By the turn of the century, women had been discouraged from using the Fourteenth Amendment to improve their legal and political status. Thus, this second period in the development of the legal status of women ended on a discouraging jurisprudential note, but with one well-established constitutional and linguistic principle that would reemerge in the third and fourth periods—namely, that women should argue in masculine terms for equal rights with men under the Constitution. While this development was a natural and laudatory option at the time, it should not be forgotten that it represented a less radical position for three reasons: first, it posited male standards for female ones; second, it narrowed the broader socioeconomic agenda Anthony and Stanton had advocated just before and after the Civil War; and, finally, focusing on equal rights with men raised to top priority an issue that had been on the bottom of the list of the more general, collective problems facing women by those who met in 1848 in Seneca Falls. Ultimately, the single individual civil right of suffrage became the most important goal of the First Women's movement rather than the restructuring of society to accommodate women more equitably through collective group action—although, as we shall see in the following chapter, some female reformers by the end of the century advocated "protecting" working women as a group.

After the Civil War, male leaders both in the victorious North and the defeated South once again reevaluated their position on women's separate estates and inheritance laws. This time the nature of economic and political dislocation associated first with Reconstruction and then with rapid growth of investment capitalism made them question whether married women's property should remain distinct from that of their families' operating budgets. As industrial development and speculation returned in the 1870s and 1880s, some courts and state legislatures decided that instead of special (equity-based) treatment, wives should be accorded more equal treatment with husbands concerning property holdings.

As noted in chapter 4, under the New York state 1848 model for Married Women's Property Acts most states simply codified equity procedures through legislation. While most of the reform of women's property rights in the 1840s "should not be perceived as an attack on coverture law," it did contain the seeds of the ultimate destruction of coverture. In practice, such legislation varied from state to state. Many states before the Civil War did not give women direct financial control over their separate estates by granting them *feme sole* status and usually only granted them lifetime tenure in realty. Some did give women absolute testamentary powers by allowing them to will or convey their real and personal property outside of their immediate families but usually after limiting the amount of property in their separate estates. Some also did away with the husband's curtesy (the automatic common-law right to a life estate in his wife's property), leaving the husband no right to contest his wife's will. Many states before the Civil War protected the wife's separate and/or inherited estates from creditors. At the same time, however, states began to limit or abolish dower rights for women that had given them claim to one-third of all property accumulated during marriage and replaced it with intestacy law granting women a one-third share only in the land held at the time of the husband's death. [82]

The Married Women's Property Acts after the Civil War were sometimes not as lenient with respect to testamentary powers. In certain states, such as Pennsylvania, for example, the legislators decided even before the Civil War that they had given wives too much power to dispose of all their property because they did not have to name their husbands as recipients. Considering this a threat to traditional family inheritance patterns, the Pennsylvania assembly gave husbands back the right to claim curtesy in their wives' separate estates, giving them larger portions of their wives' properties than widows could claim of their husbands' properties. Moreover, Pennsylvania upheld the right of husband to put property constraints on the remarriage of their widows. On the other hand, wives in more states after the Civil War were given fee simple ownership of realty (rather than the limit of lifetime tenure), except in the case of dower and homestead exceptions, with the option of *feme sole* status. However, women's separate and inherited property in some states began to be considered part of the family income. This meant such property was not protected from debts their husbands had incurred and so were subject to the claims of creditors. Thus, part of the gains that women experienced in terms of outright ownership was offset by the claims of creditors against all family wealth at the death of the husband, including any separate estates. Thus, instead of protecting widows' property, this new legislation protected the claims of creditors. [83]

Such limited equal treatment "significantly increased the ability of creditors to rely upon married women's assets as viable security." As a result, by the end of the century, the "total exemption of married women's property from family creditors became untenable as more women entered the labor force and women became the primary purchasers of family and consumer goods."[84] At the same time, by the end of the century most states had abolished dower; both unilateral and bilateral patrilineage had also disappeared; entails establishing rigid lines of inheritance patterns had disappeared along with primogeniture; and illegitimate and adopted children were now eligible to inherit, and mothers could even inherit from their children. [85] The impact of this gradual, but final victory at the end of the nineteenth century for creditors and financial interests over dower rights and protected separate property for married women cannot be understood or evaluated except in relation to succession-law changes.

Where did this array of new intestacy laws leave women, especially in light of the dramatic reduction in family size by 1900? Among other things, there was an increased trend for the first time since the early colonial time to name women as executrixes of estates and to give them more shares in those estates than required by law. Moreover, both pre– and post–Civil War Married Women's Property Acts seem to have encouraged greater testamentary behavior on the part of women. The percentage of female testators increased (from 17 percent in the 1790s to 38.5 percent in the 1890s), and the percentage of total personal testate wealth owned by women increased, at least in the limited number of counties studied to date, from 7.3 to 35.8—almost in exact proportion to the percentage increase in the number of female testators. Nonetheless, creditors could now lay claim to most property inherited by widows except in those postwar states that passed homestead legislation specifically protecting them and their children from homelessness. [86]

One has to wonder, therefore, if this move by men toward providing limited equal property rights for women, which proceeded so much faster because of economic and demographic factors than the drive on the part of women to obtain full citizenship, did not in fact leave end-of-the-century wives in a more precarious financial position than their colonial and revolutionary ancestors. Freed from both arranged (and largely economic) marriages and equity protection of their separate estates and dower rights, these women found themselves ostensibly in companionate, conjugal arrangements with no economic control over conjugal property and actually less individual economic security if their marriage should fail—all in the name of establishing a family income for purchasing consumer goods and making the conjugal unit more economically viable.

Legal, economic, and social historians have argued that the demise of coverture, more domestic and financial responsibilities, and some slight semblance of equal economic treatment by the end of the nineteenth century reflected the enhanced roles that working, but particularly middle-class, women began to play in their families' domestic and economic affairs both before and after the Civil War. [87] Thus, the question remains how much "actual" power was conveyed to women then (or is conveyed to women today) who "control" marginal family budgets, or when, during a particular time period such as after the Civil War, they begin in increasing numbers to inherit and control small personal and real property. [88]

Property ownership among free African-American women probably changed more dramatically in the course of the nineteenth century than that of white women. Although their numbers were always small, free black women in the lower South accumulated property up until the 1840s and 1850s, when sectional strife and economic conditions prevented them from expanding their holdings. After the Civil War, it took over a generation of freedom before African-American women once again began to appear in significant numbers as landowners in the upper South and North. Initially following the war, black men increased as property owners, but black women did not, as more black women chose family life and/or found it more difficult to acquire property through the legal system that had been designed to deal only minimally even with white women's desires for autonomous ownership. [89] In retrospect, it is evident that completely autonomous property rights for married women were decades away. In fact, the Supreme Court did not give "constitutional impetus" to this long, slow process of eliminating male domination over marital property until 1981, when it decided Kirchberg v. Feenstra, 450 U.S. 455 (1981). As late as February 1987, a review of married-property legislation concluded that "the laws affecting . . . woman's right[s] to marital property have reflected and perpetuated their dependence and inequality." This same review of married-property legislation urged passage of the Uniform Marital Property Act by states. As of the beginning of 1987, only Wisconsin had adopted this act, which was first recommended in 1983 by the National Conference of Commissioners on Uniform State Laws. [90]

By 1900, because the Supreme Court had begun overtly to discriminate against the professional and political desires of post–Civil War women, the best and brightest females had less reason, in fact, to rejoice about their legal status than some of their most famous leaders would have us believe. Is it any wonder that some Progressive reformers in the United States began in the early twentieth century to think that women needed protection—that is, special treatment— again, but this time not disguised as equity-court procedures but as protective legislation. The urgency and militancy of the First Feminists was gone, but their movement survived and became more assimilated into mainstream politics during the Progressive Era.

Indeed, there had been quiet statutory advances in female property rights, despite the publicity given to negative court decisions affecting women's citizenship status. For example, the most debilitating aspects of coverture had been eliminated by statute and litigation. Consequently, Susan B. Anthony could quite logically claim both victory and the need for continued struggle in 1902 as this period of constitutional discrimination was drawing to a close:

At the beginning of 1848, the English Common Law was in force practically everywhere in the United States. Its treatment of women was a blot on civilization only equalled in blackness by the slavery of the negro. The latter, technically at least, has now disappeared. The former dies slowly, because it cannot be eradicated by fire and sword. . . . An examination, doubtless, would show that in not one State does the Common Law now prevail in its entirety. In many of them it has been largely obliterated by special statutes. There has been no retrogressive legislation with respect to the status of women before the law. In the majority of the States, a married woman may now own and control property, carry on business and possess her earnings, make a will and a contract, bring suit in her own name, act as administrator and testify in the courts. In one-fifth of the States, she has equal guardianship with the father over the minor children. Where formerly there was but one cause for divorce, the wife may now obtain a divorce in almost every State for habitual drunkenness, cruelty, failure to provide and desertion on the part of the husband; and he can no longer, as of old even though the guilty party, retain sole possession of the children and the property. The general tendency of legislation for women is progressive, and there is not a doubt that this will continue to be the case.

I do not wish to be understood for a moment, however, as maintaining that woman stands on a perfect equality with man in any of the above-mentioned departments—in the industries, education, organization, public speaking or the laws. . . . Woman never will have equality of rights anywhere, she never will hold those she now has by an absolute tenure, until she possesses the fundamental right of self-representation. This fact is so obvious as to need no argument. Had this right been conceded at the start, the others would have speedily followed; and the leaders among women, instead of spending the last half-century in a constant struggle to obtain their civil and political rights, might have contributed their splendid services to the general upbuilding and strengthening of the government. The effort for this most important of rights has had to contend not only, like the rest, with the obstinate prejudices and customs of the ages, but also with the still more stubborn condition of its hard and fast intrenchment in constitutional law. [91]

Clearly, by the turn of the century Anthony understood the difference between false protection and false equality better than most of those women in the forefront of the Progressive movement—or many feminists today.

# CHAPTER SIX

# Constitutional Protection, 1908–1963

The third period in the development of the legal status of women lasted from 1908 until the early 1960s. Unlike the first period of constitutional neglect, in which women's rights as citizens were largely ignored, and the second period of constitutional discrimination, in which the courts actively discriminated against women's professional, political, and civil aspirations, this third period was characterized by several major Supreme Court decisions (originating with *Muller v. Oregon* in 1908) and a variety of state legislation aimed primarily at protecting lower-class, working women. These decisions and statutes were based on what are considered today to be debilitating stereotypical views of all women, regardless of class. Ironically, just as protective legislation began to be used to restrict job opportunities for women, the First Women's movement succeeded in obtaining passage of the Nineteenth Amendment, granting them the right to vote.

This third period is important in the legal history of women in the United States because it also is the one in which a fifty-year battle line was drawn between those female reformers who thought certain groups of women needed protection and those who thought that all women would be better off if they simply obtained equal rights with men. Nonetheless, before this debilitating split occurred in the 1920s, some middle ground was forged between the old radical militancy of the first generation of women reformers, led by Anthony and Stanton, and the conservatism of most second-generation suffragists who did not endorse their broader social and economic goals for women. This task fell to a handful of women who were leaders in the Progressive movement of the early twentieth century. In addition to being suffragists, they tried to keep the First Women's movement in the mainstream of traditional liberal reform.

Some of these female reform leaders consciously attempted to link the social welfare wing of progressivism with suffrage. They were the same women, like Jane Addams, Alice Hamilton, Lillian Wald, Grace and Edith Abbott, and Florence Kelley, who also kept avenues of communication open between working- and middle-class women and who resisted the anti-immigrant ethos so prevalent in American society at the turn of the century. Moving from individual urban-reform projects like settlement houses, such women soon realized that they needed political power to build better neighborhoods and to improve the deplorable working conditions of the urban masses. And so, along with advocating suffrage for women, they formed or supported numerous national organizations dedicated to securing state legislation to make modern society more livable for all classes of people. Specifically, they lobbied in behalf of protective-labor legislation for all workers—women, men, and children. They were also the most class-conscious of all middle-class suffrage leaders. [1]

These Progressive Era female leaders found, however, that working-class women's issues would not be positively addressed until the Supreme Court applied due process in their favor, as opposed to its application in the *Slaughter-House Cases* thirty years before when the justices had ruled that a state monopoly was procedurally constitutional (over the protests of individual butchers). Procedural due process simply did not meet the needs of most women, regardless of class, given the uniquely subordinate constitutional position they had been accorded by the courts since the American Revolution. As noted in chapter 5, by the first decade of the twentieth century the Supreme Court had used procedural due process only against the interests of women—not in their behalf. In the nineteenth century, the courts treated women differently from men primarily on the basis of "divine insight"—which judges apparently received directly from the "Creator" they so often cited. In the first half of the twentieth century, the courts began to "protect" women because of their presumed physiological deficiencies with no more evidentiary foundation than existed one hundred years before.

## The Need to Protect Working Women

The groundwork for protective legislation and Supreme Court decisions placing limits on hours and types of work in which women could engage was laid in the late nineteenth century in response to the human wreckage created by industrialization. Women who suffered under the burgeoning U.S. factory system had tried unsuccessfully since the 1820s to organize themselves in the face of discrimination, not only by male employers but also by male-dominated trade unions as well. NAWSA did little that was practical to aid women workers, although beginning in 1893 its annual convention platforms called for equal pay for equal work and its members had always assumed that working women would be better able to protect themselves in the workplace if they obtained the right to vote. It is worth noting that when working women did begin to support the suffrage movement after the turn of the century, they did so as a means to an end—that is, to improve economic conditions, not as an end in itself as so many middle-class women did. [2]

Not until 1903, however, when the national Women's Trade Union League (WTUL) was formed, did middle-class women collectively begin to assist working women in organizing themselves within the existing sex-segregated labor market and male-dominated trade unions. Led by middle- and upper-class women, they organized support for strikes by women workers and occasionally made the American Federation of Labor (AFL) consider more seriously its discriminatory practices against female laborers. By seldom questioning or attacking male dominance within either the union system or the capitalist system, the WTUL never became a radical force in American labor history. While the WTUL made no attempt to end the sex stereotyping of two-thirds of all the types of work women performed at that time, it should be noted that the same percentage of "female" jobs exists today, despite recent efforts to eradicate gender differentiation in the job market. Probably the most valuable contribution of the WTUL to the plight of working women was the support it gave to obtaining protective labor laws. Two other middle-class women's organizations participated in the protective-law effort: the General Federation of Women's Clubs and the National Consumers' League (NCL)—the latter being the major force behind lobbying for protective legislation. Most of the women in these organizations also were avid suffragists and belonged to NAWSA. [3]

By 1908 there were nineteen laws settling maximum hours for women and/or prohibiting night work for women. However, the constitutionality of such legislation was in question because three years earlier, in Lochner v. New York, 198 U.S. 45 (1905), a case involving a limit on working hours for male bakers, the Supreme Court had invalidated state protective legislation on substantive rather than procedural due-process grounds. Like Allgeyer v. Louisiana, 65 U.S. 578 (1897), almost a decade before, the decision in _Lochner_ stated in essence that such a protective restriction could not be imposed by the state (in this instance, on men) because it violated the constitutional rights of personal liberty and the liberty of contract under the due-process clause of the Fourteenth Amendment.

In 1897 when the justices had first proclaimed the "liberty-of-contract" doctrine in *Allgeyer,* they nullified a Louisiana statute that attempted to regulate not workers but insurance companies. [4] Writing for a unanimous Court, Justice Rufus W. Peckham defended the "right of the citizen to be free . . . to pursue any [lawful] livelihood or avocation, and for that purpose to enter into all contracts which may be proper, necessary and essential to his carrying [them] out to a successful conclusion." This opinion did not, however, make the freedom to contract an absolute individual right. Instead, when states attempted to assert their regulatory, that is, police powers, in this area, Peckham said that the courts should review them on a case-by-case basis.

Within a year, however, the Supreme Court ruled constitutional a Utah law setting an eight-hour workday for miners in Holden v. Hardy, 169 U.S. 366 (1898). Most important, because it would later relate to the *Lochner* decision, two justices (one of them, Peckham) dissented in *Holden* without writing opinions. Six justices, therefore, held that the state had made a "reasonable" factual determination that an exception should be made of the Utah mining industry "for the preservation of the health of employes [sic]" in unusual situations, unlike those "ordinary trades and occupations of the people." Significantly, therefore, the majority opinion in *Holden* specifically avoided any determination about other statutes limiting working hours and went so far as to assert that the Fourteenth Amendment restricted state regulatory action in the case of more inclusive *groups* of citizens, such as women or racial minorities, and in instances when the legislation would alter existing criminal proceedings. [5]

Since neither restriction was involved in *Holden* or *Lochner,* the problem for Peckham, seven years later, was to distinguish the five-to-four majority opinion of the *Lochner* case from the six-to-two one in *Holden.* In writing the *Lochner* decision, Justice Peckham first noted that the New York law could not be voided in "emergencies," as was the case in Utah, and that there was no consensus in the lower New York state courts about the dangers of working in bakeries, as there had been about working in Utah mines. Above and beyond these legal technicalities, Peckham "clearly viewed labor legislation *per se* as unconstitutional, whether or not health or welfare was protected by it." In other words, "no purely legal argument" in the future would be likely to change such a deeply held animosity toward "creeping labor protectionism" on the part of Peckham and his four associates on the Court. "It is impossible for us to shut our eyes to the fact that many of the laws of this character," Peckhman asserted, "while passed under what is claimed to be the police power for the purpose of protecting the public health or welfare, are, in reality, passed from other motives." [6]

In his dissent in *Lochner,* Justice Oliver Wendell Holmes condemned the social Darwinist and capitalist assumptions of the majority opinion, denying that the Constitution "was intended to embody particular economic theory, whether of paternalism . . . or of laissez faire." Instead, he argued that the people of New York State were experimenting in the maximum-hours law with new ways of dealing with the changed relationship between employers and employees, as well as with the growth of giant, and largely unregulated, corporations. "The right of a majority to embody their opinions in law," according to Holmes, had been violated by the majority opinion in *Lochner.* [7] Moreover, the Supreme Court's narrow five-to-four decision in *Lochner* clearly stood in the way of protective legislation for women as well as men; thus, in the next protective-legislation appeal to reach the Supreme Court, which involved a woman, a new defense had to be devised.

The justices in *Lochner* inadvertently invited a new defense by reversing "their traditional policy of assuming that state regulatory legislation was constitutional unless proven otherwise." Instead, they substituted their own socioeconomic preferences for those of the elected representatives of Illinois (and, implicitly, for those of other states who had passed similar maximum-hour legislation). They were unable to see any reasonable relationship among such statutes and public health, safety, morals, and the general welfare of employees. Even though the attorney general of New York, Julius M. Mayer, presented a "mild" statistical case in his brief on behalf of New York State, the socioeconomic biases of the justices prevailed.[8] By reversing the nature of traditional legal discourse about the presumptive constitutionality of state laws in *Lochner,* the Court placed the burden of proof on those who opposed such legislation, not on the states that only had to show a "reasonable" connection among state regulations of working conditions and employee health, safety, morals, and welfare. This shift, from determining whether a state's statute had been enacted through "fair procedures" and, therefore, was not arbitrary to determining whether it had exhibited "substantive reasonableness," tipped the Court in the direction of substantive due process and away from procedural due process in all subsequent protective-legislation decisions.[9] In 1905, when faced with a short statistical brief in *Lochner,* a majority of the justices had remained impervious on the issue of maximum hours. Three years later they changed their minds when faced with a much longer and unorthodox statistical brief.

The case turned out to be Muller v. Oregon, 208 U.S. 412 (1908). Prior to this decision a number of state supreme courts had issued decisions both validating and invalidating protective legislation for women, usually on the grounds of substantive due process. Curt Muller, for example, had been convicted under an Oregon statute when an overseer in his Portland laundry required a female employee (identified throughout the legal proceedings only by her husband's name as Mrs. Elmer Gotcher) to work more than ten hours on 4 September 1905. When Florence Kelley, as National Consumers' League (NCL) general secretary, and her associate, Josephine Goldmark, learned that Muller had appealed his misdemeanor conviction and ten-dollar fine to the Supreme Court, they decided that this should be their test case on protective legislation for women. The NCL initially tried to obtain the services of a leading New York attorney and former ambassador to Great Britain, Joseph H. Choate, but he informed Kelley and Goldmark that he saw nothing wrong with a "big husky Irishwoman . . . work[ing] more than ten hours a day in a laundry if she and her employer so desired.[10] They then turned to Goldmark's brother-in-law, Louis D. Brandeis, who agreed to take on the *pro bono publico* case only if the state of Oregon agreed that he should be its official counsel and that the NCL provide him with a massive amount of statistical data within two weeks. Both did.

Represented by Brandeis, Oregon's State's attorney general, with the NCL as co-counsel, could have argued the case against Muller in one of two ways: by trying to displace the "common-understanding" argument in *Lochner* about the lack of health dangers in bakeries or any industrial job using empirical, socioeconomic evidence to show that any such job performed steadily for more than ten hours a day was dangerous to a worker's health; or, by arguing that because women were involved there was reason to make an exception to the *Lochner* doctrine of liberty of contract, on the grounds that women needed "special protection" because there was "something special or different" about them. Unfortunately, the state chose to emphasize the latter argument, which reinforced traditional stereotypes about working women.

## The "Brandeis Brief": Myth versus Reality

Theoretically, the famous 113-page "Brandeis brief" combined both approaches by presenting statistical and sociological data from nonjudicial sources collected primarily by paralegal volunteers, such as Josephine Goldmark and her sister Pauline, secretary of NCL. Although they collected material on both women and men showing that long hours negatively affected the health and performance of both sexes, Brandeis insisted on only playing to the gender bias of the justices.[11] Consequently, the brief (and, later, the decision) focused primarily on the physical differences between men and women and, in particular, on women's biologically reproductive, rather than their economically productive, roles in society. The entire brief contained only two pages of legal argumentation, concluding:

We submit that in view of the facts above set forth and of legislative action extending over a period of more than sixty years in the leading countries of Europe, and in twenty in our States, it cannot be said that the Legislature of Oregon had no reasonable ground for believing that the public health, safety, or welfare did not require a legal limitation on women's work in manufacturing and mechanical establishments and laundries to ten hours in one day.[12]

Thus, the majority opinion did not really have to consider the individual working woman involved in the case or other American working women in terms of either their working conditions or their performance on the job. Instead, the Court was encouraged to concentrate on female physical weaknesses compared to males and their procreative functions.

In ruling in favor of the state, the Supreme Court used gendered language and attitudes reminiscent of the *Anthony, Bradwell,* and *Minor* cases. Additionally, it incorporated an argument similar to the one employed in *Dred Scott* about African-Americans—that "women as citizens" constituted a special category. Thus, the Court agreed with Brandeis and the NCL that limitations could be placed on a woman's right to contract in the interest of the "well-being of the race." Yet the justices had to be careful to avoid any direct confrontation or contradiction of the *Lochner* "liberty-of-contract" doctrine for male workers, since Brandeis relied so heavily on their opinion in that case when citing the legal precedents for the right of states to make "reasonable" regulations to protect workers. Specifically, the *Muller* decision did this with the following rationalization:

That woman's physical structure and the performance of maternal functions place her at a disadvantage in the struggle for subsistence is obvious. This is especially true when the burdens of motherhood are upon her. Even when they are not, by abundant testimony of the medical fraternity, continuance for a long time on her feet at work, repeating this from day to day, tends to injurious effects upon the body, and as healthy mothers are essential to vigorous offspring, the physical well-being of women becomes an object of public interest and care in order to preserve the strength and vigor of the race.

Still again, history discloses the fact that woman has always been dependent upon man. He established his control at the outset by superior physical strength, and this control in various forms, with diminishing intensity, has continued to the present. As minors, though not to the same extent, she has been looked upon in the courts as needing special care that her rights may be preserved . . . even with the consequent increase of capacity for business affairs it is still true that in the struggle for subsistence she is not an equal competitor with her brother. Though limitations upon personal and contractual rights may be removed by legislation, there is that in her disposition and habits of life which will operate against a full assertion of those rights. . . . Differentiated by these matters from the other sex, she is properly placed in a class by herself, and legislation designed for her protection may be sustained, *even when like legislatioin is not necessary for men and could not be sustained* (emphasis added).[13]

Had the Supreme Court simply followed the precedent set by *Holden,* the "Brandeis brief might never have been invented." Had women not been involved in *Muller,* it is unlikely that the "Brandeis brief" would have convinced the justices to make the connection between socioeconomic data and the welfare of workers. In this instance, however, they replaced one set of value judgments about the *importance of men* in the work force with another substantive due-process decision based on a related set of stereotypic views—namely, the need to protect the welfare of weaker workers and, by implication, the *lesser* importance of women in the work force.[14]

There is more gender-related constitutional scholarship on this single decision than on any other Supreme Court decision affecting women before the 1973 abortion decision. Yet until the recent works of Philippa Strum, Nancy S.

Erickson, Jennifer Friesen, and Ronald K. L. Collins, the doctrinal analysis and evaluation of the long-range legal impact of *Muller* have not been very sophisticated.[15] Strum clearly notes, for example, that the much-heralded "Brandeis brief" set a precedent for the use of economic, sociological data in arguing future cases. In fact, in a most primitive fashion, it laid the foundations for the statistical arguments employed in class-action suits beginning in the 1970s. Although Strum assigns much significance to the single sentence in the text and to the two-paragraph footnote in which Brandeis and data from his brief are cited, Erickson, Friesen, and Collins all maintain that the brief was essentially ignored in the unanimous opinion written by Justice David J. Brewer, a known opponent of both labor and the Progressive movement in the early twentieth century.

While supporting equal political rights for women, Brewer did not believe that women were, or should be, considered equal in the work place. Erickson, for example, has asserted that the decision would have been the same with or without the Brandeis "authorities" because the justices chose to base the text of their opinion on standard sex stereotyping of, and paternalistic protection toward, women as "bearers of the race." This stereotypical assumption had been a long-standing feature of American law and Supreme Court decisions in both the first and second stages in the constitutional development of women. Even Strum concludes that the legal discourse employed in "protecting" working women was so traditionally sexist that it "could not be comforting to feminists [of the period]." Additionally, Strum notes that as a belated supporter of women's suffrage, Brandeis himself was "not a feminist" but rather a Progressive concerned about achieving greater political and economic equality through legal "experimentation."[16]

The modern-sounding aspects of *Muller v. Oregon* are found today only in the brief of Curt Muller's attorney, William D. Fenton. He argued on behalf of the male employer (not the female employee who had worked longer hours than the state of Oregon allowed), pointing out that some women absolutely had to work to support themselves or their families. Thus, Fenton directly challenged the prevailing chivalrous notion that half of the members of the human race remained "sheltered in happy homes free from the exacting demands . . . [of pursuing] a living." Casting aside one fallacious assumption about women, he endorsed an equally fallacious one about employees—namely, that they can bargain or negotiate fair agreements for themselves with their employers. Relying exclusively on *Lochner v. New York,* he used the standard false-equality argument to insist that female workers did not need the "protecting arm of the legislature" any more than male workers when contracting with employers for their labor.

To his credit, Fenton anticipated that "protecting" women by limiting their working hours might turn into a general restriction of women in the workplace rather than general protection of them (as indeed happened over the next half-century). He also unsuccessfully made what today sounds like a contemporary racial analogy by arguing:

. . . if the statute had forbidden employment for more than ten hours, of all persons of white color, the statute would have had application to all of that class, . . . no one would contend that the classification was reasonable or one that could be sustained.[17]

In 1908, only isolated feminists agreed with Fenton when he predicted the potential dangers ahead in the application of the sex-stereotyped defense of protective legislation contained in the *Muller* opinion. However, they could not prevail against the avalanche of positive publicity the decision received from the press and such prominent women advocates of protective legislation as Florence Kelley and Jane Addams and the influential middle-class women's groups with which they were associated.

It is easy to denigrate the long-term deleterious impact of *Muller,* in particular, and of protective legislation, in general, on job opportunities and advancement for women. We know now that protective-labor legislation as a concept and as a body of statutes strengthened sexual segregation and stratification patterns in the labor market, for such laws were based on the assumption that women would always be cheap, temporary, unskilled labor. Protective laws also helped define patterns of discrimination against female wage-earners, limited women's economic opportunities, and reinforced stereotypic notions of women as frail, passive, and dependent. Similarly, we know that those who supported protective legislation also stressed the reproductive and nurturing characteristics of women to the exclusion of other characteristics. This bolstered a highly traditional and restrictive definition of woman's role in society generally as well as in the workplace. Beyond any doubt *Muller* opened the door to gender bias in protective legislation. At the time, however, the decision was welcomed by Progressive reformers because in the short run it did improve some of the worst conditions women faced in an unregulated factory system. Moreover, further protective legislation that followed in the wake of *Muller* convinced a number of female activists that the needs of working women were being met by the courts.

The belief in the illusory positive aspects of *Muller* actually lulled such women into a state of complacency. Only a handful of equal rights feminists in 1908 saw the potential long-term danger of the *Muller* decision: it could be used to keep women from advancement on the job and out of some occupations altogether. This is, of course, exactly what happened over the years. The AFL almost immediately in 1914 reversed its initial support of protective legislation for women, men, and children and proceeded to use the biological differences between women and men as the basis for reducing competition from women and children in certain industries. It officially banished women from so-called men's jobs, such as streetcar conducting, printing, and bartending and sanctioned unequal pay for men and women even when the work was equal. From 1908 until the initial enforcement of Title VII of the 1964 Civil Rights Act in the 1970s, the AFL and other male-dominated unions fought to keep women from competing in the labor market on an equal basis with men.

In retrospect, therefore, despite the evidentiary breakthrough it represented at the time, it is possible to question the long-term wisdom of the Brandeis approach in *Muller*. Women have continued to experience economic discrimination because the Supreme Court presumed to establish policy on the basis of quasi-scientific data and its own "common knowledge" about the nature of women. However necessary was protective legislation at the time to ameliorate the worst features of the capitalistic factory system in the United States, we can now easily perceive the antifeminist and reactionary legal and economic implications of the "Brandeis brief." As has been the case so many times before (and after) in the history of women's legal and political reform, what appeared to be such a great liberal improvement resulted in unintended negative consequences.

It is also worth noting that the famous *Muller* decision based on the "Brandeis brief" actually represented an exception to the general run of Supreme Court decisions at that time. Generally, the justices refused to accept empirical data of a nonjudicial nature and expressed extreme skepticism about so-called expert witnesses. In other words, from around the turn of the century until the 1937 *West Coast Hotel* decision, the *Lochner* precedent prevailed except in cases involving women as long as minimum wages were not an issue. Laurence Tribe has pointed out that "while the Supreme Court invalidated much state and federal legislation between 1897 and 1939 [approximately 197 cases], more statutes in fact withstood due process attack in this period than succumbed to it." Under the influence of the Progressive movement, the Court held almost three times fewer state police-power statutes unconstitutional between 1889 and 1918 than it did between 1920 and 1930. [18] In other words, a higher percentage of state statutes designed to regulate socioeconomic conditions were invalidated by the Supreme Court after 1920 than before or during the height of the Progressive movement. One study has estimated that between 1868 and 1912 the justices struck down such legislation in slightly more than 6 percent of the total number of social-justice cases that they heard, while between 1920 and 1927 they ruled against 28 percent of them. However interpreted, "Lochnerism" was less significant a constitutional concept where women were concerned than where men were because of the exceptional case-law precedent set by *Muller*.

There is, nonetheless, something positive about the position of those well-educated and often well-to-do women in the Progressive movement who supported

*also an interventionist approach*

protective legislation for working women (and men). Theirs was a social or group approach to reform—in contrast to the individualism embodied in the right to vote—even though these female reformers limited their collective protection, by and large, to lower-class women and did not apply it to themselves. Their advocacy of this modern concept of collective justice should not be dismissed simply because it is so easy to criticize the long-term negative consequences of protective legislation. The fact that so many of them chose to lead single lives (8.8 percent) should also not be lost as the percentage of single women at the end of this century once again reaches unprecedented proportions. While historians have yet to analyze definitively the many sexual and societal ramifications that this unprecedentedly high number of unmarried women had on the First Women's movement, as well as the Progressive Era and other female educational and professional endeavors from the 1890s through the 1920s, it is clear that such women formed supportive networks with one another and had more time and energy to devote both to their own careers and to the cause of reform and peace than did their married counterparts. (The percentage of never-married single women over forty in the United States fell to a low of 4 percent in the 1950s and rose to 6 percent and 7 percent, respectively, in the 1960s and 1970s. By the middle of the 1980s it had fallen again to 4.8, but the number of single women over eighteen had jumped to a record high of 18.3 percent. No doubt, never-married and divorced, single women will have had an equally significant impact on American society by the turn of this century in the year 2000, but it probably will be exactly opposite that of 1900—with the feminization of poverty outstripping educational and professional advances.

Progressive women's ideology and goals are also difficult to appreciate today because they seem contradictory and ambiguous. On the one hand, Progressive women explicitly committed themselves to women's rights—the right to equal political participation and to the opportunity for meaningful, productive, and well-paid work. On the other hand, the very same women successfully set in motion legal constraints on women's rights in the workplace. Such women as Jane Addams, Florence Kelley, Julia Lathrop, and Margaret Dreier Robins established highly visible public careers; taught themselves to lobby, speak, and organize; learned the ins and outs of political power and the workings of the political process. But they did not practice what they preached *for themselves;* instead, they promoted what seems today an idealized and dangerously romantic vision of maternity, home, and family *for other women* (not unlike Phyllis Schlafly several generations later).[19] These Progressive female reformers simultaneously insisted that some women (usually themselves) were autonomous individuals and others had to be protected because they could not take care of themselves.

Despite all their shortcomings, the middle- and upper-class Progressive women who supported protective legislation spoke in a Victorian terminology about morality, maternity, feminine sensibilities, and virtue that struck a responsive chord in all women. Their language clearly indicates that they were trying to preserve a female haven in the home and in the workplace—rooted in social and biological feminine behavior—a haven from male culture and male institutions. According to Carroll Smith-Rosenberg,[20] this peculiarly effective female form of communication was lost in the 1920s. It has only been since the late 1960s that attempts to create a similarly unifying language and to preserve the best of female socialized behavior has come back into vogue in certain feminist circles.

## The Legacy of *Muller*

In the first decade after the 1908 *Muller* decision, protective-legislation patterns affecting all workers, regardless of sex, were not uniform. Some states that had taken antiprotective stands reversed themselves; others began to extend the doctrine of sex differences to obtain all kinds of protective and often excessively restrictive laws governing work hours for women. For example, Radice v. People of the State of New York, 264 U.S. 292 (1924), set the precedent for severely restricting night work for women on the grounds that it was "substantially and especially detrimental to the health of women."[21] This was an early example of the way in which protective legislation began to be used to restrict, rather than promote, occupational opportunity and choice for women. Among other things, *Radice* prevented women from working overtime if they wanted to. Following *Muller,* still other states tried to extend the doctrine to uphold minimum-wage laws for all workers, or at least for women and minors. Only in one isolated case did the Supreme Court come close to upholding minimum wages before being forced to do so under the political and economic pressures created by the Great Depression in the 1930s. In Bunting v. Oregon, 243 U.S. 426 (1917), the justices ruled that the state could not require men to work more than ten hours per day, but allowed three hours of overtime if the workers were paid time and a half. Because opponents argued that this statute really regulated wages rather than hours, the Court's opinion completely ignored *Lochner* and deferred to "legislative judgment" in this matter, even though it noted that there was "certain verbal plausibility in the contention that [the statute] was intended to permit thirteen hours' work if there be fifteen and one-half hours' pay."[22]

Brandeis and Josephine Goldmark also prepared this *amicus* brief for the NCL, using the same arguments about health, safety, morals, and welfare as in *Muller;* but because wages were involved in *Bunting,* they added that shorter hours were also economically desirable from the standpoint of greater worker efficiency and production. Moreover, their data were much more voluminous than those in the *Muller* brief by tenfold, consisting of 1,020 pages, 35 of which were an appendix on sources. Although Brandeis and Goldmark worked on the *Bunting* brief for the first six months of 1916, by the time it came to present it to the Supreme Court Brandeis had been appointed a justice. As a result, he turned the case over to Felix Frankfurter and took no part in the five-to-three decision upholding maximum hours (and, implicitly, a wage-minimum at least for overtime work). *Bunting* notwithstanding, five years later the Supreme Court struck down an explicit attempt to establish minimum wages for women in *Adkins v. Children's Hospital*, 261 U.S. 525 (1923). Again, NCL was involved as an *amicus curiae* and used the "Brandeis approach." This time Josephine Goldmark helped Felix Frankfurter prepare still another extensive socioeconomic brief.[23] Because wages and not hours were involved, the Court appeared much more concerned with freedom of contract *for employers* than with the welfare of the employees, as they had been in *Bunting*.

The justices found in *Adkins* that, while it was unconstitutional to have women work long hours because it would inhibit their ability to produce healthy children, it was equally unconstitutional to force employers to make "an arbitrary payment" or a minimum wage to ensure the continued health of mothers and their offspring. In *Muller*, women had to pay an economic price for future generations; in *Adkins*, employers did not. Consequently in *Adkins*, the Court not only distinguished previous maximum-hour decisions from minimum wages but also suggested that the "ancient inequality of the sexes, otherwise than physical . . . has continued [but] with diminishing intensity because of the Nineteenth Amendment." Ironically, this opinion asserted that suffrage had so completely ended women's civil inferiority that they no longer needed special protection in the workplace that would infringe on "their liberty of contract." In *Adkins*, the justices made one of their strongest arguments since *Lochner* in favor of freedom of contract as "the general rule and [state regulatory] restraint the exception . . . justified only by the existence of exceptional circumstance."[24] Objective judicial neutrality unclouded by male bias and corporate favoritism should have led the justices in *Adkins* to the conclusion that substandard wages and accompanying malnutrition would damage a woman's procreative potential as much, if not more, than working too many hours—as they had proclaimed in *Muller*.

The *Muller*, *Bunting*, and *Adkins* briefs were not based on what would today be considered scientific information about women. In his *Adkins* brief, Frankfurter, following Brandeis's lead in *Muller* and *Bunting*, appended 1,138 pages of jumbled statistical and qualitative data gathered by Goldmark to his legal arguments, outdoing the brief in *Bunting* by over one hundred pages. The unorthodox briefs in these three cases prevailed because they reinforced fundamental socioeconomic values that the justices used to arrive at these decisions. *Adkins*, in particular, has to be read in light of the decision in *Radice v. New York*, handed down the following year, restricting the right of women to work at night. *Radice* had discouraged women from participation in the work force by arguing that women needed to be protected from working at night. In *Adkins,* arguments in favor of protecting women were turned down because of the economic implications of guaranteeing a minimum wage. Even though female wages remained lower than those paid men for the same job anyway, some women might have been encouraged to enter the work force if a minimum wage had been upheld in *Adkins.* In the two 1920s cases—one validating (*Radice*) and one invalidating (*Adkins*) a state statute, the justices seemed to reach contradictory conclusions that women "should be protected only so far as it did not encourage their participation in the work force."[25]

Fourteen years later under the influence of the Great Depression and New Deal legislation, the Supreme Court reversed itself and finally granted minimum wages to women and minors in West Coast Hotel v. Parrish, 300 U.S. 379 (1937). Relying on *Muller* rather than *Adkins,* which it specifically overruled, the Court simplicitly downgraded its own freedom-of-contract doctrine in *West Coast Hotel* from the fundamental constitutional right that it had so confidently proclaimed over thirty years before in *Lochner* and again in 1923 in *Adkins.* In the midst of one of the worst depressions in the country's history, the justices took "judicial notice" of the impact of the "unparallel demands for relief" and finally recognized the "exploitation of a class of workers who are in an unequal position with respect to bargaining power and are thus relatively defenceless [*sic*] against the denial of a living wage." Noting that no Brandeis-like statistical case was presented in this case, they simply assumed that the state of Washington had calculated the relationship among inadequate wages paid by "unconscionable employers," the health of female workers, and the "burden for their support upon the community." The Court denied that the legislation was arbitrary because it did not apply to men, saying that the state had the right to "recognize degrees of harm . . . and it may confine its restrictions to those classes of cases where the need is deemed to be clearest"—in this instance, women.[26]

This disclaimer notwithstanding, *West Coast Hotel v. Parrish* marked the beginning of the end of strict judicial adherence to the freedom-of-contract doctrine that disadvantaged workers. This decision laid the legal foundation for the court's holding in 1941 that minimum-wage legislation for men was constitutional. In United States v. Darby, 312 U.S. 100 (1941), the Supreme Court finally ended its use of substantive due process to distinguish between women and men when it came to setting maximum hours and minimum wages.[27] However, some federal legislation during the Great Depression continued to discriminate against married working women and encouraged wage differentials between male and female workers.[28] In general, one form of so-called judicial neutrality with respect to working women fell victim to another as Congress and the Supreme Court responded to the Great Depression. Thus, the newly proclaimed constitutionality of minimum wages misleadingly came to be viewed by the courts as somehow ensuring equality between working women and men, despite the discriminatory application of protective legislation against women. By the end of the 1930s, such discrimination was a fact of American economic life, largely due to lower-court decisions encouraged and approved by many former suffragists and most male union leaders.

## The Demise of the First Women's Movement

Another interesting aspect of *Muller* is its indirect impact on the First Women's movement. Most political activists in NAWSA had concentrated their efforts in the first two decades of the twentieth century on obtaining suffrage. While NAWSA in general supported "good laws" on behalf of women workers, it had not concentrated on influencing state- or federal-court decisions on protective legislation. Usually its individual members supported such legislation through other organizations. After achieving its greatest political triumph in 1920 with the passage of the Nineteenth Amendment, the First Women's movement succumbed to many internal divisions that, this time, proved terminal.[29] Some fragmentation within the First Women's movement was inevitable after 1920, just as it had been in the 1870s. This time, however, no Supreme Court decisions or amendments to the Constitution (as had happened during Reconstruction) or other socioeconomic incident triggered a refocusing and reuniting process among female reformers. The fragmentation was so multifaceted that it was relatively easy for many women who decided to pursue narrower avenues of reform, peace work, or professional careers in the 1920s to become singled-minded in these pursuits to the degree that they lost any sense of collective whole. At the same time, this chaotic fragmentation actually produced an apolitical atmosphere under the guise of widespread volunteer political activity and special-interest lobbying (not unlike the 1980s). Underneath the chaos that destroyed the First Women's movement lurked a fundamental legal dispute that split it hopelessly into two increasingly ineffective camps during the interwar years—the issue of special versus equal rights in the form of protective legislation and the ERA.

Harbingers of this basic legal disagreement surfaced before and during World War I with the establishment of the militant National Woman's Party (NWP). Although following its foundation in 1890 there had been numerous arguments over strategy, tactics, and leadership within NAWSA, the most serious occurred in 1913 with the formation of the Congressional Union that became the NWP under Alice Paul's leadership. When Alice Paul's followers finally broke with

NAWSA, their tactical disagreement over how to obtain suffrage masked basic political, philosophical, legal, and even language style differences among women that quickly surfaced over the ERA.[30] While some of these fundamental divisions continue to the present day, the final disintegration of the First Women's movement occurred in large measure over the Equal Rights Amendment—a battle fought not only in the United States but also at international conferences in the 1920s and 1930s.

By 1920 equal rights followers of Alice Paul viewed suffrage as only the beginning, not the end, of woman's battle to obtain full citizenship. They no longer thought the Nineteenth Amendment was a panacea for women's or society's problems, although some of them tried to use their enfranchisement to participate in two-party politics on a par with men. More typically, however, members of the NWP continued to fight the sexist implications of protective legislation that applied only to women and to urge women to run for public office as independents or members of third parties. Initially, their voices had been drowned out before World War I by a sea of more moderate suffragists and female social welfare Progressives, representing special treatment of working women. Thus it fell to a handful of feminists in the 1920s, such as Paul, Anne Henrietta Martin, and Burnita Shelton Matthews, to take a more militant stand. These members of the NWP clearly saw that the vote was at best an inefficient tool and that all inequalities in the law pertaining to jury service; property, custody, and guardianship rights; marriage; divorce; and work had to be eradicated before women could truly exercise the right to vote in any meaningful manner.[31]

Above all, these radical women realized that the vote had not eliminated sex discrimination in American life, nor had protective legislation eliminated discrimination in the workplace. But in the 1920s, too few women appreciated these radical arguments or were interested enough in third-party politics to use their suffrage effectively by voting as a bloc. There were too few former militant suffragists to reorganize the First Women's movement on a national scale to carry on the systematic legal and political battles necessary to obtain full citizenship for women in the name of justice and humanity with the same fervor they had fought for the vote.

Even after more mainstream women as Jeannette Rankin, Edith Nourse Rogers, and Mary Norton successfully used their enfranchisement to participate in two-party politics, most women found that their attempts at direct partisan participation were not welcomed by men within the Republican or Democratic parties. Consequently, when such women as Maud Wood Park, Belle Sherwin, and Marguerite Wells formed the League for Women Voters as a successor to NAWSA, it was not to support more female candidates, but primarily to educate new voters and also to attain social-welfare legislation on behalf of women and children.

They were joined in this latter cause by the National Federation of Business and Professional Women, as well as by women involved in the labor union movement, especially those represented by the Women's Bureau created within the Department of Labor in 1920. In fact, this form of indirect (and often nonpartisan) political participation constituted the major form of political activity on the part of most women reformers in the interwar years.[32]

Because women did not vote as a bloc to produce the utopian society often promised by both groups of suffragists in the last years of their long battle for the right to vote, the suffrage victory came to be unfairly regarded as a hollow one even by some of the Nineteenth Amendment's staunchest supporters. It was, of course, a hollow victory for African-American women who, like black men since 1890, were also systematically denied the right to vote after 1920. So it is not without reason that suffrage came to be looked upon in many circles as a political victory that was a major moral failure (not unlike the attitude many in that decade developed toward the classic postwar attempt to legislate morality—Prohibition).

In any case, it is unfair to continue to fault women of the 1920s for not voting as a bloc or being plagued by divisions when gender-gap politics based on political unity among women is not much more a reality in the 1990s than it was then. For example, progressive suffragists, such as Jane Addams and Florence Kelley who had worked so hard for protective legislation for women, naturally refused to support the Equal Rights Amendment when it was introduced in the 1920s by Alice Paul's NWP. In their minds, support of complete legal equality with men would have negated the recently hard-won victories in the courts and state legislatures protecting women. It would also have forced them to reconsider the crucial question of the limitations of working within established capitalistic and patriarchal parameters to reform society. This they were not prepared to do.

The interwar years were indeed a confusing time for women. They still did not have true economic independence, equal social expectations, political experience, or even the educational and professional training necessary for obtaining leadership in politics. At the same time, they were faced with the postwar reaction against socioeconomic change disguised under the superficially liberating glitter of the Jazz Age and Freudian theories on sexuality. Finally, women were confronted by a depression in 1929 that turned "flappers" back into "Gibson girls" overnight, as traditional values were once more reasserted and men were given preference for jobs. The First Women's movement would scarcely have survived even had it not been plagued by disputes over strategy and tactics and personality conflicts between the militant supporters of equal rights and the more moderate defenders of protective legislation.[33] As noted previously, these two groups also divided over how best to engage in two-party politics in the 1920s. In that decade, the supporters of the ERA tended to be identified with the Republican party, while those in favor of protective legislation were more nonpartisan. In the course of the Great Depression and New Deal, these protectionists increasingly became associated with the Democratic party.

Although this split appeared to be similar to the one that had plagued the original generation of female reformers after the Civil War, in fact, the two groups—those representing individual and collective rights—had switched positions. In the 1870s the women who single-mindedly focused on obtaining the individual right to vote were not as tactically or philosophically radical as members of the NWP became in the 1920s, when they took up a broad spectrum of individual rights pointing to the arbitrary *diversity* of state laws affecting women.[34] Conversely, social-justice progressives, representing the successors to women like Anthony and Stanton who had continued to advocate collective improvements in status for women in the 1870s, found themselves tactically on the defensive in the 1920s because they had narrowed their sights to concentrate on class-based protective legislation for working women. By either standard, however, the First Women's movement ended on a less emancipatory and, hence, "deradicalized" phase in the 1920s than it had started in the mid-nineteenth century.[35] In part, this was because the seventy-two years it took to win suffrage made suffrage an overblown and much less significant issue by the time it was achieved than when it was first proposed.

Having discovered that they could not easily win political office in the face of male indifference or outright opposition, some women, within both the Democratic and Republican parties, began to exercise effective behind-the-scenes influence in 1920s and 1930s by becoming active in their respective parties' governing bodies. Initially, the best known were Democrats. Two of them, outside of Francis Perkins and Eleanor Roosevelt who became public figures in their own right, were Belle Moskowitz and Molly Dewson. Both practiced what has been called "feminine" rather than "feminist" politics and, like Perkins and Roosevelt, neither entered politics to advance their own careers. In the tradition of the Progressive Era, these women, and others like them, entered the political fray to promote certain social ideas or economic programs. Moskowitz, for example, served behind the scenes as one of Al Smith's closest political advisers when he was governor of New York in the 1920s and when he ran for the presidency in 1928. Molly Dewson, who was to become an even more powerful behind-the-scenes force in Democratic patronage politics as head of the Women's Division of the Democratic National Committee in the 1930s, once described Moskowitz as "Al Smith's tent pole." While Dewson herself came to be thought of as the "first female American political boss," she shared with Moskowitz, Perkins, and Eleanor Roosevelt an early interest and career in social work, a personal denial of any "careerism" ambitions, and the ability to promote causes rather than herself. As secretary of labor during the New Deal, Perkins became the first woman member of a U.S. cabinet. She previously had advised Franklin Roosevelt privately and through official appointments on labor matters when he was governor of New York.[36]

None of these female political activists in either party, however, achieved the indirect power, influence, and international recognition of Eleanor Roosevelt. In the end, as discussed in chapter 9, it was Eleanor Roosevelt who determined that the Democratic party would not support the ERA until the late 1940s; and she was the only woman with enough national stature and charisma to end the feud between ERA supporters and proponents of protective legislation following World War II. But her own protectionist convictions and advice from Molly Dewson prevented this.[37]

During the interwar years, it was difficult to argue that there was a clear-cut class, generational, or racial division among pro- and anti-ERA supporters, since the leaders on both sides were middle- and upper-middle-class women claiming that they were acting in behalf of all women. Paul's followers tended to be younger than the antiratification women during the 1920s and 1930s because young women, especially those who were career oriented and/or enjoying the sexual revolution of the 1920s, gravitated toward the ERA as a symbol of the new individual opportunities that they were experiencing. For them, equal rights became a very personal, individualistic goal as well as the major focus of the NWP. To confuse matters more, the National Association of Colored Women, led by Mary Church Terrell, a wealthy black suffragist, endorsed the ERA, while the National Council of Negro Women, founded by Mary McLeod Bethune, did not.[38]

In addition to obvious partisan politics along with some generational and class-conflict overtones, it is clear, in retrospect, that the philosophical differences between these two groups of interwar feminists led to legal, political, and rhetorical battles not only at home over protective legislation and the ERA but also at international conferences. Consequently, they fought at the League of Nations, The Hague, and later at the United Nations over treaties that included broad guarantees for the equal treatment of men and women, especially with regard to independent nationality status and naturalization procedures. In part this was because Eleanor Roosevelt's views on women were not those of the NWP. As the author of the first Equal Rights Amendment submitted to Congress in 1923, Paul and her followers insisted that female equality and citizenship be on the agenda at all international conferences by repeatedly introducing an Equal Rights Treaty, which Paul also wrote. Until the late 1930s, they were more successful in creating legal texts and in arguing for equal rights at Pan-American conferences than they were in the United States. In this sense, members of the NWP, such as Doris Stevens and Jane Norman Smith, became better known and respected abroad as international feminists than they were at home. Both before and after becoming First Lady, therefore, Eleanor Roosevelt opposed the activities of the NWP on domestic and foreign affairs between the wars, out of the conviction that endorsement of a blanket Equal Rights Amendment would endanger working women around the world. However, in 1948 she finally accepted a compromise with NWP and Third World women representatives in the wording of the United Nations Declaration of Human Rights—accepting the term "all people" in place of "all men." Nonetheless, the divisiveness that the debate over equal rights created among U.S. women activists continued at home long after it had been settled at the United Nations.[39]

By 1920, women in the United States had more political, legal, educational, and economic opportunities than they had had in 1865. But they still had not achieved constitutional equality before the law with men. But, as in the past, only the more farsighted feminists of the 1920s realized that full emancipation still lay ahead and that certain achievements, like the vote, had been too little, too late. Unfortunately, the leaders of NWP, like the First Feminists of the 1870s, narrowed their initial collective approach to equal rights by focusing primarily on the ERA, while more moderate feminists fragmented their energies into a variety of male-dominated liberal causes that, at best, could only marginally improve the socioeconomic and legal status of women. Between the 1920s and the 1960s, there was no congressional legislation that made gender or full citizenship for women a central issue; the Nineteenth Amendment remains the only successful attempt to include women by sex in the Constitution. Except for the revival of support for the ERA, when the Second Women's movement emerged in the late 1960s it was not "grounded" in the issues that had caused the First Women's movement to "run aground" in the 1920s and 1930s.

Clearly the most significant aspect of the disagreement between those who supported the Equal Rights Amendment to the Constitution in the early 1920s and those who did not is that it created a "constitutional-rights-consciousness" division among women reformers that lasted for over fifty years. None of the original participants in this internecine struggle over the ERA anticipated how fundamentally legalistic or long-lasting and personally embittering their dispute would be. While both Republican and Democratic women worked side by side for reform in the Progressive Era, by the time of the Great Depression and the New Deal, reform activity (except for some very prominent and wealthy Republican women supporting Alice Paul and the ERA) increasingly became identified with the Democratic women who followed first Florence Kelley and Jane Addams and later Eleanor Roosevelt. Thus, the partisan division over the ERA was, in part, perpetuated before and after World War II by partisanship, even though both parties endorsed the amendment beginning in the 1940s. In the 1920s and 1930s, there was an increasing tendency for older (and younger) professional and business women (often Republicans) to support the ERA. Until the early 1970s, working-class women and union leaders (usually Democrats) opposed it, as did the aging generation of Progressive women reformers who had originally supported protective legislation. These partisan positions were reversed in the course of the fight for the Twenty-seventh Amendment after 1972. By and large, those who originally opposed the ERA had belonged to both the suffrage movement and the social-justice wing of the Progressive movement. This meant that for years before winning the right to vote, these women had fought long and hard through litigation and legislation to protect working women, men, and children. Their later opposition to the ERA stemmed largely from their perception that it was based too much on a selfish, individual approach to reform rather than on their own ostensibly more collective, if condescending, view of how to improve the lives of disadvantaged women. One of the few Progressive women reformers who tried to carve out a middle ground for herself and others in this debilitating debate over special versus equal rights was the historian Mary Ritter Beard.

## Mary Ritter Beard and the Origins of the ERA Debate

Until most recently Mary Ritter Beard was usually remembered as historian Charles Beard's wife who collaborated with him on a half-dozen influential textbooks from the 1920s through the 1940s. Interestingly, she did not produce the book for which she is best known, *Woman as Force in History: A Study in Traditions and Realities,* until 1946 at the end of their long collaborative career, although she wrote several other books and many articles on women.[40] As noted in chapter 4, her legal theories about equity jurisprudence in eighteenth- and nineteenth-century America have been studied more carefully by scholars since the onset of the Second Women's movement. However, Beard's specific ideas about the Equal Rights Amendment continue to be largely ignored. The relationship between her views on equity in the eighteenth and nineteenth centuries and equal rights in the twentieth century is important for understanding not only the defeat of the ERA but also the reemergence in the 1980s of the debate among feminists over special rights versus equal rights.

Born in 1876 to Eli and Narcissa Lockwood Ritter, Mary Ritter Beard was the third of six surviving children and the elder of two daughters. As a lawyer in Indianapolis, her father was active in progressive politics, especially the temperance movement. In addition to being a founder of the Anti-Saloon League, Eli Ritter also engaged in Methodist church reform activities, although he had been raised a Quaker. Mary Beard's mother taught school briefly before her marriage, but in typical late nineteenth-century fashion little else is known about her once she assumed her duties as wife and mother. Her father's progressive politics rather than his Quaker principles seem to have influenced Mary Beard most as she grew up in Indianapolis. In fact, in later life her letters reveal strongly antireligious sentiments.[41]

All the Ritter children attended DePauw University, which still is a Methodist institution, and there she met Charles Beard. She majored in German language and literature and studied Roman law before her graduation in 1897. She taught German in Greencastle, Indiana, until 1900 when she married Charles Beard, and they immediately moved to England where he had been attending Oxford University. While in London, the Beards met the Pankhursts and a variety of other Socialists and anarchists who greatly influenced their thinking, especially with respect to working-class problems and economic theories. Under the influence of Walter Vrooman and his wife Anne, all four of them contributed articles to the *Young Oxford,* a publication of the Ruskin Hall movement. Mary and Charles Beard's lifelong collaboration as authors stems from this period. Her articles from this period stressed a theme she was later to abandon and criticize other feminists for subscribing to—namely, theories about women's oppression. She was hopeful, however, that technology and education would allow women to advance and contribute a "more humane element" to society.[42]

Their first child, Miriam, was born in 1901, and the Beards returned to New York in 1902. Both of them promptly enrolled for graduate work at Columbia, but Mary discontinued her studies in 1904, never completing the degree she began in sociology. Charles received his doctorate that same year and taught history at Columbia for the next thirteen years. Their second child, William, was born in 1907. Around this time Mary became increasingly active in the suffrage movement in New York, joining first the Equality League for Self-Supporting Women (later the Women's Political Union), which tried to organize working women in behalf of suffrage. She also worked for the Women's Trade Union League of New York. By 1910 she had joined the New York City Suffrage Party and edited its magazine, *The Woman Voter,* until 1912. In 1912 and 1913, she briefly worked for the Wage Earners League, another working woman's suffrage organization, where her organizational talents were recognized by Alice Paul who, as head of the Congressional Committee of NAWSA, was then forming the Congressional Union, which later became the NWP.[43]

As a member of the executive committee of the Congressional Committee, Beard both followed and pushed Paul along the lines of militant feminism and radical politics, participating in demonstrations as only an upper-class progressive matron could. According to her late daughter's recollection:

Both Charles and Mary paraded in Washington, D.C. on March 3, 1913, in support of Suffrage. Charles walked with the men, while Mary in a green cape with gold tassels marshalled a section of Negro women, whom she had insisted in including in the demonstration. The Beard children rode on horse-drawn floats, while the cook joined Mary.[44]

Mary Beard actively supported the Congressional Union until passage of the Nineteenth Amendment, but Charles apparently prevented her from taking part in any other major demonstrations on the grounds that it was not safe. Aside from her promotion of working women in the cause of suffrage, she was most effective as a fund-raiser among wealthy women and as an adviser on politics. Ultimately, however, Beard broke with Paul and the NWP over the Equal Rights Amendment. She vociferously opposed the ERA from 1921 until four years before her death in 1954. But by the time she finally approved of it, she was too old and ill to advocate passage in any effective way.[45]

In the intervening years, however, she continued to collaborate on textbooks with her husband, to write books independently on women, and to lecture widely on the importance of women's history. Significantly, her first book on women did not appear until 1931, when she was fifty-five years old; her last was in 1953, when she was seventy-seven. Perhaps her most farsighted endeavor was the attempt she made from 1935 until 1941 to create an international Women's Center for Women's Archives (WCWA).[46] In the course of this project, she not only set in motion the first national attempt to collect and preserve women's papers regardless of race or class (ironically, she destroyed many of her own papers) but also advocated the establishment of what can only be viewed now as women's studies programs, the publication of something similar to *The Biography of Notable American Women,* a mass-circulation women's magazine, and a theory of history about women that remains as controversial as it is fruitful for discussing women's contributions to society over time.[47] The latter was not published until after most of these other farsighted projects had failed.

Mary Beard's career exhibited three basic characteristics—all of which are important for understanding her middle position in the ERA-versus-protective-legislation dispute. First, both she and her husband should be viewed as outsiders. Coming from Indiana to the eastern corridor via London, neither ever quite fit socially or politically in the radical or the conservative wealthy groups with which they came to associate. In Mary's case, she experienced this "outsideness" more acutely because she never established any permanent institutional or intellectual base of affiliation. Although Charles left Columbia in 1917, he established other, if temporary, institutional affiliations and remained in constant communication with a variety of scholarly specialists about his work.

Perhaps the greatest deficiency in Mary Beard's writing stems from the fact that her manuscripts were not subjected to constructive criticism from academic colleagues. Instead, she discussed them, if at all, with women who were usually not trained historians and who did not offer critical advice. This is especially noticeable in some of the more unintelligible passages in her writings. Hence, most of Mary Beard's public and private statements are peppered with dense, unclear passages and vague concepts. For example, her book *Woman as Force in History* was widely, but negatively, received even by women reviewers in 1946.[48] As an outsider she also seemed defensive about the fact that she had not completed her doctorate, often to the point of criticizing formal higher education for women.

A second basic characteristic of Mary Ritter Beard's career is related to the first—that is, to her sense of being an outsider. This "outsideness," or what she later referred to as her "waywardness,"[49] transformed itself into a middle political position as far as organized women's groups were concerned. Indeed, she viewed herself as a broker between the two major feuding factions of the First Women's movement that developed after 1920 over protective legislation and the original Equal Rights Amendment. As a result, Beard prided herself on belonging to neither camp. And the middle position she so carefully constructed for herself in the 1920s and 1930s became an important factor for understanding her continued opposition to the ERA following World War II.

The third influence that Charles Beard and Mary Beard had on each other's careers stems from their close intellectual collaboration. It is almost impossible to distinguish their ideas because by mutual agreement she destroyed most of their private papers. One thing is clear: Charles Beard showed little if any interest in cultural history before their collaboration on *The Rise of American Civilization* in 1927. But as Charles shifted from economic determinism to idealism and historical relativism in his own work, Mary seemed to follow suit. Despite strong circumstantial evidence to the contrary, for example, she vehemently denied that he had influenced her opposition to the ERA.[50] The impact of international politics and the Great Depression in the interwar years on the thoughts of both cannot be underestimated. But who led whom along their intellectual journey or whether it was a reciprocal course they steered cannot be proven from their existing papers or manuscripts.

These three conditions—Beard's "outsider's mentality," reinforced by lack of institutional or intellectual affiliation; her middle position with respect to women's politics; and the tangled influence she and her husband had on one another's historical interpretations—are the keys to understanding the nature and significance of her opposition to the ERA. In a 1921 letter, Mary Ritter Beard marshaled seven related arguments against a federal Equal Rights Amendment then being considered by the NWP. First, "it would overthrow all protective industrial legislation for women." Second, she stated that "I can't see why it wouldn't also conscript women for war." Third, her trip abroad following World War I had turned her against the type of "industrial equality" where the "women sweep the streets and till the land while the men drink in the cafes." Fourth, the essence of democracy [had become] that the whole nation fights as the king and barons and mercenaries once fought." She said women were rushing to recruit in Silesia and "there will be battalions of death outside Russia; but I am not interested one bit if that is all democracy has to offer." Fifth, realizing that "one must carefully word the state ERAs or the whole matter of protective legislation will be thrown into the courts," she wanted a bill that would get rid of "undisputed sex disabilities while leaving room for protective industrial legislation for those who believe in that." Sixth, Beard insisted that she was not an "ultra feminist" on equal rights "because in my mind children do add complexity to women that they cannot add to men and I see no way of removing it entirely for the best interests of both sexes as well as [the] well be[ing] of the children." Finally, in the margin of this typed letter, she handwrote: "Then too women have little sense of humor about the actions and works of men. Half [of the] goals [of] men are ridiculous[,] and pure imitation [of them by women] is both infantile and unintelligent a'ha!"[51]

## Equal Rightists versus Protectionists

As early as 1921, therefore, Mary Beard had privately opposed imitating men—a concept that became a cornerstone of her later historical works on women. Her 1921 letter captures all of the arguments she ever made against the ERA before she changed her mind in 1954. It shows that her opposition was not simply based on her support of protective legislation, as so often was the case among Progressive reformers (although this was a key element of the social feminist argument against the ERA). In contrast, Beard does not actually qualify either as a special rights or an equal rights feminist. In fact, as these two factions, which Beard referred to as the "equal rightists" and the "protectionists," became deadlocked over the ERA in the 1920s, 1930s, and 1940s, Beard thought of herself as being aloof and in the middle between them. She forcefully indicated this in a long, convoluted 1937 letter to feminist biographer Alma Lutz, who had asked Beard to contribute her opinion to the NWP's publication *Equal Rights* about the Women's Charter. This proclamation represented a defensive and unsuccessful attempt by those advocating protective legislation to substitute their own legal document for the ERA. In refusing to support the Charter, Beard replied to Lutz:

I deeply appreciate your goodwill in inviting me to state my position with respect to the Women's Charter for the readers of Equal Rights and the members of the National Woman's Party. The National Woman's Party has offered me its floor on several important occasions to "speak my piece" and this is another evidence of its consent to hear, even though what it hears may be a variant on what it defends. In accepting another invitation, I am dividing my statement into three parts with a view to being both clear and emphatic.

1) As to the past. Up to this hour I have held aloof from the factional strife within the woman movement despite the continuous attempts that have been made to smoke me out of my "ivory tower." And I have held aloof for the reason that the two major factions—the two great parties I may say—have both seemed to me very inadequate as to program. Thus the equal rightists, I have thought, ran the risk of positively strengthening anachronistic competitive industrial processes; of supporting, if unintentionally, ruthless laissez faire; of forsaking humanism in the quest for feminism as the companion-piece of manism. The women's bill of rights is, unhappily, long overdue. It should have run along with the rights of man in the eighteenth century. Its drag as to time of official proclamation is a drag as to social vision. And even if equal rights were now written into the law of our land, it would be so inadequate today as a means to food, clothing and shelter for women at large that what they would still be enjoying would be equality in disaster rather than in realistic privilege. This I have said at National Woman's Party meetings and banquets, in a voice sometimes decidedly shaky because it was emotionally hard to appear to be unsympathetic with the fierce pressure for a woman's bill of rights and emotionally hard to appear critical of many women for whom I have both affection and high regard. However I could not throw my heart and energy into the mere struggle for equality on a basis of laissez faire in the twentieth century.

Nor could I throw my heart and energy into the mere struggle for a minimum wage, even for women. The protectionists satisfied me as little as the rightists, sorry as I was to be so fussy. The minimum wage implies a wage and leaves out of account the millions of unemployed to whom a wage at all is sheer utopia. It has seemed to me to represent too complacent, too sentimental an acceptance of capitalism and to be too consistent with the economic rule of a plutocracy. Neither equal rights nor a minimum wage for women could make a dent on such an anti-social American labor system as that pictured, for instance, in Grace Hutchins' "Women Who Work."

In short, while I have always recognized the value and "justice" of the equal rights principle and lamented its historic lag, and while I have also recognized the value of restraining exploitation, since neither the one program nor the other struck at the issue of employment itself—that basis of all culture—I have lacked the zest for throwing myself into the fray of the factional dispute among women—until this hour.

2) As to the present. Now I am hurled into its center through no intention of my own. For that even Mary Vankleeck gives the explanation in a letter to the New York Times. For the inaccurate publicity with respect to the Women's Charter, she offers the correct version. I desire therefore to call a halt, as far as I am concerned, on further ill-feeling engendered by that mistake—for the sake of the future.

3) As to the future. Being thrust into this fray and kept in this fray despite Miss Vankleeck's publicity correction, from the necessity for revealing my attitude at least, to both factions of women, I offer my challenge to both factions within the woman movement. For their common inadequacy against women's and democracy's ruthless enemies—war, fascism, ignorance, poverty, scarcity, unemployment, sadistic criminality, racial persecution, man's lust for power and woman's miserable trailing in the shadow of his frightful ways—I offer the ideal of adequacy. No doubt we should have our woman's rights to equal opportunity but with them let us combine the demand for decency of life and labor all

round and security if possible to attain. Let us fight neither over the crumbs that fall from plutocratic tables nor over the right to be plutocrats dropping crumbs.

Let us demand, for example, a set-up in every industry which will carry with that industrial set-up a high minimum of labor reward without discrimination of sex, widening the laws which exist and creating the broad principle of the irreducible minimum from the start in the formulation of national codes for industry now in process of revival and development. Let us go beyond equality in the exploitive privilege to equality in social leadership designed to win security for all. Let us even go beyond equality of leadership and be creative leaders in the vanguard, if men drag along steeped in their vested interests so heavily that they cannot see humanity for seeing money profits and dictatorial power. If we will not so envisage our future, no Bill of Rights, man's or woman's, is worth the paper on which it is printed, for eventually, if not immediately, democracy will go down with plutocracy into militarism and the time will have passed when women can get together even to blow off steam about rights and protection—even about a Women's Charter. Men will win—and the cruel types of men whom no woman should desire to equal.

This letter by Beard to Lutz did not appear in *Equal Rights* during 1937. Instead, the 15 January issue simply quoted Beard's surprise at learning that she had been listed as a sponsor of the Women's Charter. Accompanying her statement was one by a New York *World-Telegram* columnist saying that it was well known that "America's most distinguished historian, who has said all along that she belongs to 'neither camp or faction to the exclusion of the other,' is not a person who changes her opinions overnight." [52]

In essence, Beard was one of the few interwar feminists who tried to break through the time-lag under which women reformers have labored since the American Revolution. She saw that both sides in the women's movement were trying for too little, too late. Or, as she once summarized the situation: "They [feminists] rejoiced to receive institutional education just at the time when it had lost its momentum and become hopelessly formalized; they got the vote when it had become least effective, owing to the power of the so-called invisible government; they entered remunerative positions at the period when big business was dropping into a deep airpocket; they made their main intellectual drive on masculine knowledge at the very stage of man's intellectual collapse." [53]

## The "Eternal Feminine Quality"

Beard suggested to women that they go "beyond equality" in her 1937 letter to Lutz. By this Beard meant that she wanted women to create the future on the basis of the "eternal feminine quality." Her definition of this phrase maintained that care giving always be at the center of things: "that is, the care of life—and, unless the growth of positive knowledge and the humane application of science during the past three hundred years are a delusion and a mistake, governments and economic institutions, all the arts of comfort and delight, will revolve around the care of life, renewing themselves at that fountain of eternal youth, whence come healing waters for despair and cynicism—the enduring belief that it is good to live, to love, to suffer and to labor." [54]

For Beard, therefore, the "eternal feminine" was the concern for the care of life. Thus, she made what is often dismissed today as an essentialist argument—namely, that women's nurturing qualities were at the very core of humanity's struggle for civilization. What appears as essentialism was more likely an early U.S. version of relational feminism because Beard perceived that women's partic-ipation in the reform activities of the Progressive Era in the early 1900s was a natural extension of their socialized roles "as givers of life, as the mothers of humanity . . . to promote the welfare of humanity." She urged women in the 1930s to take the lead in restructuring society in the midst of the Great Depres-sion by using their traditional role as care givers" through "communal organiza-tion . . . [and] through a surviving concern for primordial realities." Beard insisted that "concern for the care and protection of life [was] the primary interest of women." [55]

The idea of a community of courageous women was one of the most consistent and enduring features of Mary Ritter Beard's writings and early political activism —namely, the search for female culture, female integration into history, and the importance of female community and associationalism. Consequently, she was as opposed to the "self-interested individualism" of the equal rightists as she was to the complacent reformism of the protectionists. She never wavered in this com-mitment until the very end of her life, when she was no longer a political activist. Although Beard privately and reluctantly agreed to the ERA in a private letter written during October 1954, even her daughter remained unaware of this belated change in her position. Thus, her opposition to the ERA remained a constant even as she changed her actions and ideas on other matters. For ex-ample, in carving out a middle course for herself between the special rights and equal rights feminists during the 1920s, 1930s, and 1940s, Beard switched from being a feminist activist to a feminist historian and abandoned the subjection theory she had used to justify suffrage before World War I. [56]

All these activities and changed attitudes stemmed from Beard's enduring conviction that through communal activities women would finally find their true place and significance in history. Beard saw the potential power of community work represented in the actions of early female Progressives. In 1916 she wrote in *Woman's Work in Municipalities:*

This wider social program is now on the horizon of all those women who supplement individualistic morality by social morality and attempt to understand the causes which operate on men and women in masses. Where the women have this larger vision, they are demanding to know the facts—the plain, unvarnished facts. They will not be put off by a

"There, there, now," or "The time is not propitious." We see women everywhere backing movements for commissions to study the social evil in all its aspects, individual and social, and where such commissions are established we frequently find women serving on them or cooperating in the investigation.[57]

In the final analysis, Beard's writings display not one but two views on equality, both based on her own interpretations of history. The first was skewed by her excessively pessimistic view of post–World War I Socialist and Communist experiments in eastern Europe and later by the Great Depression and rise of fascism in Germany and Italy. These events led her to oppose "leveling" of women by any state policy, which she saw taking place in the name of industrial equality. Thus, Beard objected to the ERA *in part* because she did not believe that equality could or should be legislated. She also feared that such legislation or a constitutional amendment (such as Prohibition had demonstrated) would result in a kind of rigid, legalistic uniformity as opposed to a more fluid type of social justice based on the notion of equity, which takes into account individual differences. In the 1920s she negatively associated this "leveling" effect of industrial equality with certain Socialist and Communist theories. Later, in the 1930s, she associated "the business of leveling up the women" with the impact of the Great Depression at home and abroad, with the worst example being the repression of feminists and nonfeminists alike in Nazi Germany. In short, one reason Beard opposed the ERA involved her distrust of patriarchal states during the interwar years that promised to establish equalitarian systems.[58]

Beard also opposed the ERA because of another historical view that she held. While the first was rooted in events of the twentieth century, that second was rooted in the nineteenth. Specifically, she thought that nineteenth-century feminist ideology had become counterproductive when it began to focus on obtaining absolute equality of rights with men. Over and over again she warned against "complacency with the adequacy of sheer equality," especially in hard economic times such as the United States experienced in the 1930s. She believed that the demand for absolute equality with men, as represented by the NWP's support of the ERA, was based on an acceptance of the subjection or victim-view of history. For Beard, this constituted a perversion of the humanistic ethics symbolized in the 1848 Declaration of Sentiments. The "feminist program of 1848," Beard said in a 1940 Women's Centennial Address, had initially "reflected human values as well as a flair for rights."[59]

Because of the sensitivity of the 1848 generation of women to poverty and ignorance, Beard thought that they were concerned not only with personal rights and legal privileges but also with the general welfare as it related collectively to them as women. But as the nineteenth century drew to a close, the tyranny of a new dogma about women [as victims] had become so rigid that men and women alike were subdued to its autocracy and under its dominance women's quest for equality with men in democratic rights drove forward as the acme of intelligence about women. This was the dogma of woman's subjection to man throughout the ages of the past and in its formulation jurists, judges, and politicians were largely responsible. The more women accepted it as an interpretation of their history the more men accepted it, until in the silences of college circles and in the clamor of the marketplace for talk and writing it became a fixed idea as the truth about women in history.[60]

In summary, Beard thought that the women of 1848 had initiated a mindless pursuit of equality. Then, the NWP, without questioning that historical precedent, became more concerned with emulating male standards of power and prestige than with creating a better society (based on her own ubiquitous definition of the "eternal feminine"). Despite these reasons for opposing the ERA, Beard did not oppose all, or even most, legal rights for twentieth-century women. Accordingly, Beard told Ellen Woodward in 1939 that she realized that " 'rights' need[ed] emphasizing. I often wonder whether others believe me that rights are the clear logic of my insistence that women have always helped to make history and are indispensables in the whole process." Although she worried that her meaning of rights was being misunderstood (and it was), she, nonetheless, was determined to continue to make what she called "clear statements of the imperative of rights." What Beard opposed was any leveling system of equality that would impose juridical standarization at the expense of individual, gender, and class differences. At the same time, she opposed the "self–interested individualism in careering" of professional women.[61]

At this point, there appears to be a contradiction in her thinking if we assume that, like freedom, equality is indivisible. How could she oppose general equality and not support individual equality? In fact, it is not a contradiction because, as noted in chapter 1, according to the canons of American political, philosophical, and legal thought equality *is* a divisible concept. Beard opposed neither equality of rights nor equality of opportunity for women as long as these approaches to equality did not become ends in themselves or as long as they were not viewed as panaceas by or for women. As for equality of esteem, Beard was convinced that in the seventeenth and eighteenth centuries in America and even in earlier time periods in Europe, women had been accorded more esteem through a variety of equity procedures and collective actions than they were to experience in the nineteenth or twentieth centuries. She realized that the outer limits of "feminist" activity in any time period were determined by the degree to which women narrow the gap between themselves and equality of esteem. Ironically, equality of esteem, or respect, is a necessary prerequisite for obtaining equality of results, which, of course, Beard approved, so long as it was not defined in purely individualistic or leveling terms.

Although Mary Beard highly valued examples of equality of esteem accorded women of the past, she did not believe that simply according women the rights of men would add to their intrinsic esteem, especially on the eve of U.S. entrance into World War II when male political systems appeared to have become more violent and inhumane at the same time that they also had become more litigious. Finally, Beard categorically rejected making "man as the measure of excellence." By this she meant she could not accept equality of results based on male standards. She would, however, accept such equality if it were based on female caregiving notions of culture and community (the "eternal feminine"). In fact, her support of female standards for achieving equality of results was very radical and was at the heart of her opposition to the ERA, which she thought would result in more women becoming bad imitations of men.[62]

I have argued that these legal distinctions are rooted in Beard's study of history —in her determination, if you will, to view contemporary life as good or bad imitations of past historical phenomena. Theories about the differences between how men and women are socialized to think and behave, many of which are summarized in Carol Gilligan's book, *In a Different Voice*,[63] offer insights for understanding Beard's opposition to the ERA and even her confused language and syntax. First, Gilligan's hypothesis about moral development represents a way to explain how the ERA became associated in Beard's mind with the *uncaring indifference* represented by traditional patriarchal concepts of justice, based on individual rights and rules rather than collective care-giving responsibility and webs of interconnectedness. Second, Beard expressed her legal views in a distinctly different way from traditional legal writings on equality and equity. She literally spoke in a "different voice."

Obviously, I am making an ex post facto case in applying Gilligan's theories to Beard's ideas and writing style, but her concern with the "eternal feminine," which led to supposed contradictions in her ideas about equality, makes much more sense in light of Gilligan's and other object-relations theories about the difference between male and female psychological, moral, and linguistic development. Using Gilligan, however, it is fairly easy to reconcile Beard's social and legal arguments against the ERA with her views about female culture and community because she was clearly committed to a relational, or collective, brand of feminism. For whatever reason, however, she never recognized that the equal rights feminists of the NWP in fighting for the ERA dropped much of their earlier commitment to the subjection theory of women's history in the 1930s, just as she had. It was the special rights or protective-legislation feminists who continued to use this language of the victim after World War I. Why she did not discern this change in NWP rhetoric I simply do not know.

Nonetheless, Beard tried to bridge the legal gap between selective protectionism, on the one hand, and "self-interested" individualism, on the other—to establish a middle position for herself—because she realized that the two extreme positions were destroying what she continued all her life to call the "woman movement." Not until the 1980s have some feminist historians and laywers similarly questioned whether the contemporary single-minded pursuit of individualistic equal rights with men, as represented by the ERA, was not ultimately as reformist as was the equally single-minded pursuit of protective legislation for working women in the early twentieth century. Both, after all, represent liberal legal solutions to problems that require going beyond equality and protection to equity. Mary Ritter Beard realized this in 1958 without successfully conveying this important message to others.

Before the collective, rather than individualistic, pursuit of justice for all women (not only those designated as disadvantaged) could be fully developed or clearly enough articulated by Beard, however, the supporters of protective legislation and equal rights divided into two irreconcilable camps that fought each other to a standstill from the 1920s down to the early 1970s—thus becoming the major underlying cause of the demise of the First Women's movement and delaying the start of the Second Women's movement. Until the third and fourth periods in women's constitutional development played themselves out, few feminist reformers could think about going beyond the boundaries of liberal legalism to improve their constitutional status, as Mary Beard did so long ago. During these same decades, aside from cases involving protective legislation, there were few significant Supreme Court decisions that focused on gender; those that did usually barred women from a wide variety of activities, such as the right to tend bar and to serve on juries. Not surprisingly, arguments that had been used successfully to prevent females from practicing medicine and law in the nineteenth century were adapted between 1908 and 1963 in a last-ditch effort to confine women to their private sphere.

## The Constitutional Rights of Female Bartenders and Jurors

In 1948, for example, the Supreme Court upheld a state statute that denied women the right to be bartenders unless they were wives or daughters of male tavern owners. Although state and federal judges ignored or attempted to differentiate this opinion forbidding "all women from working behind a bar," as late as 1970 the Supreme Court again approved its 1948 position.[64] The most direct challenge issued to the Supreme Court to reconsider its sex-based discrimination in the area of liquor sales came in 1971 in a California case, *Sail'er Inn, Inc. v. Kirby*. In a most far-reaching decision, the state supreme court declared:

Today most bars, unlike the saloons of the Old West, are relatively quiet, orderly and respectable places patronized by both men and women. Even if they were not, many bars employ bouncers whose sole job is to keep order in the establishment. . . . Women must be permitted to take their chances along with men when they are otherwise qualified and capable of meeting the requirements of their employment. . . . We can no more justify denial of the means of earning a livelihood on such a basis than we could deny all women drivers' licenses to protect them from the risk of injury by drunk drivers. Such tender and chivalrous concern for the well-being of the female half of the adult population cannot be translated into legal restrictions on employment opportunities for women. . . . Laws which disable women from full participation in the political, business and economic arenas are often characterized as "protective" and beneficial. Those same laws applied to racial or ethnic minorities would readily be recognized as invidious and impermissible. *The pedestal upon which women have been placed has all too often, upon closer inspection, been revealed as a cage.* We conclude that the sexual classifications are properly treated as suspect, particularly when those classifications are made with respect to a fundamental interest such as employment (emphasis added).[65]

The Supreme Court of the United States has never ruled on an appeal of *Sail'er*. In any case, as noted in chapter 7, applications of Title VII have voided most of this kind of discriminatory legislation.

The Supreme Court has, however, revised its views on the right of women to serve on juries. Under common law, jury duty in colonial America was exclusively the preserve of white males, except in special cases when women panels examined or heard testimony from female litigants. Then, in 1879, the Supreme Court held that the exclusion of African-Americans from juries denied them equal protection and due process under the Fourteenth Amendment. In this same decision, however, the justices specifically said that states could continue to "confine selection [of jurors] to males," in keeping with their notion that the Fourteenth Amendment did not apply to sex—only to race.[66] In 1884 in *Rosencrantz v. Territory of Washington*, a female defendant who had been indicted by a grand jury in the territory of Washington charged that the presence of married women in that body was unconstitutional. The territorial supreme court ruled to the contrary, saying that since women could vote in the area and control property under the local married women's act, they were indeed both "qualified electors" and "householders."[67]

Judge Turner so strongly dissented that three years later the same court overruled its original decision and barred women from jury duty, as was the common practice in most states and territories at the time.[68] In light of its subsequent influence, Judge Turner's 1884 dissenting opinion in Rosencrantz represented a milestone in the history of male bias in judicial decisions. He argued that married women could not be either "householders" or jurors, despite the

advanced ideas of the nineteenth century, because they were unfitted by physical constitution and mental characteristics to assume and perform the civil and political duties and obligations of citizenship. . . . The liability to perform jury duty is an obligation not a right. In the case of a woman, it is not necessary that she should accept the obligation to secure or maintain her rights. If it were, I should stifle all expression of the repugnance that I feel that seeing her introduced into associations, and exposed to influences which, however others regard it, must, in my opinion, shock and blunt those fine sensibilities, the possession of which is her chiefest charm [sic], and the protection of which . . . is her most sacred right. . . . The husband was not only the head of the family at common law, because under the law he had the right to be obeyed by all the family, including the wife, but because of inherent and acquired differences between himself and wife in mental and physical constitution. . . . I believe that the facts I have mentioned obtain to this day, and that they operate and will continue to operate to give the husband paramount authority in the household . . . until an upheaval of nature has reversed the position of man and woman in the world. Legislative enactment would not make white black, nor can it provide the female form with bone and sinew equal in strength to that with which nature has provided man. No more can it reverse the law of cause and effect, and clothe a timid, shrinking woman, whose life theater is and will continue to be and ought to continue to be, primarily the home circle, with the masculine will and self-reliant judgment of a man.[69]

Not until after World War I and the passage of the Nineteenth Amendment did the question of female eligibility for jury service again appear in numerous litigations. By then women could vote; consequently, it appeared that they were finally "qualified electors" under most state statutes. However, most state legislatures did not follow this logic nor did the Supreme Court. In a series of cases in the 1920s, 1930s, and 1940s, the Court held that when a state assembly "used the word 'person' in connection with those qualified to vote [or] to describe those liable to jury service, no one contemplated the possibility of women becoming so qualified. . . . No intention to include women can be deduced from the word male."[70] And so it went. By 1942 only twenty-eight states permitted women to serve on juries, and fifteen of these allowed them to claim exemption because of their sex. Twenty other states disqualified female jurors summarily. By 1962, despite the passage of the Civil Rights Act of 1957 ensuring the right of women to sit on *federal* juries, twenty-one states still did not permit women to serve equally with men on lower-level juries. By 1973 women could sit on juries in all fifty states, but in nineteen states they were singled out for special exemptions, ranging from pregnancy and minor children to embarrassment and simple assertion of being female. Very often the rationale for these exemptions was based on

Fay v. New York, 332 U.S. 261 (1947), and Hoyt v. Florida, 368 U.S. 57 (1961). In *Fay,* the Supreme Court implied that women did not have a constitutional right to serve on juries:

The contention that women should be on the jury is not based on the Constitution, it is based on a changing view of the rights and responsibilities of women . . . in all phases of life. . . . Woman jury service has not so become a part of the textual or customary law of the land that one convicted of crime must be set free [if the jury does not include women].[71]

In *Hoyt,* fourteen years later, the Court ruled unanimously that a state law was constitutional when it automatically exempted women from jury duty— unless they expressed an affirmative desire to serve. Unlike Mollie Rosencrantz who had not wanted married women on her jury in 1884, the female defendant in this 1961 case, Gwendolyn Hoyt, insisted that she was entitled to a jury made up of both men and women. She had been convicted by an all-male jury of murdering her husband with a baseball bat. The Supreme Court ruled that the Florida statute established a "reasonable classification" when it automatically exempted women from jury duty unless they explicitly registered to serve. Realizing that this would mean underrepresentation of women on juries, the Court nonetheless maintained that such a sexual imbalance "in no way resembles those involving race or colour," because in *Hoyt* there was "neither the unfortunate atmosphere of ethnic or racial prejudices . . . nor the long course of discriminatory administrative practice." Justice Harlan did not acknowledge the existence of an "unfortunate atmosphere" created over the years by gender discrimination (resulting in the fact that only 220 women of 46,000 registered Florida voters had ever claimed their right to sit on juries). Instead, Harlan employed language reminiscent of Judge Turner's dissent in *Rosencrantz v. Territory of Washington* seventy-seven years earlier, when he said in *Hoyt:*

Despite the enlightened emancipation of women from restrictions and protections of bygone years, and their entry into many parts of the community life formerly reserved for men, woman is still regarded as the center of the home and family life.[72]

Although at least one federal court in Alabama declared in 1966 that the exclusion of women from juries was a violation of the equal-protection clause of the Fourteenth Amendment, state courts did not follow suit nor has the Supreme Court so ruled. Two 1970 opinions, issued by New York courts, once again upheld the exemption of women from jury duty as a reasonable practice. In fact, one of these decisions, Leighton v. Goodman, 311 F. Supp. 1181 (S.D.N.Y. 1970), was very much in keeping with the gendered views of both Judge Turner and Justice Harlan because it was based on assumptions about prescribed roles for women that go back to antiquity and have no "reasonable" place in the modern legal system except to perpetuate male bias. It said:

Granted that some women pursue business careers, the great majority constitute the heart of the home, where they are busily engaged in the twenty-four-hour task of producing and rearing children, providing a home for the entire family, and performing the daily household work, all of which demands their full energies. Although some women now question this arrangement, the state legislature has permitted the exemption in order not to risk disruption of the basic family unit. Its action was far from arbitrary.[73]

Not until 1975 did the Supreme Court of the United States overrule *Hoyt*. In Taylor v. Louisiana, 419 U.S. 522 (1975), the Court held that a statute denying a male defendant (ironically, in this case accused of rape) trial by a jury composed of a cross section of the community violated his rights under the Sixth Amendment. The *Taylor* decision did not specify that women had the right to serve on juries on equal terms with men. However disappointing the exact wording and ruling in this decision was, because it *did not* make sex a suspect classification under the Fourteenth Amendment, it nevertheless had the effect of invalidating all remaining state laws restricting jury duty on the basis of gender. What is amazing in this series of decisions about jury service for women is how many of them were handed down after the 1954 *Brown v. Board of Education* decision and the Civil Rights Act of 1964. They reflect how slowly traditional legal views about women's proper place in society changed even during the tumultuous decade of the 1960s, especially on the part of the liberal, activist Warren Supreme Court.

Such unexpected and often ambiguous victories over sex discrimination multiplied in the 1970s and 1980s, as noted in chapter 7. In retrospect, it is clear that, until the last twenty-five years, U.S. judges consistently upheld the constitutionality of state statutory provisions expressly excluding women from full citizenship, without taking the trouble to create "even the *appearance* of fairness or equal treatment."[74] As late as 1971, a survey made of judicial decisions in gender-based cases in the United States concluded with the observation that male-dominated courts historically followed male-dominated legislatures in exhibiting the belief that women were and ought to be confined to the social roles of homemaker, wife, and mother.[75]

Feminists in the 1960s and 1970s took up where their predecessors of the 1920s left off with the Equal Rights Amendment and the old Seneca Falls arguments against remaining vestiges of "marital bondage." Once again, white, middle-class women emerged as leaders of the Second Women's movement in the late 1960s because, as in the past, they were the first to benefit from, and hence respond to, the contradictions and frustrations of changing socioeconomic, political, and legal conditions in the United States. After thirty years of quiescence and constitutional protection, they were awakened from the post–World War II dream of the "feminine mystique" by the civil rights movement, the counterculture, further educational and professional advancements, and the Vietnam War. All these events raised, but not necessarily changed, consciousness among women in the United States. Two hundred years after the American Revolution and 120 years after Seneca Falls, the struggle continues into its fourth stage and, to date, latest stage. Will it end with too little, too late, as it has so many times in the past?

# CHAPTER SEVEN

# Constitutional Equality, 1963–1990

The legal status of women in the United States changed more rapidly in the last twenty-five years than in the previous two hundred. This fourth period in the constitutional history of the female half of the population began with the Equal Pay Act in 1963 and the addition of the word *sex* to Title VII of the 1964 Civil Rights Act. It continued with a series of executive orders, more congressional legislation, and Supreme Court decisions dating from the early 1970s through 1990. The result is that women are as close to achieving equal rights under the law with men as they ever have been. The number of legal texts relating to women and minorities mushroomed during these two and a half decades, as have their interpretations and applications.

Like the earlier periods already discussed, the question in this latest one remains: Are there collectivist changes taking place in the national and international power centers related to global economic interdependence and the "outbreak" of peace between the Soviet Union and the United States and the liberation of entire groups of people in various parts of the world that make traditional individual rights less valuable to male leaders at home and abroad and, hence, less valued by society than they were two or three decades ago? In other words, is the political economy of the United States finally heading in the direction of a global collectivism that will ultimately relegate the individual equal rights—now being accorded women—to obsolescence in the near future, as the self-contained person of modern liberalism is replaced with a "constitutive formulation of a person that better suits the global world into which we are rapidly heading"?

At first glance the answer appears to be "no" because by 1989 the Reagan administrations' attempts to undermine the application of some of these legislative and administrative equal rights and affirmative-action remedies finally began to be reflected in Supreme Court decisions. While this brand of regressive Republicanism may prove no more than a blip on the radar screen of U.S. history when viewed from the end of the next century, in the last decade of this one it has become a major concern of feminists. Even the most positive legal legacy of certain federal-court decisions in this fourth period of constitutional equality

229

remains either confusing or discouraging on a wide variety of issues affecting women—ranging from funding for abortions and attitudes toward pregnant working women, to parental leaves, child care and comparable worth, or what is now being called *pay equity*. How can we come to an understanding of whether women may be settling for too little, too late once again?

From the traditional liberal point of view of progress based on expanding individual rights for women, however, the years 1963 to 1990 are impressive, particularly given the previous two hundred years of U.S. history. From the 1860s until 1971, whenever the Supreme Court considered women's rights it upheld sex stereotyping in the law. Moreover, except for the Nineteenth Amendment, there was no congressional legislation that made gender a central issue until 1963. In the intervening years, state statutes, common-law precedents, and judicial interpretations defined the status of women primarily in terms of the rights of "the sex," not in terms of the rights of individual persons under the Constitution. The phrase "women as citizens" was almost always applied to their ascribed functions as mothers, daughters, or wives.

Ironically, the courts and Congress began to recognize women as being independent people outside of the family only in what is being called the end of the modern world, or the era of individualization. Whether women will be accorded all the attributes of liberal individualism as men move away from them into a more collectivist postmodern world will not be known until the next century. In the meantime, what is more immediately evident about the changing legal status of women since 1963 is the way in which specific legislation and litigation seemed to ebb and flow with particular presidential administrations—from John Kennedy to George Bush.

## Legislation and Litigation as Presidential Phenomena

While it is difficult to generalize about all of the congressional action and specific court decisions between 1963 and 1990 (most of which are discussed in more detail later or outlined in appendix 5), certain patterns stand out in stark relief when they are broken down into presidential periods. As noted previously, the Equal Pay Act and Title VII of the Civil Rights Act of 1964 were passed *before* the Second Women's movement had organized. In the early and mid-1960s, female activists concentrated their activities in civil rights and student or other antiwar groups dominated by black and white male leftists, just as their ancestors in the 1840s and 1850s had participated in the Temperance and Abolitionist movements. Consequently, the Second Women's movement cannot be credited with passage of either of these significant acts of Congress, any more than the

First Women's movement was responsible for the early Married Women's Property Acts. Unlike the pre– and post–Civil War periods, however, presidents and politicians since the 1960s have not been able to ignore the "women's issue," as they did in the nineteenth century.

The Kennedy administration's attitude toward women's rights can at best be characterized as one of benign neglect masquerading as pseudo concern. John F. Kennedy's record on Senate-confirmed female appointments fell below that of both Presidents Harry Truman and Dwight D. Eisenhower. And, unlike Franklin Delano Roosevelt and Eisenhower, Kennedy did not appoint any women to cabinet positions. However, because of one determined woman appointee, Kennedy's presidency marked a turning point from previous post–World War II administrations that had publicized isolated female appointments to show their concern for half the population.[2] Faced with criticism by Democratic party women for his failure to appoint a greater number of women to administrative posts, Kennedy welcomed the suggestion (and urging) of Esther Peterson, director of the Women's Bureau, to create the first national Commission on the Status of Women. The creation of the commission served the very different purposes of Kennedy and Peterson well. The president successfully silenced, or moderated, criticism from prominent Democratic women (including Eleanor Roosevelt), while promoting a public image of himself as interested in women's issues; and Peterson succeeded in promoting her own position within the administration (becoming assistant secretary of labor, as well as head of the Women's Bureau), in addition to diverting congressional attention away from the ERA.[3]

Had it not been for Vice President Lyndon Johnson, however, the commission might never have materialized. "Actually I credit him [Johnson] with the idea of setting up this commission which Kennedy bought," Peterson later recalled in an oral interview. Apparently, Johnson had specifically asked her "what are we going to do for women" right after the 1960 election.[4] The result was that it was Johnson, not Kennedy, who supported the idea of having Eleanor Roosevelt chair the commission, according to Peterson, because Johnson "liked her better than Kennedy did, so he was supportive of me in getting her to be chairman of the Commission on the Status of Women. By the way, that was another little problem I had with Jack," she added. "*I* had to ask Eleanor Roosevelt; Jack would not do it." After everything was in place and the president decided it should be a "Kennedy thing," rather than a "Johnson thing," Peterson noted that she felt conflicted over her "deep feeling of loyalty to Kennedy and . . . the feeling that I was getting so much real help from Johnson," not only on the commission but also on other women's issues as well. It was "that little subtle kind of thing that I liked about him so much . . . a sensitivity I didn't get from Kennedy on [women's issues]." It was Johnson, not Kennedy, for example, who hosted the first meeting of the commission at his home and who later helped Peterson shepherd the Equal Pay Act through Congress.[5]

Opposition to the ERA was not only a longstanding position of the Women's Bureau. Fortuitously, it also became the position of Kennedy's highly publicized commission on women whose symbolic head was Eleanor Roosevelt from 1961 until her death in 1963. One of Peterson's major reasons for recommending such a commission was to "substitute constructive recommendations for the present troublesome and futile agitation about the 'equal rights amendment.' " Consequently, under her watchful eye, commission members did not include any officials of the pro-ERA NWP or even the most loyal and prominent women members of the Democratic National Committee. Instead, Peterson saw to it that commission members shared her concern that the ERA was too divisive an issue to be given prominent consideration, let alone an endorsement.[6]

As a result, the protective-labor legislation position of the Women's Bureau prevailed under the Kennedy administration and into Lyndon Johnson's because LBJ remained more personally sympathetic and supportive of women's issues than JFK.[7] As president, Johnson reversed with great fanfare Kennedy's policy of not appointing women to high government positions, but he also quietly went on to try to follow the commission's recommendations on other civil-service appointments, raising expectations, according to Cynthia Harrison, "that he then failed to fulfill." After Johnson promoted Peterson by appointing her his special assistant on consumer affairs, she resigned from the Women's Bureau and was replaced by Mary Dublin Keyserling, who not only opposed the ERA but also the moderate recommendations made by Kennedy's Commission on the Status of Women.[8] In retrospect, this was a most unfortunate appointment that offset the others, because had ratification of the ERA been pending at the state level in the reform decade of the 1960s, its chances of passage would have been considerably greater than when it was before the states in the 1970s—the decade in which the postwar backlash began. Instead, women achieved equal pay for equal work when the work ethic began to be questioned in the 1960s.

While such women as Peterson successfully defended the Equal Pay Bill before Congress in 1962, she and her supporters viewed it as a traditional goal of the Women's Bureau in behalf of protecting working women from the perspective of their societal roles as mothers and wives—not from any inherently independent economic right. They were determined not to move women into the future. Their thinking was "stuck" somewhere in the 1920s or 1930s, but so were proponents of the ERA in the 1960s. Most important, Peterson and her supporters viewed the Equal Pay Act as a means to divert congressional attention away from the ERA. In fact, except for the chair of the NWP, Emma Guffey Miller, ✓ most of those testifying in support of equal pay were not in favor of an ERA.

Stressing individual equality rather than group equity, Peterson's forces allowed congressional critics to reword the original language, which had talked about equal pay "for work of comparable character on jobs the performance of which requires comparable skills." The final wording referred to the simpler notion of equal pay for "equal" work. This compromise avoided raising questions about women's "proper" role in society. Ironically, it was the leading ERA supporter in the House of Representatives, Katharine St. George (Republican from New York), who succeeded in narrowing the scope and meaning of the Equal Pay Act to the point that to vote against it, she said, "would be like being against motherhood."[9] At no time, however, did the supporters on either side of this linguistic debate over the first Equal Pay Act endorse today's concept of "equal pay for comparable *worth*." Consequently, from the early 1960s until the debate over comparable worth arose in the 1980s, legal and legislative attitudes toward women have theoretically broadened "equal-employment opportunities" for all women; but, in practice, this has usually meant that "women who are like men should be treated equally with men."[10]

Unlike the Equal Pay Act, which had a substantial legislative history because it had been seriously debated in Congress, the word *sex* was added to the 1964 Civil Rights Act more by accident than design, and there is every indication that Congress did not act with full knowledge of what it was doing. For example, 40 percent of members of the House absented themselves from the vote count on this bill. Less than 50 percent actually consented to this single word addition to the 1964 Civil Rights Act. To those few congressmen who were paying attention, it appeared to be only another insignificant increment. In other words, white male indifference rather than sensitivity to sex discrimination made the difference between success and failure—not organized female or male support. Moreover, most male civil rights advocates in general opposed the addition, inadvertently contributing to the formation of a Second Women's movement.[11]

Specifically, the word *sex* was introduced into the text of Title VII, which was originally intended to prohibit discrimination in employment on the basis of race, color, religion, and national origin, by the southern congressman Howard W. Smith in what appeared to be a last-minute attempt to defeat the bill. "Now I am very serious about this amendment," Congressman Smith said when introducing it, "I do not think it can do any harm to this legislation; maybe it can do some good."[12] He later denied adding the word *sex* to Title VII to delay or defeat the legislation. Smith nonetheless joked about it all through the brief debate that followed. Significantly, male (but not female) House liberals uniformly opposed

Smith's addition to Title VII with the blessing of the Women's Bureau, the Labor Department, and most women's groups at that time. In congressional history, 8 February 1964 went down as "Ladies' Day in the House."[13]

In this cavalier fashion, "one of the most profoundly redistributive [public-policy] decisions of our century" was made, according to political scientist Jo Freeman. "Why it was initially unnoticed, at least by those who passed it if not by those who were affected by it," she has later concluded, "lies in the disregard that women have normally experienced from political leaders and in the routine nature of the addition of 'sex' to the pantheon of prohibited discriminations" in the days before there was effective enforcement for the nascent concept of affirmative action. In fact, prohibiting discrimination was not the most troublesome aspect of Title VII for Congress; it was approval of an independent agency to enforce it.[14]

Although the Equal Employment Opportunity Commission (EEOC) was specifically created to enforce Title VII, it took over a decade to put teeth into the act. During that time, administrative guidelines evolved for enforcing affirmative action. Two Johnson administration executive orders were particularly important. In 1965, Executive Order No. 11246 prohibited racial, religious, and alienage employment discrimination by federal contractors; in 1967, Executive Order No. 11375 added sex to this list. Executive Order No. 11478, issued by Nixon in 1969, strongly exhorted federal agencies "to establish and maintain an affirmative action program of equal employment opportunity for all civilian employees." Nixon's administration also conducted the first compliance reviews of hiring policies toward women by institutions of higher education receiving federal grants. By August 1972, over 350 sex-discrimination suits had been brought against such schools across the country.[15]

While Presidents Kennedy and Johnson had employed the term *affirmative action,* it "did not have much bite" until the Nixon administration announced the "Philadelphia Plan" in 1969, which required federal contractors to hire a certain number of minority workers. Secretary of Labor George Shultz, who devised the plan, later extended it to nine other cities. These incentives for minority-owned firms, initiated under the Nixon administration "to improve economic fairness for . . . black construction workers," gradually evolved into what are called "set-asides" for minority businesses.[16] Shultz also issued the first guidelines requiring businesses with federal contracts to draw up "action plans" for hiring and promoting women.

Subsequently, Congress passed the 1972 educational amendments covering all employers with fifteen or more workers and allowing the EEOC to initiate suits on its own authority. The Equal Employment Opportunity Reorganization Act of 1977 amended Title VII by further broadening EEOC jurisdiction to include the

Equal Pay Act, Executiv̶ ̶.̶.̶                                    Discrimination Act.
Although the first EEOC director, Herman Edelsberg, sought to ignore the sex
provision of Title VII, saying it was a "fluke" and not the agency's first priority,
well over one-third of all complaints processed during the agency's first year
alleged sex discrimination. During the late 1960s and early 1970s, EEOC experienced increasing pressure from the National Organization for Women (NOW),
women educators, and the loose network of largely eastern corridor women inside
and outside of Congress that had emerged following the report by Kennedy's
Commission on the Status of Women.[17] This incipient network was strengthened
during the struggle over the ratification of the ERA beginning in 1972, so that
until the Reagan administration all subsequent EEOC directors became quite
sympathetic and serious about sex-discrimination complaints.

Accordingly, the accompanying chart indicates that while legislative and administrative momentum slowed down temporarily in the late 1960s, litigation over
Title VII increased. Numerous lower-court decisions by 1970 not only approved
changed EEOC guidelines but also voided a half-century of protective legislation,
with Title VII interpretations expanding equal treatment of women in the workplace. Weeks v. Southern Bell, 408 F.2d 228 (5th Cir. 1969), was the first Title
VII sex-discrimination case to reach an appellate court and to set a precedent for
using Title VII to supersede state protective legislation.[18] This and similar litigation also ended the fifty-year battle that had been going on since the early 1920s
between groups of women (and men) over whether to support protective legislation or the ERA. Thus, Title VII litigation, despite its *bona fide occupation
qualification* (BFOQ) loophole,[19] paved the way not only for several landmark
Supreme Court decisions in the early 1970s[20] but also allowed the incipient
network of professional women on the East Coast to cooperate with such key
female members of Congress as Edith Green and Martha Griffiths in outflanking
Emanuel Celler, chair of the House Judiciary Committee, to obtain approval of
the ERA in 1972.

In addition to the favorable administrative climate and presidential commission
and task force reports under Nixon, in general the spate of women's rights
legislation endorsed by the Ninety-second Congress (1971–73) can be attributed
to this coalescing of female members of congressional staffs, individual members
of Congress, and an emerging national network of professional women knowledgeable and concerned about their legal status in American society—otherwise
known as the establishment or mainstream wing of the Second Women's movement. The resulting immediate successes in Congress by the mid-1970s made the
various female leaders of this reformist feminist coalition appear to wield more
national power and influence outside of Washington, D.C., in particular, and
the eastern corridor, in general, than they actually did. Congressional lobbying

# Changing Legal Status of U.S. Women, 1963–1990

| | Legislation | Administrative Action | Women's Movement Activity | Litigation |
|---|---|---|---|---|
| 1963 | Equal Pay Act | Report of first Presidential Commission on the Status of Women | *Feminine Mystique* by Betty Friedan published | |
| 1963–66 | | | Loose East Coast network of professional women emerges following Kennedy's commission report; National Federation of Business and Professional Women's Clubs make the establishment of state commissions on the status of women their top priority | |
| 1964 | Title VII of the Civil Rights Act prohibited employment discrimination on the basis of race, color, religion, sex, or national origin with the exception of bona fide occupational qualifications (BFOQ); it also created the Equal Employment Opportunity Commission (EEOC) | | | |
| 1965 | | Executive Order No. 11246 | | *Griswold v. Connecticut* |
| 1966 | | First EEOC director refused to take sex discrimination seriously | National Organization for Women (NOW) founded | |

Kennedy/Johnson Administrations

WARREN COURT

| 1967 | Executive Order No. 11375 added "sex" to Executive Order No. 11246 prohibiting racial, religious, and alienage employment discrimination by federal contractors | First "women's liberation" group formed in Chicago; numerous state commissions on the status of women were created and issued reports; hundreds of local conscious-ness-raising and radical feminist groups organize as the Second Women's movement emerged in the late 1960s; Women's Equity Action League (WEAL) founded to attack sexism in higher education | *Loving v. Virginia* |
| --- | --- | --- | --- |
| 1968 | | | *Rosenfeld v. Southern Pacific Co.* |
| 1969 | Presidential Task Force on Women's Rights and Responsibilities; Presidential Committee on Population and Family Planning; "Philadelphia Plan" requiring federal contractors to employ a targeted number of minority workers—extended to nine other cities by Secretary of Labor George Shultz; Executive Order No. 11478 mandated affirmative-action programs of equal opportunity for the executive branch of government | Radical feminists set national agenda for transforming American society through local, regional, and national publications and begin to oppose sexism in the male-dominated civil rights and antiwar movements; women in the American Sociological Association formed the first female caucus within a professional association | *Weeks v. Southern Bell* |

WARREN COURT
Kennedy/Johnson Administrations

BURGER COURT
Nixon/Ford Administrations

**Changing Legal Status of U.S. Women, 1963–1990 (continued)**

| | Legislation | Administrative Action | Women's Movement Activity | Litigation |
|---|---|---|---|---|
| 1969–73 | | | Variety of national feminist groups formed (including the National Women's Political Caucus and the National Black Feminist Organization); socialist feminism began to replace radical feminism as a major theoretical force in the Second Women's movement, while mainstream feminism coalesced under NOW; WEAL filed the first sex-discrimination suit under Executive Order No. 11246 against the University of Maryland; *Sexual Politics* by Kate Millett published in 1970 | |
| 1971—Congress considering amendments to Title VII and addition of Title IX to 1964 Civil Rights Act | | Labor Secretary Shultz issued guidelines requiring all firms doing business with the government to create action plans for the hiring and promotion of women and authorized the first compliance reviews of female-hiring policies by educational institutions; Executive Order No. 11478 condemned sex discrimination among government agencies | | *Sail'er Inn, Inc. v. Kirby*<br>*Phillips v. Martin Marietta Corporation*<br>*Sprogis v. United Airlines*<br>*Diaz v. Pan American*<br>*Griggs v. Duke Power Company*<br>*Reed v. Reed*<br>*Eisenstadt v. Baird* |

Nixon/Ford Administrations
BURGER COURT

| Year | | | Court Cases |
|---|---|---|---|
| 1972 — Title IX and amendments to Title VII passed; ERA sent to states for ratification; U.S. Civil Rights Commission mandate extended to include sex discrimination; administration-sponsored tax deductions for child care passed; antidiscrimination provisions attached to federally supported programs included health training, revenue sharing, environment, and Appalachian redevelopment bills; Congress passed child-care legislation as amendment to OEO budget | Nixon successfully vetoed child-care legislation | Splits in the Second Women's movement temporarily overcome under the leadership of mainstream "politicos" largely under the auspices of NOW; socialist and radical feminists withheld support for the ERA until organized labor opposition to it was overcome. Twenty-two states quickly ratified the ERA with little debate by the end of 1972; eight others ratified in 1973; three in 1973; and one in 1975 | *Roe v. Wade*<br>*Roe v. Bolton*<br>*Frontiero v. Richardson*<br>*Miller v. California* |
| 1973 — End of War in Vietnam: Beginning of Conservative Postwar Era | | | *Kahn v. Shevin*<br>*Cleveland Board of Education v. LaFleur*<br>*Geduldig v. Aiello* |
| 1974 | | Antifeminist groups formed and ultimately united behind the leadership of Phyllis Schlafly's STOP ERA and Eagle Forum groups with support from political conservatives and religious Fundamentalists; these anti-ERA groups successfully linked such issues as abortion, the drafting of women, unisex toilets, and homosexuality to the ERA in the course of the late 1970s and early 1980s | *Schlesinger v. Ballard*<br>*Taylor v. Louisiana* |
| 1975 — Equal Credit Opportunity Act (ECOA) passed (effective 1977); Women's Educational Equity Act (WEEA) | | | |
| 1976 | | | *Craig v. Boren*<br>*General Electric Co. v. Gilbert*<br>*Planned Parenthood v. Danforth* |

**Changing Legal Status of U.S. Women, 1963–1990 (continued)**

| Legislation | Administrative Action | Women's Movement Activity | Litigation |
|---|---|---|---|
| | | Postwar Conservative Era Continues | |
| 1977–80—Series of Hyde Amendments passed in Congress denying poor women the right to federal funding for abortions | | | |
| 1977—EEOC jurisdiction broadened | EEOC says that it will interpret *Teamsters* narrowly | Beginning in the late 1970s radical and socialist feminists finally began to support the ERA; NOW developed strategy and tactics for its final and unsuccessful campaign to obtain ratification of the ERA at state level, heading a broad coalition of the pro-ERA groups and concentrating its lobbying efforts in a few crucial non-ERA states, such as Illinois, Florida, Virginia, and South Carolina; no more states ratified the ERA after January 1977 even though NOW made the proposed Twenty-seventh Amendment its central issue, and public opinion polls continued to indicate that a majority of the U.S. population favored the ERA | *Teamsters v. United States*<br>*Beal v. Doe*<br>*Dothard v. Rawlinson*<br>*Nashville Gas v. Satty*<br>*Mather v. Roe*<br>*Regents of University of California v. Bakke*<br>*Califano v. Goldfarb*<br>*Califano v. Webster* |
| 1978—Congress overruled *Gilbert* and extended the deadline for passage of the ERA to 1982 | | | *Cannon v. Illinois*<br>*Los Angeles Department of Water and Power v. Manhart* |
| 1979 | | | *Personnel Administrator v. Feeney*<br>*Orr v. Orr*<br>*Califano v. Westcott*<br>*Steelworkers v. Weber* |
| 1980 | | | *Harris v. McRae*<br>*Wengler v. Druggist Mutual Inc.* |

Convervative Postwar Era Exacerbated under Reagan Administrations

| Legislation | Administration/Movement | Supreme Court Cases |
|---|---|---|
| 1981—First Economic Equity Act introduced in Congress | | *Michael M. v. Sonoma County*<br>*Rostker v. Goldberg*<br>*Kirchberg v. Feenstrat*<br>*McCarty v. McCarty*<br>*Washington County v. Gunther* |
| 1982—ERA failed to be ratified at the state level; Congress overruled *McCarty* with only thirty-five out of the necessary thirty-eight states required | Justice Department's and Civil Rights Commission's statements hostile to affirmative action | *North Haven Board of Education v. Bell*<br>*Mississippi University Women v. Hogan* |
| 1983—ERA reintroduced in Congress | | Five federal circuit courts ruled that sexual harassment violates Title VII |
| | The Second Women's movement began to split in wake of the defeat of the ERA over a variety of issues reminiscent of the 1920s, with special versus equal rights being the most prominent; cultural feminism reappeared only to be attacked by post-structural feminists as essentialist; ecofeminism emerged for the first time as a viable alternative for those women with strong environmental concerns | Series of Supreme Court cases reaffirm constitutionality of abortion |
| 1984—Child-support and pension bills passed; Civil Rights Restoration Act introduced to overrule *Grove City* but defeated by filibustering | Reagan administration officials openly criticize quotas, comparable worth, class action suits, and affirmative action | The United States Supreme Court refused to hear University of Washington nurses' comparable-worth cases<br>*Roberts et al. v. U. S. Jaycees*<br>*Hishon v. King and Spaulding*<br>*Grove City College v. Ball* |

**Changing Legal Status of U.S. Women, 1963–1990 (continued)**

| | Legislation | Administrative Action | Women's Movement Activity | Litigation |
|---|---|---|---|---|
| Reagan Administration / REHNQUIST COURT | 1985—Civil Rights Restoration Act again defeated by filibustering | | Radical feminism continued to reassert itself as a significant theoretical force over such issues as sexuality, pornography, and woman and child abuse; at the same time, many socialist feminists began to move toward the apolitical poststructural theories, while mainstream feminists continued to fragment over various single issues, such as abortion and piecemeal public-policy programs aimed at improving life for women in such areas as treatment of pregnant working women, child support, and child care | *Palmer v. Shultz* *EEOC v. Sears* *AFSCME v. Washington State* *American Booksellers v. Hudnut* *Wygant v. Jackson Board of Education* *Thornburgh v. American College of Obstetricians and Gynecologists* *Meritor Savings Bank v. Vinson* *Bowers v. Hardwick* |
| | 1986—Civil Rights Restoration Act again defeated by filibustering | | | |
| | 1987—Civil Rights Restoration Act overcame filibustering and was finally sent to Senate floor for full discussion | | | *Johnson v. Transportation Agency of Santa Clara* *Guerra v. California Federal Savings and Loan Association* *Wimberly v. Labor and Industry Department* *Rotary International v. Rotary Club of Duarte* *Pope v. Illinois* |
| | 1988—Congress overrode presidential veto of Civil Rights Restoration Act, thus overruling the decision in *Grove City* | Reagan vetoed Civil Rights Restoration Act. | Second Women's movement continued to fragment and drift in a variety of directions as did Fundamentalist and conservative groups | *Hicks v. Feiock* *New York State Club Association, Inc. v. New York City* |

| | | | |
|---|---|---|---|
| 1989—Congress approved liberalized abortion funding in the District of Columbia's 1990 fiscal appropriations bill | Bush successfully vetoed District of Columbia bill expanding funding for abortions | Major Washington, D.C., rallies sponsored by NOW, the National Abortion Rights Action League (NARAL), and Planned Parenthood in the spring and fall; antiabortion groups also mobilized in anticipation of, and following, the decision in *Webster* even as the Republican party began to rethink its anti-abortion position in light of upcoming state elections | *City of Richmond v. J.A. Croson Co.* |
| Congress also passed legislation modifying the Hyde Amendment by making federal funds available for poor women in cases of incest and rape | Bush also vetoed this legislation | | *Price Waterhouse v. Hopkins* |
| Congress approved a compromise budget for the District of Columbia allowing federal funds to be used for abortions only when the life of the mother is in jeopardy, but permitting the city to use its own funds to pay for abortions for poor women | | | *Wards Cove v. Antonio* |
| | | | *Wayne Books, Inc. v. Indiana* and *Sappenfield v. Indiana* |
| Congress decided to put off action on a landmark child-care bill because of deep differences over the scope of the legislation and how to pay for it | | | *Sable Communications v. FEC* |
| | | | *Patterson v. McLean Credit Union* |
| 1989–90 Encouraged by *Webster*, a variety of state legislation was passed and is pending restricting abortions, even | | NOW and NARAL began to refocus their efforts on abortion in the wake of *Webster*, as abortion became a national is- | *Lorance v. AT&T* |
| | | | *Webster v. Reproductive Health Service* |

| | Legislation | Administrative Action | Women's Movement Activity | Litigation |
|---|---|---|---|---|
| | though state elections in the fall of 1989 saw several major opponents of abortion defeated | | sue with major political impact at the beginning of the decade of the 1990s and the possibility of revitalizing the Second Women's movement as it prepared to enter its third decade and the twenty-first century | Hodgson v. Minnesota Ohio v. Akron Center for Reproductive Health Maryland v. Craig Metro Broadcasting v. FCC |
| | Congressional attempts to override Webster fail | | | |
| | 1990—Congress passed bill requiring companies with over fifty employees to give as much as three months unpaid leave to workers with new babies or family illnesses | Bush successfully vetoed parental-leave bill | | |
| | Senate hearings on 1990 Violence Against Women bill would make gender-biased assaults against women a violation of their civil rights | | NOW in full support of 1990 Violence Against Women bill even though its language is similar to antipornography ordinances that NOW has not supported at local levels in the past | |
| | Civil Rights Act of 1990 overruled several recent Supreme Court decisions and amended 1964 Civil Rights Act more extensively than ever before, including the awarding of an unlimited amount of compensatory and punitive damages for those who prove willful bias | Bush successfully vetoed this civil rights act. | | |

Bush Administration

REHNQUIST COURT

and other highly visible national actions, including support of appeals to the Supreme Court during and after 1972, also kept the coalition's leadership from concentrating on obtaining passage of the ERA through grass-roots organizing at the state level. By the time they concentrated their attention on the ratification process in the late 1970s, their chances of overcoming the cultural and political backlash that had set across the country after the end of the Vietnam War were slim indeed. The ties of these mainstream "politicos" with radical and socialist feminist groups that had sprung up since the late 1960s had become so tenuous that no broadening of the theoretical views of the Second Women's movement took place.[21] As will be discussed in chapter 9, the ideological weakness of NOW proved problematic. It permitted the organization to reach out and somewhat opportunistically garner members from mainstream women across the country, especially in the last years of the unsuccessful campaign for the ERA, without having to think through the implications of turning the ERA into a panacean single issue.

All groups of feminists complained independently about the Nixon administration, in part from their own respective high expectations in the early 1970s but also because, emulating Kennedy, Nixon did not choose to placate female constituents with appointments or pay lip service to any feminist agenda. Instead, he created commissions dealing with a broad range of women's issues. Although many of his advisers, particularly Health, Education, and Welfare Secretary Robert Finch, urged him to follow the traditional procedure of appointing a few highly placed women to his administration, Nixon rejected this advice, saying privately, "I seriously doubt if jobs in government for women make many votes from women." Reports from the Task Force on Women's Rights and Responsibilities, the Committee on Population and Family Planning, and the Citizens' Advisory Committee on the Status of Women appointed by Nixon reinforced a wide variety of the demands of the young Second Women's movement, especially on abortion and the ERA. Nixon's aides, in turn, relied on these reports for drafting bills to Congress and for presidential messages in support of most of the legislation, including the ERA, that Nixon had sponsored in both the House and Senate in the late 1940s and early 1950s. He continued to support the ERA as vice president but less enthusiastically as president.[22]

Subsequently, Congress approved the Equal Employment Opportunity Act and Title IX of the Education Amendments Act, prohibiting sex discrimination by educational institutions receiving federal aid. Congress also approved the administration's amendments to the Revenue Act of 1971 to allow greater tax deductions for child care and, at Nixon's specific request, broadened the U.S. Civil Rights Commission mandate to include sex discrimination. In addition, Congress attached a number of anti-sex-discrimination provisions to such federally supported programs as health training, revenue sharing, Appalachian redevelopment, and environmental protection. The Ninety-second Congress also passed a child development program as part of the economic opportunity amendments of 1971, which would have provided free day care for poor families and a sliding fee scale for higher-income families. However, Nixon vetoed this legislation on budgetary and administrative grounds. Unfortunately, child care and his veto message became the political victims of a struggle between the Democratically controlled Congress and the Republican president over two other issues: welfare and the Office of Economic Opportunity (OEO). Nixon's own significant reform of the welfare system contained an annual $750 million to construct and operate day-care facilities for welfare recipients and the working poor. By calling for $2 billion in the first year, which the administration projected would mushroom into $20 billion annually, Congress went far beyond what Nixon thought was needed (since his revenue act already gave a tax break to middle-class working couples).[23]

Most of this congressional activity in behalf of women during the first Nixon administration can be considered incremental, in the sense that much of it "involved amendments to or parallels of minority civil rights legislation." The Ninety-third Congress (1973–75) under Nixon and Ford actually began to go beyond incrementalism by passing antidiscrimination legislation for women that had no racial antecedents. This included the Equal Credit Opportunity Act (ECOA), originally passed in 1975 as an amendment to the 1970 Consumer Credit Protection Act; the Women's Educational Equity Act (WEEA); creation of the National Center for the Control and Prevention of Rape; and a Foreign Assistance Act amendment favoring "programs, projects, and activities which tend to integrate women into the national economies of foreign countries." In 1975, after much pressure from women inside and outside of the government, the State Department initiated both the Mid-Level Affirmative Action Program and the Junior Office Affirmative Action Program designed to increase the number of women and minority foreign-service officers.[24]

At the same time that Congress passed such legislation or supported implementation of administrative guidelines under the Nixon and Ford administrations, an unexpected juridical metamorphosis in case law took place under the Burger Court, to which Nixon had appointed four members, including Chief Justice Warren E. Burger.[25] Of all of Nixon's appointments to the Supreme Court, Justice Harry A. Blackmun played the most crucial, if unexpected, role in changing the legal status of women because of his consistent support of abortion rights from that time to the present. This is not to say that the Burger Court was as "interventionist" in the area of sex discrimination as the Warren Court was on racial issues. It must be remembered that the Warren Court logically built on reconstruction legislation from the last century, whereas the Burger Court could

only draw on case-law precedents set in race-discrimination cases form the 1950s
and 1960s when it began to grant equal rights to women. Another factor working
against dramatic changes in women's constitutional status—then and now—is
the fact that although women are often treated like a minority group, which they
are not. Supreme Court decisions affecting them ripple more widely throughout
society at all class levels than do those regarding race. Consequently, the justices
have always realized how dangerous "redistributive" decisions affecting over 50
percent of the population could be.

These inhibiting reasons notwithstanding, the Burger Court took such significant actions against sex discrimination that it has been criticized as undemocrat-
ically "legislating" and preempting the role of Congress on national public policy
regarding women. And, indeed, by 1986 the Burger Court seemed more predisposed toward according women full equality with men based on individual rights
than any previous Supreme Court in U.S. history.[26] Ironically, this unprecedented record is now being critically reevaluated by two very different groups: (1)
radical feminists scattered around the country who are questioning whether
individual equal rights should any longer be the most important goal of the Second
Women's movement as it attempts to prepare the female half of the population
for life in the twenty-first century and (2) conservative Supreme Court justices
appointed by President Reagan who seem determined to "roll back" affirmative-
action gains for women and minorities.


## The Record of the Burger and Rehnquist Courts

By the time Warren Burger stepped down as chief justice of the United States in
1986, the transformation of women's legal status was far from complete, primarily
because the Burger Court subjected the equal-protection clause of the Fourteenth
Amendment to several levels of interpretation with respect to women, beginning
with Reed v. Reed, 404 U.S. 71 (1971). In that decision, the U.S. Supreme
Court voided an Idaho statute that automatically preferred men over women of
the same entitlement class as administrators of estates. The justices said that
when a statute accorded different treatment on the basis of sex alone, it "estab-
lishes a classification subject to scrutiny under the Equal Protection Clause,"
thus setting the stage for a middle tier, or intermediate level, of scrutiny for
women, instead of the strict scrutiny or suspect classification traditionally applied
in cases of racial discrimination.[27] With this decision, the Supreme Court invalidated *for the first time in its history* a state statute on the grounds of sex discrimination. The Idaho state law had called for the automatic appointment of a male
executor, but the justices ruled in *Reed* that when a woman and a man were

otherwise equally qualified to administer an estate, the male could not be given arbitrary preference.

This statute was declared unconstitutional under an equal-protection interpretation of due process, utilizing the rational-basis test. In delivering the unanimous opinion of the Court, Chief Justice Burger borrowed wording from a 1920 decision that had asserted that a classification "must be reasonable, not arbitrary, and must rest upon some ground of difference having a fair and substantial relation to the object of the legislation, so that all persons similarly circumstanced shall be treated alike."[28] When applied to gender, this fifty-year-old case-law precedent substantially narrowed the juridical definition of what could be considered reasonable sex-based discrimination. The *Reed* decision *did not* declare that sex was a suspect basis for classification under the Fourteenth Amendment. It merely held the Idaho law arbitrary—that is, "unreasonable."

Two years later a plurality of the justices, with William Brennan writing for the Court, came out in favor of establishing sex as a suspect classification in the case of Frontiero v. Richardson, 411 U.S. 677 (1973), when it struck down armed service regulations that had denied women the same dependents' rights as men. Unfortunately, in 1973 this position was not joined by a majority of the Court. The plurality opinion of the four justices (Brennan, Douglas, Marshall, and White), condemning statutory distinctions between the sexes, argued that they were based on " 'romantic paternalism' which in practical effects put women not on a pedestal, but in a cage . . . relegating the entire class of females to inferior legal status without regard to the actual capabilities of its individual members."[29]

The other four concurring justices (Blackmun, Burger, Powell, and Stewart) refused to subscribe to this suspect-classification argument. Since Justice Rehnquist cast the lone dissent in *Frontiero,* this meant that a majority of five prevailed against subjecting cases involving gender discrimination to strict scrutiny under the Fourteenth Amendment, meaning that there had to be a "compelling state interest" to justify such legislation. Now that the ERA has failed, it is ironic to remember that Justice Potter Stewart specifically noted in his separate concurring opinion that while he favored making sex a suspect classification, he preferred to see that come about through passage of the then-pending Twenty-seventh Amendment, which he was convinced in 1973 would be ratified. Had Stewart joined the Brennan plurality, most of the intervening debate over both strict scrutiny under the Fourteenth Amendment for women and the ERA would not have taken place.[30] Although discrimination on the basis of sex would appear to be similarly qualified for strict scrutiny as that based on race, religion, and alienage, only a plurality of Supreme Court justices have ever held this and then only once in *Frontiero,* when the prospects for passage of the ERA looked better than they did later in the decade.

Further case-law improvement took place under the Ford and Carter administrations. By 1976, with Craig v. Boren, 429 U.S. 190 (1976), the Supreme Court established a "heightened" sense of scrutiny by requiring that "classification by gender must serve important governmental objectives and must be substantially related to the achievement of these objectives."[31] The combined effect of *Reed* and *Craig* would appear to be that in a number of cases the justices have abandoned the traditional view of women as homemakers operating primarily within a private sphere. This change is most evident in decisions involving such discrete economic matters as military, social security, welfare, and worker's compensation benefits.[32]

Thus, by 1976, the justices had established a middle-level scrutiny test for sex-discrimination cases. The use of "heightened" scrutiny is all well and good because it indicates that the courts have finally recognized one demographic fact of life in the last quarter of the twentieth century—namely, that women are not only wage earners but also often the sole breadwinners as single heads of families. However, the fundamental problem in applying "heightened" scrutiny is the same as for any other standard of constitutional review—namely, that the test can be manipulated by the Supreme Court to achieve the results it wants. Both Stephanie A. Wildman and Wendy W. Williams have commented extensively on how the *Craig* standard has been variously applied through manipulation of the "dissimilarly situated" theory.[33]

Consequently, this new juridical standard for constitutional review should not be overestimated. It did not constitute a "revolution in constitutional law" as Brown v. Board of Education, 347 U.S. 483 (1954), had a dozen years before. Instead, the net effect in this middle-level scrutiny, according to Archibald Cox, "has been highly particularistic decisions resulting from shifting alliances among the Justices."[34] The limited nature of doing away with one aspect of traditional sex stereotyping about women who work (and its statutory equivalents at the state and federal levels) very quickly became evident in Supreme Court decisions with respect to poor women.[35] Hence, not all the decisions or legislative remedies since 1971 fit neatly into this new, liberal image of women because gender-based views unrelated to their roles as workers have diminished more slowly and continued to surface erratically in Supreme Court decisions and legislation.

In contrast to white women and black, native American Indian women have made much less legal progress in the last two decades. One of the most problematic discrimination cases involving a Pueblo woman was decided in May 1978. This decision declared that native American Indians cannot bring an action in federal courts under the Fourteenth Amendment when their civil rights have been violated by tribal law. The Julia Martinez case is particularly disturbing because of its blatantly sexist overtones. The Court ruled seven to one that Congress did not intend for the Indian Civil Rights Act of 1968 to authorize challenges to tribal ordinances. In this instance, Martinez had married a Navajo and was thus barred from tribal benefits because of a policy set in 1939 by an all-male tribal council. The same standard did not apply to men who married out of the tribe, apparently on the grounds that they were less likely than women to give up their native culture. As a result, Martinez's eight living children could not inherit her home, her interest in tribal land, receive federal assistance, vote, hold tribal office, or remain on the reservation after her death even though they had all been raised in the culture and spoke the tribal language. One of her terminally ill daughters was even denied federal medical aid.[36]

Yet the Court said that *Santa Clara Pueblo v. Martinez* was not a case of sex discrimination. Instead, it ruled in favor of a form of (male) tribal self-government only dating back to the New Deal when the U.S. government attempted to counter the negative socioeconomic impact the Great Depression had on many tribes. Since four-fifths of all tribal constitutions *do not* contain a bill of rights guaranteeing basic liberties to their members and since so many of the current sex-discriminatory tribal laws originated with the Indian Reorganization Acts of the 1930s, especially the General Allotment Act of 1939, it can only be hoped that more native American Indian women will begin to question this particular brand of patriarchal tribal "justice." To date, however, most legal specialists as well as tribal leaders have hailed the decision as a victory for Puebloan autonomy and sovereignty, despite its negative legal implications for this particular group of minority women. The Supreme Court seemed to be saying that this type of female discrimination was more necessary for the tribe's "survival as a cultural and economic entity" than tribal sovereignty over land, mineral, and water rights. At least this is the distinct impression left after comparing the *Martinez* decision with those in these other areas where the U.S. government has not always honored tribal sovereignty.[37]

Surprisingly, a male bastion much more powerful than tribal councils has begun to respond to women's rights. The abolition of the draft in 1973 broke down stereotypic restrictions on women in the military quicker than in society at large. Beginning in 1974, the armed services allowed women and men to enlist at the same age, and military academies began admitting women in 1975. Despite remaining limitations, military work experience prepares former service women to earn approximately $300 more a week than those who have not been in the armed services. By the end of 1987, women made up about 10 percent of the 2.2 million individuals in the armed services on active duty. In the 1970s, the military initiated what have been some of the most successful affirmative-action programs and opportunities for women in the country through a combination of independent Pentagon administrative actions, congressional amendments to existing statutes, and the 1973 Supreme Court decision in *Frontiero* striking down armed services regulations that had denied women the same dependents' benefits as men. By 1982, however, progress for women in the military began to slow down, and Congress had to intervene in order to overturn the 1981 Supreme Court decision declaring that military pensions were the sole property of the serviceman in divorce settlements. Moreover, many gender-based (and racial) problems involving recruiting, combat service, fraternization, a uniform definition of single parents, child and spousal support, medical, disability, survival benefits, and homosexuality remain to be resolved. The invasion of Panama by the United States in December 1989 once again prompted a debate over women in combat when it was revealed that a female captain, Linda L. Bray, had led thirty male soldiers into battle and that several other women who had participated under fire had not been awarded Combat Infantryman's (*sic*) Badges along with their male counterparts. Possibly the most volatile legal issue facing the U.S. military in the 1990s will revolve around the rights of homosexuals.[38]

Likewise, abortion—another private, sexually related issue—became and remains an emotionally and legally explosive concern of the Supreme Court. Despite the fact that the justices declared abortions constitutional in Roe v. Wade, 410 U.S. 113 (1973), during the last half of the 1970s a series of decisions and legislation at the state and federal levels have placed this legal medical procedure beyond the realization of most lower-class girls and women. Some of the most disturbing gender-biased decisions the Supreme Court has reached in the last seventeen years have involved pregnancy cases, as will be discussed in chapter 8. Increasingly in the 1980s, therefore, the federal and state courts began to view the related issues of pregnancy and abortion in curiously similar ways by entertaining more state interference with pregnant women's private decisions about their life styles (including personal health and sexual preference) and with their decisions about adoption or abortion, thus reflecting contemporary conservative opinion on these topics.[39]

Other recent decisions are either discouraging or disquieting for the cause of complete female equality, especially where redistributive economic issues are at stake. Because women are more than half of the population, the Supreme Court has refrained from decisions involving them that would result in significant redistribution of monies. This is particularly evident in the way the Court has avoided taking on the issue of comparable worth or pay equity for women who still largely work in a labor market that remains nearly as sex segregated as it was in 1900. For example, over half of all adult women who were in the labor force in 1984 still found work in traditional female occupations that offer few opportunities for advancement and where the wage differentials remain the greatest. Thus, the Equal Pay Act of 1963 has been unsuccessful in obtaining equality of pay in the workplace for women, except for those well-educated women who have entered such traditionally male-dominated professions and businesses as pharmaceuticals, law, engineering, medicine, personnel management, banking, and accounting.[40] The Equal Pay Act has not helped the vast majority of those blue- and pink-collar working women who remain in sex-segregated jobs, for their salaries cannot be compared with those of men in the same jobs because there are no men in these jobs.

In 1984, 53.5 percent of all adult women worked; by March 1989, 57.2 percent of all women over sixteen were part of the paid labor force, compared with 76.9 percent of all men. It is estimated that by the year 2000, between 61 and 64 percent of all adult women will be working for wages or salaries. Yet in 1984, women employed full-time routinely earned only sixty-five cents for every dollar earned by full-time working men due to the sex segregation of the labor market and unequal pay scales based on gender discrimination. By the first quarter of 1989, the median annual earnings of women working full-time all year had risen to 69.6 percent of the earnings for men, or $17,056 compared to $24,336. (In some states, the sex-based earnings gap is much larger. In Utah, for example, the figure in 1987 was fifty-two cents on the dollar.) Black women in 1950 made only half of white women's earnings, but by 1989 they had narrowed that gap by earning 88 percent of what white women earned. Historically, a higher percentage of black women have participated in the labor force than white women. In 1989, that gap had narrowed to its lowest point with 57.8 percent of black women working, compared to 56.5 percent of white women. More surprising perhaps is that the earnings gap between women and men with five years of college education remains close to the national average of 69 percent, indicating that even the increased salaries and opportunities available to college-educated women cannot overcome the factors determining that men are paid more than women at every level of employment in the United States. The Rand Corporation has predicted that full time women workers will earn only seventy-four cents on the dollar compared to men by the end of the century. Moreover, this much-publicized wage gap is primarily a differentiation between the earnings of married —not single—women and married and single men. In other words, marriage poses an economic disability for women that most of them cannot overcome. Therefore, as more married women have entered the work force, it is not surprising that the gap between the earnings of *married* women and all men nearly doubled between 1955 and 1975. It has been declining slightly since.[41]

Only comparable work can help the vast majority of minority and nonminority working women overcome gender-based wage discrimination. Comparable worth —or pay equity, as it is also known—does not address the origins of wage disparities between women and men in terms of sex discrimination; nor does it propose to eliminate the sex-segregated labor market. Comparable-worth procedures do not, for example, concentrate on comparing similar or the same jobs that women and men perform. Instead, the procedures try to establish equivalencies, or equity, among *different* jobs performed by women and men. Such comparable-worth guidelines try to recognize the "true worth" of jobs traditionally held by women and compensating them more adequately for doing stereotypically female work. At the end of the 1980s, conventional wisdom held that comparable worth threatened the free-market economy and would bankrupt most private and public employers. To date, in both Canada and the United States, the most successful attempts to establish comparable worth have been at the level of state government jobs, not in the federal or private sectors. While comparable worth would represent an advance for female workers because it would gradually improve wages in their portion of the already sex-segregated job market, there is little indication that it would end that segregation or male domination of the most prestigious positions in the economy.[42] Thus, if my "broken-barometer" theory holds true, working women should begin to be accorded comparable worth sometime in the twenty-first century when it is no longer considered an important economic concession, but rather a "reward" for fulfilling a traditional female role in the work force.

Both the Supreme Court and Congress have steered clear of the comparable-worth issue. In 1983, the Supreme Court refused to provide retroactive relief to women whose employers had offered male employees retirement options higher than those for females making the same contributions, even though the justices agreed that such a practice violated Title VII. However, in County of Washington v. Gunther, 452 U.S. 161 (1981), the justices appeared to encourage the concept of comparable worth by allowing female prison guards to claim intentional wage discrimination even though their work was different from male guards. Since then other federal judges have generally pulled back whenever they feared that retroactive payments of any kind would threaten the economic status quo. Twice in 1982 district courts refused to honor the theory of comparable worth. On 24 November 1985, the Supreme Court refused to review a ruling by the U.S. Court of Appeals for the Ninth Circuit Court in San Francisco against a comparable-worth suit brought by the nursing faculty at the University of Washington.[43] Avoiding the comparable-worth issue in the American Federation of State, County, and Municipal Employees' (AFSCME) suit against the state of Washington, the justices freed themselves to take on that question, when the time comes, with an equally conservative approach. By the end of the 1980s, the Supreme Court had not had to face this issue because in October 1985, a three-judge panel of the same federal appeals court in San Francisco reversed a 1983 decision by Federal District Judge Jack E. Tanner in Tacoma who had upheld the AFSCME claim that the state of Washington illegally maintained "a compensation system which discriminates on the basis of sex." Thus, the Burger Court let stand an interpretation of Title VII that "does not obligate" states "to eliminate an economic inequality which it did not create"—namely, uniformly lower wages for women in government jobs.[44]

During the second Reagan administration officials openly opposed congressional legislation on pay equity with such statements as it is the "looniest idea since Looney Tunes came on the screen." While the Bush administration will probably follow in the footsteps of its predecessor on this issue, comparable worth is likely to remain a lively topic of discussion in Congress for the remainder of this century. Among other things, comparable worth is being attacked by a younger generation of aspiring professional women on the grounds that "paying above-market wages for 'women's work,' . . . ensures that women stay in those jobs for good, instead of striking out into largely male fields."[45] As long as such male standards of success prevail, there is little hope that Congress or the courts can avoid endorsing more blind alleys for women in the future, as they did in the past with protective-labor legislation and equal pay for equal work.

Statements about preserving the rapidly vanishing typical American family still reverberated with increasing vigor in the Democratic Congress and the executive branch at the end of the 1980s, even though less than a quarter of all families in the United States are now composed of working husbands and nonworking, full-time housewives. Similarly, arguments about child care and parental leaves still assume that they are primarily the responsibility of working women, *not* working men. As Freeman has pointed out, legal blind alleys for women result from litigation and legislation that, despite demographic and socioeconomic profiles to the contrary, continue to accept the traditional "married couple as the basic economic unit . . . [on] the assumption that it is socially desirable for one class of adults to be economically dependent on another."[46] Blind alleys may also be lurking in any legislation or litigation on pornography, abortion, child care, and comparable worth that does not address the remaining institutionalized forms of female inequality and, hence, the continued dependency of women within marriage and the work force. There appeared little indication that even the most ardent advocates of significant socioeconomic change for women believed that they would prevail under the last years of the second Reagan administration because of increasing fragmentation within the Second Women's movement and the increasing strength of fundamentalism. Without more unity and organization among female activists, this could become a self-fulfilling prophecy under the Bush administration and, possibly, for the remainder of this century.

In this climate, it is no wonder that federal courts handed down a particularly erratic batch of decisions from 1984 through 1989. The Supreme Court, for example, in 1984 ordered the U.S. Jaycees to admit women and said that law firms may not discriminate on the basis of sex in deciding which lawyers to promote as partners. In another decisive seven-to-zero decision in May 1987, the justices rejected the argument of the Rotary International that its member clubs were more selective and service oriented than the Jaycees, and, therefore, they should be able to exclude women because the Rotarian right to private association deserved the same constitutional protection that the Court reserved for such highly intimate, highly personal relationships as marriage, childbearing, and cohabitation with relatives. Instead, in a decision similar to the one in the *Roberts v. U.S. Jaycees* case, the Court ruled that the First Amendment did not exempt Rotary clubs from state laws against sex discrimination.[47] Another bright legal light on the gender horizon in recent years has been the Supreme Court decision declaring that sexual harassment of an employee by a supervisor violated federal law against discrimination in the workplace. However, as noted in chapter 8, the June 1986 sexual-harassment decision by the Burger Court in Meritor Savings Bank v. Vinson, 477 U.S. 57 (1986), did not have any redistributive or fundamentally unsettling economic or moral impact on American society—continuing the standard pattern set in gender-related cases.

Finally, on 20 June 1988, the justices once again unanimously upheld a 1984 New York City law "requiring the admission of women to large, private clubs that play an important role in business and professional life." Specifically, the statute banned discrimination in private clubs that have more than four hundred members, provide regular meal service, and accept payment from nonmembers for meals and other services. In New York City Club Association v. New York City, 108 S. Ct. 2225 (1988), the closed-door policy of a number of New York's most prestigious, private, all-male clubs, including the Century (Club) Association, was on the line and failed to prevail. While a few other similar all-male bastions, such as the ten-thousand-member New York Athletic Club and the twenty-three-hundred-member San Francisco Bohemian Club, are still fighting in the courts on the grounds that they are strictly private and not business oriented, the forced opening of the Century Club to women encouraged cities all over the country to pass such antidiscriminatory legislation or to enforce previously approved statutes.

Unfortunately, as the list of the first twenty women asked to become members of the Century Club became known, a few responded in such stereotypically

"feminine" fashion that the significance of *New York City Club* was temporarily
lost. "At the Knickerbocker Club, where I am a member because I am the widow
of two members, I am not allowed into the dining room, the reading room and
some other rooms," remarked socialite Brooke Astor, one of those asked to join
the Century Club. "I am perfectly comfortable with that," she continued, because "older men don't want to hear women gossiping in the reading room." More
to the point, however, a number of women, including some of those initially
approached by the Century Club after the Union League Club decision, turned
down the "honor" forced by a Supreme Court decision, while others, eligible for
membership in similar clubs, have been refusing to join despite the obvious
business advantages. Generally speaking, these were older professional women
whose memories of being denied admission earlier make them less ambivalent
than younger professional women about accepting "acceptance" involuntarily
brought about by litigation.[48]

In Grove City College v. Bell, 465 U.S. 555 (1984), the justices gutted Title
IX by ruling that individual units of educational institutions could discriminate
and not endanger the federal aid received by other units. In effect, this meant
that the receipt of Basic Educational Opportunity Grants by some Grove City
College students did not require institution-wide coverage under Title IX, thereby
weakening its enforcement possibilities dramatically. On 31 May 1986, President
Reagan's nominee to be assistant education secretary for civil rights withdrew her
name from consideration because the Grove City decision made that office within
the Department of Education "impotent." The decision allowed school districts
to go back to "resegregation, rank and brutal," educational analyst, psychologist,
and lawyer Barbara Lerner said in rejecting her nomination.[49] Her words proved
prophetic because this decision did affect other civil rights laws, thus limiting
their application of Title IX to specific programs—not entire institutions.

Every year since 1984 opponents of *Grove City* introduced into Congress the
Civil Rights Restoration Bill—one segment of which would have overruled the
narrow interpretation of Title IX for schools and colleges. Until May 1987, it
died by filibuster in the Senate. With the Senate under Democratic control for
the first time in the 1980s, civil rights leaders broke this three-year stalemate and
sent the Civil Rights Restoration Act to the floor of the Senate for debate. This
bill extended civil rights protection for minorities, women, the disabled, and the
elderly. Senator Edward M. Kennedy, chair of the Senate Labor and Human
Resources Committee, which forwarded the bill after a straight twelve-to-four
bipartisan vote, declared the vote "a major victory," saying that "after years of
filibuster, the logjam is finally breaking on civil rights."[50]

By the end of 1987, both houses of Congress had approved the Civil Rights
Restoration Act even though President Reagan indicated he would veto the

measure. In March 1988, Congress overrode Reagan's veto, thus voiding the Supreme Court decision in *Grove City* and restoring Title IX to its previous potential for improving conditions on campuses around the country with respect to treatment of women, especially in the area of providing equivalent sports programs with men.[51] (Vice President George Bush refused to take a stand during the 1988 presidential campaign for or against this veto.) Although the Civil Rights Restoration Act broadened Title IX to prohibit general discrimination throughout an entire institution or agency if *any part* of that institution or agency received federal financial assistance, it contained an antiabortion amendment.[52]

The basic reason that the Civil Rights Restoration Bill had languished in Congress for four years was due to opposition from groups that refused to support it unless supporters specifically removed abortion from the scope of coverage under Title IX. Although nothing in the original Title IX had referred to abortion, regulations adopted in 1975 to implement the education law required that schools and colleges treat all pregnancy-related conditions, including the "termination of pregnancy," like any other temporary disability. Catholic, along with Protestant religious fundamentalist groups, thus prevented passage until the legislation included an antiabortion amendment permitting the exclusion of this medical procedure *even* by nondenominational educational institutions with hospital facilities. The Danforth Amendment divided supporters of equal rights for women, but not enough to prevent passage of the Civil Rights Restoration Act.

Equally disturbing were lower-court affirmative-action suits decided in 1985 and 1986. Two district court decisions negatively affected very different groups of women who failed in their attempts to show discrimination on the part of the State Department and Sears, Roebuck and Company, respectively.[53] In the first, *Palmer v. Shultz,* the U.S. District Court for the District of Columbia held that, despite overwhelming statistical evidence to the contrary, the Department of State did not discriminate against women by disproportionately assigning them to the consular division rather than to the more prestigious political division of the foreign service and denied, among other charges, that the written exam had a negatively disparate impact on female candidates for the foreign service. A similar decision was reached at the beginning of 1986 by the U.S. District Court for the Northern District of Illinois, Eastern Division, in an EEOC case against Sears claiming that it discriminated against women in high-paying, commission-sales positions.[54] Both decisions were similar in that the respective district courts pointed out flaws in the statistical evidence presented by the plaintiffs (showing greater sophistication about quantitative methodology on the part of judges than in class-action suits during the 1970s) and questioned whether a *prima facie* case of intent to discriminate can rest on statistics alone. Moreover, both cited the absence of "anecdotal" (personal) testimony on behalf of the plaintiffs and the fact that the State Department and Sears had initiated internal affirmative-action programs as factors favoring the respective defendants. Finally, in both decisions the judges ruled that the plaintiffs' lawyers failed in their reliance on "disparate-treatment" or "disparate-impact" theory to prove discriminatory intent as required by previous Title VII cases.[55]

I stress these similarities in the two decisions because, contrary to some claims, taken together in 1985 and 1986 they seem to presage how other courts might rule on similar class-action suits in the future under the influence of the conservative majority on the Rehnquist Court.[56] In particular, both cases brought into question, even if they did not constitute an outright rejection of, an earlier 1984 district court opinion in *Segar v. Smith,* in which a federal judge had accepted the reliability of statistical proof *without* personal testimony, saying that while "statistics . . . are not irrefutable . . . when a plaintiff's statistical method focuses on the appropriate pool and generates evidence of discrimination at a statistically significant level, no sound policy exists for subjecting the plaintiff to the additional requirement of either providing anecdotal evidence or showing gross disparities." Since this 1984 decision relied on the 1977 landmark Supreme Court decision in *Teamsters v. United States* and the justices refused to hear the case on appeal, both the plaintiffs in *Palmer v. Shultz* and *EEOC v. Sears* were probably assuming that their exclusively statistical approach would prevail.[57]

In this instance, the EEOC was on shakier ground because it did not have an "appropriate labor pool," in the sense that it did not have a list of potential Sears employees who could be individually identified. In contrast, women in the State Department and applicants for foreign-service jobs constituted an identifiable pool. In fact, the EEOC statisticians made a number of questionable assumptions in constructing their hypothetical pool of applicants and in calculating the expected hiring percentages that Sears should have met since 1973. So perhaps *Sears* should be distinguished from earlier federal decisions in which there were identifiable labor pools. Nonetheless, the reasoning in the *Sears* and *Palmer* decisions remained very similar. Judges in both, for example, utilized the disparate-treatment theory to bolster a decision already reached on other jurisprudential grounds. Moreover, the possible influence of these two decisions on future statistically based class-action suits cannot be lightly dismissed on the grounds that the failure of these class-action suits will automatically encourage other companies and governmental agencies to establish gender-based affirmative-action programs as Sears and the State Department had done.[58]

The *Sears* case, however, was also important because of the shock waves it sent through the national community of female historians because two of the expert witnesses testifying on opposite sides in the case were academics specializing in women's history. Neither the testimony of Rosalind Rosenberg (for Sears) nor that of Alice Kessler-Harris (for EEOC) determined the outcome of the suit, which was primarily a "pitched battle over the meaning of statistical data." Reminiscent of the "Brandeis brief" in the *Muller* decision over three-quarters of a century earlier (but without the precedent-making overtones), the historical testimonies of both Rosenberg and Kessler-Harris were relegated to two paragraphs and two footnotes in the text of the decision. Since the ruling, however, a personal and political clash between these two historians emerged at various scholarly meetings and in the columns of national newspapers and magazines.[59] Consequently, the case became an ideological football in a game between conservative and radical historians, subordinating its legal significance. The former tend to win such battles in the media because they claim to be practicing "objective" history by following their scholarship wherever it may lead—even to a negative decision in a class-action suit—while the latter always appear to be using history for some contemporary political purpose.

Neither group of historians has ever exercised a monopoly on the truth because there is no "objective" history. Unadulterated historical acts do not "lead" anyone anywhere. They have to be interpreted. Conservatives use history to justify the status quo (which was the outcome of the *Sears* cases and the thrust of Rosenberg's testimony, in which she said that women's cultural conditioning naturally led them to avoid competitive sales jobs); radicals use history to try to change the status quo (Kessler-Harris argued that Sears had not provided enough incentive or opportunity for women to take advantage of commission-sales positions). It is unfortunate that the *Sears* case devolved into a well-publicized dispute within the discipline of history that neither helped feminist attorneys (or feminist historians) better represent women the next time around in such class-action suits nor educated the general public about the legal implications of the case. In the course of this academic dispute, the technical and legal aspects of the case became lost or turned into what they were *not* about—namely, "equality-versus-difference" or "equality through sameness or difference."[60] While both briefs addressed the question of gendered discrimination, the crux of the case rested on certain relatively small statistical disparities—not on the current theoretical debate within the legal and historical professions over the meaning of equality for women of the past and present.

In its original 1979 lawsuit, the EEOC alleged forty-two major claims of sex discrimination, based primarily on its finding of statistical disparities in the sexual composition of the Sears work force. But over the next five years it abandoned most of its allegations. The case ultimately rested on whether Sears was guilty of discrimination between 1973 and 1980 in either of two areas: (1) hiring and promotion into commission sales or (2) pay within certain management jobs. In support of its allegations, the EEOC originally included thirty-five complainants in its suit, culled from the investigation of the previous six years. But it subsequently abandoned all of its individual complaints because they were not relevant to either major charge, basing its arguments solely on a statistical analysis of the Sears work force, with no individual testimony. That gender disparities existed among those hired or promoted into commission saleswork was never questioned, although the court of appeals later appeared to question whether even the EEOC's initial *prima facie* case was statistically sound.[61] Moreover, the burden of proof throughout this ten-month, $2.5 million trial rested on the EEOC *to prove discriminatory intent* on the part of Sears. As might be expected, most of that time was spent hearing statistical testimony, resulting in a transcript of over twenty thousand pages, of which only ten hours, at most, consisted of historical testimony by Rosenberg and Kessler-Harris.

For reasons that remain unclear, the EEOC chose to construct "expected hire rates," which it claimed Sears had not met, based on an artificial data base consisting of a hypothetical pool of applicants who had not actually applied for commission-sales positions but were supposedly "similar" to those who did apply.[62] All Sears had to do was to document the results of a rough affirmative-action program it had initiated in 1968 *before* the Justice Department had begun its investigation (and of the one in 1974 requiring quotas *after* the investigation began); deny any discriminatory intent; and question the validity of EEOC's statistics as evidence of proof of "significant" statistical disparities. Between 1973 and 1980, the company had hired 3 women for every 10 full-time commission-sales openings and four women for every ten part-time ones. (According to the EEOC's "expected hire rates," Sears should have employed 4 and 5.6 women, respectively, in each category.) Had those percentages been met, presumably there would have been no suit against Sears.[63] The aggregate increase in the number of women hired initially into full-time commission sales approximately doubled during the years the company was under investigation; part-time hirings in these same positions ranged from 37 to 52 percent—over half of whom had previously been part of the company's noncommission sales force. (It should be noted, however, that these are the figures the trial judge accepted; EEOC and Sears never agreed on the same set of figures in any category.)

Compounding the fact that it chose to rest its entire case on statistics that could easily be deconstructed by showing their artificial construction, EEOC magnified this error by building into its statistical analysis both a crucial and arbitrary assumption that men and women were equally interested in commission-sales jobs at Sears. This meant that EEOC based its statistical argument on the highly problematic premise that "the job interests of men and women are indistinguishable"—one that should have delighted academic poststructural historians, who stress differences among women more than between women and men.[64]

Such was not the case, however, because lawyers for the company proceeded to deconstruct this argument with Rosenberg's testimony that historically men and women had exhibited different job-preference interests. Obviously, Rosenberg's testimony contained more damaging evidence about difference and variety among workers than Kessler-Harris's, because such an approach could not injure Sears' defense. Kessler-Harris was left in the unenviable position of defending the EEOC set of statistical claims that she either did not know or did not care whether they were arbitrary at best and exaggerated at worst. In any case, she responded to cross-examination with oversimplifications of her own, by denying that personal preference influenced women's job choices and asserting that "failure to find women in so-called nontraditional jobs can thus *only* be interpreted as a consequence of employers' unexamined attitudes or preferences" (emphasis added).[65]

Although Kessler-Harris later admitted that this statement was a "mistake," prompted by courtroom inexperience, the bulk of her testimony lends itself less to the general thrust of her own historical writings on working women than Rosenberg's use of Kessler-Harris's work and the monographs of other labor historians on the question of gendered differences in the workplace. Kessler-Harris was simply not as "free" to argue on behalf of the difference between working women and men as was Rosenberg because she feared that "judicial recognition of such differences might allow employers to shift all responsibility for the prevailing allocations of gender role to women themselves." Despite all the subsequent publicity and rhetoric to the contrary, neither historian's actual written and oral testimony addressed the theoretical aspects of individual-versus-collective rights and equal-versus-special treatment of women in their pursuit of male equality. They actually argued in court over the differences between women and men in job preferences. Outside the court their supporters turned this testimony into a poststructural, personal, and political debate. Moreover, the contradictory claims about which expert witness made the best use of history or existing scholarship in her testimony is also a moot one in terms of the final outcome of the trial, although the trial judge clearly thought that Rosenberg had offered "more convincing testimony" than Kessler-Harris.[66]

In February 1986, the EEOC lost its suit against one of the largest employers of women in the country and made a weak appeal of Federal District Judge John A. Nordberg's decision on the matter of disparate-impact claims. Sears immediately cross-appealed, claiming that Nordberg should have dismissed the case initially on grounds of conflict of interest involving David A. Copus, the EEOC attorney who was in charge of investigating Sears at the same time he was involved in planning antidiscriminatory strategy for the National Organization for Women (one of whose prime targets was Sears). In its two-to-one decision affirming Nordberg's exoneration of Sears on all counts, even the one dissenting judge of the Seventh Circuit Court joined his colleagues in condemning the strong appearance of conflict of interest involving Copus, the EEOC, and NOW. Given the questionable attitudes and motivation on the part of most publicized participants and their supporters on both sides,[67] this was not the case that historians of women should have turned into a *cause célèbre* in the name of poststructural theories about the meaning of difference and equality.

A year after the *Sears* decision *Palmer* was reversed in 1987 by a U.S. court of appeals, which remanded this action for further proceedings and fact findings. As a result, in 1989, the State Department was enjoined to stop further discrimination against women in seven of the categories described by the original suit. Among other things this resulted in the cancellation of the 1989 foreign-service oral and written exams for women and men until the State Department drafted nonsexist guidelines for them. The Supreme Court also appeared to take some of the edge off the *Sears* defeat by upholding six to three, on 25 March 1987, an affirmative-action plan that promoted a woman to the position of road maintenance dispatcher ahead of a man who had scored slightly higher on a civil-service exam, in order to remedy a longstanding gender imbalance in the skilled-craft job category of a local government agency. In the decision in Johnson v. Transportation Agency of Santa Clara County, California, 480 U.S. 616 (1987), the justices ruled six to three in favor of the constitutionality of sex-conscious promotions to redress gender imbalances in the work force even when an employer had not been found guilty of discrimination. Race-conscious promotions and training programs had been upheld since 1978, and for the first time the justices in *Johnson* extended this principle to gender and to employers in the public sector. However, they used strongly preferential, if not actually protectionist, language, with little precise guidance about how to construct such voluntary affirmative programs or to evaluate the existing statistical imbalance in relation to the available pool of qualified applicants in the local area.

In summary, Justice William Brennan, writing for the majority in *Johnson,* assumed that sex was "but one of several factors" taken into consideration and that the agency's affirmative-action plan was "flexible," "temporary," and "did not unnecessarily harm male employees' rights."[68] The three dissenting justices did not make the same assumptions; in fact, they wrote opinions indicating that Title VII of the Civil Rights Act of 1964 instead of supporting such affirmative-action plans actually *forbade them.* These dissenting justices moved into the majority on the Supreme Court under the Bush administration with the predictable results, which will be discussed below.

A month earlier, in February 1987, the Supreme Court also emphatically reversed what had appeared to be a turn away from racial preferences in employment. Between 1984 and 1986, it had twice ruled that seniority rights should prevail over preserving minority hiring gains when it came to "layoffs." In *Firefighters Union v. Stotts* and *Wygant v. Jackson Board of Education,* the justices did not overrule their previous decisions upholding the use of goals, timetables, or quotas in the hiring of minorities. They drew a distinction, however, between the impact of affirmative-action hiring plans and layoff protection. "In cases involving valid *hiring* goals," Justice Lewis Powell stated in *Wygant,* "the burden to be borne by innocent individuals is diffused to a considerable extent among society generally." But, he concluded, "though hiring goals may burden some innocent individuals, they simply do not impose the same kind of injury that layoffs impose." From the beginning of the second Reagan administration, however, the Justice Department under Attorney General Edwin Meese III made a concerted effort to use both decisions to discredit "all gender-conscious or race-conscious remedies" in the hiring process, "even after discrimination has been proven."[69]

The systematic antiaffirmative-action interpretation of these two rulings by spokespersons for the executive branch (based largely on the dissenting opinions in each decision) disturbed civil rights advocates much more than the actual issues decided by the Supreme Court up until 1989. For example, the Reagan administration was dealt a double blow in this matter on 2 July 1986 when the Supreme Court handed down two decisions upholding goals and quotas for the hiring and promotion plans of a sheetmetal workers' union and a firefighters' union.[70] The position of Reagan's Justice Department was rebuked again on 25 February 1987, in United States v. Paradise, 107 S. Ct. 1053, when the justices in a close five-to-four decision ordered Alabama to promote one black state trooper for every white trooper to counter a severe pattern of past discrimination. *Paradise,* along with *Johnson,* constituted major victories for minorities and women despite (or some have suggested because of) the blatant attempts of Reagan's Justice Department under Attorney General Meese to reverse the clock on affirmative action. The dissenting opinions in all of these cases indicated, however, that Reagan's first two appointees to the Court, Justices Sandra Day O'Connor and Antonin Scalia, were increasingly concerned about the ambiguous expansiveness of affirmative-action remedies that did not require proof of intentional and systematic discrimination against women and minorities or question their practical effectiveness in relation to qualified pools of workers both in the work force and surrounding community.

These setbacks for Attorney General Meese and the Reagan administration were somewhat offset by the Rehnquist Court in the summer and fall of 1988 and during the first weeks of the George Bush presidency in 1989. On 25 April 1988, the Supreme Court decided by a slim five-to-four vote to reconsider its own twelve-year-old ruling in Runyon v. McCrary, 427 U.S. 160 (1976), when it was considering a pending North Carolina civil rights case, *Patterson v. McLean Credit Union,* even though neither side had questioned the earlier decision. In 1976, the justices held that when Congress passed the 1866 Civil Rights Act, it intended to prohibit racial discrimination in private schools. This meant that the reconstruction statute (now Section 1981 of the U.S. Code) allowed for the right of action when racial discrimination occurred in private transactions not covered by such employment discrimination statutes as Title VII. Since the 1976 *Runyon* decision, the Court has also applied this and other post–Civil War statutes to many kinds of private conduct, creating a web of affirmative-action precedents that, if overturned, would, according to Justice Stevens, undermine the faith of racial minorities in the steadfastness of the government's commitment to equal rights. When the Supreme Court heard oral arguments in *Patterson* in October 1988, some of the earlier enthusiasm on the part of those justices who originally agreed to reconsider *Runyon* back in April appeared to have waned, but this proved to be an illusion as will be noted below.[71]

Another major decision that has helped offset the setbacks experienced by antiaffirmative-action advocates in the later part of the second Reagan administration occurred in January 1989. Writing for the six-to-three majority in *City of Richmond v. J. A. Croson Co.,* Justice Sandra Day O'Connor declared unconstitutional a "set-aside" program that mandated 30 percent of all public works construction jobs to minority contractors. While the significance of this decision will not be known for several more years, it appears potentially damaging for affirmative-action programs aimed at redressing past discriminatory patterns. The Reagan administration, through the Justice Department and the U.S. Commission on Civil Rights, had been attempting since 1985 to rewrite a 1965 executive order and Labor Department guidelines developed during the Nixon administration that had given rise to these "set-asides" for minority contractors. Not all of Reagan's cabinet agreed with this approach, and one report by the U.S. Civil Rights Commission recommending a suspension of the program reserving contracts for minority companies was rejected. Then came *City of Richmond.*[72]

For the first time in its consideration of so-called reverse-discrimination cases brought by white males objecting to special benefits or special treatment of minorities and women, the Supreme Court, in this 1989 decision, made *all* racial classifications equally suspect and, therefore, subject to strict scrutiny under the equal-protection clause of the Fourteenth Amendment. Until *City of Richmond,* the most well known of the "reverse-discrimination" cases was Bakke v. Regents of University of California, 438 U.S. 265 (1978)—even though this decision did not decide the issue because the justices chose to argue on narrow statutory grounds that the University of California at Davis had to admit Allan Bakke to medical school because it had violated Title VI of the 1964 Civil Rights Act.[73]

The *Bakke* case raised a number of issues, not the least of which was the possibility that white males could systematically use the charge of "reverse discrimination," based on constitutionally guaranteed individual rights, to prevent women and minorities from obtaining redress based on the assumption that they had suffered from past discrimination. First, it is natural to be suspicious of any closely split decision. Multiple arguments represent a form of judicial individualism and "highly particularistic decisions" that connote either shifting divisions of opinion on the Court or a reluctance to establish a constitutional precedent. Thus, when nine individual justices arrive at two majority opinions through six separate written statements, it does not take any great amount of skepticism to wonder whether their conclusions determined their reasoning rather than the other way around. After all, it has been said many times that "what the Supreme Court seeks, it is apt to find," especially on controversial issues.[74] Clearly, a majority of the justices thought that Bakke should be admitted to medical school; they simply disagreed on what legal grounds to admit him. There were, after all, seven separate opinions handed down in the infamous *Dred Scott* decision—only one more than in *Bakke* and four more than in *Patterson* (discussed below). Unlike *Dred Scott,* in which all of the opinions led to a single conclusion, there were two majority (five-to-four) decisions in *Bakke,* apparently because the justices found the issues so divisive.

Neither majority settled the question of "reverse discrimination." One five-to-four opinion ordered the University of California at Davis Medical School to admit Allan Bakke; the other simultaneously held that race "may" be considered a factor in affirmative-action programs, although the Davis quota system for enrolling minorities in medical school was ruled unlawful. The most debilitating aspect of *Bakke* for all disadvantaged groups suffering from a history of discrimination would occur if the Court continued to insist, as it did in one set of the dual opinions, that racial and gender integration in hiring and admissions programs can only take place through the slow process of case-by-case, individual proof of discrimination—a definite retreat from the position taken by Chief Justice Burger in Griggs v. Duke Power Company, 401 U.S. 424 (1971), eight years earlier, in which he assigned the burden of proof in disparate-impact cases to the employer, not the employee, thus obviating the need for "individualized proof of causation."[75]

A problematic aspect of *Bakke* remains its assumption that civil rights judgments must be made individually rather than collectively on the basis of race or class. Theoretically, the Court could resurrect this aspect of the decision that did not recognize cultural or group needs, only the individual's right to find redress for discrimination. Despite *Bakke*'s potential for harming collective minority (and female) rights, all segments of the press—from the far right to the far left—hailed the decision as a victory for individualism. When in the late 1980s the justices finally applied constitutional jurisprudence in *City of Richmond* to the question of "reverse discrimination," they denied once again the collective needs of minorities suffering from discrimination.

Another "time bomb" in *Bakke* concerned the right of private parties to sue for relief under Title VI. The justices split on this point, not ruling one way or the other. One year later this indecision was settled when the Court ruled in Cannon v. the University of Chicago, 441 U.S. 677 (1979), that individuals have a private right of action under both Titles VI and IX of the 1964 Civil Rights Act.[76] Unlike *Bakke,* this ruling did not admit Geraldine Cannon to medical school; it sent the case back to the lower courts for a fuller examination of the charge that she was a victim of sex discrimination. Like *Bakke,* however, *Cannon* opened the door for more "reverse-discrimination" cases throughout the 1980s, although most civil rights attorneys in the late 1970s did not appear to question whether the stress on white male individual rights could redound to the disadvantage of women and minority groups. Instead, they seemed to think that this negative potential was more than offset by the fact that individual victims of discrimination no longer needed to rely solely on suits brought by the government to obtain redress under certain portions of civil rights legislation.[77]

At the time, most liberal legal interpretations of *Bakke* ignored the way in which individual justices utilized previous cases involving gender. Not a single opinion in *Bakke* indicated that sex, like race, should be a suspect classification subject to strict scrutiny. Thus, *Bakke* represented but one more decision in which the Burger Court backed off from *Frontiero v. Richardson.* This came to be the standard position of the Burger Court, for as Justice Powell stated in the majority opinion: "The Court has never viewed such classification [that is, gender] as inherently suspect or as comparable to racial or ethnic classifications for the purpose of equal-protection analysis."[78]

The gender cases most often cited by all the justices in *Bakke* were those connected with social security payments of one kind or another. Often, these involved male, rather than female, litigants who charged "reverse discrimination." Such cases were used by the different groupings of justices in this decision to prove diametrically opposed points. For example, even the liberally inclined Justices Brennan, White, Marshall, and Blackmun cited these cases about the unfairness of sex discrimination to show that the considerations raised in them "carry *even more force* when applied to racial classifications (emphasis added)." Thus, they stated that "race like 'gender-based classifications too often [has] been inexcusably utilized to stereotype and stigmatize politically powerless segments of society.' . . . [and] race like gender . . . is an immutable characteristic which its possessors are powerless to escape or set aside." Then they used these arguments to support the idea that "race-conscious [collective] remedial actions [not gender-conscious ones]" were legitimate and sometimes took precedent over the traditional constitutional concern for individualism.[79]

With even stronger language, Justice Powell used the very same early "reverse-discrimination" cases involving men to show that each situation was "materially different from the facts of this case" and that gender-based distinctions *were categorically not* analogous to race-based ones, because the former "are less likely to create the analytical and practical problems present in preferential programs premised on racial or ethnic criteria." His conclusion denied any collective remedy by saying that the Court has "never approved a classification that aids persons perceived as members of relatively vicitimized groups at the expense of other innocent individuals." Regardless of the arguments being justified by citing these previous gender cases, it is clear that none of the justices on the Burger Court at that time viewed sex as being a constitutional issue as important as race in the 1978 *Bakke* decision.[80] Some now argue that the Rehnquist Court may exacerbate this distinction, while at the same time retreating to proof of individual intent to discriminate in both race- and gender-based civil rights cases. If this prediction proves true, it would constitute a major setback for women and minorities in their battle for traditional equality.

The most publicized "reverse-discrimination" suit to follow Allan Bakke's was Brian Weber's against a Kaiser Aluminum factory in Gramercy, Louisiana. In 1978, Weber challenged Kaiser's voluntary affirmative-action program that established a nationwide agreement guaranteeing less-senior minority applicants half of the openings in new training programs for all skilled craft jobs. Weber also charged that Kaiser's program violated Section 703 (j) of Title VII of the Civil Rights Act of 1964 because the voluntary program was not adopted to remedy past discrimination—that is, Kaiser had not been sued, nor did it claim it had discriminated in the past. It was feared if *Steelworkers v. Weber,* 443 U.S. 193 (1979), was decided on similar grounds as *Bakke,* it would have had profoundly disruptive effects on hiring and promotion based on affirmative action in offices in factories all over the United States. Fortunately, the justices divided five to two on 27 June 1979 against Weber, saying that Congress had not intended Title VII to forbid all race-conscious affirmative-action programs on the part of private employers, as long as they were temporary in nature and "not designed to maintain racial balance, but to 'eliminate a manifest racial imbalance.' " It remained unclear whether *Weber* applied to public employees. But since the Court also reached its decision in *Weber* on narrow statutory, rather than constitutional, grounds, whether societally induced avoidance of certain "traditionally segregated jobs" by women and minorities could or should be addressed by remedial affirmative-action programs without violating the equal-protection clause and perverting the intent of Title VII remained unsettled, along with the question of "reverse discrimination."[81]

In contrast to *Bakke* and *Weber,* almost a dozen years earlier when the justices refused to define constitutional jurisprudence with respect to "reverse discrimination" and remedial race-conscious efforts, their decision in *City of Richmond* held that "an amorphous claim that there has been past discrimination in a particular industry cannot justify the use of an unyielding racial quota." It further maintained that state and local governments had been wrongly relying on a 1980 Supreme Court decision that upheld a federal 10 percent set-aside program to claim that "a city council . . . need not make specific findings of discrimination to engage in race-conscious relief" affirmative-action remedies.[82]

When the Court finally confronted the claim of "reverse discrimination" head on in 1989, it applied the legal standard called *strict scrutiny* to the Richmond program that gave members of one race preference over another. Those justices who had dissented or written highly qualified concurring opinions in *Wygant* and *Johnson* now claimed that a "wholly standardless approach to affirmative action" had been set into motion and must be curbed, since "the alteration of social attitudes" did not fall under the purvue of the Court. This means that in order to survive the charge of "reverse discrimination" by "nonminority and male victims," such programs must prove that they are based on "compelling state interest"—in this instance, the elimination and prevention of systematic and intentional racial discrimination. Since the Warren Court, strict constitutional scrutiny had usually been applied to void public statutes that overtly discriminated against minorities because it is exceedingly difficult for any local, state, or federal legislation to pass this test.[83]

In fact, the only example of a public act of racial discrimination to withstand strict-scrutiny analysis came in 1944, when the Supreme Court upheld the forcible removal and incarceration of Japanese-Americans during World War II.[84] Little wonder that Justice Thurgood Marshall (joined by Justices William J. Brennan Jr., and Harry A. Blackmun) wrote a thirty-four-page dissent in *City of Richmond,* declaring that the majority opinion constituted "a full-scale retreat from the court's longstanding solicitude to race-conscious remedial efforts, . . . scuttl[ing] one city's efforts to surmount its discriminatory past, and imperil[ing] those of dozens more localities. . . . In concluding that remedial classification warrants no different standards of review under the Constitution than the most brute and repugnant forms of state-sponsored racism," Marshall criticized the majority opinion for regarding "racial discrimination as largely a phenomenon of the past."[85]

Whether historical arguments should ever prevail in constitutional jurisprudence can always be questioned. As Lawrence Levy has noted, history has more often than not been misused by both the liberals and conservatives on the Supreme Court.[86] In *City of Richmond,* the documented history of past and present discrimination did not prevail; instead, ahistorical legal theory did. As one commentator noted: "the Court has declared that the racial playing field is now a level one," regardless of all factual evidence to the contrary. This point of view was particularly evident in Justice Scalia's separate opinion that gave no consideration to the symbolic importance of *City of Richmond* in the history of race relations. Scalia also appeared indifferent to the impact of this decision on the more than two hundred other consent agreements in effect across the country.[87] Once again minorities (and most likely women in some future decision) have been accorded equal opportunity to play a game in which the odds are overwhelmingly against them.

Since affirmative action can take many forms, ranging from recruiting and training programs to those establishing timetables, goals, and quotas, no doubt some programs will survive this new application of strict scrutiny, but many others will not. Although Justice O'Connor insisted that "nothing we say today precludes a state or local entity from taking action to rectify the effects of identified discrimination," she made it clear that only in the most extreme instances of proven intentional discrimination would "some form of narrowly tailored racial preference . . . be necessary to break down deliberate exclusion." O'Connor's words can be interpreted to mean that aggregate statistics showing racial (or gender) imbalance notwithstanding, unless "a specific person can prove a specific act of discrimination that specifically harmed him or her, there is no discrimination."[88] Individual discrimination is thus placed above group discrimination—as usual.

Unlike Justice Potter Stewart's remark about not being able to define pornography but knowing it when he saw it, newspaper columnist Tom Wicker has noted that "sadly, that's more than this Reagan Court appears able to say of racial discrimination." In fact, neither Justice Stewart nor Justice O'Connor was willing to accept the obvious negative impact of the two phenomena—racism and pornography—they insisted could not be documented with statistical or historical information. Yet, "in order to get beyond racism," Justice Blackmun correctly said in his 1978 dissent in *Bakke,* "we must first take account of race."[89] The same is true of sexism and its handmaiden, pornography. To overcome their deleterious effects on women, we must be willing to describe their historic development and to define them explicitly in the present, rather than continue to hide behind liberal or conservative legalese.

Thus, the Supreme Court would seem to have come full circle on the question of affirmative action with respect to racial discrimination in *City of Richmond*— from what Justice Stevens had called an "unambiguous" course since 1978 of permitting under Title VII "the voluntary adoption of special programs to benefit members of . . . minority groups," so long as employers are not required "to grant preferential treatment on the basis of race or gender," to what Justice Antonin Scalia (with Chief Justice Rehnquist concurring), in a dissenting opinion in *Johnson*, called a mandatory "state-enforced" system of discrimination against "predominantly unknown, unaffluent, unorganized" white males. In addition, Scalia raised once again the specter of women avoiding certain nontraditional jobs "because of longstanding social attitudes" and categorically denied that this type of self-selection was "as nefarious as conscious, exclusionary discrimination."

Since there is no "national consensus," according to Scalia in *Johnson*, on why the U.S. labor market remains so sex-segregated, it is not the duty of the court to undertake an "alteration of social attitudes" or to promote any "enormous expansion" of affirmative action in behalf of women "without the slightest justification or analysis."[90] To a degree, Scalia's remarks echo those of Chief Justice Waite in the 1875 decision denying Virginia Minor the right to vote, when he insisted that the Court's province was only to interpret the law not to presume to improve upon it. In any case, the *City of Richmond* decision and the changed composition of the U.S. Supreme Court, as the result of three Reagan appointments, does not bode well for a continuation, let alone an expansion, of affirmative-action decisions in the last decade of the twentieth century.[91]

## The Regressive Reagan Legacy

The potentially negative constitutional legacy of the Reagan administration did not begin to become a serious reality until a series of decisions following *City of Richmond*—after the fortieth president of the United States had left office. The Rehnquist Court appeared to temporarily swing into an affirmative-action mode in May 1989 with a six-to-three decision in Price Waterhouse v. Hopkins, 109 S. Ct. 1775 (1989), that stated that in some cases alleging intentional discrimination in hiring or promotion, employers—rather than employees—must prove that their decision was based on legitimate business and not discriminatory reasons. Then, in June, the other shoe fell—four shoes to be exact.

On 5 June, the first of a series of a five-to-four antiaffirmative-action decisions was handed down. In Wards Cove Packing Co., Inc. v. Atonio, 109 S. Ct. 2115 (1989), Eskimo and Asian workers in the salmon canneries in Alaska lost their fifteen-year-old suit when the justices decided to undermine the proaffirmative-action interpretation of *Griggs* by removing from employers the burden of justifying business practices, usually in the form of job requirements, that have a disparate (unfavorable) impact on employees. On the face of it, there appeared to be a conflict between the conclusion in *Price Waterhouse* and *Wards Cove.* There was not, however, because the two cases involved different categories under Title VII law. *Price Waterhouse* was brought by an individual alleging *intentional* discrimination. *Wards Cove* did not concern intent. Writing for the majority in *Wards Cove,* Justice Byron R. White arrived at a conclusion opposite to the one in *Price Waterhouse* by shifting this "persuasion" burden of proof to the plaintiffs. This reflected the concerns expressed in earlier cases by Justices O'Connor and Scalia—namely, that statistical proof of discrimination is not enough, especially if the percentage of *qualified* nonwhite job applicants and the percentage of *qualified* nonwhite population in the labor force are not significantly larger than the percentage of nonwhite workers in the most desirable or skilled jobs.[92]

Then, on 12 June the Court handed down two other decisions. One permitted white firefighters in Birmingham, Alabama, to challenge an eight-year-old affirmative-action consent-decree settlement. This "reverse-discrimination" decision in Martin v. Wilks, 109 S. Ct. 2180 (1989), placed no precise time limits on when such actions could be brought. Yet in another decision that same day, the justices, in a five-to-three vote, turned down the suit brought by three women in 1983 against AT&T's 1979 seniority program, which discriminated against women and blacks. In this five-year-old case, the Court said that the women's lawsuit was too late, ruling that such challenges must take place within three hundred days, even though the seniority system in question did not result in the women's demotion (after they lost seniority in 1979) until 1982. Scalia insisted in Lorance v. AT & T, 109 S. Ct. 2261 (1989), that cause for action under Title VII existed only *at the time* of the adoption of a discriminatory system and *not after its consequences.* "Requiring employees to sue anticipatorily or forever hold their peace," Justice Marshall retorted in his dissent, "was glaringly at odds with the purposes of Title VII."[93] White firefighters claiming "reverse discrimination" in Birmingham were not held to any such rigid time frame.

Finally, on 15 June the Court issued its long-awaited decision in Patterson v. McLean Credit Union, 109 S. Ct. 2363 (1989), reconsidering the 1866 Civil Rights Act embodied in the 1976 *Runyon* case. (See pages 263–64.) *Patterson* did not overrule *Runyon* (a majority of the justices simply damned their previous decision with faint praise by saying it was a correct decision for 1976) nor the reconstruction statute upon which it was based. But *Patterson* limited dramatically the statute's application in contemporary employment situations. The case involved a black woman teller who had claimed that after she had been hired, she was subjected to racial hazing when working as a teller at McLean Credit Union. Writing for the majority, the last Reagan appointee to the Supreme Court, Anthony M. Kennedy, wrote that Brenda Patterson had no cause for action under the 1866 Civil Rights Act (Section 1981 of the U.S. Code), whose operative words are "all peoples within the jurisdiction of the United States shall have the same right in every state . . . to make and enforce contracts . . . as is enjoyed by white citizens."[94]

Narrowly interpreting Section 1981, Kennedy insisted that the "right to make contracts does not extend, as a matter of logic or semantics, to conduct by the employer *after the contract relation has been established,* including breach of the terms of the contract or imposition of discriminatory working conditions" (emphasis added).[95] In separate dissenting opinions, both Justices Brennan and Stevens denied that the language of Section 1981 was intended to apply only to the "making" of a contract without regard for the fact that black employees may be subjected to racial harassment not experienced by similarly situated white workers. Despite Kennedy's defensive claim that "neither our words nor our decisions should be interpreted as signaling one inch of retreat from Congress' policy to forbid discrimination in the private sphere," it is difficult to interpret *Patterson* otherwise.[96]

Most important, taken together, these five U.S. Supreme Court decisions in the first six months of 1989 set a trend that is not likely to be soon reversed, given the fact that in each five-to-four decision the younger, conservative justices were in the majority; the older, liberal ones were in the minority. And in at least two instances, the Court went beyond the original position taken by the Justice Department under Reagan. In both *Patterson* and *Lorance,* the government had initially taken the side of the women plaintiffs. Additionally, in *Wards Cove* and *Patterson,* while the justices may not have completely reversed their 1971 and 1976 decisions in *Griggs* and *Runyon* and the statutes upon which these decisions were based, they have done something much more complex and difficult to correct with legislation. They have eliminated or seriously weakened the entire "superstructure of judicial interpretation" that had accrued from both these earlier civil rights decisions.[97]

Although only one of the five decisions was based on constitutional grounds (*City of Richmond*), it will not be easy for Congress to override the other four simply because interpretation of statutes is involved, as some legal commentators have suggested. After all, it took four years for Congress to overturn the *Grove City* decision. The statutes remain, but much of their interpretative significance is gone; and in *City of Richmond,* the legitimacy of hundreds of consent decrees in existence across the United States is now open to "reverse-discrimination" suits. These are issues that Congress cannot readily counter with general legislation, and the more specific Congress tries to become, the less likely is passage of countervailing statutes to overturn these antiaffirmative-action decisions.[98]

Thus, the Reagan and Rehnquist legacy had begun even before the Nixon and Burger legacy had time to resolve its somewhat ambiguous application of a "middle tier" of scrutiny. Taken as a whole, the Burger Court, in contrast to the early record of the Rehnquist Court, issued rulings that over the last fifteen years have come close to questioning most classifications based on gender—that is, to declaring sex a "suspect" category through "accumulated precedent."[99] Since 1971 the Burger Court, however, occasionally reverted to stereotypic views of women in a number of important cases (in addition to those discussed in the next chapter involving pregnant working women). For example, it forbade hiring women as guards in maximum-security prisons for men, upheld a California statutory rape law, and approved the all-male draft.[100] Moreover, there were a series of "reverse-discrimination" cases before *City of Richmond* brought by white males objecting to special benefits or affirmative-action programs for women and minorities.[101] In still another series of decisions, the justices endorsed "benign" sex discrimination in favor of women.[102] Granted, over the objections by men that certain sections of the Social Security Act or state property and divorce statutes discriminated against males, these rulings often have been aimed at redressing economic or other societal disadvantages that confront women, but the fact remains that many of them were rooted in paternalistic notions about "protecting" women through the use of special legislative treatment. This was implicitly true even in the 1987 *Johnson* ruling, as both Justices O'Connor and Scalia pointed out. In other decisions, the justices have refused to strike down certain statutes having a disparate negative impact on women as a group. For example, in 1979 they decided to uphold veterans' preferences in civil-service jobs on the grounds that although the results may be discriminatory, the intent was not.[103]

Finally, in the wake of the demise of the ERA, Congress considered a variety of relatively "safe" piecemeal measures to provide economic equality for women under what has become known as the Economic Equity Act (EEA). First introduced in Congress in 1981 by three male Republican senators, the Congressional Women's Caucus quickly endorsed this omnibus bill. It has been reintroduced every year since. Partial success occurred in 1984 with the passage of the Child Support Enforcement Amendments to facilitate child-support payments and the Retirement Equity Act to improve the terms governing the application of pension plans to women so that they better meet female life-cycle work patterns.[104] In 1987, for example, another omnibus EEA bill containing seventeen separate provisions was once again presented in both houses of Congress. The 1989 version of the EEA contained twenty-six separate provisions, ranging from pay equity to a variety of child-care programs and immigration reform so that battered women can leave abusive husbands without facing deportation.[105] While the ERA has been reintroduced each year since 1982, even its most staunch supporters are not pushing for a formal vote on it given the entrenched opposition both in Congress and in the country at large. President Reagan consistently opposed the amendment during his eight years in office, although he signed California's ERA legislation as governor. President Bush has yet to indicate whether he will support a national ERA, as he did when he was a member of the House of Representatives from 1967 to 1971.

Even this cursory summary analysis of court decisions affecting the legal status of women since 1971 indicates that it is time for women to begin to think carefully about whether they prefer equal treatment as unequal individuals (when judged by male standards) or special treatment as a protected (and thus implicitly inferior) group. Faced with these equally unattractive interpretations, the long-sought-after strict-scrutiny or suspect classification under the Fourteenth Amendment or through passage of a new Equal Rights Amendment may prove a mixed blessing. It may well be that neither option will have to be faced. After all, there is no reason to believe that an ERA will be ratified in the next ten years— anymore readily than between 1972 and 1982. At the same time, the very prevalence of women may indefinitely prevent the Supreme Court from granting a majority group suspect classification because, from a quantitative point of view, women implicitly and explicitly challenge liberal legal standards in a way that minority groups receiving strict constitutional scrutiny cannot. Whether women can turn their numerical dominance into more than outmoded demands for more traditional individual rights remains to be seen.

Despite the rapid progress in the fourth period in the changing legal status of U.S. women from 1963 to 1990, they have still not achieved complete equal rights with white males two hundred years after the drafting of the Constitution. Consequently, when assessing the relationship between the legislative and legal events affecting the lives of women in this period for the future, one must ask if they would be better off with more equality between the sexes based on prevailing masculine societal norms or with more justice between the sexes based on a recognition of equitable, but different, socialized patterns of behavior. If the political economy of the United States and the world is moving away from individuality and unilateral actions toward more cooperative global concerns, should not women be prepared for this changed state of affairs rather than once more clinging to obsolete legislation, litigation, and legal texts from several decades or several centuries past?

I return to attorney Wendy Williams's question first posed in chapter 1: "Do we want equality of the sexes—or do we want justice for two kinds of human beings who are fundamentally different?"[106] Only the rapidly changing legal status of women in the past twenty years has made it possible to ask such a question—let alone begin to answer it. If feminist leaders do not revitalize and reunify the Second Women's movement in the 1990s and resolve this question for themselves, then other groups in this continuing postwar conservative era will be quite willing to do it for them.

# CHAPTER EIGHT

# The Limits of Liberal Legalism: Marriage, Divorce, Pregnancy, and Abortion

"I feel as never before," Elizabeth Cady Stanton wrote to Susan B. Anthony in 1853, "that this whole question of women's rights turns on the pivot of the marriage relation, and, mark my word, sooner or later it will be the topic for discussion." Stanton was correct, to the degree that cohabitation problems among married and an increasing number of unmarried couples remain at the heart of domestic-relations law. In this same pre–Civil War letter, however, Stanton correctly questioned whether the "world [was] not quite willing or ready to discuss the question of marriage" in ways that would improve the good life—that is, the legal status of married women.[1]

In contrast to Alexis de Tocqueville who, two decades earlier, had described the "democratic" American family as a "haven of cooperation" because women in the United States did not look upon "conjugal authority" as a "usurpation of their rights, [but] . . . attach[ed] a sort of pride to the voluntary surrender of their own will," Stanton's generation of women reformers began to articulate the personal and professional sacrifices married women had to make for their subordination as wives. Many of them were familiar with William Thompson's 1825 work on the "white-slave code" of marriage, which stood in stark contrast to de Tocqueville's observations that the emergence of romantic love had made family life completely amicable and ostensibly democratic.[2]

In 1837, only five years after de Tocqueville visited the United States, law professor Timothy Walker described the legal relationships among husbands and wives in the United States as a "disgrace to any civilized nation."[3] I already noted in chapters 4 and 5 that the Married Women's Property Acts alleviated many of the civil disabilities faced by nineteenth-century wives because of coverture. Although the reconstruction period following the Civil War resulted in the demise of coverture restrictions that improved the contractual, testamentary, and proprietary rights of wives in the last half of the nineteenth century, one legal scholar noted as late as 1925 that "the interpretation of [Married Women's

Property Acts still] fell into the hands of judges who as young lawyers had been educated in the legal supremacy of the husband."[4]

Along with Blackstone's monogamous "marital-unity" and "civil-death" theories, de Tocqueville's idealistic and romantic view of the willingness with which women in the United States "consented" to subordinate themselves in "democratic" marriages formed the basis of the contextual model that several generations of Supreme Court justices brought to bear in cases dealing with the family well into the twentieth century. In 1878, for example, the justices ruled against the Mormon claim that polygamy was protected under religious freedom, saying that U.S. and western European law only recognized monogamous family units. A decade later, they asserted that without their stereotypic legal construction of the private (and largely middle-class Protestant) family unit, "there would be neither civilization or progress." Likewise, Lockean dominance decreed for men within the family was carried to its logical extreme when a North Carolina court in 1868 upheld wife beating on the grounds that "every household has and must have a government of its own, modeled to suit the temper, disposition and condition of its inmates. . . . and we will not interfere or attempt to control it."[5]

In the twentieth century, similarly traditional statements about the family being the foundation of society abounded even in decisions that were otherwise considered enlightened, such as Justice William O. Douglas's opinion in Griswold v. Connecticut, 381 U.S. 479 (1965), the case legalizing the use of contraceptives. Highly selective notions about noninterference with the privacy of the family unit permitted rigid parental control of children and patriarchal control of wives to continue unabated in state and federal family-law decisions until the last quarter of this century. As late as 1965, a law school casebook laconically stated: "Today the more obvious legal disabilities of married women have been eliminated, notwithstanding a determined rear-guard action by the Courts, who demonstrated a real hostility to the Married Women's Acts. Some strongholds of disability remain unconquered, however."[6]

In the mid-1960s, these remaining "strongholds of disability" for married women were formidable (to say the least), involving as they did everything from archaic marriage and divorce laws and inadequate access to contraception and abortion to almost nonexistent credit rights and literally no protection against husband battering of women and their children. By the mid-1980s, the domestic rights of women had improved significantly, but during the last two and one-half decades the basic economic disadvantages of marriage, especially for poor, minority women, are still far from resolved. In addition, new life styles, cohabitation patterns, and technology have changed and complicated domestic rights and family-court dockets by giving rise to new problems, such as rights of unwed fathers in abortion and adoption decisions and the rights of women who agree to bear children for others—the so-called surrogate mothers—and the surfacing of old problems, such as woman and child abuse exacerbated by drug abuse, especially the use of crack.[7]

In the last twenty-five years, therefore, the major legal concerns of married (and divorced) women have remained essentially the same, and almost all of them have had an economic component. Despite varying degrees of improvement, these economically related issues constitute the core of domestic rights and assume significant proportions in the lives of almost all women in the United States because 98.7 percent of them have been or are married by the age of forty-five. (Ninety percent marry by the time they are thirty years old, at a median age of twenty-three.) In this chapter I shall concentrate on only a few major categories from the following list of domestic issues that continue to concern women in the United States: (1) the right to personal support during marriage; (2) divorce reform; (3) alimony; (4) questions involving illegitimacy; (5) child custody and child support in divorce settlements; (6) property and credit rights during and after marriage; (7) reproductive control in the form of access to abortion and all forms of contraception at nominal cost and protection from state intervention during pregnancy; (8) equitable social security and other pension benefits; (9) nonpatriarchal reform of welfare; (10) pregnancy-disability insurance and parental-leave policies and benefits; (11) affordable and safe child care that does not assume that this is primarily a female responsibility; (12) rights of birth (genetic) parents versus those of adoptive parents, and (13) protection against child and woman abuse.

Of diminishing importance to women in the last two decades of the twentieth century who have decided to cohabit legally with men are such things as the assumption of the husband's surname (no state any longer requires this, but not all adequately inform women they have the right to retain their birth names); differing qualifying ages of consent for male and females to marry; the widespread refusal of states to recognize common-law marriage; and all matters arising from the lingering liberal legal assumption that the husband is automatically head of the household, such as his right to establish the marital domicile, his presumed sole responsibility for family support (which assumes the economic incapacity of the wife), and the still unrecognized and unpaid status of domestic work and child-care services of wives.[8]

## Marriage: The Contract That Isn't

Unlike most contracts, the legal marriage contract in the United States still remains unwritten, and its terms are not defined. Ostensibly, neither party knows exactly what provisions they are agreeing to because they usually do not specify through negotiation what their legal relationship will or will not be, as they would before signing a standard contract. In fact, however, marriage is an institution, not a contract, in which husbands have traditionally exercised "the power of a slave-owner" over their wives. In the past, however, the "slave wife" was required to agree to the arrangement. William Thompson and other critics of marriage in the nineteenth century were at a loss to explain why "this gratuitous degradation [of wives] swearing to be slaves" was thought necessary by society. Why did women have to be humiliated as even actual slaves were not by men who apparently did not find the "simple pleasure of commanding [as with slaves] to be sufficient, without the gratification of the additional power of taunting the victim with her pretended *voluntary* surrender of the control of her own actions"?[9] Contemporary critics of the marriage contract continue to wonder why "consensual sex" is automatically assumed to take place when heterosexual couples marry.

While Thompson's extremely negative view of marriage as a slave contract no longer prevails, the modern marriage contract continues to represent a legal fiction, as far as traditional contractual rights and consensual freedom are concerned, because the civil roles of both parties, while not usually specified in writing, have already been determined by the institutionalization of marriage in law, socioeconomic custom, or religion. Yet marriage continues to be referred to as a contract by society, in general, and the courts, in particular. Unlike normal contracts, however, only one party (the male) is automatically invested with power and domination, while the other party (the female) is expected, as in de Tocqueville's time, voluntarily to "give up the right to self-protection and bodily integrity." Even today, only the husband can decide to divest himself of marital power and "allow" the wife equal status. This renunciation of male power, as Thompson noted as far back as 1825, still has no legal standing and can be withdrawn at any time. A further complication arises in some contemporary marital situations when a woman opts for monogamous marriage in modern society because of the "fear and threat of violence implicit in promiscuous heterosexuality." According to Robin West, when this happens a woman may paradoxically find that "she gives away her own safety when she gives herself for safety." Behind all current protestations about the marriage contract permitting "equal, consensual sexual enjoyment" lies patriarchal domination in its most subtle modern form: "voluntary contractualism."[10]

It is relatively easy to criticize the defects of the marriage contract from a feminist perspective and to deconstruct its various patriarchal parts. But when some feminists then recommend more contractualism to remedy the deficiencies of this particular contract, they miss the point. Premarital, or "intimate contracts" as they are now called, do not constitute a victory over the remnants of patriarchal power within marriage as an institution. Such contracts simply represent its most modern manifestation by carrying liberal contractualism and individualism to their logical extremes. Unfortunately, many contemporary feminists have not recognized that a specific marriage contract delineating "mutual sexual use," economic equality, and other services to be rendered would represent nothing more (or less) than a form of "universal prostitution"—the ultimate in male individualism and domination. "For marriage to become merely a contract for sexual use . . . would mark the political defeat of women *as women*," according to Carole Pateman. "When contract and the individual hold full sway under the flag of civil freedom, women are left with no alternative but to (try to) become replicas of men." [11]

Surely more contractualism is not the solution to the remaining inequalities within the institution of marriage, just as I argue in chapter 9 that more pornography is not the solution for the dilemma created by the harms contemporary women experience because of the never-ending portrayal of verbal and physical violence against them in mass-distributed forms of pornography. Both recommendations simply indicate the degree to which some feminists have adopted male standards in their own most intimate relationships. Instead of confronting the fear-factor built into their everyday lives, most contemporary women naturally redefine themselves along lines that increase their already socially conditioned self-giving characteristics in order to sublimate how dangerous both married and single life in the United States has become for them. U.S. tort law does not now value or recognize emotional security as being as important as physical security and property. Therefore, it will be sometime, if ever, before laws addressing fear- or fright-based injuries are broadly enough defined to address other than a mother's fright-induced injuries when she experiences her child being harmed, as in Dillon v. Legg, 69 Cal. Rptr. 72, 441 P.2d 912 (1968). Nonetheless, it remains a legal area to be explored by feminist jurisprudence, given the increased acts of violence against women in the United States in recent years. [12]

Although requirements for establishing conjugal relationships are regulated by state law, in recent years there has been increased federal regulation of certain aspects of marriage, largely through complex interpretations of the constitutional right of privacy and due process. [13] Thus, the Supreme Court has intervened in several instances when states appeared to be infringing upon the private rights of individuals involved in intimate marital relationships; familial concerns; medical decisions; and personal, sexual activities (for example, the right of married couples to use contraceptives in Griswold v. Connecticut, 381 U.S. 479 [1965] and the right of women to abortion in Roe v. Wade, 410 U.S. 113 [1973]).

Fundamentally, however, state laws continue to determine the roles and rights of people who choose to cohabit, whether they marry or not. This is particularly true with respect to homosexual couples, as demonstrated when the Supreme Court upheld the right of a state to ban homosexual acts of sodomy in Bowers v. Hardwick, 478 U.S. 186 (1986). Increasingly, in the 1980s this also included state interference with the health practices and life styles of pregnant women.

There is some statutory uniformity across the country when it comes to restricting those who may marry. For example, most, states require parental consent if children are under eighteen years old; incestuous marriages among close blood relatives are usually prohibited, as are bigamous, polygamous, and homosexual marriages. Finally, those with certifiably severe mental defects usually cannot marry. Otherwise, however, state laws continued throughout the 1970s to vary widely in assigning privileges and obligations to men and women, because the origins of the status of husband and wife go back to common law that clearly gave higher status to men. Although Blackstone's proclamation about the civil death of married women no longer prevails, the inferior role ascribed to women under common law affected family-law decisions at the state level until recently.

In 1970, for example, the Ohio Supreme Court held that a wife was "at most a superior servant to her husband . . . only chattel with no personality, no property, and no legally recognized feelings or rights." The 1974 Georgia legislature approved a statute that defined the husband as "head of the family" with the "wife . . . subject to him; her legal existence . . . merged in the husband, except so far as the law recognizes her separately, either for her own protection, or for her benefit, or for the preservation of the public order." [14] Until the early 1980s, a Louisiana statute gave husbands exclusive control over the disposition of jointly owned community property. In Kirchberg v. Feenstra, 450 U.S. 455 (1981), a husband secured a private debt by taking out a mortgage on their house *without* telling his wife. After they separated, she refused to honor the obligation, but the district court upheld the state law. The wife appealed this decision, and the Fifth Circuit Court of Appeals found that the statute (which was changed while the appeal was pending) had violated the equal-protection clause. In 1981, the Supreme Court affirmed this decision.

As such arbitrary and gender-based statutes have increasingly been found to be unconstitutional, there have been suggestions that perhaps marriage should be converted either into a true contract relationship, where men and women would negotiate the terms as equals, or into a partnership status, where the law would mandate the same rights and responsibilities for each person. [15] Since women in the United States still experience unequal socialization, it is unlikely that most of them could negotiate a fair contract for themselves (or afford a lawyer to draw up one) at this time. This is especially true for younger people under parental or peer pressure to marry "for love"—not for economic considerations.

From the colonial period until well into the first half of the nineteenth century, however, marriage was commonly an arranged, economic matter, with daughters passing from the economic control of parents to husbands. For the wealthy, it represented a necessary negotiated agreement or arrangement about the wife's dowry and the husband's worth at the time of wedlock. In the course of the nineteenth century, this practice of protecting women's separate estates was extended through property acts to include the rising number of middle-class wives, but these new laws did not significantly improve the economic rights of working women who directly contributed to the support of their families. At the same time, romantic love began to replace parentally controlled and economic-based marriages in the name of love and "free choice" on the part of children. Even as the economic and psychological constraints of coverture diminished in the nineteenth century, giving rise to the so-called companionate marriages based on love, for most of the twentieth century women have found that they have been "free" to choose their marital dependency rather than having it arranged for them.

While some feminists are beginning to advocate a return to some form of equity in the workplace rather than continuing to single-mindedly pursue equality, many middle- and upper-middle-class women are now considering a "return" to marriage agreements. Premarital contracts were considered an avant-garde feminist idea in the 1960s and 1970s; however, by the 1980s, the concept received support from an unexpected source—yuppies who want to enjoy love and marriage without financial risk. In each decade, they represented reformist rather than radical approaches to restructuring the institution of marriage because most premarital contracts continue to benefit the financially stronger partner. The erosion of coverture in the course of the nineteenth century, discussed in chapter 5, did not resolve the "problem" of the marriage contract for twentieth-century women. On the contrary, the very "nature" of that contract remains a problem for contemporary women.

While our colonial female ancestors may have hoped for love to develop out of an arranged economic union and our nineteenth-century counterparts for economic security to materialize from love, the yuppy mentality may transform a love relationship back into an economic one on paper, leaving romance to play itself out on a financially more secure basis for both parties. However, for the remainder of this century, such an equitable improvement in the legal status of wives will only benefit those socioeconomically privileged women in U.S. society who now feel confident of their own (or their lawyers') ability to negotiate reasonable contracts (usually in the form of antenuptial agreements regarding both support and property settlements in the event of divorce).

As long as there is full disclosure of terms to both parties, all fifty states allow such contracts to be drawn up; however, only thirty states currently legally recognize such postnuptial or antenuptial agreements, and all retain the right to interpret them according to widely varying laws. Three states, for example, have refused to enforce the provisions of such agreements, "when one spouse was relieved of the responsibility to support the other." Ten others recognize only contracts involving property, not other legal relationships.[16] Moreover, under the influence of the Second Women's movement, a number of written contractual models have been drafted that would replace traditional unwritten marriage ones for those heterosexual couples who do not want to marry formally. Yet the estimated 1.8 million such unmarried couples (4 percent of all couples) have fewer rights than married men and women because even those with contracts cannot assure such things as entitlement to a family insurance plan or hospital-visitation privileges or alimony payments from a former lover.

Homosexual couples cannot legally marry in any state because no higher court has ruled that equal protection of the laws is violated by state statutes setting up "reasonable" classifications of people who can (and cannot) marry. In other words, classification by sexual orientation is not suspect under the equal-protection clause, and by the end of the 1980s the Supreme Court had not shown any inclination toward establishing new "suspect classes."[17] The only potentially significant legal concept to emerge affecting both homosexual and heterosexual unmarried couples occurred with the well-publicized 1981 "palimony" suit involving Hollywood actor Lee Marvin and the woman he lived with for six years, Michele Triola Marvin. They had no written contract forming their relationship, but a California court finally awarded her $104,000 for "rehabilitation purposes." This decision set a tenuous precedent in favor of financial obligations resulting from cohabitation previously without legal status. However, in October 1989 Sandra Jennings, a former ballet dancer, lost her palimony suit against movie star William Hurt. She sued for half of his earnings since 1984 (estimated at $5 to $7 million) on the grounds that the ten weeks they spent cohabiting in South Carolina had constituted a common-law marriage. Child support was not an issue because Hurt has paid $65,000 a year for their son. Jennings appealed the decision saying that her career suffered irreparable damage during the three years they spent together in a "spiritual marriage." An unreported, yet potentially precedent-making California case, *Conley v. Richardson,* relied on *Marvin* in ordering one lesbian to pay another "temporary support" after their relationship broke up. In this instance, the couple had both a written and oral agreement formalizing their relationship.[18]

The most significant homosexual case of the 1980s involved Sharon Kowalski of St. Cloud, Minnesota, who suffered severe brain damage and paralysis in a 1983 automobile accident. In 1985, her father denied visitation privileges to her lover, Karen Thompson, and moved his daughter to a relatively inaccessible nursing home. After a three-and-one-half-year legal battle, a Minnesota district court judge finally ruled in December 1988 that Kowalski be transferred to a rehabilitation center closer to St. Cloud and opened the possibility that Thompson would be allowed to see her. In exercising his court-appointed right as guardian over Thompson's counterclaims, Robert Kowalski has consistently denied that his daughter was involved in a lesbian relationship. In all likelihood, this case will reach the Supreme Court. Called "the love story of the century" in a 1988 television documentary, a decision in Thompson's favor could significantly change the legal status of homosexual couples because Thompson is maintaining that after buying a house together in 1979 (but in Thompson's name for secrecy), they exchanged rings and considered themselves married.[19]

Obviously, formal contracts or partnerships in lieu of marriage would allow for legal relationships among two or more people of the same or different sex not presently possible (or likely to be in the near future) under most state-regulated marriage.[20] In May 1989, for example, the Danish Parliament officially recognized secular marriages as legal partnerships between homosexuals, thus allowing limited inheritance and residence rights but no adoption rights. And in July of that same year, the New York Supreme Court ruled that a homosexual partner can take over a rent-controlled apartment when the lover who signed the lease dies. Both Berkeley and San Francisco have city ordinances providing that unmarried city employees be eligible for the same benefits as married couples. But the New York decision marks the first time a high appellate court has recognized a gay couple to be the equivalent of a family in order to comply with wording in the state's rent-control laws.[21]

An equitable partnership relationship, therefore, within traditional marriage seems to offer an immediate, if less comprehensive, societal way to mute the remaining inequalities between husbands and wives. Under a formal partnership arrangement, tacit male domination of marriage would ostensibly be replaced with an explicitly equal relationship. While partnership contracts would also represent a form of liberal contractualism, just as marriage contracts currently do, they at least would begin to rescue the prevailing misconception about marriage from the most unrealistic nineteenth-century romantic constructs. This is perhaps what Elizabeth Cady Stanton had in mind when she said in 1860 that the "one kind of marriage that has not been tried . . . is a contract made by equal parties to lead an equal life, with equal restraints and privileges on both sides."[22] The unresolved problem for Stanton, as well as twentieth-century women, remains the institutionalization of female inequality.

The likelihood of such an institutional, let alone discursive, change taking place on a wide scale is also not too great at the present time. Women's socialization and socioeconomic expectations do not make them "equal" to men as they prepare to enter the twenty-first century. Partnership marriages are, nonetheless, theoretically possible on an individual basis between well-to-do heterosexual and homosexual couples. Their legality remains questionable "because the law still prescribes sex-differentiated marital roles and male domination."[23] While the patriarchal institution of marriage protected by liberal legalism continues to place limits on the improvement of domestic rights, it is worth looking at those previously legal and debilitating aspects of family law in which considerable change (but not always resulting in improved female status) has taken place.

While the issues involved in family law—or, what I am calling the domestic rights of people who choose to cohabit with one another with or without the legal sanction of marriage—have remained somewhat constant, the field has gained prominence in the area of constitutional jurisprudence. Long considered a backwater legal specialty in which few new or controversial precedents were set, domestic rights are now in the forefront of constitutional debates because the Supreme Court, under Chief Justices Warren and Burger, has gradually expanded its own definitions of privacy, due process, and equal protection. Just as individual rights became "constitutionalized" for African-Americans in the 1950s and 1960s, domestic rights followed suit for women in the 1970s and 1980s, including more and more state interference into the previously "inviolate" private family unit.

Government involvement with the family is not disappearing; it is simply taking new forms that concentrate on the de facto aspects of cohabitation— pregnancy, child-related matters, and economic and right-to-die issues—indicating that the "right to privacy" has always been a double-edged sword. It is one that both protects the individuals and families from and encourages legal intervention into most intimate matters. The legal regulation of who can marry and court enforcement of unwritten, as well as written, marriage contracts embodying sex-stereotyped status are yielding to the amorphous bureaucratic regulation of formal and informal families through federal, state, and local agencies designed to dispense money, food, medicine, advice, comfort, nursing care, education, and child care. All of these represent services once provided in part by churches, volunteer community welfare groups, or the family itself. Thus, as some of the more traditional forms of legal control of family matters seem to be passing from the scene, less obvious ones are taking their place—often in the name of technology or hygiene.

In a word, some of the most controversial legal ferment in domestic-relations law has already been produced by technology (for example, mass distribution of effective contraceptives, surgically and chemically safe abortion procedures, new fertilization techniques, and health standards for pregnant women). Other domestic legal controversies have come about for basic economic reasons, as unprecedented numbers of married women entered the work force in the 1970s. Finally, the assertion of domestic rights by genetic fathers using DNA testing to prove paternity and in the use of frozen embryos has also been the most recent contribution of technology to this dramatic change in family law. Many predict that the battle for socioeconomic equality of women in the remainder of this century will be won or lost in the once dull and predictably gendered area of family law.

## Inheritance in Community-Property and Common-Law States

Traditionally, there have been only two ways in the United States for married couples to own property: common-law ownership and community-property ownership. Both systems contained serious economic disadvantages for women because under each system states exclusively recognized men as the heads of households, thus giving them legal privileges married women did not enjoy. Theoretically, the eight community-property states (Arizona, California, Idaho, Louisiana, Nevada, New Mexico, Texas, and Washington) appeared to offer more to women as heirs and testators than did the common-law states. In addition to any property women brought to the marriage in such states, the gifts or other property they may have acquired independently during the marriage were considered part of their separate estates, including rents, issues, proceeds, or other profit from such property. Additionally, women in community-property states could technically claim absolute ownership of one-half of any property acquired during the marriage, known as conjugal or community property, which was governed by its special set of inheritance laws.

In practice, however, in four of these eight states (California, Idaho, Nevada, and New Mexico) a wife could not will her half of the community property because if she died before her husband, he inherited *all* of their community property. But if the husband predeceased his wife, she could only claim one-half. This meant he could will his half of the community property as he saw fit, but she could not. Even divorced wives in Louisiana and California, however, could claim their half of the community property. The major disadvantage to wives in these eight community-property states was that until recently husbands traditionally had exclusive managerial control over the couple's real property (including the wife's wages) during the marriage. While in theory the community-property system was based on a partnership relationship, it did not work out that way. By 1973, five of the eight community-property states had increased the right of wives to manage the common property and to control their own earnings. Currently, all community-property states, except Louisiana where a commission is studying the issue, have made these changes. However, many of these new statutes remain ambiguous or subject to very limited interpretations.[24]

As for the women who lived in common-law states, their property rights have been traditionally based on English common law with the modifications and improvements discussed in chapters 3 and 5. Traditionally this meant that the state at best only recognized separate property brought to the marriage by either party but not property acquired during marriage. Since estates of couples usually accumulated during, not before, the marriage, community-property states seemed to be more generous to widows than common-law ones. However, improvements in the Married Women's Property Acts mitigated the worst features of inheritance for women in common-law states by 1900. By the 1980s, on the basis of a small sampling of counties on the East and West coasts, those improvements that took place by the end of the nineteenth century continued in terms of increased inheritances and testamentary behavior for women. Restricting bequests by granting only lifetime rights in property also declined in the twentieth century, except among the very wealthiest families; and shares given to children seem less subject to gender bias, except, again, among the very wealthiest of testators. The percentage of female decedents whose estates were probated between the 1890s and 1970s increased from almost 40 percent to almost 60 percent, while the probated wills of females increased from almost 19 percent to almost 40 percent. Still, it must be remembered that these are relatively small percentages since most people die without writing a will. By 1900, only 25 percent of decedents had wills; by the 1980s, around 36 percent did. Most important, perhaps, is that in the same time period the percent of probated personal wealth held by women in some parts of the United States jumped from almost 35 percent to over 50 percent by the beginning of the 1980s. However, it is unclear how much of that wealth women actually control in the sense of hands-on management because so much of it is in corporate holdings. The dramatic shift in the form of wealth inherited by 1990— from realty to financial assets—continued in the twentieth century, while increased home ownership offset the decline in family-owned farms.[25]

There was one area, however, in which neither common-law nor community-property states improved upon the general economic dependency of women within marriage and especially if they divorced: no consideration or value was placed on domestic housework and child care. Uncompensated work in the home did not entitle a wife to any interest in property acquired during marriage or any rights to her husband's income. In forty-two states, for example, divorce courts seldom ruled that women had equity in property acquired during marriage commensurate with the value of domestic work. This was especially true in rural midwestern areas where female labor was indispensable to family-farm operations but virtually unrecognized in terms of property ownership. During child-rearing years, a homemaker lost work experience and often her self-confidence as well. Many women worked (then and now) while their husbands pursued extended education without ever receiving comparable training themselves or considering repayment of the "debt" they were owed. Thus, in neither common-law nor community-property states did reform of divorce laws give women explicit financial consideration for their years of work in the home. (In the mid-1970s, Chase Manhattan Bank placed a value of $13,391 per year on housework. In the mid-1980s, the yearly domestic services of wives was valued at $46,000.)[26] Although women have almost never been compensated for years spent as homemakers, in the community-property states their contribution was at least nominally recognized at their husbands' deaths.

Finally, since women began receiving custody of children upon divorce or separation at the end of the nineteenth century, their income usually declined while their financial responsibilities increased. When a woman's marriage dissolves, she has lost her "job" as surely as a man who has been fired from his. Unfortunately, alimony, however unreliable and inadequate, remained, until the introduction of no-fault divorce, the major way of compensating women for financial disabilities aggravated or caused by marriage. Divorce insurance and "displaced-homemakers" legislation are potential, but as yet unrealized, alternatives to the remaining aspects of the institutionalized inequality for women within marriage.

For those married women who are totally dependent on their husbands for support (a rapidly vanishing breed since the runaway inflation of the 1970s), their main hope in the event of divorce remains alimony—always a very unstable source of income, but especially now with the advent of "no-fault" settlements. In actuality, neither system of property ownership—common law or community property—produced anything like economic or personal equality between spouses in any of the fifty states before the 1970s. Despite the praise and support for no-fault divorce by liberals when it was first considered in California in 1969, it has resulted, like protective legislation a half-century earlier, in "unintended" negative consequences.[27] In fact, no-fault divorce has become an almost perfect example of what happens when the legislatures and courts grant false equality to women.

## The Economics of Marriage and Divorce

Even in the increasingly sex-, love- (and violence-) oriented culture of the last twenty years, marriage in the final analysis remains more an economic than a romantic experience for all those who stay together any length of time. For example, half of all couples who marry in 1990 will divorce. However, this 50 percent divorce rate only applies to relatively recently married couples. In 1985, almost one in four black women was divorced or widowed, compared to one in five white women. Much to the surprise of researchers, those couples who engage in "trial marriages" before actually marrying divorce at a higher rate than those who marry before living together.[28] Statistically speaking, there is no way around the fact that marriage places most women at a financial disadvantage. Particularly before the 1960s, women who left the labor market to marry had not obtained enough previous work experience or education to maximize their wage-earning capacity if they decided to return to work during their marriage or after they were divorced or widowed. But in the last twenty years, more and more women have continued to work after marriage; yet, most still do not adequately prepare themselves with schooling nor choose their first jobs with the idea of making a career.[29]

Being married and having children no longer means a woman will not also work outside her home. Unless a woman marries a man already earning over $100,000, she has less than a fifty-fifty chance of not working outside the home because currently almost 60 percent of middle-income American families maintain that level of economic existence because *both* husband and wife work. Married women with children work an average of twenty years at full- or part-time jobs; those without children, an average of thirty-five years. The most rapid employment increase occurred among married women in the 1970s. In that decade, they surpassed the number of single working women. In the process, the number of working mothers increased by a stunning 500 percent between 1940 and 1978. While 58 percent of all women who are mothers (not all of whom are married) with school-age children now work, even more significant is that as of 1988, 52 percent of all *married* women with children under the age of one were in the labor force. In fact, married women with preschool children represent the fastest growing category of workers in the U.S. economy. *In 1989, only 22 percent of U.S. husband-wife families have the husband/father as the sole breadwinner in keeping with the traditional image of the nuclear family, while 49 percent have both partners working.* This contrasts dramatically with 1987 figures showing 21 percent of all children under eighteen living in households maintained by women *alone* (compared with 13 percent in 1970 and 10 percent in 1960). By the end of the century, households with a single female parent could constitute as much as 30 percent of all households. However, the participation in the work force of single-parent mothers has not significantly increased in the last decade. The greatest increase, as just noted, has been among married women.[30]

The increasing number of women who are single heads of households is not primarily due to the increased divorce rate (because the remarriage rate among divorced Americans has increased by 63 percent since 1970). Instead, this phenomenon is due to the increase in the age of marriage for both women and men and the fact that the number of births outside marriage doubled between 1970 and 1985. Thus, the meaning of "parenting" as a two-person job is rapidly becoming obsolete, except as an illusory ideal among certain lawmakers and jurists. Sadly, poverty is already a reality for single women with children. In 1986, 35 percent of such women and their children lived in poverty. By the turn of the century, this feminization of poverty will be most pronounced among single minority mothers. Between 1959 and 1986 poor, white female heads of households rose from 15 to 28 percent of the total of such households falling below the poverty line, while the percentage of poor, black female-headed families rose from 24 to 61 percent of all poverty-stricken households headed by women. In 1984, women constituted over 70 percent of all persons with incomes under $4,000 a year, while 46.1 percent of all such female-headed families were considered below the poverty level of $11,000, compared with 17.6 percent of male-headed families and 7.8 percent of married-couple families. The highest poverty rate (75 percent) can now be found among black single mothers under twenty-five years old.[31]

Clearly, as the United States prepares to enter the twenty-first century, the option of not working is only a realistic one for some middle- and upper-class married women; and even for them, support by their husbands remains *legally unenforceable* while they remain married. Traditionally, marital support did not have to be commensurate with either the wife's domestic efforts or the value of her husband's earnings or assets. It was always more accurately a right to be supported by a husband in the fashion and manner he chose. One of the most bizarre cases in this area was decided in 1953 when the Nebraska Supreme Court refused to order Charles W. McGuire to provide adequate grocery or clothing money or to supply indoor plumbing for the couple's residence, even though he owned a farm valued at $90,000 and had additional assets of $117,500. Even though the judge said that given McGuire's wealth his "attitude toward his wife . . . leaves little to be said on his behalf," he concluded that "the living standards of a family are a matter of concern to the household, and not for the courts to determine."[32] The court refused to interfere with an ongoing marital relationship on the question of what constitutes "reasonable," yet state lower courts regularly make such determinations when a marriage has ended in divorce.

All marriages do end—either in divorce or because of death. Traditionally, divorce statutes prescribed that one party had to be found responsible—that is, "at fault"—for a marriage to be dissolved. Usually, a double standard involving extramarital sexual relations also prevailed in these state laws. Regardless of how a marriage ends, the emotional and economic hardships accompanying dissolution are exacerbated by diverse state laws. This continued lack of uniformity and the resulting confusion and hardship it causes those seeking divorces would have been in part ameliorated by passage of the Equal Rights Amendment. Since 1969, however, major reforms in divorce laws have occurred in all states except South Dakota, and several national uniform marriage and divorce laws have been drafted by such groups as the National Conference of Commissioners on Uniform State Laws and the American Bar Association. All reforms have generally made divorce easier to obtain and ostensibly more sex-neutral than ever before. The economic results, however, have been anything but neutral.

## From No Divorce to No-Fault Divorce

By 1985, for example, this reform process, begun in California, had led to fourteen states adopting pure "no-fault" divorce statutes that place no blame on either spouse, but simply declare "irretrievable marital breakdown" as the major basis for dissolution of the marriage (Arizona, California, Colorado, Florida, Hawaii, Iowa, Kentucky, Michigan, Minnesota, Missouri, Montana, Nebraska, Oregon, and Washington). Most other states adopting some form of no-fault have made "irreconcilable differences" or "incompatibility" reasons for divorce, in addition to their traditionally fault-based ones. Almost all states have moved toward no-fault divorce, and it was the major form of divorce available in thirty-eight states by 1989. No-fault divorce is not a perfect solution by any means because, in practice, there is mounting evidence indicating that it reduces the amount of support allocated to needy women (and their children, if they are awarded custody), since technically no one is at fault. This is obviously not only the result of sexist court implementation of such legislation but also of granting women "false equality" under the guise of progressive, sex-neutral reform. The New York state legislature, for example, in June 1989 did not approve a no-fault divorce measure in part because of objections that it did not contain adequate protection for women given the negative impact on them from existing no-fault statutes in other states.[33]

It is difficult to exaggerate the economic problems created by no-fault reform of divorce because of lingering institutional disadvantages facing married women inside and outside the home. Some claim it is now a major factor contributing to the feminization of poverty. By the middle of the 1980s, research indicated that "the average divorced woman and the minor children in their households *experi-ence a 73 percent decline* in their standard of living in the first year of divorce. Their former husbands, in contrast, *experience a 42 percent rise* in their standard of living" (emphasis added). This is in part because judges in most no-fault divorce cases do not appear to believe that more than 25 percent of "his," rather than "their," income and property should be awarded to "her." It is also the result of these same judges according "false equality" to women in no-fault divorce settlements by refusing (1) to take into consideration job opportunities for divorced women, (2) to consider the standard of living of the family unit before the divorce, and (3) to recognize the greater economic demands on divorced women who are trying to establish a new household with children.[34]

No-fault divorce is such a depressing topic in terms of the economic conse-quences for divorced women that, in retrospect, it is not easy to understand the optimism generated in California after it was first introduced in 1963 and finally approved by the state assembly in 1969. However, the continuing popularity of no-fault divorce in most states, in view of its adverse impact on women, can no longer be defended as a misguided belief of liberal legalism that equality can be legislated. Like protective legislation, its "unanticipated, unintended, and unfor-tunate consequences" for women may prove its downfall in the long run, but unlike protective legislation, which had the strong support of women Progressives at the turn of the century, no organized female movement was responsible for no-fault divorce as it evolved in California in the 1960s *before* the formation of the Second Women's movement. Some individual feminist attorneys in California, such as Herma Hill Kay, supported it because, like all early no-fault liberal reformers, they "were so preoccupied with the question of fault and its role in both obtaining a divorce and securing a financial settlement, that few of them thought sufficiently about the consequences of the new system to foresee how its fault-neutral rules might come to disadvantage the economically weaker party."[35] This benefit of the doubt can no longer be accorded to contemporary male liberals (and conservatives) in state legislatures who advocate no-fault divorce. Until the economic inequalities of marriage are realistically confronted by courts and states, no-fault divorce will continue to make no sense for the vast majority of women subjected to it. Liberal legalism may have exceeded its own previously misogynist record with the current nationwide success of no-fault divorce and its enormous ramifications for alimony and child support.

In 1965, the first nationwide study of alimony reported that alimony awards were part of the final judgment in only 2 percent of divorce cases. Alimony was awarded temporarily in 10 percent of cases to allow the wife an opportunity to find employment. Some states (Indiana, Pennsylvania, and Texas, among others) did not then provide for permanent alimony at all. The 1975 International

Women's Year (IWY) Commission reported that only 44 percent of divorced mothers were awarded child support and that less than half of these women received their support regularly. Court-awarded payments were usually less than enough to provide half of a child's support. On the average, ten years after divorce 79 percent of husbands originally responsible for alimony are no longer making payments. By the mid-1980s, alimony was mandated in only one out of seven divorces (a little under 15 percent), only slightly lower than in the past, but the amount awarded to women by judges dropped by 25 percent between 1978 and 1981 — with the amount inadequate to support the dependent former spouse. To make matters worse, in 1985, for example, only 22 percent of divorced women who had been awarded alimony actually received any, and those payments amounted, on the average, to $3733. *This means that of all ever-divorced women less than 4 percent received any alimony in the 1980s.*[36]

A majority of states have no laws giving preference to one parent in divorce or separation proceedings involving children. Nevertheless, judges for almost a century now have preferred to award mothers custody of young children and girls and fathers custody of older boys. Most states still do place primary child-support responsibility on men. However, of the 78 percent of all divorced women with children who were awarded child support in 1985, only 48 percent of them received the full amount; 25.8 percent received partial payment; and 26 percent no payment at all. While the average amount each woman received was $2,538, it must be remembered that this figure does not include the fact that the courts are much less generous when ordering child support to poor, divorced women and never-married women. These women are much less likely to receive child-support payments even in those instances where it is awarded to them.

The 1984 Child Support Enforcement Amendments of Title IV-D of the Social Security Act have helped in the prosecution of delinquent fathers across state lines by requiring states receiving welfare funds to implement court orders for child support. Another earlier 1968 federal act, the Revised Uniform Reciprocal Enforcement of Support Act (RURESA) has been adopted by thirty-five states, and fifteen others have similar statutes. This law facilitates the collection of child-support payments across state lines with the simple filing of a no-fee petition in one's state of residence. If the defaulting parent in the other state does not pay, a citation of contempt is issued and a jail sentence can be imposed. The Child Support Enforcement Amendments have reinforced RURESA and the Supreme Court decision in Hicks v. Feiock, 485 U.S. 624 (1988), which upheld jailing fathers who failed to prove an inability to pay child support. Finally, in 1992, a federal law attaching the wages of men liable for child support will go into effect that should improve on the delinquency record of a majority of fathers who still do not comply with court orders to provide for their children.[37] Child support and women's inordinate domestic responsibilities—whether married or divorced with children—remain unresolved aspects of gender equality in the United States that public policy was nowhere near adequately addressing at the end of the 1980s.

## Whether to Punish or Protect Pregnant "Persons"

Pregnancy-disability insurance is a legal issue of increasing interest to married women in the United States because so many of them now work. Regarded as one of the most important concerns involving women's rights since the Supreme Court legalized abortion in 1973, the battle for equitable treatment of pregnant women is still going on. It began when the Supreme Court handed down a very discouraging and much-criticized decision on 7 December 1976. It represented not only one of the most gendered examples of how intransigent the Burger Court initially was when confronted by the growing number of working women, but also how making the male standard—the "nonpregnant" person—the "neutral" point of departure can lead to unequal and inequitable treatment of pregnant women under the law. In General Electric Co. v. Gilbert, 429 U.S. 125 (1976), six of nine justices ruled that employers need not compensate women for maternity-related disabilities in the same way they compensate employees for other disabilities. The insurance plan in question provided workers with 60 percent of their salaries on the eighth day of total disability (or immediately, if hospitalized), continuing up to twenty-six weeks. Sports injuries, attempted suicides, venereal disease, elective cosmetic surgery, disabilities incurred while committing a crime, prostate disease, circumcision, hair transplants, and vasectomies *were all covered* by the General Electric plan. Absences associated with pregnancy, miscarriage, childbirth, and pregnancy complicated by diseases both related and unrelated to childbearing *were excluded* from coverage.

The women suing General Electric argued that its insurance plan constituted illegal sex discrimination under Title VII of the Civil Rights Act of 1964. They also cited a 1972 Equal Employment Opportunity Commission (EEOC) guideline for Title VII, which stated that

disabilities caused or contributed to by pregnancy, miscarriage, abortion, childbirth, and recovery therefrom are, for all job-related purposes, temporary disabilities and should be treated as such under any health or temporary disability insurance or sick leave plan. . . . [Benefits] shall be applied to disability due to pregnancy or childbirth on the same terms and conditions as they are applied to other temporary disabilities.[38]

In rejecting this guideline and the opinions of six federal courts of appeal, which had found the General Electric plan discriminatory, the Supreme Court simply fell back on its earlier decision in Geduldig v. Aiello, 417 U.S. 484 (1974), involving a similar California disability plan. Justice Stewart said in *Geduldig* that since only "pregnant women and nonpregnant persons [including men]" were involved, there was no gender discrimination. Seeing no reason to distinguish *Gilbert* from *Geduldig,* two-thirds of the justices reiterated that there was no violation of the equal-protection clause of the Fourteenth Amendment because neither insurance plan excluded anyone from coverage on the basis of gender but rather merely removed one physical condition for coverage. Because Justice Rehnquist relied heavily on Stewart's classification of people in *Geduldig* into pregnant women and all others, the majority opinion in essence held that the concept of discrimination based on sex was identical under Title VII and the equal-protection clause—refusing to distinguish between the two. Moreover, the decision questioned the validity of the 1972 EEOC guideline on two grounds: (1) that the 1972 guideline contradicted a 1966 EEOC guideline and (2) that Congress in enacting Title VII "did not confer upon the EEOC authority to promulgate rules or regulations. . . . This did not mean that EEOC guidelines are not entitled to consideration in determining legislative intent." However, it did mean that courts in the mid-1970s properly may accord less weight to such guidelines. Thus, *Gilbert* summarily dismissed the "great deference" that lower courts had previously given EEOC guidelines when interpreting Title VII.[39]

Even more significant was the concluding paragraph of the majority opinion, in which it was stated: "When Congress makes it unlawful for an employer to discriminate . . . on the basis of . . . sex . . . , without further explanation of its meaning, we should not really infer that it meant something different from what the concept of discrimination has traditionally meant." At this point, the opinion referred to several earlier Supreme Court cases defining what discrimination meant. None of those cited dealt with sex discrimination. One dated from 1922, as though no legislative or litigative changes had occurred since that time to question what was meant by the traditional definition.[40]

The negative implications of *Gilbert* for married working women of the mid-1970s were enormous. At that time, the cost of bearing a child ranged between $500 and $1,500 if a woman's medical insurance did not cover it. After childbirth, there were other economic dilemmas to be faced outside of the major long-term one. In 1977, the Population Reference Bureau reported that to raise an American child required from $44,000 to $64,000, depending on the income of the average low- or middle-income family. This estimated figure jumped to $107,000 for middle-income families if the wife sacrifices a part-time job to raise the child. Ten years later, in the last half of the 1980s, the comparable figures had more than doubled. Additionally, the working mother in the mid-1970s (and today) faced inadequate and/or expensive child-care services. By the beginning of

1975, for example, less than 2 percent (326,000) of all children were in day-care centers, largely because of the high cost or absence of organized day-care facilities. "Desirable" day care cost between $300 and $500 per month a decade ago and was already beyond the means of low-income families.[41] What child care was then available was not within the reach of approximately twelve million working women whose husbands earned less than $10,000 a year in 1975. But General Electric was not concerned with the economics of pregnancy and childrearing for their employees; neither were the other large companies that submitted *amicae* briefs in this case. Instead, the companies were more impressed by the $1.4 billion a year that would be required to pay disability benefits to pregnant workers, to say nothing of what it would cost to provide adequate federal day care.[42]

Congressional reaction to *Gilbert* came immediately. Legislation was introduced into both houses of Congress in 1977 to protect the rights of pregnant workers by expanding the definition of sex discrimination in Section 701 of Title VII. The new subsection read:

The terms "because of sex" or "on the basis of sex" include, but are not limited to, because of or on the basis of pregnancy, childbirth, or related medical conditions, and women affected by pregnancy, childbirth, or related medical conditions shall be treated the same for all employment-related purposes, including receipt of benefits under fringe benefit programs, as other persons not so affected but similar in their ability or inability to work, and nothing in Section 703 (h) of this title shall be interpreted to permit otherwise.

This amendment to Title VII had the support of all major feminist and professional women's groups, the Congressional Black Caucus, and the AFL-CIO Executive Council, which went on record against *Gilbert,* saying that although "the Court may have ignored it, the facts of life are that discrimination against pregnant people is discrimination against women alone." Nonetheless, it took until 1978 for Congress to approve this legislation in response to the decisions in *Geduldig* and *Gilbert* and a related one in Nashville Gas Co. v. Satty, 434 U.S. 136 (1977)—all of which allowed companies to exclude women from the general coverage in their insurance plans or to refuse to pay for mandatory maternity leaves on the grounds that "discrimination on the basis of pregnancy isn't discrimination."[43] In that year, Congress passed the above-quoted amendment to Title VII, thus expanding the definition of sex discrimination in order to protect the rights of pregnant workers. This 1978 legislation, however, did not address the gendered legal issue at the heart of the pregnancy question and all other situations in which statutes are classified as establishing neutral classifications when, in fact, the standard used is male. As a result, the Supreme Court has continued to resort to the subterfuge that equal protection demands sexual homogeneity. For example, it upheld veterans' preferences in 1979 clearly favoring men on the grounds that nonveterans, like nonpregnant persons, included both women and men and, thus, is not a nondiscriminatory classification. Consequently, the Supreme Court has yet to recognize the "sexual specificity of pregnancy." When treating women as "different," the justices (and courts that upheld protective legislation for decades) viewed women as less than men; when treating women the same as men, or ostensibly equal, they have assiduously avoided the obvious: that "women are neither simply one or the other in terms of their sex or gender."[44]

Then, in 1978, again with the widespread support of most feminist organizations, Congress approved the Pregnancy Discrimination Act (PDA), which also does not resolve the juridical dilemma posed by the fact that pregnant women seem to defy classification as equal under same or different treatment under the law. For this reason, pregnancy has become fundamental in the ongoing debate over how to define equality. The PDA simply denies the "difference" of pregnancy by stating that under Title VII employers cannot treat pregnancy *more or less* favorably than other disabilities. However, since passage of the PDA in 1980, some states have passed legislation *distinctly favoring*—that is, protecting—women in the workplace, prompting the feminist community to divide again along the classic divisions discussed throughout this book in terms of individual-versus-group rights and equal-versus-special treatment. With passage of the PDA, Congress insisted that pregnancy was similar (equal) to other temporary nonoccupational disabilities, reaffirming what Zillah Eisenstein has called "the phallocratic discourse of duality: difference equals inequality; sameness equals equality."[45] But pregnancy is not like other illnesses or disabilities. Gestation itself may be a temporary condition; motherhood is not. Both pregnancy and motherhood are not simply biological functions but are so socially engendered that they constitute basic barriers to women ever being able to be treated the same as men.

In contrast to Wendy Williams and other liberal feminist attorneys who argue that only equal treatment of pregnancy as similar to all other sex-unique physical characteristics is the "safe" juridical way to reduce structural barriers and discrimination against women in the work force, more radical feminist attorneys have said that the specific and unique aspects of pregnancy (and, presumably, the other traditional obligations females assume with motherhood) must be recognized and treated by the law as "different."[46] This special or protectionist approach is fraught with dangers because of the history of protective legislation and the continuing tendency of the courts to make or accept "false-protectionist" arguments on the assumption of (1) a woman's inferiority and (2) her heterosexuality.

To the degree that the Supreme Court appears willing to allow state legislatures and lower courts to "protect" pregnant workers—despite the original intent of Congress when drafting the PDA—making them equal by requiring employers to provide maternity leaves can result in the firing of such women or not hiring them in the first place.[47] This tendency may be reinforced by recent statistics showing that working long hours at computer terminals may cause miscarriages.[48] Because PDA litigation has involved both special or equal rights, feminist groups could be found on both sides of two 1987 pregnancy-disability decisions. Although a Montana protectionist statute was upheld by a U.S. circuit court in the early 1980s, the Supreme Court did not decide such a case until the end of the decade. In California Federal Savings and Loan Association v. Guerra, 479 U.S. 272 (1987), the justices upheld a California law *requiring* employers to grant *unpaid* maternity leave to pregnant workers. Justice Marshall, in *Guerra,* insisted that the leave covered only "actual physical disability" during pregnancy and so was not similar to earlier protective-labor legislation. He also noted that employers were "free to give comparable benefits to other disabled employees" to avoid any preferential treatment of pregnancy.[49] In a second case, Wimberly v. Labor and Industrial Relations Commission of Missouri, 479 U.S. 511 (1987), a Missouri woman was denied unemployment benefits when she quit after not being reinstated to the same job following a maternity leave.

In both *Guerra* and *Wimberly,* the issue of treating women "specially" was raised. In the former, the Supreme Court upheld special treatment in the form of mandatory maternity leaves; in the latter, the Court refused to grant special treatment to a woman who specifically asked for it when she filed for unemployment benefits because she refused to work at the new job assigned her upon returning from having a baby. Historically we know that favorable treatment can have unfavorable results when it is rationalized in the name of "women's special procreational capacity." If history repeats itself, pregnant workers of the 1980s and 1990s might find themselves right back where their sisters were in the era of protective legislation following *Muller v. Oregon* in 1908. The protection implied in the California PDA decision plus concerns over miscarriages from long hours working on video-display terminals could lead to a disposition among employers against hiring not simply pregnant women but all women in their childbearing years, especially for low-level, sex-stereotyped jobs where teen-agers and older people can be employed for minimum wages or less. This worst-case scenario is represented by a suit against a manufacturer of batteries that has barred women from working in high lead exposure positions. In March 1990, the Supreme Court decided to review two lower-court decisions upholding the company Johnson Control, Inc.[50] Unfortunately, the Second Women's movement remains so divided on the question of special-versus-equal rights that it has not even clearly delineated for lawmakers or jurists the potential limitations of both—let alone a legal resolution of this theoretical dichotomy.

## The Right to Control One's Body

By far the most liberating aspects of female existence in the twentieth century have been the improved means of contraception and access to hygienic abortions. Until a woman has the freedom of choice to control her own reproductive functions, it is literally impossible for her to plan her private life or public career with any certainty. There are other prerequisites for full female emancipation, such as a level of urbanization, industrialization, and technology high enough to free women from traditional domestic, as well as subsistence-level, economic duties and from general immobility in a mobile society.[51] But without freedom from unwanted and unplanned pregnancies, the other prerequisites for complete emancipation lose much of their significance. Only since World War II have a majority of middle-class women in the United States gradually experienced all of these liberating material conditions.

Although abortion was not illegal under English or colonial common law, beginning in the last half of the nineteenth century and continuing into the mid-1960s, most state statutes increasingly restricted access to abortion and "banned the prescription, sale, and use of contraceptives."[52] Such restrictions were in direct conflict with the long-standing liberal principle of noninterference into family or private affairs. Once again, however, constitutional jurisprudence contradicted itself because these forms of interference primarily impacted on women's (not men's) ability to exercise private, independent control over their reproductive functions. Thus, for well over a century federal courts have turned a blind eye toward state invasion of family "privatism" when it comes to contraception and abortion. With the initiation of national social-welfare programs as a result of the Great Depression and the expansion of these programs following World War II, federal courts were faced with an increasing number of statutory and administrative questions of law concerning the family. This juridical development combined with an expansion of the constitutional meaning of due process, equal protection, and privacy rights in the 1950s and 1960s to set the stage for litigation by national groups attacking state laws interfering with private sexual activity within the family unit.[53]

In a circuitous way, therefore, Brown v. Board of Education, 347 U.S. 483 (1954), led the Supreme Court first to abolish racial classifications affecting domestic rights, such as those prohibiting interracial marriage;[54] then to void nonracial classifications, such as illegitimacy;[55] and finally to expand the right of privacy to legalize the use of contraceptives. In Griswold v. Connecticut, 381 U.S. 479 (1965), for example, the justices struck down a Connecticut law forbidding even married couples from asking for "any drug, medicinal article, or instrument for . . . preventing contraception." In Eisenstadt v. Baird, 405 U.S.

438 (1972),the justices extended the decision in *Griswold* to unmarried persons. These privacy rulings, in turn, revived substantive due process, which had originally rationalized the Supreme Court's first decision legalizing abortion in 1973. The National Association for the Advancement of Colored People (NAACP) and the American Civil Liberties Union (ACLU) had brought suit after suit against obsolete state miscegenation statutes and illegitimacy classifications in order to create a legal climate in which the justices felt justified in 1954 to overturn a half-century of legalized racism based on the separate-but-equal doctrine of *Plessy v. Ferguson*. Similarly, the Planned Parenthood Association attacked the contraceptive issue, in the face of an unprecedented number of teen-age pregnancies; and an increasing number of women's groups challenged criminal abortion laws, finally winning with Roe v. Wade, 410 U.S. 113 (1973).[56] However, the legal climate they created did not result in as "solid" legal doctrine in 1973 as in 1954, although both *Brown* and *Roe* are considered classic examples of how "hard" legal issues make for "bad" case law, especially when long-standing precedents are reversed.

It should be remembered that during the years Earl Warren was chief justice of the U.S. Supreme Court (1953–69), judicial activism in the form of strict scrutiny was the primary legal tool used to broaden (1) individual rights by reinterpreting the First Amendment; (2) the stated procedural guarantees of the Bill of Rights (incorporated into the Fourteenth Amendment); and (3) some, but not many, outright applications of the equal-protection clause of the Fourteenth Amendment. Under the Burger Court (1969–86), this liberal jurisprudential trend continued for the most part, except in the areas of criminal justice and property matters. In addition, the Burger Court also reintroduced a problematic type of judicial activism not employed widely since the first quarter of the twentieth century, known as "Lochnerism"—where due process was interpreted largely *unaided* by the specific freedoms addressed by the Bill of Rights. Some liberal legal specialists maintain that this use of the due-process clause of the Fifth and Fourteenth amendments muddled "the specificity and historic purpose that rationalized" most of the Warren Court decisions, especially with respect to the Burger Court's decisions relating to women's reproductive rights.[57]

Since the Warren Court avoided the question of abortion (let alone other civil rights for women), we will never know if it would have found a way to legalize the medical procedure without resorting to a substantive due-process definition of the fundamental "right of privacy." However, there is a body of case law, dating back to the 1920s, that accumulatively began to protect parental authority over such issues as children's education, marriage, contraception, procreation, and, most recently, the right to live or die free from "invasive" medical procedures as fundamental rights "implicit in the concept of ordered liberty." Only one of these cases, *Skinner v. Oklahoma* in 1942, specifically spoke of "marriage and procreation" as "fundamental to the very existence and survival of the race." However, as early as 1891 the Supreme Court held that "no right is held more sacred, or is more carefully guarded, by the common law than the *right of every individual to the possessions and control of his own person,* free from all restraints or interference of others, unless by clear and unquestionable authority of law" (emphasis added). Moreover, there are a series of more recent cases upholding "bodily integrity" as one of the foundations of the right to privacy.[58]

On both the contraception and abortion issues, privacy rights rather than equal protection under the law prevailed. Thus, while strengthening the idea that the state cannot interfere with personal and physical integrity or family life, the Burger Court did not do so by granting women the right to reproductive control or freedom of sexual expression. Although feminists perceived that these issues of equality were, indeed, at the heart of female sexuality,[59] the justices were more circumspect, implying in the two previous birth-control cases that the type of privacy at issue in legalizing contraception was not strictly individual liberty, but rather a matter of privacy between cohabiting adults. A similar rationale prevailed in *Roe.* This time the right of privacy was found to exist between doctor (usually male) and patient (always female). *Roe* also contained an important technological question having to do with the "viability" of the fetus during the various stages of pregnancy, granting adult women the right to abort "without any interference by the government" in the first trimester and under more limited circumstances in the second trimester.

In this manner, the Court neither diffused the abortion issue nor broke any new constitutional ground. Instead, it left the door open for a variety of countersuits and statutory restrictions on abortion even though the medical procedure was declared legal. While *Roe* and other subsequent abortion cases, such as Doe v. Bolton, 410 U.S. 179 (1973), and Planned Parenthood v. Danforth, 428 U.S. 52 (1976), left many questions unanswered, subsequent Supreme Court decisions until 1989 continued to uphold the principle that abortions during the first three months of pregnancy were exclusively matters of private conscience to be decided by women—even minors—and their physicians. In states where "right-to-life" forces were strong, states proceeded to pass restrictive legislation resulting in lengthy court battles to overturn proabortion decisions. Women in these states were temporarily denied their constitutional right to free choice and control over their own bodies indefinitely until this type of litigation reached the Supreme Court, where it was usually struck down in the 1970s and 1980s.

In light of this series of proabortion decisions, "right-to-life" groups adopted a variety of strategies, including so much physical intimidation and violence against abortion clinics that several "prolife" advocates have been prosecuted under the

1970 federal Racketeering Influenced and Corrupt Organizations Act (RICO). In March 1989, for example, the United States Court of Appeals for the Third Circuit in Philadelphia held those who attacked an abortion clinic liable for damages under RICO, and NOW is supporting this type of litigation. However, antiabortion groups across the country have continued to block entrances to abortion clinics and to picket the private homes of judges and prosecutors involved in abortion cases and those of doctors who perform abortions.[60] Initially, in the aftermath of the *Roe* decision, five states (New Jersey, Arkansas, Louisiana, Missouri, and Indiana) passed resolutions calling for a constitutional convention to consider an antiabortion amendment, and eleven others began to consider similar resolutions. This method of amending the Constitution has never been employed. Naturally, a constitutional convention raises a number of questions because there are no legal precedents or guidelines for conducting one, excepting the convention of 1787. Since other issues in addition to abortion could conceivably be considered at such a convention, the American Bar Association warned in the late 1970s that "a grave constitutional crisis" could ensue if abortion guidelines were determined in a "time of divisive controversy and confusion."[61]

Since that time, constitutional-convention resolutions to ban abortions have not made much headway, but every year since 1973 antiabortion amendments to the Constitution have been introduced into Congress. While they have all failed, in the 1980s such a constitutional amendment had the strong rhetorical backing of President Reagan. Additionally, beginning in 1984 the Reagan administration suspended foreign aid distributed by the Agency for International Development (AID) to international organizations that supported abortions. Four years later, the Reagan administration also issued new regulations for Title X family-planning programs that would bar four thousand federally funded health clinics from mentioning abortion as an option to 4.5 million largely low-income, pregnant women. Many of these antiabortion regulations were suspended by federal courts in the spring of 1988, pending the outcome of several major abortion cases before the Supreme Court.[62]

## Limiting Women's Right to Abortions

During the same decade of the 1980s, however, antiabortion forces succeeded in pressuring Congress to modify the Labor and Health Education and Welfare (HEW) appropriations bill by adding the Hyde Amendment banning Medicaid reimbursement for abortion,[63] except where the life of the mother would be endangered. Suits were immediately filed in behalf of the constitutional rights of poor women because immediately following *Roe,* Medicaid funding for abortions increased dramatically in all states. On 22 October 1976, New York Judge John

F. Dooling issued a preliminary injunction that nullified the Hyde Amendment in all fifty states until all such court challenges to it were decided. On 8 November in Califano v. McRae, 433 U.S. 916 (1976), the Supreme Court refused to back Judge Dooling's decision, and the Hyde Amendment went into effect.

Then, on 20 June 1977, the Court handed down two opinions substantially undermining the effectiveness of its earlier proabortion decisions. In Maher v. Roe, 432 U.S. 464 (1977), the justices in a six-to-three decision held that exclusion of Medicaid reimbursement for nontherapeutic abortions did not violate protection under the Fourteenth Amendment for indigent women because the Court has never ruled that financial need alone identifies a suspect class. Moreover, they held that the state's action was "rationally related" to a "constitutionally permissible" purpose. In Beal v. Doe, 432 U.S. 438 (1977), the Court specifically denied that either the Constitution or any federal statute, such as Title XIX of the Social Security Act, required states to use public funds to offer elective abortions to the poor for free. Dividing seven to two, the majority of justices declared that while states may not make abortion illegal, they may "make a value judgment favoring childbirth over abortion, and . . . implement that judgment by the allocation of public funds." Dissenting in Beal, Justice Marshall asserted that the majority opinion would in reality "impose a moral viewpoint that no State may constitutionally enforce" and "have the practical effect of preventing nearly all poor women from obtaining safe and legal abortions." Noting that public officials were already "under extraordinary pressure from well-financed and carefully orchestrated lobbying campaigns to approve more such restrictions," Marshall concluded: "the effect will be to relegate millions of people to lives of poverty and despair. When elected leaders cower before public pressure, this Court, more than ever, must not shirk its duty to enforce the Constitution for the benefit of the poor and powerless."[64]

On 29 June 1977, the Court ordered the lifting of Judge Dooling's preliminary injunction and reconsideration of Califano v. McRae, in light of Maher and Beal. While Dooling's court continued to litigate the constitutionality of the 1976 version of the Hyde Amendment, Congress remained deadlocked in the summer and fall of 1977 over the exact wording of that amendment, which was still appended to the Labor and HEW appropriations bill. The Senate wanted to "liberalize" it to read that federal funds could be used to perform abortions in case of reported rape or incest and when there would be severe and long-lasting physical damage to the mother. The House preferred the more restrictive wording of the original amendment, which allowed for termination of only life-threatening pregnancies. In the meantime, salaries for the two hundred thousand Labor and HEW employees were being voted by Congress on a month-by-month basis because $60.2 billion was tied up in the stalemate over the appropriations bill. This financial crisis finally forced a compromise on wording between the House and Senate on 7 December 1977.[65] Even the new language of the Hyde Amendment has meant that most poor women are not eligible for federally funded abortions unless their lives are at risk.

In addition to justifying such class legislation at the congressional level, *Maher* and *Beal* predictably encouraged state legislatures to initiate or continue prohibitions on the use of Medicaid or other public funds for legal abortions. These reached a high point during the 1988 elections, when three more states— Michigan, Colorado, and Arkansas—passed referenda banning state financing of abortions. This made a total of thirty-seven states that either do not have programs for funding abortions or have prohibitions against funding them. (By 1988, only nine states unequivocally endorsed the use of public funds for abortions.) Even with all these restrictions, the number of abortions fluctuated only slightly during the 1980s. As of the end of 1987, thirty of every one thousand American women between the ages of fifteen and forty-four aborted their pregnancies. In 1983 the figure was twenty-three for every one thousand, and in 1980 it was twenty-five.[66] (In contrast, the number of abortions is on the rise all over the world, regardless of state attempts to restrict or prevent them.)[67] Since many public health plans allow middle-class women in the United States to obtain abortions from tax monies, these decisions and referenda become all the harder to justify in terms of social justice.

However, *Beal* did not come as a complete surprise, nor did the 1988 referenda because in each time period, they had administrative backing. HEW Secretary Joseph A. Califano, Jr., for example, was an early supporter of the Hyde Amendment, and the Justice Department had already advised the Supreme Court that "the government has no constitutional obligation to relieve all the burdens of poverty." President Carter echoed these sentiments when he defended the *Maher* and *Beal* decisions as "adequate" and "reasonably fair," with the now-familiar words:

Well, as you know, there are many things in life that are not fair, that wealthy people can afford and poor people can't. But I don't believe that the Federal Government should take action to try to make these opportunities exactly equal, particularly when there is a moral factor involved.[68]

In 1980, the Supreme Court unequivocally declared the constitutionality of the Hyde Amendment in Harris v. McRae, 448 U.S. 297 (1980). It is estimated that the resulting federal and state cutoffs of funding have meant that 10 to 30 percent of pregnant women eligible for such funds who want abortions in any given year cannot afford to have one. In 1988, 68 percent of all women obtaining abortions said financial reasons motivated them. Only 1 percent of all the approximately three million abortions performed annually in the United States in the last decade were because of rape or incest and only 7 percent because of the mother's health. Abortion mortality has dropped from 20 percent in 1970 to less than 1 percent in 1988, while childbirth mortality remains around 12 percent in the United States—one of the highest among industrialized nations.[69] Yet, the Hyde Amendment, combined with the *Maher, Beal,* and *McRae* decisions, has placed public policy in the absurd position of saying that while abortion is safe and legal, it is immoral—but only the poor can be saved from this immorality, whether or not they want to be. Not until 1988, after the Democrats regained control of the Senate, was Medicaid financing of abortions for victims of rape and incest once again introduced and debated.[70]

To balance their antiabortion stance, both Carter and Califano endorsed a child-adoption plan under the Public Assistance Amendments of 1977 that would eventually cost more than $500 million a year, compared to the $61 million that the government paid in 1976 to fund approximately one-third of the one million legal abortions performed in the United States. For those who personally oppose abortion, this large amount of public funding to adopt unwanted children has remained preferable to the lower cost of allowing poor women the freedom to choose to have an abortion, even though funding for facilitating adoption has never been adequate. (The average cost of an illegal abortion was $500 before 1973; by 1976, the cost of a legal abortion was $280, or $42 more than the average monthly family-welfare payment. A decade later, an abortion was estimated to cost almost $230 [not adjusted for inflation], of an average monthly welfare check, which as of January 1989 was $376.) It is clear that low-income women have never been able to follow the callous advice of General Electric when it told its female workers in 1976 that "if a woman has not saved enough to get pregnant, she should get an abortion."[71]

The adoption subsidy plan of the Carter administration came under criticism not only because it drew upon Medicaid funds to pay childbirth expenses but also because in some states it amounted to twice what welfare mothers were then paid per month to support a single child. To complicate this emotional issue of abortion-versus-adoption further, an HEW study group on alternatives to abortion disbanded in November 1977, after concluding that the only real alternatives were "suicide, motherhood, and some would add, a madness."[72] Both Presidents Ronald Reagan and George Bush continued to promote adoption over abortion without adequate funding for unwanted pregnancies or adequate support to repeal federal restrictions on funding adoptions. (By the 1980s, the issue of adoption had become further complicated by the issue of surrogate motherhood.)

Numerous other attempts have also been made in court to limit the application of *Roe*. Until the late 1980s, most failed. For example, third-party "vetoes" of a woman's right to decide to have an abortion by husbands were struck down by the Supreme Court in Planned Parenthood v. Danforth, 428 U.S. 52 (1976). In a series of decisions beginning in 1979, the rights of minors to elect to have abortions without parental interference were upheld. In the course of these decisions, the Court has distinguished between "emancipated" (meaning mature) and "unemancipated" minors. In another set of decisions in the 1980s, the Supreme Court also refused to allow states to circumscribe abortions by limiting abortion counseling to physicians exclusively, by dictating the content of information distributed about abortions, and by excluding certain facilities from performing the procedure.[73]

The 1986 Supreme Court decision in Thornburgh v. American College of Obstetricians and Gynecologists, 106 S. Ct. 2169 (1986), while striking down a Pennsylvania abortion control act requiring doctors to give detailed ("intimidating") information about alternatives to women seeking abortions, was not only a close five-to-four decision but was also one in which several justices indicated they thought that the original 1973 *Roe v. Wade* case should be "re-examined."[74] Subsequently, in 1988 the Supreme Court denied a petition for rehearing the oral arguments in Harigan v. Zbaraz 108 S. Ct. 1064 (1988), originally heard in October 1986. This case involved an Illinois appeal involving notification of parents by minors seeking abortions. Before the justices finally decided not to rehear this case, they had included the procedures of notice, as well as the twenty-four-hour time period, indicating that they might be broadening their consideration of the Illinois law in order to find constitutional grounds for upholding it. The case had wide implications because in 1988 twenty other states had similar restrictions; however, half were not being enforced because of litigation. Instead of rehearing *Harigan*, the Supreme Court scheduled three other abortion cases for its 1989–90 session—two of which involved this same issue of parental notification.[75]

Additionally, the Supreme Court agreed in January 1989 to hear an appeal from the state of Missouri in Webster v. Reproductive Health Services, 109 S. Ct. 3040 (1989), concerning the constitutionality of a 1986 law prohibiting the use of public funds and public buildings for performing abortions and abortion counseling, except if the mother's life was at risk. This statute, written with the advice of the National Right to Life Committee, also required extensive testing to determine the viability of the fetus before abortions and placed restrictions on all abortions after twenty weeks of pregnancy, declaring in its preamble that "the life of each human being begins at conception," thus joining the very emotional issue of mother-versus-fetal rights. After a lower court declared the law unconstitutional, the state appealed with the backing of the Justice Department under the Reagan administration. William L. Webster, attorney general for Missouri, specifically asked the Supreme Court to overturn *Roe v. Wade* in considering this case. President Bush endorsed this recommendation, even though according to polls a majority of the public, in varying degrees, remains in favor of abortion. Significantly, on 20 March 1989 the Supreme Court agreed to the Bush administration's request to participate in the oral argument on the constitutionality of the Missouri law—something it did not grant the Reagan administration in *Thornburgh*.[76] In summary, since 1973 the Supreme Court has permitted financial consideration to limit abortions but, by narrowing margins, has struck down attempts by states to place restrictions on women's constitutional right of privacy and freedom to medical treatment when seeking abortions.

*Roe* was based not simply on privacy rights between patients and their doctors but also on an ambiguous definition—which technology may extend or make obsolete before the end of this century—of the "viability of the fetus." Consequently, between 1973 and 1989 one of the most significant aspects of many subsequent abortion rulings lies in the Supreme Court's definition of the "viability of the fetus" as that stage of development "when the life of the unborn child may be continued indefinitely outside the womb by natural or artificial life support systems." Although doctors in both *Roe* and *Danforth* wanted the Court to define viability in terms of gestational time based on the three medically determined stages (trimesters) of pregnancy, the justices refused. Instead, in the *Danforth* decision, they referred specifically back to what they had said in *Roe*, indicating that the "stage subsequent to viability" (that is, the first two trimesters of pregnancy or approximately twenty to twenty-four weeks into a pregnancy) was "purposefully left flexible for professional determination, and dependent upon developing medical skill and technical ability." After the first trimester, according to *Roe*, states could legally take action against abortions.[77] At first glance, the ambiguousness of the definition appears to open the door for future state interference with a woman's right to have an abortion after the first trimester, although fewer than 1 percent of all abortions occur after twenty-four weeks. And, indeed, this is what the Court urged the states to do in *Webster*, even though there was no change in scientific evidence or technology since 1973 indicating that fetuses are viable before twenty-four weeks of development—that is, before they weigh five hundred to six hundred grams.[78]

## From *Roe* to *Webster*

Despite its ambiguities, the *Roe* decision with its definition of viability has been attacked by antiabortionists as "the willful imposition of pure judicial preference." Even some legal scholars in favor of a woman's right to abortion have criticized *Roe* as simply being bad constitutional law because it represents an implicit return to substantive due process, or "Lochnerism."[79] On the other hand, Laurence H. Tribe persuasively argued in 1975 that the very absence of precise time limits on viability might be *Roe's* most significant constitutional contribution if it led to less dogmatic interpretations about abortion in the future. He stated that the Court's "viability" doctrine was one of the few examples of what he called "structural due process," or "structural justice," whereby the Court can structure "the process of change in constitutional principles without dictating end products." In other words, the definition of viability in *Roe*, far from reflecting arbitrary judicial preference, theoretically allowed for considerable flexibility. It could have permitted each generation, depending upon advances in medical technology, to determine when the "fetus may become viable;" ultimately, this might mean "at points ever closer to conception itself."[80]

The scientific evidence that continues to support a flexible definition of viability was ignored by a majority of the justices in the 1989 *Webster* decision. As noted throughout this work, the attempt to obtain equality of treatment for women in the late nineteenth and early twentieth centuries, as well as now, inevitably means that at various levels the courts had to abandon standard sex-stereotyped assumptions. Over time the Supreme Court has, albeit it reluctantly, abandoned some of society's or its own most simplistic sexist assumptions. When asked, however, "to identify areas of moral flux and normative transition" and "to facilitate . . . the evolution of moral and thus legal consciousness," generations of justices have been slow to respond to such juridical complexities. Tribe believed in 1975 that there was a less direct way for the Court to act as an instrument for social change in the present without dogmatically restricting the options of future generations, as has often happened with past doctrinaire decisions. The court could do this by providing the *structure* for the evolution of social values. Following "structural due process," Supreme Court decisions could become vehicles for the continuing dialogue between state regulations and those whose liberty is limited by such laws.[81] While there is the danger of individualizing each case with this approach, the risk may be outweighed by the reduction of the probability of imposing a rigid societal concept (in this case, a time-bound definition of fetal viability) that will become obsolete in light of changing opinion and/or technology.

In retrospect, it is clear that "structural justice" is not necessarily what either the "pro-choice" or "right-to-life" forces were asking of the justices before the 1989 *Webster* decision. Moreover, Tribe has retreated from his original and thought-provoking premises about "structural due process" in both a 1985 article and the 1988 edition of his case-law textbook. He now appears to tolerate much more direct state intervention "to protect fetal life" and finds "extraordinarily disturbing" feminist claims justifying abortion on the grounds that an unwanted pregnancy "is literally an invasion [of a woman's body]—the closest analogy is the difference between love-making and rape." He also seems much more willing to rely on the hope that states will "minimize the conflict between maternal and fetal rights" by providing better sex education, universal contraception, and/or more funding for prenatal care and child support. Most disturbing, however, is Tribe's precipitant conclusion (ahead of any current reproductive technology or scientific evidence of a change in the twenty-four weeks it takes a human fetus to become even minimally viable) that if, and when, "even the youngest fetus can safely be removed to another woman's womb or to some artificial incubator," then only the state and not the woman who conceived the fetus can decide whether the pregnancy should continue in someone else's body or artificial environment. As with capital punishment, only the state can legally kill; to give the woman that right would be, according to Tribe, "licensing infanticide."[82]

Despite Tribe's retreat from his own theory about "structural due process," it remains a juridically and scientifically more realistic estimation of advances in both *in vitro* and *in utero* technology. These advances will ultimately defuse the original abortion issue—namely, destruction of fetuses—more than the Supreme Court cases through the 1980s have yet done. At the same time, however, technology fuels a new issue involving ethical and legal questions about surrogate mothers and the rights of genetic versus natural parents so emphatically demonstrated in the "Baby M" case in 1987.[83] Other technological advances should also make the emotional moralism of antiabortionists more difficult to maintain by the end of the century. These include the customary practice of selectively aborting embryos when a woman taking fertility drugs ends up with more than she can carry to term. The 1988 announcement by French scientists of the drug RU-486, which induces abortion early in pregnancy, is still another example of technology pushing the question of when human life begins beyond simplistic religious rationalizations. (In September 1989 a French endocrinologist received the prestigious Lasker Award for his work in developing RU-486, possibly improving its chances of someday being made available to women in the United States.) Little wonder that antiabortionists launched an international attack against the drug's distribution and increased their physical attacks on abortion clinics.[84]

Against this legal and emotional background, pro- and antiabortion groups demonstrated in the spring of 1989 as they awaited the decision of the "Reagan" Supreme Court, under its new chief justice William H. Rehnquist in the *Webster* case. Both sides agreed that this Court would permit more rather than fewer restrictions on abortions. There were a number of reasons for this assumption. In keeping with the still-lingering postwar conservative climate, for example, many states had already shown increased interest in pregnancy questions, particularly the protection of the "potential life" of the fetus during the first trimester, or twelve weeks, by regulating the life styles and health habits of pregnant women. In contrast, by the spring of 1989 the Second Women's movement seemed more divided than ever before on the two issues of pregnancy and abortion. Its members could not agree on whether group or individual rights would restrict women's "freedom of choice about the direction of [their] lives . . . [more] than that of men."[85] The massive 300,000-person prochoice march on Washington, D.C., in April 1989 under the auspices of NOW and the National Abortion Rights Action League (NARAL) showed widespread emotional solidarity but little tactical or strategical unity on abortion. Regrettably, neither organization had made repeal of the Hyde Amendment one of its priorities in organizing this highly successful demonstration.

On the eve of the *Webster* decision, only three things were clear: (1) increasingly in the 1980s the Supreme Court viewed the related issues of pregnancy and abortion in potentially restrictive or protectionist ways, reflecting contemporary conservative opinion on these topics; (2) for over a decade, because of the Hyde Amendment most poor women in the United States could not obtain abortions even though they were legal; and (3) the Supreme Court's decision in *Webster* was awaited as anxiously by feminists abroad as it was in this country.[86]

On 3 July 1989, the Rehnquist Court handed down a five-to-four decision in *Webster v. Health Reproductive Services* in which a plurality of four justices (Rehnquist, White, Kennedy, and Scalia) indicated that they no longer believed abortion was the fundamental constitutional right of U.S. women as defined in *Roe* sixteen years before. Five justices (including O'Connor) upheld the following three provisions of a restrictive 1986 Missouri statute: (1) the barring of public employees from performing or assisting in abortions not necessary to save a woman's life; (2) the barring of the use of public buildings for performing abortions even when there is no public funding; and (3) the requirement that doctors perform tests to determine fetal viability if the woman is at least twenty weeks pregnant. Additionally, the wording of the opinion of Chief Justice Rehnquist, writing for Kennedy and White, plus the vitriolic concurring one of Justice Scalia, attacking the separate concurring opinion of Justice O'Connor as much as it did *Roe,* indicated that those four justices were prepared to uphold other state restrictions similar to those adopted by the Missouri legislature.

While this splintered *Webster* decision, with its five separate opinions, did not overturn *Roe,* it eviscerated its meaning similar to the way in which the Court's January 1989 decision in *Patterson v. McLean* undercut an earlier precedent in *Runyon* and the Reconstruction Civil Rights Act on which it was based. With respect to abortion, however, the Rehnquist Court did not need to attack a federal statute—only the Court's case-law precedent in *Roe.*

In retrospect, the plurality opinion was presaged by earlier opinions and subtle hints from individual justices. For example, in *Patterson v. McLean Credit Union,* Justice Kennedy emphasized that the Court was always more reluctant to overrule a congressional statute than a previous constitutional interpretation of its own. Such an approach would seem to indicate that the conservative members of the Court had the Missouri abortion case in mind during the discussion of this decision. Unlike *Patterson,* the question in *Webster* did not involve a federal law but the 1973 *Roe v. Wade* decision. Additionally, there were other subtle hints that the decision in *Webster* would undercut *Roe.* For example, on June 15, in *Michael H. v. Gerald D.,* 109 S. Ct. 2333 (1989), Justice Scalia in giving the judgment of the Court said that there was no historical justification for granting paternity rights to a California man who was, in all likelihood, the father of a baby conceived during an affair with a married woman who ultimately reconciled with her husband. Scalia had shown considerable interest during the 26 April 1989 oral arguments for *Webster* in whether a *historical* basis existed for a right to abortion.[87] Scalia, along with the other four conservative justices, had indicated an unusual interest in legislative social "consensus" or historical roots, in deciding the broad array of five-to-four decisions in 1989 before handing down the one in *Roe.*

Since Scalia, in particular, is prone to pontificate about whether a national consensus exists on various issues, he seems to have become the driving force on the Rehnquist Court behind "discern[ing] society's views" to find only those so rooted in history and tradition as to warrant due-process protection under the Fourteenth Amendment. The debate over consensus between old liberals and young conservatives on the Court reached a high point in *Michael H.,* with Brennan rejecting Scalia's "majoritarian" assertion that it was the duty of the justices to determine opinion at the state level before invoking the due-process clause of the Fourteenth Amendment. Such an approach, according to Brennan, would reduce the clause to a "redundancy."[88]

Much of the prepublicity about *Webster* focused on Justice Sandra Day O'Connor—the only and first woman on the Court—as the swing person who could prevent an outright rejection of *Roe.* However, it was Scalia's "derisive and intemperate" attack on O'Connor's concurring opinion that attracted the post-decision headlines. Surprisingly, Scalia did not raise the historical questions of whether there was a national consensus on abortion or whether the states had historically regulated abortion, as many predicted he would. Instead, he accused the plurality of four, but especially O'Connor, of hypocrisy for "finessing" rather than overturning *Roe.* Scalia strongly believes that in *Roe* the Court gave itself "self-awarded sovereignty over a field where it has little proper business." Declaring abortion to be a "political issue" rather than a constitutional one, Scalia condemned the "indecisive decision" of his colleagues on the Court for "preserving a chaos that is evident to anyone who can read and count." He correctly predicted that the Court would be deluged by mail and demonstrations as a result of its refusal to abandon *Roe* completely (and, presumably, the right of privacy on which that decision was partly based). "It thus appears that the mansion of constitutionalized abortion-law, constructed overnight in *Roe v. Wade*," Scalia concluded, "must be disassembled door-jamb by door-jamb, and never entirely brought down, no matter how wrong it may be."[89]

Justice Blackmun, author of the original *Roe* decision, delivered a strong dissent in which Brennan and Marshall joined, in a "weary and sorrowful tone." He accused the plurality of "implicitly invit[ing] every state legislature to enact more and more restrictive abortion regulations . . . in the hope that sometime down the line the Court will return procreative freedom to the severe limitations that generally prevailed in this country before January 22, 1973." Like Scalia, but for quite different reasons, Blackmun thought the plurality had been "deceptive" in eviscerating the precedent *Roe*, while claiming to leave it "undisturbed." He singled out the *Roe* "trimester framework," with its viability principle that Chief Justice Rehnquist, writing for the plurality, had declared could "not be found in the text of the Constitution or in any place else one would expect to find a constitutional principle," as having been developed to protect the right of privacy safeguarding women's "control over their own role in procreation."[90]

With respect to the plurality's assertion that the state of Missouri had a compelling interest in potential life "throughout pregnancy, not merely after viability," Blackmun claimed that its opinion did not contain "one word of rationale for its view of the State's interest . . . [and constituted] nothing other than an attempted exercise of brute force." He concluded that "to overturn a constitutional decision that secured a fundamental personal liberty to millions of persons would be unprecedented in our 200 years of constitutional history." To do so surreptitiously and without "special justification," as required by a departure from *stare decisis*, Blackman found unconscionable and, to say the least, irresponsible.[91] It is worth noting that the four dissenting justices in *Webster* were the same four who dissented in the antisodomy five-to-four decision in Bowers v. Hardwick, 478 U.S. 186 (1986), and who had been in the original seven-to-two majority in *Roe*.

In summary, the *Webster* decision did not directly take up the issue of abortion as a right of privacy nor rule on a portion of the preamble to the Missouri statute claiming that life begins at conception. These and several procedural issues were left to the 1989–90 session of the Court and the three abortion cases scheduled to be heard at that time.[92] Instead, with *Webster,* abortion has become fundamental in the two-hundred-year debate over what constitutes female citizenship; just as pregnancy, as noted previously, has become fundamental in the debate over what constitutes female equality. And yet there are feminists who continue to say that issues of sexuality are irrelevant or diversionary to the Second Women's movement.

## Postscript to the 1989 Abortion Decision

Women have always been second-class citizens in the United States. The Supreme Court's decision in the Missouri abortion case did not create that condition —it simply underscored it. But the plurality of justices who eviscerated *Roe v. Wade,*—Kennedy, O'Connor, Rehnquist, Scalia, and White—while claiming not to have overturned it, set a new precedent in the history of second-class citizenship for one-half of the American population. *Webster v. Reproductive Health Services* not only reaffirmed the second-class citizenship of all American women but also instilled fear in the hearts of all those pregnant women who now or in the future will want to exercise their fundamental right to have an abortion. Moreover, because it implicitly questioned the right to privacy in reproductive matters, it potentially threatened the right of all women to use certain contraceptive methods. The *Webster* decision even cast an indirect cloud over the outcome of pending right-to-die suits and raised the specter of illegal importation and distribution of the French abortion drug RU-486.[93]

For the first time, the Supreme Court took a juridically established fundamental right and said that it was up to each of the fifty states to decide how much of that right one group of citizens could exercise. No other right declared "basic" or "fundamental" by the Supreme Court has ever been turned back to the idiosyncratic whims of largely white, male legislators in the name of "majoritarianism." In fact, in its 1988–89 term in the only bona fide "majoritarian" case that the Rehnquist Court decided, Texas v. Johnson, 109 S. Ct. 2533 (1989), the justices upheld burning the U.S. flag—a decision that clearly violated majority opinion. To a lesser degree so did the pro–dial-a-porn decision in Sable Communications of California, Inc. v. Federal Communications Commission, 109 S. Ct. 2829 (1989). Both involved the First Amendment, and public-opinion polls as well as state legislatures had taken exactly the opposite "majoritarian" stand on these two issues.

Why was the overwhelming majority—the forty eight states with statutes protecting the flag—ignored? Why has the court always ignored national polls and specific city ordinances against pornography? Why is "majoritarianism" so easily resorted to in civil rights and abortion decisions by the Rehnquist Court and not in First Amendment cases? Are race and gender less important to the conservative "gang of five" in these five-to-four decisions? I suggest that this is so. When has the reproductive freedom of men been subjected to the vagarities of states' rights? When will the right of women to control their bodies as men do be argued in unequivocal, radical terms? Women must finally take a stand on what really harms them and what they really need to alleviate their suffering—instead of what mainstream politics and jurisprudence dictates—because two hundred years is too long to still be fighting for full female citizenship. Let the male commentators talk about "how abortion won't polarize the country" (William Safire) and take hope in the "constraints and hesitations" (Anthony Lewis) of the muddled *Webster* decision.[94] Pregnant women, especially those in rural areas and teen-agers, cannot afford to. For them this is an immediate private, political, and personal issue that will not be resolved until angry women show their anger and insist that only women should be able to control their reproductive functions— not states or religious groups.

In June 1990, the Supreme Court handed down two more abortion decisions— both involving notification of parents. By a vote of six to three, the justices upheld a state law in Ohio v. Akron Center for Reproductive Health, 58 L. Wk. 4979, that required teen-age girls to notify one parent before obtaining an abortion. It also provided such girls with the option of a judicial by-pass if they decided against parental notification, but the decision did not make it clear whether this option was required if only one parent (usually the custodial one) had to be informed. In a much more divided five-to-four decision in Hodgson v. Minnesota, 58 L. Wk. 4957, the Supreme Court said that a state could require that a pregnant teen-ager inform both of her parents before having an abortion as long as the law also provided the alternative of a judicial hearing. In both decisions, the high court backtracked on its longstanding resistance to third-party "vetoes" of abortions and continued its general retreat from the landmark 1973 decision in *Roe v. Wade* that established a woman's right to terminate a pregnancy on the constitutional grounds of right to privacy.

Once again, as in the 1989 *Webster* decision, Justice Sandra Day O'Connor's position proved pivotal in the close *Hodgson* case. Repeating her earlier opinions, which held that state laws restricting abortions should not impose any "undue burden" on a woman's right to abortion, O'Connor joined the slim majority of five in upholding what she called Minnesota's "unreasonable" parental-notification requirement as long as the law allowed teen-agers the option of judicial by-pass. Since O'Connor has never used her "undue-burden" standard to find a state restriction on abortion unconstitutional, it is difficult to understand (or predict) how she will apply it in future abortion cases. In *Hodgson,* she simply did not decide whether two-parent notification did, or did not, impose an "undue burden." Typically, Justice Scalia stood alone in the dissenting opinion. In it, he condemned not only the confusion created by the other justices' opinions but also the Court's "enterprise of devising an Abortion Code and . . . the illusion that we have the authority to do so."[95]

When women are denied the sexual and reproductive autonomy of men, they are relegated to second-class citizenship. In this sense, the abortion debate is, indeed, over whether women or men should control women's bodies. Perhaps less obvious, however, is the fact that both sides in the abortion debate wrap their arguments in protective and traditional rhetoric of motherhood. Proabortion advocates want to be able to decide when they want to be voluntary mothers so they can practically continue to pursue careers and act like men in most other respects. Antiabortion advocates want everyone (including themselves) to be involuntary mothers because they believe that acting like men is not as important a function for women as the moral role of motherhood. As long as the meaning of motherhood remains at the heart of the political arguments over abortion, how can we expect the courts and state legislatures to rise above this stereotypical political fray and grant women an unencumbered constitutional right as citizens (and not as voluntary, practical, or involuntary, moral mothers) to abortion? Is it any wonder that in the last decade of the twentieth century, women in the United States are once again facing the reinforcement of their second-class citizenship because certain states and the Supreme Court have undermined their fundamental right to the same reproductive freedom that men enjoy?

# CHAPTER NINE

# The Epitome of Liberal Legalism: The ERA and Pornography

Historians of American politics have long known that periods of conservative backlash follow major wars, especially in the twentieth century. That another such time of disillusionment and an attempt to return to some mythical past would ensue following the end of the Vietnam War came as no surprise, therefore, from a historical perspective. As it turned out, the profound cultural and political reaction the country began to experience in the mid-1970s exceeded that following World War I in the 1920s. Yet, the backlash triggered by Vietnam, Watergate, and "stagflation" is often ignored by those studying the achievements and failures of the Second Women's movement.

With the end to American participation in the Indochinese war in the spring of 1973, domestic issues began to emerge as targets for this backlash because they could more readily be simplistically portrayed than the senselessness of the carnage in Vietnam, the temporary moral vacuum in national leadership created by Watergate, and the problems of the economy. The major objects of this negative, national sublimation became busing, abortion, the ERA, and school prayer. By the mid-1970s, without a war to channel these frustrated emotions, conservatives and fundamentalists launched a successful grass-roots campaign aimed at all things deemed un-American, unnatural, immoral, or smacked of more New Deal government interventionism.

## Fundamentalism and Fragmentation

While it was natural to expect that momentum for reform through legislation and litigation would decline in the postwar era beginning in 1973, there have been two additional complicating factors threatening further progress of women in the United States toward equality in this dramatic fourth period of their changing legal status. The first is related to the increasing influence of antifeminist fundamentalism in the country at large, and the second is the growing evidence of the reemergence of a deep-seated split within the ranks of women activists—

316

the roots of which can be traced back in this country to the First Women's movement of the last quarter of the nineteenth century. The first factor is almost entirely due to a post-Watergate syndrome that perverted what should have been a fairly progressive brand of domestic conservatism, following the end of American participation in the war in Indochina, into a regressive conservatism under Ronald Reagan.[1]

The second factor probably poses an internal, rather than external, threat to the continued survival of the Second Women's movement. Political fragmentation among largely mainstream feminists in the wake of the defeat of the ERA in 1982 revolves around the legal question of whether public policies affecting women should be designed to treat American females and males identically (which usually means viewing women as though they are men by ignoring their socialized and cultural differences) or whether these differences should be positively recognized by Congress and the courts, thus according public status to the traditionally private-sphere female functions with their emphasis on social service and nurturing values. This conflict is currently splitting both activists and scholars over the question of "equal treatment" versus "special treatment" on such diverse questions as pregnancy-related benefits, pornography, and comparable worth. Equal versus special rights constitutes a complex and legal issue that is compounded by the plethora of dichotomous terms currently used to describe this most recent split within the Second Women's movement.[2] In retrospect, equal versus special rights will ultimately be viewed by historians of the future as a false issue if its resolution does not result in placing U.S. feminists in an anticipatory rather than a reactive mode of thought and action.

The rapidly changing legal status of women between 1963 and 1989 constituted, therefore, an unfinished "bourgeois revolution" because of (1) the ambiguity of certain Supreme Court decisions, (2) the heightened conservatism in the country at large, (3) the greater hostility toward civil rights in the 1980s, and (4) the resurfacing of an old unresolved conflict among feminists over special-versus-equal treatment of women—with neither side demonstrating an ability to go beyond liberal legalism and traditional concepts of equality to a sense of equity. As noted in the Introduction, Karen Offen has identified two basic types of feminism: the equal rights version based on "radical individualism," or "equality of sameness," and relational or familial feminism based on gender differences sometimes called "equality in difference." With the exception of protective legislation, since 1900 most female reformers in the United States have focused on the first type in their pursuit of equal rights with white males.

However, after the defeat of the ERA radical feminists resurfaced in the United States, and there was more receptivity for their arguments for equitable, rather than traditional, equal treatment of women in social legislation and litigation. As yet, the countervailing legal and socioeconomic theories offsetting the idea of equality based on individual rights have been promoted by a small number of isolated radical feminists largely outside academe, although also by feminists in other professions and disciplines. Critical Legal Studies and feminist lawyers, in particular, are taking a hard look at the limitations of *only* achieving individual equal rights with men and are considering alternatives more in keeping with the long-standing collective views of radical feminists about restructuring American society using socially constructed female gender characteristics.

For the first time since the Progressive movement of the early twentieth century, a growing number of middle-class women in the United States are thinking about the benefits of collective or relational feminism for *all* women, including themselves. As noted in chapter 6, during the height of the Progressive movement many professional women who became mainstream reformers endorsed a collective, rather than individualistic, concept of justice, but primarily for working women and others designated as disadvantaged—not for themselves or for women in general. Demanding public recognition of the private needs and, therefore, citizenship based on the equality of esteem for *all* women and not simply equal rights has been a characteristic of radical feminists, who have always been a minority within both the First and Second Women's movements in this country. The brief creative periods when radical feminists have provided the impetus at crucial historical moments to crack the boundaries of liberal legalism have been few and far between in this country's constitutional development. Usually they have occurred at the beginning, not the end, of such movements (for example, in 1848 and the late 1960s). The resurgence of radical feminism in the last decade of the twentieth century may mean that the Second Women's movement, unlike the first one, will be able to overcome its current fragmentation and the general conservatism of the country to move beyond traditional liberalism in politics and law.

## Hypotheses about Legislation and Litigation since 1963

There are several other theoretical generalizations that frequently seem to apply when talking about legislation and litigation affecting contemporary women in the United States. First, as noted in chapters 1 and 8, until most recently, women have almost always been accorded functionalist treatment—that is, the prescriptive view that female existence is largely circumscribed by a woman's role within the historical patriarchal family and political structure.[3] A second generalization is that most domestic policy making in the United States is incremental and, hence, piecemeal by nature. Incremental legislation often contains overlapping characteristics of increasing importance and controversy, which political scientists call *distributive, regulatory,* and *redistributive.*[4] In retrospect, what appears most significant about the early gender-related legislation in the 1960s is not that women benefited from incrementalism—this was inevitable given the civil rights movement—but how unconscious or indifferent Congress seemed when considering what later turned out to be significant redistributive public policy, such as adding the word sex to Title VII of the 1964 Civil Rights Act. The Supreme Court did not follow the lead of Congress by taking up gender-related cases until the early 1970s, and it proceeded more cautiously and consciously—but not always with consistency or clarity.

A third, albeit less obvious, generalization is the twentieth-century tendency for public policy based on legislation and public policy based on litigation to move in opposite directions, until such time as a new reform synthesis or consensus has emerged. For example, the Supreme Court struck down state legislation aimed at setting maximum hours for both women and men and minimum wages for women until Progressive and New Deal reformers prevailed in particular cases in the 1920s and 1930s.[5] In contrast, in the 1970s and 1980s there has not been as much clear-cut opposition between state reform legislation affecting women and Supreme Court decisions regarding them, except in certain abortion cases before 1989 in which state laws have been voided. (During these same two decades, however, on three major issues Congress has passed legislation overruling specific Supreme Court decisions.)[6]

The absence of traditional Supreme Court opposition to statutes altering the legal status of women in recent decades has possibly been due to the fact that the first federal statutes were not the product of a national reform movement, as had been the case in the Progressive Era and the New Deal period. Moreover, by the time the justices began considering cases involving the Equal Pay Act or Title VII in the early 1970s, there were numerous appellate court decisions upholding both. Additionally, most affirmative-action precedents of the 1950s and 1960s pertaining to race were fairly easily transferred to issues of gender. In essence, during the early 1970s the Burger Court was responding more to: (1) lower-court decisions invalidating sex-specific state labor laws under Title VII; (2) federal, rather than state, legislation; (3) administrative actions by the White House; (4) previous Warren Court precedents in race and privacy cases; and (5) dramatic demographic changes in family size accompanied by the massive entry of married women into the work force than to the emerging Second Women's movement, whose leaders at that time were focusing their activities on lobbying Congress for more federal legislation.

Still another generalization about legislation and litigation affecting women since 1963 is that neither Congress (except by accident) nor the Supreme Court has acted in broadly redistributive ways that would have retroactive economic impact. In fact, when faced with such a possibility, in certain social-security and pension cases or pregnancy and comparable-worth issues, the justices have come close to contradicting their own case-law precedents, which have clearly stated that "explicit sex classifications must fall whenever [they] reflect . . . the 'baggage of sexual stereotypes.' "[7] Unlike the 1963 Equal Pay Act, comparable-work legislation of the 1980s is fundamentally redistributive from an economic standpoint, and that is why all branches of government have avoided dealing squarely with this issue.

If a significant breakthrough on comparable worth (or any other issue involving collective justice for women, such as abortion, pregnancy, or pornography) occurs before the end of this century, it will probably be the result of litigation because, by definition, incremental legislation *requires* and *acquires* more "conservative" support than does litigation. When Congress outpaced the Supreme Court in the early 1960s on the question of women's individual rights, it reversed a century-old pattern of interaction between litigation and legislation, in which court cases brought by an individual or groups of women were usually more "radical" (redistributive) in intent than most of the legislation in behalf of women at the state and federal levels. This reversal of the traditional relationship between congressional and court action diminished in the 1970s—as the Burger Court began to make gender-based case-law history—only to return somewhat in the 1980s as an increasingly Democratic Congress began to assert itself over three consecutive Republican administrations. Now that the Rehnquist Court has a working conservative majority, feminists must continue to rely on federal legislation rather than litigation to protect (and advance) their hard-won legal victories of the last twenty-five years.

A final related generalization is that advances in the legal status of women have almost always been the product of conservative alliances. Perhaps because Congress appeared more progressive than the courts until the early 1970s, mainstream feminist groups, such as NOW, did not feel impelled to make the customary conservative alliances necessary to ensure passage of the ERA at the state level. Indifference to, or ignorance of, traditional brokering with conservative factions that had made possible the Married Women's Property Acts of the nineteenth century, protective legislation, passage of the suffrage amendment, and no-fault divorce proved to be a most egregious mistake in the ERA battle. Most important, the leadership of NOW did not anticipate how a postwar backlash would hinder chances for ratification in the states, making alliances with select conservative groups all the more necessary. This is particularly true on the abortion issue, in light of the negative *Webster* decision discussed in chapter 8.

It was against a background of normal postwar conservatism, compounded by a temporary loss of faith in White House leadership and Armageddon theories of the approaching millennium, that the Second Women's movement attempted to take advantage of certain fortuitous pieces of congressional legislation from the early 1960s to transform the legal and political status of half of the U.S. population. Unfortunately, the major symbol for this transformation became the Equal Rights Amendment. That the movement's attempts have not succeeded is probably less significant than the fact that it has not completely failed under such hostile conditions. As of the last decade of the twentieth century, the ERA remains a symbolic reminder of a major failure of the Second Women's movement, just as the suffrage amendment remains a symbolic reminder of a major success for the First Women's movement.

Yet, the type of individualistic equality represented by the ERA need not remain the touchstone by which future feminists (or historians) will judge the failure or success of the Second Women's movement. If the difference between equality of opportunity and equality of results is understood, then it might be possible to place the debate over progress and regression of women's legal status over time into a proper perspective. In this sense, passage of the ERA would represent for women in the United States no more than a belated ratification of the past and present Lockean liberalism—not a new legal or socioeconomic breakthrough.

## The ERA as Symbol of Equality, Not Equity

By the end of 1973, liberal reform conditions inherited from the 1960s that continued to favor a successful ERA campaign rapidly began to wane. Between March 1972 and February 1974, thirty-three states ratified the proposed Twenty-seventh Amendment to the Constitution—many without any real debate. Only three states ratified it between February 1974 and June 1982—none after 1977. An initial slowdown in ratification momentum can be perceived as early as mid-1973; it became more evident in 1974, a year after the announcement of the Paris Peace Accords in January 1973. By the presidential election of 1976, the postwar backlash was in full swing as far as the ERA was concerned. Gerald Ford's election might have made the difference between success or failure of the ERA because his wife, as First Lady, would have become a national champion of equal rights for women in a way that Rosalynn Carter did not.

At any rate, by the mid-1970s, ratification forces were so weak at the state level that they required the leadership and support of a nationally recognized and independent First Lady. The NOW leadership and famous individual feminists of the 1970s simply did not have the charismatic appeal to, or sympathy for, average women (or men) to fulfill this task. Phyllis Schlafly came closer to occupying this role for the antiratificationists than anyone on the other side. This double liability, which characterized the ERA campaign—the absence of charismatic national leadership *and* grass-roots organization (in part, because radical feminists initially withheld their support until it was too late)—contradicted the historical expertise and legacy of the First Women's movement. Neither liability had existed in the final drive for passage of the Nineteenth Amendment sixty years earlier. Since no Carrie Chapman Catts or Alice Pauls emerged in the 1970s or 1980s to capture the support of both moderate and militant feminists, only the powerful rational appeal of a First Lady activist committed to ratification might have changed the course of the ERA's history.

Eleanor Roosevelt could have altered that history following World War II, but at that time she opposed the ERA in keeping with her Progressive reform roots that had placed her in the social justice, or group equality, wing of the First Women's movement. After all, women obtained suffrage in part as a "reward" for their contributions to World War I and, in part, through astute conservative alliances. It was logical to expect that the ERA should have been the "reward" demanded in 1945. Even women outside mainstream politics sensed that the war enhanced the chances for an ERA. Georgia O'Keeffe, for example, wrote to the First Lady in 1944 saying that she should help make the ERA a reality because "it could very much change the girl child's idea of her place in the world." O'Keeffe also reminded Roosevelt that those women who had supported the ERA since the 1920s had made it possible for her "to be the power that you are in our country, to work as you work and to have the kind of public life that you have." While Alice Paul and the NWP did succeed in obtaining endorsement of the amendment by both major parties in the early 1940s, the issue was never promoted by the prominent Democratic women around Eleanor Roosevelt who could have made the difference in the late 1940s when the ERA could have been packaged as a postwar "gift" for selfless wartime work and female patriotism.[8]

Unfortunately, Roosevelt's politics and brand of relational feminism kept her from ever using her enormous power and influence to heal the wounds created by the bitter debates between the protectionists and equal rightists in the interwar years or to work publicly for passage of the ERA between 1945 and her death in 1962. Without a single leader to unite them, women continued to fight with one another until the Second Women's movement emerged in the late 1960s.

If the ratificationists were to succeed in the 1970s, they needed an Alice Paul and her followers, as well as NOW presidents Karen DeCrow and Eleanor Smeal and theirs. Just as Paul had rallied the more militant forces for suffrage during and immediately following World War I, militant activity would have made NOW seem more acceptable to Americans suspicious of the ERA, as it had the NAWSA a half-century earlier. Instead, mainstream ratificationists, led by several rela-

tively colorless NOW leaders, tried to fight the anti-ERA backlash with moderation and logic—when only the emotional charisma of an Eleanor Roosevelt or
possibly a Betty Ford could have succeeded under the adverse conditions faced by
the ERA in the last half of the 1970s and early 1980s. (By actively discouraging
the formation of militant ERA groups, NOW not only ignored a historical lesson
about the last years of the successful campaign for suffrage but also a basic
political tactic—using the fear of militancy to make reform acceptable).

There are a number of reasons for singling out Betty Ford over other First
Ladies who occupied the White House after Congress sent the ERA to the states
for ratification in 1972. Although Pat Nixon had the longest unbroken work
record of all such women since World War II (sixteen years prior to 1946 when
Tricia was born and her husband's political career began) and she had publicly
supported the Republican party's endorsement of the ERA in 1968 and 1972, she
was no longer the First Lady when the initial monumentum for it at the state
level began to wane. Richard Nixon had issued statements in favor of the ERA
his entire political career but as president was not as enthusiastic about it as his
wife and daughters, saying that it "would create a judicial Pandora's box." He
believed that the Equal Pay Act of 1963 should be used more effectively to ensure
equal treatment of women in the workplace. During his first administration,
Nixon followed his own Executive Order No. 11478, by tripling the number of
women in policy-making government jobs and replacing one thousand men in
middle-management positions with women.[9]

Of the three First Ladies following Pat Nixon before the defeat of the ERA in
1982, only Betty Ford stood out as being more liberal on issues affecting women
than her husband, especially on such issues as abortion, drug use, premarital
sex, and the ERA.[10] Betty Ford pushed her husband on all these issues in public
and private, ranging from embarrassing frankness in print and media interviews
to "pillow talk . . . when she figured he was most tired and vulnerable." On her
advice in January 1976, for example, President Ford refused to attend the annual
Gridiron Club dinner until the group elected a woman member. By her own
admission, Betty Ford "did a lot of stumping for ERA." In August 1976, she
wrote a private letter on Equality Day to Alice Paul and a public one to ERA
supporters, saying: "As your vigil outside the White House ends I assure you
mine inside the White House continues."[11]

To the degree that Betty Ford's chance to emerge as an effective ERA leader
hinged on her husband's election in his own right to the White House, the ERA
can be considered an unintended victim of Watergate. The conditions under
which Nixon resigned from office in 1974 and Ford's quick pardon of the former
president doomed Republican chances for victory in 1976. Although the ERA's
defeat is not usually associated with Ford's defeat, I believe that because of his

wife's leadership potential on the question of equal rights for women, it should, at least in part, be. Another overlooked reason for its failure is a 1980 Supreme Court decision. Some have argued that an irreversible connection between the ERA and abortion created by the Hyde Amendment and the 1980 Supreme Court decision in Harris v. McRae, 448 U.S. 297 (1980), doomed passage of the amendment two years before it officially died in 1982. The decision in *McRae* upheld the constitutionality of the Hyde Amendment, which excluded even medically needed therapeutic abortions from the federal medical-benefits program. Since *McRae* said that women were not entitled to government-subsidized abortions, only passage of the ERA offered the possibility that, by making gender a suspect classification, laws preventing poor women from exercising their constitutional rights to this medical procedure would also become subject to strict scrutiny. Since the ERA would have nullified *McRae* and the Hyde Amendment, its passage became anathema to leaders of antiabortion forces.[12] However, that this reasoning was understood by average housewives is unlikely.

Not surprisingly, under Carter's lackluster administration both legislation and litigation improving the legal status of women began to slow down, as indicated in the chart on page 240. Neither Rosalynn nor Jimmy Carter demonstrated more than interested curiosity in the passage of the ERA, either in Georgia or as First Lady and president. Passages about equal rights for women in Rosalynn Carter's autobiography are perfunctorily sandwiched between other political or cultural projects that she obviously deemed more important. Describing how her opposition to Gloria Steinem's appearance in Atlanta in 1974 prompted her governor-husband mistakenly to inform the press that his wife opposed the ERA, she laconically rationalized this incident by saying: "Georgia was not ready for the ERA in 1974." With equal dispassion, she commented on the ERA's defeat in 1982 by saying that "great progress comes slowly."[13]

This absence of charismatic First Ladies notwithstanding, momentum for the passage of the ERA declined precipitantly in the late 1970s, despite the fact that many different kinds of feminists—but particularly the more left-of-center ones who had refused to support the amendment initially—finally became belated, albeit vocal, ratificationists behind NOW's mainstream banner. In any case, by the time more left-of-center feminists joined the ERA cause and began to suggest militant action, it was probably too late to salvage the Twenty-seventh Amendment from the abyss of postwar conservatism into which it had fallen in certain key ratification states. By the late 1970s and early 1980s, too many female opponents of the ERA intuitively viewed feminist individualism and the doctrine of equal rights as a threat or danger to the traditional differences between women and men and to the dependent status accorded them by society that they assumed was protecting them as nature (or God, or both) had dictated.

It is not the purpose of a legal study such as this one to chronicle the tactical and strategic mistakes made by NOW leaders that others have already documented—except to say that until the 1989 *Webster* decision they seemed determined to repeat most of them in the battle for abortion rights.[14] The suggestion in chapter 6 about the limitations of feminist leadership in the 1920s holds true for the 1980s—namely, that liberalism, in general, and liberal legalism, in particular, have (and are) once again undermining the ability of women activists to express and organize themselves effectively out of fear of "offending" the power structure they are trying to reform.

I am not personally convinced that Phyllis Schlafly consciously realizes why those opposing the ERA intuitively fear being treated as equal, ungendered individuals. She simply capitalizes on the fact that they represent a gendered class whose fear of, and dominance by, men in their immediate lives prompt them to believe that they benefit from certain protections and differential treatment at home and on the job. Part of this fear resides in their subjective historical frame of mind and their objective contemporary condition—both of which are still based on dependence and deference arising from male-domination experiences— not unlike the fears that women opposing pornography express when talking about male violence in contemporary society. The difference is that radical feminists choose to organize against pornography and fight against male domination and violence, while more relationally oriented women choose to organize against the ERA (behind Schlafly's misleading banner) but not to fight male domination and violence. This *legitimate* fear of men by both groups of women should be a unifying force within the Second Women's movement. Instead, NOW's emphasis in its campaign for the ERA on middle-class political and professional issues rather than sexual issues, such as rape, spousal abuse, and daily harassment in factories and in other low-paying jobs, prevents either group from recognizing their common fear of men because its manifestation across class lines takes distinctly different forms.

Ironically, Schlafly's personal historical frame of mind made her perception of her personal subjective and objective condition (as a wealthy woman with a law degree) quite different from that of her followers, but they either did not know this or did not care about it. The important thing was she spoke their common language—something feminist leaders of the First Women's movement had abandoned in the 1920s and those of the Second Women's movement have yet to learn. The average fearful housewife resented the fact that pro-ERA groups seemed determined to break the cultural solidarity of women's "rightful" place in society, based upon their "special nature." Such women feared what would happen to them as mothers, wives, and workers if they were treated "just like" men. In southern and northern cities with large ghetto populations, these women's largely unarticulated fear of men at home and in the workplace was exacerbated by racial prejudice. For example, the argument against *unisex* toilets really was one about *integrated* toilets and was often associated with school integration in many areas of the country. Even when race was not an issue, washrooms restricted by sex (and race) represented "safe space," especially in industrial-work situations.[15]

The emotional, gender, sex, and sometimes racial conflict raised by the ERA in certain conservative states combined with NOW's liberalism to defeat the ERA, not the more esoteric political-science arguments sometimes offered. Such intangibles as the perception of two Supreme Court decisions in *Harris v. McRae*, in 1980, and in *Rostker v. Goldberg*, in 1981, by the fundamentalists opposing the ERA surely played a role that cannot be precisely calibrated or understood through social-science jargon. The first decision, as noted here and in chapter 8, on the surface represented a victory for antiabortion forces because the justices upheld the Hyde Amendment, which forbids the use of federal funds for abortion. Since the decision was based on the due-process clause of the Fifth Amendment, conservative religious leaders correctly, but in the most emotional terms possible, argued that passage of the ERA would make such funds available to the poor. Then, when the decision in *Rostker* held that the draft was legal but limited to men only, another long-held emotional claim of the anti-ERA forces became more tangibly urgent: the ERA would take away this female exception to the draft. By the early 1980s, state ERA statutes made a national ERA both *less* important as a tool to already liberated women and *more* important as a threat to those who remained victims of no-fault divorce, unpaid alimony and child support, and the feminization of poverty in general. Finally, Watergate played another intangible role (in addition to the defeat of Gerald Ford in 1976) by giving Sam Ervin, an irascible opponent of the ERA, more national power and prestige than he had had before in the wake of the Senate impeachment hearings.[16]

All these emotional intangibles paled, however, beside the one least analyzed and most quickly dismissed: the imponderable "opposition of traditionalist housewives." Their fears—almost invisible on the surface of the ERA debate—provided the antiratification leaders with an emotional foundation that the ratification leaders could not generate or fight with their logical, liberal arguments and tactics in behalf of the ERA. These immediate fears of those forgotten women who opposed the ERA were bolstered by a vague sense of resentment that NOW and other national ERA groups had used "tricks" or "unfair" political procedures in getting the amendment and other federal legislation through Congress for most of the 1970s.[17]

But mainly it was the "traditionalist housewife's" fear of men and of being forced to be like men that galvanized them behind anti-ERA leaders who no more appreciated the internal qualities of their lives than the pro-ERA ones. "I am a widow, have three children, and work to make ends meet," wrote one of these women. "I am still against the ERA. I am a woman—and I want to be treated as a woman—not a man!" When this deeply held sentiment combined with equally traditional views about the family, there was no room in these women's private lives for liberation, let alone emancipation. As one told Senator Ervin even before the ERA passed Congress: "He [her husband] works for me, takes care of me and our three children, doesn't make me do things that are hard for me (drive in town), loves me and doesn't smoke, drink, gamble, run around or do anything that would upset me. I do what he tells me to do. I like this arrangement, it's the only way I know how to live."[18]

From this perspective, the ERA was an assault on womanhood and the institution of marriage—the security most women were raised to know, however tenuous their marital rights were under the law. The "scare tactics" employed in behalf of the traditional, if rapidly disappearing, family unit by the anti-ERA leaders worked because their followers were afraid—afraid of the draft, afraid of losing spousal support, afraid of raising girl children to have abortions, afraid of the decriminalization of rape and other sex crimes, afraid of blacks. "You do not and cannot know what the [blue collar] working woman has to put up with," one white North Carolina millworker said when writing of her opposition to the ERA to her state senator. She then recounted how she was lying down in the "ladies washroom" at the plant where she worked because she didn't feel well, and a black man thrust his arm into the room. She had told him to go away, which he did. However, she was convinced that if the ERA were ratified he would have come in over her protestations.[19]

It is at this level of sexual (and racial) vulnerability that the ERA failed because there was no way liberal legalism could counter, even if it had understood, that "the ladies room was [as much] a haven and sanctuary" to factory women as the "home" had once been to working men. Male toilets were only latrines and urinals, and under the ERA that is all women's would be too.[20] At most, the "traditionalist housewife" could only understand equality and individualism in terms of work outside the home, but not in many of the other terms served up to them by NOW. Even in the workplace, however, equality was fearful because it meant more direct competition with men, whom these women already knew were superior to them.

Little wonder that the very language of the ERA could be vulgarized by its opponents. "On account of sex" was translated by male antiratificationists and by their fearful female supporters to mean "on account of the manner in which and the partner with whom you have sexual relations." Jane De Hart and Donald Mathews have presented the most empathetic and sophisticated interpretation of the views of the "traditionalist housewives" within the antiratificationist ranks. At one level, their descriptions of these women approach the gender consciousness of the familial or relational feminists described by Offen, but only on the most primitive physical and spacial levels. Unless the female cultural identity of the members of the anti-ERA forces is recognized and distinguished from the conservative leadership that converted that identity into irrational antifeminism during the battle over the ERA, women who advocate complete equal rights with men will not succeed in obtaining passage of a new version of the ERA in the near or distant future. And perhaps it is best that they do not, since the amendment is another example of too little, too late—now "represent[ing] a symbolic gesture . . . the unfinished business" of "another era."[21]

Despite a somewhat inconsistent record, the courts have undoubtedly improved the legal status of women in the last twenty years without an Equal Rights Amendment. Ratification of the ERA would have contributed significantly, but only slowly over time, to this ongoing process. It would not have immediately produced uniform treatment of women under the law or guaranteed consistently favorable court decisions; but, in the long run, it would have ensured that women, regardless of the accident of birth or residence, would have had the same rights in all states. In the wake of the ERA's defeat, we are disposed to forget that this amendment, like the Fourteenth Amendment before it and all subsequent civil rights acts, was designed not to change values but to modify the behavior of mainstream citizens by forcing the Supreme Court to grant suspect classification to women as a group. By guaranteeing that cases involving sex discrimination would have been subjected to strict constitutional scrutiny, the ERA would have finally provided meaningful, as opposed to illusory, equality of opportunity for those women who want to realize full personal and professional expectations with men and by being assimilated into male mainstream America. What the ERA would have done *for* feminism in the United States and the other more collectivistic goals of the Second Women's movement remains unclear.

Had the ERA been ratified, it would have been absolutely noncoercive when it came to individual life styles because its enforcement powers were directed only against state and federal agencies or public officials, not against private citizens. It also would not automatically have changed public policy based on remaining sexist assumptions about women. Nonetheless, passage of the ERA in 1982 gradually would have promoted legal uniformity in the treatment of females in state and federal statutes in a way that no previous acts of Congress, executive orders, or Supreme Court decisions could.

As a symbol of how far women still have to go to obtain true constitutional equity in American society, the ERA may be more important in defeat than in victory. Its defeat has forced advocates of civil rights for women to seek creative legislation and judicial solutions in their continuing struggle for full and equal status with men. It already has resulted in a greater questioning of public policy that continues to discriminate against women, such as the lack of comparable pay scales, or to inconvenience them, such as the incompatibility of the working hours of banks, post offices, and schools with the typical nine-to-five shifts of working mothers. Most important, the defeat of the ERA has forced the debate over the question of special versus equal rights into the public arena once again because it theoretically embodied both concepts. Without the strained unity among feminists that the unsuccessful battle for passage of the Twenty-seventh Amendment provided, old factions within the Second Women's movement have reemerged to do battle. This is not necessarily an unhealthy development unless the rampant fragmentation and cooptation of the 1920s is repeated, and the widespread fear of men by two distinct groups of women—average housewives and radical feminists—continues to go unanalyzed, let alone utilized, for future feminist organizational purposes.

## Mary Beard—Once Again

In the 1930s and 1940s, historian Mary Beard similarly questioned the complex meaning of the ERA and the efficacy of egalitarian legislation in general in ways that most contemporary feminists have yet to address. Perhaps it is true that educated women have come to think more like men than we care to admit. In any case, Beard was concerned with questions that many women activists have suppressed or forgotten. Before World War II, Beard raised hard questions about women's attitudes toward themselves and the world; defeat of the ERA has finally forced us to consider those questions in the 1980s. For example, she asked, What do women really mean by equality of results? Is it primarily the demand "for equal opportunity at acquisition in the madness of the market place," as she strongly suspected? Does it inevitably mean supporting oppressive political regimes in the name of nationalism or national security? Does this indiscriminate demand for equality on male terms usually result in a loss of "distinct function[s] as women" and the "masculinism of politics and economics" as she feared? In other words, what happens to female sensibilities, relationships, and culture when women finally achieve complete equality with men? Perhaps because she always felt somewhat defensive about not having completed her own graduate education, Beard was particularly critical of college-educated women who "after they had won a large measure of equality . . . showed an inclination to settle back in its illusory security and to forget about women, that is, [to forget] about society as an organism in the process of evolution" and the role of the "eternal feminine" in this process.[22]

In the 1970s, women reformers did not show much concern over this hypothetical line of thinking because there has never been a political or socioeconomic movement in this country that has espoused equality of results at the expense of individualism that had any chance of succeeding. But Mary Beard did think about such things. We should at least use her concern to sharpen our own thinking about what we mean by the word *equality* in relation to *equity*. Beard also recognized the inertia that almost inevitably sets in after legal safeguards and political victories are won. Thus, Beard's legal legacy has become more relevant in the wake of the defeat of the ERA because of her suggestion that the concept of justice through equity or fairness and a sense of collective responsibility more nearly "fits" women's "real" societal position and needs than the pursuit of masculinist justice through individual rights and impersonal application of rules and regulations.

It may well be that we will come to see the value of Mary Beard's contention that women should not simply advocate equality of results based on traditional male values but instead advocate equity based on female values. This is what she demanded of nineteenth-century and pre–World War II reformers. Otherwise, as she argued, women will never be viewed as an independent collective force in history—"indispensables to the whole process."[23] She asked no less of herself as she struggled to understand the immediate meaning and long-term ramifications of equality for women. Should we ask or expect any less of ourselves in the last decade of the twentieth century?

The overriding philosophical consideration of some of today's postmodern legal theorists is whether or not society should now consciously strive for collective *equality of results* and group freedoms, in contrast to the "natural" or actual inequality in the distribution of society's benefits to the individual that has attended the pursuit of variegated equality in America throughout its history. Beard would have disagreed with this exact formulation of the problem, but she, too, envisioned a more collective, cooperative society coming out of the Great Depression and the New Deal. She called it "socialized democracy" in a "collective age." She clearly opposed state-enforced equality of results without using the term because she realized that it created people who were "routineers," contributing little to the humanizing of society. Instead, Beard supported equality of opportunity *and* equality of esteem for women because only by combining these two types of equality could women maintain their collective identity. She opposed the ERA because its words—no discrimination "on account of sex"—embodied a form of equality that history had shown to be counterproductive.[24] While her formulations were not systematically thought out, she sensed what the Critical Legal Studies movement has revealed by demystifying liberal theories of equality

—namely, that citizenship in modern civilizations was (and is) more than equality. It is "membership in the sense of belonging and acceptance."[25]

At first, the success of the Nineteenth Amendment lulled into complacency many in the First Women's movement. Later, in the 1920s and 1930s, the perceived "failure" of the Eighteenth and Nineteenth amendments and the counterproductive results of protective legislation further reified and increased ambivalence about the Constitution and other legal texts. Perhaps the actual failure of the Twenty-seventh Amendment will inspire those in the Second Women's movement to think more about the criticisms of the ERA Mary Beard raised over a half-century ago. This could mean continuing the struggle not only for the remaining legal rights that still elude them but also for public-policy changes that will positively affect the everyday lives of women, as well as for group identity through citizenship that both accords equality of opportunity and equality of esteem to them. Then, and only then, will they be in a position to restructure society to meet their needs and to become a part of the history that Mary Beard envisioned for them.

Just as suffrage and then protective legislation appeared as avant-garde reforms, they were not achieved until they no longer threatened the dominant white, male power structure. In turn, these issues were replaced with others that appeared radical at first, such as equal pay for equal work in the 1960s and the Equal Rights Amendment in the late 1970s. These were then replaced in the late 1980s by speculation as to whether Congress would finally endorse a national child-care program, whether the Supreme Court would take a progressive stand on comparable worth and pregnancy disability, or whether it would regress on affirmative action and on the legality of abortion. Above all, however, the impact on women of mass-distributed violent pornography loomed largest as the most radical issue.

## Pornography as Liberation, Not Emancipation

At the end of the 1980s, feminists divided bitterly over sexual violence in audiovisual and print media. Of all the problems facing the Second Women's movement in the last fifteen years of the twentieth century, pornography is potentially the most divisive and debilitating since the fifty-year debate over protective legislation and the ERA. In all likelihood, pornography will become *the* civil rights issue for the remainder of the century. Whether it can be resolved (as it is most commonly described) as a conflict between liberal values of equality and free speech is another matter. Nonetheless, the battle lines have already been clearly drawn, and the disagreement appears to have reached a stalemate. Some pluralists have allied themselves with fundamentalists in advocating the banning of such material through antipornography ordinances; most assimilationists have allied themselves with the purveyors of pornography, arguing that such material is protected by the First Amendment. The First Amendment absolutists also insist that pornography is an unnecessarily devisive issue for the Second Women's movement to address. Using poststructural arguments, others have relativistically dismissed the issue as an unimportant diversion, despite the disproportionately negative impact violent pornography has on the most disadvantaged classes of women.[26]

For all that has been written about pornography, especially since the indiscriminate distribution of it becomes possible with video cassettes, it has passed from obscurity in antiquity to a present-day mass phenomenon without acquiring either a history or a legal definition. The 1986 Attorney General's Commission on Pornography (AGCP) was forced to conclude that "the history of pornography still remains to be written." This same report stated that "to understand the phenomenon of pornography, it is necessary to look at the history of the phenomenon itself . . . [but] commissioning independent historical research was far beyond our mandate, our budget, and our time constraints." The 1970 President's Commission on Obscenity and Pornography, which had a budget sixteen times larger than the AGCP's (after taking into account the impact of inflation on the difference between $500,000 and $2 million), also did not authorize such a historical study.[27]

Why? Simplistic and often contradictory answers abound—ranging from the implicit notion that it is too trivial (or too dangerous) a subject to the explicit assertion that existing histories of sexual practices and of attempts to regulate such practices and writings about them are sufficient. Several basic reasons belie these standard ahistorical rationalizations. One of them has to do with the liberal bias of most legal and historical research discussed throughout this work. Feminist opposition to pornography represents the ultimate antithesis of traditional liberal legalism and historicism because it directly challenges the First Amendment doctrine and maintains that pornography so degrades women that it denies them the esteem or respect necessary for full citizenship.[28] To date, however, historians and lawyers have tended to bring their respective talents to bear primarily on opposing the variety of attempts to censor pornography, rather than on understanding it as a social phenomenon that violates women's civil rights.

Historically we know that despite state and religious proscriptions, the authority of both institutions had tolerated a wide range of sexually explicit representations from antiquity up to the nineteenth century. In colonial America, for example, there were some statutes that criminalized immorality, blasphemy, and heretical actions associated with them, but they did not primarily focus on materials dealing with sex. This remained true during the first decades of the new republic after the Constitution of 1787 officially separated church and state, because "pure sexual explicitness, while often condemned, was not . . . taken to be a matter of governmental concern."[29] Beginning in the nineteenth century, private organizations and individuals supporting social concepts about decency and obscenity dominated attempts to regulate sexually explicit material. Before then protection of state authority and religious values formed the basis for such erratic regulation of immoral material—the bulk of which was sex-oriented.[30]

In the course of the last century, certain individuals, such as Anthony Comstock, decided to ban all sexually explicit materials on grounds unrelated to state security or religious integrity. Instead, Comstock and others argued that sexually explicit materials were lewd, indecent, and obscene. Even after the passage of the federal Comstock Law in 1873 and similar state statutes, courts quickly became confused over what obscenity meant, thus enforcement remained highly idiosyncratic and only as effective as fanatics like Comstock could make it. During the progressive reform period of the early twentieth century, Margaret Sanger ran afoul of the Comstock Law in her attempt to disperse birth-control information to private individuals. Ironically, both the Comstock Law and Sanger can be seen in retrospect to have strengthened, rather than weakened, the sexualization of society. They did this by encouraging the capitalistic, patriarchal, and pseudoscientific principles upon which nineteenth-century concepts of sexuality were based.[31] Such campaigns (then and now) have futilely attempted to solve a sexual societal problem through behavior modification of *individuals*—not through structural or collective attitudinal change. Moreover, the early sex-reform crusades in the United States—whether for or against obscene materials—also failed to curb the simultaneous development of "acceptable" public forms of pornography under the guise of nineteenth-century versions of the grotesque, which accompanied the increase in pornographic representations at private levels of society.[32]

Then gradually during this century, such individual crusades gave way as the legal system and government focused on sexually explicit material more systematically than ever before. But this time it was not at the instigation of secular or religious zealots. Instead, the current government and juridical interest in obscene materials originated with the free expression of concerns of the "lost generation" of post–World War I writers and liberal lawyers. Beginning in the 1920s and 1930s, intellectuals in the United States began to make highly subjective distinctions between erotica and pornography that had no historical or etymological rationale. They automatically assigned a reputable (and, primarily, heterosexual) past to the former but not to the latter. Although the attempt to distinguish between the two is at most an arbitrary and artificial product of three generations of writers, literary and theater critics, and journalists, it has so captured the imagination of the liberal establishment that its relatively recent arbitrary and self-interested origins have been obscured.[33]

These private literary definitions, having little to do with moral purity or sex education, were soon thrust into the public arena of the courts, as all literature became more professionalized and academicized between the two world wars. From the time that intellectuals successfully separated pornography from erotica, the statutory definition of obscenity narrowed, and enforcement of laws regulating obscene materials diminished.[34] Two common themes linked the opinions of the literary giants and academic experts of these decades to the nineteenth-century moral reform movements and legislation: one was the acceptance of objectification and, hence, subordination of women in most sexually explicit material; the other was the continuing focus of the courts on obscenity, not on pornography per se. (Some feminists also now maintain that "true" erotica consists of "sexually explicit materials premised on equality" and thus advocate the creation of a feminist erotica.[35] Unfortunately, all the examples of this type of material available in contemporary American society could fit on the head of a pin. They also do not address the immediacy of the harm that the flood of violent pornography now represents by perpetuating the subordination of women.)

It has only been in this century, therefore, that private, social concepts about decency and obscenity have dominated the attempts to regulate sexually explicit material. Previously, protection of state authority and religious values formed the basis for such erratic regulation as existed. This move from public censorship of sexual writings and practices by governmental and religious groups was largely replaced by private censorship efforts in the course of the last century. Then in this century, both public *and* private censors have erratically combined forces in what represents a complicated historical process that has not yet been completely reconstructed—let alone deconstructed.[36]

During the late 1960s and early 1970s, the cultural and legal climate was such that pornographic fantasy and erotic realism merged with a vengeance in literature and films into what I call *pornrotica,* happily escaping both definition and prosecution under obscenity laws. Pornrotica is any representation of persons that sexually objectifies them and is accompanied by actual or implied violence in ways designed to encourage readers or viewers to assume that such sexual subordination of women (and children or men) is acceptable behavior, an innocuous form of sex education, or necessary to achieve orgasms. I prefer this definition because it more accurately conveys the historical blurring or merging of the meanings of erotica and pornography rather than the conventional wisdom about the differences between them. It is also essential in the 1980s that any definition of pornrotica recognize the close association in mass-distributed movies and videocassettes between sex and violence—most of which is directed *against* women *by* men.

Until the late 1970s, authors of books about sex practices made little attempt to come up with a historically comprehensive or accurate definition of pornography because, among other things, none of them was concerned about gender as a category of analysis.[37] Without gender analysis, there could be no redefinition of pornography exposing its basic misogyny and function as an ideological representation of patriarchy. Since pornography has come to represent "a practice of power and powerlessness" because of its mass-distributed publications and video forms, it no longer can be neglected through adequate regulation and prosecuted using statutes and legal interpretations about proof, discovery, and immunity meant to apply in criminal obscenity cases.[38] It quite literally must be redefined for political and juridical purposes.

Obscenity and pornography are two quite different concepts. Obscenity laws are meant to cover sexually explicit material when it promotes "excessive" arousal or excitement through candid portrayals of nudity, prurient appeal, and illegal or unnatural acts. Even the Meese commission's report noted that obscene material is probably not very harmful to women or society. From a radical feminist perspective, the same cannot be said of pornography, especially its more virulent forms because the "thought" or "speech" aspects of pornography cannot be separated from violent action against women. Thus, pornography has become "sex forced on real women so that it can be sold at a profit to be forced on other real women; women's bodies trussed and maimed and raped and made into things to be hurt and obtained and accessed and this presented as the nature of women in a way that is acted on and acted out over and over."[39]

In a word, pornography is "injurious speech as far as women are concerned." Radical feminist attorneys insist, therefore, that pornography resembles other categories of unprotected speech under the First Amendment, such as group libel along the lines upheld in Beauharnais v. Illinois, 343 U.S. 250 (1952), or the more narrow "fighting-words" doctrine of Chaplinsky v. New Hampshire, 315 U.S. 568 (1942). The courts have consistently refused to apply either precedent to pornography, in part because both decisions were premised on the male assumption that such words or depictions must carry the strong potential for inciting "an immediate breach of the peace" leading to public disorder and violence.[40] Presumably, until women begin to riot over degrading pornographic representations of them, the legal system will not see any compelling state interest for protecting them from such "injurious speech."

In part, it is the absence of, or callousness toward, gender analysis that has contributed to the obsession among members of the legal community for defining obscenity from a male perspective, while refusing to define pornography from a female perspective. Using gender analysis, radical feminists began to question not only the sexist assumptions of these legal distinctions but also the implicitly and explicitly harmful societal effects of mass-distributed pornography on women. For these reasons, Catharine MacKinnon and Andrea Dworkin began in 1983 to draft antipornography ordinances.[41] Although the courts have declared these ordinances unconstitutional violations of the First Amendment guarantee of free speech, to a surprising degree the ordinances have brought academic respectability to research on pornography and raised political consciousness on the topic, even though they have failed to change U.S. laws regulating it.[42]

This disagreement between radical feminist and civil libertarians over First Amendment doctrine is the most dramatic but by no means the only rift between the two groups over the much-heralded legal fiction that civil liberties are indivisible. Although U.S. legal history is replete with contrary examples, contemporary liberals maintain that civil liberties, especially those represented in the First Amendment, must protect (and apply to) everyone or they will protect (and apply to) no one. Obviously, when two civil liberties clash (in this case, women's liberties versus free speech) only one can prevail, thus violating the indivisibility postulate. As of the mid-1980s, the free-speech rights of pornographers under the First Amendment had prevailed in the courts over women's equality and esteem as citizens, on the grounds that pornography cannot be prosecuted unless it falls under the criminal-law definition of obscenity. MacKinnon and Dworkin have insisted that pornography should be removed from the absolutist intervention of the First Amendment and prosecuted under civil law.[43]

In the 1980s, civil suits increasingly succeeded against drug dealers, terrorist organizations, anti-Semitic or white-supremacist groups, corrupt politicians, white-collar criminals, and antiabortion demonstrations at the same time that legal decisions continued to deny that pornography was a violation of the civil rights of women. In all these other areas where the possibility of criminal prosecution exists, as it does for pornography under obscenity laws, the government and individuals have found successful cause for action using civil law. Thus, the 1970 federal Racketeering Influenced and Corrupt Organizations Act (RICO) has been increasingly broadly interpreted by U.S. courts in the 1980s, much to the consternation of civil libertarians—*except in pornography cases.*[44] However, one 1989 Supreme Court decision implored Congress to limit, or at least clarify, the RICO statute. In H. J. Inc. v. Northwestern Bell Telephone Co., 109 S. Ct. 2839 (1989), for example, the justices refused to narrow the scope of RICO, but they also refused, in this case, to apply it to a telephone company accused of manipulating the state's rate-setting process. Justice Brennan, writing for the narrow majority of five, dismissed the private civil suit brought by telephone customers in Wisconsin on the grounds that the law required proof of at least two separate fraudulent "schemes." This was in keeping with the Court's 1984 decision in Sedima v. Imrex, 473 U.S. 479 (1985), in which it insisted that RICO could be used to prosecute legitimate as well as illegitimate businesses but also that these racketeering offenses must be related to one another—that is, show "continuity" as "part of an ongoing entity's regular way of doing business." Representatives of the business community had hoped that the Court in *Sedima* would hold that a violation under RICO was warranted only when evidence *proved* a connection with organized crime.[45]

Several months prior to the close 1989 *Northwestern Bell* decision involving the application of RICO against a telephone company, the Supreme Court ruled unanimously in February that the First Amendment barred law-enforcement officials from seizing the entire inventory of adult bookstores (and, presumably video outlets) before the materials involved had been proven to be obscene. In Wayne Books Inc. v. Indiana and Sappenfield v. Indiana, 109 S. Ct. 916 (1989), the justices had no trouble distinguishing the seizure of the "assets" of a book dealer, arguing that this was a form of "prior constraint." Thus, for the first time the Supreme Court limited the application of RICO, although lower appeals courts continued with impunity to use the statute to collect damages from anti-abortion demonstrators who destroyed abortion clinic property, denying the free-speech and right-to-assembly arguments made by the National Rights to Life Committee. The adult book dealers in *Wayne Books* had challenged the constitutionality of the Indiana RICO statute on grounds of its "inherent" vagueness and "Draconian" application. The justices agreed, saying "if we are to maintain the regard for the First Amendment values expressed in our prior decisions dealing with interpreting the flow of expressive materials," the application of RICO in this instance had to be denied. By six to three in this same opinion, Justice White, writing for the majority, rejected the idea that antiracketeering laws should never be constitutionally applied to obscenity-law violations, as Justices Stevens, Brennan, and Marshall insisted in their dissents.[46]

RICO has proven effective when criminal procedures have not because of significant differences between civil and criminal suits in the areas of burden of proof, the power to grant immunity, "discovery" procedures, and availability of remedies (to say nothing of allowing successful plaintiffs to collect triple damages). As of 1989, however, RICO civil suits against pornographers have failed because pornography has tacitly become one of the many legal texts of modern patriarchy. Under pressure from business groups, in the fall of that year the Justice Department and Congress began to consider such drastic revisions of RICO that even some of its former critics questioned them.[47] If successful, it will be all the easier for contemporary American Civil Liberties Union (ACLU) attorneys to maintain that the right of pornographers to freedom of expression under the First Amendment takes precedence over any harmful impact that this form of protected speech may have on women, even though it is difficult to understand how such material can be considered legitimate political expression since no exchange of ideas takes place in most pornographic representations of women.

In 1988, Congress attempted to protect children from access to sexually explicit dial-a-porn messages, which represent a two-billion-dollar-a-year industry that began in the 1980s. By specifically prohibiting all indecent and obscene interstate commercial telephone communications (regardless of the age of the caller) in a general education bill, Congress invited negative opinions from the Supreme Court on the grounds the legislation was not narrowly enough tailored "to serve the compelling interest of preventing minors from being exposed to indecent telephone messages." Subsequently, Justice White wrote the opinion in the so-called dial-a-porn cases. Handed down in June 1989, Sable Communication Commission of California v. FCC, and FCC v. Sable, 109 S. Ct. 2829 (1989), did not involve RICO. Consequently, the opinion of the Court was straightforward in striking down the "total ban Congress had placed on both obscene and indecent telephone communications," saying: "Because the statute's denial of adult access to telephone messages which are indecent but not obscene far exceeds that which is necessary to limit the access of minors to such messages, we hold that the ban does not survive constitutional scrutiny."[48]

Only Justice Scalia in his concurring opinion in Sable noted a troublesome inverse relationship between obscenity and pornography. By striking down the FCC regulations because they included indecent speech, which is protected under the First Amendment, in contrast to obscene speech, which is not, Scalia said: "The more narrow the understanding of what is "obscene," and the more pornographic what is embraced within the residual category of "indecency," the more reasonable it becomes to insist upon greater assurancy of insulation from minors." Falling back on what are becoming his obviously ultratraditional views about the family, adultery, affirmative action for women, and now sex, Scalia concluded that not all sexual activity portrayed over the phone would continue to fall outside the current definition of obscenity. At best, he said, even under the vague indecency guidelines of the Court only portrayals of "normal, healthy sexual desires," as opposed to "shameful or morbid" ones, would be acceptable if it could be shown that more than a "few" children gained access to such dial-a-porn messages in future suits.[49]

The more narrow (limited) the Court's interpretation of what is obscene— that is, unprotected speech—the more all-encompassing and protected pornographic speech becomes. But even Justice Scalia (like Congress and the FCC) is only concerned about this expanding area of protected speech, represented by pornographic materials, in relation to its potential impact on children, not women. Obviously, many feminists would not want such a comparison between children and women made for fear of returning to a patriarchally protective approach to women's rights. This is why the antipornography ordinances have attempted to remove the debate over such materials from the purview of First Amendment and criminal prosecutions by redefining pornography as a violation of the civil rights of adult women.

As if being an orphan of history and literature was not enough, pornography has been assigned bastard status as well because lawyers have claimed since the 1960s that the term cannot be legally defined. The hegemonic hypocrisy of this civil-libertarian stance with respect to pornography is revealed by the fact that male intelligentsia in the United States has not hesitated to define illicit or illegitimate sexual behavior for themselves (and their readers) in the name of erotica. This proves once again Karl Mannheim's (and Antonio Gramsci's) axioms: "intellectuals exist to provide an interpretation of the world for that society," and political power rests less on coercion than on "the control of the intellectual life of society by purely cultural means."[50] In this case, liberal academics and legal theorists have consciously chosen both to invent the word *erotica* and to accord it privileged status, while claiming no similar responsibility for pornography.

Instead, since World War II pornography has obtained an official position within the legal system as one of the forms of speech absolutely protected under the First Amendment and an unofficial position as one of the most powerful texts of patriarchy. Additionally, by the end of the 1980s, the ACLU insisted that a legal definition of pornography would be an exercise in both futility and folly given the current conservative climate in the United States. This places the ACLU in direct opposition to those feminists who argue that the violent and misogynistic nature of modern pornography makes it a major cause of continued sex discrimination and battering of women (and children). While pornography has become a litmus test of free expression for liberals, radical feminists claim that its very existence harms women and contributes to maintaining a patriarchal status quo by equating violence with virility for men and pain with pleasure for women.[51]

Regardless of which side one favors in this legal debate, the fact remains that pornographic material dealing with sexuality has, from its invention in the nineteenth century down to the present, served the interests of the patriarchal state. Pornography functions as a vehicle for hegemonic male dominance because its pervasiveness in contemporary society makes its subordination of women appear all the more "natural" and "acceptable." Like the other patriarchal legal texts discussed in this book, pornographic texts are seldom recognized for what they are—vehicles for preserving, not protesting, the status quo. This "conservative" function of pornography was less evident in the past when the distribution of such materials, particularly the most violent ones, was much less than it is today with mass means of distribution and promotion at the disposal of the pornographic industry. Now with the law currently on its side, pornography has definitely become the handmaiden of the state, constantly reminding women of their proper subordinate roles in society. The evolution of this legalization of pornography can be traced back to the nineteenth century and corresponds almost too coincidentally with the "invention" of sexuality as a social construct.

For over a century—from the broad Queen's Bench meaning of obscenity in Regina v. Hicklin, (1868) LR 3 QB 360, to Pope v. Illinois, 107 S. Ct. 1918 (1987)—the legal definition of obscenity gradually narrowed in both English and American common law.[52] The *Hicklin* test (like the Comstock Law) had been intended to apply to other than *sexually* explicit materials because the ruling labeled as obscene anything that would corrupt the minds of youth—particularly young men.[53] Legal obscenity under *Hicklin* focused on acts or writings that violated prevailing standards of propriety. But this proved too broad and imprecise after the invention of sexuality and the resurrection of the word *pornography*. In the course of the next one hundred years, attempts to diminish the scope of similar decisions and legislation prevailed in the United States until, by the 1960s, "the range of permissible regulation [of obscene materials] could properly be described as 'minimal.' "[54]

The success in narrowing the definition of obscenity was the result in no small measure of the influence of lawyers who, relying on the private literary definitions, made sexually explicit pictures, words, and films subject to protection under the First Amendment. A few famous cases involving major literary works and films were won in the 1930s and 1940s, but the major U.S. case-law precedents (until *Pope*) occurred in the 1950s and 1970s. In Roth v. United States, 354 U.S. 476 (1957), and other subsequent decisions, the Supreme Court declared that only obscene material "utterly without redeeming social importance" fell outside the jurisdiction of the First Amendment. In terms of constitutional jurisprudence, this ultimately meant that most ideas, however hateful and controversial, were protected if they demonstrated "even the slightest redeeming social importance."[55] Anything deemed legally obscene is not, therefore, considered to be "speech" under the First Amendment.

In 1973, the justices came as close as they ever have to a comprehensive definition. Miller v. California, 413 U.S. 15 (1973), set three conditions for determining whether visual or printed material is obscene. This tripartite definition held that obscenity exists when (1) an average person using "contemporary community standards" concludes that the work in its entirety appeals to "prurient interest" in sex; (2) the work is "patently offensive," as defined by state or federal laws; and (3) when the entire work "lacks serious literary, artistic, political, or scientific value." The third point constituted the so-called LAPS test. While Supreme Court decisions between 1973 and 1987 paid lip service to "community standards," actual prosecutions of obscenity declined. In any case, as Catharine MacKinnon noted, this definition turns obscenity into a "moral idea" based on the application of good and bad literary standards, while pornography remains a "political practice."[56]

Then, in *Pope v. Illinois*, the Supreme Court further narrowed the definition of obscenity by negating entirely the idea that the value of any particular work could "vary from community to community based on the degree of local acceptance it has won." Throwing out the "average person" reference in *Miller*, the justices ruled that the "LAPS test" could only be determined by a "reasonable person," not an "ordinary person."[57] This decision appears to have eliminated community standards for determining legal obscenity, thus rendering the remaining portions of the *Miller* definition even less applicable to the undefinable— pornography. Ironically, as the depiction of sexual violence proliferated beyond all reason, a "reasonable" gender-neutral person is now sought to determine the overall value of material alleged to be obscene.

Long before the 1987 *Pope* decision, however, leading members of the Second Women's movement had divided over how to respond to the increased violence and availability of contemporary pornography. Battle lines had already been clearly drawn by the beginning of the 1980s.[58] This stalemate placed some radical feminists ostensibly on the side of Fundamentalists in advocating the banning of such material through antipornography ordinances. At the same time, many reformist and socialist feminists appeared to have allied themselves with the purveyors of pornography, arguing that such material is protected by the First Amendment and that, in addition, consenting adults have the sexual right to engage in all intimate acts short of murder.

In actuality, the debate is both more complex and significant than it sometimes appears on the surface. The two groupings are misaligned for a variety of reasons, the most important being that of the four groups, only one is attempting to "desexualize" society by banning or severely regulating the production and distribution of pornography—namely, the radical feminists. The other three groups— members of the radical right, producers and distributors of pornography, and reformist feminists—are all advocating a "resexualizing" of society through the promotion of pornography behind the banner of the First Amendment and sexual rights. They are, in a word, trying to reinforce, albeit with some minor modifications, the idea that male-dominated views about sexuality should continue to determine gender identity and sexual activity. This is particularly true of heterosexual and homosexual sadomasochists. Since resexualizing represents nothing more nor less than an extension of the nineteenth-century construct of sexuality, it cannot liberate women or men. Only desexualization can do that, as Michel Foucault pointed out almost twenty years ago.[59]

Foucault's works, especially the last two volumes of his trilogy, *The History of Sexuality,* emphasize the ascribed gender roles of women more than either those of Marx or Freud, especially because of his earlier conviction that middle-class women were the first to be "sexualized" in the nineteenth century—that is, invested with sexuality and "assigned a new destiny charged with conjugal and parental obligations," in order to be of value in the new bourgeois order of things. With this "invention of sexuality," as he called it, sex had been transformed into a vehicle of social control rather than a form of freedom of expression.[60] In fact, by the early 1970s, Foucault believed in the potential of the Second Women's movement for "desexualizing" society by demystifying the pseudoscientific discourse that clouded and controlled twentieth-century attitudes about sex, saying:

> . . . the real strength of the women's liberation movement is not that of having laid claim to the specificity of their sexuality and the rights pertaining to it, but that they have actually departed from the discourse conducted within the apparatuses of sexuality. Ultimately, it is a veritable movement of desexualization, a displacement effected in relation to the sexual centering of the problem, formulating the demand for forms of culture, discourse, language and so on which are no longer part of that rigid assignation and pin-down to their sex which they had initially in some sense been politically obliged to accept in order to make themselves heard.[61]

Yet, some feminists currently dismiss or disparage his work, while others endorse Marxian or Freudian theories that are much less relevant for demonstrating the importance of pornography as a misogynistic text of patriarchy.[62]

For all of these reasons, I can no longer accept the standard liberal defense of pornography in the name of freedom of expression nor the assertions of the Feminist Anti-Censorship Taskforce (FACT) that when women publish male examples of pornography it automatically is sexually liberating. In terms of the difference between resexualizing or desexualizing society, the exact opposite is true. FACT's pornographic publication *Caught Looking* and Susie Bright's (a.k.a. "Suzie Sexpert") *On Our Backs* are no better or worse than the male standards of individuality and sexuality that they imitate so well by stigmatizing all those who speak out against pornrotica as sexually inhibited. Most important, both publications and the porn movies produced by the "self-proclaimed feminist" pornographers further silence the suffering of women from pornrotica by not encouraging the type of honest dialogue that is necessary about the "quality of women's internal lives." *Caught Looking,* for example, with its random assortment of "genital engagements" from homosexual, heterosexual, and autoerotic perspectives, is really a pictorial throwback to the "money shots" of early pornographic films, as is Bright's defense of sadomasochistic sex as "fun" and necessary for women to achieve satisfying orgasms. The articles in *Caught Looking* interspersed among the genitalia contain false equality arguments (that is, sexual liberation of women through more pornography), ignoring, as do the graphics, the increasing association between violence and sex in the mass media that is designed to keep women in their "proper places."[63]

Statistics indicate that "legal leaders" (and *both* conservative and liberal Supreme Court justices) are far "ahead" of mass opinion and more influential than average citizens in determining public policy on this highly controversial sexual issue. Yet on almost all other social problems, the legal profession traditionally follows, rather than leads, public opinion. As of the mid-1980s, for example, 52 percent of the public in a *Newsweek* poll felt that magazines showing nudity should not be publicly displayed; 47 percent wanted magazines picturing adults having sexual relations banned; 73 percent wanted magazines depicting sexual violence censored; and over 60 percent wanted both movies and videocassettes featuring sexual violence banned. At the same time, leaders in local communities and in the legal profession generally disagreed with the censorious views held by the public respondents (many of whom were, no doubt, consumers of the material they wanted to restrict). Forty-eight percent of community leaders and 67 percent of lawyers polled thought that the majority of pornographic films (regardless of how distasteful their content) were "mostly harmless"; and only 35 percent of the community leaders and 20 percent of the lawyers questioned believed that there was any connection between violent sex crimes and pornography, compared to 53 percent of the general public.[64]

Such wide divergences between public and elite opinion account for the difficulty of recommending widely acceptable policy to deal with the dilemma posed by violent pornrotica. Privileged male views that cut across political and class lines on sexuality offer the best explanation for the fact that conservative and liberal men (and their male-oriented female supporters) seem so comfortable with one another in hiding behind an ahistorical interpretation of the First Amendment to prevent serious consideration of the relationship in our time among degradation, violence, sex, and technology. Understanding and resolving the significance of the interconnectedness of these issues for the quality of American female life for the remainder of this century will not be achieved by further legal debates among such liberals or conservatives within the legal profession. As long as both sides continue to ignore the sexist history and discriminatory function of pornography, conservatives will continue to pay lip service to regulating it and liberals will continue to claim that *more* pornrotica is the answer to the problems created *by* pornrotica. (If this were true, then sex crimes and violence against women in the United States should have decreased since the 1970s; instead, women are more fearful than ever about being victims of violent personal assaults from men. Increased sexual assaults on women finally prompted the Senate Judiciary Committee in June 1990 to begin hearings on a Violence Against Women Act, which among other things, would make gender-motivated violence a civil rights violation.[65]

Approximately one hundred years after the original invention of sexuality, according to Foucault, with all of its hypocritical and repressive elements, the most conservative and most liberal factions in U.S. society are unwittingly in a sexual alliance, despite their different intentions and goals. The radical right wants to ban pornography in order to resexualize society by returning to repressive sexuality along the lines that Margaret Atwood carries to its logical and frightening extremes in *The Handmaid's Tale*.[66] The pornography industry wants to resexualize society with violent pornrotica simply to keep the profits flowing. And FACT, along with the ACLU, wants to resexualize society in the name of the First Amendment because it is easier than rethinking liberal legalism, thus ensuring that the least emancipated areas in America will remain the millions of bedrooms across the country, regardless of sexual preference. Only a handful of radical feminists are attempting to desexualize society by exposing standard legal and cultural debates over sexuality for what they really are: sexist social-control tactics disguised as sexual liberation.

Contrary to conventional wisdom, therefore, the current debate over what I call *pornrotica* is not a question of heterosexual-versus-homosexual preferences; nor is it a question of sexual liberation versus sexual inhibition. It is a question of desexualizing (and thereby endorsing nonviolent sex) or resexualizing (with all of its violent, degrading elements) society at the end of the twentieth century. The "more-is-better" approach of FACT and the ACLU is typical of the dangerously shallow and uncritical liberal response to the increase in violence against women and children in contemporary society and stems in part from the fear of not being liberal in a conservative era.

This confusing and misunderstood set of misalliances reached a dramatic legal climax on 11 June 1984, when the city of Indianapolis adopted a statute that defined pornography as a form of sex discrimination and, hence, a violation of women's civil rights. Largely the creation of Catharine MacKinnon and Andrea Dworkin, the brief of the supporters of the Indianapolis ordinance, citing a section of *Roth v. United States*, argued that pornographic material should be removed from the purview of the First Amendment because its content does not permit the "unfettered interchange of ideas for the bringing about of political and social changes desired by the people."[67] Since the primary function of the First Amendment is to protect speech as a form of communication, the supporters of the statute maintained that pornography "is no more the communication of ideas than segregation is." Carrying this analogy further, they argued that while it is still possible in the United States to advocate "separate-but-equal" treatment as an example of protected speech, the practice of segregation is not a form of protected speech. Thus, espousing the subordination of women to men is protected, but the "practice of subordinating women through pornography is not and can be validly proscribed."[68]

Although several other cities—such as Los Angeles, Minneapolis, and Cambridge—have considered similar antipornography legislation since Indianapolis adopted a statute making pornography a violation of women's civil rights, only Bellingham, Washington, has followed suit. Although supporters of the 1988 antipornography initiative in Bellingham thought they were distinguishing their statute from the Indianapolis ordinance, in February 1989 it was declared unconstitutional by U.S. District Court Judge Carolyn Dimmick. In *Village Books v. The City of Bellingham,* she simply issued summary judgment for the plaintiffs, saying that the previous decisions in the Indianapolis suits were controlling. "It is indisputed," Judge Dimmick concluded, "that many societal harms are caused by pornography"; but, in her opinion, the Bellingham initiative did not present a constitutional way to address this important public-policy issue. No appeal was filed.[69]

While these debates have forced FACT and ACLU attorneys to admit that a variety of societal harms "may" accrue to women from pornography, they still contend that the term cannot (and should not) be redefined. This is not an insignificant achievement from the standpoint of legal argumentation. However, the discussion over antipornography ordinances has not removed the issue from the confining boundaries of liberal legalism and traditional discourses about sexuality. Until this is done, the modern dilemma that violent pornography poses for society will not be addressed in ways that go beyond, rather than simply continue to restate, the issue within standard legal paradigms that protect and, thus, encourage a wide variety of acceptable grotesque disguises.

The various decisions in *American Booksellers Association, Inc. v. Hudnut, Mayor of Indianapolis*[70] did not by any means settle the issue of pornrotica for the various participants. They simply demonstrated the epitome of liberal legalism and the limits of absolutist First Amendment doctrine. While accepting the premises of the Indianapolis ordinance—namely, that "depictions of subordination tend to perpetuate subordination"—the various judges held that no legal definition of pornography had been put forth that did not violate free speech under the Constitution; hence, the legal system was powerless to remedy the harm that it purported to understand. *Hudnut* remains a classic example of the rigidity of liberal principles when they address issues that fundamentally challenge the hegemony of male dominance. Since *Hudnut*, the Attorney General's Commission on Pornography issued in July 1986 a report that has only exacerbated the debate among scholars and feminists alike, by declaring categorically that pornography does play a leading role in causing "sexual violence, sexual aggression or unwanted sexual coercion," despite the ambiguity of social-science research and the raised political consciousness on this causal relationship. To its credit, however, the Meese Report abandoned the absolutist sociological "cathartic" model that dominated the propornography conclusions of the 1970 President's Commission on Obscenity and Pornography.[71] In fact, the Meese Report clearly documented that a difference of kind, not simply degree, has occurred in the pornographic depictions of women over the last fifteen to twenty years. This change has taken place in basically a conservative era, dating roughly from the end of the Vietnam War with its heightened and intensified sexualization of society. Although conservative groups, like the Victorians of the late nineteenth century, are in the forefront of the current antipornography campaign, the public displays of sex and sexually explicit material they oppose have exponentially increased under their political and economic, if not cultural, tutelage.

Since the Meese Report, but by no means because of it, there have been expressions of fear about and concern over the increased random violence against women and children in U.S. society. The 1989 "wilding" assault on a woman jogger in New York City's Central Park, gang and date rapes of younger and younger girls by teen-age boys, and the sexual abuse and battering of female children by adult males have been given widespread publicity in recent years. "No matter how equal the opportunities in our schools and workplace," President George Bush told American Association of University Women (AAUW) women in June 1989, "women will never have the same opportunities as men if a climate of fear leaves them justifiably concerned about walking to the campus library at night or reluctant to work late hours for fear of getting out of some parking lot safely."[72] The reasons for these violent crimes against American women vary from crack use and perverse rock lyrics reinforced by music videos to a steady diet of murder, rape, and mayhem on television and in popular movies and "slasher" videocassettes, which erotically depict the torture, rape, and murder of women. Yet the fear engendered in women by this pornographic media barrage and the pyschic damage caused by their attempts to accommodate such dangers by "consenting" and "giving" themselves in marriage or other private contractual arrangements in return for a modicum of safety are not discussed as much as why men are increasingly motivated to victimize women.[73]

Even though most experts agree that the presentations in the media linking sex and violence are a major part of the cause of the physical battering of women, none of this expert advice or the legitimate fears of women for their safety seems to get translated into any effective litigation or legislation, although there is a body of case law allowing women (and men) to sue for such fright-based injuries as emotional harm.[74] Such precedents have been long accumulating and most often are connected with pregnancy complications, as noted in chapter 8. Harm from fear of invasion, whether it be in the form of an unwanted pregnancy, rape, or other violent invasions of women's bodies, continues to increase while the fight against pornography as a violation of women's civil rights is thwarted by the courts.

Liberal legalism has been most innovative in responding to the harm men fear most—physical annihilation—to the point of using civil rights legislation in cases of murders that cannot be criminally prosecuted. When will the legal system begin to address systematically what women fear most: physical invasion in all of its myriad modern forms? How high does violence against women and their fear-factor have to rise before the courts address this issue? "For too long we have ignored the right of women to be free from the fear of attacks based on their gender," Senator Joseph Biden (Democrat of Delaware) said in opening hearings on legislation that designates sexual assaults as bias related and, therefore, a violation of female civil rights (since "97 percent of such assaults in this country are against women"). The language of his 1990 Violence Against Women Act is encouragingly similar to that of the various antipornography ordinances. Even President Bush has noted that "women will never have equal opportunities as long as they have unequal fear."[75] When will the ACLU and FACT add female fear in modern U.S. society to its list of legitimate legal grievances by redefining pornography? Obviously, not as long as they continue to protect violent pornographic representations of women with the First Amendment.

While historians and lawyers leisurely wax eloquent and disagree over the meaning and legal status of pornography, more and more social-science and literary studies express a sense of immediacy and emergency, suggesting that pornography is rapidly becoming the new opiate of the masses. Thus, the "raptures and bliss of the cosmic fuck" are replacing both religion and science as ways to attain heaven on earth in our sex-and-violence–obsessed era.[76] Other studies maintain that pornography has always been a "frontier" literature,[77] presaging or predicting future sexual relationships. Indeed, sexual practices considered perverse or bizarre in explicit representations are now largely accepted as normal behavior among consenting adults. Until women speak out about the dangers and fears they experience on a daily basis and recognize that their apparently limitless capacity to "consent to their misery," whether it be in the form of unwanted pregnancies, abusive personal relationships, or sexual harassment, has created an untenable division between their objective sexuality and subjective selves, there will be no limit to so-called consensual sexual violence in the United States; it will simply remain open season on human females.

While the "frontier" function of pornography appears to be a valid generalization about the past, it may not be for the future. It is possible that violent pornography has a demographic profile. By the end of the twentieth century, it may not be as much in demand and prevalent as the population significantly ages. The current AIDS epidemic constitutes another reason why pornography may not continue to live up to its previous reputation as a self-fulfilling sexual prophecy. Until a cure or prevention for AIDS is found, unrestricted and indiscriminate sexual relations may become voluntarily or involuntarily a thing of the past—at least temporarily. Demography and disease may ultimately be the determining factors in the battle over whether to resexualize or desexualize society on the eve of the twentieth-first century. This is another reason why Atwood's book, about a fascistic future in which impotent male leaders pervert feminist principles beyond recognition in order to control the reproductive capacities of women, should be read carefully by all concerned about the potential impact of pornrotica on U.S. society and its relationship to contemporary genetic engineering at women's expense.

In any case, until pornography receives adequate historical and legal gender analysis by liberals, from which we can draw lessons and new paradigms for the future rather than the past, I can only agree with David Holbrook, who has said that "our failure to discriminate against pornography . . . marks a deep failure in our intellectual life."[78] Even more important, as long as pornography continues not to have a history, the longer its negative importance will be denied and the variety of its acceptably sexist and violently grotesque disguises will increase. We know this to be true of rape. By denying its historical gender implications, men have long refused to "see rape as a physical and mental attack on the body and soul of another human being, but rather as a crime against property."[79] When people, events, and issues are without histories, they are taken less seriously than otherwise would be the case. Thus, until the history of pornography is written and it is redefined in legal terms as a violation of women's civil rights, those who would resexualize U.S. society can use its ahistorical and juridically privileged status to serve their own disparate interests with impunity. But most important, without a history, contemporary pornrotica will continue to silence women when it comes to thinking and speaking the truth about the meaning of their own sexual lives.

The June 1986 Supreme Court decision in Bowers v. Hardwick, 478 U.S. 186 (1986), upholding a Georgia antisodomy law also added to the volatility of the national discussion about sexual issues and privacy rights.[80] Clearly, alliances with conservatives on questions of sexuality, in general, and sexual violence, in particular, are no less dangerous than previous ones in the past have proven to be. This is all the more reason to make the redefinition of pornography a major goal of the Second Women's movement for the remainder of this century under radical, rather than mainstream, feminist leadership. Hiding behind the First Amendment does not guarantee that some form of censorship will not ultimately be devised by conservatives that will be declared constitutional to the dismay of both types of feminists. It is not without reason that I have linked the ERA and pornography in this chapter as the epitome of liberal legalism. The first, as a political failure, represents the ongoing too little, too late pursuit by women in the United States of equal rights with men; the second, as legally protected and largely male speech, symbolizes why women in this country will never be equal until they are "fear-less." Some women feared the ERA because they feared men; most women fear contemporary society because they fear men.

# CHAPTER TEN

# Beyond Liberal Legalism:
# From Equality to Equity

In the 1980s, some contemporary feminist historians and lawyers began, more than ever before, to question whether women's long-sought-after goal of obtaining equality based primarily on individual, male rights as embodied in the U.S. Constitution and the Bill of Rights should be pursued to its logical conclusion. Such women looked back on a quarter-century of dramatic improvement in their legal status and began suggesting ways to recognize the limits of, and ways to go beyond, liberal legalism as they entered a fifth period in their constitutional development—the one I hope will be viewed by legal historians of the future as a period of constitutional equity. However, during that same decade just when radical feminist historians and lawyers began to assert that sexuality was a common "crucial factor in the construction of gender relationships" and the "linchpin of gender inequality," deconstructionists began to emphasize the differences among women and among groups of women.[1] Initially, this emphasis on differences among women sounded innocuous and familiar—nothing more than the diversity within a commonly shared set of socially conditioned female characteristics. It soon became evident that for some deconstructionists, *difference* meant that *"the female subject of feminism"* consisted of "each woman's consciousness and subjective limits." Thus, according to Teresa de Lauretis, women were defined by their differences rather than any commonality derived from subordination under patriarchy over time. Differences among women, de Lauretis has asserted, will prevent feminism from ever again being represented as a "coherent ideology." In this sense, deconstruction represents an attack on radical political feminism in the United States. Yet this point of view is what Joan W. Scott has praised in reviewing de Lauretis's work as a "crucial breakthrough for feminist theorizing" because it articulated "the connection many of us have been seeking between individual subjectivity and collective consciousness."[2]

This interpretative (and possibly political) divergence among feminist historians has always been present but not always analyzed. Initially, I labeled these tendencies the *minimizing* and the *maximizing* schools of interpretation, not realizing that the dispute over how to use gender analysis would manifest itself even more clearly with the influence of poststructuralism on U.S. women's history in the late 1980s.[3] Both major interpretative schools initially used the category of gender to analyze individual and group identities. *Minimizers* employed a more traditional analysis of class and race based on material conditions in order to determine experiential identity, while *maximizers* analyze the ways in which multiple discourses socially construct identity and experience. On these shifting sands of individual female selfhood and collective consciousness the most productive narrative and theoretical work took place among historians until the advent of poststructural gender analysis. Then material experiences became abstract representations drawn from textual analysis; personal identities or agency became subjects constructed by discourses; and flesh-and-blood women became social constructs—with no "natural" or physiological context except as a set of symbolic meanings connoting sexual difference. Feminist politics, according to the poststructuralists, no longer could be used to alleviate conditions of oppression because "identity is not an objectively determined sense of self defined by needs" any more than "politics is . . . the collective coming to consciousness of similarly situated individual subjects."[4]

If experience could not be based on relatively unchanging socioeconomic categories or on the diversity and variability of common gender identities, then there could be no objective, visionary history from which contemporary feminist activists could draw sustenance and advice for opposing and critiquing the obvious oppression of women in the United States or other countries. Thus, instead of remaining simply another useful methodological innovation for studying women's history and making it more relevant to radical political feminism, poststructuralism became a potentially politically paralyzing and intellectually irrelevant exercise for endlessly analyzing myriad representations of cultural forms and discourses. Women's history became in the 1980s more and more removed from the political and legal arena in which the battle for the rights of women and minorities was being waged. Contrary to the claim of poststructural historians that women's history has lost its identity or their predictions that it is about to "dissolve," it is their deliberate depoliticization of power through representations of it as totally diffuse and decentered that has created their own private identity crisis and sense of lack of agency that they now attribute to the profession as a whole. If women's history is "dissolving," it is only doing so in a sea of relativity created on the head of a semiotic pin by deconstructionists, not because the field itself has nothing to offer contemporary feminism.[5]

Therefore, there is still another danger represented by the methodological innovation that took place within the field of women's history in the 1980s. In a word, those feminist historians who are now most eager to maximize differences among women are also usually those who earlier minimized differences between women and men. First, as I have noted, deconstructionist theories tend to minimize men's dominance of women and to maximize differences among women. Some poststructural historians, for example, "acknowledge, celebrate and support the instigation of all differences that divide and constitute both men and women" to the point that they no longer identify their work as being *about women.*" Yet difference and dominance go hand in hand in the sense that both continue to be defined in America and other societies by male criteria. Simply because gender differences can be variously interpreted by researchers so that they are found to be "historically and culturally specific" and that they are social rather than biological does not mean that they are also benign, neutral, or noncategorical.[6] To the contrary, their very historical and cultural diversity often mask their oppressive commonality—namely, that gender is, in fact, about the power of men over women. Simone de Beauvoir captured the historical significance of female oppression when she proclaimed in 1949: "Throughout history [women] have always been subordinated to men, and hence their dependency is not the result of a historical event or a social change—it was not something that occurred."[7]

## Gender Analysis: Breakthrough or Breakdown?

The growing acceptance of the word *gender* and its use as an analytical category among historians of women may, unfortunately, sanction the study of masculinity before the study of femininity—let alone the history of women—is anywhere near complete. Another historiographical difficulty posed by gender analysis is that it delineates an impersonal structure of society rather than personal experience. This very abstractness has the advantage of allowing researchers to see socioeconomic patterns more clearly. Gender analysis is useful, for example, in studying changes in female legal status because such changes sometimes anticipate, but usually follow, significant cultural, political, or economic trends. Moreover, this kind of analysis reminds us that gender is a social, rather than an essential, category. Despite the extremes to which it can be carried interpretively and politically, gender analysis will remain a significant, albeit controversial, methodological tool in the field of history for the remainder of this century as historians explore the idea that just as sexuality informs gendered power identities, so gendered power relations permeate all socioeconomic and racial classes.

However, some feminist historians who attack both male and female essentialism appear on the verge of advocating a particularized version of reality, in which "the voice of gender risks being lost entirely." This implication is present in Joan W. Scott's assertion that "once you grant that men and women in particular times and in particular places differ, you undercut the possibility of any kind of universal theory of gender identity."[8] Clare Dalton has suggested three reasons that draw some feminists "away from specific questions about gender oppression and the mechanisms through which it operates." They are anger, fear, and denial over being stereotyped by the same socially constructed gender differences that such feminists purport to study. Hence, these feminists have stressed the factors that divide women in order to avoid stigmatizing themselves and other women as "only" the cultural creations of a male world. Dalton suggests that these are really three deconstructionist responses to Carol Gilligan's thesis about a female moral system based on the "ethic of care."[9]

The first response, *anger,* leads some feminists "to reject (the existence or the value of) attributes, like caring, or sensitivity to others" that women develop because our culture insists they do. Thus, some feminists have opposed Gilligan's work by "underscor[ing] the differences among and between women without ever returning to ask whether those differences entirely undercut" her idea about the ethics of caring "or only complicate and modify it." The second response, *fear,* makes some feminists reluctant to acknowledge that women possess the attributes of caring, lest men demand that they exercise these attributes. The third response, *denial,* allows us "to hide from ourselves the extent to which we do, in fact, submit to male demands for care and attention."[10] All three responses use deconstructionist techniques in their repudiation of a female ethic of care to deny the objective experiences of women as well as the existence of attributes that commonly delineate women as a gendered class.

Since deconstruction can also lead to an antiessentialist particularism and political paralysis, it should be viewed primarily as a methodological tool for historical research—nothing more and nothing less. Even with this caveat, some women of color are justifiably concerned that a "race for theory" now exists among academic humanists in the United States, based largely on French poststructural hypotheses that radical feminists consider dangerous.[11] Their concern about deconstruction is twofold: first, they suspect that deconstruction may become the hegemonic practice in elite academic circles, thereby displacing the collective understanding of racism that women of color have struggled to obtain by using African or rationalist modes of analysis; and second, they suspect that feminists who use deconstructionist techniques may be unintentionally racist because deconstruction prompts them to suggest that race, like gender, is a discursively constructed binarism. Gerda Lerner has suggested a much more constructive approach in her reconceptualization of a "holistic" history—one that would understand "interrelated aspects of the system of patriarchal dominance" rather than continuing "to regard class, race and gender dominance as separate, though intersecting and overlapping systems."[12]

Nonetheless, it is becoming increasingly common among poststructural and socialist feminists to deny both categories of "woman" and "women" because they represent a false or fictive "universalization of sex class that does not focus on specificity and only recognizes the homogeneity of women." This denial is too simplistic. While it is desirable to avoid imposing a "false sense of commonality" on different groups of women in specific time periods, it is equally desirable to recognize that women are perceived in all societies as "an always-already constituted group" because of the specific prevailing "discourse of engendered sex 'difference,' " which presumes that sex and gender are the same thing. Rather than deny any "specific unity" among women, therefore, we should try to identify it historically along with a description of their differences. In other words, as Zillah Eisenstein has noted, "the tension between diversity and unity" must become the focus.[13] Linda Gordon has described this as tension between writing history with the "mythic power" to inspire moral and political action and writing accurate history, which, even if it cannot contain the absolute truth in the way "grand" partiarchal history purported to, will at least point out the "objective lies" from the past about women's public and private lives. "There may be no objective canon of historiography," according to Gordon, "but there are degrees of accuracy; there are better and worse pieces of history. The challenge is precisely to maintain this tension between accuracy and [the] mythic power [of history]." To the degree that historians of women exclusively emphasize one or the other, their writings will disserve the cause of political and legal reform on behalf of women in the United States and abroad.[14]

So what are we to make of Joan W. Scott's idealist poststructural assertion that "once you grant that men and women in particular times and in particular places differ, you undercut the possibility of any kind of universal theory of gender identity" or the dismissal by some socialist feminists of the early radicalness of the early middle-class leadership of both the First and Second Women's movements, on the grounds that it did not reflect the diversity among even women of their own class, let alone any "systematic critique of American class relations"?[15] Both are examples, to a large degree, of an anachronistic imposition of contemporary ideas about diversity and differences and lack of identity and agency on the past due to (1) the current fragmentation within the Second Women's movement; (2) disturbing figures indicating ever-widening discrepancies between rich and poor in the United States;[16] and (3) and the trendiness of applying the poststructural relativism of the 1980s to other time periods.

In reality, women and men do not enter into past and present socioeconomic and political systems as decentered, genderless individuals. They enter *first* as gendered groups and are perceived and treated accordingly. To argue otherwise is simply to give a poststructural glaze to Lockean and Hobbesian theories about diverse individuals existing with benevolence or malevolence toward one another before the creation of the state. To argue that class divisions obliterate gender identification not only is a throwback to sexist Marxism but also flies in the face of all successful (and unsuccessful) forms of woman-identified-woman movements of the past—long before the particular social construction of gender from the nineteenth century from which we are still trying to free ourselves.[17]

Analyses denying the historicity of female identity, whether based on post-structural or socialist theories, have not resulted in accurate descriptions of the past or present contributions of radical and collective—as opposed to liberal and individualistic—feminism in the United States since the nineteenth century; nor are they adequately explaining the debilitating theoretical fragmentation that exists within the Second Women's movement of the 1990s, let alone contributing to its resolution. Most important for this book, the extreme emphasis placed by poststructuralist and socialist historians on diversity does not contribute to our understanding of the masculinist nature of case law, to which all women are still subjected regardless of their socioeconomic status.[18] Instead, such historians have chosen to impose the fragmentation of the present on the past by using methodologies based on sophisticated materialistic and deconstructionist techniques, insisting that class interests and/or diversity always prevailed over any common patriarchal oppression women experienced. Curiously, this contemporary insistence on finding the same diversity in the past that is currently evident in the present is usually confined to groups of white women, with women of color being portrayed as much more monolithically united by racial and class discrimination than other groups of women. By implication, at least, such an analysis leaves socialist feminists (as well as poststructuralists) uncomfortably vulnerable to the same charge of racism they so readily use against white, bourgeois feminist leaders of the past and present.[19]

In summary, gender is central to relationships of power. But, as Joan W. Scott's theoretical articles reveal, it is much easier to assert that "gender is a primary way of signifying relationships of power" than it is to set up a research design that allows us to observe how gendered power is expressed in actual experiences of men and women.[20] The recommendation that we deconstruct the binary opposition on which most gender analyses rest will, in effect, stress the differences among women at the expense of their commonalities. It also has the apolitical and particularistic implications of poststructuralism in appearing (1) to undermine the political potential of feminism for restructuring U.S. society and (2) to preclude generic historical definitions of feminism that can be compared historically and cross-culturally. While the Second Women's movement played a major role in stimulating feminist historical writing, historians of women now appear on the verge of ignoring their original political and moral origins by hopelessly complicating or denying the gender categories and definitions that make the most historical and common sense.

The Second Women's movement in the United States is now faced with the most convoluted legal debates in its history. This debate is over whether to continue to pursue equal treatment or whether to insist on being treated as an equal based on female, or what are considered special, standards because male standards still constitute what most of us think as normal equality. In a word, mainstream feminist attorneys and activists are bitterly divided over equal rights versus special rights. By the beginning of the 1990s, this debate had prevented the Second Women's movement from moving beyond liberal legalism to more radical considerations about equitable constitutional treatment. Unless the current dispute is resolved, the Second Women's movement may end up as hopelessly fragmented for the remainder of this century as the First Women's movement did beginning in the 1920s—over what appears to be the same issue of whether to improve the legal status of women collectively, as women, or individually, as imitations of men. In reality, however, a much more sophisticated and hopeful theoretical discussion has surfaced than did fifty years ago. At least this appears to be the case among radical lawyers and legal scholars, if not historians.

*→ is this even possible w/ US state structures?*

## Assimilation versus Pluralism

To understand the meaning of equal (meaning individual) rights versus special (meaning group or collective rights) since World War II, it is necessary to ask how discriminated groups have gone about obtaining some equality for themselves in modern America. In other words, How do they begin to work their way up the four steps or stages of equality, discussed in chapter 1, toward equity? First, they must determine who does have equality in society and then try to obtain at least part of the equality of that privileged group. After all, white males have not shown much inclination in "reverse-discrimination" cases to date to assume the status of racial minorities or women in U.S. society.[21] In general, it is up to the group(s) discriminated against to try to emulate or become like the privileged group—not vice versa. Thus, both the early civil rights movement in the United States as well as the First and now the Second Women's movements naturally focused their attention on obtaining equal individual rights with white men. Following the example set by African-Americans, political feminists (both mainstream and socialist) initially adopted what is called the *assimilationist* approach. This means that they advocated (as did early African-American civil rights advocates) that the law should treat *only* individual women and men (and blacks and whites) as though they were interchangeable.[22] This belief initially fostered what is known as the melting-pot theory about American society—namely, the traditional liberal notion of homogeneity based on individual rights, not heterogeneity based on equity, as the ultimate good life in the United States.

Assimilationism is the equivalent of saying that biological and racial characteristics should be ignored or minimized because they are not important for job performance or the general distribution of rights or responsibilities—no more important, for example, than eye color might be. The assimilationist ideal, according to Sylvia Law, posits that "characteristics—race, sex, eye color—do not describe differences that should ever be allowed to matter in any significant way."[23] The assimilationist, or equal-individual rightest, approach for improving women's legal status has been a popular one in the United States among politicians for some time because it does not threaten the status quo, and among constitutional lawyers since World War II "because it builds up [obvious] analogies [or comparisons] between race- and sex-based discrimination." The most commonly cited analogies are that "sex, like race, is an immutable and highly visible characteristic";[24] women and African-Americans suffer from obvious economic and political inferiority and powerlessness; and, as a plurality of the Supreme Court said in 1973, sex, like race, "frequently bears no relation to ability to perform or contribute to society."[25]

While there is no rational scientific or moral justification for believing "that white and black people are inherently different in any way that should ever be allowed to matter under the law. . . . Men and women, by contrast are different in significant sex-specific physical ways . . . [primarily those] relating to reproductive capacity." One of the different characteristics between the sexes that cannot be ignored under the law relates to the fact that in the childbearing process there are two functions only women can perform: *in utero* pregnancies and breastfeeding.[26] Until technology offers *acceptable* substitutes for these unique physical functions of the female half of the population, most women and no men will continue to possess the capacity physically to reproduce the species. I stress the word *acceptable* because an increasing number of contemporary radical feminists maintain that most biomedical reproductive technologies, especially those emphasizing sex predetermination but also including *in vitro* fertilization, surrogate motherhood, embryo transfer, forced Caesarean births, and other mandatory medical treatment of pregnant women, are turning the female body into the "biological laboratory of the future"—often under the benign guise of aiding infertile women to reproduce or of providing married and single women and men with a baby purchased from some "happy breeder." Just as women have made some gains over controlling their lives by controlling their reproductive functions, medical techniques are manipulating and experimenting with their bodies more than ever, carrying on the nineteenth-century tradition of "medicalization of female existence." Ultimately, this may not only result in many more male babies but also the removal of reproductive control (and possibly of reproduction itself) from women without any compensating increase in their other socioeconomic or legal status.[27]

At the moment, however, reproductive capacity is *not* a false sex-based question of difference. It is one of the few physical differences between women and men that is irreducible under the laws of nature and current state of science. And so the assimilationist approach to equal rights, which is based on comparing what are called "similarly situated individuals," falls apart every time legitimate reproductive sex-based differences arise—that is, when there are no males with whom females can be compared, for example, when the latter are pregnant or lactating. Assimilationism also fundamentally falls apart because it often assumes that discrimination against racial minorities and women makes them completely analogous groups or classes. Not until 1987 did a majority of Supreme Court justices categorically maintain that cases involving discrimination against white women (and, sometimes, white men) were as important as those involving discrimination cases involving racial minorities.[28] In particular, white women cannot fairly be compared to African-Americans when it comes to the question of which group has suffered most from the stigmata of discrimination. Conversely, because the stigmata have been and are less for white women, sex discrimination is still "more firmly embedded in American law than race discrimination."[29]

While enforcement of civil rights for racial minorities has somewhat stagnated in the 1980s, racial slurs are no longer acceptable in American public life (as the 1987 firings of a sports commentator and a baseball executive demonstrated, even if neither incident was handled in ways designed to educate the public about remaining pockets of racial discrimination in professional sports).[30] Similar gender slurs against women are still quite commonplace on television, *especially* in sports and talk-show broadcasts. Moreover, there are fewer statements applying specifically to women, like the following 1987 one issued by Princeton president Harold T. Shapiro when he was president of the University of Michigan: "Discrimination, harassment, abusive language, threats of personal violence, or similar manifestations of bigotry or racism are unacceptable and will be dealt with as serious violations of University policy." If the word *sexism* had been substituted for *racism* in this statement, I am quite sure many reading it would have thought it excessive or irrelevant. In a word, discrimination against women, especially in the subtle areas of sexual harassment, abusive language, and threats of violence, is still not taken completely seriously by the public at large or by the courts. The unanimous 1986 Supreme Court decision in Meritor Savings Bank v. Vinson, 477 U.S. 57 (1986), on sexual harassment was encouraging, but the treatment of the female employee in this case was so blatant that it will be difficult to apply to "normal," on-the-job examples of gender-biased harassment of female employees in the workplace. Moreover, the Court ruled in this decision that in sexual-harassment cases, unlike rape cases, evidence showing possible seductive or provocative behavior is permissible.

In recent years, laws and court decisions disadvantaging women have diminished; but cultural perceptions about women, especially with respect to "harms" accruing to them because of their sexuality, still do not strike most men as being real, let alone detrimental or offensive. Thus, another defect in the comparison analysis of the assimilationist approach is that it is inherently "gendered" from a male legal and social perspective. Therefore, the assimilationist approach is deficient not simply because there are limitations to the number of legitimate comparisons that can be made in job-related cases but also because in those cases involving rape, military combat, pregnancy, abortion, sexual harassment, and pornography no real serious comparison can be made. Yet, these cases will all remain major legal issues in the U.S. for at least the rest of this century.

Finally, assimilation *means* assimilation—that is, "equality in sameness," which is based on the assumption that the current reality of different cultural characteristics among ethnic and racial groups and "socially developed concepts of gender defin[ing] different expectations and value different qualities in males and females can somehow be (or already are) eliminated."[31] Would that it were true. Assimilation more often than not means acceptance of white, male norms, at the expense of specific cultural, behavioral, and value attributes associated with nonwhite male groups. All groups who have suffered from discrimination in the United States have had to face this fact sooner or later. How do individuals obtain equality without losing their group identity, and in the long run do they want to? Most immigrant groups who came to the United States in the nineteenth and early twentieth centuries since World War II opted for assimilation at the expense of their ethnicity. Native Americans, African-Americans, Hispanics, and now some women have questioned whether the price of assimilation is worth the loss of legitimate racial or sexual differences.

Even though there are only a few irreducible physical differences between many minorities and most whites, based on skin color and physiognomy, and between women's and men's reproductive systems, these differences continue to manifest themselves in distinct socialization and disparate treatment of minorities and women in U.S. society despite claims to the contrary. Activist members of these groups also logically argue that they have collective characteristics worth preserving from assimilation. Granted, most of these groups did not question the assimilationist game until they had been quite successful at it. This is particularly true of certain white, middle-class women reformers, for whom assimilation has always been more seductive because of their determination to obtain equal rights with men and because they do not usually view themselves as an oppressed class. Consequently, political or assimilationist feminists represented largely by NOW, the National Women's Political Caucus, and the ACLU have successfully advocated this "equality-in-sameness" approach since the early 1970s.

Pluralist feminists, however, have less successfully advocated another model —based on what is commonly (and somewhat misleadingly) called special rights based on the unique physical and/or behavioral characteristics of women. Since the defeat of the ERA in 1982, this group of feminists has adopted a pluralistic approach to politics and women's legal status that stresses differences. Instead of demanding exact or traditional equality with men, they want to prevent discrimination through procedures that take into consideration certain basic differences between women and men. By the mid-1980s, the pluralist feminists had acquired other names as well. Questioning the assimilationist model for obtaining equality, they are often referred to as special righters because of their "respect for difference" and their belief in "equality in difference." This pluralistic model has also been called the participatory perspective or the positive-action approach. In its most extreme form, it is known as radical pluralism.

The fact that feminists in favor of a pluralistic approach have been (and are) being called by more than one name is an indication that their views have not been as understood or accepted by women at large as the assimilationist approach. In large measure this is because pluralist feminism is associated with advocating special rather than equal treatment for disadvantaged people in U.S. society. The notion of special rights has a negative connotation not only for most white males but also for many minorities and women because, in their respective pursuits of equal rights, everytime they have been granted special treatment it usually has meant inferior status. For example, separate-but-equal schools for African-Americans meant inferior schools as a result of *Plessey v. Ferguson,* until the 1950s with the decision in *Brown v. Board of Education.* Protective legislation for women, beginning with the case *Muller v. Oregon* in 1908, meant that women were ultimately relegated to sex-segregated inferior jobs. Special treatment has also meant that women were kept out of a number of positions, ranging from bartending to jury duty or those requiring certain weight, height, or other physical requirements on the grounds that their special nature as women and bearers of the race did not permit or qualify them for all the benefits of citizenship of equality in the workplace.

Historically speaking, special rights have a bad reputation among African-Americans and women—and with good reason. In other words, arbitrarily implemented pluralism, meaning the arbitrary application of special rights to disadvantaged groups, has led to unintended injustices—just as the single-minded pursuit of equal individual rights has. Nonetheless, there are feminists in the United

States, particularly since the defeat of the ERA (which publicly embodies traditional equal rights), who are arguing that "the life experiences of men and women in relation to biology, psychology, and moral development" are, after all, different and that difference should be recognized without relegating women to uniquely inferior positions. Hence, the phrase "equality in difference" has been used to describe this juridical and cultural approach. In fact, pluralists argue that there is no other way to change American society than to take this group point of view, while the assimilationists strongly imply that giving women (and minorities) the individual right to act like white males contributes to the creation of an androgynous society. Pluralists insist that the ERA would have simply given more women the right to act like men, without changing the status quo. This part of the pluralist approach is also advocated by radical feminists who believe strongly in the existence of attitudinal differences based on female and male cultural values. However socially conditioned these cultural differences may be, radical feminists want them brought to bear when evaluating laws affecting women and men. Along with pluralist attorneys, they oppose any further use of such strained analogies made between the sexes as the one that compared hernias to pregnancies.[32]

Instead, pluralists want the frank admission of differences between women and men—not only the basic biological ones mentioned earlier but cultural ones as well, such as conceptions about ethics and interpersonal relationships. They urge juridical recognition of both socially conditioned and physiological differences. Under such a system of justice, laws that do not empower and respect women would automatically be considered suspect or unconstitutional using female-based standards. Feminists advocating a pluralist rather than assimilationist view of equality say that is time to admit that "[most] women and *not* [most] men are the victims of sex discrimination, just as [most] African-Americans and *not* [most] whites are the victims of race discrimination." Since women and African-Americans have been treated differently by society, their argument continues: "If people have been treated differently in society, they will [naturally] appear in dissimilar positions when they are compared [to white males]. Therefore, they cannot be similarly situated for purposes of equal protection review."[33]

This point of view strikes at the very heart of liberal legalism and is why some assimilationist feminists fear that it would result in abandoning or undermining entirely the comparative, or equality-based-on-"sameness," approach. They argue that when contrasted with equality based on differences between the sexes, which are socially constructed and, hence, ultimately ephemeral, they see little wrong with continuing to support the comparison model. Assimilationists argue that such a model can be used to promote the "normalization" of pregnancy if it is combined with another legal theory that has arisen in some affirmative-action cases, known as the disparate-impact or disparate-effects doctrine. This has been applied in some cases involving black voters and workers, and it "goes beyond assessment of discrimination against individuals to identify the group effects of particular rules" or regulations that appear neutral but that, in actuality, discriminate (for example, height, weight, or certain culturally biased exams).[34] Pluralists respond that this is not enough and that disparate impact has been manipulated too much by judges to be a reliable legal tool in the future. In fact, the 1989 Supreme Court decision in *Wards Cove v. Atonio,* which undermined the disparate-impact rules established by *Griggs v. Duke Power Company* in 1971, seemed to prove the pluralists correct.[35] Radical feminists go beyond both arguments by insisting that most issues involving sexuality, such as pornography, are not only *noncomparable* and, therefore, defy any more assimilation but also cannot be resolved by making a virtue out of difference, as the moderate pluralists tend to do.

The moderate pluralists who advocate "equality in difference" also maintain that the achievement of equal justice between women and men ultimately requires not ignoring their differences but understanding them. They are critical of Supreme Court decisions that "have looked at how women have been treated in relation to how men have been treated rather than looking at the treatment of women generally." This approach has led to decisions where actions that discriminated against both sexes have been said not to violate the equal-protection clause because both groups are "similarly situated." In other decisions, when there is no example of males being discriminated against, the Court has ruled that there is no discrimination against women because no adequate comparison with men can be made. They also note that the Constitution *does not mandate the comparison approach*—it is just a legal convention or interpretation. Moreover, comparative analogies allow the courts to "maintain an ambivalent attitude toward ending sex discrimination that reflects the ambivalence in society and in our Constitution."[36] In the final analysis, the pluralist approach is more progressive than the assimilationist one, in that it clearly and unequivocally advocates changes in the status quo. Such change cannot take place through more assimilation.

This is the most serious political, philosophical, legal, and feminist debate. By the beginning of the 1990s, the assimilationists remain by far the most numerous and vocal under the auspices of NOW and the ACLU. Yet the pluralists are gaining ground (or at least publicity) for a very ironic reason. The fundamentalist New Right has attempted to coopt or ride on the coattails of some radical pluralists on certain cultural issues involving the family or "protection" of women, especially on the issue of pornography in the various ways discussed in chapter 9. These conservative groups have appeared to join the ranks of the pluralists by adopting their rhetoric without understanding, and hence ignoring, their critical analysis of traditional patriarchal power. Obviously, this is a marriage of convenience and not love because the groups agree on practically nothing else.

During the same time that this strange coalition emerged, so has another one. Socialist and poststructuralist feminists also seem to have made an inadvertent alliance by maintaining that the solution to the phallocratic duality (since both sameness and difference are argued using the male as the norm) is to posit radical pluralism or multiple differences as the basis of equality. Joan Scott has denied that her historical use of poststructuralism is "a simple substitution of multiple for binary differences [because] it is not a happy pluralism." Yet both Scott and feminist socialist Zillah Eisenstein advocate "an equality that rests on difference" or "how difference constitutes the meaning of equality."[37] I have difficulty distinguishing either of these two positions from each other and from the "radical individualism" of classical liberalism.

Is there no way out of the virtual stalemate that currently exists in the United States among these groups of feminists, attorneys, and historians? Or is the Second Women's movement doomed to the same internecine split that occurred in the 1920s in the First Women's movement? At the moment, the situation does not look good. There are a few feminist attorneys, for example, trying to find a middle ground between what were (and are) the old equal righters and the special righters. Like Mary Beard and her small circle of friends before them, these legal specialists are too few in number and too scattered across the country. Moreover, they have not yet given themselves a recognizable name. For the time being I am calling them middle of the roaders. Like the Mugwumps of the mid-nineteenth century, the middle of the roaders argue that both assimilationism and pluralism are too extreme. The first because when asked if "men and women are essentially similar," they come up with the liberal knee-jerk answer "yes," while the pluralists come up with the equally radical knee-jerk response of "no."

Two attorneys, Sylvia Law and Stephanie Wildman, have posited the idea that it is not possible to give a "simple yes or no answer to the question whether men and women are essentially similar or different." Instead, they argue "that there are biological differences between men and women in relation to reproduction. [But] these differences have been used to justify sex-based legal and cultural limitations on human potential that do not reflect any real difference between men and women and that enforce the inferiority of women and the dominance of men." (Note that Law and Wildman seem to be saying that culturally conditioned differences are not really differences, only biological ones are. However, they imply that the latter have been used more by the courts to create differences between women and men that do not actually exist.) They further insist that the comparison approach can be carried no further on the major issues that remain to be resolved in women's pursuit—not of simplistic notions about obtaining absolute equality with men but of the more complicated concept of obtaining equity for themselves and others. At the same time, they note that it is dangerous to use nonbiologically based differences—that is, conditioned female virtues or values —as a standard for rewarding women or granting them collective equality.[38] Since men do not generally want what women represent—biologically or culturally—this Mugwump position represents only the most moderate attempt at resolving this legal stalemate. As noted in chapter 7, through some "reverse-discrimination" suits, men have occasionally attempted to obtain the same rights as women under laws favoring the latter, but it has been the contention of this work that the liberal legal system operates in such a way as to give women what men don't want or no longer value. Therefore, this "half-the-loaf" approach by the Mugwumps becomes part of the problem rather than the solution.

## Toward a Feminist Jurisprudence and History

Although radical feminists tended to dominate both theoretical and organizational concepts of the Second Women's movement in its early years, from roughly 1967 to 1972, they were overshadowed by assimilationist feminists during the 1970s and could not often be distinguished from the pluralist feminists in the 1980s and at the beginning of the 1990s. Only recently have they once again emerged as a major voice of U.S. feminism. One of these radical feminist attorneys has urged a legal standard "that would ask simply whether laws challenged as sex-discriminatory empower women and enable them to participate as full members of the society."[39]

Thus, the revolution in the legal status of women in the United States remains not only unfinished and bourgeois but also one that is stalemated at the moment —with assimilationists and pluralists talking past one another, for the most part, and the Mugwumps talking only to one another. Although a number of Critical Legal Studies and radical feminist lawyers have talked about breaking this current political and legal stalemate by constructing a model for feminist jurisprudence, only a few of them have proceeded very far theoretically. The formulation I find most plausible has been offered by Robin West. However, Catharine MacKinnon and Rhonda Copelon have also contributed to my thinking on this topic. MacKinnon, for example, has for a number of years been the leading spokesperson for the brand of radical legal feminism that most separates itself from liberal and Marxist legalism. She insists that in the "zero-sum" game that the adversarial system of justice in the United States represents, women always lose because they are the ultimate victims of male legitimization of power and sexuality because the law functions to rationalize only the liberal or Marxist versions of reality as constructed by men. Somehow, and MacKinnon never quite makes this clear, women must begin to come together and assert their critical consciousness by analyzing their own privatization and substituting experience in the face of the ahistorical and false reality that characterizes the current legal system. To engage in the "practice of politics of all women in the face of its theoretical impossibility" seems to pose an almost hopeless agenda. Yet MacKinnon insists that words like *hope* and *despair* are outside of her analysis because she seems to think that reorientation of theory alone will begin to ameliorate the powerlessness of women in contemporary society. And, indeed, her 1979 theoretical work on the sexual harassment of women has had practical, legal results in the courts.[40]

Rhonda Copelon, on the other hand, deals more optimistically and specifically with constitutional ideas about equality and suggests specific legal strategies for exposing historical and legal fictions that have blamed the victims of patriarchal political economies, rather than demystifying and transforming those systems through what she calls "constitutionalization." Much of her argument for the liberation of women is for them to refuse any longer to subscribe to the separation between the public and private spheres of human existence in order to begin to bring about this new constitutionalism. She argues, for example, that the much-touted "right of privacy" as currently interpreted by the courts, especially in the struggle for abortion rights, does not represent women's best interests. Hence, women's (and men's) personal lives must be authenticated differently by the legal system and public policy in order for the state to take responsibility for the disadvantaged groups or individuals in society, rather than continuing to blame them for their lack of self-sufficiency. Both MacKinnon and Copelon, like other radical feminist legal theorists, are concerned with providing some kind of meaningful legal and socioeconomic autonomy for women that their past and present socioeconomic conditioning does not instill in them. Thus they argue that male legal doctrines about autonomy and privacy, as those in abortion case law, are not as positive or self-empowering for women as a feminist jurisprudence or constitutionalism would have made them.[41]

The search for collective female empowerment is central both to feminist jurisprudence and to feminist history, and each requires a moral as well as a political vision. The greatest weakness of both MacKinnon's and Copelon's approaches to it is that neither proceeds very far, if at all, for suggesting solutions for women's past and present inequality *outside* of the law. They seem to be saying that since the law is the problem, the law must also be the solution. Robin West's analytical approach to a feminist jurisprudence contains some of the elements of both MacKinnon's and Copelon's writings, but her search for female autonomy and authenticity sometimes takes her outside the letter and the institution of the law. Likewise, poststructural relativism is threatening to either discredit or destroy the type of feminist history devoted to analyzing and combating the oppression of women.

After analyzing what it means to be a *human being* from the point of view of four intellectual groupings—liberal legalism, critical legal theory, cultural feminism, and radical feminism—West ultimately concludes that "the subjectivity of human existence told by feminist theory and legal theory contrast at every point. There is no overlap."[42] She arrives at this conclusion by using four-celled typologies to differentiate legal theory and feminist theory. She describes the liberal and critical legal theorists' ideas about separateness and contrasts them with the cultural and radical feminists' ideas about difference. Then she categorizes these respective theories in terms of what she considers to be their most relevant overt and covert meanings: VALUE (or longing) and HARM (or dread). After that she creates an eight-celled typology by combining what she finds common or underlying in the "official stories" and "unofficial stories" about value and harm on the part of her original four subject groupings. She does this, however, by collapsing liberal legalism and critical legalism into one category and doing the same thing with cultural and radical feminism. By cross-tabulating these unofficial and official stories, she is then able to show contradictions in both legal and feminist theory at the unofficial, or "subterranean," level of existence but also shows how more alike critical legalism and radical feminism are to each other at the official, or "conscious," level of existence. Conversely, she demonstrates in what areas liberalism and cultural feminism also are alike and yet different. Therefore, the following charts allow West to indicate where she believes all four groupings fail to provide a sound basis for a feminist jurisprudence and to offer her own.

West begins to construct a feminist jurisprudence by noting that the "official" and "unofficial" responses of individual women and men, as described by these four groups, contrast in terms of substance if not structure. All deny the "subterranean desires that permeate their lives" *out of fear* that if they are expressed, they "will be met by either violence or rejection by the dominant culture." Thus, according to West, "men deny their need for attachment and women deny their need for individuation." Although both Critical Legal Studies and radical feminists appear to have similar descriptions of subjectivity, in fact they do not. Critical Legal Studies theorists depict individuals wanting connection and fearing alienation, while radical feminists claim that women want intimacy and fear separation. All they share is their "outsider's status," from the point of view of mainstream liberals (both legal and cultural) whose rhetoric reflects the status quo.[43]

Borrowing from Roberto Unger and Duncan Kennedy (but primarily the latter), West goes on to assert that the human being who, according to liberal legalism, "values autonomy and fears annihilation" "precludes the women described by feminism [and necessary] for the development of feminist jurispru-

|  | Cultural feminism | Radical feminism |
|---|---|---|
| Value, (or Longing): | Intimacy | Individuation; Integrity |
| Harm, (or Dread): | Separation | Invasion; Intrusion |

|  | The Official Story (Liberal legalism and cultural feminism) | | The Unofficial Story (Critical legalism and radical feminism) | |
|---|---|---|---|---|
|  | Value | Harm | Longing | Dread |
| Legal Theory (human beings) | Autonomy | Annihilation; Frustration | Attachment; Connection | Alienation |
| Feminist Theory (women) | Intimacy | Separation | Individuation | Invasion; Intrusion |

Source: Robin West, "Jurisprudence and Gender," University of Chicago Law Review 55, no. 1 (Winter 1980), p. 37.

dence." West notes that the "fundamental contradiction" that explains these diametrically opposed interpretations is an *experiential,* not a logical, one. To create a feminist jurisprudence capable of going beyond the liberal legalism of those advocating special rights versus equal rights, radical feminists must begin systematically to expose this experiential contradiction—namely, the "women's (and men's) existential and material circumstance . . . is itself one of contradiction."[44] According to West:

The potentiality for physical connection with others that uniquely characterizes women's lives has within it seeds of *both* intimacy and invasion, and therefore women rightly value the former while we dread and fear the latter, just as the necessity of physical separation, for men, carries within it the seeds of *both* intimacy and alienation, and men rightly value the former and dread the latter. If this is right, then *all four* accounts of human experience —liberal legalism, critical legalism, cultural feminism and radical feminism—are saying something true about human experience. Liberal legalism and critical legalism both describe something true about male experience, and cultural feminism and radical feminism both describe something true about female experience. If Kennedy is right, then men simply live with an experiental contradiction. In a parallel fashion, cultural feminism and radical feminism may both be *true* although contradictory. The contradiction between them may be experiential rather than logical. Women may both value intimacy and dread the intrusion and invasion which intimacy implies; and women may both fear separation and long for the individualization which separation would bring.[45]

From this premise, West then suggested the following way to create a "reconstructive feminist jurisprudence" that would finally make "feminist reform rational."[46] By "rational" West does not mean "male," as most assimilationists and even some moderate pluralists do, but "rational" from a radical feminist point of view. If different groups of women do legitimately "fear" men, the law must be redesigned to alleviate these fears without resorting to male legal rationales or by deconstructing these fears into illusions. Thus, West believes that neither equality through more (male) choice, as advocated by the assimilationists, nor equality through obtaining (male) power, as advocated by some radical pluralists, may reflect or result in achieving the subjective well-being of women because they are outwardly rather than inwardly directed. West goes so far as to claim that the goals of both liberal legalism and pluralist legalism "have the potential to backfire —badly—against women's true interests," which she insists remain largely ignored or silenced in their subjective, hedonic lives. "My substantive claim is that woman's happiness or pleasure—as opposed to women's freedom or equality —should be the ideal toward which female legal criticism and reform should be pressed," concludes West, "and that women's misery, suffering and pain—as opposed to women's oppression or subordination—is the evil we should resist."[47]

While West has taken the "fundamental-contradiction" theories of Unger and Kennedy further than any other radical legal theorist by trying to construct a feminist jurisprudence that does not automatically assume, as both assimilationists and pluralists do, that an improvement in objective conditions will improve the subjective reality of most women's lives, she does not connect her own and their analysis of this contradiction with the interconnection between the passing of the modern era and the incoherency of liberal individualism. It is not simply that liberalism with all its inconsistencies was suited to the modern era of individualization, promoted first by commercial and then by capitalistic development with its emphasis on male equality, rationality, and superiority in the family and state. It is also that liberalism has not been able to offer an alternative to the "nature of persons [or, to use West's term, "human beings"] that is better suited to a global, linked world system."[48] The "fundamental contradiction" is liberalism itself, now that the era of globalization—especially with respect to the relation of persons to community and culture—is emerging.

In these great historic sea changes from premodernism to modernism and now to postmodernism, the social construction of women probably was (and is) more in tune with first and third societal transformations rather than our own modern time. This is because both pre- and postmodernism stress that persons (human beings) are members of communities first and not simply isolated individuals who operate as sovereign agents.[49] It is for this reason that relational feminist jurisprudence cannot build upon the increasingly obvious contractions of past and present liberal legalism, but it can begin to ride the crest (and needs) of the future of postmodern globalism. Already, psychologists are suggesting that feminist perspectives of women today probably will form the basis for the human psychology of the postmodern future. Why should any less be true of feminist jurisprudence, since it also rests on the inter- and intraconnected constitutive persons that women have been socialized to be?

Individual rights only make sense in a Lockean society based on the belief that "persons are understood to be an antecedent to any kind of constitutive community," rather than the other way around. If persons of the future are to be those "whose very identities are constituted by social locations," then women already possess many of the constitutive perspectives necessary for developing this new postmodern human self protected by human rights. In a globally relational setting, feminist jurisprudence would appear both more rational and necessary than it does now, at the end of the postmodern era with its excesses of individualization. The fundamental contradiction of the liberal individualist view of human nature—whether in its female or male versions—is not the basis upon which to build a feminist jurisprudence, as West maintains. Instead, even the contradictions about human nature projected by radical feminism must be rejected in the name of community identity based on fairness and equity. Otherwise, remnants of liberal individualism and liberal legalism will continue to confound indefinitely women's civil rights and sexuality.

Nonetheless, analyses like West's offer the hope that the 1980s and 1990s will not become the 1920s and 1930s for female activism if a feminist jurisprudence becomes reality and if a common woman's language can once again be identified and utilized by reformers rather than reactionaries. While these tasks will be difficult to accomplish (unlike the interwar years in which the First Women's movement drowned in the sea of largely unreflective fragmentation accompanied by the illusory adoption of male language to achieve female goals),[50] at least the correct questions are now being asked and a few tentative and provocative answers are being suggested.

Perhaps before the end of this century, women in the United States will reunite behind a more relational approach to improving their status and society; but by the beginning of the 1990s, there was every indication that the equal rights approach of liberal legalism will remain intact for the rest of the century. To the degree that radical feminists anticipate and transform the future of the U.S. political economy rather than continue to react to its ever-changing contemporary manifestations, they will ultimately be judged as the true visionaries. My own resolution to the problem of how to move from liberation to emancipation is through radical feminism. However, as the preceding chapters have indicated, the liberal historical and legal barriers have kept most women in the United States of the past and present from endorsing practicing this brand of feminism, let alone constructing a feminist jurisprudence.[51] As Catharine MacKinnon has said: "justice [for women] will require change, not [simply more] reflection . . . [but] new jurisprudence, a new relation between life and law."[52]

## If the Future Is Not to Be What It Was

As I noted in chapter 7, the trend in Supreme Court decisions under Chief Justice Rehnquist at the end of the 1980s was away from encouraging collective class-action suits and back to emphasizing the responsibility of isolated individuals to prove they have been the victims of discrimination. When the lone person, regardless of class, sex, or race, is left to sue for individual or human rights without group identification, this represents a return to the harsh liberal ideal of extending equal protection to unequal individuals. As such, it also represents a turn away from the affirmative-action approach for minorities and women of the Warren and Burger courts. Once again American women are faced with the inadequacy of the concepts of citizenship and equality as they apply to themselves and all minorities. Once again they must decide whether to accept too little, too late or to continue their struggle to become full citizens, based on equitable, rather than equal, legal treatment and on female, rather than male, standards for "life, liberty, and happiness."

Of course, there remains the distinct possibility that relational global concepts are being and will be increasingly coopted by the male legal establishment of the future as international economic interests experience forced change. As the decade of the 1990s begins, however, this does not seem to be the path charted by the Supreme Court under Chief Justice William Rehnquist. If anything, the five justice conservative majority appears to be a last bastion of modern individual rights on the eve of postmodern globalization. In fact, these justices may well represent an endangered species if the legal system follows (as it always has in the past) the basic economic developments already in progress, which appear to be collective and interdependent. Unlike during the early dawning of the modern period several centuries ago, women's socialization, based on lingering forms of dependency and deference under liberalism, now seems more suited for human existence in a postmodern era than does men's socialization—if it can be translated into an autonomous alternative at all levels of society. Also, there is a women's movement that could possibly take advantage of this fortuitous situation —if it could divorce itself of its too little, too late liberal legal mentality.

Any feminist jurisprudence, therefore, would have to continue to reemphasize the necessity of class actions and congressional legislation to redress group "wrongs" and to question the basically regressive rash of five-to-four Rehnquist Court decisions in the late 1980s. Moreover, it must deny the idea that if there is "no national consensus" on some issues of extreme importance to disadvantaged

groups—such as blacks, the young, the mentally retarded, and women—as
Justice Scalia is so fond of noting,[53] then the states should continue to legislate
idiosyncratically on such matters. Women and minorities should be able to live
and travel *anywhere* in the United States without fear that their fundamental
rights will be honored in only some of them.

But a feminist jurisprudence must go beyond the obvious support of class-
action suits, the precedent for which has already been established under civil
rights law. It must fight to give legal standing to particular societal "harms"
against women and disadvantaged groups world-wide in the name of human
rights.[54] Some advances along these lines can be seen in the MacKinnon and
Dworkin antipornography ordinances and in some of NARAL's arguments in
favor of a woman's right to abortion using metaphors about pregnancy as an
invasion of women's bodies. Most importantly, there are steps being taken to
internationalize female relational concepts and to develop a collective feminist
definition of human rights for the twenty-first century. Much more remains to be
done to recast legal arguments. Most important, perhaps, is that feminist jurisprudence in conjunction with radical feminist political action must work to
reconstruct values and the legal system so that women in the United States can
live in freedom without fear. A "fear-less" society in women's terms would not
conform to past and present macho ideas about the (post) modern state or (post)
modern sexuality. Instead, the state would assume its responsibility for the
protection of the fundamental or basic rights of all of its people based on their
respective collective identities, rather than selectively denying them such rights
based on obsolete and contradictory views about women's role in civil society and
as human beings.

Most important, both feminist jurisprudence and history must recognize the
limitations inherent in any legal system but especially one dominated by the
current conservative majority on the Supreme Court that seems to reflect a
political and legal climate based on a return to social Darwinism, whereby those
who succeed are judged as deserving of juridical favoritism, in contrast to those
who have not. The Court has always exercised a "disproportionate influence . . .
on the much-touted neutral concept of rights"and has usually ended up supporting the "haves" more than the "have-nots" when it comes to issues of national
security, corporate polluters, white-collar criminals, a multibillion-dollar pornography and prostitution industry, and powerful establishment lobby groups. Is it
any wonder that the courts in this lingering postwar backlash era can see no way
out of this dilemma created by both liberals and conservatives clinging to neutrality and fixed rules of law to avoid what they consider to be a dangerous, but
different, set of personal pluralistic preferences? These same limitations would
ultimately apply to any feminist jurisprudence that accepted the idea that the

"time is not right" to attack the "unresolved dilemma of neutrality that lies at the heart of American law."[55] The time has never been right for women and minorities to assert themselves against the sexist constraints of the U.S. legal system. The time has never been right for the nation's legal and political system to address the socioeconomic needs of women and their legitimate concerns over the wanton violence they fear and experience everyday.

Feminist jurisprudence alone cannot change a "fearful" society into a "fearless" one, if for no other reason than the law usually follows rather than leads the nation in changing societal values—except on those very issues, such as pornography and antiabortion, that bolster the most vicious strongholds of hatred toward women. Therefore, a feminist jurisprudence cannot redefine what it means to be a human being or citizen unless such a definition is integrally connected to radical feminist political activism carried on in the name of women as women, not as individuals who happen to meet the patriarchal, poststructural standards of the period.

Radical feminist activism is non-neutral by definition and outside the boundaries of the law because it recognizes without qualification the fearfully harmful results of female oppression, whether in the form of unwanted pregnancies, surrogate motherhood, prostitution, pornography, discrimination in hiring and promotion, or sexual harassment on the job. Such radical feminist activism also must insist all more in the face of poststructural abstractions that the patriarchal contradictions about human nature, sexuality, and the liberal state continue in more and more sophisticated forms to dominate the public and private lives of women in the United States. "High talk about language, meaning, sign, process, and law can mask racist and sexist ugliness [more than ever before]," according to attorney Mari J. Matsuda, "if we never stop to ask: 'Exactly what are you talking about and what is the implication of what you are saying for my sister who is carrying buckets of water up five flights of stairs in a welfare hotel?' "[56]

These contradictions have been exposed by radical feminism for some time, but it is clear that they cannot be overcome exclusively by reform of the present U.S. legal system. A feminist jurisprudence that did not honor the alleged neutrality of the law or the alleged "sameness" of women and men in postmodern society would be a step forward, but without a political and social movement it cannot succeed because the legal system seldom leads when it comes to restructuring society. As a democracy, we clearly cannot legislate and litigate equality and morals or force society to grant equality of esteem to women and minorities. But at the same time, we can no longer adhere to the increasingly rigid, regressive, and defensive interpretation of the Constitution that does not address the needs of contemporary women—whether by conservatives or liberals. In June

1978, Aleksandr Solzhenitsyn delivered a controversial commencement address at Harvard in which he criticized among other things the Western, Anglo-Saxon, patriarchal system of law.

A society which is based on the letter of the law and never reaches any higher is taking very scarce advantage of the high level of human possibilities. The letter of the law is too cold and formal to have a beneficial influence on society. Whenever the tissue of life is woven of legalistic relations, there is an atmosphere of moral mediocrity, paralyzing men's noblest impulses. And it will be simply impossible to stand through the trials of this threatening century with only the support of a legalistic structure.

It is, therefore, of the utmost importance for women in the United States to continue to stretch the outer limits of the letter of the law until the legal system finally addresses their long-ignored socioeconomic concerns. This could prove especially effective in the 1990s when new interpretations of old laws seem to be becoming a reality in an unprecedented short period of time in the Soviet Union, Eastern Europe, and even South Africa. Women here and abroad should take advantage of these propitious times to ensure that they are not left out, as they have been so many times in the past, of the momentous legal, political, and economic revolutions going on simultaneously in so many parts of the world. Only when women in this country, for example, decide to transform the Constitution of 1787, the Bill of Rights, and other legal texts that continue to grant them too little, too late will the Second Women's movement, unlike the first one, go beyond the pursuit of individual rights to human rights—from equality to equity. Attitudes can be modified through public-policy measures that address the societal harms that continue to deny women and minorities full citizenship and membership in society. But this will mean confronting the deficiencies of equality, as defined by liberal legalism. Not until such attitudinal changes, corresponding to the transformation now occurring in the world's economic and ideological systems, take place can women collectively end both their self-imposed and societally prescribed silence about the conflation of their legal and sexual existence in the eyes of the law.[57]

If the future is not to be what the past was, socially conditioned female culture and hedonic experiences must be accorded equity with socially conditioned male culture and hedonic experiences. Otherwise, like the hypothetical frog who keeps jumping half the space each time—never theoretically reaching its destination—women will continue to become progressively more liberated by male standards without being effectively emancipated. When both women and men can finally speak of patriarchy and its attendant versions of constitutionalism under socialism and capitalism as historical phenomena, then—and only then—will women truly be liberated and free from their multidimensional levels of subordination. It is only when alleged female inferiority becomes a normative factor of the past rather than the present that women will be accorded equal socioeconomic and constitutional expectations that are not based on male standards. Until then, they will continue to be unequal citizens under the law and within the various patriarchal systems they have internalized and "consented" to so well.

As I noted in the Introduction, political, socioeconomic, and legal-reform activity on the part of women is only one component, however a necessary one, of any definition of feminism.[58] It is even more essential in the last decade of the twentieth century to maintain a strong sense of female consciousness and culture (that is, the philosophical validity of relational feminism), if the doctrine of "equality in difference" is to take its rightful place alongside "equality in sameness" in the United States. Only then will a concept of equity ultimately subsume both types of equality in the pursuit of justice for U.S. women; only then will liberation become emancipation. It goes without saying that a large proportion of new social and new legal historians consider themselves feminists, as do most activists in the Second Women's movement. But just as some people are more equal that others, some feminists are more feminist than others. Their level of feminism is directly proportional to the degree that they challenge the limits of liberalism in economics, politics, history, and law. Yet most women scholars and reformers usually define themselves and their goals from well within the present status quo—perpetuating their "broken-barometric" function in relation to U.S. history as it is reflected in their legal status.

The potential of the Constitution and other legal texts to perpetuate the sexual and psychological domination of women in contemporary society is alive and well because equality and most other legal concepts are still largely based on male standards. Unless members of the Second Women's movement move beyond current "unisex" liberal arguments in their pursuit of "life, liberty, and [male] happiness," they will come proportionally no closer to altering the material (objective) and personal (subjective) conditions of women at the end of the twentieth century than did their predecessors in the First Women's movement at the end of the nineteenth. But any theoretical synthesis resolving the current issues of special rights versus equal rights, assimilation versus pluralism, reproductive versus structurally and culturally imposed differences between women and men will be meaningless if it takes place in a political vacuum of poststructural relativism. Political and moral commitment on the part of activists and scholars is necessary for the successful creation of a feminist jurisprudence that finally puts women *into* the Constitution on female rather than male terms.

Unless attitudes among legal elites are changed by feminist lawyers and historians to reflect and accommodate female needs and characteristics as basic to the successful globalization of the future, our counterparts in 2087 may well still be pondering yet another reexamination of women's legal status during the tercentenary of the U.S. Constitution. And, like us, they might also be wondering why the long-sought-after "one-size-fits-all" equality with men has proven both illusory and disillusioning, despite obvious improvements in the juridical treatment of women in the last quarter of the twentieth century.

# APPENDIX ONE

# Married Women's Property Acts, 1800–1900

**Laws Affecting the Legal Status of Married Women, 1800–1900, Northeastern and Mid-Atlantic States, by Percentage**

| Year | Wills | Estates freed from debts of husbands | Feme sole status abandoned | Widow's access to husband's personal estate | Separate estates for married women | Earnings act passed |
|------|-------|--------------------------------------|----------------------------|---------------------------------------------|-----------------------------------|---------------------|
| 1820 | 8  | —  | —  | 8  | —   | —  |
| 1830 | 25 | —  | 8  | 25 | —   | —  |
| 1840 | 33 | 8  | 25 | 33 | —   | —  |
| 1850 | 50 | 67 | 50 | 50 | 50  | —  |
| 1860 | 58 | 75 | 50 | 50 | 83  | 33 |
| 1870 | 67 | 75 | 50 | 50 | 100 | 42 |
| 1880 | 75 | 75 | 58 | 50 | 100 | 58 |
| 1890 | 75 | 75 | 58 | 50 | 100 | 58 |
| 1900 | 75 | 75 | 58 | 50 | 100 | 58 |

**Laws Affecting the Legal Status of Married Women, 1800–1900, Southern States, by Percentage**

| Year | Wills | Estates freed from debts of husbands | Feme sole status abandoned | Widow's access to husband's personal estate | Separate estates for married women | Earnings act passed |
|------|-------|--------------------------------------|----------------------------|---------------------------------------------|-----------------------------------|---------------------|
| 1820 | —  | —  | —  | 8  | —  | —  |
| 1830 | 8  | —  | 8  | 23 | —  | —  |
| 1840 | 8  | 15 | 8  | 31 | —  | —  |
| 1850 | 15 | 46 | 23 | 31 | 31 | —  |
| 1860 | 23 | 46 | 23 | 31 | 31 | —  |
| 1870 | 39 | 69 | 31 | 39 | 54 | 23 |
| 1880 | 39 | 77 | 31 | 54 | 77 | 46 |
| 1890 | 46 | 77 | 31 | 54 | 77 | 46 |
| 1900 | 54 | 92 | 62 | 54 | 85 | 46 |

## Laws Affecting the Legal Status of Married Women, 1800–1900, Midwestern States, by Percentage

|      | Wills | Estates freed from debts of husbands | Feme sole status abandoned | Widow's access to husband's personal estate | Separate estates for married women | Earnings act passed |
|------|-------|--------------------------------------|----------------------------|---------------------------------------------|-------------------------------------|---------------------|
| 1820 | 11    | —                                    | 11                         | 11                                          | —                                   | —                   |
| 1830 | 11    | —                                    | 11                         | 22                                          | —                                   | —                   |
| 1840 | 11    | —                                    | 22                         | 44                                          | —                                   | —                   |
| 1850 | 33    | 67                                   | 33                         | 44                                          | 33                                  | —                   |
| 1860 | 44    | 67                                   | 33                         | 44                                          | 44                                  | 22                  |
| 1870 | 55    | 78                                   | 33                         | 56                                          | 67                                  | 33                  |
| 1880 | 67    | 100                                  | 56                         | 56                                          | 78                                  | 78                  |
| 1890 | 67    | 100                                  | 56                         | 56                                          | 78                                  | 78                  |
| 1900 | 67    | 100                                  | 56                         | 56                                          | 78                                  | 78                  |

## Laws Affecting the Legal Status of Married Women, 1800–1900, Western States, by Percentage[a]

|      | Wills | Estates freed from debts of husbands | Right to vote by 1911 | Feme sole status abandoned | Separate estates for married women | Earnings act passed |
|------|-------|--------------------------------------|-----------------------|----------------------------|-------------------------------------|---------------------|
| 1850 | —     | 8                                    | —                     | —                          | —                                   | —                   |
| 1860 | 8     | 8                                    | —                     | —                          | 8                                   | —                   |
| 1870 | 8     | 8                                    | 8                     | 8                          | 8                                   | 8                   |
| 1880 | 33    | 50                                   | 8                     | 17                         | 42                                  | 25                  |
| 1890 | 58    | 83                                   | 8                     | 67                         | 92                                  | 58                  |
| 1900 | 75    | 83                                   | 50                    | 92                         | 100                                 | 75                  |

[a]Widows' access to their husbands' personal estates not calculated for Western States because so few provided for it by statute. See chart on page 129.

**Laws Affecting the Legal Status of Married Women, 1800–1900, Northeastern and Mid-Atlantic States, by State**

| State | Wills | Debt-free estates | Feme sole status | Personal estate access | Separate estates | Earnings acts |
|---|---|---|---|---|---|---|
| Connecticut | 1809 | 1845, 1849 | — | — | 1849, 1869, 1872 | — |
| Delaware | — | — | — | — | 1865 | 1871,[c] 1873 |
| Maine | — | 1844 | 1828 | 1849[a] | 1844 | 1860 |
| Maryland | 1843[d] | 1843 | — | 1798 | 1853[b] | 1860 |
| Massachusetts | 1818, 1842,[d] 1855 | 1833 | 1833, 1846 | 1833, 1835[a] | 1845 | 1855 |
| New Hampshire | 1841,[d] 1854 | 1846 | 1840 | 1822 | 1846, 1850,[b] 1871 | — |
| New Jersey | 1864 | 1852 | — | — | 1852, 1874 | 1878[c] |
| New York | 1829,[c] 1849 | 1848 | — | — | 1848, 1849,[b] 1887 | 1860 |
| Pennsylvania | 1833,[d] 1848 | 1848 | — | 1833 | 1848 | 1855,[c] 1872 |
| Rhode Island | 1856 | — | 1841 | — | 1848 | — |
| Vermont | — | 1845 | 1846 | 1821 | 1867 | 1866[b] |

[a] Based on case law, not statutes.
[b] Removed trustee necessity.
[c] Limited earnings statutes; only protected married women who were no longer living with their husbands.
[d] Women could write wills with husbands' consent or other restrictions applied.
[e] Limited wills acts.

# Laws Affecting the Legal Status of Married Women, 1800–1900, Midwestern States, by State

| State | Wills | Debt-free estates | Feme sole status | Personal estate access | Separate estates | Earnings acts |
|---|---|---|---|---|---|---|
| Illinois[d] | 1872 | 1874 | 1874 | 1861, 1868, 1874 | 1861, 1869, 1874 | 1869, 1874 |
| Indiana | 1847,[c] 1859 | 1847 | — | 1831 | 1879 | 1879 |
| Iowa | — | 1846 | 1840 | — | — | 1866,[b] 1870 |
| Kansas | 1858, 1868 | 1868 | — | — | 1859, 1868 | 1858, 1868 |
| Kentucky | — | 1846 | 1843 | 1811[a] | — | 1873 |
| Michigan | 1850 | 1844 | — | 1825 | 1844, 1855 | — |
| Minnesota | 1869 | 1876, 1878 | 1874 | — | 1860, 1869 | 1860[b] |
| Ohio | 1808, 1810, 1840, 1852 | 1804, 1846 | 1811 | 1840 | 1846, 1861, 1874 | 1871 |
| Wisconsin | — | 1850 | — | — | 1850 | — |

[a] Based on case law, not statutes.
[b] Limited earnings statutes; only protected married women who were no longer living with their husbands.
[c] Women could write wills with husbands' consent or other restrictions applied.
[d] Also followed 1845 Texas community-property laws.

## Laws Affecting the Legal Status of Married Women 1800–1900, Southern States, by State

| State | Wills | Debt-free estates | Feme sole status | Personal estate access | Separate estates | Earnings acts[c] |
|---|---|---|---|---|---|---|
| Alabama | 1846[d] | 1846 | 1846 | 1812 | 1845, 1848 | 1868[c] |
| Arkansas | 1868 | 1835, 1846 | 1868[a] | — | 1846, 1848, 1873 | 1873 |
| Florida | 1823, 1825 | 1845 | — | — | 1845, 1855[b] | — |
| Georgia | 1867 | — | — | 1870 | 1866, 1868 | 1870 |
| Louisiana | — | 1869 | 1894 | 1839 | — | — |
| Mississippi | — | 1839 | — | 1825, 1838[a] | 1873,[b] 1881 | 1871 |
| Missouri | — | 1849 | — | | 1849 | — |
| North Carolina | — | 1868 | 1828 | 1828, 1872 | 1850[b] | 1868, 1872 |
| South Carolina | — | 1866 | 1868, 1870, 1891 | 1870 | 1868, 1870, 1882, 1891, 1895 | — |
| Tennessee | 1852 | 1850 | 1850 | — | 1870 | — |
| Texas[e] | 1895 | 1895 | 1845 | — | 1845 | — |
| Virginia | — | 1877 | — | — | 1877 | — |
| West Virginia | 1882 | 1891, 1893 | 1891, 1893 | 1866, 1891, 1893 | 1875, 1882, 1891, 1893 | 1879,[c] 1891, 1893 |

[a] Based on case law, not statutes.

[b] Removed trustee necessity.

[c] Limited earnings statutes; only protected married women who were no longer living with their husbands.

[d] Women could write wills with husband's consent or other restrictions applied.

[e] "The 1845 Texas Constitution provided that 'all property, both real and personal, of the wife, owned or claimed by marriage, and that acquired afterwards by gift, devise, or descent, shall be her separate property; and laws shall be passed more clearly defining the rights of the wife in relation as well as to her separate property, as to that held with her husband. Laws shall also be passed providing for the registration of the wife's separate property.' This provision established the community-property system and provided for women's separate property. Identical language was adopted by California and Nevada" (Mari Matsuda, "The West and the Legal Status of Women: Explanations of Frontier Feminism." Journal of the West 24, no. 1 [January 1985]: 56).

# Laws Affecting the Legal Status of Married Women 1800–1900, Western States, by State

| State | Wills | Debt-free estates | Personal estate access | Right to vote by 1911 | Feme sole status | Separate estates | Earnings acts |
|---|---|---|---|---|---|---|---|
| California[a] | 1876 | by 1911 | — | 1900 | 1874[b] | — | — |
| Colorado | 1874 | 1876 | — | by 1911 | 1876 | 1876 | 1876 |
| Idaho[a] | 1887 | — | — | by 1911 | 1887 | 1887 | 1889 |
| Montana | — | 1889 | 1889[c] | — | 1889 | 1889 | 1889 |
| Nebraska | 1897 | 1875 | — | — | 1882 | 1889, 1897 | — |
| Nevada[a] | 1873 | 1879 | 1881, 1883[c] | — | 1867 | 1873[b] | 1861[b] |
| North Dakota | 1877, 1893, 1899 | — | — | 1899 | 1899 | 1899 | — |
| Oregon | 1853 | 1850 | — | — | 1859, 1866, 1878, 1880 | — | 1880 |
| South Dakota | 1887 | 1889 | — | — | 1889 | 1889 | 1887 |
| Utah | 1895 | 1885, 1896 | — | by 1911 | 1895 | 1895 | 1895 |
| Washington | 1889 | 1889 | 1889[c] | by 1911 | 1889 | 1888, 1889[b] | 1889 |
| Wyoming | 1876 | — | — | 1869 | 1882 | 1876 | — |

[a] Adopted 1845 Texas community property laws.

[b] All of these states had some form of Married Women's Property Acts written into their state constitutions by 1921.

[c] Washington, Montana, and Nevada are the only western states to provide for a widow's access to her husband's personal estate by statute. Other western states may have found it unnecessary to provide for access to the husband's personal estate due to community-property legislation, such as what was in effect in California, Nevada, and Idaho. (Other community-property states, such as New Mexico and Arizona, were not admitted to the Union as states until 1912 and, thus, are not under consideration in the nineteenth century.)

# 1848 Declaration of Sentiments

*This Declaration of Sentiments was written and adopted at the first Women's Rights Convention in the United States, held in Seneca Falls, New York, the nineteenth and twentieth of July 1848.*

**When, in the course of human events, it becomes necessary for one** portion of the family of man to assume among the people of the earth a position different from that which they have hitherto occupied, but one **to which the laws of nature and of nature's God entitle them, a decent respect to the opinions of mankind requires that they should declare the causes that impel them** to such a course.

We hold these truths to be self-evident; that all men and women are created equal; that they are endowed by their Creator with certain inalienable rights; that among these are life, liberty, and the pursuit of happiness; that to secure these rights governments are instituted, deriving their just powers from the consent of the governed. Whenever any form of Government becomes destructive of these ends, it is the right of those who suffer from it to refuse allegiance to it, and to insist upon the institution of a new government, laying its foundation on such principles, and organizing its powers in such form as to them shall seem most likely to effect their safety and happiness. Prudence, indeed, will dictate that governments long established should not be changed for light and transient causes; and accordingly, all experience hath shown that mankind are more disposed to suffer, while evils are sufferable, than to right themselves, by abolishing the forms to which they are accustomed. But when a long train of abuses and usurpations, pursuing invariably the same object, evinces a design to reduce them under absolute despotism, it is their duty to throw off such government, and to provide new guards for their future security. Such has been the patient sufferance of the women under this government, and such is now the necessity which constrains them to demand the equal station to which they are entitled.

**The history of mankind is a history of repeated injuries and usurpations on the part of man toward woman, having in direct object the establishment of an**

absolute tyranny over her. To prove this, let facts be submitted to a candid world.

He has never permitted her to exercise her inalienable right to the elective franchise.

He has compelled her to submit to laws, in the formation of which she had no voice.

He has withheld from her rights which are given to the most ignorant and degraded men—both natives and foreigners.

Having deprived her of this first right of a citizen, the elective franchise, thereby leaving her without representation in the halls of legislation, he has oppressed her on all sides.

He has made her, if married, in the eye of the law, civilly dead.

He has taken from her all right in property, even to the wages she earns.

He has made her, morally, an irresponsible being, as she can commit many crimes with impunity, provided they be done in the presence of her husband. In the covenant of marriage, she is compelled to promise obedience to her husband, he becoming, to all intents and purposes, her master—the law giving him power to deprive her of her liberty, and to administer chastisement.

He has so framed the laws of divorce, as to what shall be the proper causes of divorce; in case of separation, to whom the guardianship of the children shall be given, as to be wholly regardless of the happiness of women—the law, in all cases, going upon the false supposition of the supremacy of man, and giving all power into his hands.

After depriving her of all rights as a married woman, if single and the owner of property, he has taxed her to support a government which recognizes her only when her property can be made profitable to it.

He had monopolized nearly all the profitable employments, and from those she is permitted to follow, she receives but a scanty remuneration.

He closes against her all the avenues to wealth and distinction, which he considers most honorable to himself. As a teacher of theology, medicine, or law, she is not known.

He has denied her the facilities for obtaining a thorough education—all colleges being closed against her.

He allows her in Church as well as State, but a subordinate position, claiming Apostolic authority for her exclusion from the ministry, and, with some exceptions, from any public participation in the affairs of the Church.

He has created a false public sentiment, by giving to the world a different code of morals for men and women, by which moral delinquencies which exclude women from society, are not only tolerated but deemed of little account in man.

He has usurped the prerogative of Jehovah himself, claiming it as his right to assign for her a sphere of action, when that belongs to her conscience and her God.

He has endeavored, in every way that he could to destroy her confidence in her own powers, to lessen her self-respect, and to make her willing to lead a dependent and abject life.

Now, in view of this entire disfranchisement of one-half the people of this country, their social and religious degradation,—in view of the unjust laws above mentioned, and because women do feel themselves aggrieved, oppressed, and fraudulently deprived of the most sacred rights, we insist that they have immediate admission to all the rights and privileges which belong to them as citizens of these United States.

In entering upon the great work before us, we anticipate no small amount of misconception, misrepresentation, and ridicule; but we shall use every instrumentality within our power to effect our object. We shall employ agents, circulate tracts, petition the State and national Legislatures, and endeavor to enlist the pulpit and the press in our behalf. We hope this Convention will be followed by a series of Conventions, embracing every part of the country.

Firmly relying upon the final triumph of the Right and the True, we do this day affix our signatures to this declaration.

Signers of the Declaration of Sentiments, Seneca Falls, New York, July 19-20, 1848.

Caroline Barker, Eunice Barker, William G. Barker, Rachel D. (Mitchell) Bonnel, Joel D. Bunker, William Burroughs, E.W. Capron, Jacob P. Chamberlain, Elizabeth Conklin, Mark Conklin, P.A. Culvert, Cynthia Davis, Thomas Dell, William S. Dell, Elias J. Doty, Susan R. Doty, Frederick Douglass, Julia Ann Drake, Harriet Cady Eaton, Elisha Foote, Eunice Newton Foote, Mary Ann Frink, Cynthia Fuller, Experience Gibbs, Mary Gilbert, Lydia Gild, Sarah Hallowell, Mary H. Hallowell, Henry Hatley, Sarah Hoffman, Charles L. Hoskins, Jane C. Hunt, Richard P. Hunt, Margaret Jenkins, John Jones, Lucy Jones, Phebe King, Hannah J. Latham, Lovina Latham, Elizabeth Leslie, Eliza Martin, Mary Martin, Delia Mathews, Dorothy Mathews, Jacob Mathews, Elizabeth W. McClintock, Mary McClintock, Mary Ann McClintock, Thomas McClintock, Jonathan Metcalf, Nathan J. Milliken, Mary S. Mirror, Pheobe Mosher, Sarah A. Mosher, James Mott, Lucretia Mott, Lydia Mount, Catharine C. Paine, Rhoda Palmer, Saron Phillips, Sally Pitcher, Hannah Plant, Ann Porter, Amy Post, George W. Pryor, Margaret Pryor, Susan Quinn, Rebecca Race, Martha Ridley, Azaliah Schooley, Margaret Schooley, Deborah Scott, Antoinette E. Segur, Henry Seymour, Henry W. Seymour, Malvina Seymour, Catharine Shaw, Stephen Shear, Sarah Sisson, Robert Smallbridge, Elizabeth D. Smith, Sarah Smith, David Spalding, Lucy Spalding, Elizabeth Cady Stanton, Catharine F.

Stebbins, Sophronia Taylor, Betsey Tewksbury, Samuel D. Tillman, Edward F. Underhill, Martha Underhill, Mary E. Vail, Isaac Van Tassel, Sarah Whitney, Maria E. Wilbur, Justin Williams, Sarah R. Woods, Charlotte Woodward, S.E. Woodworth, Martha C. Wright.

The following resolutions were discussed by Lucretia Mott, Thomas and Mary Ann McClintock, Amy Post, Catharine A. F. Stebbins, and others, and were adopted:

WHEREAS, The great precept of nature is conceded to be, that "man shall pursue his own true and substantial happiness." Blackstone in his Commentaries remarks, that this law of Nature being coeval with mankind, and dictated by God himself, is of course superior in obligation to any other. It is binding over all the globe, in all countries and at all times; no human laws are of any validity if contrary to this, and such of them as are valid, derive all their force, and all their validity, and all their authority, mediately and immediately, from this original; therefore,

*Resolved,* That such laws as conflict, in any way, with the true and substantial happiness of woman, are contrary to the great precept of nature and of no validity, for this is "superior in obligation to any other."

*Resolved,* That all laws which prevent woman from occupying such a station in society as her conscience shall dictate, or which place her in a position inferior to that of man, are contrary to the great precept of nature and therefore of no force or authority.

*Resolved,* That woman is man's equal—was intended to be so by the Creator, and the highest good of the race demands that she should be recognized as such.

*Resolved,* That the women of this country ought to be enlightened in regard to the laws under which they live, that they may no longer publish their degradation by declaring themselves satisfied with their present position, nor their ignorance, by asserting that they have all the rights they want.

*Resolved,* That inasmuch as man, while claiming for himself intellectual superiority, does accord to woman moral superiority, it is pre-eminently his duty to encourage her to speak and teach, as she has an opportunity, in all religious assemblies.

*Resolved,* That the same amount of virtue, delicacy, and refinement of behavior that is required of woman in the social state, should also be required of man, and the same transgressions should be visited with equal severity on both man and woman.

*Resolved,* That the objection of indelicacy and impropriety, which is so often brought against woman when she addresses a public audience, comes with a very ill-grace from those who encourage, by their attendance, her appearance on the stage, in the concert, or in feats of the circus.

*Resolved,* That woman has too long rested satisfied in the circumscribed limits which corrupt customs and a perverted application of the Scriptures have marked out for her, and that it is time she should move in the enlarged sphere which her great Creator has assigned her.

*Resolved,* That it is the duty of the women of this country to secure to themselves their sacred right to elective franchise.

*Resolved,* That the equality of human rights results necessarily from the fact of the identity of the race in capabilities and responsibilities.

*Resolved, therefore,* That being invested by the Creator with the same capabilities, and the same consciousness of responsibility for their exercise, it is demonstrably the right and duty of woman, equally with man, to promote every righteous cause by every righteous means; and especially in regard to the great subjects of morals and religion, it is self-evidently her right to participate with her brother in teaching them, both in private and in public, by writing and by speaking, by any instrumentalities proper to be used, and in any assemblies proper to be held; and this being a self-evident truth growing out of the divinely implanted principles of human nature, any custom or authority adverse to it, whether modern or wearing the hoary sanction of antiquity, is to be regarded as a self-evident falsehood, and at war with mankind.

*Resolved,* That the speedy success of our cause depends upon the zealous and untiring efforts of both men and women, for the overthrow of the monopoly of the pulpit, and for the securing to woman an equal participation with men in the various trades, professions, and commerce.

# 1876 Declaration of Rights

While the nation is buoyant with patriotism, and all hearts are attuned to praise, it is with sorrow we come to strike the one discordant note, on this one-hundredth anniversary of our country's birth. When subjects of kings, emperors, and czars, from the old world join in our national jubilee, shall the women of the republic refuse to lay their hands with benedictions on the nation's head? Surveying America's exposition, surpassing in magnificence those of London, Paris, and Vienna, shall we not rejoice at the success of the youngest rival among the nations of the earth? May not our hearts, in unison with all, swell with pride at our great achievements as a people; our free speech, free press, free schools, free church, and the rapid progress we have made in material wealth, trade, commerce and the inventive arts? And we do rejoice in the success, thus far, of our experiment of self-government. Our faith is firm and unwavering in the broad principles of human rights proclaimed in 1776, not only as abstract truths, but as the corner stones of a republic. Yet we cannot forget, even in this glad hour, that while all men of every race, and clime, and condition, have been invested with the full rights of citizenship under our hospitable flag, all women still suffer the degradation of disfranchisement.

The history of our country the past hundred years has been a series of assumptions and usurpations of power over woman, in direct opposition to the principles of just government, acknowledged by the United States as its foundation, which are:

*First*—The natural rights of each individual.

*Second*—The equality of these rights.

*Third*—That rights not delegated are retained by the individual.

*Fourth*—That no person can exercise the rights of others without delegated authority.

*Fifth*—That the non-use of rights does not destroy them.

And for the violation of these fundamental principles of our government, we arraign our rulers on this Fourth day of July, 1876,—and these are our articles of impeachment:

*Bills of attainder* have been passed by the introduction of the word "male" into all the State constitutions, denying to women the right of suffrage, and thereby making sex a crime—an exercise of power clearly forbidden in article I, sections 9, 10, of the United States constitution.

*The writ of habeas corpus,* the only protection against *lettres de cachet* and all forms of unjust imprisonment, which the constitution declares "shall not be suspended, except when in cases of rebellion or invasion the public safety demands it," is held inoperative in every State of the Union, in case of a married woman against her husband—the marital rights of the husband being in all cases primary, and the rights of the wife secondary.

*The right of trial by a jury of one's peers* was so jealously guarded that States refused to ratify the original constitution until it was guaranteed by the sixth amendment. And yet the women of this nation have never been allowed a jury of their peers—being tried in all cases by men, native and foreign, educated and ignorant, virtuous and vicious. Young girls have been arraigned in our courts for the crime of infanticide; tried, convicted, hanged—victims, perchance, of judge, jurors, advocates—while no woman's voice could be heard in their defense. And not only are women denied a jury of their peers, but in some cases, jury trial altogether. During the war, a woman was tried and hanged by military law, in defiance of the fifth amendment, which specifically declares: "No person shall be held to answer for a capital or otherwise infamous crime, unless on a presentment or indictment of a grand jury, except in cases . . . . of persons in actual service in time of war." During the last presidential campaign, a woman, arrested for voting, was denied the protection of a jury, tried, convicted, and sentenced to a fine and costs of prosecution, by the absolute power of a judge of the Supreme Court of the United States.

*Taxation without representation,* the immediate cause of the rebellion of the colonies against Great Britain, is one of the grievous wrongs the women of this country have suffered during the century. Deploring war, with all the demoralization that follows in its train, we have been taxed to support standing armies, with their waste of life and wealth. Believing in temperance, we have been taxed to support the vice, crime and pauperism of the liquor traffic. While we suffer its wrongs and abuses infinitely more than man, we have no power to protect our sons against this giant evil. During the temperance crusade, mothers were arrested, fined, imprisoned, for even praying and singing in the streets, while men blockade the sidewalks with impunity, even on Sunday, with their military parades and political processions. Believing in honesty, we are taxed to support a dangerous army of civilians, buying and selling the offices of government and sacrificing the best interests of the people. And, moreover, we are taxed to support the very legislators and judges who make laws, and render decisions adverse to woman. And for refusing to pay such unjust taxation, the houses, lands, bonds, and stock of women have been seized and sold within the present year, thus proving Lord Coke's assertion, that "The very act of taxing a man's property without his consent is, in effect, disfranchising him of every civil right."

*Unequal codes for men and women.* Held by law a perpetual minor, deemed incapable of self-protection, even in the industries of the world, woman is denied equality of rights. The fact of sex, not the quantity or quality of work, in most cases, decides the pay and position; and because of this injustice thousands of fatherless girls are compelled to choose between a life of shame and starvation. Laws catering to man's vices have created two codes of morals in which penalties are graded according to the political status of the offender. Under such laws, women are fined and imprisoned if found alone in the streets, or in public places of resort, at certain hours. Under the pretense of regulating public morals, police officers seizing the occupants of disreputable houses, march the women in platoons to prison, while the men, partners in their guilt, go free. While making a show of virtue in forbidding the importation of Chinese women on the Pacific coast for immoral purposes, our rulers, in many States, and even under the shadow of the national capitol, are now proposing to legalize the sale of American womanhood for the same vile purposes.

*Special legislation for woman* has placed us in a most anomalous position. Women invested with the rights of citizens in one section—voters, jurors, office-holders—crossing an imaginary line, are subjects in the next. In some States, a married woman may hold property and transact business in her own name; in others, her earnings belong to her husband. In some States, a woman may testify against her husband, sue and be sued in the courts; in others, she has no redress in case of damage to person, property, or character. In case of divorce on account of adultery in the husband, the innocent wife is held to possess no right to children or property, unless by special decree of the court. But in no State of the Union has the wife the right to her own person, or to any part of the joint earnings of the co-partnership during the life of her husband. In some States women may enter the law schools and practice in the courts; in others they are forbidden. In some universities girls enjoy equal educational advantages with boys, while many of the proudest institutions in the land deny them admittance, though the sons of China, Japan and Africa are welcomed there. But the privileges already granted in the several States are by no means secure. The right of suffrage once exercised by women in certain States and territories has been denied by subsequent legislation. A bill is now pending in congress to disfranchise the women of Utah, thus interfering to deprive United States citizens of the same rights which the Supreme Court has declared the national government powerless to protect anywhere. Laws passed after years of untiring effort, guaranteeing married women certain rights of property, and mothers the custody of their children, have been repealed in States where we supposed all was safe. Thus have our most sacred rights been made the football of legislative caprice, proving that a power which grants as a privilege what by nature is a right, may withhold the same as a penalty when deeming it necessary for its own perpetuation.

*Representation of woman* has had no place in the nation's thought. Since the incorporation of the thirteen original States, twenty-four have been admitted to the Union, not one of which has recognized woman's right of self-government. On this birthday of our national liberties, July Fourth, 1876, Colorado, like all her elder sisters, comes into the Union with the invidious word "male" in her constitution.

*Universal manhood suffrage,* by establishing an aristocracy of sex, imposes upon the women of this nation a more absolute and cruel despotism than monarchy; in that, woman finds a political master in her father, husband, brother, son. The aristocracies of the old world are based upon birth, wealth, refinement, education, nobility, brave deeds of chivalry; in this nation, on sex alone; exalting brute force above moral power, vice above virtue, ignorance above education, and the son above the mother who bore him.

*The judiciary above the nation* has proved itself but the echo of the party in power, by upholding and enforcing laws that are opposed to the spirit and letter of the constitution. When the slave power was dominant, the Supreme Court decided that a black man was not a citizen, because he had not the right to vote; and when the constitution was so amended as to make all persons citizens, the same high tribunal decided that a woman, though a citizen, had not the right to vote. Such vacillating interpretations of constitutional law unsettle our faith in judicial authority, and undermine the liberties of the whole people.

These articles of impeachment against our rulers we now submit to the impartial judgment of the people. To all these wrongs and oppressions woman has not submitted in silence and resignation. From the beginning of the century, when Abigail Adams, the wife of one president and mother of another, said, "We will not hold ourselves bound to obey laws in which we have no voice or representation," until now, woman's discontent has been steadily increasing, culminating nearly thirty years ago in a simultaneous movement among the women of the nation, demanding the right of suffrage. In making our just demands, a higher motive than the pride of sex inspires us; we feel that national safety and stability depend on the complete recognition of the broad principles of our government. Woman's degraded, helpless position is the weak point in our institutions to-day; a disturbing force everywhere, severing family ties, filling our asylums with the deaf, the dumb, the blind; our prisons with criminals, our cities with drunkenness and prostitution; our homes with disease and death. It was the boast of the founders of the republic, that the rights for which they contended were the rights of human nature. If these rights are ignored in the case of one-half the people, the nation is surely preparing for its downfall. Governments try themselves. The recognition of a governing and a governed class is incompatible with the first principles of freedom. Woman has not been a heedless spectator of the events of this century, nor a dull listener to the grand arguments for the equal rights of humanity. From the earliest history of our country woman has shown equal devotion with man to the cause of freedom, and has stood firmly by his side in its defense. Together, they have made this country what it is. Woman's wealth, thought and labor have cemented the stones of every monument man has reared to liberty.

And now, at the close of a hundred years, as the hour-hand of the great clock that marks the centuries points to 1876, we declare our faith in the principles of self-government; our full equality with man in natural rights; that woman was made first for her own happiness, with the absolute right to herself—to all the opportunities and advantages life affords for her complete development; and we deny that dogma of the centuries, incorporated in the codes of all nations—that woman was made for man—her best interests, in all cases, to be sacrificed to his will. We ask of our rulers, at this hour, no special favors, no special privileges, no special legislation. We ask justice, we ask equality, we ask that all the civil and political rights that belong to citizens of the United States, be guaranteed to us and our daughters forever.

# Constitutional Amendments

### Amendment XIII.

Section 1. Neither slavery not involuntary servitude, except as a punishment for crime whereof the party shall have been duly convicted, shall exist within the United States, or any place subject to their jurisdiction.

Section 2. Congress shall have power to enforce this article by appropriate legislation.

### Amendment XIV.

Section 1. All persons born or naturalized in the United States and subject to the jurisdiction thereof, are citizens of the United States and of the State wherein they reside. No State shall make or enforce any law which shall abridge the privileges or immunities of citizens of the United States; nor shall any State deprive any person of life, liberty, or property, without due process of law; nor deny to any person within its jurisdiction the equal protection of the laws.

Section 2. Representatives shall be apportioned among the several States according to their respective numbers, counting the whole number of persons in each State, excluding Indians not taxed. But when the right to vote at any election for the choice of electors for President and Vice President of the United States, Representatives in Congress, the Executive and Judicial offers of a State, or the members of the Legislature thereof, is denied to any of the male inhabitants of such State, being twenty-one years of age, and citizens of the United States, or in any way abridged except for participation in rebellion, or other crime, the basis of representation therein shall be reduced in the proportion which the number of such male citizens shall bear to the whole number of male citizens twenty-one years of age in such State.

Section 3. No person shall be a Senator or Representative in Congress, or elector of President and Vice President, or hold any office, civil or military, under the United States, or under any State, who, having previously taken an oath, as a member of Congress, or as an officer of the United States, or as a member of any State legislature, or as an executive or judicial officer of any State, to support the Constitution of the United States, shall have engaged in insurrection or rebellion against the same, or given aid or comfort to the enemies thereof. But Congress may by a vote of two-thirds of each House remove such disability.

Section 4. The validity of the public debt of the United States, authorized by law, including debts incurred for payment of pensions and bounties for services in suppressing insurrection or rebellion, shall not be questioned. But neither the United States nor any State shall assume or pay any debt or obligation incurred in aid of insurrection or rebellion against the United States, or any claim for the loss or emancipation of any slave; but all such debts, obligations and claims shall be held illegal and void.

Section 5. The Congress shall have power to enforce, by appropriate legislation, the provisions of this article.

## Amendment XV.

Section 1. The right of citizens of the United States to vote shall not be denied or abridged by the United States or by any State on account of race, color, or previous condition of servitude.

Section 2. The Congress shall have power to enforce this article by appropriate legislation.

# Summary of Litigation and Legislation, 1963–1990*

## 1963

The Equal Pay Act forbade discrimination in wages on the basis of race, color, religion, sex, or national origin for those engaged in the same work.

## 1964

The Civil Rights Act through Title VII prohibited employment based on race, color, religion, sex, or national origin. The same ace created the Equal Employment Opportunity Commission (EEOC).

## 1965

Executive Order No. 11246 prohibited employment discrimination by federal contractors on the same grounds as Title VII, except sex was not included.

Griswold v. Connecticut, 381 U.S. 479 (1965). The Supreme Court struck down a state law forbidding the use of contraceptives. This decision, along with the following one, laid the groundwork for later decisions extending access to contraceptives and the right to privacy in procreative matters that ultimately included abortion.

## 1967

Loving v. Virginia, 388 U.S. 1 (1967). This decision invalidated violations of the equal-protection clause and held that the "freedom to marry" was a "basic civil right of man."

* Not all of the cases or statutes mentioned in the text are summarized here. See the Index for a complete listing.

Executive Order No. 11375 added sex to the categories of people who could not be discriminated against by institutions with federal contracts over $10,000.

## 1969

Executive Order No. 11478 ordered federal agencies "to establish and maintain an affirmative-action program of equal opportunities for all civilian employees."

## 1971

Sail'er Inn, Inc. v. Kirby, 5 Cal. 3d 1. 20585 P. 2d 329 (1971). The California Supreme Court declared that women could tend bar equally with men.

Phillips v. Martin Marietta Corporation, 400 U.S. 542 (1971). The Supreme Court tentatively struck down the exclusion of women with preschool children from holding certain jobs.

Reed v. Reed, 404 U.S. 71 (1971). The Supreme Court for the first time invalidated state legislation that classified on the basis of sex by finally declaring that women were "persons" and that males could not arbitrarily be given preference as executors of estates. It established a middle or intermediate tier of scrutiny under the equal-protection clause for statutes discriminating solely on the basis of sex.

Griggs v. Duke Power Company, 401 U.S. 424 (1971). The Supreme Court held that under Title VII an employer may not use ostensibly "neutral" screening tests resulting in a disparate (unfavorable) impact on blacks if the tests do not demonstrate a reasonable indication of job performance, that is, "business necessity." The employer's intent to discriminate through the use of such tests does not need to be proven. The *Griggs* disparate-impact precedent was seriously undermined in the 1989 *Wards Cove v. Atonio* decision.

## 1972

Additional amendments extended Title VII to include all employers with fifteen or more workers and gave the EEOC greater power by allowing it to initiate suits.

Title IX of the Educational Amendments Act made it illegal to discriminate on the grounds of sex in all public undergraduate institutions and in most private and public graduate and vocational schools receiving federal monies.

After passing in the House of Representatives 354 to 23, and in the Senate 84 to 8, Congress sent the Equal Rights Amendment (ERA) to the states for ratification.

## 1973

Roe v. Wade, 410 U.S. 113 (1973). By a margin of seven to two, for the first time the Supreme Court legalized abortions during the first three months of pregnancy, based on the right of privacy between a woman and her doctor. This decision was reconsidered by the Court and undermined in the 1989 *Webster v. Reproductive Health Services* decision.

Frontiero v. Richardson, 411 U.S. 677 (1973). The Supreme Court struck down armed service regulations that had denied women the same dependents' benefits as men. However, only a plurality of the justices declared sex to be a suspect classification requiring close scrutiny.

Miller v. California, 413 U.S. 15 (1973). With this decision, the justices created the so-called LAPS test, saying that material is legal obscenity '(a) whether 'the average person, applying contemporary community standards' would find that the work, taken as a whole, appeals to the prurient interest . . . ; (b) whether the work depicts or describes, in a patently offensive way, sexual conduct specifically defined by the applicable state law; and (c) whether the work, taken as a whole, lacks serious literary, artistic, political, or scientific value."

## 1974

Cleveland Board of Education v. LaFleur, 414 U.S. 632 (1974). The Supreme Court held that a law requiring mandatory unpaid maternity leave was in violation of the due process of pregnant women.

Geduldig v. Aiello, 417 U.S. 484 (1974). The Supreme Court upheld a California disability insurance program denying benefits for pregnancy-related disabilities.

## 1975

Taylor v. Louisiana, 419 U.S. 522 (1975). The Supreme Court invalidated all remaining state laws restricting jury duty on the basis of gender.

## 1976

Craig v. Boren, 429 U.S. 190 (1976). With this case the Supreme Court heightened the "middle-tier" interpretation established in *Reed*, by declaring that sex-based classification must bear "substantial" relationship to an "important" government purpose.

General Electric Co. v. Gilbert, 429 U.S. 125 (1976). Relying heavily on *Geduldig,* the Supreme Court held that employers need not compensate women for maternity-related disabilities under employee insurance plans. Congress overruled this and similar decisions in 1977.

Runyon v. McCrary, 427 U.S. 160 (1976). The Supreme Court ruled that the 1866 Civil Rights Act (now 42 Section 1981 of the U.S. Code) permitted the right of action in private transactions involving racial discrimination. In 1989 this decision was reconsidered by the Court in *Paterson v. McLean Credit Union.*

Planned Parenthood v. Danforth, 428 U.S. 52 (1976). The Supreme Court continued to deny state challenges to first-trimester abortions as proclaimed in Roe v. Wade, 410 U.S. 113 (1973).

## 1977

International Brotherhood of Teamsters v. United States, 431 U.S. 324 (1977). In a series of related decisions, the Supreme Court undermined all affirmative-action programs and class-action lawsuits by upholding seniority plans in effect before July 1965.

Beal v. Doe, 432 U.S. 438 (1977). The Supreme Court ruled that states were not required to use public funds to perform abortions, thereby making it more difficult for poor women to benefit from *Roe* and other proabortion decisions.

The Equal Opportunity Reorganization Act further amended Title VII and broadened EEOC jurisdiction to include the Equal Pay Act, Executive Order No. 11246, and the Age Discrimination Act.

The Equal Credit Opportunity Act (ECOA), originally passed in 1975 as an amendment to the 1970 Consumer Credit Protection Act, finally became effective and should eliminate remaining credit discrimination against women if enforced upon states that have not already passed affirmative-action legislation extending equal credit to women.

The EEOC announced that it would narrowly interpret *Teamsters* in order not to undermine existing affirmative-action programs.

Legislation introduced in Congress to expand the definition of sex discrimination under Title VII in order to protect the rights of pregnant workers negatively affected by *Gilbert.*

Legislation introduced in Congress to provide better protection for victims of rape, aid for displaced homemakers, and retirement benefits for divorced or widowed spouses married at least twenty years.

## 1978

Congress extended the time limitation on the ERA, or the Twenty-seventh Amendment to the U.S. Constitution to 30 June 1982.

Bakke v. Regents of the University of California, 438 U.S. 265 (1978). The Supreme Court, in addressing but failing to settle the issue of "reverse discrimination," held that an absolute admissions quota was unlawful and, therefore, ordered Allan Bakke admitted to medical school, but it also held that race (and, presumably, gender) "may" be a factor considered in affirmative-action admissions programs.

Legislation introduced in Congress amending the Title VII definition of "sex" to include pregnancy and requiring that employers provide the same fringe benefits for pregnancy-related disabilities as for other disabilities, in an attempt to overrule *Gilbert*. This amendment, called the Pregnancy Discrimination Act (PDA), finally passed in 1978.

Los Angeles Department of Water and Power v. Manhart, 435 U.S. 702 (1978). The Supreme Court ruled that men and women must be treated equally with regard to retirement benefits. Women cannot be required to make larger monthly contributions in order to receive the same monthly benefits as men.

Santa Clara Pueblo v. Martinez, 436 U.S. 49 (1978). The Supreme Court ruled that tribal benefits were a matter of tribal sovereignty, and discrimination resulting from their application was not subject to constitutional jurisprudence under the Fourteenth Amendment.

## 1979

Personnel Administration of Massachusetts v. Feeney, 442 U.S. 256 (1979). The Supreme Court upheld an absolute lifetime veterans' preference in civil-service jobs, even though the Court knew that there had been a 2 percent quota on women in the military until 1967 and that the veterans' preference had a devastating impact on the employment opportunities of women.

Cannon v. The University of Chicago, 99 S. Ct. 1946 (1979). The Supreme Court held that there was a private right of action under Title VI and Title IX allowing individuals alleging discrimination by an educational institution to assert their rights through litigation.

## 1980

Harris v. McRae, 448 U.S. 297 (1980). The Supreme Court ruled that the Constitution does not require Medicaid to pay for medically necessary abortions, even though Medicaid pays for all other medically necessary procedures.

Pregnancy Discrimination Act (PDA) passed by Congress in 1978, stating somewhat ambiguously that employers cannot treat pregnancy *more or less* favorably than other worker disabilities. The interpretation of this wording has led different states and feminist groups to disagree over how the act should be applied.

## 1981

Michael M. v. Superior Court, 450 U.S. 464 (1981). This decision upheld the California statutory rape law making such intercourse a crime for men but not for women, on the grounds that it would prevent teen-age pregnancies and that since women were more at risk, that is, not "similarly situated," with men in sexual relations, the statute need not meet the more rigorous *Craig* standard.

Sandra Day O'Connor became the first female member of the Supreme Court of the United States.

Rostker v. Goldberg, 453 U.S. 57 (1981). The Supreme Court held that Congress's decision to authorize military draft registration of only men did not violate the due-process clause of the Fifth Amendment and that the exemption of women was closly related to the congressional purpose of providing combat troops, since women were not available for combat duty.

Kirchberg v. Feenstra, 450 U.S. 455 (1981). The Supreme Court invalidated a Louisiana statute making the husband "head and master" with sole control of community property owned jointly with his wife.

McCarty v. McCarty, 453 U.S. 210 (1981). The Supreme Court held that Congress designed the military pension to be the property of the serviceman, thereby denying the military wife any claim to it as part of a divorce settlement. Congress overruled this decision in 1982.

Economic Equity Act introduced in Congress. This was an omnibus bill proposing broad reforms in public and private pension law, in tax policy, and in insurance and government regulations to improve the economic status of women.

County of Washington v. Gunther, 452 U.S. 161 (1981). The Supreme Court for the first time narrowly acknowledged that comparable worth was a valid legal theory in finding that Title VII coverage applied even to situations in which no male employees performed substantially equal work for higher wages. Specifically, the Court held that the Bennett Amendment did not limit sex-based wage discrimination claims under Title VII (in this instance, on the part of female guards who were paid less than male guards) to equal-work claims.

## 1982

The Equal Rights Amendment officially died when the extended deadline ran out on 30 June, with only thirty-five out of the required thirty-eight states having ratified it.

Congress approved legislation that allowed state courts to divide military retirement benefits between the serviceperson and spouse in divorce settlements, thereby reversing the effect of *McCarty*.

By 1982, five federal circuit courts of appeal had held that sexual harassment that affects the terms and conditions of a woman's employment violates Title VII.

North Haven Board of Education v. Bell, 102 S. Ct. 1912 (1982). The Supreme Court ruled that Title IX bars six bias against employees of educational institutions as well as against students.

Mississippi University for Women v. Hogan, 102 S. Ct. 3331 (1982). The Supreme Court held that the university's refusal to let men into the school of nursing was unconstitutional because the policy "tends to perpetuate the stereotyped view of nursing as an exclusively woman's job" rather than compensation for discriminatory barriers faced by women.

## 1983

In January, Democrats reintroduced the ERA in Congress.

In a series of cases, the Supreme Court reaffirmed the constitutionality of the right to obtain an abortion and struck down an array of local legislative restrictions on access to abortions.

AFSCME v. State of Washington, 578 F. Supp. 846 (1983); rev., 770 F.2d 1401 (9th Cir. 1985). A federal district court ruled that the state had to compensate women for having been paid less than men in jobs of comparable worth.

## 1984

Grove City College v. Ball, 465 U.S. 555 (1984). The Supreme Court held that Title IX applied only to those departments or programs in a school that directly received federal funds—not to the entire institution—thus exempting many sports and other educational programs from equal-opportunity laws. Congress overruled this decision in 1988.

Hishon v. King and Spalding, 467 U.S. 69 (1984). The Supreme Court held for the first time that under Title VII law firms may not discriminate on the basis of sex in decisions as to which lawyers to promote as partners.

Roberts et al. v. United States Jaycees, 104 S. Ct. 3244 (1984). The Supreme Court ruled (seven to zero) that accepting women as members did not "abridge either the male members' freedom of intimate association or their freedom of expressive association." Any incidental abridgement of the Jaycees' protected speech was no greater than necessary in order for the government to exercise its compelling interest to prevent discrimination causing "unique evils."

In August, Congress approved both the Retirement Equity Act and the Child Support Enforcement Amendment. Both originated with the Economic Equity Act of 1981 and represented attempts to improve women's ability to receive retirement benefits under their husbands' or their own pension programs and to obtain court-ordered child-support benefits.

In October, the Civil Rights Restoration Act died by filibuster in the Senate. One segment of it would have overruled the narrow application of Title IX to schools and colleges set forth in *Grove City*. It has been reintroduced every year since 1984 and finally passed over a presidential veto in May 1988.

In November, the ERA failed again to obtain the necessary two-thirds vote in the House of Representatives.

Spaulding v. University of Washington, 676 F.2d 1232; 740 F.2d 686. At the end of the year, the Supreme Court refused to review a lower court (9th Cir. Court of Appeals) decision striking down a "comparable-worth" claim by the nursing faculty at the University of Washington.

## 1985

Palmer et al. v. Shultz, Civil 616 F. Supp. 1540, *rev'd.*, 815 F.2d 84 (D.C. Cir. 1987). The District Court for the District of Columbia ruled that female foreign-service officers failed to show by a preponderance of the evidence that the State

Department had practiced sexual discrimination in the assignments, promotions, performance evaluations, awards, and class-at-hire of women. The U.S. Court of Appeals for the District of Columbia Circuit reversed this decision in 1987 and remanded the case for further consideration. In 1989, the State Department was found guilty of discrimination against women.

EEOC v. Sears, Roebuck and Company, 504 F. Supp. 241; 628 F. Supp. 1264 (31 January 1986). The U.S. District Court for the Northern District of Illinois, Eastern Division, held that Sears had not demonstrated a pattern or practice of discrimination against women in hiring, promotion, or pay and that alleged statistical disparities between rank or salary of women and men were the result of "legitimate non-discriminatory reasons."

AFSCME v. State of Washington, 578 F. Supp. 846 (1983); revised, 770 F.2d 1401 (9th Cir. 1985). In a cursory opinion, the Ninth Circuit Court in San Francisco reversed the 1983 district court's decision that held the state liable under both disparate-treatment and disparate-impact analyses across the entire labor force and ordered the implementation of a comparable-worth plan as the remedy to this Title VII violation. In contrast, the Ninth Circuit said that the female plaintiffs had not proven discriminatory intent on the part of the state and that impact analysis could not apply to a compensation scheme based on the free market.

## 1986

American Booksellers Association, Inc. v. William H. Hudnut, III, Mayor, City of Indianapolis, 598 F. Supp. 1316 (1985), 771 F.2d 323 (7th Cir. 1985); aff'd., 175 U.S. 1001 (1986). Without issuing an opinion, the Supreme Court upheld two federal court rulings in 1984 and 1985 that dismissed the claim that pornography violated women's civil rights and declared the Indianapolis antipornography ordinance unconstitutional because it violated free speech under the First Amendment.

Wygant v. Jackson Board of Education, 476 U.S. 267 (1986). The Supreme Court rejected as unconstitutional an affirmative-action plan protecting less-senior minorities against job layoffs, without evidence of prior discrimination by the employer.

Thornburgh v. American College of Obstetricians and Gynecologists, 476 U.S. 747 (1986). The Supreme Court narrowly struck down (five to four) a Pennsylvania law, on the grounds that some of its provisions were designed to deter women from having abortions and others would require doctors to risk the health of pregnant women to save late-term fetuses.

Meritor Savings Bank v. Vinson, 477 U.S. 57 (1986). The Supreme Court ruled unanimously that sexual harassment of an employee by a supervisor violated the federal law against sex discrimination in the workplace. In this instance, a female bank employee had been forced by her supervisor to have repeated sexual relations, and the justices overruled a lower court that claimed this was not discrimination under Title VII.

Bowers v. Hardwick, 478 U.S. 186 (1986). Closely dividing five to four, the Supreme Court ruled that the Constitution does not protect homosexual relations between consenting adults in the privacy of their own homes, thus upholding a Georgia antisodomy law that imposed criminal penalties for homosexual sodomy. Justice Powell apparently joined the majority at the last moment after first indicating he was not in favor of such a statute.

## 1987

United States v. Paradise, 480 U.S. 149 (1987). In a close five-to-four decision, the Supreme Court ordered Alabama to promote one black state trooper for each white one to compensate for the state's previously extreme pattern of past discrimination.

Johnson v. Transportation Agency of Santa Clara County, California, 107 S. Ct. 1442 (1987). With this (six-to-three) decision, the Supreme Court approved sex-conscious promotions to redress gender imbalances in the work force, thus extending the same principle that had been applied to race-conscious promotions almost a decade earlier in Steelworkers v. Weber, U.S. 443 (1979), at 193.

California Federal Savings and Loan Association v. Guerra, 107 S. Ct. 683 (1987). In the first Pregnancy Disability Act case to be decided by the Supreme Court, the justices upheld a California law *requiring* employers to grant *unpaid* maternity leave to pregnant workers, thereby sanctioning "special treatment" of women.

Wimberly v. Labor and Industry Department, 107 S. Ct. 821 (1987). In this instance, the Supreme Court ruled against a Missouri woman who specifically requested "special treatment" by asking for unemployment benefits after she did not receive her old job back following a maternity leave.

Rotary International v. Rotary Club of Duarte, 107 S. Ct. 1940 (1987). In a decision reminiscent of the 1984 *Jaycees* case, the Supreme Court ruled (seven to zero) that Rotary International could not revoke the charter of the Rotary Club in Duarte, California, for admitting three women as members in 1977.

Pope v. Illinois, 107 S. Ct. 1918 (1987). This five-to-four decision (with its five separate opinions) eliminated one of the three component parts of the 1973 *Miller v. California* test for determining whether material is obscene—namely, community standards. Instead, the opinion stated that "the proper inquiry is not whether an ordinary member of any given community would find serious literary, artistic, political or scientific value in allegedly obscene material, but whether a reasonable person would find such value in the material, taken as a whole." Neither *Miller* nor *Pope* addressed the question of violent pornography.

## 1988

In March, Congress overrode a presidential veto to finally pass the Civil Rights Restoration Act overruling the 1984 Supreme Court decision in *Grove City*. This legislation broadened Title IX to generally prohibit discrimination throughout an entire institution or agency if any part of that institution or agency receives federal financial assistance. Although this law does prohibit discrimination by such institutions or agencies against persons who have had abortions, it contains an amendment allowing universities and hospitals receiving federal funds to refuse to perform or pay for abortions or abortion-related services.

Hicks v. Feiock, 485 U.S. 624 (1988). This eight-to-zero decision placed the burden of proof in all civil contempt-of-court cases involving child support on fathers who claimed that they were unable to pay.

New York State Club Association, Inc. v. New York City, 108 S. Ct. 2225 (1988). The Supreme Court upheld the New York City Human Rights Law prohibiting discrimination in certain private clubs found to be sufficiently nonprivate in nature.

Harigan v. In Zbaraz, *reh'g. denied,* 108 S. Ct. (1988). First heard in 1986, this case involved notice to parents of minors seeking abortions in Illinois. Instead of rehearing it, the justices decided to consider three other abortion cases they accepted after *Webster* in the fall term of the 1989–90 session (nos. 88-790, 88-805, and twin appeals 88-1125 and 88-1309). See chapter 8, note 92, and the decisions for 1990 below.

## 1989

City of Richmond v. J. A. Croson Co., 109 S. Ct. 706 (1989). By six to three, the justices declared unconstitutional a Richmond, Virginia, ordinance setting aside 30 percent of public-works contract spending for minority contractors. Such "set-aside" had been initiated twenty-five years before by executive order during the Nixon administration.

Price Waterhouse v. Hopkins, 109 S. Ct. 1775 (1989). In this six-to-three ruling involving a partnership denial, the Supreme Court ruled that in some cases alleging intentional discrimination, employers have the burden of proving that their refusal to hire or promote someone is based on legitimate and not discriminatory reasons. In the retrial a federal district judge in 1990 ordered Price Waterhouse to give a partnership to Ann B. Hopkins—a position denied her in 1983. Price Waterhouse appealed this decision.

Wards Cove Packing Co, Inc. v. Atonio, 109 S. Ct. 2115 (1989). By five to four, the Supreme Court reversed the eighteen-year-old "disparate-impact" precedent set by *Griggs v. Duke Power Company* in 1971 and ruled that employees, not employers, have the burden of proving whether a job requirement that is shown statistically to screen out minorities or women is a "business necessity."

Lorance v. AT&T, 109 S. Ct. 2261 (1989). In a five-to-three decision involving a 1979 seniority program, the justices ruled that the female employees had brought their suit too late. For the first time, a limit of three hundred days was placed on filing complaints under Title VII.

Wayne Books, Inc. v. Indiana and Sappenfield v. Indiana, 109 S. Ct. 916 (1989). In these two decisions, the justices unanimously said that state Racketeer Influenced and Corrupt Organizations Act (RICO) statutes could not be used to seize entire inventories of adult book stores before such material had been found to be obscene. This decision marks the first time the Supreme Court had significantly limited the application of federal or state antiracketeering statutes that have been increasingly used in a wide variety of civil prosecutions since first enacted in 1970.

Sable Communications of California, Inc. v. Federal Communications Commission et al., 109 S. Ct. 2829 (1989). In a unanimous decision involving two cases challenging the 1988 congressional amendment to the 1934 communications act banning both obscene and indecent dial-a-porn messages, the Supreme Court declared that the statute was unconstitutionally broad.

Patterson v. McLean Credit Union, 109 S. Ct. 2363 (1989). In this case, the justices reconsidered *Runyon v. McCrary*. In a five-to-four decision, they decided to uphold their earlier (1976) decision but to limit the 1866 civil rights statute upon which it was based to only the "making" of private contracts, not their discriminatory implementation.

Webster v. Reproductive Health Services, 109 S. Ct. 3040 (1989). In this case involving public funding in Missouri for abortions and abortion counseling, the justices were asked to reconsider *Roe v. Wade*. In a split five-to-four decision with five different opinions, a plurality of the Court recognized the state's compelling interest in life from conception, eviscerated *Roe*'s trimester structure, and women's fundamental right of privacy to abortion by encouraging states to pass restrictive legislation, which, like Missouri's in this case, would make it more difficult for poor, rural women and teen-agers to obtain abortions.

## 1990

Hodgson v. Minnesota, No. 89-1125, 58 L. Wk. 4957 (1990). This five-to-four ruling produced five different opinions, with the Supreme Court ruling that a Minnesota law requiring that two parents be notified before a teen-ager could obtain an abortion was constitutional as long as the state provided the option of a judicial hearing in lieu of parental consent.

Ohio v. Akron Center for Reproductive Health, No. 88-805, 58 L. Wk. 4979 (1990). The justices held that the state law requiring notification of one parent before a teen-ager could obtain an abortion was constitutional, without addressing the issue of whether a judicial alternative (which the Ohio law cantained) was a necessary prerequisite for constitutionality.

Maryland v. Craig, No. 89-478 5 L. Wk. 5044 (1990). In this and a related decision in Idaho v. Wright, No. 89-260, 58 L. Wk. 5036, the Supreme Court held in five-to-four decisions that states may shield victims of child abuse by permitting them to testify on closed-circuit television rather than face in court those accused of abusing them.

Metro Broadcasting v. Federal Communications Commission (FCC), 58 L. Wk. 5053 (1990). The justices ruled in this five-to-four decision that two federal affirmative-action programs aimed at increasing minority (and, presumably, female) ownership of broadcast licenses were "benign race-conscious measures" and, therefore, constitutional. Additionally, the majority underscored its approval of a 1980 decision reserving 10 percent of federal funds for a public works program. The decision in Fullilove v. Klutznick, 448 U.S. 448 (1980) had been seriously questioned in the Court's 1989 *City of Richmond* ruling. In coming to this conclusion, the justices seemed to be saying that federally sponsored "special opportunities" were less likely to be struck down than city or state ones.

# 1989 Declaration of Interdependence

**When in the Course of Human Events,** it becomes necessary to create a new bond among the peoples of the earth, connecting each to the other, undertaking equal responsibilities under the laws of nature, a decent respect for the welfare of humankind and all life on earth requires us to Declare our Interdependence.

We recognize that humankind has not woven the web of life; we are but one thread within it. Whatever we do to the web, we do to ourselves. Whatever befalls the earth befalls also the family of the earth.

We are concerned about the wounds and bleeding sores on the naked body of the earth: the famine; the poverty; the children born into hunger and disease; the destruction of forests and fertile lands; the chemical and nuclear accidents; the wars and deaths in so many parts of the world.

It is our belief that man's dominion over nature parallels the subjugation of women in many societies, denying them sovereignty over their lives and bodies. Until all societies truly value women and the environment, their joint degradation will continue.

Women's views on economic justice, human rights, reproduction and the achievement of peace must be heard at local, national, and international forums, wherever policies are made that could affect the future of life on earth. Partnership among all peoples is essential for the survival of the planet.

If we are to have a common future, we must commit ourselves to preserve the natural wealth of our earth for future generations.

**As women we accept our responsibility and declare our intention to:**
- Link with others—young and old, women and men, people of all races, religions, cultures and political beliefs—in a common concern for global survival;
- Be aware in our private, public and working lives of actions we can take to safeguard our food, fresh water, clean air and quality of life;
- Make women's collective experiences and value judgments equal to the experiences and value judgments of men when policies are made that affect our future and future generations;

- Expose the connections between environmental degradation, greed, uncontrolled militarism and technology devoid of human values. Insist that human and ecological values take absolute precedence when decisions are made in national affairs;
- Change government, economic and social policies to protect the well-being of the most vulnerable among us and to end poverty and inequality;
- Work to dismantle nuclear and conventional weapons, build trust among peoples and nations, and use all available international institutions and networks to achieve common security for the family of earth.

We also declare that, whenever and wherever people meet to decide the fate of the planet, it is our intention to participate on an equal footing, with full and fair representation, equivalent to our number and kind on earth.

*Drawn from the words and philosophies of: The drafters of the U.S. Declaration of Independence (July 4, 1776); Chief Seattle to President Franklin Pierce (1855); Wangari Maathai, founder, Green Belt Movement, and Chair, National Council of Women of Kenya (1988); The UN Population Fund (1988); Women's Foreign Policy Council; The World Commission on Environment and Development (1987); Spiritual and Parliamentary Leaders Global Survival Conference, Oxford (April 1988).*

# Notes

## Introduction: Toward a Theory of Women's Legal History

1. See chapter 10 of this volume for more details about poststructural history discussed later in the Introduction and for a review of the theoretical debates over constructing a feminist jurisprudence that led me to this conclusion.
2. Ruth H. Bloch, "The Gendered Meanings of Virtue in Revolutionary America," *Signs* 13, no. 1 (Autumn 1987): 37–58. For further discussions of virtue and republicanism, see chapters 1, 2, and 3 of this volume.
3. Kathleen Barry, *Susan B. Anthony: A Biography of a Singular Feminist* (New York: New York University Press, 1988), p. 132.
4. Elizabeth Pleck, "Feminist Responses to 'Crimes Against Women,' 1868–1896," *Signs* 8, no. 3 (Spring 1983): 465–70 (quotation).
5. Joan Hoff, "Why Is There No History of Pornography?" in Susan Gubar and Joan Hoff, eds., *For Adult Users Only: The Dilemma of Violent Pornography* (Bloomington: Indiana University Press, 1989), pp. 17–46. In this essay on pornography I relied extensively on Michel Foucault's three-volume *History of Sexuality* and theories developed by radical feminists in the Critical Legal Studies movement.

   According to Michel Foucault, beginning in the seventeenth century a sense of sexuality slowly emerged until in the course of the nineteenth century, women (and to a lesser degree, children) became institutionalized objects of study as repositories of sexuality (not necessarily sex) from medical, psychological, legal, and socioeconomic points of view. As a result, sexuality (and adolescence) become problematized for society, and the word *pornography* (the word *erotica* did not yet exist) came into common usage. This transformation of sex into sexuality through pseudoscientific discourse meant that the more freedom that certain nineteenth- and twentieth-century privileged individuals had to speak about sex was, in fact, not a form of freedom of expression but rather only the freedom to speak about sexuality in ways that allowed them first to subordinate and relegate sex to purely biological functions, while alienating themselves physically from one another, and then allowing those in charge of socioeconomic and political institutions to turn private attitudes about sexuality into conduits of control. The most important of these was the invention of sexuality by male psychiatrists beginning with Freud. See Michel Foucault, *The History of Sexuality*, Vol. 1: *An Introduction* (New York: Vintage, 1980), pp. 115–31. (The original work was published in 1976.)
6. Foucault, *History of Sexuality*, 1: 53–73; and Elizabeth Lunbeck, " 'A New Generation of Women': Progressive Psychiatrists and the Hypersexual Female," *Feminist Studies* 13, no. 3 (Fall 1987): 513–44. While Estelle B. Freedman and John D'Emilio

document individual examples of capitalism's responsibility first for sexual repression in the nineteenth century and then for sexual liberation in the twentieth century, they do not deal specifically with the psychological or legal impact on women that accompanied the gradual transformation of sex into sexuality. Paying only lip service to Foucauldian theories about power and dissent, they almost always implicitly equate manifestations of sexual liberation with forms of social protest, instead of discussing them as subtle forms of social control with significant negative implications for women. See John D'Emilio and Estelle B. Freedman, *Intimate Matters: A History of Sexuality in America* (New York: Harper & Row, 1988), pp. 139–274. Moreover, the tenaciousness of male domination over sexual mores disguised as sexual liberation has become increasingly evident in recent years with the widespread distribution of violent pornographic representations of women. See chapter 9 of this volume; Hoff, "Why Is There No History of Pornography?" pp. 27–36; and Catharine A. MacKinnon, *Feminism Unmodified: Discourses on Life and Law* (Cambridge: Harvard University Press, 1987), pp. 51–61, 143–62.

7. For the function that fear plays in the consciousness of contemporary women, see chapters 9 and 10 in this volume. See also Robin L. West, "The Difference in Women's Hedonic Lives: A Phenomenological Critique of Feminist Legal Theory," *Wisconsin Women's Law Journal* 3 (1987): 90–93, 144 (quotation). For other examples of the silencing of women, see MacKinnon, *Feminism Unmodified,* pp. 16, 41, 130, 140, 181, 188–89, 190, 193–95, 209. See also chapter 3 in this volume for a discussion of how problematic the legal concept of "consensual freedom" has been for women, beginning with the colonial practice of private consultations with wives to obtain their consent to a variety of legal procedures, such as dower renunciations, and chapter 9 for a discussion of the "silencing" and the fearful aspects of contemporary pornography.

8. Paula Baker, "The Domestication of Politics: Women and American Political Society, 1780–1920," *American Historical Review* 89 (June 1984): 620–47. I do not accept Baker's general thesis in this article that women's participation in politics as nonvoters had domesticated the electoral process by 1920. However, the significant incremental changes in election procedures, which were largely the result of actions taken by male, not female, progressive reformers, combined with the initial introduction of packaged candidates, through print and radio media, that ultimately reduced the importance of grass-roots politics and, hence, the value of individual votes for both women and men during the interwar years.

9. Jan Zimmerman, *Once upon the Future: A Woman's Guide to Tomorrow's Technology* (London: Pandora, 1986); and *Washington Post,* 9 December 1988, p. A10 (miscarriages among video-display terminal [VDT] users); *New York Times,* 2 August 1988, pp. A1, A10 (employers' use of "protective exclusion" of pregnant and/or childbearing women from certain jobs), 13 June 1989, pp. A1, D5 (computers replacing human phone operators).

10. See chapter 9 in this volume.

11. For a discussion of how the moral and political vision of feminist women's history is being threatened by poststructural scholarship, see Judith M. Bennett, "Feminism and History," *Gender and History* 3 (Autumn 1989): 251–72; and chapter 10 of this volume.

12. Robert W. Gordon, "J. Willard Hurst and the Common Law Tradition in American Legal Historiography," *Law and Society Review* 10, no. 2 (Fall 1975): 51.

13. J. Willard Hurst, "Legal History: A Research Program," *Wisconsin Law Review* 3 (May 1942): 331.

14. Hurst himself acknowledged as much in a 1982 essay, in which he reviewed the current problems facing those writing what he was then calling the "social history of law" and what Robert W. Gordon has referred to "as the historical sociology of law." James Willard Hurst, "The State of Legal History," *Reviews in American History* 10, no. 4 (December 1982): 298; and Robert W. Gordon, "Historicism in Legal Scholarship," *Yale Law Review* 90 (1981): 1052.

15. Nancy F. Cott and Elizabeth H. Pleck, *A Heritage of Her Own: Toward a New Social History of American History* (New York: Simon & Schuster, 1979), p. 17.

16. Annette K. Baxter and Louise L. Stevenson, eds., *Women's History: Selected Reading Lists and Course Outlines from American Colleges and Universities* (New York: Markus Wiener, 1987), p. 3 (quotation). For a review of changes in the writing of women's history, see Nancy A. Hewitt, "Beyond the Search for Sisterhood: American Women's History in the 1980s." *Social History* 10, no. 3 (October 1985): 299–321; Linda K. Kerber, "Separate Spheres, Female Worlds, Woman's Place: The Rhetoric of Women's History," *Journal of American History* 75 (June 1988): 9–39; and Bennett, "Feminism and History," pp. 251–72.

17. A review of the development of feminist theory in the legal profession and law schools can be found in Clare Dalton, "Where We Stand: Observations on the Situation of Feminist Legal Thought," *Berkeley Women's Law Journal* 3 (1987–88): 1–13; and Christina Spaulding, "Anti-Pornography Laws as a Claim for Equal Respect: Feminism, Liberalism, and Community," *Berkeley Women's Law Journal* 4 (1988–89): 128–65. For more details, see chapters 1 and 10 of this volume.

18. Dalton, "Where We Stand," pp. 1–13; and Frances Olsen, "From False Paternalism to False Equality: Judicial Assaults on Feminist Community, Illinois, 1869–1895," *Michigan Law Review* 84, no. 7 (June 1986): 1522, n. 16 (quotation).

19. *Ms.*, May 1988, p. 12; and *New York Times*, 10 September 1987, p. 27, and 12 November 1988, p. 16.

20. Joan Wallach Scott, "Gender: A Useful Category of Historical Analysis," *American Historical Review* 91, no. 5 (December 1986): 1053–75; idem, "Deconstructing Equality-versus-Difference: Or, the Uses of Poststructural Theory for Feminism," *Feminist Studies* 14, no. 1 (Spring 1988): 36 (first quotation); idem, "Rewriting History," in Margaret Randolph Higonnet et al., eds., *Behind the Lines: Gender and the Two World Wars* (New Haven, Conn.: Yale University Press, 1987), p. 22 (second quotation); Lois Banner, "A Reply to 'Culture et Pouvoir' from the Perspective of United States Women's History," *JOURNAL OF WOMEN'S HISTORY* 1, no. 1 (Spring 1989): 104 (third and fifth quotations); Myra Dinnerstein, "Questions for the Nineties," *Women's Review of Books*, February 1989, p. 13; and Dalton, "Where We Stand," p. 11 (fourth and sixth quotations). For details, see also chapter 10 of this volume.

21. Karen Offen, "Defining Feminism: A Comparative Historical Approach," *Signs* 14, no. 1 (Autumn 1988): 119–57.

22. Ibid., p. 139.

23. Feminist attorneys usually refer to these differences as equal treatment and special

treatment. See Wendy W. Williams, "The Equality Crisis: Some Reflections on Culture, Courts, and Feminism," *Women's Rights Law Reporter* 7, no. 3 (Spring 1982): 175–200; and idem, "Equality's Riddle: Pregnancy and the Equal Treatment/Special Treatment Debate," *New York University Review of Law and Social Change* 13, no. 2 (1984–85): 325–80. See chapter 10 for details.

24. This is my interpretation of Donald G. Mathews and Jane Sherron de Hart, *ERA and the Politics of Cultural Survival: North Carolina* (New York: Oxford University Press, 1990).

25. Hewitt, "Beyond the Search for Sisterhood," p. 316. Like so many labor and economic historians, Hewitt believes that material conditions produce more diversity among women than gender characteristics produce commonality.

26. Offen, "Defining Feminism," p. 152. My current definition of feminism has also been informed by Janice G. Raymond, *Passion for Friends: Toward a Philosophy of Female Affection* (Boston: Beacon, 1986), pp. 207–9. For my original three-part definition, see Joan Hoff-Wilson, "The Illusion of Change: Women and the American Revolution," in Alfred F. Young, ed., *The American Revolution: Explorations in the History of American Radicalism* (De Kalb: Northern Illinois University Press, 1976), pp. 391–92. Nancy Cott has arrived at a similar tripartite definition in *The Grounding of Modern Feminism* (New Haven, Conn.: Yale University Press, 1987), pp. 4–5.

27. Offen, "Defining Feminism," p. 152.

28. For a discussion of "false paternalism" and "false equality," see Olsen, "From False Paternalism to False Equality, pp. 1518–41. Olsen uses the term *false paternalism* instead of *false protection* to describe arguments in decisions that purport to be taken on the basis of protecting women, when, in fact, they do not. (See also chapters 5 and 6 in this volume.) I believe that the word *protection* is a better illumination of this conservative ploy of liberal legalism than the word *paternalism,* but I have drawn heavily upon Olsen's article for the general idea, however, and have applied it to other than a thirty-year period in Illinois's legal history (as, indeed, Olsen encouraged her readers to do).

29. Michelle Perrot, "The New Eve and the Old Adam: Changes in French Women's Condition at the Turn of the Century," in Higonnet et al., *Behind the Lines,* p. 57.

30. Quoted in Anne E. Simon, "The Politics of Law: A Progressive Critique," *Women's Rights Law Reporter* 8, no. 3 (Summer 1985): 202–3. See chapter 1 in this volume for details about the current debate within historical circles over whether the "separate-sphere" concept remains a useful analytical tool.

31. For example, women since the *Bradwell* decision in 1873 to the 1981 draft decision in McCarty v. McCarty, 453 U.S. 210 (1981), have been sporadically falsely protected and, on occasion, accorded false equality as in Ritchie v. People, 155 Ill. 98, 40 N.E. 454 (1895), and in Adkins v. Children's Hospital of the District of Columbia, 261 U.S. 525 (1923). (See chapter 6 of this volume for details.) The Adkins decision not only distinguished enforcing maximum-hour legislation to protect women's health from guaranteeing them a minimum wage but also asserted that suffrage had so completely ended female inferiority that women no longer needed additional protection in the workplace. For the negative economic impact on women of no-fault divorce, see Lenore J. Weitzman, *The Divorce Revolution: The Unexpected Social and Economic Consequences for Women and Children in America* (New York: Free Press, 1985), pp. 323–56. For details on the equality question, see chapters 4, 7, 8, and 9 in this

volume and Kathleen A. Lahey, "Feminist Theories of (In)Equality," Elizabeth B. Clark, "Religion, Rights, and Difference in the Early Woman's Rights Movement," Diana Majury, "Strategizing in Equality," and Christine A. Littleton, "Equality across Difference: A Place for Rights Discourse"—all in *Wisconsin Women's Law Journal* 3 (1987): 5–58, 169–212.

32. Kenneth L. Karst, "Woman's Constitution," *Duke Law Journal* 3 (June 1984): 472 (quotation), 476.

33. Betty Friedan, "How To Get the Women's Movement Going Again," *New York Times Magazine*, 3 November 1985, p. 26; and Fox-Genovese, "Women's Rights," p. 354. For a discussion of radical pluralism from a socialist, but also a sexual, point of view, see Eisenstein, *Female Body and the Law*, pp. 4–5, 10–15, 23–24, 35–36, 157–58, 172, 191–200, 222–23.

34. See Carole Pateman, *The Sexual Contract* (Cambridge: Polity, 1988), pp. 1–18, 219–34. For different reasons why citizenship has been neglected in contemporary feminist theory, see Mary G. Dietz, "Context Is All: Feminism and Theories of Citizenship," *Daedalus* 116 (Fall 1987): 1–24. See also chapters 3, 5, 6, and 9 of this volume for a discussion of the meaning of both citizenship and consent for women in the United States since 1787.

35. I first developed this reperiodization for a Project '87 summer seminar in 1984. See Joan Hoff-Wilson, "Women and the Constitution," APSA *News for Teachers of Political Science* 46 (Summer 1985): 10–16; reprinted in Bertell Ollman and Jonathan Birnbaum, eds., *The United States Constitution: Two Hundred Years of Anti-Federalist, Abolitionist, Feminist, Muckraking, Progressive, and Especially Socialist Criticism* (New York: New York University Press, 1990).

## 1. The Masculinity of U.S. Constitutionalism

1. "Women and the Constitution: The Challenge," 11 February 1988, address by Barbara Jordan at First Ladies' Women and the Constitution Conference in Atlanta, Georgia. For the full text of Justice Marshall's address to the San Francisco Patent and Trademark Law Association in Maui, Hawaii, see *Signs* 13, no. 1 (Autumn 1987): 2–6. Historian Peter S. Onuf has concluded that "the historians' major function throughout the Bicentennial hoopla . . . has been to ward off the most egregious misuses of the past." Two other historians, Michael Kammen and Louis Harlan, have also criticized the excessively eulogistic nature of the work of Burger's Commission on the Bicentennial of the U.S. Constitution. See *OAH Newsletter*, May 1988, p. 4; and *New York Times*, 22 December 1987, p. 10.

2. Morton J. Horwitz, *The Transformation of American Law, 1780–1860* (Cambridge: Harvard University Press, 1977); idem, "The Rise of Legal Formalism," *American Journal of Legal History* 19, no. 4 (October 1975): 251–64; Robert Samuel Summers, *Instrumentalism and American Legal Theory* (Ithaca, N.Y.: Cornell University Press, 1982), pp. 11–38, 255–81 passim; Robert W. Gordon, "Historicism in Legal Scholarship," *Yale Law Journal* 90 (1981): 1017–56; Mark Tushnet, "Legal Scholarship: Its Causes and Cure," *Yale Law Journal* 90 (1981): 1205–23; Lawrence Meir Friedman, *A History of American Law* (New York: Simon & Schuster, 1973), pp. 567–95; Harry N. Scheiber, "American Constitutional History and the New Legal History: Comple-

mentary Themes in Two Modes," *Journal of American History* 68, no. 2 (September 1981): 337–50.

3. The best theoretical review of the critical-theory interpretation of U.S. law can be found in Roberto Mangabeira Unger, *The Critical Legal Studies Movement* (Cambridge: Harvard University Press, 1986). For individual examples of the ideas of this New Left school of thought, see David Kairys, ed., *The Politics of Law* (New York: Pantheon, 1982), Introduction, pp. 1–7, 281–309; a special double issue of the *Stanford Law Review* 36 (1984): 1–674; and Robert W. Gordon and William Nelson, "An Exchange of Critical Legal Studies," *Law and History Review* 6 (Spring 1988): 139–86. The critical legal theory movement contains four basic elements: (1) a rejection of the notion that an idealized juridical model exists from which only "bad" decisions deviate; (2) a recognition that democracy in the United States seldom exists for most people outside of the public sphere and that the public/private debate often masks control of the society by corporate or other powerful, but not popularly (or democratically) based interests; (3) a denial that the law is neutral or objective and disconnected from socioeconomic, cultural, and political forces; and (4) an insistence that the basic function of the law is to serve and rationalize the dominant ideology and political economy. Except for those who have been influenced by the critical legal studies movement, few legal historians have systematically analyzed the implications for women of a legal system that supports not only capitalism but also sexism. For a radical feminist critic of both liberal legalism and critical legal theory, see Robin West, "Jurisprudence and Gender," *The University of Chicago Law Review* 55, no. 1 (Winter 1988): 1–12, 50–58.

4. In addition to those liberal and radical feminist legal scholars cited in chapter 9 of this volume, see Isabel Marcus, "Feminist Legal Strategies: The Shoe that Never Fits," unpublished paper delivered at the Sixth Berkshire Conference on the History of Women, 1984, p. 11 (quoted with permission of author); Ann C. Scales, "Towards a Feminist Jurisprudence," *Indiana Law Journal* 56, no. 3 (1981): 375–444; Wendy W. Williams, "The Equality Crisis: Some Reflections on Culture, Courts, and Feminism," *Women's Rights Law Reporter* 7, no. 3 (Spring 1982): 175–200; and Heather Ruth Wishik, "To Question Everything: The Inquiries of Feminist Jurisprudence," *Berkeley Women's Law Journal* 1, no. 1 (Fall 1985): 64–77.

5. Judith Shklar, *Legalism* (Cambridge: Harvard University Press, 1964), p. 10.

6. Marcus, "Feminist Legal Strategies," p. 9 (first quotation); Anne E. Simon, "The Politics of Law: A Progressive Critique," *Women's Rights Law Reporter* 8, no. 3 (Summer 1985): 199 (second quotation). According to Marcus, to be "cognizable," that is, a legal case on claim "must be made by someone or something which has a 'legal personality.' " Moreover, if the case "will not lie," using traditional juridical standards, the action will be dismissed.

7. Robin West, "Pornography as a Legal Text: Comments from a Legal Perspective," in Susan Gubar and Joan Hoff, eds., *For Adult Users Only: The Dilemma of Violent Pornography* (Bloomington: Indiana University Press, 1989), p. 110 (quotations). Although West is primarily addressing pornography as a legal text in this essay, I believe some of her generalizations apply to all legal texts, as she indicates briefly on pages 118, 120 passim.

8. Ibid., pp. 112 passim; and idem, "Gender and Jurisprudence," p. 4 (quotation). Most socialist feminists continue to insist that men are constitutionally more sovereign than

women because of their class rather than their gender, ignoring the irrefutable masculinity of past and present U.S. jurisprudence so convincingly argued by radical feminist attorneys. An exception to this generalization can be found in Zillah R. Eisenstein, *The Female Body and the Law* (Berkeley: University of California Press, 1988), pp. 16–22, 42–78.

9. Carole Pateman, *The Sexual Contract* (Cambridge: Polity, 1988), pp. 19–117; Monique Wittig, "On the Social Contract," in Anja van Kooten Niekerk et al., eds., *Homosexuality, Which Homosexuality?* (London: GMP, 1989), pp. 239–49; Susan Moller Okin, *Women in Western Political Thought* (Princeton, N.J.: Princeton University Press, 1979), pp. 199–201; Lorenne M. G. Clark, "Women and John Locke: Who Owns the Apples in the Garden of Eden?" in Lorenne M. G. Clark and Lynda Lange, eds., *The Sexism of Social and Political Theory: Women and Reproduction from Plato to Nietzsche* (Toronto: University of Toronto Press, 1979), pp. 16–40; Melissa Butler, "Early Roots of Feminism: John Locke and the Attack on Patriarchy," *American Political Science Review* 72 (March 1979): 135–50; Kathleen A. Lahey, "The Canadian Charter of Rights and Pornography toward a Theory of Actual Gender Equality," *New England Law Review* 20 (1984–1985): 653–59; and Linda J. Nicholson, *Gender and History: The Limits of Social Theory in the Age of the Family* (New York: Columbia University Press, 1986), pp. 152–66.

10. Pateman, *Sexual Contract,* pp. 3, 11–12, 76–115, especially 82–100 (quotation at 90); and Gayle Graham Yates, ed., *Harriet Martineau on Women* (New Brunswick, N.J.: Rutgers University Press, 1985), p. 134. See chapter 10 of this volume for a discussion of this fundamental gender contradiction in Lockean contract theory as it relates to other basic contradictions of liberal legalism in general and is so cogently argued by Michael J. Sandel, *Liberalism and the Limits of Justice* (Cambridge: Cambridge University Press, 1982). The theoretical importance of recognizing such fundamental contradictions, rather than continuing to deny or ignore them, cannot be underestimated if women in the United States are to move beyond equality to equity in their legal status.

11. All U.S. courts now have equity jurisdiction stemming from equity procedures inherited from England during the colonial period. See chapters 3 and 4 of this volume for details. Equity as a form of justice has long been used as a way to reform or humanize substantive common law. It is in this broad sense of obtaining justice, therefore, that I am using the term here and not simply in the traditional sense of a form of jurisprudence largely concerned with making changes in the legal procedures that under common law have become unworkable and/or unjust. See Peggy A. Rabkin, *Fathers to Daughters: The Legal Foundation of American Emancipation* (Westport, Conn.: Greenwood, 1980), pp. 25–28.

12. See, for example, Michael Kammen, *A Machine that Would Go of Itself: The Constitution in American Culture* (New York: Knopf, 1986); and Leonard Levy, *Original Intent and the Framers of the Constitution* (New York: Macmillan, 1988).

13. Catharine A. MacKinnon, "Feminism, Marxism, Method, and the State: Toward Feminist Jurisprudence," in Sandra Harding, ed., *Feminism and Methodology* (Bloomington: Indiana University Press, 1987) (first quotation at 139); *New York Times,* 8 November 1987, p. A27, Op-Ed piece by New York University law professor Stephen Gillers and board member of New York ACLU; and *New York Times,* 24 November 1987, p. A22 (second quotation), letter to editor criticizing Gillers's Op-Ed piece by Laura Anne Silverstein, New York University Law Women Steering Committee;

Ellen Carol DuBois, "Outgrowing the Compact of the Fathers: Equal Rights, Woman's Suffrage, and the U.S. Constitution, 1820–1878," *Journal of American History* 74 (December 1987): 837 (third quotation); and Elizabeth Fox-Genovese, "Women's Rights, Affirmative Action, and the Myth of Individualism," *George Washington Law Review* 54 (January–March 1986): 354.

14. For a discussion of the most moderate of these alternatives, see Kenneth L. Karst, "Woman's Constitution," *Duke Law Journal* 3 (June 1984): 480–508. See also chapter 10 of this volume for a discussion of feminist jurisprudence.

15. Barbara Jordan, address to First Ladies Conference on the Constitution, Atlanta, 11 February 1988; and Eleanor Holmes Norton, "Equality and the Court," *Constitution*, Fall 1989, p. 19.

16. Eva R. Rubin, *The Supreme Court and the American Family: Ideology and Issues* (Westport, Conn.: Greenwood, 1986), pp. 66–67.

17. David Benjamin Oppenheimer, "Distinguishing Five Models of Affirmative Action," *Berkeley Women's Law Journal* 4 (1988–1989): 42–61; and Wendy W. Williams, "Equality Crisis," p. 180, n. 35.

18. J. R. Pole, *The Pursuit of Equality in American History* (Berkeley: University of California Press, 1978), pp. xii, 112–47, 289, 358; H. N. Hirsch, "The Threnody of Liberalism," *Political Theory* 14 (August 1986): 423–44, especially 423, 425; Kenneth Karst, "The Supreme Court 1976 Term-Forward: Equal Citizenship under the Fourteenth Amendment," *Harvard Law Review* 91 (1977): 1–5; and Christina Spaulding, "Anti-Pornography Laws as a Claim for Equal Respect: Feminism, Liberalism, and Community," *Berkeley Women's Law Journal* 4 (1988–1989): 151–54, 158–60.

19. Archibald Cox, *The Court and the Constitution* (Boston: Houghton Mifflin, 1987), pp. 327, 355–58.

20. Ibid., pp. 177 (quotation), 178, 306–7, 341.

21. Ibid., pp. 126, 317 (quotation), 326. For the complex reasons distinguishing fundamental rights from other kinds of suspect classifications, see John Hart Ely, "The Wages of Crying Wolf: A Comment on *Roe v. Wade*," *Yale Law Journal* 82, no. 5 (April 1973): 932; and Ruth Bader Ginsburg, "Women as Full Members of the Club: An Evolving American Ideal," *Human Rights* (American Bar Association) 6, no. 1 (1976): 1–21.

22. John Rawls, *A Theory of Justice* (Cambridge: Belknap Press of Harvard University Press, 1971), p. 302; James S. Coleman, "Rawls, Nozick, Educational Equality," *The Public Interest* 43 (Spring 1976): 121–22; Pateman, *Sexual Contract*, pp. 12, 41–43, 79, 205, 223. Pateman, in particular, points out how traditional Rawls's discussion of contract theory is in that, like others before him, Rawls accepts "patriarchal relations of subordination" (p. 42). For other evidence of the incoherence and contradiction in Rawls's liberal-individualist theory of the person, see Sandel, *Liberalism and the Limits of Justice*, pp. 60–67, 116–20, 147–52 passim.

23. Fox-Genovese, "Women's Rights," p. 359, n. 64; and Karst, "Woman's Constitution," p. 503, n. 216 (quotation).

24. Williams, "Equality Crisis," pp. 179–80, n. 35.

25. Ibid., pp. 488–89. United States v. Carolene Products Co., 304 U.S. 152 (1938), n. 4.

26. Pole, *Pursuit of Equality in American History*, pp. 287, 288; and Plessy v. Ferguson, 165 U.S. 537 (1896).

27. Pole, *Pursuit of Equality*, pp. 250, 293–324. By 1988 Pole had modified his views considerably about the efficacy of the "principle of interchangeability" for racial minorities but not necessarily for women. See idem, "Equality: An American Dilemma," in Leslie Berlowitz et al., eds., *America in Theory* (New York: Oxford University Press, 1988), pp. 69–83.

28. Joan Hoff-Wilson, "The Pluralistic Society," in The New York Public Library, *Censorship: Five Hundred Years of Conflict* (New York: Oxford University Press, 1984), pp. 110–12.

29. Clayton Koppes, "From New Deal to Termination," *Pacific Historical Review* 47 (March 1978): 564, n. 37 (quotation); Hugh Graham, *The Civil Rights Era: Origins and Development of National Policy, 1960–1972* (New York: Oxford University Press, forthcoming). Graham emphasizes the differences between the African-American and women's liberation movements, arguing that the feminist leadership by 1972 was demanding equal treatment for men and women, while black leaders called increasingly for racially different (what is often called "special") treatment to compensate for past discrimination. Although I agree with Graham's distinction for the 1970s, I believe that African-Americans and other racial groups started their post–World War II civil rights movements (like women) demanding the individual equal rights enjoyed by white males; only after some initial successes did they turn to a more collective and cultural approach to civil rights.

30. Kathleen A. Lahey, "Feminist Theories of (In)Equality," *Wisconsin Women's Law Journal* 3 (1987): 5 (second quotation), 23 (first quotation).

31. For example, "women's issues," according to Robin West, have reached a point where they "are crazy issues."

> Arguments for reproductive freedom, for example, are a little insane: pro-choice advocates can't explain the difference between reproductive freedom and infanticide; or how this right can possibly be grounded in the Constitution; or how it is that women can claim to be "nurturant" and at the same time show blatant disregard for the rights and feelings of fetuses. In fact . . . the abortion issue is increasingly used in ethics as well as constitutional law classrooms to exemplify the "irrationality" of individual moral commitment. Rape reform efforts are also a little insane. Rape reform efforts that aim to expand the scope of the defined harm are also perceived . . . as insane. Why would anyone possibly object to non-violent sex? Isn't sex always pleasurable? Feminist pornography initiatives are viewed as irrational, and the surrogate motherhood issue is no better. There's an air of irrationality around each of these issues.
>
> That air of irrationality is both real and feigned. The reason for the air of irrationality around particular, substantive feminist legal reform efforts . . . is that feminist legal reforms are by necessity advocated in a form that masks rather than reflects women's true subjective nature. This is hardly surprising: language, of course, constrains our descriptive options. But whether or not surprising, the damage is alarming, and we need to understand its root. . . . [W]e have tried to explain feminist reform efforts through the use of analogies that don't work and arguments that are strained. The result . . . is internally inconsistent, poorly reasoned, weak, and then vulnerable legal doctrine. (Robin West, "Jurisprudence and Gender," *University of Chicago Law Review*) 55, no. 1 [Winter 1988]: 69–70)

32. Theodore Stanton and Harriot Stanton Blatch, eds., *Elizabeth Cady Stanton as Revealed in Her Letters, Diary, and Reminiscences*, 2 vols. (New York: Harper & Brothers, 1922), 1:148 (quotation), 2:18–22.

33. Susan B. Anthony, "Homes of Single Women," October 1877, Anthony Papers,

Library of Congress; excerpts reprinted in Ellen Carol DuBois, ed., *Elizabeth Cady Stanton and Susan B. Anthony: Correspondence, Writings, Speeches* (New York: Schocken, 1981), pp. 146–51, quotations at 148. For representative statements by Mary Beard, see "A New Task for Social Democracy," *Equal Rights*, 6 July 1935, p. 140; and idem, *Woman as Force in History: A Study in Traditions and Realities* (New York: Macmillan, 1946), p. 151.

34. Robin West, "The Difference in Women's Hedonic Lives: A Phenomenological Critique of Feminist Legal Theory," *Wisconsin Women's Law Journal* 3 (1987): 90–93, 144 (quotation). For other examples of the silencing of women, see Catharine MacKinnon, *Feminism Unmodified: Discourses on Life and Law* (Cambridge: Harvard University Press, 1987), pp. 16, 41, 130, 140, 181, 188–89, 190, 193–95, 209. See also Carroll Smith-Rosenberg, *Disorderly Conduct: Visions of Gender in Victorian America* (New York: Knopf, 1985), pp. 252–305, 358, n. 127; and chapter 9 in this volume for the communication problems women had in the 1920s and still have today.

35. Karst, "Woman's Constitution," pp. 471, 472 (quotation), 475, 480, 487, 494, 501, 506; and Mary G. Dietz, "Context Is All: Feminism and Theories of Citizenship," *Daedalus* 116 (Fall 1987): 3–6.

36. Simon, "Politics of Law," p. 203. See also Joan Wallach Scott, "Deconstructing Equality-versus-Difference: Or, the Uses of Poststructural Theory for Feminism," *Feminist Studies* 14, no. 1 (Spring 1988): 33–50.

37. Robert W. Gordon, "New Developments in Legal Theory," in David D. Kairys, ed., *The Politics of Law: A Progressive Critique,* (New York: Pantheon, 1982), pp. 286–93 (quotation at 286, paraphrasing Antonio Gramsci's views on "hegemony" and at 287, discussing the law and other nonlegal "clusters of belief," which "convince people that all the many hierarchical relations in which they live and work are natural and necessary").

38. Richard D. Heffner, ed., Alexis de Tocqueville, *Democracy in America* (New York: Mentor, 1956): pp. 244, 246; and Linda K. Kerber, "Separate Spheres, Female Worlds, Woman's Place: Rhetoric of Women's History," *Journal of American History* 75 (June 1988): 9–10, 37–39. In this article, Kerber concluded that de Tocqueville's remarks about separate spheres were no longer considered valid by historians because he did not perceive that "political systems and systems of gender relations are reciprocal social constructions" (p. 39). I cannot think of any nineteenth-century social commentator who would pass this late twentieth-century poststructural test.

39. Mary Beth Norton, "The Evolution of White Women's Experience in Early America," *American Historical Review* 89 (June 1984): 617 (quotation). See also chapter 3 of this volume.

40. Ruth H. Bloch, "The Gendered Meanings of Virtue in Revolutionary America," *Signs* 13, no. 1 (Autumn 1987): 37–58; Karst, "Woman's Constitution," pp. 494 (quotation), 451–60.

41. Bloch, "Gendered Meanings of Virtue," pp. 38–47; Jan Lewis, "The Republican Wife: Virtue and Seduction in the Early Republic," *William and Mary Quarterly,* 3d ser., 44 (1987): 699, 701.

42. Linda K. Kerber, "The Republican Ideology of the Revolutionary Generation," *American Quarterly* 37, no. 4 (Fall 1985): 484, 486; idem, *Women of the Republic: Intellect and Ideology in Revolutionary America* (Chapel Hill: University of North Carolina Press), pp. 284–85; idem, "Can a Woman Be an Individual? The Limits of Puritan

Tradition in the Early Republic," *Texas Studies in Literature and Language* 25, no. 4 (Winter 1983): 171–76; Joan R. Gunderson, "Independence, Citizenship, and the American Revolution," *Signs* 13, no. 1 (Autumn 1987): 72–77; Kerber, "Separate Spheres," pp. 19–26, 37–39; and Linda Grant De Pauw, "The American Revolution and the Rights of Women: The Feminist Theory of Abigail Adams," in Larry R. Gerlach et al., eds., *Legacies of the American Revolution* (Logan: Utah State University Press, 1978), pp. 199–219.

43. Linda J. Nicholson, "Feminist Theory: The Private and the Public," in Carol C. Gould, ed., *Beyond Domination: New Perspectives on Women and Philosophy* (Towata, N.J.: Rowman & Allanheld, 1983), p. 228 (quotation); and Pateman, *Sexual Contract*, pp. 77–115. As Marilyn Arthur has noted, "this praise of women in the marriage relationship does not invalidate the idea that the fundamental attitude of the Greeks toward women remained misogynistic. As social beings, women in the polis entered into a partnership with men that fostered civilization, and only in this relationship did women gain favor." See Marilyn Arthur, " 'Liberated' Women: The Classical Era," in Renate Bridenthal and Claudia Koonz, eds., *Becoming Visible: Women in European History* (Boston: Houghton Mifflin, 1977), p. 73. See chapter 3 of this volume for a discussion of revolutionary praise for republican wives and mothers.

44. Arthur, " 'Liberated' Women," pp. 60–89; and Nicholson, *Gender and History,* pp. 51–56, 120 (quotation).

45. Lewis, "Republican Wife," pp. 689 (quotation), 690, 701.

46. I use modernization theories in my discussion of the changing legal and socioeconomic status of women in chapters 2 and 4. Modernization theories were first applied to developing nations in an attempt to anticipate changes and reactions to modern technology and the introduction of Western social and political concepts. For bibliographies and explanations of these theories, see *A Conference Report on the Role of Ideas in American Foreign Policy* (Hanover, N.H.: University Press of New England, 1971), pp. 54–58; Nancy F. Cott, *The Bonds of Womanhood* (New Haven, Conn.: Yale University Press, 1977), p. 3; Richard Jensen, "Modernization and Community History" (unpublished Newberry Paper), January 1978. These theories were critically scrutinized when first applied generally to broad periods of early American history. See James A. Henretta, "Modernization: Toward a False Synthesis," *Reviews in American History* 5 (December 1977): 445–52, for a critical analysis of Richard D. Brown, *Modernization: The Transformation of American Life, 1600–1863* (New York: Hill & Wang, 1976). For general surveys of modernization theories in relation to Third World women, see Irene Tinker and Michele B. Bramsen, eds., *Women and World Development* (Washington, D.C.: American Association for the Advancement of Science, 1976); and Mayra Bivinic, *Women and World Development: An Annotated Bibliography* (Washington, D.C.: American Association for the Advancement of Science, 1976). For recent studies portraying Third World women as victims of modernization, see Lucy E. Creevey, ed., *Women in Africa: Rural Development in Mali and the Sahel* (Syracuse, N.Y.: Syracuse University Press, 1986); Marja-Lisa Swantz, *Women in Development* (London and New York: C. Hurst, 1985); Regina Smith Oboler, *Women, Power, and Economic Change: The Nandi of Kenya* (Stanford, Calif.: Stanford University Press, 1985); and E. Frances White, *Sierra Leone's Settler Women Traders: Women on the Afro-European Frontier* (Ann Arbor: University of Michigan Press, 1987).

47. Nicholson, "Feminist Theory," p. 229 (quotation); Kenneth A. Lockridge, "Social Change and the Meaning of the American Revolution," *Journal of Social History* 6 (Summer 1973): 403–39; and Gordon Wood, "Rhetoric and Reality in the American Revolution," *William and Mary Quarterly* 23 (January 1966): 3–31.

48. The term *deputy husband* is discussed in Laurel Thatcher Ulrich, *Good Wives: Image and Reality in the Lives of Women in Northern New England, 1650–1750* (New York: Knopf, 1982), pp. 35–49.

49. Kathleen Barry, *Susan B. Anthony: A Biography of a Singular Feminist* (New York: New York University Press, 1988), p. 260. For a discussion of the various meanings of "the personal is political," see Carol C. Gould, "Private Rights and Public Virtues: Women, the Family, and Democracy," and Nicholson, "Feminist Theory," both in Carol C. Gould, *Beyond Domination*, pp. 3–18, 221–30, especially at 9 and 225–26; and see also chapters 2, 3, 4, and 5 of this volume.

50. Karst, "Woman's Constitution," pp. 475, 480, 487, 494, 501, 506; and Dietz, "Context Is All," pp. 3–6.

51. Kerber, "Separate Spheres," pp. 9–39, especially 37–39; and Joan Wallach Scott, "Gender: A Useful Category of Analysis," *American Historical Review* 91, no. 5 (1986): 1061–66.

52. See the latest assessments on these issues by Arlie Hochschild, *The Second Shift* (New York: Viking, 1989); Sara M. Evans and Barbara J. Nelson, *Wage Justice: Comparable Worth and the Paradox of Technocratic Reform* (Chicago: University of Chicago Press, 1989); and *New York Times*, 20, 21, 22 August 1989, pp. 1, A6, 1, A14, 1, A18 (women's work inside and outside the home).

53. I find the works of de Beauvoir, Foucault, and Kappeler more enlightening for a common-sense appreciation of self-other and object-relations theories than the studies by psychologists.

54. Carol Gilligan, *In a Different Voice: Psychological Theory and Women's Development* (Cambridge: Harvard University Press, 1982); Mary Daly, *Pure Lust: Elemental Feminist Philosophy* (Boston: Beacon, 1984); West, "Jurisprudence and Gender," pp. 68–70; and idem, "Women's Hedonic Lives," pp. 90–93. The most extensive use of Gilligan's theories about female moral development and its potential for restructuring the constitutional jurisprudence of rights can be found in Karst, "Woman's Constitution," pp. 448, n. 5, 486–508 passim.

55. Scott, "Gender," p. 1065 (quotation). For the best discussion of the strengths and weaknesses of Gilligan's book and her contention that there are significant differences between male and female moral development due to socialization, see Irene Diamond and Lee Quinby, eds., *Feminism and Foucault: Reflections on Resistance* (Boston: Northeastern University Press, 1988). See especially essays by Martin, Jones, Woodhull, and Diamond and Quinby. Also useful are Elizabeth Spellman, *Inessential Woman: Problems of Exclusion in Feminist Thought* (Boston: Beacon, 1988); "On *In a Different Voice*: An Interdisciplinary Forum," *Signs* 11, no. 2 (Winter 1986): 304–33; James C. Walker, "In a Diffident Voice: Cryptoseparatist Analysis of Female Moral Development," *Social Research* 50, no. 3 (Autumn 1983): 665–95; Judy Auerbach, "Commenting on Gilligan's *In a Different Voice*," *Feminist Studies* 11, no. 1 (Spring 1985): 149–161; and Karst, "Woman's Constitution," pp. 461–62, 483–84, 487–90, 494–96.

56. See the Introduction and chapter 10 in this volume, pp. 350–56.

57. Marcus, "Feminist Legal Strategies," p. 6 (first quotation); Scott, "Deconstructing

Equality-versus-Difference," p. 36 (second quotation); West, "Jurisprudence and Gender," pp. 1–72, especially pp. 4–42; Gilligan, *In a Different Voice*, pp. 16, n. 56, 18–23, 62; and West, "Women's Hedonic Lives," pp. 94, 100, 105. Feminist jurisprudence is discussed in chapter 10 of this volume.

58. Karst, "Woman's Constitution," pp. 481 (first quotation), 482 passim; Simon, "Politics of Law," pp. 200, 203 (second and third quotations); Diane Polan, "Toward a Theory of Law and Patriarchy," in Kairys, ed., *Politics of Law*, p. 298; and West, "Jurisprudence and Gender," pp. 15–20.

59. Karst, "Woman's Constitution," pp. 480–508; Carrie Menkel-Meadow, "Portia in a Different Voice: Speculations on a Woman's Lawyering Process," *Berkeley Women's Law Journal* 1, no. 1 (Fall 1985): 39–63; West, "Jurisprudence and Gender," pp. 58–72; and idem, "Love, Rage, and Legal Theory," *Yale Journal of Law and Feminism* 1, no. 1 (Spring 1989): 101–10.

60. Hilda L. Smith, "Are We Ready for a Comparative Historiography of Women?" *JOURNAL OF WOMEN'S HISTORY* 1, no. 1 (Spring 1989): 99. See also chapter 10 of this volume for details about feminist jurisprudence. Some male lawyers in the Critical Legal Studies movement are not optimistic that disadvantaged groups can ever rise above "legal traps" through "legal rights" to obtain equality of results. See Duncan Kennedy, "Legal Education as Training for Hierarchy"; Alan D. Freeman, "Antidiscrimination Law: A Critical Review"; Robert W. Gordon, "New Developments in Legal Theory," all in Kairys, ed., *The Politics of Law*, pp. 40–64, 96–116, 281–93.

61. I am using the terms "are" and "have" in the way that Sandel uses them to describe the constitutive conception of community that I believe women already possess to a large degree in contrast to the liberal male sense of community.

> . . . to say that the members of a society are bound by a sense of community is not simply to say that a great many of them profess communitarian sentiments and pursue communitarian aims, but rather that they conceive their identity—the subject and not just the object of their feeling and aspirations—as defined to some extent by the community of which they are a part. For them, community describes not just what they *have* as fellow citizens but also what they *are*, not a relationship they choose (as in a voluntary association) but an attachment they discover, not merely an attribute but a constituent of their identity. In contrast to the instrumental and sentimental conceptions of community, we might describe this strong view as the constitutive conception. (Sandel, *Liberalism and the Limits of Justice*, p. 150)

62. Marcus, "Feminist Legal Strategies," p. 10.
63. Williams, "Equality Crisis," p. 200.
64. Marcus, "Feminist Legal Strategies," pp. 12–16; Alice Kessler-Harris, "The Debate over Equality for Women in the Workplace: Recognizing Differences," in Laurie Larwood et al., eds., *Women and Work: An Annual Review* (Beverly Hills: Sage, 1985), 1:153–54.
65. Marcus, "Feminist Legal Strategies," p. 15.

## 2. Women and the American Revolution

Segments of this chapter first appeared in Joan Hoff-Wilson, "The Illusion of Change: Women and the American Revolution," in Alfred F. Young, ed., *The American Revolution: Explorations in the History of American Radicalism* (De Kalb: Northern Illinois University

Press, 1976), pp. 383–445; and Joan Hoff-Wilson and Sharon L. Bollinger, "Mercy Otis Warren: Playwright, Poet, and Historian of the American Revolution," in J. R. Brink, ed., *Female Scholars: A Tradition of Learned Women Before 1800* (Montreal: Eden, 1980), pp. 161–82.

1. Kenneth J. Vandevelde, "The New Property of the Nineteenth Century: The Development of the Modern Concept of Property," *Buffalo Law Review* 29, no. 2 (Spring 1980): 329–30; Cathy Matson and Peter Onuf, "Toward a Republican Empire: Interest and Ideology in Revolutionary America," *American Quarterly* 37, no. 4 (Fall 1985): 498 (second quotation); and Joan R. Gunderson, "Independence and Citizenship: Ideology and Women during the Era of the American Revolution," *Signs* 13, no. 1 (Autumn 1987): 72–74.

2. Linda K. Kerber, *Women of the Republic: Intellect and Ideology in Revolutionary America* (Chapel Hill: University of North Carolina Press, 1980), pp. 269–88; idem, "The Republican Mother: Women and the Enlightenment—An American Perspective," *American Quarterly* 28 (Summer 1976): 187–205; and Jan Lewis, "The Republican Wife," *William and Mary Quarterly*, 3d ser., 44 (1987): 689–721.

3. Ruth H. Bloch, "The Gendered Meanings of Virtue in Revolutionary America," *Signs* 13, no. 1 (Autumn 1987): 37–58.

4. Jane Abray, "Feminism and the French Revolution," *American Historical Review* 80 (February 1975): 43–62; Carol R. Berkin and Clara M. Lovett, eds., *Women, War, and Revolution* (New York: Holmes & Meier, 1980), pp. 79–258; Marie Marmo Mullaney, *Revolutionary Women: Gender and the Socialist Revolution Role* (New York: Praeger, 1983), pp. 1–11, 243–75; and Margaret Randolph Higonnet et al., eds., *Behind the Lines: Gender and the Two World Wars* (New Haven, Conn.: Yale University Press, 1987), pp. 51–60, 99–113, 260–71, 272–84.

5. For information on the roles played by camp followers who may have numbered as many as twenty thousand, see Charles Royster, *A Revolutionary People at War: The Continental Army and the American Character, 1775–1783* (Chapel Hill: University of North Carolina Press, 1979), pp. 59–61; Barton C. Hacker, "Women and Military Institutions in Early Modern Europe: A Reconnaissance," *Signs* 6 (Summer 1981): 643–71; Walter Hart Blumenthal, *Women Camp Followers of the American Revolution* (Philadelphia: George S. McManus, 1952), pp. 58–66, 72–79; and Sally Smith Booth, *Women of '76* (New York: Hastings House, 1973), pp. 181–88.

6. For a general review of the varied roles played by women during the American Revolution, see Linda K. Kerber, " 'History Can Do It No Justice': Women and the Reinterpretation of the American Revolution," in Ronald Hoffman and Peter J. Alpert, eds., *Women in the Age of the American Revolution* (Charlottesville: University Press of Virginia, 1989), pp. 3–42. For the devastating impact of war, inflation, and depression on colonial and revolutionary America, see Billy G. Smith, "The Material Lives of Laboring Philadelphians, 1750 to 1800," *William and Mary Quarterly*, 3d ser., 38 (1981): 163–202; Carole Shammas, "The Female Social Structure of Philadelphia in 1775," *Pennsylvania Magazine of History and Biography* 107 (1983): 69–84; and Gary B. Nash, *The Urban Crucible: Social Change, Political Consciousness, and the Origins of the American Revolution* (Cambridge: Harvard University Press, 1979), pp. 59–83, 246–56, 325–36. See also Virginia Bever Platt, "The Working Women of Newport,

Rhode Island," paper delivered at 1975 Conference on Women in the Era of the American Revolution, pp. 8, 11, 13; Elizabeth Cometti, "Inflation in Maryland," *William and Mary Quarterly*, 3d ser., 8 (1951): 228–33, 234; L. H. Butterfield and Marc Friedlander, eds., *Adams Family Correspondence*, 4 vols. (Cambridge: Harvard University Press, Belknap, 1963) (hereafter cited as *AFC*), 2:212, 4:7, 296; and "Extracts from the Journal of Mrs. Henry [Elizabeth] Drinker, of Philadelphia, from September 25, 1777, to July 4, 1778," *Pennsylvania Magazine* 13 (1889): 300, 301.

7. The role and attitude about war on the part of women has generally been misinterpreted in twentieth-century reproductions of this woodcut of an armed female partisan, which, according to Laurel Ulrich, probably is more a religious artifact of the war than a patriotic one. It is not even exclusively a product of the American Revolution, having been used on other broadsides before 1776—sometimes derisively, sometimes seriously, as a depiction of female resolve on a variety of issues. For more details about it, see Laurel Thatcher Ulrich, " 'Daughters of Liberty': Religious Women in Revolutionary New England," in Hoffman and Alpert, eds., *Women in the Age of the American Revolution*, pp. 228–36 (quotation at 235).

8. Kenneth A. Lockridge, "Social Change and the Meaning of the American Revolution," *Journal of Social History* 6, no. 1 (Summer 1973): 404, 424, 426–27, 433, 435.

9. Three excellent examples of a gendered analysis of revolutionary rhetoric can be found in Bloch, "Gendered Meanings of Virtue," and Gunderson, "Independence and Citizenship," pp. 37–78; and Ulrich, "Daughters of Liberty," pp. 211–43.

10. Lockridge, "Social Change and the Meaning of the American Revolution," p. 424 (quotations); Gordon S. Wood, "Rhetoric and Reality in the American Revolution," *William and Mary Quarterly* 23 (January 1966): 31 passim; Bernard Bailyn, *The Ideological Origins of the American Revolution* (Cambridge: Harvard University Press, Belknap, 1967), pp. viii–ix, 160–229; Edwin G. Burrows and Michael Wallace, "The American Revolution: The Ideology and Psychology of National Liberation," *Perspectives in American History* 7 (1972): 268–94.

11. Bloch, "Gendered Meanings of Virtue," p. 38 (first quotation); and Thomas Paine, "An Occasional Letter on the Female Sex," *Pennsylvania Magazine*, 1 August 1775, p. 364 (second quotation).

12. Barbara H. Solomon and Paula S. Berggren, eds., *A Mary Wollstonecraft Reader* (New York: New American Library, 1983), pp. 289, 290–97, 364.

13. Bloch, "Gendered Meanings of Virtue," p. 54 (quotation) passim; and Matson and Onuf, "Toward a Republican Empire," pp. 496–516.

14. *AFC*, 1:85–87, 2:93–94, 391–92, 3:52–55, 4:75, 184, 328–31, 344; Anne H. Sherrill, "Abigail Adams and the American Enlightenment," paper delivered at University of San Francisco Symposium, August 1974, p. 23; Susan Groag Bell and Karen M. Offen, eds., *Women, the Family, and Freedom: The Debate in Documents* (Stanford, Calif.: Stanford University Press, 1983), p. 71; and Margaret Fisher, "Eighteenth-Century Theorists of Women's Liberation," in Carol V. R. George, ed., *"Remember the Ladies": New Perspectives on Women in American History* (Syracuse, N.Y.: Syracuse University Press, 1975), p. 40.

15. Mercy Otis Warren, *History of the Rise, Progress, and Termination of the American Revolution: Interspersed with Biographical, Political, and Moral Observations* (Boston: Manning and Loring, 1805), 3 vols. passim, but especially 3:413–36; Thomas Woody,

A *History of Women's Education in the United States* (New York: Science Press, 1929), 1:135; Mary Sumner Benson, *Women in Eighteenth-Century America: A Study in Usage and Opinion* (London: P. S. King & Son, 1966), p. 263.

16. *AFC*, 1:87; Mercy Otis Warren to Rebecca Otis, n.d., 1776, "Letter-Book," Mercy Otis Warren Papers, Massachusetts Historical Society, Boston (hereafter cited as "Letter-Book," Warren Papers); Lucy Martin Donnelly, "The Celebrated Mrs. Macauley," *William and Mary Quarterly*, 3d ser., 40 (1949): 181–82.

17. James A. Henretta, "Society and Republicanism: America in 1787," *this Constitution* 15 (Summer 1987): 22–23. Jan Lewis has also noted the tendency of historians to overstate Kerber's original thesis about republican motherhood. See Lewis, "Republican Wife," p. 690, n. 2.

18. Winthrop Jordan, "On the Bracketing of Blacks and Women in the Same Agenda," p. 280 (quotations); Elaine F. Crane, "Dependence in the Era of Independence," pp. 256–58; both in Jack P. Greene, ed., *The American Revolution: Its Characters and Limits* (New York: New York University Press, 1987); and Linda K. Kerber, " 'May All Our Citizens Be Soldiers, and All Our Soldiers Citizens': The Ambiguities of Female Citizenship in the New Nation," in Joan R. Challinor and Robert L. Beisner, eds., *Arms at Rest: Peacemaking and Peacekeeping in American History* (Westport, Conn.: Greenwood, 1987), p. 16.

19. Amelia Day Campbell, "Women in New York State in the Revolution," *Quarterly Journal of the New York State Historical Association* 3 (July 1922): 155.

20. Lockridge, "Social Change and the Meaning of the American Revolution," p. 426.

21. Bloch, "Gendered Meanings of Virtue," p. 57.

22. Eliza Southgate Bowne, *A Girl's Life Eighty Years Ago* (New York: Charles Scribner's Sons, 1887), pp. 60–61; Carol Ruth Berkin, "Conjurer's Circle: Women in Colonial America," University Programs Modular Studies (Morristown, N.J.: General Learning Press, 1974), p. 17; Linda K. Kerber, "Daughters of Columbia: Educating Women for the Republic, 1787–1805," in Stanley Elkins and Eric McKitrick, eds., *The Hofstadter Aegis: A Memorial, 1916–1970* (New York: Knopf, 1974), pp. 49–55; and idem, "Ambiguities of Female Citizenship," pp. 15–17. For descriptions of woman's "proper sphere" according to theories of the Enlightenment based on natural law, see Holt Carleton Marlow, "The Ideology of the Woman's Movement, 1750–1860" (Ph.D. dissertation, University of Oklahoma, 1966), pp. 7–15, 100–123; Benson, *Women in Eighteenth-Century America*, pp. 11–33, 100–103; Abray, "Feminism and the French Revolution," p. 52. For women's fears about exceeding their "proper spheres," see *AFC*, 2:109–10; Elizabeth F. Ellet, *The Women of the American Revolution* (New York: Baker & Scribner, 1848–50), 1:84–85; Katherine Anthony, *First Lady of the Revolution: The Life of Mercy Otis Warren* (Garden City, N.Y.: Doubleday, 1958), pp. 32–33, 188; Charles F. Adams, ed., *Correspondence between John Adams and Mercy Warren* (New York: Arno Press, 1972), p. 485; and Caroline Gilman, ed., *Letters of Eliza Wilkinson*, (Samuel Colman edition, 1839; reprint, New York: Arno, 1969), pp. 61, 66.

23. Alice Morse Earle, *Home Life in Colonial Days* (New York: Macmillan, 1898), p. 253; Royster, *Revolutionary People at War*, pp. 30–31, 135–36, 201, 295–97; Miriam Schnier, "Women in the Revolutionary Economy," paper delivered April 1975, Organization of American Historians Convention, pp. 15–17; and Hoff-Wilson, "Illusion of Change," pp. 410–11, 419–26.

24. *Pennsylvania Gazette*, 6 June 1787, p. 2; Lockridge, "Social Change and Meaning of the Revolution," p. 425. See also *Pennsylvania Packet*, 7 August 1775, p. 1.

25. *AFC*, 3:380; William Raymond Smith, *History as Argument: Three Patriot Historians of the American Revolution* (The Hague: Mouton, 1966), p. 117 (quotation); Mollie Somerville, *Women and the American Revolution* (Judd & Detweiler, 1974), pp. 18–22; Alice Morse Earle, *Colonial Dames and Good Wives* (1895; reprint, New York: Frederick Ungar, 1962), pp. 251–53; Eugenie Andruss Leonard, *Dear-Bought Heritage* (Philadelphia: University of Pennsylvania Press, 1965), pp. 548–59, 555–59.

26. Chalmers Johnson, *Revolutionary Change* (Boston: Little, Brown, 1966), pp. 44–45, 80–81, 106–7; Anthony F. C. Wallace, *Culture and Personality* (New York: Random House, 1961), pp. 143–44. For a discussion of the preconditions necessary for feminist emancipation, see Lerner, "Women's Rights and American Feminism," *American Scholar* 40 (1971): 237; and Joan Hoff-Wilson, "Woman as a Declining Force in American History," in Betty Chmaj, ed., *Image, Myth, and Beyond: American Women and American Studies* (Philadelphia: Know, Inc., 1974), pp. 224–38.

27. Adrienne Koch, ed., *The American Enlightenment: The Shaping of the American Experiment in a Free Society* (New York: George Braziller, 1965), pp. 19–45; idem, *Power, Morals, and the Founding Fathers: Essays in the Interpretation of the American Enlightenment* (Ithaca, N.Y.: Cornell University Press, Great Seal Books, 1961), pp. 3–5; Keith E. Melder, "Beginnings of the Women's Rights Movement in the United States, 1800–1940" (Ph.D. dissertation, Yale University, 1964), pp. 7–13; and Linda Grant De Pauw, "The American Revolution and the Rights of Women: The Feminist Theory of Abigail Adams," in Larry R. Gerlach et al., eds., *Legacies of the American Revolution* (Logan: Utah University Press, 1978), pp. 199–202.

28. *AFC*, 1:370; and Benson, *Women in Eighteenth-Century America*, p. 247.

29. *AFC*, 1:382.

30. Peter H. Smith, ed., *Letters of Delegates to Congress* (Washington, D.C.: Government Printing Office, 1979), 4:72–75.

31. It should be noted, however, that John Adams was the "only delegate to Congress under the Articles of Confederation to discuss the issue of women's rights" between 1775 and 1789. Other revolutionary leaders, such as Jefferson, did not give the matter any serious consideration even in private letters because they thought that women's natural dependency disqualified them as voters. See Gunderson, "Independence and Citizenship," pp. 63–65, especially n. 13 (quotation) and 17; and Crane, "Dependence in the Era of Independence," pp. 254–57.

32. *AFC*, 1:397.

33. *AFC*, 1:402–3.

34. *AFC*, 4:328.

35. De Pauw, "American Revolution and the Rights of Women," p. 205 (for Lee quotation); *AFC*, 3:372, 4:328; and Stewart Mitchell, ed., *New Letters of Abigail Adams, 1788–1801* (Boston: Little, Brown, 1947), pp. 96 (second quotation to Cranch), 103, 112 (first quotation to Cranch), 116–17.

36. *AFC*, 1:369–70. Other independent and influential positions taken by Abigail Adams include her private opposition to the institution of slavery, her indirect responsibility for the fact that John Adams's first draft of a constitution for the new state of Massachusetts did not specify "male" for citizen, and her decisive role in his negotiations of a new loan with the Dutch in 1799. See *AFC*, 1:162, 332, 369, 380, 400,

2:15, 24, 37, 45–48, 50, 3:226–28; Page Smith, *John Adams,* 2 vols. (Garden City, N.Y.: Doubleday, 1962–63), 2:727–30, 1006 (quotation); Anthony, *First Lady of the Revolution,* pp. 186–89; Janet Whitney, *Abigail Adams* (Boston: Little, Brown, 1974), pp. 155, 290.

37. Warren to Hannah Lincoln, 3 September 1774; Warren to Macauley, 29 December 1774. "Letter-Book," Warren Papers.

38. De Pauw, "American Revolution and the Rights of Women," pp. 217–18. De Pauw suggests that it is anachronistic to apply the term *feminism* to American women before 1900. For its first usage in the United States, see Nancy F. Cott, *The Grounding of Modern Feminism* (New Haven, Conn.: Yale University Press, 1987), pp. 13–16.

39. Gilman, *Letters of Eliza Wilkinson,* pp. 17, 61.

40. Ibid., p. 66.

41. Julia Cherry Spruill, *Women's Life and Work in the Southern Colonies* (University of North Carolina Press, 1938; reprint, New York: W. W. Norton, 1972), pp. 51–53, 232–54; Benson, *Women in Eighteenth-Century America,* pp. 232–73.

42. See, in particular, "An Occasional Letter on the Female Sex" and "Reflections on Unhappy Marriages." Both appeared originally in *Pennsylvania Magazine,* 1 August 1775, pp. 364, 365. Solomon and Berggren, *A Mary Wollstonecraft Reader,* pp. 31–44, 264–364. See also Augusta Genevieve Violette, *Economic Feminism in American Literature prior to 1848* (Orono: University of Maine Press, 1925), pp. 18–29.

43. Sherrill, "Abigail Adams," pp. 3, 5–7; Michael Paul Rogin, *Fathers and Children: Andrew Jackson and the Subjection of the American Indians* (New York: Knopf, 1975), p. 71.

44. For biographical details see Alice Brown, *Mercy Warren* (New York: Scribner's, 1896; reprint, Spartanburg, S.C.: Reprint Co., 1968), pp. 1–66 passim; Anthony, *First Lady,* pp. 19–61 passim; Jean Fritz, *Cast for a Revolution, 1728–1814* (Boston: Houghton Mifflin, 1972), pp. 6–32 passim; Annie Russell Marble, "Mistress Mercy Warren: Real Daughter of the American Revolution," *New England Magazine* 28 (1903): 163–74; Maud Macdonald Hutcheson, "Mercy Warren, 1728–1814," *William and Mary Quarterly* 10 (1953): 379–402; Ellet, *Women of the American Revolution,* 1:91–126.

45. Mary Beard, ed., *America through Women's Eyes* (New York: Macmillan, 1935), p. 59; Lawrence J. Friedman and Arthur H. Shaffer, "Mercy Otis Warren and the Politics of Historical Nationalism," *New England Quarterly* 48 (1975): 206; Ellet, *Women of the Revolution,* 1:94; Hutcheson, "Mercy Warren," p. 384; Anthony, *First Lady,* pp. 77–78; Charles F. Adams, *Correspondence between John Adams and Mercy Warren* (1878; reprint, New York: Arno, 1972), p. 482.

46. AFC, 1:338–39, 423–24, 2:377.

47. Unless otherwise noted, all references to Warren's poetry (including her two long blank-verse tragedies) are taken from Mrs. M. Warren, *Poems, Dramatic and Miscellaneous* (Boston: I. Thomas & E. T. Thomas, 1790), pp. 188–94, quotation at 192.

48. Ibid., p. 205.

49. Hutcheson, "Mercy Warren," pp. 386–87; Ellet, *Women of the American Revolution,* 1:113; AFC, 1:91–94, 97–99.

50. Hutcheson, "Mercy Warren," pp. 378, 386, 395; Ellet, *Women of the American Revolution,* 1:104–5; Friedman and Shaffer, "Mercy Otis Warren," p. 209; Anthony, *First Lady,* p. 202.

51. Warren, *Poems*, pp. 225, 246, 249, 250.

52. For comments on her prose and poetic style, see Benjamin Franklin, ed., *The Plays and Poems of Mercy Otis Warren* (Delmar, N.Y.: Scholars Reprints and Facsimiles, 1980), pp. xvii–xxx; AFC, 3:290, n. 1; Hutcheson, "Mercy Warren," pp. 339–40; Brown, *Warren*, pp. 67–70; Anthony, *First Lady*, pp. 78–80, 148–49.

53. Only two scholars categorically deny she wrote either *The Blockheads* or *The Motley Assembly*. See Worthington Chauncey Ford, "Mrs. Warren's 'The Group,' " *Massachusetts Historical Society Proceedings* 62 (1928–29): 20–21; and Fritz, *Cast for a Revolution*, pp. 318–19. Most of her biographers, especially Anthony, simply assume she did write both plays or indicate that the evidence is not conclusive on one side or the other.

54. Mercy Warren, *The Blockheads; or, the Affrighted Officers, a Farce* (Boston: John Gill, 1776), pp. 4, 10, 11, 17–19.

55. Franklin, *Plays and Poems*, p. xx.

56. Ibid., p. xiv.

57. AFC, 1:xiv.

58. AFC, 1:186, n. 5; Hutcheson, "Mercy Warren," p. 388; Anthony, *First Lady*, pp. 94–95; Brown, *Warren*, p. 165; Ford, "Mrs. Warren's 'The Group,' " pp. 15–22.

59. AFC, 1:185; Ford, "Mrs. Warren's 'The Group,' " pp. 15–19; and Anthony, *First Lady*, pp. 95–96.

60. Letter quoted in Brown, *Warren*, pp. 174–75.

61. Warren, *Poems*, p. 101.

62. Ibid.

63. Ibid., pp. 10–11, 95.

64. Ibid., pp. 94, 178. For another analysis of *The Ladies of Castile*, see Kerber, *Women of the Republic*, pp. 269–71.

65. Charles Warren, "Elbridge Gerry, James Warren, Mercy Warren, and the Ratification of the Federal Constitution in Massachusetts," *Massachusetts Historical Society* 64 (1932): 143–64. It is this article that attributes the authorship of *Observations* to Mercy Warren. Although Charles Warren's arguments have been accepted by most scholars, it should be noted that he was a direct descendant of the Warren family. In addition to the original pamphlet, the *Observations* can be found reprinted in Richard Henry Lee, ed., *An Additional Number of Letters from the Federal Farmer to the Republican* (1788; reprint, Chicago: Quadrangle Books, 1962).

66. *Observations on the Constitution and on the Federal and State Conventions by a Columbian Patriot* (Boston: N.p., 1788), pp. 1–9.

67. Ibid., pp. 9–22.

68. Friedman and Shaffer, "Mercy Otis Warren," pp. 194–215; and Lester H. Cohen, "Explaining the Revolution: Ideology and Ethics in Mercy Otis Warren's Historical Theory," *William and Mary Quarterly* 37 (April 1980): 200–218. Unless otherwise noted, all references to Warren's *History* are taken from Mercy Otis Warren, *History of the Rise, Progress, and Termination of the American Revolution* (1805; reprint, New York: AMS, 1970), pp. vi–vii, 1:2, 3, 26, 70, 3:8, 279, 309, 322, 324–26, 330, 424, 429 passim; and Cohen, "Explaining the Revolution," p. 202, n. 5.

69. Anthony, *First Lady*, pp. 204–10.

70. Warren, *History of the American Revolution*, 1:iv.

71. Ibid.

72. Ibid.
73. Hutcheson, "Mercy Warren," pp. 396, 399.
74. Sandra Gilbert and Susan Gubar, *Mad Woman in the Attic: The Woman Writer and the Nineteenth-Century Literary Imagination* (New Haven, Conn.: Yale University Press, 1979), pp. xi–xii.
75. Charles and Mary Beard, *The American Spirit: A Study of Civilization in the United States* (New York: Macmillan, 1942), pp. 120–22. For detailed criticisms and interpretations of the work, see Judith B. Markowitz, "Radical and Feminist: Mercy Otis Warren and the Historiographers," *Peace and Change* 4 (1977): 15–19; and Friedman and Shaffer, "Mercy Otis Warren," pp. 194–215.
76. *AFC*, 3:191, n. 5; Warren, *History of the American Revolution*, 3:206, 330. See also Cohen, "Explaining the Revolution," pp. 206–7.
77. Markowitz, "Radical and Feminist," pp. 10–15.
78. Lockridge, "Social Change and the Meaning of the American Revolution," pp. 425–26; Smith, *History as Argument*, pp. 118–19; Friedman and Shaffer, "Mercy Otis Warren," pp. 197–99; Markowitz, "Radical and Feminist," pp. 13–14, 19.
79. Warren, *History of the American Revolution*, 2:120–22.
80. Ibid., 3:206.
81. Smith, *History as Argument*, pp. 73–75; Adams, *Correspondence between Adams and Warren*, p. 463; and Cohen, "Explaining the Revolution," pp. 214–15.
82. Smith, *History as Argument*, pp. 100–119.
83. Warren, *History of the American Revolution*, 3:340–43, 356–57.
84. Ibid., 3:336–37.
85. Adams, *Correspondence between Adams and Warren*, p. 392. For other historical details over which they disagreed, see Hoff-Wilson and Bolinger, "Mercy Otis Warren," pp. 175–77.
86. Adams, *Correspondence between Adams and Warren*, p. 423.
87. Mary Beth Norton, *Liberty's Daughters: The Revolutionary Experience of American Women, 1750–1800* (Boston: Little, Brown, 1980), pp. 121–24 (John Adams quoted at 123).
88. Adams, *Correspondence between Adams and Warren*, p. 350.
89. Kerber, *Women of the Republic*, pp. 82–85; Friedman and Shaffer, "Mercy Otis Warren," p. 208; Smith, *John Adams*, p. 225; and Abigail Adams to Mary Cranch, 4 July 1797, in Stewart Mitchell, ed., *New Letters of Abigail Adams, 1788–1801* (Boston: Little, Brown, 1947), p. 112.
90. Mercy Otis Warren to Rebecca Otis, 1776; Mercy Otis Warren to Lincoln Hannah, 12 June and 3 September 1774, "Letter-Book," Warren Papers; and James Warren to Mercy Otis Warren, 6 June 1779, in *Warren-Adams Letters: Being Chiefly the Correspondence among John Adams, Samuel Adams, and James Warren, 1743–1814* (Boston: Massachusetts Historical Society, 1917–25), 2 vols. in *Collections of the Massachusetts Historical Society* 73 (1923), 2:101.
91. "The Rights of the British Colonies Asserted and Proved," in Bernard Bailyn, ed., *Pamphlets of the American Revolution, 1750–1776* (Cambridge: Harvard University Press, 1965), 1:420.
92. Kerber, *Women of the Republic*, pp. 73–80, 85; Gunderson, "Independence and Citizenship," p. 76 (quotation).

### 3. From British Subjects to U.S. Citizens

1. James H. Kettner, "The Development of American Citizenship in the Revolutionary Era: The Idea of Voluntary Allegiance," *American Journal of Legal History* 18 (1974): 208–42; Joan R. Gunderson, "Independence, Citizenship, and the American Revolution," *Signs* 13, no. 1 (Autumn 1987): 59–77 (quotation at 62).

2. Gunderson, "Independence, Citizenship, and the American Revolution," pp. 60–65; and Linda K. Kerber, *Women of the Republic: Intellect and Ideology in Revolutionary America* (Chapel Hill: University of North Carolina Press, 1980), pp. 121–23; and Cornelia Hughes Dayton, "Women, Political Membership, and Constitutional Language in Early America," 1988 paper delivered at Women and the Constitution: Two Hundred Years' Conference, American University, p. 14.

3. Kenneth Karst, "The Supreme Court 1976 Term-Forward: Equal Citizenship under the Fourteenth Amendment," *Harvard Law Review* 91 (1977): 5 (quotation); and Christina Spaulding, "Anti-Pornography Laws as a Claim for Equal Respect: Feminism, Liberalism, and Community," *Berkeley Women's Law Journal* 4 (1988–89): 151–54, 158–60.

4. Linda K. Kerber, " 'May All Our Citizens Be Soldiers, and All Our Soldiers Citizens,': The Ambiguities of Female Citizenship in the New Nation," in Joan R. Challinor and Robert L. Beisner, eds., *Arms at Rest: Peacemaking and Peacekeeping in American History* (Westport, Conn.: Greenwood, 1987), pp. 5, 11.

5. Mary G. Dietz, "Context Is All: Feminism and Theories of Citizenship," *Daedalus* 116 (Fall 1987): 2–6, 18. For an application of male republican views about the family and work, see Michael Grossberg, *Governing the Hearth: Law and the Family in Nineteenth-Century America* (Chapel Hill: University of North Carolina Press, 1985); Steven Hahn, *The Roots of Southern Populism: Yeoman Farmers and the Transformation of the Georgia Upcountry* (New York: Oxford University Press, 1983); and Sean Wilentz, *Chants Democratic: New York City and the Rise of the American Working Class, 1788–1850* (New York: Oxford University Press, 1984).

6. Peggy A. Rabkin, *Fathers to Daughters: The Legal Foundations of Female Emancipation* (Westport, Conn.: Greenwood, 1980), p. 21.

7. Peggy A. Rabkin, "The Silent Feminist Revolution: Women and the Law in New York State from Blackstone to the Beginning of the American Women's Rights Movement" (Ph.D. dissertation, State University of New York, Buffalo, 1975), pp. 31, 40–52 passim; idem, *Fathers to Daughters*, pp. 19–30; Joseph H. Smith and Leo Hershkowitz, "Courts of Equity in the Province of New York: The Cosby Controversy, 1732–1736," *American Journal of Legal History* 16 (1972): 1–50; Mary Ritter Beard, *Woman as Force in History: A Study in Traditions and Realities* (New York: Macmillan, 1946), pp. 133–44, 158–59; Marylynn Salmon, "Equity or Submersion? *Feme Covert* Status in Early Pennsylvania," in Carol Ruth Berkin, ed., *Women of American History* (Boston: Houghton Mifflin, 1979), pp. 92–113; and idem, *Women and the Law of Property in Early America* (Chapel Hill: University of North Carolina Press, 1986), pp. 11–12, 14–80, 86, 120–23.

8. Carole Shammas, "Early American Women and Control over Capital," and Marylynn Salmon, "Republican Sentiment, Economic Change, and the Property Rights of Women in American Law," both in Ronald Hoffman and Peter J. Albert, eds., *Women in the Age of the American Revolution* (Charlottesville: University of Virginia Press,

1989), pp. 137–38, and n. 5, p. 448; and Salmon, *Women and the Law of Property in Early America*, p. 185 (quotation).

9. Carole Shammas, Marylynn Salmon, and Michel Dahlin, *Inheritance in America from Colonial Times to the Present* (New Brunswick, N.J.: Rutgers University Press, 1987), pp. 27–35; and Salmon, "Property Rights of Women," p. 448.

10. Edmund S. Morgan, *American Slavery, American Freedom: The Ordeal of Colonial Virginia* (New York: W. W. Norton, 1975), pp. 164–68, 304; Smith, "Inheritance and the Position and Orientation of Colonial Women," pp. 6, 10, 11, 13, 425–26, n. 9; and Shammas et al., *Inheritance in America*, pp. 59–61.

11. Shammas et al., *Inheritance in America*, pp. 3–79, especially table 2.12 on pp. 59–60. Richard B. Morris, *Studies in the History of American Law* (New York: Columbia University Press, 1930), pp. 126–200; Alexander Keyssar, "Widowhood in Eighteenth-Century Massachusetts: A Problem in the History of the Family," *Perspectives in American History* 8 (1974): 101, 118; George Lee Haskins, *Law and Authority in Early Massachusetts: A Study in Tradition and Design* (New York: Macmillan, 1960), pp. 180–82; George Athan Billias, ed., *Selected Essays: Law and Authority in Colonial America* (Barre, Mass.: Barre Publishing, 1965), pp. 23–26; Allan Kulikoff, "The Progress of Inequality in Revolutionary Boston," *William and Mary Quarterly* 28 (July 1971): 388.

12. Shammas et al., *Inheritance in America*, pp. 114–22, 179–206 (quotations at 114 and 196). The reader who is interested in details of these changing intestacy patterns based on studies of scattered colonies and states should consult this work.

13. Ibid., pp. 35–39; Salmon, *Women and the Law of Property*, pp. 3–13, 185–93; and Elizabeth Bowles Warbasse, *The Changing Legal Status of Married Women, 1800–1861* (New York: Garland, 1987), p. 42.

14. For a bibliographical review of the status of *feme sole* and *feme covert*, see G. S. Rowe, "*Femes Covert* and Criminal Prosecution in Eighteenth-Century Pennsylvania," *American Journal of Legal History* 332 (April 1988): 138–56, especially 138–41, nn. 1–11; Warbasse, *Changing Legal Status of Married Women*, pp. 7–56; and Salmon, *Women and the Law of Property*, pp. 44–57.

15. Neil H. Cogan, " 'Standing' before the Constitution: Membership in the Community," *Law and History Review* 7 (Spring 1989): 1–22. Cogan notes that the most common Latin phrase to describe enemies, minors, married women, clerics, the insane, and other disparate groups who lacked "standing" before the law was *persona standi*, but "it is not clear how well American lawyers of the 1780s knew of the civil law's [historical] use of 'standing' with married women." Under Roman law, women were members of the community but only partial members of the judicial community. In German-Dutch law, "women simply were not members [of the judicial] community at all." In all likelihood, colonial attorneys generally followed the more restrictive English and German-Dutch legal tradition about who had "standing" to sue and be sued in courts when it came to married women. (See pp. 7–9, 10–11, 14–15.)

16. For examples of the traditional and nontraditional jobs held by colonial women, see Gary B. Nash, *The Urban Crucible: Social Change, Political Consciousness, and the Origins of the American Revolution* (Cambridge: Harvard University Press, 1979), pp. 106–8, 176–96, 227, 333–36; Mary P. Ryan, *Womanhood in America: From Colonial Times to the Present* (New York: New Viewpoints, 1983), pp. 34, 73, 86–87, 91–99; Elaine Forman Crane, *A Dependent People: Newport, Rhode Island, in the Revolutionary*

*Era* (New York: Fordham University Press, 1985), pp. 71–75; idem, "When More Means Less: Women and Work in Colonial American Seaports," paper delivered at 1984 Berkshire Conference on the History of Women; and Virginia Bever Platt, "The Working Women of Newport, Rhode Island," paper delivered at 1975 Conference on Women in the Era of the American Revolution. According to Platt's figures, female laborers in Newport (whether free, indentured, or hired out as slaves and regardless of race) were paid approximately 30 percent less than the lowest paid unskilled, free, white male workers and 20 percent less than hired-out male slaves. These figures have since been confirmed upward by Billy G. Smith, "The Material Lives of Laboring Philadelphians, 1750 to 1800," *William and Mary Quarterly,* 3d ser., 38 (1981): 163–202; and Carole Shammas, "The Female Social Structure of Philadelphia in 1775," *Pennsylvania Magazine of History and Biography* 107 (1983): 69–84. For general gendered-economic functions in the colonial period, see Edith Abbott, *Women in Industry: A Study in American Economic History* (New York: Source Book Press, 1970; reprint of 1910 edition), pp. 13–20, 149–56; Frances May Manges, "Women Shopkeepers, Tavernkeepers, and Artisans" (Ph.D. dissertation, University of Pennsylvania, 1958), pp. xxxi–xxxii, 40–41, 44, n. 101, 69–117, n. 290; Carl Bridenbaugh, *The Colonial Craftsman* (New York: New York University Press, 1950; reprint, Chicago: University of Chicago Press, Phoenix Books, 1961), pp. 105–8; Alice Morse Earle, *Colonial Dames and Good Wives,* (Boston: Houghton Mifflin, 1895) pp. 45–87; Carl Holliday, *Women's Life in Colonial Days* (New York: Frederick Ungar, 1922), pp. 291–312; and Elisabeth Anthony Dexter, *Colonial Women of Affairs: Women in Business and the Professions in America before 1776,* 2d ed., rev. (Boston: Houghton Mifflin, 1931), passim.

17. Keyssar, "Widowhood in Eighteenth-Century Massachusetts," pp. 101, 118; (quotation); Haskins, *Law and Authority,* pp. 180–82; Billias, *Law and Authority in Colonial America,* pp. 23–26; and Kulikoff, "Progress of Inequality in Revolutionary Boston," p. 388.

18. Morris, *Studies in the History of American Law,* pp. 128–30; Nash, *Urban Crucible,* pp. 19–22, 59–65, 74, 115, 127, 171–74, 182, 188–89, 195–96, 246, 253–54, 325; Kerber, *Women of the Republic,* pp. 139–55; Salmon, *Women and the Law of Property,* pp. 15–57, 81–140; and Richard H. Chused, "Married Women's Property and Inheritance by Widows in Massachusetts: A Study of Wills Probated between 1800 and 1850," *Berkeley Women's Law Journal* 2 (Fall 1986): 48–58.

19. Gunderson, "Independence and Citizenship," pp. 59–67 (quotations at 66–67); Kettner, "Development of American Citizenship," pp. 222–31 (first quotation at 225).

20. Gunderson, "Independence and Citizenship," pp. 67–68; and Kerber, *Women of the Republic,* pp. 115–36.

21. Gunderson, "Independence and Citizenship," pp. 68–71.

22. Hilda Smith, "Masculinity and Citizenship," 1987 unpublished paper; and Linda Kerber, "Can a Woman Be an Individual? The Limits of the Puritan Tradition in the Early Republic," *Texas Studies in Literature and Language* 25, no. 4 (Winter 1983): 165–77; idem, "Ambiguities of Citizenship," pp. 1–5.

23. Dayton, "Women, Political Membership, and Constitutional Language," p. 14. For treason cases and confiscation laws, see Kerber, *Women of the Republic,* pp. 121–36; and Gunderson, "Independence and Citizenship," pp. 68–70.

24. *Acts of the General Assembly of New Jersey* [5th Session] (Trenton, 1781), p. 14. As I

note later, New Jersey continued to use male and female pronouns in other postrevolutionary statutes governing voting rights because New Jersey was the only state that temporarily allowed women to vote. Most states, however, in redrafting their hastily passed state constitutions, dropped all references to "she" or "her," as all citizens became male by definition. One other exception can be found in an 1787 New York "act concerning the rights of the citizens of this state," in which the generic "he" was dropped in favor of "his" or "her." See *Laws of the State of New York* [10th Session], 26 January 1787, pp. 344–45.

25. Quoted in Kerber, "Ambiguities of Citizenship," p. 14.

26. Quoted in ibid., pp. 14, 15.

27. Quoted in ibid., p. 21, citing Kempe's Lessee v. Kennedy, et al., February 1809, *U.S. Supreme Court Reports* 5 (Cranch), pp. 173–86; and Kerber, *Women of the Republic*, pp. 130–32.

28. Kerber, *Women of the Republic*, pp. 59–183 (first quotation at 85); and idem, " 'I Have Dun . . . Much to Carrey on the Warr': Women and the Shaping of Republican Ideology after the American Revolution," in *Women and Politics in the Era of the French Revolution* (Ann Arbor: University of Michigan Press, forthcoming) (second quotation).

29. This is especially true in Western European countries, England, and the United States with their increasing emphasis on the rule of law and respect for individual rights in the last two to three hundred years.

30. The periodization cited here is from Hendrik Hartog, "Public Law of a County Court: Judicial Government in Eighteenth-Century Massachusetts," *American Journal of Legal History* 20 (1976): 327.

31. Lawrence Meir Friedman, *A History of American Law* (New York: Simon & Schuster, 1973), pp. 35, 37; James W. Ely Jr., "American Independence and the Law: A Study of Post-Revolutionary South Carolina Legislation," *Vanderbilt Law Review* 26 (1973): 958–62; Hartog, "Public Law of a County Court," pp. 282–329.

32. Friedman, *History of American Law*, p. 35.

33. For the importance of defamation cases to colonial women, see Mary Beth Norton, "Gender and Defamation in Seventeenth-Century Maryland," *William and Mary Quarterly*, 3d ser., 44 (1987): 3–39. For other examples of women testifying or bringing actions at the county-court level, see A. G. Roeber, "Authority, Law, and Custom: The Rituals of Court Day in Tidewater, Virginia, 1720–1750," *William and Mary Quarterly*, 3d. ser., 37 (1980): 29–52.

34. Richard B. Morris, "Legalism versus Revolutionary Doctrine in New England," *New England Quarterly* 4 (April 1931): 195–215. Roscoe Pound wrote his first work on *The Formative Era of American Law* in 1938. See also idem, *Administrative Law* (Pittsburgh: University of Pittsburgh Press, 1942). For detailed descriptions about the differences between "a modern positivist jurisprudence that considers law the command of a sovereign and unitary state" and the local legal institutions of the colonial period, which were "regarded as independent recipients of constitutional power and authority," see Hartog, "Public Law of a County Court"; David Roper, "Society and Law before the Formative Era," *Reviews in American History* 5 (June 1977): 180–85; Harry N. Scheiber, "Back to 'The Legal Mind'? Doctrinal Analysis and the History of Law," *Reviews in American History* 5 (December 1977): 458–65; and Friedman, *History of American Law*, pp. 32–49, 93–137.

35. Dayton, "Women before the Bar: Gender, Law, and Society in Connecticut, 1710–1790," (Ph.D. dissertation, Princeton University, 1986), chap. 2; and idem, "Women, Political Membership, and Constitutional Language," pp. 10 (quotation), 17.

36. Hartog, "Public Law of a County Court," pp. 284, 328, 329.

37. Ibid., p. 323.

38. Morton J. Horwitz, "The Emergence of an Instrumental Concept of American Law, 1780–1820," in Donald Fleming, ed., *Law in American History* (Cambridge: Harvard University Press, 1971), pp. 24–25, 74, 291, 452–57.

39. Augusta Genevieve Violette, *Economic Feminism in American Literature prior to 1848* (Orono: University of Maine Press, 1925), pp. 12–29; Linda K. Kerber, "The Republican Mother: Women and the Enlightenment—an American Perspective," *American Quarterly* 28 (Summer 1976): 187–205; idem, *Women of the Republic,* pp. 15–32; and Marguerite Fisher, "Eighteenth-Century Theorists of Women's Liberation," in Carol V. R. George, ed., *"Remember the Ladies": New Perspectives on Women in American History* (Syracuse, N.Y.: Syracuse University Press, 1975), pp. 39–47.

40. Morton J. Horwitz, *The Transformation of American Law, 1780–1860* (Cambridge: Harvard University Press, 1975), pp. 17–18 passim; Peggy A. Rabkin, "The Silent Feminist Revolution: Women and the Law in New York State from Blackstone to the Beginnings of the American Women's Rights Movement" (Ph.D. dissertation, State University of New York, Buffalo, 1975), pp. 31, 147; and William E. Nelson, *Americanization of the Common Law: The Impact of Legal Change on Massachusetts Society, 1760–1830* (Cambridge: Harvard University Press, 1975), pp. 165–74.

41. Sophie H. Drinker, "Votes for Women in Eighteenth-Century New Jersey," *Proceedings of the New Jersey Historical Society* 80 (January 1962): 31, 35–43.

42. See, for example, Lucy Stone's 1858 statement refusing to pay her taxes because she could not vote, quoted by William A. Whitehead in "A Brief Statement: Of the Facts Connected with the Origin, Practice, and Prohibition of Female Suffrage in New Jersey," *Proceedings of the New Jersey Historical Society,* 1st. ser., 8 (1858): 105; and idem, "Reasons Why the Women of New Jersey Should Vote: As Shown from the Constitution and Statutes of New Jersey, March 1, 1863," statement approved by the Executive Committee of the New Jersey State Woman Suffrage Association. As late as 1912, the New Jersey Supreme Court decided against a woman contending that since the 1776 state constitution had given suffrage to women, subsequent state laws in 1807, 1820, 1839, and the revised constitution of 1844 were all invalid because women had been excluded from participating in these deliberations because they could not vote. See Edward Raymond Turner, "Women's Suffrage in New Jersey, 1790–1807," *Smith College Studies in History* 1 (July 1916): 186; and Richard P. McCormick, *The History of Voting in New Jersey* (New Brunswick, N.J.: Rutgers University Press, 1953), pp. 203–5, n. 63. See also references to women voting in Minor v. Happersett, 88 U.S. 162 (1875), in chapter 5 of this volume.

43. Nancy Woloch, *Women and the American Experience* (New York: Knopf, 1984), pp. 39–42; Mary Philbrook, "Woman's Suffrage in New Jersey prior to 1807," *Proceedings of the New Jersey Historical Society* 57, no. 1 (1939): 87–88; Albert Edward McKinley, *The Suffrage Franchise in the Thirteen English Colonies* (Philadelphia: University of Pennsylvania Press, 1905), pp. 255–56; Drinker, "Votes for Women," pp. 35–36.

44. Drinker, "Votes for Women," pp. 31, 35–43 (first quotation at 35–36); Turner,

"Women's Suffrage in New Jersey," p. 166, n. 6 (second quotation); and Philbrook, "Woman's Suffrage in New Jersey," p. 87.

45. Drinker, "Votes for Women," p. 43; and Philbrook, "Woman's Suffrage in New Jersey," p. 88, n. 6 (quotation).

46. McCormick, *History of Voting in New Jersey,* p. 93; Drinker, "Votes for Women," pp. 43–44; Philbrook, "Woman's Suffrage in New Jersey," p. 89; and Turner, "Women's Suffrage in New Jersey," pp. 169–70 (quotation from n. 23).

47. Philbrook, "Woman's Suffrage in New Jersey," pp. 88–89 (quotation); and Turner, "Women's Suffrage in New Jersey," pp. 170, n. 23, 175.

48. McCormick, *History of Voting in New Jersey,* p. 99 (second quotation, n. 23); Turner, "Women's Suffrage in New Jersey," pp. 170, 172 (first and third quotations).

49. Turner, "Women's Suffrage in New Jersey," p. 172; and Philbrook, "Woman's Suffrage in New Jersey," pp. 93–94 (quoting from March 1801 issues of the *Sentinel of Freedom*).

50. Philbrook, "Woman's Suffrage in New Jersey," p. 94.

51. Ibid., pp. 95–96.

52. Turner, *"Women's Suffrage in New Jersey,"* pp. 181–83. For a video docudrama of the battle over the county courthouse that resulted in the disfranchisement of New Jersey women, see Elizabeth F. Defeis and Joan Hoff-Wilson, *Experiment in Equality: The Woman's Vote,* available through WTL Productions, P.O. Box 351, Primos, PA 19018.

53. Philbrook, "Woman's Suffrage in New Jersey," p. 97 (first quotation from the *True American* for 19 November 1807); and Turner, "Women's Suffrage in New Jersey," pp. 184–85 (second quotation).

54. Harriet Martineau, *Society in America* (New York: Sauders & Otley, 1937), 1:148–154, 2:125; Linda K. Kerber, "Can a Woman Be an Individual? The Limits of Puritan Tradition in the Early Republic," *Texas Studies in Literature and Language* 25, no. 4 (Winter 1983): 176.

55. Patrick H. Hutton, "The Print Revolution of the Eighteenth Century and the Drafting of Written Constitutions," *Vermont History* 56 (Summer 1988): 155. This is not generally the position taken by Marylynn Salmon in *Women and the Law of Property.*

56. Joseph Story, *Commentaries on Equity Jurisprudence as Administered in England and America* (Boston: Charles C. Little and James Brown, 1839), 1:62. *Dedimus protestatem* literally means "we have given power." In English law, it meant a writ or commission issuing out of chancery that empowered the persons named in them to perform certain acts, such as administering oaths to defendants in chancery and taking their answers and administering oaths to justices of the peace.

57. Stanley N. Katz, "The Politics of Law in Colonial America: Controversies over Chancery Courts and Equity Law in the Eighteenth Century," in Fleming, ed., *Law in American History,* pp. 259, 282. For a more positive assessment of the meaning of divorce for postrevolutionary women, see Nancy F. Cott, "Divorce and the Changing Status of Women in Eighteenth-Century Massachusetts," *William and Mary Quarterly,* 3d ser., 33 (1976): 586–614; and idem, "Eighteenth-Century Family and Social Life Revealed in Massachusetts Divorce Records," *Journal of Social History* 10 (Fall 1976): 20–43.

58. Dartmouth College v. Woodward, 17 U.S. 518 (1819). See the quotations and sections on divorce at 600–601, 650, 696–97. For data on prerevolutionary divorce, see Helena Mast Robinson, "The Status of the *Feme Covert* in Eighteenth-Century Virginia" (M.A. thesis, University of Virginia, 1971), pp. 19–21; idem, " 'Under Greet Temp-

tations Heer': Women and Divorce in Puritan Massachusetts," *Feminist Studies* 2 (1975): 183–93; Norbert B. Lacy, "The Records of the Court Assistants of Connecticut, 1665–1701" (M.A. thesis, Yale University, 1937).

59. *Dartmouth College v. Woodward,* at 697.
60. Kerber, *Women of the Republic,* pp. 59–183 (quotation at 173). Marylynn Salmon appears to agree with Kerber's assessment that postrevolutionary women did not benefit in any unqualified way from the increased instances of divorce. See Salmon, *Women and the Law of Property,* pp. 58–80. See also Michael S. Hindus and Lynne E. Withey, "The Law of Husband and Wife in Nineteenth-Century America: Changing Views of Divorce," in D. Kelly Weisberg, ed., *Women and the Law: A Social Historical Perspective* (Cambridge, Mass.: Schenkman, 1982), 2:133–50.
61. Grossberg, *Governing the Hearth,* pp. 64–195, 289–307; and Christine Stansell, *City of Women: Sex and Class in New York, 1789–1860* (New York: Knopf, 1986), pp. 214–16.
62. For the importance of informal settlements of most civil disputes and the demise of a sense of community with an increase in formal litigation around 1800, see William E. Nelson, *Dispute and Conflict Resolution in Plymouth County, Massachusetts, 1725–1825* (Chapel Hill: University of North Carolina Press, 1981), pp. 76–152. Unfortunately, this valuable study does not attempt any gender analysis.
63. For the relatively small number of criminal cases, see Michael Stephen Hindus, *Prison and Plantation: Crime, Justice, and Authority in Massachusetts and South Carolina, 1767–1878* (Chapel Hill: University of North Carolina Press, 1980); and Douglas Greenburg, *Crime and Law Enforcement in the Colony of New York, 1691–1776* (Ithaca, N.Y.: Cornell University Press, 1976).
64. John James Park, *A Treatise on the Law of Dower; Particularly with a View to the Modern Practice of Conveyancing* (Philadelphia: John S. Littell, 1836), p. 3 (quotation). See also Rabkin, "Women and the Law in New York State," pp. 1–90 passim; Albie Sachs and Joan Hoff-Wilson, *Sexism and the Law: A Study in Male Beliefs and Legal Bias in Britain and the United States* (New York: Free Press, 1979), pp. 77–125, 210–224.
65. 25 *Am. Jur.* 2d (1966), "Dower and Curtesy," Sec. 1, p. 80 (quotation); George Lee Haskins, "Reception of Common Law in Seventeenth-Century Massachusetts: Case Study [of Dower Rights]," in Athan Billias, ed., *Selected Essays: Law and Authority in Colonial America* (Barre, Mass.: Barre Publishers, 1965), pp. 19–23; Charles M. Scribner, *A Treatise on the Law of Dower* (Philadelphia: N.p., 1864–67), 2 vols., passim; and Robinson, "Status of the *Feme Covert,*" pp. 23–26.
66. Salmon, *Women and the Law of Property,* pp. 17–75, 234, nn. 98 and 106 (first quotation). Dower decisions cited in Horwitz, *Transformation of American Law,* pp. 56–58; and Nelson, *Americanization of the Common Law,* pp. 9, 48, 228, n. 175, 249, n. 34, 253, n. 100.
67. Salmon, *Women and the Law of Property,* pp. 163–68, 181 (quoting Conner v. Shephard), 15 Mass. 164 [1818]).
68. Ibid., pp. 163–68.
69. Ibid., p. 164.
70. Graff v. Smith's Administrations, 1 Dallas 481 (1789).
71. 25 *Am. Jur.* 2d (1966), "Dower and Curtesy," sec. 3, p. 83.
72. Salmon, *Women and the Law of Property,* pp. 164–68 (quoting *Conner v. Shephard*).
73. *Conner v. Shephard,* at 167–68.

74. Herbert v. Wren, 7 Cranch 368, 3 L. Ed. 374 (1813), at 373, 375, 378, 381.
75. Ibid., at 371, 378, 381; 3 L. Ed. 374 (1813), at 377–78; and 25 *Am. Jur. 2d* (1966), "Dower and Curtesy," sec. 156, p. 202.
76. Stelle v. Carroll, 12 Pet. 200, at 205; 9 L. Ed. 1056 (1838), at 1057.
77. Ibid., at 203.
78. Mayburry v. Brien, 15 Pet. 21, at 22, 25, 31, 37; 10 L. Ed. 646 (1841), at 646, 648, 650, 652.
79. Ibid., 15 Pet. 21, at 31; 10 L. Ed. 646 (1841), at 650.
80. Ibid.
81. Ibid.
82. Dolton v. Cain (U.S.), 14 Wall 472, 20 L. Ed. 830 (1871); Sykes v. Chadwick (U.S.), 18 Wall 144, 21 L. Ed. 824 (1873); and Randall v. Krieger (U.S.), 23 Wall 137, 23 L. Ed. 124 (1874).
83. 25 *Am. Jur. 2d* (1966), "Dower and Curtesy," sec. 6, p. 85 (all quotations in paragraph).
84. Dowries usually took the form of livestock, household items, or cash. While such goods look impressive when subjectively compared to lands given to sons, they fell far short of constituting equal economic distribution between the sexes, contrary to the claims of a few demographers. See Narrett, "Preparation for Death," p. 422.
85. South Carolina dower records can be found in the South Carolina Department of Archives and History in the record of the Court of Common Pleas, Columbia.
86. Kerber, *Women of the Republic*, p. 145.
87. Ibid., p. 147.
88. 25 *Am. Jur. 2d* (1966), "Dower and Curtesy," sec. 6, p. 85.

## 4. Constitutional Neglect, 1787–1872

1. Linda K. Kerber, " 'Ourselves and Our Daughters Forever': Women and the Constitution, 1787–1876," *this Constitution* 6 (Spring 1985): 29; Ronald Dworkin, "The Bork Nomination," *New York Review of Books*, 13 August 1987, p. 8; and Patrick Hutton, "The Print Revolution of the Eighteenth Century and the Drafting of Written Constitutions," *Vermont History* 56 (Summer 1988): 161–62.
2. Joan Gunderson, "Independence, Citizenship, and the American Revolution," *Signs* 13, no. 1 (Autumn 1987): 64, n. 13. For a discussion of the Founding Fathers and Locke's views on women, see Carole Pateman, *The Sexual Contract* (Cambridge: Polity, 1988), pp. 19–38, 84–85, 91–94.
3. Linda J. Nicholson, "Feminist Theory: The Private and the Public," in Carol C. Gould, ed., *Beyond Domination: New Perspectives on Women and Philosophy* (Totowa, N.J.: Rowman & Allanheld, 1983), pp. 224–26 (quotation).
4. Clinton Rossiter, ed., *Federalist Papers* (New York: Mentor, 1961), pp. 54–55. See chapters 1 and 2 of this volume for examples of positive, rather than negative, references to postrevolutionary women.
5. Blackstone had said: "By marriage, the husband and wife are one person in law: that is, the very being or legal existence of woman is suspended during marriage." See also Norma Basch, *In the Eyes of the Law: Women, Marriage, and Property in Nineteenth-Century New York* (Ithaca, N.Y.: Cornell University Press, 1982), pp. 42–46, 168–69. This common-law position was not officially abandoned until the decision in

Eisenstadt v. Baird, 405 U.S. 438 (1972), which stated that "the marital couple is not an independent entity . . . but an association of two individuals." As late as 1966, Justice Hugo Black insisted in a dissenting opinion that "husband and wife are one . . . and that one . . . is the husband." See U.S. v. Yazell, 382 U.S. 341 (1966). After surveying marriage laws in fifty states, Shana Alexander concluded as late as 1975 that "when two people marry they become in the eyes of the law one person, and that one person is the husband! . . . When a woman marries she legally to some degree ceases to exist. Only the loss of her husband through death or divorce can bring about the full restoration of her legal self." See Shana Alexander, *State-by-State Guide to Women's Legal Rights* (Los Angeles: Wollstonecraft, 1975), p. 10.

6. For the complicated proprietary situations facing most postrevolutionary women who had mainly moral, but not financial, authority in their families, see Joy Day and Richard Buel Jr., *The Way of Duty: A Woman and Her Family in Revolutionary America* (New York: W. W. Norton, 1984), pp. 212–25; and for an assortment of Alice Izard's postrevolutionary letters commenting on her family's finances, especially during 1807 when she was trying to get her son to explain the details of the estate settlement and what her annual annuity would be, see the Ralph Izard Papers, 1765–1955, Manuscript Division of the South Carolinian Library, University of South Carolina, Columbia. See also Marylynn Salmon, "Republican Sentiment, Economic Change, and the Property Rights of Women in American Law," in Ronald Hoffman and Peter J. Albert, eds., *Women in the Age of the American Revolution* (Charlottesville: University Press of Virginia, 1989), pp. 447–52. Unless I am misreading this article by Salmon, she seems to be contradicting the conclusion reached for the period from the 1790s to the 1830s by her coauthors, Carole Shammas and Michel Dahlin, in *Inheritance in America: From Colonial Times to the Present* (New Brunswick, N.J.: Rutgers University Press, 1987), where several charts and accompanying text make it clear that the "1790s marked a nadir in the fortunes of testators' wives" with little improvement until after 1820. In addition, there was "deterioration in the widow's position between the colonial period and the 1790s" that was not resolved with the "alteration in intestacy laws—changes made them [daughters] equal to their elder brothers. . . . the problem was that it all went to their husbands when they wed. . . . The Revolution does not seem to have produced any immediate increase in the amount of capital women owned or controlled" (pp. 121, 149, 151). No evidence of any meaningful statutory improvement in the inheritance laws is provided by Shammas until the 1830s, using Salmon's own research for that decade with no indication of significant change cited for the years between 1800 and 1830. The charts in appendix 1 in this volume show some regional, but little national increase in laws designed to increase property rights until the 1820s.

7. Peggy A. Rabkin, *Fathers to Daughters: The Legal Foundations of Female Emancipation* (Westport, Conn.: Greenwood, 1980), pp. 40–49, 52–58; Eric Foner, "Get a Lawyer!" *New York Review of Books,* 14 April 1977, p. 38; and George Dargo, *Life in the New Republic: Private Law and Public Estate* (New York: Knopf, 1983), pp. 7–59.

8. Shammas et al., *Inheritance in America,* pp. 63, 87, 94–97; Marlene Stein Wortman, ed., *Women in American Law: From Colonial Times to the New Deal* (New York: Holmes & Meier, 1985), pp. 8 (quotation), 59–196; Linda E. Speth, "The Married Women's Property Acts, 1839–1865: Reform, Reaction, or Revolution?" in D. Kelly Weisberg, ed., *Women and the Law: A Social Historical Perspective* (Cambridge, Mass.:

Schenkman, 1982), 2:69–91; Elizabeth Bowles Warbasse, *The Changing Legal Rights of Married Women,* 1800–1861 (New York: Garland, 1987), pp. 57–87; and John D'Emilio and Estelle B. Freedman, *Intimate Matters: A History of Sexuality in America* (New York: Harper & Row, 1988), pp. 59, 63–66, 137, 145–47.

9. Wortman, *Women in American Law,* p. 120 (first quotation); Richard H. Chused, "Married Women's Property and Inheritance by Widows in Massachusetts: A Study of Wills Probated between 1800 and 1850," *Berkeley Women's Law Journal* 2 (Fall 1986): 43 (second quotation).

10. Shammas et al., *Inheritance in America,* pp. 84–87; Richard H. Chused's articles contain the best documentation for this complicated economic and legal process. See Chused, "Married Women's Property and Inheritance," pp. 42–88; and idem, "Married Women's Property Law: 1800–1850," *Georgetown Law Journal* 71 (1983): 1359–84.

11. For a discussion of the loss of equity procedures, see Rabkin, "Women and the Law in New York State," pp. 27–52; Marylynn Salmon, "Protecting the Widow's Share: Equity Law and Women's Property Rights in Early Pennsylvania"; Norma Basch, "Equity versus Equality: Emerging Concepts of Women's Political Status in the Age of Jackson," *Journal of Early Republic* 3 (Fall 1983): 297–318. For declining female inheritance patterns, see Joan Hoff-Wilson, "The Illusion of Change: Women and the American Revolution," in Alfred F. Young, ed., *The American Revolution: Explorations in the History of American Radicalism* (De Kalb: Northern Illinois University Press, 1976), pp. 416–17, nn. 91–92; and Shammas et al., *Inheritance in America,* pp. 112–22.

12. Shammas et al., *Inheritance in America,* pp. 103–22; and Chused, "Married Women's Property and Inheritance," pp. 42–88.

13. Joseph Story, *Commentaries on Equity Jurisprudence as Administered in England and America* (Boston: Charles C. Little and James Brown, 1839), 2:654–55.

14. In particular, I have in mind the statements made by Elisabeth Anthony Dexter in the 1920s and 1930s about the greater economic opportunities available to colonial women in comparison to women of the nineteenth century. See Dexter, *Colonial Women of Affairs: Women in Business and the Professions in America before 1776,* 2d ed., rev. (Boston: Houghton Mifflin, 1931), pp. 34–35, 37–38, 162–65; idem, *Career Women of America, 1776–1840* (Francestown, N.H.: M. Jones, 1950; reprint, Clifton, N.J.: A. M. Kelley, 1972 [Houghton Mifflin reprint editions]; N.Y.: Schocken, 1976), p. 139.

15. Marylynn Salmon, "The Legal Status of Women in Early America: A Reappraisal," *Law and History* 1 (Spring 1983): 129–51; Berenice Carroll, "Mary Beard's Woman as Force in History: A Critique," in Lee R. Edwards, Mary Heath, and Lisa Baski, eds., *Woman: An Issue* (Boston: Little, Brown, 1972), pp. 125–43; Ann J. Lane's introductory comments in *Mary Ritter Beard: A Source Book* (New York: Schocken, 1977; reprint, Boston: Northeastern University Press, 1988); and Barbara K. Turoff's even briefer remarks in *Mary Beard as Force in History,* Monograph Series Number 3 (Dayton: Wright State University, 1979) represent early attempts to analyze her work but do not concentrate on her extensive comments on women's legal rights beyond what is found in her book *Woman as Force in History.* More recent essays that also neglect Beard's legal theories include Bonnie G. Smith, "Seeing Mary Beard," *Feminist Studies* 10, no. 3 (Fall 1984): 395–416; and Nancy F. Cott, "How Weird Was

Beard? Mary Ritter Beard and American Feminism," paper presented at the 1987 Berkshire Conference on the History of Women.

16. Mary Ritter Beard, *Woman as Force in History: A Study in Traditions and Realities* (New York: Macmillan, 1946) pp. 113–21 (also 1962 Collier Books reprint, which unlike the 1987 Persea reprint does not retain the original pagination of the first edition).

17. Ibid., pp. 82–88.

18. Ibid., pp. 122–44, 158–66.

19. Ibid., pp. 81–95; Rabkin, *Fathers to Daughters*, pp. 75, 76–77.

20. Beard, *Woman as Force in History*, pp. 198–201.

21. Ibid., pp. 113, 115 (quotations).

22. Ibid., pp. 115–121, 155–58.

23. Ibid., pp. 158–59.

24. Salmon, *Women and the Law of Property*, p. 82. See also note 11 above.

25. Beard, *Woman as Force in History*, pp. 120, 127, 132; and Rabkin, *Fathers to Daughters*, pp. 5–7, 36, 75–77.

26. Beard, *Woman as Force in History*, pp. 122–28.

27. Ibid., pp. 160 (quotation), 161–65. One of the best brief analyses of Beard's legal thought can be found in Basch, *In the Eyes of the Law*, pp. 30–37, 109, 168–69, 198.

28. Rabkin, *Fathers to Daughters*, pp. 106–7; Chused, "Married Women's Property Inheritance," pp. 42–88; idem, "Late Nineteenth-Century Married Women's Property Law: Reception of the Early Married Women's Property Acts by Courts and Legislatures," *American Journal of Legal History* 29 (January 1985): 3–35. The texts of various New York Married Women's Property Acts can be found in Basch, *In the Eyes of the Law*, pp. 233–37.

29. Quotations are from Barbara Allen Babcock, Ann E. Freedman, Eleanor Holmes Norton, and Susan C. Ross, *Sex Discrimination and the Law: Causes and Remedies* (Boston: Little, Brown, 1975), pp. 593, 594. See also Peggy A. Rabkin, "Silent Feminist Revolution: Women and the Law in New York State from Blackstone to the Beginnings of the American Women's Right Movement" (Ph.D. dissertation, State University of New York, Buffalo, 1975), pp. 176–86; and Keith E. Melder, *Beginnings of Sisterhood: The American Woman's Rights Movement, 1800–1850* (New York: Schocken, 1977), pp. 4–6, 143–44.

30. In addition to case law and published state statutes and codes, data for these charts came from Chused, "Married Women's Property Law," pp. 1366–1424, nn. 27, 165, 172, 192, 200, 206–9, 233, 239, 244, 263, 361; idem, "Late Nineteenth-Century Married Women's Property Law," pp. 3–35; Warbasse, *Changing Legal Rights of Married Women*, 137–247; Suzanne Lebsock, "Radical Reconstruction and the Property Rights of Southern Women," *Journal of Southern History* 43 (May 1977): 195–216; Mari Matsuda, "The West and the Legal Status of Women: Explanations of Frontier Feminism," *Journal of the West* 24, no. 1 (January 1985): 47–56; Michael B. Dougan, "The Arkansas Married Woman's Property Law," *Arkansas Historical Quarterly* 46 (Spring 1987): 3–26; and where applicable data from charts in Shammas et al., *Inheritance in America*, pp. 85, 224–58 passim.

31. Gary B. Nash, Julie Roy Jeffrey, John Howe, Peter Frederick, Allen Davis, and Allan Winkler, eds., *The American People: Creating a Nation and Society* (New York: Harper & Row, 1986), table A–17; and Elyce Rotella, "Fact Sheet: Women in the U.S.

Economy," in Sheila Ruth, ed., *Issues in Feminism* (Boston: Houghton Mifflin, 1980; revised 1990 edition forthcoming).

32. Figures on single women are from Ethel Klein, *Gender Politics: From Consciousness to Mass Politics* (Cambridge: Harvard University Press, 1984), p. 70; and Paula Rayman, "The Meaning of Work in Women's Lives," *Radcliffe Quarterly* (June 1990): 11.

33. Michael Grossberg, *Governing the Hearth: Law and the Family in Nineteenth-Century America* (Chapel Hill: University of North Carolina Press, 1985), pp. 84–86, 200–215, 248–53, 281–307, quotation at page 304; and Wortman, *Women in American Law*, pp. 87–88, 140–48, 182–93. See also Michael Grossberg, "Drawing Lines: The d'Hauteville Case and the Creation of a Feminine Sphere in Nineteenth-Century American Law." Paper delivered at 1988 Conference on Women and the Law in Washington, D.C., pp. 44–45 (quotations); and Michael S. Hindus and Lynne E. Withey, "The Law of Husband and Wife in Nineteenth-Century America: Changing Views of Divorce," in D. Kelly Weisberg ed., *Women and the Law: A Social Historical Perspective* (Cambridge, Mass.: Schenkman, 1982), 2:133–53.

34. Elizabeth Pleck, "Feminist Responses to 'Crimes against Women,' 1868–1896," *Signs* 8, no. 3 (Spring 1983): 465–69.

35. Speth, "Married Women's Property Acts," pp. 70–72.

36. Ibid., pp. 76–85; and Shammas et al., *Inheritance in America*, pp. 171–75, 195–204.

37. Rabkin, *Fathers to Daughters*, pp. 110–111 (quotations); and Speth, "Married Women's Property Acts," pp. 77–82.

38. Judith Wellman, "Women's Rights, Republicanism, and Revolutionary Rhetoric in Antebellum New York State," *New York History* (July 1988): 353–84.

39. Ibid. See also Wellman's articles cited in notes 42 and 43 below. Quotations are from the 1940 Women's Centennial address of Mary Beard, "Changes in the Intellectual, Ethical, Spiritual Climate," Marjorie White Collection, MC184, Box 26, Folder 150b, Schlesinger Library, Radcliffe College.

40. Ellen Carol DuBois, "Outgrowing the Compact of the Fathers: Equal Rights, Woman Suffrage, and the United States Constitution, 1820–1878," *Journal of American History* 74 (December 1987): 841. DuBois uses elipses in the following quotation to argue that the declaration "had as its central idea" protest against the denial to women of "this first right of a citizen, the elective franchise, thereby leaving her without representation in the halls of legislation, . . . oppressed on all sides." This allows her to turn the original phrase "he has oppressed her on all sides" misleadingly into apposition with the term "elective franchise," when, in fact, it is a transitional phrase leading to a listing of the other—that is, to the *nonpolitical* list of grievances in the declaration. See appendix 2 for the complete text of the Declaration of Sentiments.

41. Melder, *Beginnings of Sisterhood*, p. 146. For details about the intellectual and economic ferment in Seneca Falls, see Whitney R. Cross, *The Burned-Over District: The Social and Intellectual History of Enthusiastic Religion in Western New York, 1800–1850* (New York: Harper & Row, 1950), pp. 3–6, 55–56, 237. Cross coined the phrase "psychic highway" in referring to those in this area of New York who were "devoted to crusades aimed at the perfection of mankind and the attainment of millennial happiness." The term "burned-over," or "burnt," district refers to the analogy between forest fires and fires of the spirit. The evangelist Charles Grandison Finney applied these terms to the region. The Erie Canal, completed in 1825, aided economic

development of the region. Its completion also marked the beginning of major, significant religious revivals.

42. Judith Wellman, "The Mystery of the Seneca Falls Women's Rights Convention: Who Came and Why?" 31 May 1985 (unpublished manuscript), pp. 13–26, referred to in chapter 1 of U.S. Department of the Interior, National Park Service, "Special History Study, Women's Rights National Historical Park, New York," prepared by Sandra S. Weber, Denver Service Center, Denver, Colorado, 1985, to be published by the state of New York, 1990; Glenn C. Altschuler and Jan M. Saltzgaber, *Revivalism, Social Conscience, and Community in the Burnt-Over District: The Trial of Rhoda Bement* (Ithaca, N.Y.: Cornell University Press, 1983), pp. 89–140; Ross Evans Paulson, *Women's Suffrage and Prohibition: A Comparative Study of Equality and Social Control* (Glenview, Ill.: Scott, Foresman, 1973), p. 37; and Judith Wellman, "Women's Rights, Free Soil, and Quakerism: The Seneca Falls Women's Rights Convention," paper delivered at SHEAR Conference July 1981, pp. 26–27.

43. Judith Wellman, "The Seneca Falls Women's Rights Convention: A Study in Social Networks," *JOURNAL OF WOMEN'S HISTORY,* forthcoming; and Theodore Stanton and Harriot Blatch, eds., *Elizabeth Cady Stanton as Revealed in Her Letters, Diary, and Reminiscences,* 2 vols. (New York: Harper & Brothers, 1922), 1:142–43, 145.

44. Elizabeth Cady Stanton, Susan B. Anthony, and Matilda Joslyn Gage, eds., *History of Woman Suffrage,* 6 vols. (Rochester, N.Y.: Charles Mann, 1881; reprint, New York: Source Book, 1970), 1:50 (first quotation), 68 (second quotation). For a discussion of what the Enlightenment meant to Stanton and Anthony, see Kathleen Barry, *Susan B. Anthony: A Biography of a Singular Feminist* (New York: New York University Press, 1988), pp. 114–45, especially 126–33.

45. See appendix 2. When compared word for word with the Declaration of Independence, only 152 of the 1,071 words in the original were duplicated exactly in 1848. (These are bold-faced in appendix 2.) Although the format is that of the Declaration of Independence, it is the general Enlightenment natural-law theories that the First Feminists borrowed more than the precise Jeffersonian wording or phraseology.

46. Stanton to Anthony, 1 March 1853, quoted in Stanton and Blatch, *Stanton Revealed,* 2:48.

47. *The Revolution,* 27 October 1870, p. 264.

48. DuBois, "Outgrowing the Compact of the Fathers," p. 843. Stanton quoted at the Tenth National Woman's Rights Convention, May 1860, in Mary Jo Buhle and Paul Buhle, eds., *The Concise History of Woman Suffrage* (Urbana: University of Illinois Press, 1978), p. 171.

49. Stanton to Anthony, 20 July 1857, quoted in Elizabeth B. Clark, "Religion, Rights, and Difference in the Early Woman's Rights Movement," *Wisconsin Women's Law Journal* 3 (1987): 51.

50. Barry, *Anthony,* pp. 137–45; Elizabeth Cady Stanton, *Eighty Years and More: Reminiscences, 1815–1897* (New York: Schocken, 1971; reprint of 1898 T. Fisher Unwin Edition), pp. 215–33 (quotations at 230–31).

51. Leonard W. Levy and Harlan B. Phillips, "The *Roberts* Case: Source of the 'Separate-but-Equal' Doctrine," *American Historical Review* 56 (April 1951): 510–18.

52. Ibid., p. 511; and Roberts v. The City of Boston, 59 Mass. 198 (1849), at 201.

53. Levy and Phillips, "*Roberts* Case," pp. 513, 514.

54. Ibid., pp. 517–18, nn. 35–43.

55. *Roberts v. The City of Boston,* at 206, 209–10.

56. Stanton, Anthony, and Gage, *History of Woman Suffrage,* 2:1–89; Ida Husted Harper, *The Life and Work of Susan B. Anthony* (Indianapolis: Bowen-Merrill, 1898), pp. 207–24; Catherine Clinton, *The Other Civil War: American Women in the Nineteenth Century* (New York: Hill & Wang, 1984), pp. 81, 85–86, 90–92. Suzanne Lebsock, *The Free Women of Petersburg: Status and Culture in a Southern Town, 1784–1860* (New York: W. W. Norton, 1984), pp. 244–46.

57. Clinton, *Other Civil War,* pp. 81–89; Gerda Lerner, *The Woman in American History* (Menlo Park, Calif.: Addison-Wesley, 1971), pp. 95–105; Stanton, Anthony, and Gage, *History of Woman Suffrage,* 2:80–89; Harper, *Anthony,* pp. 225–240; Barry, *Anthony,* pp. 152–54.

58. Quoted in Andrew Sinclair, *The Better Half: The Emancipation of the American Woman* (New York: Harper & Row, 1965), p. 185.

59. Ibid.

60. Barry, *Anthony,* pp. 169–72.

61. The first section of the Fourteenth Amendment reads: "All persons born or naturalized in the United States and subject to the jurisdiction thereof, are citizens of the United States and of the State wherein they reside. No State shall make or enforce any law which shall abridge the privileges or immunities of citizens of the United States; nor shall any State deprive any person of life, liberty, or property, without due process of law; nor deny to any person within its jurisdiction the equal protection of the laws." The Fifteenth Amendment reads: "The right of citizens of the United States to vote shall not be denied or abridged by the United States or by any State on account of race, color, or previous condition of servitude." See appendix 4 for the full text of the Fourteenth and Fifteenth amendments.

62. Michael Les Benedict, "Preserving the Constitution: The Conservative Basis of Radical Reconstruction," *Journal of American History* 61 (June 1974): 87 (quoting the New York *Tribune* of 1 December 1868).

63. Ibid., p. 87 (first quotation); and Michael Kammen, *A Machine that Would Go of Itself: The Constitution in American Culture* (New York: Knopf, 1986), p. 117 (second quotation).

64. Barry, *Anthony,* pp. 174–94.

65. For various descriptions of this schism and its resolution, see Stanton, Anthony, and Gage, *History of Woman Suffrage,* 2:345–406, 2:756–862, 3:1–149; Harper, *Anthony,* pp. 241–94; Barry, *Anthony,* pp. 195–224; Ellen Carol DuBois, *Feminism and Suffrage: The Emergence of an Independent Women's Movement in America, 1848–1869* (Ithaca, N.Y.: Cornell University Press, 1978), pp. 53–125; and Israel Kugler, *From Ladies to Women: The Organized Struggle for Women's Rights in the Reconstruction Era* (Westport, Conn.: Greenwood, 1987), pp. 135–72.

66. Barry, *Anthony,* pp. 146–94.

67. Lerner, *Woman in American History,* pp. 95–105; Stanton, Anthony, and Gage, *History of Woman Suffrage,* 2:443–82; Barry, *Anthony,* pp. 195–248; and Harper, *Anthony,* 1:379 (quotation).

68. Barry, *Anthony,* pp. 146–224.

69. Benedict, "Preserving the Constitution," pp. 85, 86.

70. Kenneth L. Karst, "Woman's Constitution," *Duke Law Journal* 3 (June 1984): 487 passim.

## 5. Constitutional Discrimination, 1872–1908

1. I am referring to the works of Kathleen Barry, Norma Basch, Steven Buechler, Richard H. Chused, Ellen DuBois, Michael Grossberg, Hendrik Hartog, Israel Kugler, Suzanne Lebsock, Nancy E. McGlen, Karen Berger Morello, Karen O'Connor, Frances Olsen, Peggy A. Rabkin, and Marlene Wortman—I have found the legal research of Basch, Hartog, Lebsock, and Olsen particularly useful in writing this chapter.
2. Hendrik Hartog, "The Constitution of Aspiration and 'the Rights that Belong to Us All,' " *Journal of American History* 74 (December 1987): 1021, 1023 (quotations).
3. Elizabeth Cady Stanton, Susan B. Anthony, and Matilda Joslyn Gage, eds., *History of Woman Suffrage* (Rochester, N.Y.: Charles Mann, 1881; reprint, New York: Source Book, 1970), 2:627.
4. Details of Anthony's arguments for her own and other women's right to vote can be found in ibid., 2:627–715.
5. Ibid., 2:635.
6. Ibid., 2:638.
7. Ibid., 2:639–40.
8. Ibid., 2:640–41.
9. Ibid., 2:641.
10. Ibid., 2:642, 643–44.
11. Silver v. Ladd, 74 U.S. (7 Wall.) 219 (1868), at 219.
12. Stanton, Anthony, and Gage, *History of Woman Suffrage*, 2:647.
13. Ibid., 2:647–80, quotations at 647, 689. There remains some confusion over whether Hunt was procedurally correct in directing a guilty verdict in this criminal trial. Today, directed verdicts in criminal suits usually occur only with a "judgment of acquittal," but there may be no directed verdict of conviction because this would be a due-process violation of the defendant's right to trial by jury. Hunt defended his decision to direct a verdict of guilty when he denied Anthony's attorney's request for a retrial. Citing New York State law precedents in *both* civil and criminal cases, "where the facts are conceded, or where they are contradicted by evidence, it has always been the practice of the Courts to take the case from the jury and decide it as a question of law." Since "every fact in the case was undisputed"—that is, Anthony was, after all, a woman who admitted to voting—Hunt denied the motion for a new trial because the duty of a jury was to decide on the facts of the case and these were not in dispute, leaving it to "the court to determine whether, according to the law, the defendant is guilty." Since he had done this and the facts had not changed, Hunt concluded that there was no reason for a retrial according to late nineteenth-century constitutionalism and the laws of New York State. See U.S. v. Anthony, 24 Fed. Cas. (C.C.N.D.N.Y. 1873), at 832–33.
14. Stanton, Anthony, and Gage, *History of Woman Suffrage*, 2:678–80; and *U.S. v. Anthony*, at 829–33 (quotations).

15. Stanton, Anthony, and Gage, *History of Woman Suffrage*, 2:658. Seldon had confirmed this advice to Anthony in writing. See Seldon to Anthony, 27 November 1872. The complete text of this letter can be found in ibid., 2:935.
16. Ibid., 2:660–61.
17. Ibid., 2:675.
18. Ibid., 2:687–88.
19. Ibid., 2:689, 690–91, 947–49.
20. Ibid., 2:691–714.
21. Ibid., 2:701.
22. Ibid., 2:934–35. This letter is quoted with slightly different wording and with less exuberance and emphasis in Ida Husted Harper, *The Life and Work of Susan B. Anthony* (Indianapolis: Bowen-Merrill, 1899), 2:424.
23. See appendix 3 for the text of the 1876 Declaration of Rights.
24. For a discussion of the futility of using history to document "original-intent" arguments, see Leonard W. Levy, *Original Intent and the Framers of the Constitution* (New York: Macmillan, 1988), pp. 284–321.
25. Konigsberg v. State Bar, 353 U.S. 252 (1957); and Schware v. Board of Examiners, 353 U.S. 232 (1957).
26. For other examples of women studying the law and attempting to become attorneys before 1908, see Karen Berger Morello, *The Invisible Bar: The Woman Lawyer in America, 1638 to the Present* (Boston: Beacon, 1986), pp. 3–87.
27. Quoted in Dorothy Thomas, ed., *Women Lawyers in the United States* (New York: Scarecrow, 1957), p. vii. See also Morello, *Invisible Bar*, pp. 11–14.
28. Ibid.
29. Quoted in Janette Barnes, "Women and Entrance to the Legal Profession," *Journal of Legal Education* 23 (1970): 283; and Morello, *Invisible Bar*, pp. 44–49.
30. Morello, *Invisible Bar*, pp. 22–38, 49–65; and State v. Goodell, 39 Wisc. 232 (1875), at 245–46.
31. *In re Goodell*, 48 Wisc. 693 (1879), at 694.
32. Morello, *Invisible Bar*, pp. 14–18; and Nancy T. Gilliam, "A Professional Pioneer: Myra Bradwell's Fight to Practice Law," *Law and History Review* 5 (Spring 1987): 105–9; and Frances Olsen, "From False Paternalism to False Equality: Judicial Assaults on Feminist Community, Illinois 1869–1895," *Michigan Law Review* 84 (June 1986): 1523–25.
33. Bradwell v. Illinois, 83 U.S. (16 Wall.) 130 (1873), at 141–42; and Morello, *Invisible Bar*, pp. 18–23.
34. *Bradwell v. Illinois*, at 143.
35. Ibid., at 142.
36. Olsen, "From False Paternalism to False Equality," pp. 1531–44, quotations at 1531–32.
37. Ritchie v. People, 155 Ill. 98, 40 N.E. 458 (1895), quoted in ibid., p. 1534.
38. Barbara Allen Babcock, Ann E. Freedman, Eleanor Holmes Norton, and Susan C. Ross, *Sex Discrimination and the Law: Causes and Remedies* (Boston: Little, Brown, 1975), pp. 7–8 (quotation); Gilliam, "A Professional Pioneer," pp. 117–23.
39. Slaughter-House Cases, 16 Wall 36 (1873), at 81.
40. Ibid.

41. Ibid., at 122; *Bradwell v. Illinois,* 133–37.
42. Olsen, "From False Paternalism to False Equality," pp. 1527–28.
43. Charles Fairman, *History of the Supreme Court of the United States* (New York: Macmillan, 1971), Vol. 7: *Reconstruction and Reunion, 1864–1888,* p. 1365 (quotation). See also Morello, *Invisible Bar,* pp. 21–22.
44. Stanton, Anthony, and Gage, *History of Woman Suffrage,* 2:946.
45. *American Law Review* 28 (1894): 278–83.
46. Stanton, Anthony, and Gage, *History of Woman Suffrage,* 2:406–26, 716 (quotation), and 4:3–5.
47. See ibid., 2:406–10, for the texts of Francis Minor's original letter and resolutions and for Virginia Minor's address to the Missouri Suffrage Association. Both were published in *The Revolution,* 5 January 1870. Ten thousand extra copies were printed and distributed to members of Congress and others across the country. See also Stanton, Anthony, and Gage, 2:715–34, for the Minors' original petition to the Circuit Court of St. Louis after Virginia Minor was denied the right to vote and for their brief to the state of Missouri.
48. I am grateful to Norma Basch for questioning the "intent" and tone of the Minors' brief. See Basch, "Reconstructing Female Citizenship: *Minor v. Happersett,*" paper delivered at Conference on Women and the Constitution at American University in April 1988.
49. Harold M. Hyman and William M. Wiecek, *Equal Justice under the Law: Constitutional Development, 1835–1875* (New York: Harper & Row, 1982), pp. 495–96.
50. Philip B. Kurland and Gerhard Casper, eds., *Landmark Briefs and Arguments of the Supreme Court of the United States: Constitutional Law* (Arlington, Va.: University Publications, 1975), pp. 214–48.
51. Minor v. Happersett, 88 U.S. 162 (1875), at 163–64, 165, 167, 170.
52. Ibid., at 177–79.
53. Ibid., at 176ff.; and Basch, "Reconstructing Female Citizenship."
54. Ibid., at 173, 176; and Basch, "Reconstructing Female Citizenship."
55. Basch, "Reconstructing Female Citizenship."
56. Michael Kammen, *A Machine that Would Go of Itself: The Constitution in American Culture* (New York: Knopf, 1986), p. 28.
57. W. William Hodes, "Women and the Constitution: Some Legal History and a New Approach to the Nineteenth Amendment," *Rutgers Law Review* 25 (1970): 35, 43–46.
58. Anthony quoted in Anthony, Stanton, and Gage, *History of Woman Suffrage,* 2:641. Two of the earliest Supreme Court cases denying black men the vote were U.S. v. Reese, 92 U.S. 214 (1876); and U.S. v. Cruikshank, 92 U.S. 542 (1876).
59. Hall v. De Cuir, 95 S. Ct. 485 (1877), at 489, 490. (See chapter 4 of this volume for a discussion of Roberts v. The City of Boston, 59 Mass. 198 [1849].)
60. *Hall v. De Cuir,* at 503, 505.
61. For other representative transportation and school cases, see Mary Frances Ward v. Noah F. Flood, U.S. S. Ct. 36 (1874); Chicago & Northwest Railway Company v. Anna Williams, North Carolina S. Ct. 185 (1853). For representative samples of specific domestic rights cases involving former slaves in South Carolina, see Davenport v. Caldwell, 10 S. Ct. 317 (1877), State v. Whaley, 10 S. Ct. 500 (1878), James v.

Mickey, 26 S. Ct. 270 (1886), and Knox v. Moore, 41 S. Ct. 355 (1893). See Hyman and Wiecek, *Equal Justice under the Law*, pp. 473–515, for other decisions in the 1870s and 1880s that set in motion "the judicial avalanche that buried adherents of race equality" (p. 496).

62. *Minor v. Happersett*, at 178.
63. Stanton, Anthony, and Gage, *History of Woman Suffrage*, 2:952.
64. Archibald Cox, *The Court and the Constitution* (Boston: Houghton Mifflin, 1987), p. 316; and Hyman and Wiecek, *Equal Justice under the Law*, pp. 386–413.
65. Stanton, Anthony, and Gage, *History of Woman Suffrage*, 2:407–8, 411, 443–82; and 4:3–4; and Kathleen Barry, *Susan B. Anthony: A Biography of a Singular Feminist* (New York: New York University Press, 1988), pp. 231–37.
66. Stanton, Anthony, and Gage, *History of Woman Suffrage*, 2:407–520, 745 (quotation from Matilda Gage's critique of *Minor*).
67. See appendix 3 for the text of the 1876 Declaration of Rights and for all other quotations from it in the text.
68. Ellen Carol DuBois, "Outgrowing the Compact of the Fathers: Equal Rights, Woman Suffrage, and the United States Constitution, 1820–1878," *Journal of American History* 74 (December 1987): 841.
69. Hartog, "Constitution of Aspiration," pp. 1016–17.
70. Ibid., p. 1018.
71. Barry, *Anthony*, pp. 275–303.
72. DuBois, "Outgrowing the Compact of the Fathers," pp. 836–62.
73. Ibid.; and Elizabeth Cady Stanton, *Eighty Years and More: Reminiscences, 1815–1897* (1898; reprint, New York: Schocken, 1971), p. 150; and Hartog, "Constitution of Aspiration," p. 1018.
74. Quoted in Madeline Stern, *We the Women: Career Firsts of Nineteenth-Century America* (New York: Schulte, 1963), p. 211.
75. Reed v. Reed, 404 U.S. 71 (1971).
76. Quoted in Gerda Lerner, *The Female Experience: An American Documentary* (Indianapolis: Bobbs-Merrill, 1977), pp. 418–19.
77. Kammen, *A Machine that Would Go*, pp. 119, 398; and Michael Les Benedict, "Preserving the Constitution: The Conservative Basis of Radical Reconstruction," *Journal of American History* 61 (June 1974): 86.
78. Hartog, "Constitutional Aspiration," pp. 1016–25; and Kammen, *A Machine that Would Go*, p. 119.
79. Kammen, *A Machine that Would Go*, p. 398.
80. Babcock et al., *Sex Discrimination and the Law*, p. 19.
81. Cox, *Court and the Constitution*, pp. 120–31, 322–34, 336–38, 339–400. See also chapters 1 and 8 of this volume.
82. Richard H. Chused, "Married Women's Property Law: 1800–1850," *Georgetown Law Journal* 71 (1983): 1397–1425 (quotation); and Carole Shammas, Marylynn Salmon, and Michel Dahlin, *Inheritance in America: From the Colonial Times to the Present* (New Brunswick, N.J.: Rutgers University Press, 1987), pp. 83–101, 103–22, especially tables 4.1, 5.8, 5.9, 5.11, 5.12. See also charts in appendix 1 of this volume.
83. Shammas et al., *Inheritance in America*, pp. 88–101; and Richard H. Chused, "Late Nineteenth-Century Married Women's Property Law: Reception of the Early Married Women's Property Acts by Courts and Legislatures," *American Journal of Legal History*

29 (January 1985): 24–34; and idem, "Married Women's Property Law," pp. 1392–1421.

84. Chused, "Married Women's Property Law," pp. 24, 34.

85. Shammas et al., *Inheritance in America*, pp. 85–86.

86. Ibid., pp. 86, 119, table 5.12, 167.

87. Richard H. Chused, "Married Women's Property and Inheritance by Widows in Massachusetts: A Study of Wills Probated between 1800 and 1850," *Berkeley Women's Law Journal* 2 (Fall 1986): 42–88 (a review of the research of others can be found in this article); Michael B. Dougan, "Arkansas Married Woman's Property Law," *Arkansas Historical Quarterly* 46 (Spring 1987): 2–26; Marlene Stein Wortman, ed.; *Women in American Law: From Colonial Times to the New Deal* (San Francisco: Holmes & Meier), pp. 13–105, 213–85; and Shammas et al., *Inheritance in America*, pp. 83–122.

88. Research on contemporary working-class women indicates that when there is little discretionary money, women pay the family bills; when there is a surplus, men manage the money. Therefore, there is little evidence today that when women pay the bills "they wield a great deal of power and influence in the family," although this claim is often made. Whether it is any more valid for the nineteenth century remains to be proven because post–World War II evidence indicates that no real decision-making power (or very little) is involved in managing low family incomes or those that are just beginning to rise. See Lillian Breslow Rubin, *Worlds of Pain: Life in the Working-Class Family* (New York: Basic Books, 1975), pp. 105–13.

89. Loren Schweninger, "Property-Owning Free African-American Women in the South," *JOURNAL OF WOMEN'S HISTORY* 1, no. 3 (February 1990): 13–45.

90. Chused, "Late Nineteenth-Century Married Women's Property Law," p. 3 (first quotation); and Carol H. Lefcourt, ed., *Women and the Law* (New York: Clark Boardman, 1987), 3A-15 and 3A-25 (second quotation).

91. Susan B. Anthony, "Woman's Half-Century of Evolution," *North American Review* 175, no. 553 (December 1902): 804, 808–9.

## 6. Constitutional Protection, 1908–1963

1. For general works on the labor and suffrage activities of Progressive women, see the bibliographies contained in Steven M. Buechler, *The Transformation of the Woman Suffrage Movement: The Case of Illinois, 1850–1920* (New Brunswick, N.J.: Rutgers University Press, 1986); Susan Ware, *Modern American Women: A Documentary History* (Chicago: Dorsey, 1989); and Susan Lehrer, *Origins of Protective Labor Legislation for Women, 1905–1925* (Albany, N.Y.: State University of New York, 1987).

2. Equal pay for equal work was first proposed at the National Labor Union Convention of 1868 and first introduced in Congress in 1870. It did not become a significant federal issue until World War I and did not become law until the 1963 Equal Pay Act —ninety-five years after it was first conceptualized and seventy years after it was taken up by the First Women's movement. See also Lehrer, *Origins of Protective Legislation*, pp. 95–114.

3. See note 1 above, especially Lehrer, *Origins of Protective Legislation*, pp. 19–40, 115–68; and Buechler, *Transformation of Woman Suffrage*, pp. 148–68.

4. Allgeyer v. Louisiana, 165 U.S. 578 (1897).

5. Holden v. Hardy, 169 U.S. 366 (1898), at 383–84 (first quotation), 393–98; and Lochner v. New York, 198 U.S. 45 (1905), at 63 (second quotation).

6. *Lochner v. New York,* at 45, 50, 54–58, 63, 64; Philippa Strum, *Louis D. Brandeis: Justice for the People* (Cambridge: Harvard University Press, 1984), p. 118 (first three quotations, not from opinion itself).

7. From Holmes's dissent in *Lochner v. New York,* at 74–76.

8. Strum, *Brandeis,* pp. 120 (quotation), 119, 121.

9. Barbara Allen Babcock et al., *Sex Discrimination and the Law: Causes and Remedies* (Boston: Little, Brown, 1975), pp. 19–20 (quotation). Babcock and her coauthors note that one method used by the Court in giving "substance" to due process was to take "judicial notice" of "common understanding" or "common knowledge" to determine if a state statute was "reasonable." "Initially at least," according to Babcock, " 'common knowledge' was virtually indistinguishable from the personal world view of the justices" (p. 20).

10. Strum, *Brandeis,* pp. 115–16 (quotation).

11. Ibid., p. 128. To his credit, Brandeis did later insist that all of the findings gathered by the two Goldmark sisters be published by the Russell Sage Foundation as a book in 1912, entitled *Fatigue and Efficiency.*

12. *Woman in Industry: Decision in Muller and Brief for the State of Oregon* (New York: National Consumers League, 1908), n.p.

13. Muller v. Oregon, 208 U.S. 412 (1908), at 421–22.

14. Strum, *Brandeis,* pp. 118 (quotation), 119–21.

15. In addition to Strum, *Brandeis,* pp. 44–131, see Nancy S. Erickson, "Historical Background of 'Protective' Labor Legislation: *Muller v. Oregon,*" in D. Kelly Weisberg, ed., *Women and the Law: A Social Historical Perspective* (Cambridge, Mass.: Schenkman, 1982), 2:155–86; Jennifer Friesen and Ronald K. L. Collins, "Looking Back on *Muller v. Oregon,*" *American Bar Association Journal* 69 (March–April 1983): 294–98, 472–77.

16. Strum, *Brandeis,* p. 127 (quotations at 128, 131).

17. *Muller* brief, p. 24. Erickson notes that this analogy was similar to one used by Mathew Carpenter in defending Myra Bradwell's right to practice law in Bradwell v. Illinois, 83 U.S. 130, 134 (1873).

18. Laurence H. Tribe, *American Constitutional Law* (Mineola, N.Y.: Foundation Press, 1978), p. 435; and Babcock, *Sex Discrimination,* p. 49, n. 78.

19. Donald G. Mathews and Jane Sherron De Hart, *ERA and the Politics of Cultural Conflict: North Carolina* (New York: Oxford University Press, 1990); and Buechler, *Transformation of Woman Suffrage,* pp. 168–82.

20. Carroll Smith-Rosenberg, *Disorderly Conduct: Visions of Gender in Victorian America* (New York: Knopf, 1985), pp. 252–305, 358 (n. 127); and idem, "Discourses of Sexuality and Subjectivity: The New Woman, 1870–1936," in Martin Bauml Duberman et al., eds., *Hidden from History: Reclaiming the Gay and Lesbian Past* (New York: NAL, 1989), pp. 277–94.

21. Radice v. People of the State of New York, 264 U.S. 292 (1924), at 294.

22. Bunting v. Oregon, 243 U.S. 426 (1917), at 436.

23. Babcock et al., *Sex Discrimination and the Law,* p. 41. In addition to the Frankfurter and Goldmark brief in *Adkins,* another equally long statistical brief was filed by Frankfurter with Molly Dewson, then secretary of the NCL.

24. Adkins v. Children's Hospital, 261 U.S. 525 (1923), at 546, 553, 558.

25. Marlene Stein Wortman, ed., *Women in American Law: From Colonial Times to the New Deal* (San Francisco: Holmes & Meier, 1985), p. 335 (quotation). See also Judith A. Baer, *The Chains of Protection: The Judicial Response to Women's Labor Legislation* (Westport, Conn.: Greenwood, 1976), pp. 75–135.

26. West Coast Hotel v. Parrish, 300 U.S. 379 (1937), at 397, 399–400 (quotations).

27. Babcock et al., *Sex Discrimination and the Law*, p. 53; and Wortman, *Women in American Law*, pp. 332–36.

28. Lois Scharf, "ER and Feminism," in Joan Hoff-Wilson and Marjorie Lightman, eds., *Without Precedent: The Life and Career of Eleanor Roosevelt* (Bloomington: Indiana University Press, 1984), pp. 234–36; idem, *Female Employment, Feminism, and the Great Depression* (Westport, Conn.: Greenwood, 1980), pp. 86–138.

29. Nancy F. Cott, *The Grounding of Modern Feminism* (New Haven, Conn.: Yale University Press, 1987), pp. 66–77 passim; and Lehrer, *Origins of Protective Legislation*, pp. 99–105.

30. Christine A. Lunardini, *From Equal Suffrage to Equal Rights: Alice Paul and the National Woman's Party, 1910–1929* (New York: New York University Press, 1986), pp. 71–103; Cott, *Grounding of Modern Feminism*, pp. 53–81.

31. Lunardini, *Equal Suffrage to Equal Rights*, pp. 150–70; Cott, *Grounding of Modern Feminism*, pp. 75–81, 107–14 passim; Susan D. Becker, *The Origins of the Equal Rights Amendment: American Feminism between the Wars* (Westport, Conn.: Greenwood, 1981), pp. 15–42, 47–70; Burnita Shelton Matthews, "Women Should Have Equal Rights with Men: A Reply," *American Bar Association Journal* 12 (1926): 117–20; and Amelia Fry, "Alice Paul and the ERA," and Kathryn Kish Sklar, "Why Were Most Politically Active Women Opposed to the ERA in the 1920s?"—both in Joan Hoff-Wilson, ed., *Rights of Passage: The Past and Future of the ERA* (Bloomington: Indiana University Press, 1986), pp. 8–35.

32. Cott, *Grounding of Modern Feminism*, pp. 85–107, 126–30; Susan Ware, *Partner and I: Molly Dewson, Feminism, and New Deal Politics* (New Haven, Conn.: Yale University Press, 1987), pp. 148–57; Elisabeth Israels Perry, *Belle Moskowitz: Feminine Politics and the Exercise of Power in the Age of Al Smith* (New York: Oxford University Press, 1987), pp. 150–67.

33. For details of divisions in two states, see Buechler, *Transformation of Woman Suffrage*, pp. 199–228 passim; and Felice D. Gordon, *After Winning: The Legacy of the New Jersey Suffragists, 1920–1947* (New Brunswick, N.J.: Rutgers University Press, 1986), pp. 33–123.

34. One has only to compare the 1930 publication by the National League of Women Voters, *A Survey of the Legal Status of Women in the Forty-eight States*, with NOW's 1987 publication, *The State-by-State Guide to Women's Legal Rights*, to see how much more uniform the laws affecting women have become across the country.

35. For a detailed study of how fragmentation led to a "deradicalization" within the First Women's movement in one state, but also for a theoretical delineation of three distinct phases and leadership in the struggle for the vote, see Buechler, *Transformation of Woman Suffrage*, pp. 37–55, 217–28 passim.

36. Elisabeth Israels Perry, "Training for Public Life: ER and Women's Political Networks in the 1920s," and Susan Ware, "ER and Democratic Politics: Women in the Postsuffrage Era"—both in Hoff-Wilson and Lightman, *Without Precedent*, pp. 28–

60; Perry, *Moskowitz*, pp. xii, 160 (quotations) passim; Ware, *Partner and I*, p. xi–xix, 158–95 passim.

37. Ware, *Partner and I*, pp. 95–97, 154–55, 162–63, 188–92; Martha H. Swain, "ER and Ellen Woodward: A Partnership for Women's Work: Relief and Security"; Tamara K. Hareven, "ER and Reform"; and Lois Scharf, "ER and Feminism"—all in Hoff-Wilson and Lightman, *Without Precedent*, pp. 135–51, 201–13, 226–37.

38. Cynthia E. Harrison, *On Account of Sex: The Politics of Women's Issues, 1945–1968* (Berkeley: University of California Press, 1988), pp. 6–12; and Becker, *Origins of the Equal Rights Amendment*, pp. 75–111, 121–51.

39. Blanche Wiesen Cook, " 'Turn Toward Peace': ER and Foreign Affairs," and Scharf, "ER and Feminism"—both in Hoff-Wilson and Marjorie Lightman, *Without Precedent*, pp. 108–21, 239–45; and Paula Pfeffer, "Eleanor Roosevelt versus the National Women's Party: A Study in Conflict," unpublished conference paper delivered at 1984 Fifth Berkshire Conference on Women's History.

40. For a complete list of Mary Beard's writings, see Barbara K. Turoff, *Mary Beard as Force in History*, Monograph Series No. 3 (Dayton, Ohio: Wright State University, 1979), pp. 76–78.

41. Ibid., pp. 7–13; Loretta E. Zimmerman, "Mary Beard: An Activist of the Progressive Era," *University of Portland Review* 26 (Spring 1974): 17. Author's interview with Miriam Beard Vagts, 12 September 1982.

42. Microfilm of *The Beard Material*, as provided by William Beard and Miriam B. Vagts, *Vita*, Film No. 139, Part 3, DePauw University, Greencastle, Indiana (hereafter cited as DePauw Film No. 139, *Vita*). Author's interview with Miriam Beard Vagts, 12 September 1982; Vagts to author, 13 August 1982; Zimmerman, "Mary Beard," pp. 18–20; Turoff, *Mary Beard*, pp. 12–17, 38 (quotation).

43. DePauw Film No. 139, *Vita*; Zimmerman, "Mary Beard," pp. 20–25; Turoff, *Mary Beard*, pp. 19–29.

44. DePauw Film No. 139, *Vita* (quotation). Between 1913 and 1916 Alice Paul and Mary Beard wrote each other over eighty times. See NWP Microfilm, Reel No. 2, Library of Congress.

45. Zimmerman, "Mary Beard," pp. 24–31; author's interview with Miriam Beard Vagts, 12 September 1982; Beard to Florence Kitchell, 16 October 1954, Kitchelt Collection, Box 5, Folder 13, Schlesinger Library, Radcliffe College, Cambridge.

46. Material on this international archive project can be found in the Smith College Sophia Smith Collection of Mary Beard's papers.

47. Material on these projects can be found in the Smith College Sophia Smith and Schlesinger Library collections relating to Mary Beard.

48. For the most complete set of reviews, see DePauw Film No. 139, Part 3, Mary Beard File, Part 2—Book Reviews. Other reviews can be found in Beard to Marjorie White, 3 April 1946, commenting on one critical review by Lewis Gannett in the New York *Herald Tribune Weekly Book Review*, 17 March 1946. Gannett did not understand her use of the word *force*. Included in this section of White's papers are copies of her own favorable review, plus a very negative one by Stephen Peabody in the *Daily Worker*, 14 April 1946, and assorted other reviews and notices of the book—all in the Marjorie White Collection on John Braeman Film MC 184, Box 26, Folder 150a, Schlesinger Library. See also Beard to James Putnam, her editor at Macmillan, 24 April and 1

May 1946, 1945–1954 Folder of Letters from Charles and Mary Beard, in Macmillan Company Papers, New York Public Library; and Beard to Ellen S. Woodward, 17 May 1946, Woodward Papers, Box 2, Folder 15, Manuscript Collections, Mississippi Department of Archives and History, Jackson.

49. Beard to Wilbur K. Jordan, 23 June 1944, Mary Beard Collection, A-9, Box 2, Folder 29, Schlesinger Library.

50. Eugene D. Genovese, "Beard's Economic Interpretation of History," in *Charles A. Beard: An Observance of the Centennial of His Birth* (Greencastle, Ind.: DePauw University, 1976), pp. 28–37; author's interview with Miriam Beard Vagts, 12 September 1982; and Beard to Jane Norman Smith, n.d., A-116, Boxes 1–2, Folders 47, 55, 60; and Beard to Elsie M. Hill, 19 July 1921, National Woman's Party Papers (hereafter cited as NWPP), 1913–1974, Reel No. 9. Charles Beard lacked "modern" views on women, to the point that he could not see any prominent role for women in business, according to his daughter. It was not entirely coincidental, therefore, that his first public opposition to the ERA was published in 1921—the same year that Mary Beard privately began to oppose it.

51. Beard to Hill, 19 July 1921, NWPP, Reel No. 9.

52. Beard to Alma Lutz, 29 January 1937, NWPP, Reel No. 58. This letter by Beard did not appear in any issue of *Equal Rights* for 1937. *Equal Rights* published many other anti-Women's Charter articles after the *New York Times* first announced its formulation and supporters at the end of December 1936. See, for example, *Equal Rights*, 15 January, 1 and 15 February, and 1 March 1937, NWPP, Reel No. 156. For private Beard letters denying she supported the Women's Charter, see Beard to Florence Bayard Hilles, 5 and 21 January 1937, NWPP, Reel No. 58.

53. Mary Ritter Beard, "Test for the Modern Woman," *Current History* 37 (November 1932): 183. Although this article was written as a general critique of what the Great Depression had done to feminism, in 1932 it was directed more at the views of the NWP than of those supporting protective legislation. See Becker, *Origins of the Equal Rights Amendment*, pp. 60–62.

54. Mary Ritter Beard, *On Understanding Women* (Westport, Conn: Greenwood, 1968; reprint of original 1931 Longmans edition), pp. 522–23.

55. Ibid., pp. 513–14 (first quotation), 522; idem, *Woman's Work in Municipalities* (New York: D. Appleton, 1916), p. 226 (second quotation); and idem, ed., *America through Women's Eyes* (New York: Macmillan, 1933), pp. 2–7 (third quotation).

56. Beard to Woodward, 18 November 1938, Woodward Papers, Box 2, Folder 15, Mississippi Department of Archives and History; Beard to Florence Kitchelt, 16 October 1954, Kitchelt Collection, Box 5, Folder 13, Schlesinger Library; Miriam Beard Vagts to author, 13 August 1982; Ann J. Lane, ed., *Mary Ritter Beard: A Sourcebook* (Boston: Northeastern University Press, 1988; reprint of 1977 Schocken edition), p. 29; and Turoff, *Mary Beard*, pp. 19–30.

57. Beard, *Woman's Work in Municipalities*, p. 101.

58. Beard, *America through Women's Eyes*, pp. 5–6; Berenice Carroll, "Mary Beard's *Woman as Force in History*: A Critique," *Massachusetts Review* 13 (Winter–Spring 1972): 125–43; and *Equal Rights*, 6 July 1935, p. 140, NWPP, Reel No. 157.

59. *Equal Rights*, 6 July 1935, p. 140, NWPP, Reel No. 157 (first quotation); and Beard, "Changes in the Intellectual, Ethical, Spiritual Climate," Marjorie White Collection, MC 184, Box 26, Folder 150b, Schlesinger Library (second quotation).

60. Beard, "The Historical Approach To Learning about Women," Beard Collection, A-9, Box 1, Folder 5c, Schlesinger Library.
61. Beard to Woodward, 18 November 1938, 18 September 1939, 3 October 1939, Woodward Papers, Box 2, Folder 15, Mississippi Department of Archives and History. My thanks to Martha H. Swain for bringing these Beard letters to my attention.
62. Beard, *Woman as Force in History*, pp. 29, 151 (quotation).
63. Carol Gilligan, *In a Different Voice: Psychological Theory and Women's Development* (Cambridge: Harvard University Press, 1982).
64. Goesaert v. Cleary et al., Members of the Liquor Control Commission of Michigan, 335 U.S. 464 (1948). *Goesaert* was not overruled until Sail'er Inn, Inc. v. Kirby, 5 Cal. 3d 1. 20 585 P. 2d 329 (1971); Baindridge v. Williams, 397 U.S. 471 (1970).
65. *Sail'er*, at 585 P. 2d 329 (1971).
66. Strauder v. West Virginia, 100 U.S. 303 (1879), at 310.
67. Rosencrantz v. Territory of Washington, 2 Wash. Terr. 267, 5 P. 305 (1884), at 272 and 306.
68. Harland v. Territory, 3 Wash. Terr. 131, 13 P. 453 (1887).
69. John D. Johnston Jr., and Charles L. Knapp, "Sex Discrimination by Law: A Study in Judicial Perspective," *New York University Law Review* 46, no. 4 (October 1971): 709–10.
70. Ibid., p. 711.
71. Ibid., pp. 714–15.
72. Quoted in ibid., p. 717.
73. Quoted in ibid., p. 719.
74. Eva R. Rubin, *The Supreme Court and the American Family* (Westport, Conn.: Greenwood, 1986), pp. 1–9.
75. Johnston and Knapp, "Sex Discrimination by Law," pp. 736–47.

## 7. Constitutional Equality, 1963–1990

Segments of this chapter first appeared in Joan Hoff-Wilson, "The Unfinished Revolution: Changing Legal Status of U.S. Women," *Signs* 13, no. 1 (Winter 1987): 7–36.

1. Edward E. Sampson, "Globalization and Psychology's Theory of the Person," *American Psychologist* 44, no. 6 (June 1989): 919.
2. Cynthia E. Harrison, "A 'New Frontier' for Women: The Public Policy of the Kennedy Administration," *Journal of American History* 67, no. 3 (December 1980): 635, 644–45.
3. Katie Louchheim, *By the Political Sea* (New York: Doubleday, 1970), p. 245; *Congressional Record*, 9 August 1961, pp. 15258–60; and Lois Scharf, "ER and Feminism," in Joan Hoff-Wilson and Marjorie Lightman, eds., *Without Precedent: The Life and Career of Eleanor Roosevelt* (Bloomington: Indiana University Press, 1984), p. 247.
4. Oral History Interviews of Esther Peterson, 25 November 1968, 1:27. Lyndon Baines Johnson Library, Austin, Texas.
5. Ibid., 1:28; and 29 October 1974, 2:13–17. Contrary to the impression conveyed by Cynthia E. Harrison in *On Account of Sex: The Politics of Women's Issues, 1945–1968* (Berkeley: University of California Press, 1988), Peterson did not have to move "quickly to identify Johnson with the Kennedy policy initiatives on women" (p. 173).

Johnson had already identified himself with these issues, as Peterson's oral-history interviews clearly indicate.

6. Harrison, " 'New Frontier' for Women," pp. 638–39. For example, India Edwards, executive director of the Women's Division of the Democratic National Committee, was not appointed to the commission. See India Edwards, *Pulling No Punches* (New York: G. P. Putnam's Sons, 1977), p. 231.

7. *American Women: Report of the President's Commission on the Status of Women, 1963* (Washington, D.C.: Government Printing Office, 1963), pp. 76–77; Oral History Interviews of Esther Peterson, 2:13–16; and Nancy Kegan Smith, "Women and the White House: A Look at Women's Papers in the Johnson Library," *Prologue* 18, no. 2 (Summer 1986): 123–29.

8. Harrison, *On Account of Sex*, pp. 174–76.

9. U.S. Congress, House Select Subcommittee on Labor, *Hearings on H.R. 8898 and H.R. 10226*, 87th Cong., 2d Sess. (Washington, D.C.: Government Printing Office, 1962), Pt. 1, pp. i–v, 24–26, 141–42, and Pt. 2, pp. ii–iv; *Congressional Record*, 14 June 1962, p. 10501 (St. George quotation), 25 July 1962, pp. 14768–69, 14782, 17 May 1963, pp. 8914–17, 23 May 1963, pp. 9193–217, 9761; U.S. Congress, House Select Subcommittee on Labor, *Hearings on H.R. 4269 and H.R. 3861*, 88th Cong., 1st Sess. (Washington, D.C.: Government Printing Office, 1963), pp. 7–10; and Harrison, *On Account of Sex*, pp. 31–32, 35, 177.

10. Jo Freeman, "Women and Public Policy: An Overview," in Ellen Boneparth, ed., *Women, Power, and Policy* (New York: Pergamon, 1982), p. 63. Freeman is critical of this point of view because it still "accepts as standard the traditional male lifestyle, and that standard in turn assumes that one's primary responsibility should and can be one's job, because one has a spouse (or spouse surrogate) whose primary responsibility is the maintenance of house and family obligations" (p. 63).

11. Gilbert Steiner, *Constitutional Inequality: The Political Fortunes of the Equal Rights Amendment* (Washington, D.C.: Brookings Institution, 1985), pp. 12–13; Freeman, "Women and Public Policy," pp. 52–53. Increasing disillusionment with male-dominated antiwar and civil rights movements were also factors contributing to the emergence of the Second Women's movement. Other nationally organized activist groups included the Women's Equity Action League (WEAL); Federally Employed Women (FEW); Human Rights for Women, Inc. (HRW)—all formed in 1968; Professional Women's Political Caucus (NWPC), formalized in 1971; and the National Black Feminist Organization of 1973.

12. Congressman Howard W. Smith, quoted in Caroline Bird, *Born Female: The High Cost of Keeping Women Down* (David McKay, 1968; reprint, New York: Pocket Books, 1969), pp. 2–3.

13. Ibid., pp. 3–7; Robert Stevens Miller Jr., "Sex Discrimination and Title VII of the Civil Rights Act of 1964," *Minnesota Law Review* 51 (1967): 883, n. 34.

14. Jo Freeman, *The Politics of Women's Liberation* (New York: David McKay, 1975), pp. 177–84; and idem, "Women and Public Policy," p. 52.

15. *Federal Register*, 34:12985; "White House Fact Sheet: Women in the Federal Government," 18 August 1972, Robert Finch Papers, Occidental College, Los Angeles (hereafter cited as Finch Papers).

16. Samuel H. Beer, "In Search of a New Public Philosophy," in Anthony King, ed., *The New American Political System* (Washington, D.C.: American Enterprise Institute for

Public Policy Research, 1978), p. 35 (first quotation); Joan Hoff-Wilson, "Nixon," in Frank N. Magill, ed., *American Presidents* (Englewood Cliffs, N.J.: Prentice Hall, 1986), pp. 762–63; "White House Fact Sheet," 18 August 1972, Finch Papers; and Tom Wicker, *New York Times*, 27 January 1989, p. A31 (second quotation). See pp. 268–70 in this volume for the recent Supreme Court decision negatively affecting "set-asides."

17. Herman Edelsberg, quoted in *Labor Relations Reporter* 61 (August 1966): 253–55; Steiner, *Constitutional Inequality*, p. 13; Freeman, *Politics of Women's Liberation*, pp. 54–55; idem, "Women and Public Policy," p. 53; and Harrison, " 'New Frontier' for Women," pp. 645–46.

18. Baer notes that beginning in 1969 every sex-specific state law (including most protective legislation) fell when litigated under Title VII. See Judith A. Baer, *Chains of Protection: The Judicial Response to Women's Labor Legislation* (Westport, Conn.: Greenwood, 1978), p. 167.

19. The bona fide occupation qualification (BFOQ) has proven particularly cumbersome, even though EEOC guidelines technically limit it to physical attributes crucial to job performance and sexual attributes necessary for authenticity, such as in modeling or acting careers. In practice, a heavy burden of persuasion is placed on the individual litigant to overturn a BFOQ exception claimed by an employer. Litigation under Title VII first focused primarily on the BFOQ, then moved to protective legislation at the state level, and most recently has concentrated on pregnancy-related health and employment practices. See Malvina H. Guggenheim and Elizabeth F. Defeis, "United States Participation in International Agreements Providing Rights for Women," *Loyola of Los Angeles Law Review* 10, no. 1 (December 1976). The BFOQ provision allows "an employer to hire and employ employees . . . on the basis of his [sic] religion, sex, or national origin in occupational qualification reasonably necessary to the normal operation of that particular business or enterprise" (pp. 51–52). It was originally thought that the BFOQ would be interpreted so broadly that it would undermine any meaningful application of Title VII. In fact, initial litigation under Title VII did concentrate on the BFOQ exception with disturbing results. Phillips v. Martin-Marietta Corporation, 400 U.S. 542 (1971), for example, was the first Title VII case based exclusively on sex discrimination. The decision only narrowly and tentatively struck down a company policy that insisted that BFOQ allowed it to establish one hiring policy for women with preschool children and another for men similarly situated. This decision strongly implied that such a sex-based BFOQ might apply in the future if it could be demonstrated that it was more important for mothers than fathers to spend time with preschool children. This is known as "sex-plus" discrimination because it linked women's eligibility for jobs with either a condition of pregnancy or the presence of small children in the home. Since *Phillips*, however, courts have generally followed EEOC guidelines requiring a narrow interpretation of the BFOQ exception, but the issue has been raised again in suits over whether employers can bar women from certain jobs during the women's childbearing years. See United Auto Workers v. Johnson Controls, Inc., 866 F.2d 871 (7th Cir. 1989). See Baer, *The Chains of Protection*, pp. 149–56; and Malvina Halbertson and Elizabeth F. Defeis, *Women's Legal Rights: International Covenants, an Alternative to ERA?* (Dobbs Ferry, N.Y.: Transnational, 1987), pp. 66–76.

20. Sprogis v. United Air Lines, 444 F.2d 1194 (7th Cir.), *cert. denied*, 404 U.S. 999

(1971); and Diaz v. Pan American World Airways, 442 F.2d 385 (5th Cir.), *cert. denied*, 404 U.S. 950 (1971). Both tested the scope of the BFOQ section of Title VII (which did not apply to race discrimination) by successfully challenging standard sexual stereotypes about airline cabin attendants.

21. Kathryn Kish Sklar, "Why Were Most Politically Active Women Opposed to the ERA in the 1930s?" in Joan Hoff-Wilson, ed., *Rights of Passage: The Past and Future of the ERA* (Bloomington: Indiana University Press, 1986), pp. 3–4, 25–35; Freeman, "Women and Public Policy," pp. 53–54; Ruth Bader Ginsburg, "The Burger Court's Grapplings with Sex Discrimination," in Vincent Blasi, ed., *The Burger Court: The Counter-Revolution that Wasn't* (New Haven, Conn.: Yale University Press, 1983), pp. 133–34; Steiner, *Constitutional Inequality*, pp. 13–23; Baer, *Chains of Protection*, pp. 149–69. Some early radical feminist groups were Radical Women (1967), the Jeanette Rankin Brigade (1967), the Berkeley Women's Sociology Caucus (1967), Sudsofloppen (1968), WITCH (1968), Redstockings (1969), The Feminists (1969), and New York Radical Feminists (1969). There were also numerous consciousness-raising groups all over the country, and many feminist journals and newspapers were founded in the late 1960s and early 1970s.

22. Confidential memorandum from Jon M. Huntsman to Finch, 5 May 1971 (Nixon quotation); H. R. Haldeman to Finch, 8 September 1970; Nixon memorandum to heads of executive departments and agencies, n.d., 1970; Finch to Office of Staff Secretary, 17 October and 4 December 1970; Finch to Nixon, 15 April 1971—all in Finch Papers; "Recommendations of the Committee on Population Growth and the American Future," Box 6, RG 148, National Archives; *New York Times,* 21 January 1972, p. 20; Nixon to Josephine Terrill, 14 November 1946, to Katharine St. George, 1 February 1949, and statement as vice president, 26 August 1960—all in the National Women's Party Papers, 1913–74, Reel Nos. 94 and 104.

23. "Veto of Economic Opportunity Amendments of 1971," 10 December 1971, Document No. 387, *The Public Papers of Richard Nixon, 1971* (Washington, D.C.: Government Printing Office, 1972), pp. 1174–78. Two-thirds of Nixon's final veto message dealt with the child development program, which had been attached to the OEO bill as a deliberate ploy to make the president appear to be an opponent of child care, since there was every indication that he would veto Congress's OEO legislation. However, the extremely conservative profamily tone of the veto was substituted at the last minute when Pat Buchanan and Charles Colson prevailed over Elliot Richardson and Nixon's more moderate speech writers. See News Conference Transcript No. 1274, 9 December 1971; transcript of Frank Carlucci and Stephen Kurzman press conference, 9 December 1971; Charles Colson to H. R. Haldeman, 8 December 1971, Pat Buchanan to Haldeman, 9 December 1971, Box 87, Haldeman Papers, White House Special Files, Nixon Presidential Materials Project, Alexandria, Virginia. See chapter 9 of this volume for Nixon's reservations about the ERA when he was president.

24. Freeman, "Women and Public Policy," pp. 57–59; Joan Hoff-Wilson, "Of Mice and Men," in Edward P. Crapol, ed., *Women and American Foreign Policy: Lobbyists, Critics, and Insiders* (Westport, Conn.: Greenwood, 1987), pp. 177–78.

25. Nixon's other appointments were Justices Harry A. Blackmun, William H. Rehnquist, and Lewis Powell.

26. Ginsburg, "Burger Court's Grapplings with Sex Discrimination," pp. 151–52.

27. Reed v. Reed, 404 U.S. 71 (1971), at 75.

28. Royster Guano Co. v. Virginia, 253 U.S. 412 (1920), at 415.

29. Frontiero v. Richardson, 411 U.S. 677 (1973), at 684.

30. Steiner, *Constitutional Inequality*, pp. 38–39; Bob Woodward and Scott Armstrong, *The Brethren: Inside the Supreme Court* (Simon & Schuster, 1979), pp. 253–55.

31. Craig v. Boren, 429 U.S. 190 (1976), at 197.

32. For example, see *Frontiero v. Richardson;* Califano v. Goldfarb, 430 U.S. 199 (1977); Califano v. Westcott, 433 U.S. 76 (1979); Wengler v. Druggists Mutual Insurance Co., 446 U.S. 142 (1980).

33. Stephanie M. Wildman, "The Legitimation of Sex Discrimination: A Critical Response to Supreme Court Jurisprudence," *Oregon Law Review* 63 (1984): 287–94; Wendy W. Williams, "The Equality Crisis: Some Reflections on Culture, Courts, and Feminism," *Women's Rights Law Reporter* 7, no. 3 (spring 1982): 178–83, n. 50.

34. Archibald Cox, *The Court and the Constitution* (Boston: Houghton Mifflin, 1987), pp. 250–68, 316–21 (quotations at 257, 321). Although *Brown* only involved school desegregation, it set into motion decisions striking down discrimination on the basis of sex, nationality, length of residence, illegitimacy, and sometimes even ability to pay.

35. Robert W. Bennett, "The Burger Court and the Poor," in Blasi, *Burger Court,* pp. 46–61. See also the special issue of *Signs* 10 (1984), which was entirely devoted to women and poverty.

36. Santa Clara Pueblo v. Martinez, 436 U.S. 49 (1978), at 71–72. David Matas, "Indian Women's Rights," *Manitoba Law Journal* 6 (1974): 195–209; Douglas Sanders, "Indian Women: A Brief History of Their Roles and Rights," *McGill Law Journal* 21 (1975): 656–72. For a more critical point of view, see Catharine A. MacKinnon, *Feminism Unmodified: Discourses on Life and Law* (Cambridge: Harvard University Press, 1987), pp. 65–69.

37. *Santa Clara Pueblo v. Martinez,* at 54 (quoting Martinez v. Santa Clara Pueblo, 402 F. Supp. 5, 15 (D.N.M. 1975); *"Martinez v. Santa Clara Pueblo* (540 F.2d 1039): The Scope of Indian Equal Protection," *Utah Law Review,* no. 3 (1976): 547–57; Susan Sanders Molander, "Case Notes: Indian Civil Rights Act and Sex Discrimination," *Arizona State Law Journal* 1 (1977): 227–39; and *Pueblo News* 6, nos. 6–7 (June–July 1978): 1–2.

38. Freeman, "Women and Public Policy," p. 59; NOW Legal Defense and Education Fund and Dr. Renée Cherow-O'Leary, *The State-by-State Guide to Women's Legal Rights* (New York: McGraw-Hill, 1987), pp. 87–92. In 1982, Congress approved legislation allowing state courts the right to divide equitably military retirement benefits in long-term marriages ending in divorce, thereby overruling McCarty v. McCarty, 453 U.S. 210 (1981), which had declared that military pensions were the sole property of the serviceman, not his spouse. For references to continuing gender problems in the military, see Martin Binkin and Shirley J. Bach, *Women and the Military* (Washington, D.C.: The Brookings Institution, 1977), pp. 22–72 passim; Dorothy Schneider and Carl J. Schneider, *Sound Off! American Women Speak Out* (New York: Dutton, 1988); *New York Times,* 25 October 1987, p. 28 (right of military spouses to take private jobs), 2 February 1988, p. A17 (41 percent of pregnant enlisted women in the navy not married), 3 February 1988, pp. 1, A23 (Pentagon adds military jobs for women and criticizes sexual harassment), 8 February 1988, p. A11 (adultery and fraternization charges against a female air force officer for having an affair with an enlisted male), 5 December 1988, p. 12 (heterosexual crews assigned to control

rooms of air force underground missile control rooms), 23 February 1989, p. A24 (army agrees to discharge soldier with baby rather than assign her abroad) 7 January 1990, p. 25 (Captain Linda L. Bray leads platoon in Panama fighting); *Washington Post*, 4 January 1989, p. A3 (navy admits black officers face more obstacles than black enlisted personnel), 3 February 1988, p. A17 (Carlucci orders air force and marines to expand opportunities for women), 29 April 1988, p. A19 (soldiers having babies bring complaints about parental-leave policies), 31 May 1989, p. A2 (Supreme Court rules that ex-spouses of divorced military veterans cannot share disability payments), 7 January 1990, p. 25, 31 January 1990, p. A1 (women soldiers in Panama invasion not getting same recognition as men), 10 February 1990, p. A22 (Combat Infantryman's Badge being denied women who participated in Panama invasion). For the homosexual issue within the military, see: *New York Times*, 11 February 1988, pp. 1, B10 (federal appeals court ruled army's ban on homosexuals unconstitutional), 23 February 1988, p. A23 (marines considering suspending or discharging lesbians at boot camp), 25 February 1988, p. A20 (two female marines charged with "fraternization and indecent acts" with other women), 10 June 1988, p. A10 (federal appeals court to nullify its ruling and rehear case stating that the army can exclude homosexuals); and *Washington Post,* 18 February 1988, p. A23 (James J. Kilpatrick stating that military arguments against homosexuals are the same ones once used against blacks).

39. *Washington Post*, 13 December 1988, pp. D1, D2 (maternal-fetal conflict in court-ordered medical procedures); *New York Times*, 4 September 1988, p. 23 (court-ordered birth control reversed), 9 January 1989, pp. 1, 9 (whether drug abuse during pregnancy can be considered child abuse), 8 February 1989, p. 13 (husband denied right to authorize abortion for comatose wife), 12 March 1989, p. 27 (court limits divorced woman's right to overnight male guest when her children are at home), 10 May 1989, p. A18 (mother charged in baby's death from her cocaine habit during pregnancy), 11 June 1989, p. 28 (charges dropped against mother for son belonging to a gang), 10 August 1989, p. B6 (woman sentenced to six months in jail for abandoning baby born in airplane bathroom); *The Nation*, 1 May 1989, pp. 585–88 (jailing mothers for drug abuse), 10 July 1989, p. 38 (letter-to-editor about attempts to control behavior of pregnant women). See chapter 8 of this volume for more detailed discussions of pregnancy, abortion, and adoption.

40. Alice Kessler-Harris, "The Debate over Quality for Women in the Workplace: Recognizing Differences," in Laurie Larwood et al., eds., *Women and Work: An Annual Review* (Beverly Hills: Sage, 1985), pp. 153–54.

41. Elyce Rotella, "Fact Sheet: Women in the U.S. Economy," in Shelia Ruth, ed., *Issues in Feminism* (Boston: Houghton Mifflin, 1980; revised 1990 edition forthcoming); *New York Times*, 25 November 1984, p. 1 (report on Rand Corporation study); Lenore J. Weitzman, *The Marriage Contract: Spouses, Lovers, and the Law* (New York: Free Press, 1981), p. 171; *U.S. News & World Report*, 6 August 1982, pp. 46–48; Victor R. Fuchs, *Women's Quest for Economic Equality* (Cambridge: Harvard University Press, 1988), pp. 84–89, 92–93; Susan Ware, *Modern American Women: A Documentary History* (Chicago: Dorsey, 1989), p. 377. See also *The State of Families, 1984–85* (New York: Family Service America, 1984), pp. 7–15; and Heather McLeod, "Women in the Twenty-first Century," *Radcliffe Quarterly*, March 1989, pp. 2, 3.

42. Sara M. Evans and Barbara J. Nelson, *Wage Justice: Comparable Worth and the Paradox*

*of Democratic Reform* (Chicago: University of Chicago Press, 1989); M. Anne Hill and Mark R. Killingsworth, eds., *Comparable Worth: Analysis and Evidence* (Ithaca, N.Y.: Cornell University Press, 1989), pp. 1–10; Note, "Equal Pay, Comparable Work, and Job Evaluation," *Yale Law Journal* 90 (1981): 657–80.

43. Hill and Killingsworth, *Comparable Worth*, pp. 4–5, 54–56; Halbertson and Defeis, *Women's Legal Rights*, pp. 73–74. See also Laura N. Gasaway, "Comparable Worth: A Post-Gunther Overview," *Georgetown Law Journal* 69 (1981): 1123–69; Comment, "Sex-Based Wage Discrimination Claims after *County of Washington v. Gunther*," *Columbia Law Review* 81 (October 1981): 1333–47; Note, "Gender-Based Wage Discrimination," *Harvard Law Review* 95 (November 1981): 300–310; Note, "Women, Wages, and Title VII: The Significance of *County of Washington v. Gunther*," *University of Pittsburgh Law Review* 43 (Winter 1982): 467–99; Note, "Comparable Worth," *Harvard Women's Law Journal* 8 (Spring 1983): 201–8.

44. AFSCME v. State of Washington, 578 F. Supp. 846 (1983); *rev'd.*, 770 F.2d 1401 (9th Cir. 1985); Mary Frances Berry, *Why the ERA Failed: Politics, Women's Rights, and the Amending Process* (Bloomington: Indiana University Press, 1986), pp. 112–13. AFSCME finally settled with the state of Washington in an agreement providing for "substantial pay increases for workers in female-dominated jobs." See NOW and Cherow-O'Leary, *State-by-State Guide*, pp. 62–63; and Diana Stone, "Comparable Worth in the Wake of *AFSCME v. State of Washington*," *Berkeley Women's Law Journal* 1, no. 1 (Fall 1985): 78–114.

45. Berry, *Why the ERA Failed*, pp. 110–11; and *New York Times*, 24 May 1986, p. 17 (Op-Ed piece by a woman law student at Yale).

46. Freeman, "Women and Public Policy," p. 64.

47. See Roberts et al. v. United States Jaycees, 104 S. Ct. 3244 (1984); Hishon v. King and Spalding, 467 U.S. 69 (1984); Board of Directors of Rotary International v. Rotary Club of Duarte, 107 S. Ct. 1940 (1987); and *Washington Post*, 5 May 1987, pp. 1, 12. See chapter 9 of this volume for the relevance of *Roberts* with respect to pornography litigation.

48. *New York Times*, 21 June 1988, pp. 1 (first quotation), 12, 30, 14 September 1988, pp. Y19, Y26, 27 November 1988, p. 40 (second quotation). Some of the first twenty nominated for membership in the Century Club were former First Lady Jacqueline Onassis, opera singer Beverly Sills, and actress Marian Seldes. Among the women who have eschewed membership in other formerly all-male clubs were such bona fide businesswomen as Muriel Siebert, the first woman to buy a seat on the New York Stock Exchange; Judy Hendren Mello, owner of a small New York investment company; and Shirley J. Cheramy, a partner at Price Waterhouse in Los Angeles.

49. *Washington Post*, 31 May 1986, p. A6; and *Chronicle of Higher Education*, 11 June 1986, pp. 31, 38.

50. *Washington Post*, 21 March 1987, p. 18, 5 May 1987, pp. 1, 12; and *Update* 7, no. 4 (May 1987): 1, 13.

51. *Washington Post*, 29 January 1988, pp. A1, A12, 17 March 1988, pp. A1, A14; and *New York Times*, 23 March 1988, pp. A1, D26, and 10 February 1988, p. A28.

52. *Chronicle of Higher Education*, 22 June 1988, pp. A1, A33. Indeed, many educational institutions had not been consistently enforcing Title IX against sex discrimination on campuses since the decision in *Grove City College*. As early as June 1988, however, Temple University settled an eight-year-old sex-discrimination lawsuit out of court by

agreeing to give more than 40 percent of its athletic scholarships to women. This belated action was a clear indication that Title IX had been on the "back of the front burner" with respect to discriminatory athletic programs at educational institutions while *Grove City College* was in effect. The antiabortion amendment of the Civil Rights Restoration Act has yet to prove effective or be tested in court.

53. Palmer et al. v. Shultz, and Cooper et al. v. Shultz, Civil 616 F. Supp. 1540 (D.D.C. 1985), *rev'd.*, 815 F.2d 84 (D.C. Cir. 1987); and EEOC v. Sears, Roebuck and Co., 628 F. Supp. 1264 (N.D. Ill. 1986), *aff'd.*, 839 F.2d 302 (7th Cir. 1988).

54. Sears, Roebuck and Company had been investigated by the EEOC since 1973. In 1977, it found "reasonable cause" to charge Sears with employment-practice violations under Title VII and, on 26 January 1979, notified Sears of "failure to conciliate." But before the Justice Department formally filed against the company in October 1979, Sears brought a class-action suit against nine federal agencies for having fostered much existing racial and sexual discrimination. Technically, the Sears suit on behalf of other major retailers was not a "reverse-discrimination" case, but Sears insisted at the time that the government must eliminate all contradictions in its own rules and regulations before it prosecuted any more private businesses. Given the number of women employed by Sears, this constituted a serious challenge to continued affirmative-action programs among the nation's largest retailers—many of which have never done anything about fair employment except to fight it.

In May 1979, Sears's preemptive suit was dismissed. That same month the company announced that it would conduct no more business with the federal government because it was being harassed by the Office of Federal Contract Compliance Programs. In May, it was also reported that Sears's sales were down for the first quarter of 1979, primarily due to excessive centralization of its organization not the loss of $20 million worth of goods to the government out of its eighteen-billion-dollar-a-year retailing business. The U.S. Chamber of Commerce initially filed amicus briefs on Sears's behalf, as did the International Organization of Women Executives. See *Newsweek*, 7 May 1979, p. 78; *Los Angeles Times*, 25 January 1979, 25 April 1979, 22 May 1979; *New York Times*, 28 March 1979, p. A19, 6 April 1979, p. D12, 16 May 1979, pp. A1, D18; and *New Republic*, 10 March 1979, pp. 18–21.

55. *Disparate treatment* is the intentional "treat[ment] of some people less favorably than others because of their race, color, religion, sex or national origin." *Disparate impact* involves "employment practices that are facially neutral in their treatment of different groups but that in fact fall more harshly on one group than another and cannot be justified by business necessity." See International Brotherhood of Teamsters v. United States, 431 U.S. 324 (1977), at 335, n. 15, and at 336, n. 15. See also Herma Hill Kay, "Models of Equality," *University of Illinois Law Review* 1 (1985): 57–61, n. 131. For more details about *Palmer*, see Hoff-Wilson, "Of Mice and Men," pp. 177–79.

56. For an example of the assertion that *Sears* "does no damage to affirmative action," see Thomas Haskell and Sanford Levinson, "Academic Freedom and Expert Witnessing: Historians and the *Sears* Case," *Texas Law Review* 66 (1988): 301–31, quotation at 328, nn. 128, 129. At the beginning of this article, the authors seem less dogmatic about Sears's doctrinal impact than they become at the end of it (see p. 302, n. 6). Because they appear unaware of the similarities with *Palmer* before it was reversed, because they do not take the dissenting opinions in *Johnson v. Transportation Agency of*

*Santa Clara County* seriously enough (discussed later), and because they wrote this article before the *City of Richmond* decision (also discussed later) and before the voting majority of five conservative justices on the Rehnquist Court had materialized, their underestimation of the potential precedent set in *Sears* is understandable. This is a superb article, however, for placing into perspective the statistical and tactical mistakes made by EEOC in this suit against Sears.

57. The district court opinion was delivered by Judge Skelly Wright in Segar v. Smith, 738, F.2d 1249 (D.C. Cir. 1984), at 1278–79, *cert. denied,* 471 U.S. 1115 (1985). Wright relied on *International Brotherhood of Teamsters v. United States,* and the Supreme Court refused to hear an appeal of the *Segar* decision. For contrary decisions, see Haskell and Levinson, "Academic Freedom and Expert Witnessing," pp. 310–11, nn. 56–58.

58. Haskell and Levinson, "Academic Freedom and Expert Witnessing," pp. 307–9, quotation at 308.

59. Ruth Milkman, "Women's History and the *Sears* Case," *Feminist Studies* 12 (Summer 1986): 375–400; *CCWHP Newsletter* 17, no. 1 (February 1986): 4–6; *Chronicle of Higher Education,* 5 February 1985, pp. 1, 8, 12 March 1986, pp. 44–45, 23 April 1986, pp. 43–44, 2 July 1986, p. 22; *Ms.,* July 1986, pp. 48–51, 86–91; *The Nation,* 7 September 1985, pp. 161, 176–80, 26 October 1985, p. 394; *New Directions for Women* 14, no. 6 (November-December 1985): 1, 11, (September-October 1986): 1, 8; *New York Times,* 4 February 1985, p. A21, 9 February 1986, p. 6, 27 February 1986, p. A23, 6 June 1986, pp. B1, B4, 28 June 1986, p. A28; *Philadelphia Enquirer,* 15 June 1986, p. 15A, 22 July 1986, p. 9A; *Radical History Newsletter* 49 (May 1986): 7; *Radical History Review* 35 (1986): 57–79; *Savvy,* October 1986, pp. 73–75, 83; *Signs* 11, no. 4 (Summer 1986): 751–79; *Time,* 18 August 1986, pp. 63–64; *Washington Post,* 8 February 1986, p. A20, 9 June 1986, p. A20, 16 June 1986, p. C2; *AHA Perspectives,* January 1987, p. 20; and Zillah R. Eisenstein, *The Female Body and the Law* (Berkeley: University of California Press, 1988), pp. 108–16.

60. For examples of how a rather straightforward legal question was turned into an academic one, see Joan Wallach Scott, "Deconstructing Equality-versus-Difference: Or, the Uses of Poststructural Theory for Feminism," *Feminist Studies* 14, no. 1 (Spring 1988): 37–48; Eileen Boris, "Looking at Women's Historians Looking at 'Difference,' " *Wisconsin Women's Law Journal* 3 (1987): 213–16, 236–38; Carol Sternhell, "Life in the Mainstream: What Happens When Feminists Turn Up on Both Sides of the Courtroom?" *Ms.,* July 1986, 48 ff.; and Milkman, "Women's History and the *Sears* Case," pp. 394–95 passim. Only Haskell and Levinson in "Academic Freedom and Expert Witnessing," pp. 321–28, relate what Rosenberg and Kessler-Harris actually said in court to the points of law involved in the case. While this itself does not explain all the sensationalism and misrepresentation surrounding the case, it does illuminate how various factions within the historical profession ignored the facts of the case and used it for their own ideological and historiographical purposes.

61. Haskell and Levinson, "Academic Freedom and Expert Witnessing," pp. 305–10, n. 38; EEOC v. Sears, 839 F2d.302, at 309; Milkman, "Women's History and the *Sears* Case," pp. 377–85.

62. Haskell and Levinson, "Academic Freedom and Expert Witnessing," pp. 310–11, 315–20.

63. Ibid., pp. 316, nn. 77–80.
64. Ibid., pp. 318–21 (quotation). See the Introduction and chapter 10 to this volume for poststructural concepts about differences that are influencing some academic historians.
65. Ibid., pp. 306–7, n. 43, 325–26.
66. Ibid., p. 321 (quotation); EEOC v. Sears, 628 F. Supp. 1264 (N.D. Ill., 1986), at 1314, nn. 62, 63 (dismissing Kessler-Harris's testimony). See also notes 59 and 60 above.
67. Haskell and Levinson, "Academic Freedom and Expert Witnessing," pp. 305, 309–10, n. 53. For example, they point out that academics in favor of the EEOC's case not only ignored the points of law at issue in the case but also demonstrated a questionable tolerance for the serious appearance of conflict of interest on the part of EEOC attorney David A. Copus, and well as an indifference to the academic and free-speech rights of historian Rosalind Rosenberg, who testified in favor of Sears (pp. 302–4, 310). Haskell and Levinson also note that Rosenberg's former husband "was associated with Sears's outside counsel" and that this probably accounted for the inside information she obviously possessed about the defects in EEOC's overblown statistical claims, making her a much more knowledgeable expert witness than Kessler-Harris. However, Haskell and Levinson do not indicate that Rosenberg must have been initially aware of the potentially negative impact of a Sears's victory on already poorly paid saleswomen working in the retail industry. Instead, they stress her later claims that if a single female employee had testified against Sears, the largest retail employer of women in the country, she would not have appeared in the company's behalf (pp. 315, 321, 322, n. 99). Moreover, the authors underemphasize the extent to which the motivation and attitude of Charles Morgan, Sears's counsel, toward affirmative action for women was also not above suspicion. Morgan left his position as director of the Washington ACLU office in 1976 to go into private practice. Haskell and Levinson leave no doubt that his first big case was *Sears,* but one has to turn to other sources to find out that when asked about how he reconciled his former career at ACLU with this suit, Morgan responded that he had "always been against the Government . . . [and for making] the Government use the law for the purposes for which it was intended." In this instance, he did not believe the EEOC should have been prosecuting sex-discrimination cases because "there's just no equation between minorities and women." See *New York Times,* 29 January 1979, p. D9; and Milkman, "Women's History and the *Sears* Case," pp. 378–79, 392–93.
68. Johnson v. Transportation Agency of Santa Clara County, California, 480 U.S. 616 (1987), at 637–41.
69. Firefighters Local Union No. 1784 v. Stotts, 467 U.S. 561 (1984); Wygant v. Jackson Board of Education, 467 U.S. 267 (1986), at 281–82; and Berry, *Why the ERA Failed,* p. 114.
70. Local No. 28 Sheet Metal Workers v. EEOC, 106 S. Ct. 3019 (1986); and Local No. 93, International Association of Firefighters, AFL-CIO v. Cleveland, 106 S. Ct. 3036 (1986).
71. *Washington Post,* 27 April 1988, p. A20; *New York Times,* 7 June 1988, p. 26 (letter-to-the-editor criticizing civil rights decisions "favoring nonwhites," particularly Jones v. A. H. Mayer, 392 U.S. 409 (1968), which laid the groundwork for *Runyon's* extension of the private right for action if an individual or institution refused to enter

into a contract with another person because of that person's race; and *New York Times,* 13 October 1988, pp. 1, 14.

72. *New York Times,* 27 October 1985, p. E5, 11 November 1985, p. 9, 11 April 1986, p. 22, 12 April 1986, p. 1.

73. The Supreme Court muddled another "reverse-discrimination" case earlier when, in Vochheimer v. School District of Philadelphia, 430 U.S. 703 (1977), affirming by an equally divided court, 532 F.2d 880 (3d Cir. 1976) (2-1), reversing 400 F. Supp. 326 (E. D. Pa. 1975). Dividing four to four, the justices could not decide for or against Philadelphia's sex-segregated secondary schools for gifted children and, thus, by default upheld the system and judgment of the court of appeals. Most "reverse-discrimination" cases have involved social security benefits, union seniority questions, or voluntary affirmative-action programs undertaken by schools, cities, or industries. See notes 69 and 70 above and notes 76, 81, 82, and 101 below.

74. Cox, *Court and the Constitution,* p. 321 (first quotation); and J. R. Pole, *The Pursuit of Equality in American History* (Berkeley: University of California Press, 1978), pp. 153, 178.

75. Griggs v. Duke Power Company, 401 U.S. 424 (1971); and Baer, *Chains of Protection,* pp. 156–58. The importance of *Griggs* (until undermined by *Wards Cove v. Atonio* in 1989) was the fact that ostensibly neutral standards used to evaluate workers must be job-relevant to comply with Title VII.

76. Bakke sued under Title VI of the Civil Rights Act of 1964, which states: "No person in the U.S. shall, on the ground of race, color, or national origin, be excluded from participation in, be denied the benefits of, or be subjected to discrimination under any program or activity receiving Federal financial assistance." Cannon sued under Title IX of the educational amendments of 1972. Title IX was expressly patterned after Title VI, except that the former covers employment as well as admissions at educational institutions. The original wording of both Title VI and Title IX left unresolved whether private parties, like Bakke and Cannon, had the right to go to court and seek enforcement of civil rights statutes. In *Bakke,* the Court *did not* hold that private parties could go to court for relief under Title VI. Four justices merely assumed a right for this case alone; four others agreed the right was implied under the 1964 act; only one—Justice White—took an unequivocal stand on the the issue, arguing strongly that Title VI *did not* grant a private right of action. This indecision in *Bakke* cast a cloud over Cannon's right to sue (in her initial suit) under Title IX. Had the issue of a private right of action been decided in *Bakke,* Cannon's first action would have been on much stronger statutory grounds.

77. Cannon subsequently filed suit against the original seven defendant medical schools in September of 1984. See Cannon v. Loyola University of Chicago, 606 F. Supp. 1010 (N. D. Ill. 1985), *cert. denied,* 107 S. Ct. 880 (1987). Under the same material facts in her previous suits, Cannon claimed breach of contractual duties precipitated by violations of Title IX. The schools allegedly violated their contractual obligations, created by the application fee, when they evaluated Cannon's application based on a criterion that was against public policy—the age requirement. Cannon also claimed that the schools created a contractual agreement with the federal government to abide by Title IX when they accepted federal funds. As a third-party beneficiary to this contract, Cannon sought injunctive relief and damages because the schools allegedly violated Title IX by denying her admission. The suit was dismissed under

the doctrine of *res judicata,* and the court awarded the defendants reasonable costs and fees.

78. Bakke v. Regents of the University of California, 438 U.S. 265 (1978), at 303.

79. Ibid., at 359–60, 364–69.

80. Ibid., at 302–3, 307, nn. 408–21.

81. Weber v. Kaiser Aluminum and Chemical Corporation, 47 *U.S. Law Week* 3408 (1978); consolidated with Steelworkers v. Weber, 443 U.S. 193 (1979), at 204. One of the most recent and ironic "reverse-discrimination" situations arose in 1988 when the 130-year-old Young Women's Christian Association (YWCA) threatened to disaffiliate a chapter in Washington State for having a male executive director. YWCA by-laws permit only females as "voting members" to occupy such positions. The local chapter sued the national association on behalf of Alan Tiger to prevent his ouster, arguing that it would violate the state's antidiscrimination laws. This suit was filed in June 1988—the same month that the Supreme Court unanimously upheld a New York City ordinance requiring the admission of women to large, private clubs. See New York City Club Association v. New York City, 108 S. Ct. 2225 (1988); and *New York Times,* 12 July 1988, p. A22 (YWCA suit).

82. City of Richmond v. J. A. Croson Co., 109 S. Ct. 706 (1989), citing *Fullilove v. Klutznick,* 448 U.S. 448 (1980).

83. *Johnson v. Transportation Agency, Santa Clara County, California,* first quotation (O'Connor concurring) at 3 and other quotations (Scalia dissenting) at 12, 20.

84. Korematsu v. United States, 323 U.S. 214 (1944).

85. *City of Richmond v. J. A. Croson Co.,* at 752, 757.

86. Lawrence Levy, *Original Intent and the Framers' Constitution* (New York: Macmillan, 1988), pp. 284–321; and Paul Finkelman, "The Constitution and the Intentions of the Framers: The Limits of Historical Analysis," *University of Pittsburgh Law Review* 50, no. 2 (1989): 349–98.

87. *City of Richmond v. J. A. Croson Co.,* at 735–39 (Scalia opinion). For example, in Richmond, symbolic still as the capital of the Confederacy, "only two-thirds of 1 percent of the city's construction contracts had been awarded to black firms in the five years before the set-aside." Moreover, set-aside programs promoting, but not setting, fixed quotas in New York State have resulted in 6.1 percent of all private contract money going to minority businesses and 1.9 percent going to businesses run by women. In some individual state departments, the figure is as high as 17 percent. While in Atlanta, where minorities make up 67 percent of the population, the 1973 nonquota affirmative-action program has resulted in raising the percentage of city-financed construction going to minority contractors from less than 1 percent to 37 percent by 1989. See *New York Times,* 24 January 1989, pp. A1, A19, 25 January 1989, pp. A1, A18, 27 January 1989, pp. A10, A31 (second quotation in text and first quotation in this footnote), 29 January 1989, sect. 3, p. 1; and *Washington Post,* 24 January 1989, pp. A1, A5.

88. *City of Richmond v. J. A. Croson Co.,* at 929; and *New York Times,* 27 January 1989, p. A31.

89. *New York Times,* 27 January 1989, p. A31; and *Bakke v. Regents of the University of California,* at 407.

90. *City of Richmond v. J. A. Croson Co.,* quoting Stevens at 644; and *Johnson v. Transportation Agency of Santa Clara County, California,* quoting Scalia at 668, 677.

91. *City of Richmond v. J. A. Croson Co.* was initially publicized as such an extreme antiaffirmative-action decision that liberal constitutional experts met at Harvard and issued a statement trying to mitigate the impression that the decision forbade "any race-conscious [affirmative-action] remedy." See *New York Times,* 6 April 1989, p. A19. Reagan's appointments were Sandra Day O'Connor, Antonin Scalia, and Anthony M. Kennedy.

92. Wards Cove Packing v. Atonio, 109 S. Ct. 2115 (1989), at 2126; and *New York Times,* 13 May 1989, p. 1, 6 June 1989, pp. 1, 24, 7 June 1989, pp. 1, 22. See also note 75 above and appendix 5 for *Griggs v. Duke Power Company.*

93. Lorance v. AT&T, 109 S. Ct. 2261 (1989), quoting Marshall at 2270.

94. Patterson v. McLean Credit Union, 109 S. Ct. 2363 (1989), at 2368–79 (Kennedy's opinion); and *New York Times,* 13 June 1989, pp. A1, B5.

95. *Patterson v. McLean Credit Union,* at 2373; and *New York Times,* 13 June 1989, p. B5.

96. *Patterson v. McLean Credit Union,* Kennedy quoted at 2379, Brennan's and Stevens's opinions at 2379–96; and *New York Times,* 16 June 1989, pp. 1, 12, 26.

97. *New York Times,* 16 June 1989, p. 13.

98. *Washington Post,* 17 June 1989, p. A19; and *New York Times,* 13 June 1989, p. B5, 18 June 1989, sect. 4, p. 1.

99. Ginsburg, "Burger Court's Grapplings with Sex Discrimination," p. 156.

100. Dothard v. Rawlinson, 433 U.S. 321 (1977); Michael M. v. Superior Court, 450 U.S. 464 (1981); and Rostker v. Goldberg, 453 U.S. 57 (1981).

101. Weinberger v. Wiesenfeld, 420 U.S. 636 (1975); Vorchheimer v. School District of Philadelphia, 430 U.S. 703 (1977); Califano v. Goldfarb, 430 U.S. 199 (1977); Orr v. Orr, 44 U.S. 268 (1979); and Caban V. Mohammed, 441 U.S. 380 (1979).

102. For example, see Kahn v. Shevin, 416 U.S. 351 (1974); Schlesinger v. Ballard, 419 U.S. 498 (1975); Califano v. Webster, 430 U.S. 313 (1977); Fiallo v. Bell, 430 U.S. 787 (1979); and Parham v. Hughes, 441 U.S. 347 (1979).

103. Personnel Administration of Massachusetts v. Feeney, 442 U.S. 256 (1979). Part of the Court's reasoning was that since the state statute distinguished between veterans and nonveterans rather than between women and men, there was no discriminatory intent. See *Gilbert v. General Electric* and other pregnancy cases in chapter 8 of this volume for similar reasoning about pregnant and nonpregnant persons.

104. *Washington Post,* 8 April 1981, pp. C1, C6; Berry, *Why the ERA Failed,* pp. 118–20. In April 1988, the Supreme Court reinforced child-support legislation by ruling eight to zero in Hicks v. Feiock, 485 U.S. 624 (1988), that in state proceedings for civil contempt of court against fathers who violate child-support orders, such men had to bear the burden of proof for proving their financial inability to pay—if they made that claim as a legal defense. In other words, if fathers cannot prove they do not have the money for delinquent child-support payments, they may be jailed. See *New York Times,* 28 April 1988, p. A23; and *Washington Post,* 28 April 1988, p. A5. See also chapter 8 of this volume for figures on child-support payments. For a summary of the 1987 EEA bill, see *Update* 7, no. 4 (May 1987): 7–11.

105. For details of the 1989 Economic Equity Act, see *Update* 9, no. 6 (August 1989): 7–12.

106. Williams, "Equality Crisis," p. 200. Williams has since answered "no" to her own question because of her insistence that since pregnancy is comparable to other unique-sex characteristics, equality should continue to be based on the "sameness"

rather than the "difference" between women and men. See also chapters 8 and 10 in this volume.

## 8. The Limits of Liberal Legalism

1. Theodore Stanton and Harriot Stanton Blatch, eds., *Elizabeth Cady Stanton as Revealed in Her Letters, Diary, and Reminiscences* (New York: Harper & Brothers, 1922), 2:48–49. See chapter 4 of this volume for an explanation of why women placed collective reform of the institution of marriage ahead of individual rights before the Civil War.
2. F. L. Morton, "Sexual Equality and the Family in Tocqueville's *Democracy in America*," *Canadian Journal of Political Science* 17 (June 1984): 311 (quotation); Richard D. Heffner, ed., *Alexis de Tocqueville, Democracy in America* (New York: Mentor, 1956), p. 245; William Thompson, *Appeal of One-Half of the Human Race, Women, Against the Pretensions of the Other Half, Men, to Retain Them in Political, and Thence in Civil and Domestic, Slavery* (1825; reprint, New York: Source Book, 1970), pp. 60–70 (quotation at 66) passim.
3. Timothy Walker, *Introduction to American Law* (Boston: Charles C. Little and James Brown, 1837), p. 260.
4. Joseph Warren, "Husband's Rights to Wife's Services," *Harvard Law Review* 38 (February 1925): 421, 423.
5. Reynolds v. United States, 98 U.S. 244 (1878); Maynard v. Hill, 125 U.S. 190 (1888); and State v. Rhodes, 61 N.C. 453 (1868).
6. Quoted in Leo Kanowitz, *Women and the Law: The Unfinished Revolution* (Albuquerque: University of New Mexico Press, 1969), p. 263, n. 48.
7. *New York Times*, 2 September 1988, "Family Law: Battle Ground in Social Revolution," p. 19, 9 February 1989, "Breaking up Families, Crack Besieges a Court," pp. 1, 12; and Stephanie Coontz, *The Social Origins of Private Life: A History of American Families, 1600–1900* (London: Verso, 1988), pp. 354–65.
8. See Lenore J. Weitzman, "Legal Regulation of Marriage: Tradition and Change," *California Law Review* 62, no. 4 (July–September 1974): 1173–97 for the remaining implications of the husband's traditional role as head of the family; idem, *The Marriage Contract: Spouses, Lovers, and the Law* (New York: Free Press, 1981), pp. 5–59.
9. Thompson, *Appeal of One-Half of the Human Race*, pp. 65–66. The explanation that Carole Pateman offers to Thompson's inquiry is based on the historical and philosophical relationship between the "social" contract and the marriage contract. See Carole Pateman, *The Sexual Contract* (Cambridge: Polity, 1988), pp. 154–88.
10. Pateman, *Sexual Contract*, pp. 158, 159 (third quotation), 161, 163 (first quotation); Thompson, *Appeal of One-Half of the Human Race*, pp. 79, 84, 89; Robin L. West, "The Difference in Women's Hedonic Lives: A Phenomenological Critique of Feminist Legal Theory," *Wisconsin Women's Law Journal* 3 (1987): 101, 105; and Christine Delphy, *Close to Home: A Materialist Analysis of Women's Oppression* (Amherst: University of Massachusetts Press, 1984). Delphy has cogently underscored that male power within marriage remains even if it is renounced because "the particular individual man [may] not play a personal role in this general oppression, which occurs before his appearance on the scene: but, reciprocally, no personal initiative on his part can undo or mitigate what exists before and outside his entrance" (p. 116).
11. Pateman, *Sexual Contract*, pp. 155–56, 184–87.

12. West, "Women's Hedonic Lives," pp. 93–108; and Martha Chamallas with Linda Kerber, *Women, Mothers, and the Law of Fright: A History* (Madison, Wis.: Institute for Legal Studies, 1989), pp. 1–107. See also chapter 9 of this volume for a further discussion of the fear experienced by American women.

13. Barbara Allen Babcock et al., *Sex Discrimination and the Law: Causes and Remedies* (Boston: Little, Brown, 1975), pp. 151–52.

14. Quoted in *The Spokeswoman*, 15 January 1977, p. 11.

15. Weitzman, "Legal Regulation of Marriage," pp. 1249–50. An informal trend toward "more equitable relationships" has been most pronounced in the 1980s. See *U.S. News & World Report*, 6 August 1984, p. 50.

16. NOW Legal Defense and Education Fund and Dr. Renée Cherow-O'Leary, *The State-by-State Guide to Women's Legal Rights* (New York: McGraw-Hill, 1987), pp. 14–15.

17. As of 1988, only California courts had subjected laws discriminating on the basis of sexual orientation to strict scrutiny. The trend in Supreme Court cases away from establishing new "suspect classes" can be seen in Cleburne v. Cleburne Living Center, 473 U.S. 432 (1985), a case involving the mentally retarded.

18. NOW, *State-by-State Guide*, pp. 15–18 (*Conley v. Richardson*, cited on p. 17); Ellen Goodman column, 27 June 1989, *Centre Daily Times;* Marvin v. Marvin (3) 122 Cal. App. 3d 871 (176 Cal. 555, 1981); and *New York Times*, 26 June 1989, p. B4, and 4 October 1989, p. B3.

19. For *Thompson v. Kowalski*, see *New York Times*, 7 August 1988, p. 13; and *Washington Post*, 15 December 1988, p. A21. See also Karen Thompson and Julie Andrzejewski, *Why Can't Sharon Kowalski Come Home?* (San Francisco: Spinsters/Aunt Lute, 1988).

20. Weitzman, "Legal Regulation of Marriage," pp. 1250–58, 1278–88.

21. *Le Monde*, 30 Mai 1989, p. 18; *Los Angeles Times*, 7 July 1989, p. 24; *Washington Post*, 24 June 1989, p. A27; and *New York Times*, 4 March 1989, p. 27, 31 May 1989, p. A17, 31 August 1989, pp. C1, C6. The San Francisco Domestic Partners Bill permits homosexual couples to enter into a "domestic partnership," similar to the Danish statute, but its application is limited to unmarried homosexual or heterosexual city employees. The same is true of the Berkeley city ordinance. To date, more straight than gay couples have taken advantage of it. Laws discriminating against homosexuals affect gay males as well as lesbians. For a general review of evolving homosexual rights in the last decade, see Alissa Friedman, "The Necessity for State Recognition of Same-Sex Marriage: Constitutional Requirements and Evolving Notions of the Family," *Berkeley Women's Law Journal* 3 (1987–88): 134–70; Elvia Rosales Arriola, "Sexual Identity and the Constitution: Homosexual Persons as a Discrete and Insular Minority," *Women's Rights Law Reporter* 10 (Winter 1988): 143–76. See also Note: "Substantive Due Process Comes Home to Roost: Fundamental Rights, *Griswold to Bowers*," *Women's Rights Law Reporter* 10 (Winter, 1988): 177–208.

22. Stanton, quoted in Elizabeth Griffith, *In Her Own Right: The Life of Elizabeth Cady Stanton* (New York: Oxford University Press, 1984), p. 104.

23. Weitzman, "Legal Regulation of Marriage," pp. 1258–66 (quotation at 1260). For more details, see idem, *Marriage Contract*, pp. 227–359.

24. NOW, *State-by-State Guide*, pp. 12, 22; and Carole Shammas, Marylynn Salmon, and

Michel Dahlin, *Inheritance in America from Colonial Times to the Present* (New Brunswick, N.J.: Rutgers University Press, 1987), p. 83.

25. Herma Hill Kay, *Sex-Based Discrimination in Family Law* (St. Paul: West Publishing, 1981), pp. 117–30; Babcock et al., *Sex Discrimination and the Law*, pp. 609–19; and Riane Tennenhaus Eisler, *Dissolution: No-Fault Divorce, Marriage, and the Future of Women* (New York: McGraw-Hill, 1977), pp. 20–40; Shammas et al., *Inheritance in America*, p. 84, 179–206; and Carole Shammas, "Early American Women and Capital," in Ronald Hoffman and Peter J. Albert, eds., *Women in the Age of the American Revolution* (Charlottesville: University Press of Virginia, 1989), pp. 139–40.

26. Weitzman, "Legal Regulation of Marriage," pp. 1180–97; Malvina H. Guggenheim and Elizabeth F. Defeis, "United States Participation in International Agreements Providing Rights for Women," *Loyola of Los Angeles Law Review* 10, no. 1 (December 1976): 59–65.

27. Kay, *Sex-Based Discrimination in Family Law*, 163–479; Eve Cary and Kathleen Willert Peratis, *Woman and the Law* (Skokie, Ill.: National Textbook, 1977), pp. 145–77; Eisler, *Dissolution*, pp. 10–13 passim; and Lenore J. Weitzman, *The Divorce Revolution: The Unexpected Social and Economic Consequences for Women and Children in America* (New York: Free Press, 1985), pp. ix–xiv passim.

28. *U.S. News & World Report*, 29 January 1990, p. 50; Heather McLeod, "Women in the Twenty-first Century," *Radcliffe Quarterly* 75, no. 1 (March 1989): 2; Lawrence Stone, "The Road to Polygamy," *New York Review of Books*, 2 March 1989, p. 12; and *New York Times* (federal survey of premarital cohabitation), 9 June 1989, pp. A1, A28.

29. Victor R. Fuchs, *Women's Quest for Economic Equality* (Cambridge: Harvard University Press, 1988), pp. 58–64.

30. Elyce Rotella, "Fact Sheet: Women in the U.S. Economy," in Sheila Ruth, ed., *Issues in Feminism* (Boston: Houghton Mifflin, 1980; revised edition, forthcoming); Weitzman, *Marriage Contract*, p. 171; *U.S. News & World Report*, 6 August 1984, pp. 46–48; Fuchs, *Women's Quest for Economic Equality*, pp. 84–89, 92–93; Susan Ware, *Modern American Women: A Documentary History* (Chicago: Dorsey, 1989), p. 377; and *The State of Families, 1984–85* (New York: Family Service America, 1984), pp. 7–15. See also chapter 7 of this volume for data on the earnings of working women, pp. 252–53.

31. See note 30 above.

32. McGuire v. McGuire, 157 Neb. 226, 59 N.W. 2d 336 (1953); and Babcock et al., *Sex Discrimination and the Law*, pp. 619–26 (quotations at 621).

33. Weitzman, *Divorce Revolution*, pp. 41–42; NOW, *State-by-State Guide*, pp. 18–19; and *New York Times*, 18 June 1989, p. 29.

34. Weitzman, *Divorce Revolution*, pp. ix–xii (quotation), xiii–xxiv, 337–56 passim.

35. Ibid., pp. 19 (second quotation), 15–51 (first quotation), 364–65; Herma Hill Kay, "Equality and Difference: A Perspective on No-Fault Divorce and Its Aftermath," *University of Cincinnati Law Review* 56 (1987): 1–90; and idem, "An Appraisal of California's No-Fault Divorce Law," *California Law Review* 75 (January 1987): 291–319.

36. NOW, *State-by-State Guide*, pp. 20–25; and *U.S. News & World Report*, 21 November 1983, p. 39; Rotella, "Fact Sheet."

37. Rotella, "Fact Sheet"; NOW, *State-by-State Guide*, pp. 23–25. See also appendix 5 for *Hicks v. Feiock*.

38. Quoted in *The Spokeswoman*, 15 January 1977, p. 1.

39. General Electric Co. v. Gilbert, 429 U.S. 125 (1976), at 140–41.

40. *General Electric Co. v. Gilbert*, at 145; and Ozawa v. U.S., 260 U.S. 178 (1922).

41. *Boston Evening Globe*, 3 May 1977, p. 9; and *Women's Newsletter* (Winter 1977): 11 (a publication of the National Commission on Women's Oppression [NCWO] of the National Lawyer's Guild).

42. *General Electric Co. v. Gilbert*, at 134, 141, 142.

43. Quoted in *The Spokeswoman*, 15 April 1977, pp. 1–2.

44. Zillah R. Eisenstein, *The Female Body and the Law* (Berkeley: University of California Press, 1988), pp. 68–69 (quotations) and Eva R. Rubin, *The Supreme Court and the American Family: Ideology and Issues* (Westport, Conn.: Greenwood, 1986), pp. 76–83, 90–95. Although it is difficult to rationalize the Supreme Court's resistance in the mid-1970s to extend the equal-protection doctrine unequivocally to gender issues, Rubin has offered the following explanation:

> . . . [it] probably reflected the view that this change should come through the proposed Equal Rights Amendment rather than through judicial decision-making. The justices may also have realized, subconsciously, that the treatment of pregnancy as a temporary disability, even in the context of employment practices, rather than as a condition that inexorably defined the female role, removed another key support to the structure of the traditional family. Pregnancy leave rules force women to return home and assume responsibility for child-raising; refusal to cover pregnancy under health insurance schemes makes working conditions for women less attractive (pp. 93–94).

45. Eisenstein, *Female Body and the Law*, pp. 98–100 (quotation). See also chapter 10 of this volume.

46. Miller-Wohl Co. v. Commissioner of Labor and Industry, 515 F. Supp. 1264 (D. Mont. 1981), vacated, 685 F.2d 1088 (9th Cir. 1982). Miller-Wohl defended firing Tamara Buley, who was pregnant, on the grounds that all new employees were told they would be fired if they missed work because the company allowed no leave of absence during the first year of employment, regardless of reasons. Miller-Wohl argued that the Montana Maternity Leave Act (MMLA) requiring special treatment of women was illegal under the 1980 congressional PDA. After the Ninth Circuit Court dismissed the case, a Montana judge said that the state law conflicted with Title VII. However, the Montana Supreme Court reversed this opinion in 1984, and the employer's appeal to the U.S. Supreme Court was not accepted.

47. Wendy W. Williams, "The Equality Crisis: Some Reflections on Culture, Courts, and Feminism," *Women's Rights Law Reporter* 7, no. 3 (Spring 1982): 190–93. See Ann C. Scales, "Towards a Feminist Jurisprudence," *Indiana Law Journal* 56, no. 3 (1981): 375–444, for a general review of Supreme Court cases on pregnancy.

48. *Washington Post*, 9 December 1988, pp. A1, A10; *U.S.A. Today*, 15 December 1988, pp. 10, 20; and *New York Times*, 2 August 1988, pp. 1, 10.

49. California Federal Savings and Loan Association v. Guerra, 449 U.S. 272 (1987), at 290–91.

50. Williams, "Equality Crisis," pp. 194–96; idem, "Equality's Riddle: Pregnancy and the Equal Treatment/Special Treatment Debate," *New York University Review of Law*

*and Social Change* 13, no. 2 (1984–85): 325–80; and United Auto Workers v. Johnson Controls, 886 F.2d 871 (7th Cir. 1989). *En blanc,* affirming 680 F. Supp. 309 (E.D. Wisc. 1988).

51. Gerda Lerner, "Women's Rights and American Feminism," *American Scholar* 40 (Spring 1971): 237.
52. Sylvia Law, Amicus Brief of 279 American Historians (title says 281, but two names were subsequently withdrawn) in *Webster v. Reproductive Health Services,* February 1989, pp. 1–30; and NOW, *State-by-State Guide,* p. 27 (quotation).
53. Rubin, *Supreme Court and the American Family,* pp. 12–13, 63–64; and Archibald Cox, *The Court and the Constitution* (Boston: Houghton Mifflin, 1987), pp. 257–58, 332–34.
54. Loving v. Virginia, 388 U.S. 1 (1967).
55. Levy v. Louisiana, 391 U.S. 68 (1968).
56. Cox, *Court and the Constitution,* pp. 255–60; Rubin, *Supreme Court and the American Family,* pp. 97–103; and NOW, *State-by-State Guide,* p. 27.
57. Cox, *Court and the Constitution,* pp. 322–25 (quotation). See also chapters 5 and 6 of this volume for a discussion of "Lochnerism" in relation to male workers' freedom of contract and protective legislation for women.
58. Union Pacific Railway Co. v. Botsford, 141 U.S. 250 (1891). The cases prior to *Griswold* in 1965 and *Eisenstadt* in 1972—the only ones to deal with birth control and/or the right of association and education as an aspect of privacy protected by both the First Amendment and due process—perhaps closest to reasoning in *Roe* were Meyer v. Nebraska, 262 U.S. 399 (1923) (constitutionality of teaching German to children); Pierce v. Society of Sisters, 268 U.S. 510 (1925) (constitutionality of sending children to Catholic schools); Skinner v. Oklahoma, 316 U.S. 535 (1942), at 541 (second quotation) (sterilization of "habitual criminals" declared unconstitutional under the equal-protection clause of the Fourteenth Amendment); Loving v. Virginia, 388 U.S. 1 (1967) (interracial marriage declared constitutional under the equal-protection clause of the Fourteenth Amendment); Stanley v. Georgia, 394 U.S. 557 (1969) (constitutionality of using pornographic materials in the privacy of one's home); Winters v. Miller, 46 F.2d 65 (2d Cir. 1971) (compulsory medical treatment constitutes assault and battery); McFall v. Schimp, unpub. opinion, Ct. 51 Common Pleas, Allegheny County, Pennsylvania, Civil Div. (26 July 1978) (first quotation) (right to refuse to donate organ to save another's life); and Rochin v. California, 342 U.S. 165 (1951) (against forcible stomach pumping). See also chapter 1 of this volume for a discussion of fundamental rights; and Rhonda Copelon, "Testimony on Constitutional Amendments To Negate *Roe v. Wade* Given before the Subcommittee on the Constitution of the Senate Judiciary Committee, March 7, 1983," reprinted in *Women's Rights Law Reporter* 8 (Summer 1985): 179 (third quotation).
59. For a review of feminist legal arguments on abortion, see Nancy Stearns, *"Roe v. Wade:* Our Struggle Continues," and Gayle Binion, "Reproductive Freedom and the Constitution: The Limits of Choice," both in *Berkeley Women's Law Journal* 4 (1988–89): 1–11, 12–41; Copelon, "Testimony," pp. 179–83; and Eisenstein, *Female Body and the Law,* pp. 184–90.
60. See chapter 9 of this volume for a discussion of other applications of RICO. In the case of attacks on abortion clinics, the U.S. Court of Appeals for the Third Circuit in Philadelphia has held that those responsible were liable for damages to the clinic

under RICO, and NOW is supporting this type of litigation. See *New York Times*, 4 March 1989, pp. 1, 9, 24, 28 September 1989, pp. A25, A40.

61. American Bar Association, quoted in *The Spokeswoman*, 15 April 1977, p. 3.

62. *Ms.*, February 1978, pp. 46–49, 97–98; *New York Times*, 4 September 1987, p. 18, 11 November 1988, p. 13, 23 January 1989, p. A24; *Washington Post*, 16 February 1988, p. A19, 4 March 1988, p. A3, 9 November 1989, p. A22.

63. Title XIX established the Medical Assistance Program (Medicaid), under which participating states could provide federally funded medical assistance to needy persons.

64. Beal v. Doe, 432 U.S. 438 (1977), at 455, 462; and NOW, *State-by-State Guide*, pp. 30–31.

65. The compromise language of the Hyde Amendment permitted a poor woman to have a Medicaid abortion only if her life was threatened by the pregnancy *or* if she had been a rape or incest victim and had reported the incident to proper federal authorities *within* sixty days. See *Los Angeles Times*, 8 December 1977, pp. 1, 18, 27 January 1978, p. 4.

66. *New York Times*, 25 August 1987, p. 9, 10 November 1988, p. 13; and *Washington Post*, 27 November 1988, p. F2, 21 March 1989, pp. A1, A6.

67. *Washington Post*, 23 January 1988, p. A12 (England), 24 January 1989, p. A16 (Soviet Union), 23 March 1989, pp. A29, A33 (Italy); *New York Times*, 22 February 1987, p. 6 (Canada), 26 November 1988, pp. 1, 6 (Latin America); and *International Herald Tribune*, 30 May 1989, p. 6 (Poland).

68. *The Spokeswoman*, 15 November 1976, pp. 3–4, 15 December 1976, p. 3; "Congress Restricts Medicaid Payment for Abortion," *Clearinghouse Review* 10 (December 1976): 700–703; Jimmy Carter, quoted in *New York Times*, 13 July 1977, pp. 1, 10.

69. *Washington Post*, 21 March 1989, pp. A1, A6; and *Ms.*, April 1989, pp. 90, 93. The greater medical risks of childbirth compared with abortion prompted the American Bar Association to file an amicus brief in *Webster v. Reproductive Health Services*. See *Washington Post*, 5 April 1989, p. A23.

70. *Washington Post*, 28 July 1988, pp. A1, A18.

71. *Boston Globe*, 13 July 1977, p. 2; General Electric, quoted in *Women's Newsletter* (Winter 1977): 2.

72. Quotation from *New York Times*, 27 November 1977, p. 1. For the estimates of the financial impact of the Hyde Amendment in the 1970s and 1980s, see *The Spokeswoman*, 15 October 1977, pp. 3–4; and Susan Tenenbaum, "Will America Bribe Poor To Breed for Adoptions?" *Los Angeles Times*, 15 September 1977, part 2, p. 7; *Washington Post*, 21 March 1989, pp. A1, A6; and *Ms.*, April 1989, pp. 87–95.

73. Belliotti v. Baird, 443 U.S. 622, 99 S. Ct. 3035 (1979); H. L. v. Matheson, 450 U.S. 398 (1981); City of Akron v. Akron Center for Reproductive Health, 462 U.S. 416 (1983); and Planned Parenthood Association v. Ashcroft, 462 U.S. 476 (1983).

74. *New York Times*, 12 June 1986, pp. 1, 12, 13, 15 June 1986, sect. 4, p. 1, 16 April 1989, p. 28; and Lynn Paltrow, "Amicus Brief: *Richard Thornburgh v. American College of Obstetricians and Gynecologists*," *Women's Rights Law Reporter* 9, no. 1 (Winter 1986): 3–24.

75. *New York Times*, 4 September 1986, p. 15, 1 September 1987, p. A22, 9 September 1987, p. 13, 12 February 1988, p. A10, 13 August 1988, p. 6 (Courts' rulings against

Arizona, Colorado, Minnesota, Georgia, and Ohio restrictions on abortions and/or abortion counseling). See note 92 below for a description of the three new cases.

76. *New York Times,* 9 April 1987, p. 13, 10 May 1988, p. A20, 30 June 1988, p. 11, 13 October 1988, p. 19, 10 January 1989, pp. 1, 9, 22 January 1989, p. 21, 21 March 1989, p. A19; *Washington Post,* 28 July 1988, p. A21, 24 January 1989, pp. A1, A10; and *Ms.,* April 1989, pp. 89–90. Over two thousand Justice Department employees signed petitions protesting Attorney General Thornburgh's involvement in this appeal on behalf of the Bush administration. See *New York Times,* 5 April 1989, p. 43.

77. Planned Parenthood v. Danforth, 428 U.S. 52 (1976), at 61; and *Roe v. Wade,* at 164–65.

78. *Washington Post,* 21 March 1989, pp. A1, A6; *New York Times,* 8 May 1989, pp. 1, B6, 4 July 1989, p. 11, 3 August 1989, p. A18.

79. Laurence H. Tribe, "Structural Due Process," *Harvard Civil Rights–Civil Liberties Law Review* 10, no. 2 (Spring 1975): 269–321; and John Hart Ely, "The Wages of Crying Wolf: A Comment on *Roe v. Wade,*" *Yale Law Journal* 82, no. 5 (April 1973): 920–49.

80. Tribe, "Structural Due Process," p. 297.

81. Ibid., pp. 319, 321.

82. Laurence H. Tribe, *American Constitutional Law* (Mineola, N.Y.: Foundation Press, 1988, 2d revised edition), pp. 1356 (first quotation), 1359 (third quotation); and idem, "The Abortion Funding Conundrum: Inalienable Rights, Affirmative Duties, and the Dilemma of Dependence," *Harvard Law Review* 99 (1985): 330 (second quotation).

83. For a review of the legal and moral questions of surrogate motherhood, see Martha Field, *Surrogate Motherhood: The Ethics of Using Human Beings* (Crossroads, N.Y.: Crossroads, 1988); and Rochelle Sharpe, *The Case of Baby M and the Facts of Life* (Englewood Cliffs, N.J.: Prentice-Hall, 1989).

84. *New York Times,* 25 January 1988, pp. 1, 15, 22 February 1988, pp. A1, A13, 28 October 1988, pp. 1, 4, 26, 28 September 1989, p. A24. Information packets about RU-486 can be obtained from the Reproductive Health Technologies Project, 1601 Connecticut Ave., N.W., Suite 801, Washington, D.C. 20009, or calling (202) 328-2208. On 29 June 1990, the AMA endorsed testing RU-486 in the United States.

85. Williams, "Equality Crisis," p. 196.

86. *New York Times,* 28 June 1989, pp. A1, A9 (Western Europe's interest in *Webster*).

87. In his oral presentation of the majority decision in *Michael H.,* Scalia left no doubt that he favored preserving the sanctity of traditional marriage from the "unique" facts of this case and from what he called "disruptive adulterers" (and, presumably, from disruptive women who want abortions). It was left to Justice Brennan, at the age of eighty-three, to defend the natural father's right to have his day in court and to point out that it was "make-believe" to view the California love triangle as a "situation [that] does not repeat itself every day in every corner of the country." Michael H. v. Gerald D., 109 S. Ct. 2333 (1989), at 2336–46 (Scalia's opinion), and 2349–59 (Brennan's opinion, quotation at 2359).

88. *New York Times,* 2 July 1989, sect. 4, pp. 1, 4. See chapter 7 of this volume, p. 270, for Scalia's national-consensus remarks in Johnson v. Transportation Agency, 107 S. Ct. 1442 (1987). It was also Scalia's "majoritarian" point of view that prevailed in the Court's decisions in *Stanford v. Kentucky* and *Wilkins v. Missouri,* which allow states

to execute sixteen-year-olds and the mentally retarded. See *New York Times*, 27 June 1989, pp. 1, A18, and 28 June 1989, p. A22.

89. *Webster v. Reproductive Health Services*, at 3064–67 (Scalia); and *Washington Post*, 5 July 1989, pp. A1, A10.

90. *Webster v. Reproductive Health Services*, at 5030 (Rehnquist), 5035–39 (Blackmun's quotations).

91. Ibid., at 5035–39 (Blackmun).

92. The three original cases were *Ragsdale v. Turnock, Ohio v. Akron Center for Reproductive Health,* and *Hodgson v. Minnesota, Minnesota v. Hodgson.* While the Missouri case concerned restrictions on the use of public services for abortions, Ragsdale v. Turnock, 841 F.2d 1358, involved state regulation of private abortion clinics. In March 1990 the Court of Appeals for the Seventh District decided that the state statute was too restrictive and held in favor of the doctor running an abortion clinic. Consequently, this case was removed from the 1989–90 Supreme Court docket. In *Ohio v. Akron Center for Reproductive Health,* the subject of the second case, No. 88-805, is the right of teen-age girls to obtain abortions without involving their parents. A 1985 Ohio law required that doctors notify at least one parent. The Court of Appeals for the Sixth Circuit, in Cleveland, declared the law unconstitutional, citing Supreme Court precedents that have limited states' discretion to place obstacles in the path of teen-agers seeking abortions. Finally, the third case, *Hodgson v. Minnesota, Minnesota v. Hodgson,* involved twin appeals, Nos. 88-1125 and 88-1309 respectively, concerning Minnesota's requirement that both parents be notified before a teen-age girl can receive an abortion. The law applies even in situations of divorce or parental desertion, requiring notification to the parent who does not have legal custody. The Court of Appeals for the Eighth Circuit, in St. Paul, upheld the law in most respects. Supreme Court appeals were filed both by a group of doctors and the state of Minnesota.

93. *New York Times*, 25 July 1989, pp. 1, A15 (right to die and privacy), 7 July 1989, p. A20 (illegal importation of RU-486), 26 June 1990, pp. A1, A12 (Supreme Court decision in Nancy Cruzan case).

94. *New York Times*, 6 July 1989, p. A21.

95. *New York Times*, 4 July 1989, pp. 1, 10–14, 28, 31, 23 July 1989, p. 18 (NOW national convention), 26 June 1990, pp. A1, A13; and *Washington Post*, 4 July 1989, pp. 1, A5, A10.


## 9. The Epitome of Liberal Legalism

A longer version of the pornography segment of this chapter first appeared in Susan Gubar and Joan Hoff, eds., *For Adult Users Only: The Dilemma of Violent Pornography* (Bloomington: Indiana University Press, 1989), pp. 17–46.

1. Joan Hoff-Wilson, "Richard M. Nixon," in Frank N. Magill, ed., *American Presidents* (Englewood Cliffs, N.J.: Salem, 1986), 3:761–64.

2. For a review of this terminology, see chapter 1 of this volume, p. 9–16. For a review of various feminist factions of the past and present, see Olive Banks, *Faces of Feminism: The Study of Feminism as a Social Movement* (New York: St. Martin's, 1981); and Hester Eisenstein, *Contemporary Feminist Thought* (London: Unwin Paperbacks,

1984); Carol McMillan, *Women, Reason, and Nature: Some Philosophical Problems with Feminism* (Princeton, N.J.: Princeton University Press, 1982); and Elizabeth Hankins Wolgast, *Equality and the Rights of Women* (Ithaca, N.Y.: Cornell University Press, 1980). For a review of the legal underpinnings of the current fragmentation among feminist attorneys and scholars, see Isabel Marcus, "Feminist Legal Strategies: The Shoe that Never Fits," unpublished paper presented at the Sixth Berkshire Conference on the History of Women, 1984, p. 15; Ann C. Scales, "Towards a Feminist Jurisprudence," *Indiana Law Journal* 56, no. 3 (1981): 375–444; Wendy W. Williams, "The Equality Crisis: Some Reflections on Culture, Courts, and Feminism," *Women's Rights Law Reporter* 7, no. 3 (Spring 1982): 175–200; Herma Hill Kay, "Models of Equality," *University of Illinois Law Review* 1 (1985): 39–88; Stephanie M. Wildman, "The Legitimation of Sex Discrimination: A Critical Response to Supreme Court Jurisprudence," *Oregon Law Review* 63 (1984): 265–307; and Sylvia A. Law, "Rethinking Sex and the Constitution," *University of Pennsylvania Law Review* 132 (1984): 954–1040.

3. Susan Moller Okin, *Women in Western Political Thought* (Princeton, N.J.: Princeton University Press, 1979), pp. 10–11; Carole Pateman, *The Sexual Contract* (Cambridge: Polity, 1988), pp. 1–153; and Monique Wittig, "On the Social Contract," in Anja van Kooten Niekerk and Theo van der Meer et al., eds., *Homosexuality, Which Homosexuality?* (London: GMP, 1989), pp. 239–49.

4. Theodore J. Lowi, "Distribution, Regulation, Redistribution," in Randall B. Ripley, ed., *Public Policies and Their Politics* (New York: W. W. Norton, 1966), pp. 27–40. For a discussion of the limitations of these categories when discussing legislation affecting women, see Ellen Boneparth, "A Framework for Policy Analysis," in Boneparth, ed., *Women, Power, and Policy* (Elmsford, N.Y.: Pergamon, 1982), pp. 11–13; and Maren Lockwood Carden, *Feminism in the Mid-1970s* (New York: Ford Foundation, 1977), pp. 40–43. Increasingly, feminists are using the terms *role equity* and *role change* to describe women's issues. While the former can involve redistribution of power, such issues do not change gender relationships or stereotypes, while the latter does. Consequently, legislation or litigation involving role change are much more controversial and generate more opposition than do role-equity questions.

5. The notable New Deal decision upholding minimum wages for women and minors was West Coast Hotel v. Parrish, 300 U.S. 379 (1937). While the Supreme Court upheld maximum hours for women in Muller v. Oregon, 208 U.S. 412 (1908), it did not set a similar precedent for men because it had earlier ruled in Lockner v. New York, 198 U.S. 45 (1905), that to "protect" men with maximum working hours would violate their right of personal liberty and liberty of contract. For a review of the legal ramifications of protective legislation, see chapter 6 of this volume; Susan Lehrer, *Origins of Protective Legislation for Women, 1905–1925* (Albany: State University of New York Press, 1987), pp. 41–93; Judith A. Baer, *The Chains of Protection: The Judicial Response to Women's Labor Legislation* (Westport, Conn.: Greenwood, 1978), pp. 3–106; Nancy S. Erickson, "Historical Background of 'Protective' Legislation: Muller v. Oregon," in D. Kelly Weisberg, ed., *Women and the Law: A Social Historical Perspective* (Cambridge, Mass.: Schenkman, 1982), 2:155–86; and Jennifer Friesen and Ronald K. L. Collins, "Looking Back on Muller v. Oregon," *American Bar Association Journal* 69 (March–April 1983): 294–98, 472–77.

6. This occurred specifically in 1978 when Congress passed legislation amending the

Title VII definition of the word *sex* to include pregnancy-related disabilities, thereby overruling the decision in General Electric Co. v. Gilbert, 321 U.S. 125 (1976); again, in 1982, when it approved legislation allowing state courts the right to divide equitably military-retirement benefits in long-term marriages ending in divorce, thereby overruling McCarty v. McCarty, 453 U.S. 210 (1981), which had declared that military pensions were the sole property of the serviceman not his spouse; and still again, in 1988, when Congress overturned Grove City College v. Bell, 465 U.S. 555 (1984)—a decision undermining enforcement of Title IX, which had proven effective, among other things, for obtaining funding for women's sports programs in secondary schools and colleges.

7. Ruth Bader Ginsburg, "The Burger Court's Grapplings with Sex Discrimination," in Vincent Blasi, ed., *The Burger Court: The Counter-Revolution that Wasn't* (New Haven, Conn.: Yale University Press, 1983), pp. 133–34, 139–40; Freeman, "Women and Public Policy," in Boneparth, *Women, Power, and Policy,* pp. 54–57.

8. Georgia O'Keeffe, *Art and Letters* (Boston: Little, Brown, 1987), p. 235; Joan Hoff-Wilson, ed., *Rights of Passage: The Past and Future of the ERA* (Bloomington: Indiana University Press, 1986), pp. 3–4, 94; Susan Ware, "ER and Democratic Politics: Women in the Postsuffrage Era," and Lois Scharf, "ER and Feminism"—both in Joan Hoff-Wilson and Marjorie Lightman, eds., *Without Precedent: The Life and Career of Eleanor Roosevelt* (Bloomington: Indiana University Press, 1984), pp. 46–60, 238–46.

9. Julie Nixon Eisenhower, *Pat Nixon: The Untold Story* (New York: Simon & Schuster, 1986), pp. 321–22; author's 27 January 1983 interview with Nixon. See also chapter 7 of this volume for details about women's rights during the Nixon administration.

10. First Lady's Staff Files, O'Neill Subject File, Boxes 1 and 2, Gerald Ford Presidential Library, Ann Arbor, Michigan; and Betty Ford with Chris Chase, *The Times of My Life* (New York: Harper & Row, 1978), pp. 151, 194, 201–10.

11. First Lady's Staff Files, Pullen Working File, 1975–77, Box 2, Gerald Ford Presidential Library; and Ford, *Times of My Life,* pp. 201 (first quotation), 204 (second quotation).

12. Gilbert Steiner, *Constitutional Inequality: The Political Fortunes of the Equal Rights Amendment* (Washington, D.C.: Brookings Institution, 1985), pp. 96–103. See also chapter 8 of this volume for other abortion cases.

13. Rosalynn Carter, *First Lady from Plains* (Boston: Houghton Mifflin, 1984), pp. 100, 288.

14. Susan D. Becker, *The Origins of the Equal Rights Amendment: American Feminism between the Wars* (Westport, Conn.: Greenwood, 1981); Mary Frances Berry, *Why the ERA Failed: Politics, Women's Rights, and the Amending Process* (Bloomington: Indiana University Press, 1986); Janet K. Boles, "Building Support for the ERA: A Case of 'Too Much Too Late,'" *Political Science* 15 (Fall 1982): 572–77; idem, *The Politics of the Equal Rights Amendment* (White Plains, N.Y.: Longman, 1979); Jane J. Mansbridge, *Why We Lost the ERA* (Chicago: University of Chicago Press, 1986); Donald G. Mathews and Jane Sherron De Hart, *ERA and the Politics of Cultural Survival: North Carolina* (New York: Oxford University Press, 1990); Loretta J. Blahna, "The Rhetoric of the Equal Rights Amendment" (Ph.D. dissertation, University of Kansas, 1973); and David George Ondercin, "The Compleat Woman: The Equal Rights Amendment

and Perceptions of Womanhood, 1920–1972" (Ph.D. dissertation, University of Minnesota, 1973).

15. The following discussion in the text is my interpretation of material in Mathews and De Hart, *ERA and the Politics of Cultural Survival,* chapter 6. (Page references are to the manuscript version of the book.)

16. Ibid., Introduction.

17. Ibid., p. xi.

18. Ibid., p. 329.

19. Ibid., pp. 359–60.

20. Ibid., p. 359.

21. Ibid., p. 362 (first quotation); and Elizabeth Fox-Genovese, "Women's Rights, Affirmative Action, and the Myth of Individualism," *George Washington Law Review* 54, nos. 1, 2 (January–March 1986): 368 (second quotation).

22. Mary Ritter Beard, *America through Women's Eyes* (New York: Macmillan, 1933), pp. 3, 5–6 (quotations); idem, *Woman as Force in History: A Study in Traditions and Realities* (New York: Macmillan, 1946; reprint, New York: Persea, 1987), pp. 7–46.

23. Beard, *Woman as Force in History,* pp. 199–218, 270–332; and Beard to Ellen Woodward, 3 October 1939, Woodward Papers, Box 2, Folder 15 (hereafter cited as Woodward Papers), Manuscript Division of the Mississippi Department of Archives and History, Jackson. I want to thank Martha H. Swain for bringing these letters to my attention.

24. Beard to Ellen Woodward, 18 November 1938, Woodward Papers, Box 2, Folder 15; *Equal Rights,* 6 July 1935, p. 141.

25. The degree to which membership or esteem is an integral part of citizenship is still a subject for debate. See H. N. Hirsch, "The Threnody of Liberalism," *Political Theory* 14 (1986): 425, 431; and Kenneth L. Karst, "The Supreme Court 1976 Term-Forward: Equal Citizenship under the Fourteenth Amendment," *Harvard Law Review* 91 (1977): 50.

26. For a review of the technical aspects of this stalemate, see Christina Spaulding, "Anti-Pornography Laws as a Claim for Equal Respect: Feminism, Liberalism, and Community," *Berkeley Women's Law Journal* 4 (1988–89): 128–65, especially n. 3. For a more general discussion of the stalemate over pornography, see Andrea Dworkin, *Pornography: Men Possessing Women* (New York: Perigee, 1984); Catharine A. MacKinnon, "Not a Moral Issue," *Yale Law and Policy Review* 11, no. 2 (1984): 321–45; Lisa Duggan, Nan Hunter, and Carol S. Vance, "False Promises: New Antipornography Legislation in the U.S.," *SIECUS Report* 13, no. 5 (May 1985): 1–5; Walter Kendrick, *The Secret Museum: Pornography in Modern Culture* (New York: Viking, 1987), pp. 213–39; and Betty Friedan, "How To Get the Women's Movement Moving Again," *New York Times Magazine,* 3 November 1985, pp. 26–27, 66. Friedan remains a leading proponent of the idea that "pornography is dividing the women's movement" and that it "and other sexual diversions . . . do not affect most women's lives."

27. Attorney General's Commission on Pornography (AGCP), *Final Report [Meese Report]* (Washington, D.C.: Government Printing Office, 1986), 1:222–25, 233 (quotations).

28. Spaulding, "Anti-Pornography Laws," pp. 128–29, 152–53, 158–60.

29. AGCP, *Final Report,* 1:242 (quotation); and John D'Emilio and Estelle B. Freedman, *Intimate Matters: A History of Sexuality in America* (New York: Harper & Row, 1988), pp. 36–52.

30. AGCP, *Final Report,* 1:233–44.

31. Joan Hoff, "Why Is There No History of Pornography?" in Susan Gubar and Joan Hoff, eds., *For Adult Users Only: The Dilemma of Violent Pornography* (Bloomington: Indiana University Press, 1989), pp. 26–27; and D'Emilio and Freedman, *Intimate Matters,* pp. 60–66, 147–64, 232–33, 242, 277.

32. Leslie Fiedler, *Freaks: Myths and Images of the Secret Self* (New York: Simon & Schuster, 1978), pp. 13–36, 114–53. For a description of the modern grotesque based on a loose interpretation of Mikhail Bakhtin's original definition, see Hoff, "Why Is There No History of Pornography?" pp. 19–26.

33. For details, see Hoff, "Why Is There No History of Pornography?" pp. 21–30.

34. Kendrick, *Secret Museum,* pp. 125–57.

35. Marian Leslie Klausner, "Redefining Pornography as Sex Discrimination: An Innovative Civil Rights Approach," *New England Law Review* 20, no. 4 (1984–85): 734 (quotation); Kathy Myers, "Towards a Feminist Erotica," in Hillary Robinson, ed., *Visibly Female: Feminism and Art: An Anthology* (London: Camden, 1987), pp. 283–96; and Laura Fraser, "Nasty Girls," *Mother Jones,* February–March 1990, pp. 32ff. Even this article in *Mother Jones* comments on the small quantity and poor quality of so-called feminist pornography.

36. Joan Hoff-Wilson, "The Pluralistic Society," in the New York Public Library, *Censorship: Five Hundred Years of Conflict* (New York: Oxford University Press, 1984): 103–15; D'Emilio and Freedman, *Intimate Matters,* pp. 36–84, 275–360.

37. For representative examples of this point of view, see Paul J. Gillette, *An Uncensored History of Pornography* (Los Angeles: Holloway House, 1965); Peter Michelson, *The Aesthetics of Pornography* (New York: Herder and Herder, 1971); Roger Thompson, *Unfit for Modest Ears: A Study of Pornographic, Obscene, and Bawdy Works Written or Published in England in the Second Half of the Seventeenth Century* (London: Macmillan, 1979); Douglas A. Hughes, ed., *Perspectives on Pornography* (New York: St. Martin's, 1970); Ove Brusendorff and Poul Henningsen, *The Complete History of Eroticism* (Secaucus, N.J.: Castle, 1983; originally published in six volumes between 1961 and 1963).

38. Spaulding, "Anti-Pornography Laws," pp. 137–38; and Catharine A. MacKinnon, "Pornography, Civil Rights, and Speech," *Harvard Civil Rights–Civil Liberties Law Review* 20 (1985): 21 (quotation).

39. MacKinnon, "Pornography, Civil Rights, and Speech," pp. 21–22 (quotation); AGCP, *Final Report,* 1:277–351, 355; Klausner, "Redefining Pornography," pp. 733–35; Spaulding, "Anti-Pornography Laws," pp. 132–33.

40. Chaplinsky. v. New Hampshire, 315 U.S. 568 (1942), at 572–73. Collin v. Smith, 578 F.2d 1197 (7th Cir. 1978), *cert. denied,* 439 U.S. 916 (1978), invalidated the Skokie, Illinois, city ordinance banning pro-Nazi demonstrations in a largely Jewish community. Since the Seventh Circuit so narrowly construed the group-libel issue, the avenue of redress against "injurious speech" has been considerably reduced, although the Supreme Court has not yet overruled *Beauharhais.*

41. For their latest defense of this approach, see Andrea Dworkin and Catharine A. MacKinnon, *Pornography and Civil Rights: A New Day for Women's Equality* (Minneapolis: Organizing against Pornography: A Resource Center for Education and Action, 1988).

42. *Chronicle of Higher Education,* 14 June 1989, p. A4; and Spaulding, "Anti-Pornography Laws," pp. 128–129.

43. Stephen Gillers, *New York Times,* 8 November 1987, p. A27. In this Op-Ed piece, Gillers upheld the indivisibility principle. See also chapter 1 of this volume. The notion that there is a body of protected political speech under the First Amendment that warrants absolute protection is largely a post–World War II development. See Alexander Meiklejohn, *Free Speech and Its Relation to Self-Government,* (New York: Harper, 1949), pp. 93–94.

44. For examples of opposition to RICO, see *New York Times,* 30 January 1989, pp. A16, A17, 20 June 1989, p. 12, and 26 June 1989, pp. D1, D23.

45. Ibid., 3 February 1989, pp. 1, 9, and 12 March 1989, p. 4. There were 19 civil RICO suits in 1981; in the year ending 30 June 1988, there were 959.

46. Wayne Books Inc. v. Indiana, 109 S. Ct. 916 (1989), at 924–925, 930; and *Washington Post,* 22 February 1989, p. A13.

47. In addition to radical feminists, public-interest groups defend RICO's broad application. See *New York Times,* 1 September 1987, p. A23, Op-Ed piece by G. Robert Blakely (one of the drafers of RICO). Ralph Nader and the Public Citizen's Congress Watch also support RICO's "watchdog" civil applications. For revisions of RICO, see *New York Times,* 27 August 1989, p. 18, 24 October 1989, pp. A26, 1, and D5.

48. *Washington Post,* 20 April 1989, p. A16, 21 April 1989, pp. A7, A22; Sable Communication Commission of California v. FCC, 109 S. Ct. 2829, at 4923, 4924.

49. *Sable Communication Commission of California v. FCC,* at 4924 (quoting Scalia).

50. Mannheim, quoted in Mikhail Bakhtin, *Rabelais and His World* (Bloomington: Indiana University Press, 1984; translation of original 1965 edition), p. xiii. For a discussion of Gramsci's views, see Edward Greer, "Legal Hegemony," in David Kairys, ed., *The Politics of Law: A Progressive Critique* (New York: Pantheon, 1982), p. 304; and Spaulding, "Anti-Pornography Laws," p. 143, nn. 69, 70.

51. For a review of both sides, see Robin L. West, "Pornography as a Legal Text: Comments from a Legal Perspective," in Gubar and Hoff, *For Adult Users Only,* pp. 108–32; Ann Russo, "Conflicts and Contradictions among Feminists over Issues of Pornography and Sexual Freedom," *Women's Studies International Forum* 10, no. 2 (1987): 103–12; *Caught Looking: Feminism, Pornography, and Censorship* (Seattle: Real Comet Press, 1988); *Humanities in Society* ("Special Issue on Sexuality, Violence, and Pornography") 7, nos. 1, 2 (1984): 1–101; A. Snitow, Christine Stansell, and Sharon Thompson, eds., *Powers of Desire: The Politics of Sexuality* (New York: Monthly Review, 1983); and Kathleen Barry, *Female Sexual Slavery* (Englewood Cliffs, N.J.: Prentice-Hall, 1979), pp. 174–214.

52. Kendrick, *Secret Museum,* pp. 120–24; and David Copp and Susan Wendell, eds., *Pornography and Censorship* (New York: Prometheus, 1983), pp. 26–55.

53. AGCP, *Final Report,* 1:277–351, 355; Klausner, "Redefining Pornography," pp. 733–35.

54. AGCP, *Final Report,* 1:253–54.

55. Klausner, "Redefining Pornography," p. 733; and Joel B. Grossman, "The First Amendment and the New Anti-Pornography Statutes," APSA *News for Teachers of Political Science* 4 (Spring 1985): 16.

56. MacKinnon, "Pornography, Civil Rights, and Speech," p. 21.

57. Pope v. Illinois, 107 S. Ct. 1918 (1987), at 1921.
58. For the best summary of these positions, see Russo, "Conflicts and Contradictions among Feminists," pp. 103–12.
59. Biddy Martin, "Feminism, Criticism, and Foucault," *New German Critique* 27 (1982): 3–30.
60. Michel Foucault, *History of Sexuality*, Vol. 1: *An Introduction* (New York: Vintage, 1980), p. 121.
61. Michel Foucault, *Power/Knowledge: Selected Interviews and Other Writings, 1972–1977*, Colin Gordon, ed. (New York: Pantheon, 1980), pp. 219–20.
62. See Alan Soble, *Pornography: Marxism, Feminism, and the Future of Sexuality* (New Haven, Conn.: Yale University Press, 1986); and Teresa de Lauretis, *The Technologies of Gender* (Bloomington: Indiana University Press, 1988). The most well-rounded assessment of Foucault's positive influence on feminism can be found in Irene Diamond and Lee Quinby, eds., *Feminism and Foucault: Reflections on Resistance* (Boston: Northeastern University Press, 1988).
63. Robin L. West, "The Difference in Women's Hedonic Lives: A Phenomenological Critique of Feminist Legal Theory," *Wisconsin Women's Law Journal* 3 (1987): 144 (first quotation); *Humanities in Society* 7, nos. 1, 2 (1984): 1–101; ("Special Issue on Sexuality, Violence, and Pornography"); Joyce Hollyday, "An Epidemic of Violence: Manifestations of Violence against Women," *Sojourners Magazine* 13, no. 10 (1984): 10–12; Ginny Soley, "Our Lives at Stake: The Cultural Roots of Sexual Violence," *Sojourners Magazine* 13, no. 10 (1984): 13–15; and Linda Williams, "Fetishism and Hard Core: Marx, Freud, and the Money Shot," in Gubar and Hoff, *For Adult Users Only*, pp. 198–217.
64. Grossman, "First Amendment and the New Anti-Pornography Statutes," pp. 16–21; and *Newsweek*, 18 March 1985, pp. 58–66 (chart citing poll at 60).
65. For sources, see Hoff, "Why Is There No History of Pornography?" pp. 31–34; and *New York Times*, 21 June 1990, p. A12.
66. Margaret Atwood, *The Handmaid's Tale* (Boston: Houghton Mifflin, 1986).
67. Roth v. United States, 354 U.S. 476 (1957), at 484.
68. Dworkin and MacKinnon, unpublished city of Indianapolis brief, p. 19.
69. *Village Books et al. v. The City of Bellingham*, U.S. District Court for the Western District of Washington, No. C88-1470. The Bellingham antipornography initiative was in court even before the election, and a superior court judge ruled that the ordinance must appear on the ballot even though he questioned its constitutionality. At the time, Civil Rights Organization for Women (CROW) attorney Jan Bianchi had said that since the Supreme Court in 1986 had given no reasons for rejecting the Indianapolis ordinance, the ruling had not set a precedent. Judge Dimmick disagreed, citing a Supreme Court case that said that a summary affirmation on the question of a statute's constitutionality cannot be disregarded by lower courts. The judge declared that the Bellingham ordinance was "virtually identical" to the 1984 Indianapolis statute. She further ruled that the argument in the 1985 Seventh Circuit Court's decision in *Hudnut* was wrong because it did "not establish that a different statute was at issue or that different issues were presented." Dimmick also rejected the defendant intervenors' argument that the issues in *Village Books* could be distinguished from *Hudnut* because the state of Washington, unlike Indiana, had ratified the Equal Rights Amendment and, therefore, had voiced a strong public policy to

eradicate sex discrimination. The intervenors had called for a hearing to document the harms to women caused by pornography, but the judge ruled that Washington's commitment to ending sex discrimination did not differentiate the two city ordinances.

70. American Booksellers Association, Inc., et al. v. William H. Hudnut, Mayor, City of Indianapolis et al., 598 F. Supp. 1316 (1985), 771 F.2d 323 (7th Cir. 1985), aff'd., 475 U.S. 1001 (1986); and New York Times, 25 February 1986, pp. 1, 26.

71. American Booksellers v. Hudnut, 598 F. Supp. 1316 (1985), at 1327; New York Times, 14 May 1986, pp. 1, 11, 15 May 1986, p. 14, 18 May 1986, pp. 1, 7, E8, 19 May 1986, p. 13, and 20 May 1986, p. 6; and AGCP, Final Report, 1:87. For a discussion of all these issues, including the July 1986 attorney general's report on pornography, see Linda Williams, "Sexual Politics: Strange Bedfellows," In These Times (October–November 1986): 18–20; and Gubar and Hoff, For Adult Users Only, pp. 87–107.

72. New York Times, 27 June 1989, p. A17.

73. Time, 5 June 1989 (teen-agers and sex crimes), p. 6; New York Times, 10 May 1989, pp. 1, B5 (crack use); Katha Pollitt, "Violence in a Man's World," New York Times Magazine, 18 June 1989, pp. 16, 20, 30 May 1989, pp. 1, A16 (sex abuse of children); and Washington Post, 9 April 1989, pp. B1, B4 (global war against women), 21 June 1989, p. G7 (violent and antifemale contents of popular music lyrics and album jackets). For a succinct reiteration of how women sublimate the constant fear from violence they experience, see West, "Difference in Women's Hedonic Lives," pp. 94–108.

74. Martha Chamallas with Linda Kerber, "Women, Mothers, and the Law of Fright," Legal History Programs, Working Paper Series 3:1 (Madison, Wisc.: Institute for Legal Studies, 1989), pp. 1–4, 78–91. The California Supreme Court decision, Dillon v. Legg, 69 Cal. Rptr. 72, 441 P.2d 912 (1968), set the precedent for a mother to recover damages for fright-induced injuries after witnessing the injury of her child.

75. West, "Jurisprudence and Gender," pp. 59–60; New York Times, 27 June 1989, p. A17 (paraphrasing Bush's remarks to the AAUW), and 21 June 1990, p. A12 (quoting Senator Biden). See chapter 10 of this volume for a discussion of differences between women's and men's experiential lives.

76. Rousas J. Rushdoony, The Politics of Pornography (New Rochelle, N.Y.: Arlington House, 1974), p. 33.

77. Michael Leach, I Know It When I See It (Philadelphia: Westminster, 1975), pp. 17–26.

78. David Holbrook, The Case against Pornography (La Salle, Ill.: Library Press, 1973), p. 2.

79. Semiotica ("Special Issue: The Rhetoric of Violence") 54, nos. 1, 2 (1985): 1–266 (quotation at 39).

80. Bowers v. Hardwick, 478 U.S. 186 (1986).

## 10. Beyond Liberal Legalism

1. Clare Dalton, "Where We Stand: Observations on the Situation of Feminist Legal Thought," Berkeley Women's Law Journal 3 (1987–88): 1–13. Quotations are from Linda J. Nicholson, Gender and History: The Limits of Social Theory in the Age of the Family (New York: Columbia University Press, 1986), p. 206; and Catharine A.

MacKinnon, "Feminism, Marxism, Method, and the State: An Agenda for Theory," *Signs* 7, no. 3 (Spring 1982): 533.

2. Teresa de Lauretis, ed., *Feminist Studies/Critical Studies* (Bloomington: Indiana University Press, 1986), p. 14 (emphasis in original quotation); Joan Wallach Scott, "Critical Tensions," *Women's Review of Books* 5, no. 1 (October 1987): 17.

3. Before poststructuralism had an impact on the writing of U.S. history, *minimizers* viewed patriarchy, like capitalism, as relentlessly self-correcting. In consequence, they accepted modernization theories and, therefore, saw linear progress in the lives of American women from the colonial period to the present. *Minimizing* the cultural differences between women and men, they sometimes overemphasized the biological ones. More often than not, therefore, *minimizers* cited biological reasons to rationalize the unequal treatment of all women over time, and they generally assumed that members of both sexes experience historical events similarly. In contrast, *maximizers* viewed the history of American women as an uneven progression in which gender has been only one factor in a complex interaction of economic, political, legal, and cultural considerations. Refusing to adopt a male standard of progress for women, they measured progress in terms of women's own values and their own estimates of their potential. In placing less emphasis on biological differences and more on socially constructed ones, they are more likely than the *minimizers* to criticize periodization, which corresponds to male standards of achievement or change. Most important, *maximizers* stressed that cultural distinctions in the experiences of different socioeconomic groups, as well as among women of the same class, religion, or ethnic background, lead to quite different perceptions of the same historical event or period.

4. Joan Wallach Scott, *Gender and the Politics of History* (New York: Columbia University Press, 1988), pp. 2–5 (quotation).

5. Judith M. Bennett, "Feminism and History," *Gender and History* 1, no. 3 (Autumn 1989): 259 passim; and Karen J. Winkler, "Scholars of Women's History Fear the Field Has Lost Its Identity," *Chronicle of Higher Education,* 5 July 1990, pp. A4, A6.

6. Dalton, "Where We Stand," p. 9 (first quotation); and Jeffrey Weeks, "Questions of Identity," in Pat Caplan, ed., *The Cultural Construction of Sexuality* (London: Tavistock, 1987), p. 31 (second quotation).

7. Simone de Beauvoir, *The Second Sex* (New York: Bantam, 1961), p. xviii. For standard rationalizations about the harshness and hopelessness of de Beauvoir's assumptions, see Mary Daly, *Pure Lust: Elemental Feminist Philosophy* (Boston: Beacon, 1984), pp. 137–38.

8. Scott, quoted in Karen Winkler, "Women's Studies after Two Decades: Debates over Politics, New Directions for Research," *Chronicle of Higher Education,* 28 September 1988, p. A6.

9. For detailed extrapolations of Gilligan's thesis about how women's moral development differs from men's, see Eva Feder Kittay and Diana T. Meyers, eds., *Women and Moral Theory* (New York: Rowman & Littlefield, 1987).

10. Dalton, "Where We Stand," pp. 9–10.

11. Barbara Christian, "The Race for Theory," *Feminist Studies* 14, no. 1 (Spring 1988): 67–79. This issue of *Feminist Studies* addresses the problems when feminists in the United States adapt French poststructural thought for academic and political purposes, as does "Learning about Women: Gender, Politics, and Power," a special issue of *Daedalus* 116, no. 4 (Fall 1987): 1–210. For a discussion of the Afro-feminist

analytical model, see Rosalyn Terborg-Penn, Sharon Harley, and Andrea Benton Rushing, eds., *Women in Africa and the African Diaspora* (Washington, D.C.: Howard University Press, 1988). See also Gloria I. Joseph and Jill Lewis, *Common Differences: Conflicts in Black and White Feminist Perspectives* (Boston: South End, 1981; reprint, New York: Doubleday, 1986); Chandra Talpade Mohanty, "Under Western Eyes: Feminist Scholarship and Colonial Discourses," *Boundary 2: A Journal of Post Modern Literature and Culture* 12–13 (1984): 333–58; and Maxine Molyneux, "Mobilization without Emancipation? Women's Interests, the State, and Revolution in Nicaragua," *Feminist Studies* 11 (Summer 1985): 227–54.

12. Gerda Lerner, "Placing Women in History: A Theoretical Framework," unpublished 1988 paper. Hegemonic and racist implications of deconstruction are discussed in Kathleen Barry, "Biography and the Search for Women's Subjectivity," *Women's Studies International Forum* 12, no. 6 (November 1989): 561–77. Mary Poovey criticizes the ahistorical and apolitical strains of deconstruction in "Feminism and Deconstruction," *Feminist Studies* 141 (Spring 1988): 60–63.

13. Zillah R. Eisenstein, *The Female Body and the Law* (Berkeley: University of California Press, 1988), pp. 3, 39–40.

14. Linda Gordon, "What's New in Women's History," in Lauretis, *Feminist Studies/ Critical Studies,* pp. 22 (quotation), 30 passim.

15. Joan W. Scott, *Gender and the Politics of History* (New York: Columbia University Press, 1988), p. 2; and Elizabeth Fox-Genovese, "Women's Rights, Affirmative Action, and the Myth of Individualism," *George Washington Law Review* 54, nos. 1, 2 (January–March 1986): 351–52 (second quotation). For a critique of Scott's avoidance of class analysis from an economic point of view, see the review of her book *Gender and Politics* by Claudia Koonz, "Postscript," *Women's Review of Books,* January 1989, pp. 19–20.

16. Report by the National League of Cities in *New York Times,* 12 March 1989, p. 22 (poor getting poorer), 19 April 1989, p. A27 (rich, richer), 16 July 1989, pp. 1, 23 (report of growing poverty by U.S. House Ways and Means Committee); and "The New Permanence of Poverty," *Ford Foundation Letter* 19, no. 2 (June 1988): 1–3, 8–9.

17. Karen Offen, "The Use and Abuse of History," *Women's Review of Books,* April 1989, p. 16; and idem, "Defining Feminism: A Comparative Historical Approach," *Signs* 14, no. 1 (Autumn 1988): 119–57. For a review of Michael T. Sandel's and others' criticism of the mythical Lockean "self-contained" individual, see Edward E. Sampson, "Globalization and Psychology's Theory of the Person," *American Psychologist* 44 (June 1989): 914–21.

18. For a representative sample of the kind of criticism of the white, middle-class leaders of both the First and Second Women's movements that contains too little gendered analysis of the common legal dilemmas shared by such women, see Fox-Genovese, "Women's Rights," pp. 338–74. For a less-sophisticated version of Fox-Genovese's critique of the lack of class consciousness and, hence, diversity in previous scholarship on women, see Hewitt, "Beyond the Search for Sisterhood," pp. 299–321; and Lori Ginsberg, " 'Moral Suasion Is Moral Balderdash': Women, Politics and Social Activism in the 1850s," *Journal of American History* 73 (December 1986): 601–22.

19. Elizabeth Fox-Genovese provides an example of this type of scholarship in *Within the Plantation Household: Black and White Women of the Old South* (Chapel Hill: University

of North Carolina Press, 1988). While this book has been deservedly praised for its copious research, Fox-Genovese concentrates primarily on showing diversity (and hypocrisy) among white plantation mistresses, denying that even the most sympathetic of them "bonded" with the plight of black women or men. When dealing with black women, she implies that they did not develop any sense of "sisterhood" with either their white female owners or among themselves, because slavery denied them an ideological sense of womanhood. Thus, average black women emerge as less diverse among each other (and, by implication, less human) than white women for the same reason—class interests that prevail over all other values, especially those related to gender, even those that clearly crossed class lines, such as motherhood. To rationalize this extreme genderless portrayal of black women, Fox-Genovese must portray exceptional black women, such as Harriet Jacobs (and, presumably, Harriet Tubman whom she ignores), as "loners" who only faked a sense of gender solidarity to obtain acceptance in the North in their fight against slavery, with little authentic community or group support among whites or blacks. Black women leaders become implicitly, therefore, the very personification of the iron-willed liberal individualism that Fox-Genovese has criticized generally in American society and specifically among middle-class leaders of the First and Second Women's movements. See also note 18 above.

20. Joan Wallach Scott, "Gender: A Useful Category of Historical Analysis," *American Historical Review* 91, no. 5 (December 1986): 1067 (quotation); and idem, "Deconstructing Equality-versus-Difference: Or, the Uses of Poststructural Theory for Feminism," *Feminist Studies* 14, no. 1 (Spring 1988): 39–47.

21. Herma Hill Kay, "Models of Equality," *University of Illinois Law Review* 1 (1985): 39–88. Kay argues in this article that there is a "two-way" model of equality between women and men, with women "asking to be treated like men in the public sphere and men asking to be treated like women in the private sphere." However, she believes that only a "one-way" model of equality exists between whites and blacks, with white litigants using the charge of "reverse discrimination" to obtain "limited opportunity made available to blacks" (pp. 45–46). While I agree whites seldom sue to obtain the legal status or race roles of minority groups, I do not believe that men sue to be treated like women in either the public or private spheres, except where they think that women enjoy a statutory or monetary advantage, as in social security cases. As I argued in chapter 1, men occasionally want what women "have" but do not generally want what women represent, anymore than they want to be treated like blacks—both being generally disadvantaged groups.

22. Ibid., pp. 41–43, 48ff. Stephanie M. Wildman, "The Legitimation of Sex Discrimination: A Critical Response to Supreme Court Jurisprudence," *Oregon Law Review* 63 (1984): 267–69; Sylvia A. Law, "Rethinking Sex and the Constitution," *University of Pennsylvania Law Review* 132 (1984): 963–69; and J. R. Pole, *The Pursuit of Equality in American History* (Berkeley: University of California Press, 1978), pp. 293–94, 295.

23. Law, "Rethinking Sex and the Constitution," p. 963.

24. Ibid., pp. 963–64.

25. Frontier v. Richardson, 411 U.S. 677, 686 (1973) (plurality opinion).

26. Law, "Rethinking Sex and the Constitution," p. 965 (quotation); and Ann C. Scales, "Towards a Feminist Jurisprudence," *Indiana Law Journal* 56, no. 3 (1980–81): 435.

27. Gena Corea et al., *Man-Made Women: How New Reproductive Technologies Affect Women* (Bloomington: Indiana University Press, 1987; reprint of 1985 Hutchinson

edition), p. 12 (first and third quotations); Lynda Birke, *Women, Feminism, and Biology: The Feminist Challenge* (New York: Methuen, 1986); and Gena Corea, *The Mother Machine: Reproductive Technologies from Artificial Insemination to Artificial Wombs* (New York: Harper & Row, 1985), p. 213 (second quotation).

28. Until (and even after) Johnson v. Transportation Agency of Santa Clara County, California, 480 U.S. 616 (1987), there were many in the legal profession and in society at large who continued to agree with the attorney in the *Sears* case, who said: "There's just no equation between minorities and women. . . . I know who the Thirteenth, Fourteenth, and Fifteenth Amendments were intended for and that's still the priority" (*New York Times*, 29 January 1979, p. D9). See also chapter 7 of this volume, pp. 266–67, nn. 79–80, for examples of justices saying that race discrimination was more important than gender discrimination in Bakke v. Regents of California, 438 U.S. 265 (1978).

29. Kay, "Models of Equality," p. 47.

30. For reports on the 1987–88 firings of Al Campanis and Jimmy ("the Greek") Snyder, see *Washington Post,* 17 January 1988, pp. A1, A16, 19 January 1988, p. A15; and *Washington Post National Weekly,* 25–31 January 1988, p. 37.

31. Law, "Rethinking Sex and the Constitution," pp. 966–97.

32. Ibid., pp. 1005–09; Scales, "Towards a Feminist Jurisprudence," pp. 437–38; and Robin West, "Jurisprudence and Gender," *University of Chicago Law Review* 55, no. 1 (Winter 1988): 70.

33. Kay, "Models of Equality," pp. 85–86; Wildman, "Legitimation of Sex Discrimination," pp. 269 (quotation), 304 (quotation).

34. Wendy W. Williams, "Equality's Riddle: Pregnancy and the Equal Treatment/Special Treatment Debate," *New York University Review of Law and Social Change* 13, no. 2 (1984–85): 361–63 (quotation at 362).

35. See chapter 7 of this volume, pp. 265, 270–71, for details.

36. Wildman, "Legitimation of Sex Discrimination," pp. 268 (first quotation), 271, 305 (second quotation).

37. Joan Wallach Scott, "Deconstructing Equality-versus-Difference: Or, the Uses of Poststructuralist Theory for Feminism," *Feminist Studies* 14, no. 1 (Spring 1988): 46, 48; and Zillah R. Eisenstein, *The Female Body and the Law* (Berkeley: University of California Press, 1988), pp. 222 passim.

38. Law, "Rethinking Sex and the Constitution," pp. 968–69 (quotations); Wildman, "Legitimation of Sex Discrimination," pp. 304–6.

39. Law, "Rethinking Sex and the Constitution," p. 968 (paraphrasing MacKinnon); West, "Jurisprudence and Gender," p. 37.

40. Catharine A. MacKinnon, *Feminism Unmodified: Discourses on Life and Law* (Cambridge: Harvard University Press, 1987), pp. 1–17, 32–62, 103–16, 215–28; Kenneth Karst, "Woman's Constitution," *Duke Law Journal* 1984, no. 3 (June 1984): 448, 455, 473–77.

41. Rhonda Copelon, "Beyond the Liberal Idea of Privacy: Toward a Positive Right of Autonomy," in Michael W. McCann and Gerald L. Houseman, eds., *Judging the Constitution: Critical Essays in Judicial Lawmaking* (Glenview, Ill.: Scott, Foresman, 1989), pp. 291–320; and Sarah Slavin, "Authenticity and Fiction in Law: Contemporary Case Studies Exploring Radical Feminism," *JOURNAL OF WOMEN'S HISTORY* 1, no. 3 (February 1990): 123–31.

42. In her own words in "Jurisprudence and Gender," this is how West describes the concepts in the charts on pp. 367:

> First, and most obviously, the "official" descriptions of human beings' subjectivity and women's subjectivity contrast rather than compare. According to liberal theory, human beings respond aggressively to their natural state of relative physical equality. In response to the great dangers posed by their natural aggression, they abide by a sharply anti-naturalist morality of autonomy, rights, and individual spheres of freedom, which is intended to and to some extent does curb their natural aggression. They respect a civil state that enforces those rights against the most egregious breaches. The description of women's subjectivity told by cultural feminism is much the opposite. According to cultural feminism, women inhabit a realm of natural *inequality*. They are physically stronger than the fetus and the infant. Women respond to their natural inequality over the fetus and infant not with aggression, but with nurturance and care. That natural and nurturant response evolves into a naturalist moral ethic of care which is consistent with women's natural response. The substantive moralities consequent to these two stories, then, unsurprisingly, are also diametrically opposed. The autonomy that human beings value and the rights they need as a restriction on their natural hostility to the equal and separate other are in sharp contrast to the intimacy that women value, and the ethic of care that represents not a limitation upon, but an extension of, women's natural nurturant response to the dependent, connected other.
>
> The subterranean descriptions of subjectivity that emerge from the unofficial stories of radical feminism and critical legalism also contrast rather than compare. According to the critical legalists, human beings respond to their natural state of physical separateness not with aggression, fear and mutual suspicion, as liberalism holds, but with longing. Men suffer from a perpetual dread of isolation and alienation and a fear of rejection, and harbor a craving for community, connection, and association. Women, by contrast, according to radical feminism, respond to their natural state of material connection to the other with a craving for individuation and a loathing for invasion. Just as clearly, the subterranean dread men have of alienation (according to critical legalism) contrasts sharply with the subterranean dread that women have of invasion and intrusion (according to radical feminism) (pp. 38–39).

43. Ibid., p. 42.
44. Ibid., pp. 43, 53 (quotations).
45. Ibid., p. 53.
46. Ibid., pp. 68–70.
47. Robin West, "The Difference in Women's Hedonic Lives: A Phenomenological Critique of Feminist Legal Theory," *Wisconsin Women's Law Journal* 3 (1987): 87–90 (quotations at 89–90).
48. Edward E. Sampson, "Globalization and Psychology's Theory of the Person," *American Psychologist* 44 (June 1989): 914–15, 917 (quotation).
49. Ibid., pp. 918–19 (quotations). Sampson goes on to note that the "personal being" who is "clearly constituted within the social world" learns this through psychological symbiosis. The best example can be found in the way "mothers do not talk *about* the child's wishes and emotions; they *supply* the wishes, needs, intentions, wants and the like, and interact with the child as if it had them" (Sampson quoting R. Harre, *Personal Being* [Cambridge: Harvard University Press, 1986], pp. 105, 720).
50. Carroll Smith-Rosenberg, *Disorderly Conduct: Visions of Gender in Victorian America* (New York: Knopf, 1985), pp. 252–305, 358, n. 127; and idem, "Discourses of Sexuality and Subjectivity: The New Woman, 1870–1936," in Martin B. Duberman

et al., eds., *Hidden from History: Reclaiming the Gay and Lesbian Past* (New York: NAL, 1989), pp. 277–94.

51. West, "Jurisprudence and Gender," pp. 68–70.

52. Catharine A. MacKinnon, "Feminism, Marxism, Method, and the State: Toward Feminist Jurisprudence," in Sandra Harding, ed., *Feminism and Methodology* (Bloomington: Indiana University Press, 1987), p. 149.

53. See chapter 7 of this volume, p. 270, and notes 83 and 90 for Scalia's national-consensus remarks in Johnson v. Transportation Agency, 107 S. Ct. 1442 (1987). It was also Scalia's "majoritarian" point of view that prevailed in the Court's decisions in *Stanford v. Kentucky* and *Wilkins v. Missouri,* which allow states to execute sixteen-year-olds and the mentally retarded. See also *New York Times,* 27 June 1989, pp. 1, A18, and 28 June 1989, p. A22.

54. See appendix 6 for the text of the 1989 Declaration of Interdependence. It was issued by the Women's Foreign Policy Council in April 1989. See also Kathleen Barry, "The Prostitution of Sexuality," unpublished 1989 paper, for a discussion of a feminist version of international human rights, and information published by the Non-Governmental Organization (NGO) of the United Nations on the Trafficking in Women, for which Barry is the executive director.

55. Eleanor Holmes Norton, "Equality and the Court," *Constitution,* Fall 1989, p. 19; Mari J. Matsuda, "When the First Quail Calls: Multiple Consciousness as Jurisprudential Method," *Women's Rights Law Reporter* 11, no. 1 (Spring 1989): 7–10; and Marjorie Heins, *Cutting the Mustard: Affirmative Action and the Nature of Excellence* (Boston: Faber & Faber, 1987), p. 10.

56. Matsuda, "When the First Quail Calls," p. 9.

57. Sampson, "Globalization and Psychology's Theory of the Person," p. 916.

58. See the Introduction for my definition of feminism, pp. 12–16.

# Bibliography

Articles printed in edited editions are not cited separately unless there is only one essay on women in the collection. Otherwise, authors referred to in the notes are simply cited by last name following the publication information about the anthology in which they appear.

Akers, Charles W. *Abigail Adams, An American Woman*. Boston: Little, Brown, 1980.

Alexander, Shana. *State-by-State Guide to Women's Legal Rights*. Los Angeles: Wollstone-craft, 1975.

Allen, David Grayson. *In English Ways: The Movement of Societies and the Transferral of English Local Law and Custom to Massachusetts Bay in the Seventeenth Century*. Chapel Hill: University of North Carolina Press, 1982.

*American Women: Report of the President's Commission on the Status of Women, 1963*. Washington, D.C.: Government Printing Office, 1963.

"Answering Opponents of Equal Rights." *Independent Woman* 26 (October 1947): 302.

Anthony, Susan B. "The 'Equal Rights' Amendment; An Attack on Labor." *Lawyer's Guild Review*, January 1943, 12–17.

*Antisexism Newsletter*. Formerly *Women's Newsletter*, a publication of the National Commission of Women's Oppression (NCWO) of the National Lawyers' Guild, Anti-Sexism Task Force.

Arriola, Elvia Rosales. "Sexual Identity and the Constitution: Homosexual Persons as a Discrete and Insular Minority." *Women's Rights Law Reporter* 10, (Winter 1988): 143–76.

Auerbach, Jerold. *Unequal Justice: Lawyers and Social Change in Modern America*. New York: Oxford University Press, 1976.

Babcock, Barbara Allen, Ann E. Freedman, Eleanor Holmes Norton, and Susan C. Ross. *Sex Discrimination and the Law: Causes and Remedies*. Boston: Little, Brown, 1975, supplement 1978.

Baer, Judith A. *The Chains of Protection: The Judicial Response to Women's Labor Legislation*. Westport, Conn.: Greenwood, 1978.

———. *Equality under the Constitution: Reclaiming the Fourteenth Amendment*. Ithaca, N.Y.: Cornell University Press, 1983.

Banks, Olive. *Faces of Feminism: A Study of Feminism as a Social Movement*. New York: St. Martin's, 1981.

Barry, Kathleen. *Female Sexual Slavery*. Englewood Cliffs, N.J.: Prentice-Hall, 1979.

———. *Susan B. Anthony: A Biography of a Singular Feminist*. New York: New York University Press, 1988.

Basch, Norma. *In the Eyes of the Law: Women, Marriage, and Property in Nineteenth-Century New York*. Ithaca, N.Y.: Cornell University Press, 1982.

Bayles, George James. *Woman and the Law*. New York: Century, 1901.

Beard, Mary Ritter. *Woman's Work in Municipalities*. New York: D. Appleton, 1916.

———. *On Understanding Women*. New York: Longmans, 1931. Reprint. Westport, Conn.: Greenwood, 1968.

———. *America through Women's Eyes*. New York: Macmillan, 1933.

———. *Woman as Force in History: A Study in Traditions and Realities*. New York: Macmillan, 1946. Reprint. New York: Persea, 1981.

Becker, Susan D. *The Origins of the Equal Rights Amendment: American Feminism between the Wars*. Westport, Conn.: Greenwood, 1981.

Benson, Mary Sumner. *Women in Eighteenth-Century America: A Study in Usage and Opinion*. 1935. Reprint. London: P. S. King & Son, 1966.

Berger, Margaret A. *Litigation on Behalf of Women*. New York: Ford Foundation, 1980.

Berger, Raoul. *Government by Judiciary: The Transformation of the Fourteenth Amendment*. Cambridge: Harvard University Press, 1977.

Bergmann, Barbara R. *The Economic Emergence of Women*. New York: Basic Books, 1986.

*Berkeley Women's Law Journal*. A quarterly publication produced by law students of Boalt Hall School of Law, University of California, Berkeley.

Berry, Mary Francis. *Why the ERA Failed: Politics, Women's Rights, and the Amending Process*. Bloomington: Indiana University Press, 1986.

Biemer, Linda Briggs. *Women and Property in Colonial New York: The Transition from Dutch to English Law, 1643–1727*. Ann Arbor: UMI Research Press, 1983.

Binion, Gayle. "Reproductive Freedom and the Constitution: The Limits of Choice." *Berkeley Women's Law Journal* 4 (1988–89): 12–41.

Binkin, Martin, and Shirley J. Bach. *Women and the Military*. Washington, D.C.: Brookings Institution, 1977.

Bird, Caroline. *Born Female: The High Cost of Keeping Women Down*. New York: David McKay, 1968. Reprint. New York: Pocket Books, 1969.

Bittenbender, Adam. "Woman in Law." In *Women's Work in America*, edited by Annie Nathan Meyer, 218–44. New York: H. Holt, 1891.

Blahna, Loretta J. "The Rhetoric of the Equal Rights Amendment." Ph.D. diss., University of Kansas, 1973.

Blasi, Vincent. ed. *The Burger Court: The Counter-Revolution that Wasn't*. New Haven, Conn.: Yale University Press, 1983. (See especially Burt and Ginsburg.)

Bloch, Ruth H. "The Gendered Meanings of Virtue in Revolutionary America." *Signs* 13, no. 1 (Autumn 1987): 37–58.

Blumenthal, Walter Hart. *Women Camp Followers of the American Revolution*. 1952. Reprint. New York: Avon, 1974.

Boggan, E. Carrington, Marilyn G. Haft, Charles Lister, and John P. Rupp. *The Rights of Gay People: A Basic ACLU Guide to a Gay Person's Rights*. New York: Avon, 1975.

Boles, Janet K. *The Politics of the Equal Rights Amendment*. White Plains, N.Y.: Longman, 1979.

———. "Building Support for the ERA: A Case of 'Too Much Too Late.'" *Political Science* 15 (Fall 1982): 572–77.

Boneparth, Ellen, ed. *Women, Power, and Policy*. Elmsford, N.Y.: Pergamon, 1982. (See especially Boneparth, Freeman, and Moulds.)

Boxer, Marilyn J. "Protective Legislation and Home Industry: The Marginalization of Women Workers in Late Nineteenth–Early Twentieth Century France." *Journal of Social History* 20 (Autumn 1986): 45–66.

Brady, David W., and Kent L. Tedin. "Ladies in Pink: Religion and Political Ideology in the Anti-ERA Movement." *Social Science Quarterly* 56 (March 1976): 564–75.

Brown, Barbara A., Thomas I. Emerson, Gail Falk, and Ann E. Freedman. "The Equal Rights Amendment: A Constitutional Basis for Equal Rights for Women." *Yale Law Journal* 80 (April 1971): 871–985.

Brown, Marvin Luther Jr., trans. and ed. *Baroness Von Riedesel and the American Revolution: Journal and Correspondence of a Tour of Duty, 1776–1783.* Chapel Hill: University of North Carolina Press, 1965.

Buechler, Steven M. *The Transformation of the Woman Suffrage Movement: The Case of Illinois, 1850–1920.* New Brunswick, N.J.: Rutgers University Press, 1986.

Buel, Joy Day, and Richard Buel Jr. *The Way of Duty: A Woman and Her Family in Revolutionary America.* New York: W. W. Norton, 1984.

Burns, Haywood. "Black People and the Tyranny of American Law." *The Annals of the American Academy of Political and Social Science* 407 (May 1973): 156–66.

Butler, Melissa. "Early Roots of Feminism: John Locke and the Attack on Patriarchy." *American Political Science Review* 72 (March 1979): 135–50.

Butterfield, L. H., and Marc Friedlander, eds. *Adams Family Correspondence.* 4 vols. Cambridge: Harvard University Press, 1963.

Campbell, Karlyn Kohrs. "The Rhetoric of Women's Liberation: An Oxymoron." *Quarterly Journal of Speech* 59 (February 1973): 74–86.

Carden, Maren Lockwood. *Feminism in the Mid-1970s.* New York: Ford Foundation, 1977.

Carr, Lois Green, and Lorena S. Walsh. "The Planter's Wife: The Experience of White Women in Seventeenth-Century Maryland." *William and Mary Quarterly,* 3d ser., 34 (1977): 542–71.

Cary, Eve, and Kathleen Willert Peratis. *Woman and the Law.* Skokie, Ill.: National Textbook, 1977.

Cassidy, James J. *The Legal Status of Women.* New York: National American Woman Suffrage Association, 1897.

Chafe, William H. *The American Woman: Her Changing Social, Economic, and Political Role, 1920–1970.* New York: Oxford University Press, 1972.

———. *Women and Equality: Changing Patterns in American Culture.* New York: Oxford University Press, 1978.

Chalou, George C. "Women in the American Revolution: Vignettes or Profiles?" In *Clio Was a Woman: Studies in the History of American Women,* edited by Mable Deutrich and Virginia C. Purdy, 73–90. Washington, D.C.: Howard University Press, 1980.

Chapman Jane R., and Margaret Gates, eds. *Women into Wives: The Legal and Economic Impact of Marriage.* New York: Sage Books, 1977.

Childs, Marjorie. *Fabric of the ERA: Congressional Intent.* Smithtown, N.Y.: Exposition, 1982.

Chused, Richard H. "Married Women's Property Law: 1800–1850." *Georgetown Law Journal* 71 (1983): 1359–1425.

———. "The Oregon Donation Act of 1850 and Nineteenth-Century Federal Married Women's Property Law." *Law and History Review* 2, no. 1 (Spring 1984): 44–78.

———. "Late Nineteenth-Century Married Women's Property Law: Reception of the

Early Married Women's Property Acts by Courts and Legislatures." *American Journal of Legal History* 29 (January 1985): 3–35.

————. "Married Women's Property and Inheritance by Widows in Massachusetts: A Study of Wills Probated between 1800 and 1850." *Berkeley Women's Law Journal* 2 (Fall 1986): 42–88.

Clark, Barbara A. "The Rhetoric of Women's Rights: A Study of the Controversy Surrounding the Proposed Equal Rights Amendment." Master's thesis, University of Kansas, 1973.

Clark, Judith Freeman. *Almanac of American Women in the Twentieth Century.* Englewood Cliffs, N.J.: Prentice-Hall, 1987.

Clark, Lorenne M. G. "Women and John Locke: Who Owns the Apples in the Garden of Eden?" In *The Sexism of Social and Political Theory: Women and Reproduction from Plato to Nietzsche,* edited by Lorenne M. G. Clark and Lynda Lange, 16–40. Toronto: University of Toronto Press, 1979.

Clavert, Karin. "Children in American Family Portraiture, 1670 to 1810." *William and Mary Quarterly,* 3d ser., 39 (1982): 87–113.

Clinton, Catherine. *The Other Civil War: American Women in the Nineteenth Century.* New York: Hill & Wang, 1984.

Cometti, Elizabeth. "Women in the American Revolution." *New England Quarterly* 20 (1947): 329–46.

*Congressional Record.* 18 July 1946, 9225 (ERA).

*Congressional Record.* 7 March 1950, A2054 (ERA).

*Congressional Record.* 10 September 1970, 31132 (ERA).

*Congressional Record.* 2 March 1972, 6765 (ERA).

*Congressional Record.* 28 March 1972, 10450–56 (ERA).

Coontz, Stephanie. *The Social Origins of Private Life: A History of American Families, 1600–1900.* London: Verso, 1988.

Copelon, Rhonda. "Beyond the Liberal Idea of Privacy: Toward a Positive Right of Autonomy." In *Judging the Constitution: Critical Essays on Judicial Lawmaking,* edited by Michael W. McCann and Gerald L. Houseman. Glenview, Ill.: Scott, Foresman, 1989.

Corea, Gena, et al. *Man-Made Women: How New Reproductive Technologies Affect Women.* London: Hutchinson, 1985. Reprint. Bloomington: Indiana University Press, 1987.

Cott, Nancy F. "Divorce and the Changing Status of Women in Eighteenth-Century Massachusetts." *William and Mary Quarterly,* 3d ser., 33 (1976): 586–614.

————. "Eighteenth-Century Family and Social Life Revealed in Massachusetts Divorce Records." *Journal of Social History* 10 (Fall 1976): 20–43.

————. *The Grounding of Modern Feminism.* New Haven, Conn.: Yale University Press, 1987.

Cox, Archibald. *The Court and the Constitution.* (Boston: Houghton Mifflin, 1987).

Crable, E. C. "Pros and Cons of the Equal Rights Amendment." *Women Lawyers Journal* 35 (Summer 1949): 7–9.

Crane, Elaine Forman. *A Dependent People: Newport, Rhode Island, in the Revolutionary Era.* New York: Fordham University Press, 1985.

Crapol, Edward P., ed. *Women and American Foreign Policy: Lobbyists, Critics, and Insiders.* Westport, Conn.: Greenwood, 1987.

Crozier, Blanche. "Constitutionality of Discrimination Based on Sex." *Boston University Law Review,* 15, no. 4 (November 1935): 723–55.

Dalton, Clare. "Where We Stand: Observations on the Situation of Feminist Legal Thought." *Berkeley Women's Law Journal* 3 (1987–88): 1–13.

Daniels, M. R., and J. W. Westphal. "The ERA Won—At Least in the Opinion Polls." *Political Science* 15 (Fall 1982): 578–84.

Dargo, George. *Life in the New Republic: Private Law and Public Estate.* New York: Knopf, 1983.

Davidson, Kenneth, Ruth Bader Ginsburg, and Herma Hill Kay. *Text, Cases, and Materials on Sex-Based Discrimination.* St. Paul: West Publishing, 1974, 1981.

Dayton, Cornelia Hughes. "Woman before the Bar: Gender, Law, and Society in Connecticut, 1710–1790." Ph.D. diss., Princeton University, 1986.

Deckard, Barbara Sinclair. *The Women's Movement: Political, Socioeconomic, and Psychological Issues.* New York: Harper & Row, 1975.

DeCrow, Karen. *Sexist Justice.* New York: Vintage, 1975.

Degler, Carl. *At Odds: Women and the Family in America from the Revolution to the Present.* New York: Oxford University Press, 1980.

Dekeuwer-Defossez, Françoise. *Droits des Femmes.* Paris: Dalloz, 1985.

D'Emilio, John, and Estelle B. Freedman. *Intimate Matters: A History of Sexuality in America.* New York: Harper & Row, 1988.

Demos, John. *Past, Present, and Personal: The Family and Life Course in American History.* New York: Oxford University Press, 1986.

De Pauw, Linda Grant. "The American Revolution and the Rights of Women: The Feminist Theory of Abigail Adams." In *Legacies of the American Revolution,* edited by Larry R. Gerlach et al., 199–219. Logan: Utah State University Press, 1978.

Deutchman, I. E., and S. Prince-Emburg. "Political Ideology of Pro- and Anti-ERA Women." *Women and Politics* 2 (Spring–Summer 1982): 39–55.

Diamond, Irene, and Lee Quinby, eds. *Feminism and Foucault: Reflections on Resistance.* Boston: Northeastern University Press, 1988. (See especially essays by Martin, Jones, Woodhull, and Diamond and Quinby.)

Dobash, R. Emerson, and Dobash, Russell. *Violence against Wives.* New York: Free Press, 1979.

Dorsen, Norma, and Susan Deller Ross. "The Necessity of a Constitutional Amendment." *Harvard Civil Rights–Civil Liberties Law Review* 6, no. 2 (March 1971): 216–24.

Dougan, Michael B. "The Arkansas Married Woman's Property Law." *Arkansas Historical Quarterly* 46 (Spring 1987): 3–26.

Downs, Donald Alexander. *The New Politics of Pornography.* Chicago: University of Chicago Press, 1989.

Duberman, Martin Bauml, Martha Vicinus, and George Chauncey Jr., eds. *Hidden from History: Reclaiming the Gay and Lesbian Past.* New York: NAL, 1989.

DuBois, Ellen Carol. *Feminism and Suffrage: The Emergence of an Independent Women's Movement in America, 1848–1869.* Ithaca, N.Y.: Cornell University Press, 1978.

———, ed. *Elizabeth Cady Stanton and Susan B. Anthony: Correspondence, Writings, Speeches.* New York: Schocken, 1981.

———. "Outgrowing the Compact of the Fathers: Equal Rights, Woman Suffrage, and the United States Constitution, 1820–1878." *Journal of American History* 74 (December 1987): 836–62.

Dunshee, Esther. "Miss Dunshee on 'Equal Rights.'" *Woman Citizen,* March 1924, 19.

Dworkin, Andrea. *Pornography: Men Possessing Women.* New York: Perigee, 1981.

Dworkin, Andrea. *Intercourse*. New York: Free Press, 1987.

Dworkin, Robert. *A Matter of Principle*. Cambridge: Harvard University Press, 1985.

Eastwood, Mary. "The Double Standard of Justice: Women's Rights under the Constitution." *Valparaiso University Law Review* 5 (1971): 281–317.

Eisenstein, Hester. *Contemporary Feminist Thought*. London: Unwin Paperbacks, 1984.

Eisenstein, Zillah R. *The Female Body and the Law*. Berkeley: University of California Press, 1988.

Eisler, Riane Tennenhaus. *Dissolution: No-Fault Divorce, Marriage, and the Future of Women*. New York: McGraw-Hill, 1977.

Ellet, Elizabeth F. *The Women of the American Revolution*. 3 vols. New York: Baber & Scribner, 1848–50. Micropublished in "History of Women." New Haven, Conn.: Research Publication, 1975. Reprint. Williamstown, Mass.: Corner House, 1980.

Ely, John Hart. "The Wages of Crying Wolf: A Comment on *Roe v. Wade*." *Yale Law Journal* 82, no. 5 (April 1973): 920–49.

Epstein, Cynthia Fuchs. *Woman's Place: Options and Limits in Professional Careers*. Berkeley: University of California Press, 1971.

———. *Women in Law*. New York: Basic Books, 1982.

"Equality of Women." *America* 109 (October 1963): 473.

"Equal Rights." *Women's Home Companion*, April 1939, 2.

"Equal Rights Amendment." *Ave Maria* 65 (February 1947): 133.

"Equal Rights Amendment." *Social Justice Review* 37 (March 1945): 383–84.

"Equal Rights Amendment and the Woman Worker." *Catholic Action* 25 (February 1943): 18.

"The Equal Rights Amendment: Is It the Next Step to Women's Freedom?" *Graduate Woman* 47 (October 1953): 20–27.

"Equal Rights for Women?" *New Republic* 94 (February 1938): 34.

"Equal Rights for Women: A Symposium on the Proposed Constitutional Amendment." *Harvard Civil Rights–Civil Liberties Law Review* 6 (March 1971): 215–87.

"Equal Rights for Women? Things May Never Be the Same." *U.S. News and World Report*, 24 August 1970, 29–30.

"Equal Rights for Women Workers: A New Push." *U.S. News and World Report*, 3 August 1970, 51–52.

"Equal Rights NOW." *Newsweek*, 2 March 1970, 75.

Erickson, Nancy S. "Historical Background of 'Protective' Labor Legislation: *Muller v. Oregon*." In Vol. 2 of *Women and the Law: A Social Historical Perspective*, edited by D. Kelly Weisberg, 155–86. Cambridge, Mass.: Schenkman, 1982.

Evans, Sara M. *Born for Liberty: A History of Women in America*. New York: Free Press, 1989.

Evans, Sara M., and Barbara J. Nelson. *Wage Justice: Comparable Worth and the Paradox of Technocratic Reform*. Chicago: University of Chicago Press, 1989.

Faragher, John. "Old Women and Old Men in Seventeenth-Century Wethersfield, Connecticut." *Women's Studies* 4 (1976): 11–31.

Faux, Marian. *Roe v. Wade: The Untold Story of the Landmark Supreme Court Decision that Made Abortion Legal*. New York: Macmillan, 1988.

Felsenthal, C. *The Sweetheart of the Silent Majority*. Garden City, N.Y.: Doubleday, 1981.

Finkelman, Paul. "The Coming of Age of American Legal History: A Review Essay." *Maryland Historian* 16 (Fall–Winter 1985): 1–11.

Flaherty, David H. "Law and the Enforcement of Morals in Early America." *Perspectives in American History* 5 (1971): 203–53.

Flexner, Eleanor. *Century of Struggle: The Woman's Rights Movement in the United States.* New York: Atheneum, 1968.

Folbre, Nancy. "Patriarchy in Colonial New England." *Review of Radical Political Economies* 12 (1980): 4–13.

Forbus, Lady Willie. "The Lucretia Mott Amendment." *Equal Rights,* 26 April 1924, 85.

Foss, Karen Ann. "Ideological Manifestations in the Discourse of Contemporary Feminism." Ph.D. diss., University of Iowa, 1976.

Foss, Sonja Kay. "A Fantasy Theme Analysis of the Rhetoric of the Debate on the Equal Rights Amendment, 1970–1976: Toward a Theory of the Rhetoric of Movements." Ph.D. diss., Northwestern University, 1976.

———. "The Equal Rights Amendment Controversy: Two Worlds in Conflict." *Quarterly Journal of Speech* 65, no. 3 (1979): 275–88.

Fox-Genovese, Elizabeth. "Women's Rights, Affirmative Action, and the Myth of Individualism." *George Washington Law Review* 54, nos. 1, 2 (January–March 1986): 338–74.

Franklin, Benjamin V. *The Plays and Poems of Mercy Otis Warren.* Delmar, N.Y.: Scholars Reprints and Facsimiles, 1980.

Freeman, Alan D. "Truth and Mystification in Legal Scholarship." *Yale Law Journal* 90 (1981): 1228.

Freeman, Jo. *The Politics of Women's Liberation.* New York: David McKay, 1975.

———. "Women and Public Policy: An Overview." In *Women, Power, and Policy,* edited by Ellen Boneparth, 47–71. New York: Pergamon, 1982.

Freund, Paul. "The Equal Rights Amendment Is Not the Way." *Harvard Civil Rights–Civil Liberties Law Review* 6, no. 2 (March 1971): 234–42.

Friedman, Lawrence Meir. *A History of American Law.* New York: Simon & Schuster, 1973; 2d ed., 1985, 1986.

Friesen, Jennifer, and Ronald K. L. Collins. "Looking Back on *Muller v. Oregon.*" *American Bar Association Journal* 69 (March–April 1983): 294–98, 472–77.

Fry, Amelia R. *Conversations with Alice Paul.* Oral history prepared for the Regional Oral History Office, The Bancroft Library, University of California, Berkeley, 1972–73.

Fuchs, Victor R. *Women's Quest for Economic Equality.* Cambridge: Harvard University Press, 1988.

Gallman, James M. "Determinants of Age at Marriage in Colonial Perquimans County, North Carolina." *William and Mary Quarterly,* 3d ser., 39 (1982): 176–91.

Gallup, George. "Public Support for the ERA Reaches New High." *Gallup Poll,* 9 August 1981.

Gardner, Jane F. *Women in Roman Law and Society.* Bloomington: Indiana University Press, 1986.

George, Carol V. R., ed. *"Remember the Ladies": New Perspectives on Women in American History.* Syracuse, N.Y.: Syracuse University Press, 1975. (See especially Donegan, Fisher, O'Neill, and Scruggs.)

Gilligan, Carol. *In a Different Voice: Psychological Theory and Women's Development.* Cambridge: Harvard University Press, 1982.

Gilsinan, James F., Lynn Obernyer, and Christine A. Gilsinan. "Women Attorneys and the Judiciary." *Denver Law Journal* 52, no. 4 (1975): 881–909.

Ginsburg, Ruth Bader. "The Need for the Equal Rights Amendment." *American Bar Association Journal* 59 (September 1973): 1013–19.

———. *Text, Cases, and Materials on Constitutional Aspects of Sex-Based Discrimination.* St. Paul: West Publishing, 1974.

———. "The Burger Court's Grapplings with Sex Discrimination." In *The Burger Court: The Counter-Revolution that Wasn't,* edited by Vincent Blasi, New Haven Conn.: Yale University Press, 1983, pp 132–56.

Giraldo, Z. I., ed. *Women and American Law: New Deal to the Present.* San Francisco: Holmes & Meier, forthcoming.

Glendon, Mary Ann. "Marriage and the State: The Withering Away of Marriage." *Virginia Law Review* 62, no. 4 (May 1976): 663–720.

———. *Abortion and Divorce in Western Law: American Failures, European Challenges.* Cambridge: Harvard University Press, 1987.

Glynn, Edward. "How To Unnerve Male Chauvinists." *America* 123 (12 September 1970): 144–46; (10 October 1970): 247.

Goldstein, Leslie Friedman. *The Constitutional Rights of Women: Cases in Law and Social Change.* 1979. 2d ed. New York: Longman, 1988.

Goodman, Robert. "Note: Substantive Due Process Comes Home To Roost: Fundamental Rights, *Griswold* to *Bowers.*" *Women's Rights Law Reporter* 10, nos. 2, 3 (Winter 1988): 177–208.

Graham, Hugh. *The Civil Rights Era.* New York: Oxford University Press, 1989.

Greathouse, Rebekah S. "The Effect of Constitutional Equality on Working Women." *American Economic Review,* suppl. (March 1944): 227–36.

Greenberg, Douglas. *Crime and Law Enforcement in the Colony of New York, 1691–1776.* Ithaca, N.Y.: Cornell University Press, 1976.

Greenberg, Hazel, and Anita Miller, eds. *The Equal Rights Amendment: A Bibliographic Study.* Westport, Conn.: Greenwood, 1976.

Greene, Jack P., ed. *The American Revolution: Its Character and Limits.* New York: New York University Press, 1987. (See especially Albanese, Bonomi, Crane, Frey, and Jordan.)

Griswold, Robert L. *Family and Divorce in California, 1850–1890: Victorian Illusions and Everyday Realities.* Albany: State University of New York Press, 1982.

Grossberg, Michael. "Who Gets the Child? Custody, Guardianship, and Rise of Judicial Patriarchy in Nineteenth-Century America." *Feminist Studies* 9 (1983): 235–60.

———. *Governing the Hearth: Law and the Family in Nineteenth-Century America.* Chapel Hill: University of North Carolina Press, 1985.

Grossblat, Martha, and Bette H. Sikes, eds. *Women Lawyers: Supplementary Data to the 1971 Lawyer Statistical Report.* Chicago: American Bar Foundation, 1973.

Gubar, Susan, and Joan Hoff, eds. *For Adult Users Only: The Dilemma of Violent Pornography.* Bloomington: Indiana University Press, 1989. (See especially Einsiendel, Hoff, Robel, and West.)

Guggenheim, Malvina H., and Elizabeth F. Defeis. "United States Participation in International Agreements Providing Rights for Women." *Loyola of Los Angeles Law Review* 10, no. 1 (December 1976): 1–71.

Gunderson, Joan, and Gwen Victor Gampel. "Married Women's Legal Status in Eighteenth-Century New York and Virginia." *William and Mary Quarterly,* 3d ser., 39 (1982): 114–34.

Halbertson, Malvina, and Elizabeth F. Defeis. *Women's Legal Rights: International Covenants an Alternative to ERA?* Dobbs Ferry, N.Y.: Transnational, 1987.

Hale, Judith, and Ellen Levine. *Rebirth of Feminism.* New York: Quadrangle, 1971.

Hamilton, Alice. "The 'Blanket' Amendment—A Debate—Protection for Women Workers." *The Forum* 72 (August 1924): 152–60.

Harris, Louis. "Public Support for ERA Soars as Ratification Deadline Nears." *The Harris Survey,* 6 May 1982.

———. "Support Increasing for Strengthening Women's Status in Society." *Harris Survey,* 17 August 1982.

Harrison, Cynthia E. "A 'New Frontier' for Women: The Public Policy of the Kennedy Administration." *Journal of American History* 67, no. 3 (December 1980): 630–46.

———. *On Account of Sex: The Politics of Women's Issues, 1945–1968.* Berkeley: University of California Press, 1988.

Haskins, George Lee. *Law and Authority in Early Massachusetts: A Study in Tradition and Design.* New York: Macmillan, 1960.

———. "Reception of the Common Law in Seventeenth-Century Massachusetts: Case Study [of Dower Rights], in *Selected Essays: Law and Authority in Colonial America,* edited by George Athan Billias, 17–31. Barre, Mass.: Barre Publishers, 1965.

Helmes, Winifred. "Equal Rights, Where Do We Stand?" *Graduate Woman* 46 (March 1953): 165.

Hershowitz, Leo, and Milton M. Klein, eds. *Courts and Law in Early New York: Selected Essays.* Port Washington, N.Y.: Kennikat, 1978.

Hill, Anne Corinne. "Protection of Women Workers and the Courts: A Legal Case History." *Feminist Studies* 5, no. 2 (Summer 1979): 247–73.

Hill, M. Anne, and Mark R. Killingsworth, eds. *Comparable Worth: Analysis and Evidence.* Ithaca, N.Y.: Cornell University Press, 1989.

Hiller, Dana V., and Robin Ann Sheets, eds. *Women and Men: The Consequences of Power.* Cincinnati: Office of Women's Studies, University of Cincinnati, 1977.

Hindus, Michael Stephen. *Prison and Plantation: Crime, Justice, and Authority in Massachusetts and South Carolina, 1767–1878.* Chapel Hill: University of North Carolina Press, 1980.

Hochschild, Arlie. *The Second Shift.* New York: Viking, 1989.

Hoffman, Ronald, and Peter J. Albert. *Women in the Age of the American Revolution.* Charlottesville: University Press of Virginia, 1989. (See especially Kerber, Salmon, Shammas, Smith, Norton, and Ulrich.)

Hoff-Wilson, Joan. "The Illusion of Change: Women and the American Revolution." In *The American Revolution: Explorations in the History of American Radicalism,* edited by Alfred F. Young, 383–441. De Kalb: Northern Illinois University Press, 1976.

———. "The Legal Status of Women in the Late Nineteenth and Early Twentieth Centuries." *Human Rights* (American Bar Association) 6, no. 2 (Winter 1977): 125–34.

———. "Hidden Riches: Legal Records and Women, 1750–1825." In *Women's Being, Woman's Place: Female Identity and Vocation in American History,* edited by Mary Kelley, 7–25. Boston: G. K. Hall, 1979.

———. "The Pluralistic Society." In the New York Public Library, *Censorship: Five Hundred Years of Conflict,* 103–15. New York: Oxford University Press, 1984.

———, and Marjorie Lightman, eds. *Without Precedent: The Life and Career of Eleanor*

*Roosevelt.* Bloomington: Indiana University Press, 1984. (See especially Cook, Perry, Scharf, and Ware.)

————, ed. *Rights of Passage: The Past and Future of the ERA.* Bloomington: Indiana University Press, 1986.

————. "The Unfinished Revolution: Changing Legal Status of U.S. Women." *Signs* 13, no. 1 (Winter 1987): 7–36.

Holmes, Oliver Wendell. *The Common Law.* Boston: Little, Brown, 1881.

Hornaday, M. "Showdown on Equal Rights: Amending the Constitution." *Christian Science Monitor,* 9 October 1943.

Horwitz, Morton J. "The Rise of Legal Formalism." *American Journal of Legal History* 19, no. 4 (October 1975): 251–64.

————. *The Transformation of American Law, 1780–1860.* Cambridge: Harvard University Press, 1977.

————. "The Historical Contingency of the Role of History." *Yale Law Journal* 90 (1981): 1057–59.

Hyman, Harold M., and William M. Wiecek. *Equal Justice under the Law: Constitutional Development, 1835–1875.* New York: Harper & Row, 1982.

" 'I Didn't Raise My Girl To Be a Soldier': Sense and Nonsense About the ERA." *Christian Century,* 25 October 1972, 1056–58.

Irwin, Inez Haynes. "Why the Woman's Party Is for It." *Good Housekeeping* 78 (March 1924): 18, 158–61.

Isaac, Rhys. *The Transformation of Virginia, 1740–1790.* Chapel Hill: University of North Carolina Press, 1982.

James, Janet Wilson, ed. *Women in American Religion.* Philadelphia: University of Pennsylvania Press, 1978.

Johnston, John D. and Charles L. Knapp. "Sex Discrimination by Law: A Study in Judicial Perspective." *New York University Law Review* 46, no. 4 (1971): 675–747.

Kairys, David, ed. *The Politics of Law: A Progressive Critique* New York: Pantheon, 1982. (See especially Freeman, Gordon, Kennedy, Polan, Schneider, and Taub.)

Kalman, Laura. *Legal Realism at Yale, 1927–1960.* Chapel Hill: University of North Carolina Press, 1986.

Kammen, Michael. *A Machine that Would Go of Itself: The Constitution in American Culture.* New York: Knopf, 1986.

Kanowitz, Leo. *Women and the Law: The Unfinished Revolution.* Albuquerque: University of New Mexico Press, 1969.

Karlsen, Carol F., and Laurie Crumpacker, eds. *The Journal of Esther Edwards Burr, 1754–1757.* New Haven, Conn.: Yale University Press, 1984.

Karst, Kenneth L. "Woman's Constitution." *Duke Law Journal* 1984, no. 3 (June 1984): 447–508.

Kay, Herma Hill. *Sex-Based Discrimination in Family Law.* St. Paul: West Publishing, 1974.

————. "Models of Equality." *University of Illinois Law Review* 1985, no. 1: 39–88.

————. "An Appraisal of California's No-Fault Divorce Law." *California Law Review* 75 (January 1987): 291–319.

————. "Equality and Difference: A Perspective on No-Fault Divorce and Its Aftermath." *University of Cincinnati Law Review* 56, no. 1 (1987): 1–90.

Kelley, Florence. "The New Woman's Party." *Survey* 45 (March 1921): 827–28.

————, comp. *Twenty Questions about the Federal Amendment Proposed by the National Woman's Party*. New York: National Consumer's League, 1922.

————. "Why Other Women's Groups Oppose It." *Good Housekeeping* 78 (March 1924): 19, 162–65.

Kelley, Mary, ed. *Women's Being, Women's Place: Female Identity and Vocation in American History*. Boston: G. K. Hall, 1979. (See especially Bolin, Chambers-Schiller, Griffiths, Hersh, Hoff-Wilson, and Rogers.)

Kendrick, Walter. *The Secret Museum: Pornography in Modern Culture*. New York: Viking, 1987.

Kenton, E. "Ladies' Next Step: The Case for the Equal Rights Amendment." *Harper's* 152 (February 1926): 366–74.

Kerber, Linda K. "The Republican Mother: Women and the Enlightenment—An American Perspective." *American Quarterly* 28 (Summer 1976): 187–205.

————. *Women of the Republic: Intellect and Ideology in Revolutionary America*. Chapel Hill: University of North Carolina Press, 1980.

————. "The Republican Ideology of the Revolutionary Generation." *American Quarterly* 37, no. 4 (Fall 1985): 474–95.

————. " 'May All Our Citizens Be Soldiers, and All Our Soldiers Citizens': The Ambiguities of Female Citizenship in the New Nation." In *Arms at Rest: Peacemaking and Peacekeeping in American History*, edited by Joan R. Challinor and Robert L. Beisner, 1–22. Westport, Conn.: Greenwood, 1987.

————. "Separate Spheres, Female Worlds, Woman's Place: The Rhetoric of Women's History." *Journal of American History* 75 (June 1988): 9–39.

————, and Jane De Hart-Mathews. *Women's America: Refocusing the Past*. 2d ed. New York: Oxford University Press, 1987. (See especially Banner, Cook, Kessler-Harris, Koehler, and Mohr.)

Kessler-Harris, Alice. *Out to Work: A History of Wage-Earning Women in the United States*. New York: Oxford University Press, 1982.

————. "The Debate over Equality for Women in the Workplace: Recognizing Differences." In *Women and Work: An Annual Review*, edited by Laurie Lorwood et al., vol. 1, 141–61. Beverly Hills: Sage, 1985.

Keyssar, Alexander. "Widowhood in Eighteenth-Century Massachusetts: A Problem in the History of the Family." *Perspectives in American History* 8 (1974).

Kirp, David L., Mark G. Yudof, and Marlene Strong Franks. *Gender Justice*. Chicago: University of Chicago Press, 1986.

Kittay, Eva Feder, and Diana T. Meyers. *Women and Moral Theory*. New York: Rowman & Littlefield, 1987. (See especially Feder, Meyer, Gilligan, and Hasse.)

Klausner, Marian Leslie. "Redefining Pornography as Sex Discrimination: An Innovative Civil Rights Approach." *New England Law Review* 20, no. 4 (1984–85): 721–57.

Klein, Ethel. *Gender Politics: From Consciousness to Mass Politics*. Cambridge: Harvard University Press, 1984.

Knight, Holford. "Women and the Legal Profession." *Contemporary Review* 103 (May 1913): 689–96.

Koehler, Lyle. *A Search for Power: The "Weaker Sex" in Seventeenth-Century New England*. Urbana: University of Illinois Press, 1980.

Kraditor, Aileen S. *The Ideas of the Woman Suffrage Movement, 1890–1920*. Garden City, N.Y.: Anchor, 1971.

Kraditor, Aileen S., ed. *Up from the Pedestal: Selected Writings in the History of American Feminism*. Chicago: Quadrangle, 1970.

Krichmar, Albert. *The Women's Rights Movement in the United States, 1848–1970: A Bibliography and Source Book*. Metuchen, N.J.: Scarecrow, 1972.

Kugler, Israel. *From Ladies to Women: The Organized Struggle for Women's Rights in the Reconstruction Era*. New York: Greenwood, 1987.

Kurland, Philip B. "The Equal Rights Amendment: Some Problems of Construction." *Harvard Civil Rights–Civil Liberties Law Review* 6 no. 2 (March 1971): 243–52.

"Ladies' Day." *Newsweek* 76 (24 Aug. 1970): 15–16.

Lahey, Kathleen A. "The Canadian Charter of Rights and Pornography toward a Theory of Actual Gender Equality." *New England Law Review* 20 (1984–85): 653–59.

———. "Feminist Theories of (In)Equality." *Wisconsin Women's Law Journal* 3, no. 4 (1987): 649–85.

Land, Aubrey, Lois G. Carr, and Edward C. Papenfuse, eds. *Law, Society, and Politics in Early Maryland*. Baltimore: Johns Hopkins University Press, 1977.

Law, Sylvia A. "Rethinking Sex and the Constitution." *University of Pennsylvania Law Review* 132 (1984): 954–1040.

Lebsock, Suzanne. *The Free Women of Petersburg: Status and Culture in a Southern Town, 1784–1860*. New York: W. W. Norton, 1984.

Lee, Rex E. *A Lawyer Looks at the Equal Rights Amendment*. Provo, Utah: Brigham Young University Press, 1980.

Le Grand, Camille. "Rape and Rape Laws: Sexism in Society and Law." *California Law Review* 61, no. 3 (May 1973): 919–41.

Lehrer, Susan. *Origins of Protective Legislation for Women, 1905–1925*. Albany: State University of New York Press, 1987.

Leites, Edmund. "The Duty to Desire: Love, Friendship, and Sexuality in Some Puritan Theories of Marriage." *Journal of Social History* 15 (Spring 1982): 383–408.

Lemons, J. Stanley. *The Woman Citizen*. Urbana: University of Illinois Press, 1971.

Leonard, Eugenie Andruss, Sophie Hutchinson Drinker, and Miriam Young Holden. *The American Woman in Colonial and Revolutionary Times: 1565–1800. A Syllabus with Bibliography*. 1962. Reprint. Philadelphia: University of Pennsylvania Press, 1975.

Lerner, Gerda. *The Creation of Patriarchy*. New York: Oxford University Press, 1986.

Levin, Phyllis Lee. *Abigail Adams: A Biography*. New York: Ballantine, 1987.

Levy, Leonard W. *Original Intent and the Framers' Constitution*. New York: Macmillan, 1988.

Lewis, Jan. "The Republican Wife." *William and Mary Quarterly*, 3d ser., 44 (1987): 689–721.

Lilie, Joyce R., Roger Handberg Jr., and Wanda Lowney. "Women State Legislators and the ERA: Dimensions of Support and Opposition." *Women and Politics* 2, nos. 1–2 (Spring–Summer 1982): 23–28.

Lockridge, Kenneth A. *Literacy in Colonial New England: An Enquiry into the Social Context of Literacy in the Early Modern West*. New York: W. W. Norton, 1974.

Lorvan, Sidney. "Dower and Curtesy." In *American Jurisprudence: A Modern Comprehensive Text Statement of American Law, State and Federal*. Rochester, N.Y.: Jurisprudence Publishers, Lawyers Cooperative Publishing, 1966.

Lunardini, Christine A. *From Equal Suffrage to Equal Rights: Alice Paul and the National Woman's Party, 1910–1928*. New York: Columbia University Press, 1986.

Lutz, Alma. "Why Bar Equality?" *Christian Science Monitor*, 22 July 1944.
———. "Only One Choice." *Independent Woman*, July 1947, 199–205.
MacKinnon, Catharine A. "Not a Moral Issue." *Yale Law and Policy Review* 11, no. 2 (1984): 321–45.
———. "Pornography, Civil Rights, and Speech." *Harvard Civil Rights–Civil Liberties Law Review* 20, no. 1, (Winter 1985): 1–70.
———. *Feminism Unmodified: Discourses on Life and Law*. Cambridge: Harvard University Press, 1987.
Mann, Bruce H. "Law, Legalism, and Community before the American Revolution." *Michigan Law Review* 84 (June 1986): 1415–39.
Mansbridge, Jane J. *Why We Lost the ERA*. Chicago: University of Chicago Press, 1986.
Mansfield, Edward. *The Legal Rights, Liabilities, and Duties of Women*. Salem, Mass.: Jewett, 1845.
Marcus, Isabel. "Feminist Legal Strategies: The Shoe that Never Fits." Paper presented at the Sixth Berkshire Conference on the History of Women, 1984.
Martin, Del. *Battered Wives*. San Francisco: Glide Publications, 1976.
Masson, Margaret. "The Typology of the Female as a Model for the Regenerate: Puritan Preaching, 1690–1730." *Signs* 2 (1975–76): 305–15.
Mathews, Donald G., and Jane Sherron De Hart. *ERA and the Politics of Cultural Survival: North Carolina*. New York: Oxford University Press, 1990.
Matson, Cathy, and Peter Onuf. "Toward a Republican Empire: Interest and Ideology in Revolutionary America." *American Quarterly* 37, no. 4 (Fall 1985): 496–531.
Matthaei, Judith A. *An Economic History of Women in America: Women's Work. The Sexual Division of Labor and the Development of Capitalism*. New York: Schocken, 1982.
———. *Dispute and Conflict Resolution in Plymouth County, Massachusetts, 1725–1825*. Chapel Hill: University of North Carolina Press, 1981.
Melder, Keith E. *Beginnings of Sisterhood: The American Woman's Rights Movement, 1800–1850*. New York: Schocken, 1977.
"Men and Women: Equality or Equity?" *America* 123 (September 1970): 167–68.
Meyer, Carol Finn. "Attitudes toward the Equal Rights Amendment." Ph.D. diss., City University of New York, 1979.
Michelman, Frank I. "Politics as Medicine: On Misleading Legal Scholarship." *Yale Law Journal* 90 (1981): 1224–28.
Mintz, Steven, and Susan Kellogg. *Domestic Revolutions: A Social History of American Family Life*. New York: Free Press, 1988.
Mohr, James C. *Abortion in America*. New York: Oxford University Press, 1978.
Moran, Gerald F. and Maris Vinovskis. "The Puritan Family and Religion: A Critical Reappraisal." *William and Mary Quarterly*, 3d ser. 39 (1982): 29–63.
Morello, Karen Berger. *The Invisible Bar: The Woman Lawyer in America, 1638 to the Present*. Boston: Beacon, 1986.
Morris, Richard B. *Studies in the History of American Law*. 1930. Reprint. New York: Octagon, 1974.
Murray, Pauli. "The Negro Woman's Stake in the Equal Rights Amendment." *Harvard Civil Rights–Civil Liberties Law Review* 6 (March 1971): 253–59.
Nash, Gary B. *The Urban Crucible: Social Change, Political Consciousness, and the Origins of the American Revolution*. Cambridge: Harvard University Press, 1979.
National Organization for Women. "Bill of Rights for 1969." Reprinted in *Herstory: A*

*Woman's View of American History,* edited by June Sochen, 435–36. New York: Alfred Publishing, 1974.

Nelson, William E. *Americanization of the Common Law: The Impact of Legal Change on Massachusetts Society, 1760–1830.* Cambridge: Harvard University Press, 1975.

———, and John Phillip Reid. *The Literature of American Legal History.* New York: Oceana, 1985.

"New Victory in an Old Crusade." *Time* 96 (August 1970): 10–12.

"Next Step in the Emancipation of Women—An Equal Rights Amendment?" *Graduate Woman* 31 (April 1938): 160–64.

Nicholson, Linda J. *Gender and History: The Limits of Social Theory in the Age of the Family.* New York: Columbia University Press, 1986.

Norton, Mary Beth. *Liberty's Daughters: The Revolutionary Experience of American Women, 1750–1800.* Boston: Little, Brown, 1980.

———. "The Evolution of White Women's Experience in Early America." *American Historical Review* 89 (June 1984): 593–619.

NOW Legal Defense and Education Fund and Dr. Renée Cherow-O'Leary. *The State-by-State Guide to Women's Legal Rights.* New York: McGraw-Hill, 1987.

Offen, Karen. "Defining Feminism: A Comparative Historical Approach." *Signs* 14, no. 1 (Autumn 1988): 119–57.

Okin, Susan Moller. *Women in Western Political Thought.* Princeton, N.J.: Princeton University Press, 1979.

———. *Justice, Gender, and the Family.* New York: Basic Books, 1989.

Olsen, Frances. "From False Paternalism to False Equality: Judicial Assaults on Feminist Community, Illinois, 1869–1895." *Michigan Law Review* 84, no. 7 (June 1986): 1518–43.

Ondercin, David George. "The Compleat Woman: The Equal Rights Amendment and Perceptions of Womanhood, 1920–1972." Ph.D. diss., University of Minnesota, 1973.

O'Neill, William L. *The Woman Movement: Feminism in the United States and England.* London: Allen & Unwin, 1969; Chicago: Quadrangle, 1969, 1971.

"Only One Choice." *Independent Woman* 26 (July 1947): 199.

Oppenheimer, David Benjamin. "Distinguishing Five Models of Affirmative Action." *Berkeley Women's Law Journal* 4 (1988–89): 42–61.

"Organizations Supporting the Equal Rights Amendment." *National NOW Times,* 13 May 1980.

Pascal, Harold J. *Battered Wives: The Secret Scandal.* Canfield, Ohio: Alfa, 1977.

Pateman, Carole. *The Sexual Contract.* Cambridge: Polity, 1988.

Paul, Alice. *Congressional Record* 20 (April 1943): 107.

Peak, Mayme Ober. "Women in Politics." *Outlook* 136 (January 1924): 147–50.

Petchesky, Rosalind P. *Abortion and Woman's Choice: The State, Sexuality, and Reproductive Freedom.* New York: Longman, 1984.

Pinckney, Elise, ed. *The Letterbook of Eliza Lucas Pinckney.* Chapel Hill: University of North Carolina Press, 1972.

Pole, J. R. *The Pursuit of Equality in American History.* Berkeley: University of California Press, 1978.

Portnow, Billie. "What's Wrong with the Equal Rights Amendment?" *Jewish Currents* 25 (July–August 1971): 4–9.

Puller, Edwin S. "When Equal Rights Are Unequal." *Virginia Law Review* 13 (June 1927): 619–30.

Purcell, Susan Kaufman. "Ideology and the Law: Sexism and the Supreme Court Decisions." In *Women in Politics*, edited by Jane Jaquette, 131–53. New York: John Wiley & Sons, 1974.

Rabkin, Peggy A. *Fathers to Daughters: The Legal Foundations of Female Emancipation.* Westport, Conn.: Greenwood, 1980.

Randall, Susan Louise. "A Legislative History of the Equal Rights Amendment, 1923–1960." Ph.D. diss., University of Utah, 1979.

Rawls, John. *A Theory of Justice.* Cambridge: Belknap Press of Harvard University Press, 1971.

"Rights for Women." *Newsweek* 28 (July 1946): 17.

Robinson, Donald Allen. "Two Movements in Pursuit of Equal Opportunities." *Signs* 4 (Spring 1979): 413–33.

Roeber, A. G. "Authority, Law, and Custom: The Rituals of Court Day in Tidewater, Virginia, 1720 to 1750." *William and Mary Quarterly*, 3d ser., 37 (1980): 29–52.

Ross, Susan C. *The Rights of Women: The Basic ACLU Guide to a Woman's Rights.* New York: Sunshine, 1973.

Rossi, Alice S., ed. *The Feminist Papers: From Adams to de Beauvoir.* New York: Columbia University Press, 1973. Reprint. New York: Bantam, 1974.

Rothman, Barbara Katz. *Recreating Motherhood.* New York: W. W. Norton, 1989.

Rowbotham, Sheila. *Hidden from History: Three Hundred Years of Women's Oppression and the Fight against It.* 2d ed. London: Pluto, 1974.

Rubin, Eva R. *The Supreme Court and the American Family: Ideology and Issues.* Westport, Conn.: Greenwood, 1986.

Russell, Diana E. H., and Nicole Van de Ven, eds. *The Proceedings of the International Tribunal on Crimes against Women.* Milbrae, Cal.: Les Femmes, 1976.

Russo, Ann. "Conflicts and Contradictions among Feminists over Issues of Pornography and Sexual Freedom." *Women's Studies International Forum* 10, no. 2 (1987): 103–12.

Ruth, Sheila, ed. *Issues in Feminism.* Boston: Houghton Mifflin, 1990.

Ryan, Mary P. *Womanhood in America: From Colonial Times to the Present.* 1975. 3d ed. New York: New Viewpoints, 1983.

Sachs, Albie, and Joan Hoff-Wilson. *Sexism and the Law: A Study in Male Beliefs and Legal Bias in Britain and the United States.* New York: Free Press, 1979.

Salmon, Marylynn. "The Legal Status of Women in Early America: A Reappraisal." *Law and History Review* 1 (Spring 1983): 129–51.

———. *Women and the Law of Property in Early America.* Chapel Hill: University of North Carolina Press, 1986.

Sandel, Michael J. *Liberalism and the Limits of Justice.* Cambridge: Cambridge University Press, 1982.

Sassower, Doris L. "Women and the Judiciary: Undoing 'The Law of the Creator.'" *Judicature: Journal of the American Judicature Society* 57, no. 7 (February 1974): 282–88.

———. "Women, Power, and the Law." *American Bar Association Journal*, 1976.

Scales, Ann C. "Towards a Feminist Jurisprudence." *Indiana Law Journal* 56, no. 3 (1980–81): 375–444.

Scheiber, Harry N. "American Constitutional History and the New Legal History: Complementary Themes in Two Modes." *Journal of American History* 68, no. 2 (September 1981): 337–50.

Schlafly, Phyllis. "The Case against ERA." *Radcliffe Quarterly* 6 (March 1982): 18–20.

*Schlafly Report* 5, no. 7 (February 1972).

*Schlafly Report* 9, no. 11 (June 1976).

Scholten, Catherine M. *Childbearing in American Society: 1650–1850*. New York: Columbia University Press, 1985.

Schwartz, Herman, ed. *The Burger Court: Rights and Wrongs in the Supreme Court*. New York: Viking Penguin, 1987. (See especially Burns, Rosenberg, and Williams.)

Schwarzchild, Hannah. "Same-Sex Marriage and Constitutional Privacy: Moral Threat and Legal Anomaly." *Berkeley Women's Law Journal* 4 (1988–89): 94–127.

Scott, Anne Firor. *The Southern Lady: From Pedestal to Politics, 1830–1930*. Chicago: University of Chicago Press, 1970.

———. *Making the Invisible Woman Visible*. Urbana: University of Illinois Press, 1984.

———, and Andrew M. Scott. *One Half the People: The Fight for Woman Suffrage*. Philadelphia: Lippincott, 1975.

Scott, Joan Wallach. "Gender: A Useful Category of Historical Analysis." *American Historical Review* 91, no. 5 (December 1986): 1053–75.

———. "Critical Tensions." *The Women's Review of Books* 5, no. 1 (October 1987): 17.

———. "Deconstructing Equality-versus-Difference: Or, the Uses of Poststructural Theory for Feminism." *Feminist Studies* 14, no. 1 (Spring 1988): 33–50.

———. *Gender and the Politics of History*. New York: Columbia University Press, 1988.

Seager, Joni, and Ann Olson. *Women in the World: An International Atlas*. London: Pan, 1986.

*Sex Bias in the United States Code: A Report of the U.S. Commission on Civil Rights*. Washington, D.C.: Government Printing Office, April 1977.

Shalhope, Robert. "Republicanism and Early American Historiography." *William and Mary Quarterly*, 3d ser., 39 (1982): 334–56.

Shammas, Carole. "The Domestic Environment in Early Modern England and America." *Journal of Social History* 14 (1980): 3–24.

———, Marylynn Salmon, and Michel Dahlin. *Inheritance in America from Colonial Times to the Present*. New Brunswick, N.J.: Rutgers University Press, 1987.

Sherrill, R. "That Equal Rights Amendment: What Exactly Does It Mean?" *New York Times Magazine*, 20 September 1970.

Shiels, Richard D. "The Feminization of American Congregationalism, 1730–1835." *American Quarterly* 33 (1981): 46–62.

Shklar, Judith. *Legalism*. Cambridge: Harvard University Press, 1964.

Simon, Anne E. "The Politics of Law: A Progressive Critique." *Women's Rights Law Reporter* 8, no. 3 (Summer 1985): 199–204.

Sinclair, Andrew. *The Better Half: The Emancipation of the American Woman*. New York: Harper & Row, 1965.

Slavin, Sarah. *Gender and the Politics of Constitutional Principles*. Washington, D.C.: American Political Science Association, 1985.

Smith, Daniel Blake. "Mortality and Family in the Colonial Chesapeake." *Journal of Interdisciplinary History* 8 (1978): 403–27.

———. *Inside the Great House: Planter Life in Eighteenth-Century Chesapeake Society*. Ithaca, N.Y.: Cornell University Press, 1980.

————. "The Study of the Family in Early America: Trends, Problems, and Prospects." *William and Mary Quarterly*, 3d ser., 39 (1982): 3–28.

Smith, Daniel Scott. "Parental Power and Marriage Patterns: An Analysis of Historical Trends in Higham, Massachusetts." *Journal of Marriage and the Family* 3, no. 3 (August 1973): 419–28.

————. "The Estimates of Early American Historical Demographers: Two Steps Forward, One Step Back, What Steps in the Future?" *Historical Methods* 12 (1979): 24–38.

Smith, Ethel M. "Equal Rights and Equal Rights: What Is Wrong with the Woman's Party Amendment?" Chicago: National Women's Trade Union League of America, [1925].

Smith, Nancy Kegan. "Women and the White House: A Look at Woman's Papers in the Johnson Library." *Prologue* 18, no. 2 (Summer 1986): 123–29.

Smith-Rosenberg, Carroll. *Disorderly Conduct: Visions of Gender in Victorian America*. New York: Knopf, 1985.

Solomon, Martha. "The Rhetoric of Stop ERA: Fatalistic Reaffirmation." *Southern Speech Communication Journal* 44, no. 1 (1978): 42–59.

Soule, Bradley, and Kay Standley. "Perceptions of Sex Discrimination in Law." *American Bar Association Journal* 59 (October 1973): 1144–47.

Spaulding, Christina. "Anti-Pornography Laws as a Claim for Equal Respect: Feminism, Liberalism, and Community." *Berkeley Women's Law Journal* 4 (1988–89): 128–65.

Speth, Linda. "More Than her 'Thirds': Wives and Widows in Colonial Virginia." *Women and History* 4 (1982): 5–41.

*The Spokeswoman*. A monthly newsletter published in Chicago, Illinois, by the Urban Research Corporation beginning in June 1970.

Spruill, Julia Cherry. *Women's Life and Work in the Southern Colonies*. 1938. Reprint. Chapel Hill: University of North Carolina Press, 1972.

Stanton, Elizabeth Cady, Susan B. Anthony, and Matilda Joslyn Gage, eds. *History of Woman Suffrage*. 6 vols. Rochester, N.Y.: Charles Mann, 1881. Reprint. New York: Source Books, 1970.

Steele, E. Boyd. "The Legal Status of Women." In Council of State Governments, *The Book of the States, 1972–1973*, 401–11.

Steiner, Gilbert. *Constitutional Inequality: The Political Fortunes of the Equal Rights Amendment*. Washington, D.C.: Brookings Institution, 1985.

Stephen, James Fitzjames. *Liberty, Equality, Fraternity*. London: Smith, Elder, 1873.

Stevens, Doris. "The 'Blanket' Amendment—A Debate: Suffrage Does Not Give Equality." *Forum* 60–62 (August 1924): 151.

Stone, Deborah A. *Policy, Paradox, and Political Reason*. Glenview, Ill.: Scott, Foresman, 1988.

Summers, Robert Samuel. *Instrumentation and American Legal Theory*. Ithaca, N.Y.: Cornell University Press, 1982.

Switzer, Ellen. *The Law for a Woman: Real Cases and What Happened*. New York: Charles Scribner's Sons, 1975.

Tedin, Kent L. "If the Equal Rights Amendment Becomes Law: Perceptions of Consequences among Female Activists and Masses." Midwest Political Science Association, 1980.

Tedin, K. L., D. W. Brady, M. E. Buxton, B. M. Gorman, and J. L. Thompson. "Social

Background and Political Differences between Pro- and Anti-ERA Activitist." *American Politics Quarterly* 5 (1977): 395–408.

———. "Religious Preference and Pro and Anti Activism on the Equal Rights Amendment Issue." *Pacific Sociological Review* 21 (1978): 55–66.

Temple, M. L. "Is Your Representative among Those Present?" *Independent Woman* 33 (June 1954): 223–24.

Thomas, Dorothy, ed. *Women Lawyers in the United States.* New York: Scarecrow, 1957.

". . . To Form a More Perfect Union." In *Justice for American Women: Report of the National Commission on the Observance of International Women's Year.* Washington, D.C.: Government Printing Office, 1976.

Tong, Rosemarie. *Women, Sex, and the Law.* Totowa, N.J.: Rowman & Allenheld, 1984.

Tribe, Laurence H. *American Constitutional Law.* 1976. 2d rev. ed. Mineola, N.Y.: Foundation Press, 1988.

Tushnet, Mark. "The American Law of Slavery, 1810–1860: A Study in the Persistence of Legal Autonomy." *Law and Society Review* 10 (Fall 1975): 120–84.

———. "Legal Scholarship: Its Causes and Cure." *Yale Law Review* 90 (1981): 1205–23.

Ulrich, Laurel Thatcher. *Good Wives: Image and Reality in the Lives of Women in Northern New England, 1650–1750.* New York: Knopf, 1982.

Unger, Roberto Mangabeira. *The Critical Legal Studies Movement.* Cambridge: Harvard University Press, 1986.

United States Citizens Advisory Council on the Status of Women. "Report of the Committee on Civil and Political Rights." Washington, D.C.: Government Printing Office, 1963.

*Update.* Informational bulletin published monthly during congressional sessions by the Congressional Caucus for Women's Issues beginning in 1982.

Violette, Augusta Genevieve. *Economic Feminism in American Literature prior to 1848.* Orono: University of Maine Press, 1925. Reprint New York: B. Franklin, 1975.

Warbasse, Elizabeth Bowles. *The Changing Legal Rights of Married Women, 1800–1861.* New York: Garland, 1987.

Ware, Susan. *Modern American Women: A Documentary History.* Chicago: Dorsey, 1989.

Watson, Alan D. "Household Size and Composition in Prerevolutionary North Carolina." *Mississippi Quarterly* 31 (Fall 1978): 551–69.

———. "Women in Colonial North Carolina: Overlooked and Underestimated." *North Carolina Historical Review* 58 (1981): 1–22.

Weir, Robert M. " 'The Harmony We Were Famous For': An Interpretation of Pre-Revolutionary South Carolina Politics." *William and Mary Quarterly,* 3d ser., 26 (1969): 473–501.

Weisberg, D. Kelly, ed. *Women and the Law: A Social Historical Perspective.* 2 vols. Cambridge, Mass.: Schenkman, 1982. (See especially Erickson, Hindus, Speth, Weisberg, and Withey.)

Weitzman, Lenore J. "Legal Regulation of Marriage: Tradition and Change." *California Law Review* 62, no. 4 (July–September 1974): 1169–1288.

———. *The Marriage Contract: Spouses, Lovers, and the Law.* New York: Free Press, 1981.

———. *The Divorce Revolution: The Unexpected Social and Economic Consequences for Women and Children in America.* New York: Free Press, 1985.

Wells, Robert V. *Revolution in Americans' Lives: A Demographic Perspective on the History of Americans. Their Families, and Their Society.* Westport, Conn.: Greenwood, 1982.

West, Robin L. "The Difference in Women's Hedonic Lives: A Phenomenological Critique of Feminist Legal Theory." *Wisconsin Women's Law Journal* 3 (1987): 81–145.

———. "Jurisprudence and Gender." *University of Chicago Law Review* 55, no. 1 (Winter 1988): 1–72.

Whalen, Charles, and Barbara Whalen. *The Longest Debate: A Legislative History of the 1964 Civil Rights Act.* Washington, D.C.: Seven Locks, 1985.

White, James J. "Women in the Law." *Michigan Law Review* 65, no. 5 (March 1967): 1051–1122.

White, Luise. "Prostitutes, Reformers, and Historians." *Criminal Justice History* 6 (1985): 201–28.

Wildman, Stephanie M. "The Legitimation of Sex Discrimination: A Critical Response to Supreme Court Jurisprudence." *Oregon Law Review* 63 (1984): 265–307.

Williams, Wendy W. "The Equality Crisis: Some Reflections on Culture, Courts, and Feminism." *Women's Rights Law Reporter* 7, no. 3 (Spring 1982): 175–200.

———. "Equality's Riddle: Pregnancy and the Equal Treatment/Special Treatment Debate." *New York University Review of Law and Social Change* 13, no. 2 (1984–85): 325–80.

Wilson, Jennie L. *The Legal and Political Status of Women in the United States.* Cedar Rapids, Iowa: Torch, 1912.

*Wisconsin Women's Law Journal* 3 (1987): 1–274. Special issue of papers from the 1985–86 Feminism and Legal Theory Conference at the University of Wisconsin. (See especially Boris, Clark, Lahey, Littleton, and West.)

Wishik, Heather Ruth. "To Question Everything: The Inquiries of Feminist Jurisprudence." *Berkeley Women's Law Journal* 1, no. 1 (Fall 1985): 64–77.

Wohl, Lisa Cronin. "Phyllis Schlafly: The Sweetheart of the Silent Majority." *Ms.* 2 (March 1974): 55–57.

———. "White Gloves and Combat Boots: The Fight for ERA." *Civil Liberties Review* 1 (Fall 1974): 77–86.

Woloch, Nancy. *Women and the American Experience.* New York: Knopf, 1984.

*Women Law Reporter.* A bimonthy legal service reporting exclusively on sex-discrimination cases.

*Women Lawyers Journal.* A trimester publication of the National Association of Women Lawyers.

*Women's Newsletter.* See *Antisexism Newsletter.*

Women's Research and Education Institute. *The American Woman, 1987–1988.* New York: W. W. Norton, 1987.

*Women's Rights Law Reporter.* A quarterly publication produced by law students at Rutgers Law School, Rutgers University.

Wortman, Marlene Stein, ed. *Women in American Law: From Colonial Times to the New Deal.* San Francisco: Holmes & Meier, 1985.

Wythey, Lynne. *Dearest Friend: A Life of Abigail Adams.* New York: Free Press, (1981).

Yates, Gayle Graham. *What Women Want: The Ideas of the Women's Movement.* Cambridge: Harvard University Press, 1975.

Zimmerman, Jan. *Once upon the Future: A Woman's Guide to Tomorrow's Technology.* London: Pandora, 1986.

# Index

Child Support Enforcement Amendments of Title IV-D, 273, 402

Child support, 133, 273, 278, 283, 292–93, 309, 326, 402, 405, 466 n. 104

Childbirth mortality, 305

Children, 4, 10, 24, 30, 39, 52, 55, 60–63, 85–86, 106, 108, 110, 114, 131–33, 142–43, 154, 156, 172, 187, 189, 191, 193, 200, 204, 207, 216, 225, 227, 250, 277–78, 281–82, 287–94, 296, 300, 305, 327, 334, 338–39, 344, 346, 396; custody, 132, 288; orphans, 144; "unemancipated minors," 306. *See also* Child care; Parental leaves

China, 14

Choate, Joseph H., 197

Chodorow, Nancy, 43

Citizens' Advisory Committee on the Status of Women, 245

Citizenship, 16–19, 22, 28, 30, 38–40, 50, 80–81, 87, 90, 91–94, 96, 98, 102, 103, 106, 116, 118, 152–59, 165–68, 170–75, 184–86, 190, 192, 196, 199, 210, 225, 230, 245, 272, 312–15, 318, 328, 331, 336, 343, 360, 370, 374; and esteem, 477 n. 25; female, 7, 18, 170, 221, 314; full, 1, 16–19, 36, 40, 49, 61, 80, 81, 94, 117, 139, 146, 149, 151, 152, 170, 173–75, 182, 207, 211, 227, 332, 373; more than equality, 331; private/public, 4; second-class, 36, 81, 151, 154, 175, 313, 315

City of Richmond v. J. A. Croson Co., (109 S. Ct. 706 (1989), 264, 266, 268–70, 272, 273, 405–7; set aside programs, 264, 406, 465 n. 87

Civil liberties, 25, 28, 300, 336, 337, 474, 479

Civil Rights Act (1866), 264, 271, 272, 398

Civil Rights Act (1870), 153, 156, 157, 160

Civil Rights Act (1957), 225, 227

Civil Rights Act (1964), 163, 201, 225, 227–30, 233, 250, 262, 265–67, 271, 272, 294, 319, 395, 398, 464 n. 76

Civil Rights Commission, 245, 264

Civil rights movement, 18, 33, 185, 228, 319, 356

Civil Rights Restoration Act, 256, 257, 402, 405, 462

Civil Rights Restoration Bill, 256, 257

Civil War, 4–6, 18, 21, 28, 39, 98, 105, 112, 113, 120–24, 126–32, 134, 135, 140–44, 146–49, 152, 154, 155, 161, 162, 170, 173–79, 181, 184–90, 219, 231, 264, 276

Clark, Amy, 144

Class-action suits, 30, 33, 200, 258, 259, 370

Cleburne v. Cleburne Living Center, 473 U.S. 432 (1985), 468 n. 17

Cleveland Board of Education v. LaFleur, 414 U.S. 631 (1974), 397

Clifford, Nathan, 176

Codification, 1, 110, 112–14, 120–24

Cohabitation, 255, 276, 277, 283, 285

Collin v. Smith, 578 F.2d 1197 (7th Cir. 1978), cert. denied, 439 U.S. 916 (1978), 478 n. 40

Collins, Ronald K. L., 199

Combs v. Young, 12 Tenn. (4 Yerg.) 218 (1833), 109

Commerce Clause, 29, 176

Commission on Civil Rights, 264

Commission on the Status of Women, 231, 232, 235

Common law, restrictions, 50, 62, 78, 88, 151

Commonwealth v. Addicks, 5 Benney (Pa.) 519 (1813), 132

Community, constitutive conception of, 369, 423 n. 61

Community standards, 340, 341, 397, 405

Comparable work, 252

Comparable worth, 4, 7, 8, 230, 233, 251, 253, 254, 317, 320, 331, 401, 403. *See also* Pay equity

Comstock, Anthony, 333; law, 333, 340

Condict, John, 100, 102

Congress, Ninety-second, 235, 246; Ninety-third, 246

Congressional Black Caucus, 296

Congressional Union, 206, 213–14. *See also* National Woman's Party (NWP)

Congressional Women's Caucus, 273

Conkling, Roscoe, 153

Conley v. Richardson, unreported California decision, 283

Conner v. Shephard, 15 Mass. 164 (1818), 108, 109

Consent(ing), 18, 19, 24, 35, 80, 81, 87, 176, 277, 346–48; tacit, 87, 176; as voluntary surrender, 276, 279

Consensual acts on part of women, 6, 18, 19, 37, 43, 279

Constitution of 1787, 4, 31, 38, 50, 54, 72, 74, 333, 373

Constitutionalism, 14, 21, 25, 42, 46, 151, 174, 175, 177, 184, 365, 373; first period of (1787–1872), 117–50; feminist, 185; fifth period of (1990–?), 350; fourth period of

Constitutionalism (*continued*)
(1963–1990), 229–75, 316; masculinity of,
14, 21–43, 177; second period of (1872–
1908), 151–91; third period of (1908–1963),
191–228; reperiodization of, 16, 19, 42
Consumer Credit Protection Act, 246, 398
Continental Congress, 63, 90, 94, 98, 99; Second, 98, 99
Contraception, 7, 182, 277, 278, 299–301, 309
Contraceptives, 277, 280, 286, 299–300, 313,
395
Contract: doctrine of, 24, 206; marital, 141,
278–80, 285; social, 24; theory of, 24, 417 n.
10
Contractualism, 24, 25, 42, 279–84, 284, 346;
voluntary, 279
Copus, David A., 261, 464
Corbin, Hanna Lee, 62
County of Washington v. Gunther, 452 U.S.
161 (1981), 253, 401
Courts, chancery, 84 (*see also* Equity courts);
county, 82, 84, 94–97, 106, 126, 127
Couzins, Phoebe, 163
Coverture, 3, 87–90, 93, 106, 113, 116, 119,
121, 122, 129, 134, 187, 189, 190, 276, 282;
erosion of, 282
Cox, Archibald, 249
Craig v. Boren, 429 U.S. 190 (1976), 249, 397,
400
Cranch, Mary, 63, 431
Crane, William, 100
Critical Legal Studies (CLS), 2, 22, 44, 318,
330, 364, 366–67; definition of theory,
416 n. 3
Crowley, Richard, 157
Cult of domesticity, 42
Cult of true womanhood, 3, 39
Culture, 9, 16, 36, 44, 59, 79, 93, 118, 137,
139, 153, 203, 217, 219, 222, 250, 289, 329,
342, 353, 366, 368, 373–74
Curtis, George William, 148

d'Hauteville, Daniel, 133
Dalton, Clare, 352
Daly, Mary, 43
Danforth Amendment, 257
Dartmouth College v. Woodward, 17 U.S. 518
(1819), 103, 104
Daughters of Liberty, 51, 52, 58
Day care, 246. See also Child care
de Beauvoir, Simone, 43, 352
de Condorcet, Marquis, 97

De Cuir, Mrs., 175, 447 n. 95
de Lauretis, Teresa, 350
de Tocqueville, Alexis, 37, 276
Deane, Joseph, 109
Declaration of Independence, 136, 138, 145,
178
Declaration of Rights, 142, 161, 177–81
Declaration of Sentiments, 4, 34, 136, 138,
139, 178–81, 219
Deconstructionist, 2, 11, 12, 44, 352, 353,
355; methodology, 44
DeCrow, Karen, 322
Defeis, Elizabeth, x
Democracy, 4, 6, 18, 19, 30, 33, 41, 77, 102,
121, 122, 153, 179, 215, 216, 330, 372; participatory, 18, 19
Democratic National Committee, 208, 232, 455
Democratic party, 155, 298, 209, 231
Democrats, 137, 147, 148, 163, 168, 207–8,
211, 305, 322, 401
Den ex dem. Davidson v. Frew, 14 N.C. (3
Dev. L.) 1 (1831), 108
Department of State, 257
Dependency of women, 40, 79, 80, 90–92, 94–
95, 105, 117, 134, 254, 282, 287–88, 293,
324
Dewson, Molly, 208–9
Dial-a-porn, 280, 313, 338, 406
Dimmick, Carolyn, 345, 481 n. 69
Disabilities, common law, 60, 82, 104, 151, 165
Discrimination, against homosexuals, 468 n.
21; group, 269; individual, 269; within military, 250–51, 458–59 n. 38; racial, 29, 175,
247, 264, 268–70, 358, 398; reverse, 264–
68, 271–73, 356, 364, 399, 461 n. 54,
464 n. 73, 465 n. 81, 484 n. 21; sex, 9, 10,
29, 206, 226, 233, 235, 245–47, 250, 253,
255, 259, 266, 273, 294–96, 328, 339, 344,
358, 361, 362; sex-based, 223, 248, 357; sexual, 403
Disparate impact, 257–58, 261, 265, 273, 362,
462, 396, 403, 406, 461 n. 55
Disparate treatment, 258, 359, 461 n. 55
Diversity, 14, 27, 31, 53, 56, 88, 208, 350–52,
354, 355, 483–84 nn. 18, 19; of state laws
affecting women, 209
Divorce, 3, 4, 7, 32, 35, 95, 103–5, 121, 132–
34, 139–41, 146, 174, 180, 182, 191, 206,
251, 273, 276–78, 283, 288–93, 320, 326,
370; alimony, 132, 133, 278, 283, 288, 292,
293, 326; no-fault reform, 291; no-fault, 4,
7, 35, 134, 288, 291, 292, 320, 326

Doe v. Bolton, 410 U.S. 179 (1973), 301

Domestic partnerships, 281, 284–85, 287, 468 n. 21

Domestic relations law, 276–94. *See also* Family law; Rights, domestic

Domination, male, 7, 14, 22, 36, 59, 133, 136, 149, 158, 175, 190, 192–93, 200, 210, 226, 252, 253, 280, 284, 285, 325, 341, 374, 455 n. 11, 467 n. 10

Dooling, John F., 303

Douglas, William O., 248, 277

Dower, 1, 3, 82–86, 88–89, 91–93, 102–3, 105–15, 122–24, 188, 189; renunciation, 103, 105, 107, 113, 114, 123

Dower rights, 1, 82, 85–86, 88–89, 91, 93, 102–3, 105–8, 110–11, 112–15, 122, 123, 188, 189

Dowry, 88, 114, 124, 282, 438 n. 84

Draft, conscription of women, 216

Dred Scott v. Sandford, 60 U.S. 394 (1857), 141, 154, 173, 175, 185, 197, 265

Drinker, Elizabeth, 57

DuBois, Ellen, 137, 442 n. 40

Due process: procedural, 186, 193–95; structural, 308, 309, 474; substantive, 186–87, 194–96, 300; and judicial notice of common knowledge or common understanding, 197, 201, 450 n. 9

Dworkin, Andrea, 19, 336, 344

Dworkin, Ronald, 30

Earnings, 129–32, 191, 252, 283, 287, 290, 470. *See also* Wages

Earnings acts, 129

Economic Equity Act (EEA), 273, 467, 400, 402

Edelsberg, Herman, 235

Edmonds, Sarah Emma, 144

Educational Amendments Act, 396

EEOC v. Sears Roebuck and Company, 504 F. Supp. 241; 628 F. Supp. 1264 (31 January 1986), 133, 257–62, 403, 461–63 nn. 54, 56, 57, 59, 60, 66, 67

Eighteenth Amendment, 331

Eisenhower, Dwight D., 231

Eisenstadt v. Baird, 405 U.S. 438 (1972), 299

Eisenstein, Zillah, 297, 354, 363

Elshtain, Jean Bethke, 43

Emancipation (as opposed to liberation), 9, 15, 25, 34, 59, 121, 135, 137, 141, 144, 210, 225, 299, 327, 331, 369, 374; collective, 121, 137, 141

Embryos, 286, 309. *See also* Fetal viability

Enlightenment, 5, 11, 39, 42, 53, 59, 65, 76, 96, 120, 126, 138, 141, 179, 246

Equal Credit Opportunity Act (ECOA), 246, 398

Equal Employment Opportunity Act, 245

Equal Employment Opportunity Commission (EEOC), 234, 235, 257–62, 294, 295, 395, 396, 398, 403, 457, 462–64

Equal Employment Opportunity Reorganization Act, 234

Equal Opportunity Reorganization Act, 398

Equal opportunity, 27, 31, 33, 217, 269, 329, 398, 402

Equal Pay Act, 6, 228, 230, 232, 233, 235, 252, 319, 320, 323, 395, 398. *See also* Pay equity; Comparable worth

Equal pay, 4, 6, 15, 134, 182, 192, 228, 230, 232, 233, 235, 252, 254, 319, 320, 323, 331

Equal protection, 27, 29, 31, 32, 154, 167, 176, 184, 223, 247, 283, 285, 296, 299, 301, 361, 370, 470 n. 44; demands sexual homogeneity, 296

Equal Rights Amendment (ERA), 4, 6, 13–15, 17, 18, 26, 36, 43, 53, 98, 103, 119, 122, 169, 182, 186, 190, 192, 201, 205–11, 213–15, 218–22, 226, 230–33, 235, 245, 248, 249, 273–75, 291, 298, 316, 317, 319–31, 344, 346, 347, 349, 360, 361, 368–71, 397, 399, 401, 402, 470 n. 44

Equal Rights Treaty, 209

Equal rights, 6, 7, 11–16, 19, 32, 33, 42, 43, 48, 57, 116, 145, 146, 178, 182, 183, 185, 187, 191, 199, 205–7, 209–11, 213–16, 218, 221, 222, 226, 228, 232, 247, 257, 264, 274, 291, 298, 317, 318, 321, 324, 328, 329, 331, 349, 356, 358–61, 367, 369, 374

Equal treatment, 8, 9, 13, 25, 43, 187, 188, 209, 226, 235, 274, 297, 317, 323, 356, 360; versus special treatment, 261, 297, 317, 329, 356

Equality Day, 323

Equality League for Self-Supporting Women, 213

Equality, 1–4, 8–13, 15, 17–21, 24–35, 37, 39, 40, 46–48, 56, 57, 59, 60, 63, 64, 75, 76, 78, 96, 112, 136, 137, 139, 140, 142, 146, 149–52, 180, 181, 185, 205, 207, 209, 210, 212, 215–17, 228, 247, 252, 261, 262, 267, 274, 280, 286, 301, 313, 316–18, 323, 327–31, 334, 336, 359–65, 368, 370, 372–75; divisibility of concept, 26–28, 31; "false,"

Noninterference, legal principle of, 277, 299
Nordberg, John A., 261
North Haven Board of Education v. Bell, 102 S. Ct. 1912 (1982), 401
Norton, Eleanor Holmes, 27
Norton, Mary, 207

Obscenity, 7, 332–38, 340, 341, 346, 397; "LAPS" test as part of tripartite definition, 341, 397. *See also Miller v. California*
O'Connor, Sandra Day, 263, 264, 269, 271, 273, 310, 311, 313, 314
Offen, Karen, 12, 15, 317, 328
Office of Economic Opportunity (OEO), 246, 457 n. 23
Ohio v. Akron Center for Reproductive Health, No. 88-805, 58 L. Wk. 4979 (1990), 314, 407, 474 n. 92
O'Keeffe, Georgia, 322
Olsen, Frances, 109, 166, 167
Orwell, George, 26
Otis, James, 79
Otis, Rebecca, 55

Paine, Thomas, 53, 65
Palimony, 283
Palmer et al. v. Shultz, Civil 616 F. Supp. 1540, rev'd., 815 F.2d 84 (D.C. Cir. 1987), 258
Pankhursts, 212
Parental leaves, 7, 230, 254. *See also* Child care
Paris Peace Accords, 321
Park, Maud Wood, 206
Parker, Isaac, 107–8
Parsons, Theophilus, 93
Pateman, Carole, 19, 24, 280
Paternalism, 108, 163, 166, 194, 248; "false," 108, 166. *See also* Protection, "false"
Paternity, 286, 311
Patriarchy, 1, 9, 12, 14–16, 20, 22, 23, 28, 35, 132, 335, 337, 339, 342, 350, 373
Patriotism, 4, 41, 52, 54, 56, 143, 322
Patterson v. McLean Credit Union, 109 S. Ct. 2363 (1989), 264, 265, 271, 272, 310, 311, 406
Patterson, Brenda, 272
Paul, Alice, 205–7, 208, 210, 212, 213, 322, 323
Pay equity, 230, 251, 253, 254, 273. *See also* Comparable worth
Peabody, Elizabeth Shaw, 63

Peckham, Rufus W., 194–95
Pension benefits, 278
Perkins, Francis, 208, 209
Personnel Administration of Massachusetts v. Feeney, 442 U.S. 256 (1979), 466 n. 103
Persons, legal use of term, 116
Peterson, Esther, 231–33
Phillips v. Martin Marietta Corporation, 400 U.S. 542 (1971), 396
Phillips, Wendell, 146
Pillsbury, Parker, 148
Planned Parenthood Association, 300, 473
Planned Parenthood v. Danforth, 428 U.S. 52 (1976), 301, 306, 307, 398
Pleck, Elizabeth, 5
Plessy v. Ferguson, 163 U.S. 537 (1896), 32, 142, 173, 300, 360
Pluralism, 17, 19, 33, 356, 360, 363, 374; radical, 360, 363
Pluralist and pluralists, 1, 13, 20, 360–62, 364, 368
Pole, J. R., 32, 209
Polis, 40
Politicos, 245
Pope v. Illinois, 107 S. Ct. 1918 (1987), 66, 340, 341, 405
Population Reference Bureau, 295
Pornography, 6–8, 19, 23, 25, 34, 254, 269, 280, 313, 316, 317, 320, 325, 331, 332–49, 359, 362, 371, 372, 403, 405; feminist, 334, 419 n. 31, 478 n. 35
"Pornrotica," 334, 342–45, 348
Postfeminist, 13
Postmodern society, 7, 372
Poststructural analysis, 11; gender analysis, 11, 12, 351; theories about, 2, 11, 43, 44, 262
Poststructuralist and poststructuralists, 13, 15, 45, 355, 363
Powell, Lewis, 248, 263, 266, 267, 404
Poverty, the feminization of, 202, 290, 291, 326
Power, male, 23, 25, 135, 279, 331
Pregnancy Discrimination Act (PDA), 297, 298, 399, 400, 404, 470 n. 46
Pregnancy, 4, 8, 23, 224, 251, 257, 276, 278, 285, 294–98, 306, 307, 309, 310, 312–14, 317, 320, 331, 347, 359, 361, 371, 397, 399, 400; and equality, 296–98
Pregnancy-disability acts, 4
Pregnancy-disability insurance, 278, 294–96
President's Commission on Obscenity and Pornography, 332, 346

Presidential administrations, 230; Bush, 254, 255, 262, 307; Carter, 249, 304, 305, 324; Johnson, 234, 454–55; Kennedy, 231–32; Nixon, 234, 245, 246, 264, 406; Reagan, 235, 254, 263, 264, 270, 302, 307
Price Waterhouse v. Hopkins, 109 S. Ct. 1775 (1989), 270, 271, 406
Prior constraint, 337
Privatization, 4, 38, 42, 137, 365
Privatized morality, 4, 135
Privilege and immunity, 165, 172, 173, 182; clause, 164, 165, 167, 169, 170, 176, 184, 186
Pro-life, 301
Probate, 82, 94, 114
Progressive Era, 13, 17, 169, 182, 186, 190, 192, 201, 208, 210, 218, 319
Progressive female reformers, 201
Progressive movement, 187, 191, 198, 200, 211, 318
Progressive reformers, 190, 199, 215
Progressives, 6, 13, 17, 18, 29, 136, 169, 182, 184, 186, 187, 190–92, 198–201, 206, 208, 210–11, 215, 218, 291, 317, 318, 319, 320, 322, 331, 333, 362
Progressivism, 22, 191
Prohibition, 155, 207, 221
Property, commercialized, 123; common law, 124, 286–88; community, 286–88; defeudalization of, 81–82, 97, 123; real, 81, 85, 86, 88, 106, 120, 131, 190, 287
Protection, false, 17, 108, 166, 167, 191
Protectionism, 33, 194, 222
Protective legislation, 4, 13, 182, 187, 190, 191–93, 195, 199–202, 205, 206, 207–9, 211, 214–16, 221–23, 235, 254, 288, 292, 297, 298, 317, 320, 331, 360
Protective-labor legislation, 192, 199, 232, 254, 298
Public Assistance Amendments, 305
Purvis, Robert, 148, 149

Quaker and Quakers, 97, 98, 102, 444
Queen's Bench, 340

Racism, 19, 148–50, 163, 175, 185, 268, 269, 300, 353, 355, 358
Racketeering Influenced and Corrupt Organizations Act (RICO), 302, 336–38, 406, 479 n. 47
Radice v. People of the State of New York, 264 U.S. 292 (1924), 203–5

Ramsay, David, 74
Rankin, Jeannette, 207
Rape, statutory, 273, 400
Rawls, John, 30, 418 n. 22
Raymond, Janice, 15
Reconstruction Civil Rights Law, 310
Reed v. Reed, 404 U.S. 71 (1971), 247–49, 396, 397
Regina v. Hicklin (1868) LR 3 QB 360, 340
Rehnquist, William, 247, 248, 258, 263, 267, 270, 273, 295, 309–13, 320, 370; court, 258, 263, 267, 270, 273, 310, 311, 313, 320, 370
Republicanism, 38, 39, 55, 75, 77, 78, 81, 103, 173, 174, 229
Republican and Republicans, 323, faction, 98, 100, 102; radical, 76, 148, 149
Republican party, 148, 149, 155, 209, 323
Retirement Equity Act, 273, 402
Revenue Act of 1971, 245
Revised Uniform Reciprocal Enforcement of Support Act (RURESA), 293
Right, of citizenship, 17, 18, 30, 36, 38, 93, 116, 154, 174; fundamental, 166, 191, 313, 315, 407; to die, 285, 313; to life, 301, 308; to privacy, 285, 299–301, 306, 307, 312, 313–15, 323, 341, 361, 371, 395, 401, 471 n. 58
Rights: civil, 12, 17, 22, 25, 32–34, 63, 81, 118, 148, 149, 153, 156, 157, 160, 163, 175, 179, 185, 186, 189, 201, 225, 227, 228, 230, 233, 245, 246, 250, 256, 257, 262–67, 271, 272, 294, 300, 310, 313, 317, 319, 328, 331, 332, 336, 339, 344, 345, 347, 348, 356, 358, 371, 395, 398, 402, 403, 405, 406; collectivist, 30; domestic, 276–78, 285–88; individual, 3, 7, 9, 13, 28, 32, 33, 50, 80, 136–41, 148, 150, 152, 169, 173, 209, 228, 230, 247, 265, 266, 274, 285, 300, 310, 330, 356, 357, 360, 369, 370, 373; individual-versus-group or collective, 261, 297, 310, 330; interchangeability principle of, 32; of dependents, 105; and privacy, 299, 300–301, 307, 348, 471 n. 58; veterans, 273, 466 n. 103
Ritchie v. People, 155 Ill. 98, 40 N.E. 458 (1895), 166
Ritter, Eli, 212
Ritter, Narcissa Lockwood, 212
Roberts et al. v. United States Jaycees, 104 S.Ct. 3244 (1984), 255, 402, 404
Roberts v. The City of Boston, 59 Mass. 198 (1849), 141–43
Roberts, Benjamin, 141, 177; Sarah, 142
Robins, Margaret Dreier, 202

Roe v. Wade, 410 U.S. 113 (1973), 251, 280,
300–303, 306–8, 310–14, 397, 398, 407
Rogers, Edith Nourse, 207
Roosevelt, Eleanor, 209–11, 231, 232, 322, 323
Roosevelt, Franklin Delano, 210, 231
Rose, Ernestine, 134
Rosenberg, Rosalind, 36, 203, 258–61
Rosencrantz, Mollie, 226
Rosencrantz v. Territory of Washington, 2
(Wash. Terr.) 267, 5 p. 305 (1884), 224–26
Rostker v. Goldberg, 453 U.S. 57 (1981), 326
Rotarians, 255, 404, 405
Rotary International v. Rotary Club of Duarte,
107 S.Ct. 1940 (1987), 404
Roth v. United States, 354 U.S. 476 (1957),
340, 344
Rousseau, Jean-Jacques, 24, 55
RU-486, 309, 313
Runyon v. McCrary, 427 U.S. 160 (1976), 264,
271, 272, 310, 398, 406
Ruskin Hall, 213
Ryan, C. J., 163

Sachs, Albie, x, 1
Sail'er Inn, Inc. v. Kirby, 5 Cal. 3d I.20585 P.
2d 329 (1971), 224, 396
St. George, Katharine, 233
Salmon, Marylynn, 120, 439 n. 6
Sanitary Commission, 144
Santa Clara Pueblo v. Martinez, 436 U.S. 49
(1978), 250
Sargent, A. A., 160
Scalia, Antonin, 263, 269–71, 273, 310–14,
338, 371, 473–74 nn. 87, 88, 487 n. 53
Schlafly, Phyllis, 202, 321, 325
Scott, Joan Wallach, 350, 352, 354, 355, 363,
483 n. 15
Scrutiny: heightened, 249; middle-level, 249;
strict, 29, 30, 247, 248, 264, 266, 268, 269,
300, 324
Sears, Ellen, 133
Section 1981, 264, 272, 398
Section 701 of Title VII, 296
Section 703 (j) of Title VII of the Civil Rights
Act of 1964, 267, 296
Self-giving, 44, 47
Selfness, 43, 47
Self/other, 43–48
Self-regarding, 44, 47
Sedima v. Imrex, 473 U.S. 479 (1985), 337
*Segar v. Smith* 738, F. 2d 1249 (D.C. Cir.

1984), at 1278–79 cert. denied, 471 U.S.
1115 (1985), 258
Senate Judiciary Committee, 160, 344
Seneca Falls, 6, 134–40, 143, 145, 179, 187,
227, 228; Convention, 6, 134, 136, 138, 140,
143
Separate-but-equal, 141, 142, 300, 345, 360
Sexism(ist), 19, 41, 135, 163, 168, 269, 291,
308, 328, 358
"Sexpert, Suzie," 342. *See also* Bright, Susie
Sexual contract, 418, 419, 422, 439, 468, 475
Sexual harassment, 25, 255, 347, 358, 359,
365, 372, 404
Sexuality, 2, 5, 19, 23, 25, 26, 81, 121, 181,
208, 301, 313, 333, 339, 340, 341–45, 348–
50, 352, 359, 362, 364, 369, 371, 372
Shammas, Carole, 86
Shapiro, Harold T., 358
Shaw, Lemuel, 141–42
Sherwin, Belle, 207
Shipton, Clifford K., 70, 176, 397
Shklar, Judith, 22
Shultz, George, 234
Simon, Anne E., 36
Sixth Amendment, 227
Skinner v. Oklahoma, 301
Slaughter-House Cases, 16 Wall 36 (1873), 157,
165–70, 172, 174, 186, 193
Smeal, Eleanor, 322
Smith, Al, 210
Smith, Gerrit, 148
Smith, Hilda, 46
Smith, Howard W., 233
Smith, Jane Norman, 211
Smith-Rosenberg, Carroll, 36, 204
Social contract, 24
Social Darwinism, 371
Social justice, 82, 210, 221, 304, 322
Social Security Act, 273, 293, 303
Social Security, 249, 266, 273, 278, 293, 303
Spaulding v. University of Washington, 676
F.2d 1232; 740 F. 2d 686, 402
Special righters, 360, 363
Special treatment, 8, 13, 17, 34, 122, 123, 130,
134, 190, 207, 261, 264, 274, 297, 298, 317,
360, 404
Special treatment versus equal treatment, 8
Special versus equal rights, 207, 213, 329
Sphere: private, 4, 8, 17, 18, 38, 41–43, 45, 47,
50, 57, 59, 79, 81, 133, 139, 223, 249, 272;
public, 8, 17, 18, 24, 36, 38–43, 45, 70, 74,
139, 140

Spheres, separate, 10, 15, 17, 22, 31, 38, 39, 44, 46–50, 54, 59, 63, 64, 82–84, 87, 89–91, 93, 103, 108, 115, 119, 121–23, 126–33, 141, 142, 165, 185, 187–89, 248, 265, 269, 272, 273, 282, 286, 287, 300, 310, 336, 345, 353, 360, 405, 420 n. 38

Springer, Francis, 163

Stanton, Elizabeth Cady, 4, 35, 134, 135, 137–41, 143, 145–49, 161, 181, 187, 191, 209, 276, 284, 285

Steelworkers v. Weber, 443 U.S. 193 (1979), 267, 404

Steinem, Gloria, 324

Stelle, Beulah, 111–13

Stelle, Pontius D., 111

Stelle v. Carroll, 12 Pet. 200, 9 L. Ed. 1056 (1838), 111–13

Stevens, Doris, 211

Stevens, John Paul, 264, 270, 272, 337

Stewart, Potter, 248, 269, 295

Stockton, Richard, 93

Stone, Lawrence, 40, 269

Stone, Lucy, 135, 143, 147

Story, Joseph, 124

Structural justice, 308

Strum, Phillipa, 198–99

Subjectivity, 350, 366, 486 n. 42

Subjectship, 80–81, 96

Succession, law, 84–86; primogeniture, 84, 86, 189

Suffrage movement, 4, 6, 15, 17, 18, 21, 63, 79, 98–99, 101, 103, 130, 131, 134, 135, 137, 140, 143, 145–49, 153, 155, 157, 161, 164, 168, 171, 172, 174–77, 180–82, 187, 191, 193, 199, 204, 206–9, 212–14, 219, 320–23, 331

Sullivan, James, 61, 62, 101

Sullivan, John, 101

Sumner, Charles, 142

Suspect classification, 30, 227, 247, 248, 266, 274, 324, 328, 397

Swayne, Noah, 169

Taney, Roger B., 111, 154

Tanner, Jack E., 254

Task Force on Women's Rights and Responsibilities, 245

Taylor, Susie, 144

Taylor v. Louisiana, 419 U.S. 522 (1975), 144, 227, 397

Temperance, 5, 39, 42, 56, 135–38, 212, 230; movement, 5, 56, 230

Terrell, Mary Church, 210

Texas v. Johnson, 109 S. Ct. 2533 (1989), 313

Thaxter, John, 54

Thirteenth Amendment, 143, 144, 155, 172, 173

Thompson v. Morrow, 5 Serg. & R. 289 (PA) (1819), 108, 276, 279, 284, 468

Thompson, Karen, 284

Thompson, William, 276, 279

Thornburgh v. American College of Obstetricians and Gynecologists, 476 U.S. 747 (1986), 306, 307, 403

Tilton, Theodore, 146, 148

Title IX of the 1964 Civil Rights Act, 245, 256, 257, 396, 399, 401, 402, 405

Title VI of the 1964 Civil Rights Act, 265, 266, 399

Title VII of the 1964 Civil Rights Act, 224, 228, 230, 233–35, 253, 254, 258, 262, 264, 267, 268, 270, 271, 294–97, 319, 395, 396, 398, 399, 401–4, 406

Title X of family-planning programs, 302

Title XIX of the Social Security Act, 303, 473

Tory, 70, 90–91. See also Loyalist and Loyalists

Trade unions, 193, 195

Train, George Francis, 147

Tribe, Laurence H., 60, 201, 250, 308, 309

Truman, Harry, 231

Truth, Sojourner, 135, 149

Tubman, Harriet, 144

Turner, Frederick Jackson, 75; Judge, 224–26

Turnicliffe, William, 111

Twenty-seventh Amendment, 6, 212, 248, 321, 324, 329, 331, 399

Unger, Roberto, 366, 368

Uniform Marital Property Act, 190

Union League Club, 256

United Nations, 210–211; Declaration of Human Rights, 211

United States of America v. Susan B. Anthony, 152–61, 164, 169–71, 173–75, 178, 183, 186, 190–91, 198, 209, 272, 276, 314, 333

United States v. Darby, 312 U.S. 100 (1941), 205

United States v. Paradise, 480 U.S. 149 (1987), 263, 404

U.S. Department of Labor, 234, 264

U.S. Department of State, 246, 257, 258, 262, 403; foreign service, 257, 402

U.S. Jaycees, 255

U.S. Supreme Court: decisions overturned, 475–76 n. 6; judicial interference, 17, 22, 28, 29, 45, 88, 91, 93–97, 105, 108, 120, 128, 132, 147, 151, 164, 168–70, 184, 185, 204–5, 225, 227, 230, 261, 265, 272, 300, 307, 308, 314, 323, 329, 407; "majoritarian" point of view, 473–74 n. 88; 487 n. 53; majoritarianism, 313
USSR, 2, 14, 228, 373

Vankleeck, Mary, 217
Vietnam war, 33, 228, 245, 316, 346
Violence Against Women Act, 347
Violence, male, 325. *See also* Women, violence against
Virtue, civic, 50; disinterested public, 4, 54; male, 4, 78; maternal, 39, 198, 309; patriotic, 38; public, 4, 37–39, 50, 57, 65; republican, 50, 53–55

Wage Earners League, 213
Wages, minimum, 201, 203–6, 217, 298, 319, 475 n. 5
Wages (*see also* Earnings acts), 43, 51, 88, 95, 124, 128, 130, 139, 156, 201, 203–6, 252–54, 287, 293, 298, 319, 395, 401; sex-based differential, 89, 124, 252, 298
Waite, Morrison, 172
Wald, Lillian, 192
Walker, Timothy, 276
Wallace, Anthony F. C., 59
War of Independence, 1, 4, 39, 42, 49, 51, 52, 54, 59, 62, 68, 71, 77, 80, 90–94, 120, 143. *See also* American Revolution
War, and women, 88, 98, 105, 111, 208, 217, 231, 290, 362; camp followers, 51, 143
Wards Cove Packing Co., Inc. v. Atonio, 109 S. Ct. 2115 (1989), 270–72, 362, 396, 406
Warren, Earl, 300
Warren, James, 66, 70, 74
Warren, Mercy Otis, 21, 39, 55–58, 62–64, 66–79, 227, 246, 247, 268, 285, 300, 319, 370
Warren Court, 227, 246, 268, 300, 319
Washington, George, 71, 77
Watergate, 316, 317, 323, 326
Wayne Books, Inc. v. Indiana and Sappenfield v. Indiana, 109 S. Ct. 916 (1989), 337, 406
Weber, Brian, 267
Webster, William L., 307

Webster v. Reproductive Health Services, 109 S. Ct. 3040 (1989), 306–14, 320, 325, 397, 405, 407
Weeks v. Southern Bell, 408 F.2d 228 (5th Cir. 1969), 235
Wells, Marguerite, 207
Wells, Rachel, 94
West Coast Hotel v. Parrish, 300 U.S. 379 (1937), 201, 205
West, Robin, x, 19, 23, 35, 44, 130, 131, 165, 201, 205, 224, 279, 287, 364, 365–69
White, Byron R., 271
Wicker, Tom, 269
"Wilding," 346
Wildman, Stephanie A., x, 249, 363
Wilkinson, Eliza, 64
Williams, Wendy W., 31, 47, 249, 274, 297, 466–67 n. 106
Wills, 83–85, 89, 93, 109, 112, 115, 123, 128, 129, 287
Wilson, Franny, 144
Wimberly v. Labor and Industrial Relations Commission of Missouri, 479 U.S. 511 (1987), 298, 404
Winthrop, Hannah, 67
Winthrop, John, 67
Wollstonecraft, Mary, 24, 54, 65, 78, 97
Woman's National Loyal League, 144
Women: and "crazy," or insane, or irrational legal issues, 34–35, 44, 82, 87, 91, 135; and the Constitution, 21; and fear, 346–47, 366–67, 371–72; and happiness, 25, 58, 60, 76, 133, 136, 139–41, 178–82, 368, 370, 374; and revolution, 49–55, 425 n. 7; as care givers, 219, 222; as second-class citizens, 1, 3, 10, 14–16, 18, 19, 24, 30, 34, 37, 40, 43, 45, 47, 52, 57, 78, 91, 99, 106, 118, 124, 140, 152, 153, 162, 173, 179, 183, 187, 189, 196, 198–202, 207, 221, 230, 232, 249, 273, 280, 286, 297, 310, 315, 317, 327, 328, 353, 365, 372, 402, 405; battering of, 42, 277, 339, 346; collective pursuit of justice, 223; Democratic, 211, 231, 322; divorced, 132, 202, 278, 286, 287, 289, 290, 292–94, 399, 460; doctors, 14, 144, 374; full citizenship for, 94, 207, 211; lower-class, 203; married, 3, 22, 36, 39–42, 49, 50, 56, 60, 62, 63, 78, 82–84, 86–94, 100–2, 104–5, 113, 115–16, 119–32, 134, 135–38, 146, 152, 154–57, 162, 164, 165, 180, 182, 187, 188–90, 224–26, 231, 252, 276, 277, 281, 286–91, 293, 294, 319, 320; middle-class, 36, 39, 88, 122, 128, 129,

# About the Author

**JOAN HOFF**, former Executive Secretary of the Organization of American Historians and currently Professor of History at Indiana University Bloomington, is a specialist in twentieth-century U.S. diplomacy and politics and the constitutional history of U.S. women. She has written *American Business and Foreign Policy, 1920–1933* and coauthored *For Adult Users Only: The Dilemma of Violent Pornography in the United States* in addition to books and articles on Herbert Hoover, Eleanor Roosevelt, and Richard Nixon.